COLLISION COURSE

COLLISION COURSE

RONALD REAGAN, THE AIR TRAFFIC CONTROLLERS, AND THE STRIKE THAT CHANGED AMERICA

★

JOSEPH A. McCARTIN

OXFORD
UNIVERSITY PRESS

OXFORD
UNIVERSITY PRESS

Oxford University Press, Inc., publishes works that further
Oxford University's objective of excellence
in research, scholarship, and education.

Oxford   New York
Auckland   Cape Town   Dar es Salaam   Hong Kong   Karachi
Kuala Lumpur   Madrid   Melbourne   Mexico City   Nairobi
New Delhi   Shanghai   Taipei   Toronto

With offices in
Argentina   Austria   Brazil   Chile   Czech Republic   France   Greece
Guatemala   Hungary   Italy   Japan   Poland   Portugal   Singapore
South Korea   Switzerland   Thailand   Turkey   Ukraine   Vietnam

Copyright © 2011 by Joseph A. McCartin

Published by Oxford University Press, Inc.
198 Madison Avenue, New York, NY 10016

www.oup.com

Oxford is a registered trademark of Oxford University Press

Library of Congress Cataloging-in-Publication Data
McCartin, Joseph Anthony.
Collision course : Ronald Reagan, the air traffic controllers, and the strike that
changed America / Joseph A. McCartin.
p.   cm.
Includes bibliographical references and index.
ISBN 978-0-19-983678-9 (hardcover : alk. paper)
1. Reagan, Ronald.   2. Professional Air Traffic Controllers Organization
(Washington, D.C.)United States.   3. Federal Labor Relations Authority.
4. Air Traffic Controllers' Strike, U.S., 1981.   5. Collective bargaining—
Aeronautics—United States.   6. Collective bargaining—United States.   I. Title
HD5325.A4252   2011
331.892—dc22   2011016420

Printed in the United States of America
on acid-free paper

The start of strife is like the opening of a dam;
therefore, check a quarrel before it begins!
PROVERBS 17:14

For Diane, Mara, and Elisa,
and all those who work in the dark places,
whose good labor goes unseen

CONTENTS

★

COLLISION COURSE

GETTING THE PICTURE

Roger, that appears to be jet traffic off your right now, three
o'clock, at one mile, northeast bound.
— WILLIAM L. SMITH, DEC. 16, 1960

Well, Jackie, we got to the end of the road. It's all over now.
— MIKE ROCK, AUG. 4, 1981

It was a warm, sunlit August morning in 1981. But as he awoke from a rest-less night's sleep at his home in Aiken, South Carolina, retired air traffic controller Jack Maher's thoughts turned once again to a cold, gray December day in New York more than twenty years earlier, replaying an event that had haunted his dreams ever since.

Fog and low clouds had shrouded the New York City skyline on Friday morning, December 16, 1960. Snow squalls threatened. It was poor flying weather. Even so, New York's three major airports, LaGuardia, Newark, and New York International—popularly known as Idlewild—were expected to handle a total of nearly seventeen hundred flights. Later, Maher would only remember two of them: United Airlines Flight 826, a Douglas DC-8 jet, carrying eighty-four people from Chicago's O'Hare Airport to Idlewild in southeast Queens, and Trans World Airlines (TWA) Flight 266, a four-engine turboprop Lockheed Super Constellation, carrying forty-four people from Dayton and Columbus, Ohio, to LaGuardia Airport, on Flushing Bay at the north end of Queens.

Below, the New York Air Route Traffic Control Center, a facility of the Federal Aviation Agency (FAA) known as New York Center, buzzed with a murmur that betrayed the faintest hint of strain. Tucked away in Hangar 11 at Idlewild, Maher was among the dozens of air traffic controllers talking crisply into radio transmitters, placing or answering calls on telephones connected directly to the control towers at Idlewild, LaGuardia, and Newark airports, or to the control centers housed in similar hangars at airports in Boston, Cleveland, and Washington. The hangar floor was divided into sectors. Radar scopes tracked arrivals, departures, and over flights within an eighty-mile radius of the airport. The controllers who worked the radar screens were responsible for all traffic operating on instrument flight rules (IFR) within range of their scopes. As they toiled in their regulation white shirts, top buttons undone and ties loosened, World War II–vintage flat radar screens lit their faces with a green glow. Packs of cigarettes rested in their front pockets and coffee cups sat nearby, but the controllers had no time for breaks on this morning. It was not yet 10:30 a.m., but on days like this, with such bad weather, controllers lost all sense of time. More than one hundred flights were taking off or landing at Idlewild, LaGuardia, and Newark each hour. With poor visibility and a cloud ceiling at just six hundred feet, controllers were acting as the pilots' eyes, keeping aircraft separated and on their proper course.

As usual, controllers worked in teams of two to five, depending upon the sector and the volume of traffic. One member of the team, known as the A-side, or assistant, managed flight data regarding the planes entering the sector. On a strip of paper inserted into a metal holder, the assistant would write codes indicating an aircraft's origin, destination, airline, flight number, aircraft type, altitude, and the time it was estimated to reach its next checkpoint. The D-side, or manual controller, worked the telephones communicating with tower controllers. Meanwhile, the R-side, or radar-man, transferred airline and flight number information from the strips lined up by the assistant to smaller paper strips that he inserted into plastic markers called "shrimp boats." The radar controller then lined up the shrimp boats on the side of the radar screen in the order in which he expected them to enter his sector. Once he identified the appropriate "target" as it became visible on the edge of his screen, he would place the identifying shrimp boat next to it. With every few pulses from the radar signal's origin point, or "main bang," the controller moved the shrimp boats along with their targets, tracking the progress of the flights under his direction. All the while, the radarman kept in his head the altitude, speed, and heading of the target, communicating with the aircraft, giving them new directions—known as "vectors"—when appropriate, and preserving their separation in airspace. When a target was ready to move from one sector to the next, a coordinator who stood between the two adjacent sectors helped facilitate the "handoff" from one to the other. Once they accepted the handoff, the second team assumed control of the target.

On this morning, a coworker of Maher's named Ronald DiGiovanni was the R-side handling incoming traffic on a route called Airway Victor 30 that crossed New Jersey twenty miles north of Trenton. John Fisher and Harold Brown were working as DiGiovanni's A and D men. At about 10:27 a.m., DiGiovanni took a handoff of United 826, which was streaking east along Victor 30. Picking up the target on his radar, DiGiovanni confirmed that it was United 826, piloted by Captain Robert H. Sawyer. DiGiovanni marked the blip with a shrimp boat. He then radioed United 826 to proceed east, using the signal of an omnidirectional radio beacon in Yardley, Pennsylvania, to help it maintain its course along Victor 30. As United 826 passed over Freehold, New Jersey, he instructed Sawyer to turn seventy degrees left and proceed northeast toward New York on Airway Victor 123, using another radio transmitter at Colts Neck to align his heading. Once Captain Sawyer turned onto Victor 123, DiGiovanni directed him to descend to five thousand feet and approach a holding area over the north Jersey coast called Preston. Preston's navigation "fix" was determined by the intersecting signals of two ground radio transmitters. DiGiovanni warned Sawyer that he might be held up at Preston and "stacked" in an elliptical pattern until Idlewild was ready for him to land. Preparing Sawyer for that possibility, the controller radioed, "United 826, if holding is necessary at Preston, southwest one minute pattern right turns on the zero radial of Robbinsville. The only delay will be in descent." Once United 826 confirmed the instructions, DiGiovanni signed off, telling Captain Sawyer to contact Idlewild approach controllers to direct him from there. Then DiGiovanni turned to address three other flights in his sector, while Captain Sawyer switched frequencies and radioed Idlewild approach controller Herbert Rausch that he was headed to the Preston holding area. It was 10:33:20 a.m. When

Rausch looked on his radar screen a few seconds later, he could not find the United DC-8.

Less than a minute earlier, in the radar room at LaGuardia on the north side of Queens, approach controller William L. Smith had accepted the handoff of TWA 266 from another team of controllers at New York Center. Smith radioed its pilot, Captain David A. Wollam, to confirm that he was using a radio signal at Linden as a guide across New Jersey on Airway Victor 6, which would put him on course to cross Staten Island five miles south of Newark Airport. Smith instructed the TWA to slow its approach speed and descend to five thousand feet as it followed Victor 6. Just after Smith radioed these directions, he noticed an unexpected target six miles south of the TWA on a northeast heading. He quickly radioed a warning. "Trans World Two Six Six, traffic at two-thirty, six miles northeast bound." "Trans World Two Six Six," responded Captain Wollam, indicating that he had heard Smith. Smith instructed Wollam to descend further to fifteen hundred feet. A few long seconds passed as the radar completed another sweep. The distance between the targets was closing rapidly, the unidentified blip was moving at twice the speed of the TWA. Smith radioed another warning. "Roger, that appears to be jet traffic off to your right now, three o'clock, at one mile, northeast bound," he called at 10:33:26 a.m. "Trans World Two Six Six, turn further left one zero zero." There was no response. His heart racing, Smith tried to stay calm. Situations like this happened every day in New York's skies, he knew. Targets converged on a radar screen, creating what appeared to be a "confliction" or near collision, when in reality they were separated by at least one thousand feet in altitude, as was required on all intersecting flight paths. But the next radar sweep felt like a kick in the gut. Smith's target had not moved. "Trans World Two Sixty-Six, this is LaGuardia, er, Approach Control, one, two, three, four, five, five, four, three, two, one, how do you read?" Smith tried again. Getting no answer, he called for help. A supervisor rushed over. Staring at the scope, he picked up the phone that connected to the LaGuardia control tower cab: "I think we have trouble here with a T.W.A. Connie," he said. "There's something wrong. He's not moving or anything. He might have got hit by another plane."

A few seconds after Smith instructed Wollam to turn further to the left, United 826, having overshot the Preston holding area, sliced through TWA 266. The collision tore an engine off of the DC-8 and broke the TWA Super Constellation's fuselage into pieces, raining victims and wreckage from the TWA on New Dorp and Miller Field near Staten Island's eastern shore. Its wing fatally damaged, the United DC-8 plunged through the clouds toward the streets of Brooklyn. Staten Island florist Paul Kleinauman looked up when he heard the sound of the collision. "Oh my God!" he screamed. The crippled jet he saw hurtling through the sky reminded him of "a big shark, just like a shark when you're fishing."

Across the harbor in Brooklyn, Brother Conrad Barnes was teaching at St. Augustine Catholic School on Sterling Place and Sixth Avenue in the crowded neighborhood of Park Slope when the panicked look on the face of one of his students caused him to turn and look out the window. Brother Barnes froze. A jet trailing smoke was plummeting from the sky and bearing down on the school. Gasping, he told his students to put their heads on their desks and say a prayer. Before he got all the words out, he saw the jet bank hard to the east. Captain Sawyer was trying to reach Prospect Park.

He did not quite make it. The DC-8 clipped the steeple off of a church and exploded in a ball of fire at the intersection of Seventh Avenue and Sterling Place, one block from Brother Barnes's school where more than one thousand students sat doing their lessons. Not realizing what kind of crash had occurred, a stunned priest from St. Augustine's made his way outside with holy oils to minister to the dying. But the inferno was too intense for anyone to approach. Within minutes it consumed ten brownstones, several small businesses, and a Pentecostal church prophetically named Pillar of Fire.

Miraculously, rescuers found one survivor amid the carnage, a badly burned boy lying in a snow bank near the flaming wreckage. Initially, they believed he was a Park Slope resident wounded by falling debris. After he regained consciousness they discovered that he was eleven-year old Stephen Baltz, a passenger on the DC-8. His father had placed him on the flight in Chicago. His mother and sister were to meet him at LaGuardia for a holiday visit with his grandparents. That evening the semiconscious boy told officials about the final minutes of his doomed flight. The last thing he remembered was looking out on the snow-dusted rooftops of New York as his plane broke through the clouds. "It looked like a picture out of a fairy book," he said. He died the next day. The boy's death brought the total number of fatalities, including those on the ground, to 134, making it the worst air disaster in U.S. history up to that time.[1]

More than twenty years later, retired from air traffic control and living in South Carolina, Jack Maher could still not shake the memories of that dreadful morning. He had been working in Hangar 11 that day, and had directed Captain Wollam's TWA for a few minutes as it crossed Eastern Pennsylvania before handing it off to other controllers. He knew Ronnie DiGiovanni. The events of that December day were forever seared into his consciousness. Those memories came flooding back again on the morning of August 3, 1981, when Maher awoke and turned on his radio to hear the news: over twelve thousand air traffic controllers, three-quarters of the workforce of the Federal Aviation Administration (FAA), had walked off their jobs. The men and women who normally directed aircraft to and from more than four hundred airports in the largest air traffic system in the world were defying laws that made it illegal for federal workers to strike, pledging not to return until the government raised their pay, shortened their work-week, and took other measures to reduce the stress of their jobs.[2]

The walkout was more than a news story to Maher. The strikers were members of the Professional Air Traffic Controllers Organization (PATCO), a union that had grown out of the persistent efforts of Maher and other vet-erans of Hangar 11 to organize in the aftermath of the 1960 air disaster. It took several years and some abortive efforts to build that union. Maher was its cofounder. He gave it its name. In 1981, he was no longer formally connected to PATCO, having resigned from its staff in a squabble with its president a year earlier. He had decided then to move south and confront his alcoholism, but in truth Maher's heart was still with the union he had helped to found. During the spring and summer of 1981 he had closely followed its contract talks with the administration of President Ronald Reagan. The announcement that negotiations had broken down and PATCO was striking did not surprise him. He knew the 1981 contract negotiation would be diffi-cult. The union had prepared for three years for this moment, and long before decided that, if the government did not address its demands, it would organize something unprecedented: a coordinated national strike. Maher had led the effort to design that strike plan. He had recruited and trained the key strike organizers. He understood every aspect of the union's strategy. Maher knew that if PATCO was calling a strike its leaders believed they were in a position to shut down the nation's air traffic.

As Maher digested the news and reflected on the twenty years of struggle that had led to this moment, his thoughts turned to his longtime friend and partner in the founding of PATCO, Mike Rock, another veteran of Hangar 11. Maher knew exactly where Rock would be at that moment: in the union's strike headquarters, a secret "safe house" Maher himself had picked out on a rundown street near the Capitol. From that location Rock was helping to direct something never before seen: a carefully planned, illegal strike, stretching from Puerto Rico to Guam, from Key West to Anchorage, against the most powerful government in the world. Maher resolved at that moment that he had to go to Washington. He was determined to stand in solidarity with Rock and his other friends. Jumping in his car, he sped north on I-95.[3]

As the miles rolled by, the car radio carried frequent bulletins on the walkout. Announcers reported that scheduled flights had been cut by more than half that morning and a skeleton crew of nonstrikers, supervisors, and hastily deployed military air traffic controllers was scrambling to handle the remaining flights. Rental car agencies and train and bus depots were swarming with worried travelers; analysts were offering staggering predictions of the strike's potential cost if it continued for more than a few days. It seemed to Maher that the plan was working. There was no way the government could refuse to improve its contract offer in the face of this strike, he thought.

Maher's optimism was not diminished by the live broadcast of President Reagan's statement from the White House Rose Garden at 11 a.m. Reagan announced to the assembled press corps and millions watching on television that his administration would not negotiate with controllers engaged in an illegal strike. If the strikers failed to return to work within forty-eight hours, he explained, they would be terminated from their jobs and permanently replaced. "What lesser action can there be?" Reagan asked. "The law is very explicit. They are violating the law." Maher thought Reagan was posturing, talking tough for the cameras while behind the scenes negotiators were probably discussing the details of a possible settlement at that very moment. That was how PATCO's previous (albeit smaller-scale) confrontations with the federal government had gone, Maher remembered. There was no reason to believe that pattern would not be repeated now with three-quarters of the nation's air traffic controllers out on strike. Maher was sure Reagan would not fire more than ten thousand skilled specialists that the government had spent hundreds of millions of dollars and many years to train—not when they were seeking only improved working conditions and fair compensation after years of seeing their salaries lag behind inflation, and when dismissing them would ultimately be far more costly than meeting their demands.[4]

Yet as Maher sped toward Washington, the ironies of the situation in which his friends and former colleagues found themselves were obvious. Air traffic controllers tended to love their work as much as they hated the FAA's management style, complained about government pay scales, and griped about their stressful workplaces. On this hot August morning, thousands of them were risking the careers that they had hoped would guarantee them a middle-class lifestyle. Although they were breaking federal law in an unprecedented effort to shut down the nation's air travel, they were hardly radicals. On the contrary, the vast majority of them were suburb-dwelling military veterans who, like Maher, had first learned air traffic control while in the service. The strike's field coordinator, handpicked by Maher before his departure, was a decorated Vietnam War hero. Most of the thousands of Vietnam-era veterans in the union's ranks had not been drafted. They had willingly enlisted in the service. After their discharge they applied for jobs with the FAA because they found the work better paying than their other options, because it was exciting, and because it offered them something otherwise unavailable to Americans who lacked college degrees as most controllers did: the chance to become white-collar professionals. They were striking now because they felt they had to protect their profession from the degradation of diminished real earnings and increased stress. "I don't even think air traffic controllers should have the right to strike," explained Jim Stakem, the thirty-three-year-old strike leader at the FAA's huge air route traffic control center in Leesburg, Virginia. "We're striking against the federal government now because for ten years we have exhausted every means at our disposal with the government. At this point, we have been forced into this strike," Stakem said. A Marine veteran of the siege of Con Thien, one of the bloodiest fire fights of the Vietnam War, Stakem was not intimidated by the president's ultimatum. "I'm standing up for something I believe in and I'm not about to fold," he added. As Maher well knew, strikers like Stakem meant what they said. Maher found the irony of the situation almost too excruciating to contemplate: Ronald Reagan, past president of the Screen Actors Guild, the only former union official ever to occupy the Oval Office, a man whose election PATCO had endorsed only nine months earlier, condemning good people like Stakem as lawbreakers and threatening them with dismissal, perhaps even jail.[5]

But in many ways it was not surprising that the striking air traffic controllers and Reagan found themselves in a showdown on August 3, 1981. In a sense, the conflict had long been in the making. Both Ronald Reagan and PATCO were in important respects products of the 1960s—although disparate products to be sure. The seeds of Reagan's political career and PATCO's formation were both sown during the presidency of John F. Kennedy. A New Deal liberal in the days when he led the Screen Actors Guild after World War II, Ronald Reagan gradually drifted rightward during the 1950s as his movie career faded. But he remained nominally a Democrat until the Kennedy administration's policies convinced him to leave the party of his youth. Kennedy's liberalism appalled Reagan. Writing to Richard Nixon, the man Kennedy had defeated in the 1960 election, Reagan lashed out at the sitting president and his policies. "Under the tousled boyish hair cut it is still old Karl Marx—first launched a century ago. There is nothing new in the idea of a government being Big Brother to us all," he wrote. Switching his registration to the Republican Party in 1962, Reagan began to map out the political career that would eventually carry him to the White House.[6]

The same year Reagan switched parties, Kennedy signed Executive Order 10988, which allowed millions of federal workers to join unions and bargain collectively with the U.S. government over many of the conditions of their work. Kennedy's order inspired many states and localities to also allow their workers to join unions and bargain, prompting a massive wave of unionization across all levels of government in the 1960s and 1970s. It was the Kennedy order that cleared the way for a union organizing drive among aggrieved air traffic controllers—among them PATCO cofounders Maher and Rock—a drive that would eventually lead to PATCO's founding in 1968 in a hotel ten miles from the site of the 1960 Brooklyn crash. Both the conservative movement, with which Reagan was identified, and the public sector union movement that produced unions like PATCO gathered strength as the 1960s gave way to the 1970s. In a sense, these two 1960s-spawned forces had been on a collision course for years. On August 3, 1981, the day of reckoning arrived.[7]

The confrontation came at a crucial moment in American political and economic history. As the "Reagan revolution" began refashioning the role of government in American life in 1981, cutting back regulations and spending on social programs, American workers were entering a period of enormous vulnerability. Already the economy was sliding into a recession that would push the unemployment rate up to over 10 percent in 1982, its highest level since before World War II. Income growth had stagnated for most workers; indeed, inflation-adjusted hourly pay had begun to decline in the formerly vibrant manufacturing sector. Moreover, the labor movement, once the bulwark of the liberal order, seemed unable to resist these political and economic trends. Unions had been severely weakened by the economic developments of the 1970s, as container ships began disgorging imports in bulk on American waterfronts, oil prices skyrocketed, "stagflation" appeared, factories closed in waves, and employers began fighting unions with a level of determination unseen since the New Deal. As the share of workers organized in unions slipped to under 22 percent in 1981, down from its high point of 35 percent after World War II, the labor movement was losing clout.[8]

One indicator of the shift, little noticed at the time, was a subtle change in strike activity. Statistics showed that employers were more likely to try to break strikes after 1975 than they had been for the first thirty years after World War II. Increased employer resistance was making an impact by the spring of 1981: the annual number of major work stoppages registered by the Bureau of Labor Statistics fell by 20 percent in 1980. It seemed that workers' confidence in their ability to win strikes was wavering, just as the controllers' walkout began.[9]

That this most significant strike of the late twentieth century was unfolding in the public sector was itself ironic. The rise of public employees' unions in the years after 1962 had been the happiest development for organized labor since the New Deal. The growing numbers of unionized government workers, like the air traffic controllers of PATCO, had partially offset the falling rate of private sector unionization. But, on August 3, 1981, the tables suddenly turned. The public sector union movement that had buoyed labor's fortunes for nearly two decades was now the source of a potentially devastating blow. An illegal and unpopular strike by PATCO's federal employees, erupting just as employers' resistance to strikes was rising across the board, threatened to place all of organized labor on the defensive.[10]

PATCO's walkout was freighted with enormous implications that reached far beyond the ranks of striking air traffic controllers who placed their jobs on the line on the morning of August 3, and far beyond 1981. Carried out on a national stage and covered incessantly by both national and local media outlets, the strike would capture the attention of the nation like no other labor conflict of the post–World War II era. Both labor and its opponents realized even in its first hours that the future direction of American labor relations might be affected by the outcome of this momentous walkout. Indeed, while Jack Maher drove toward Washington, leaders of America's federation of labor unions, the AFL-CIO, were locked in a closed-door meeting in Chicago, where they received updates on the controllers' strike and Reagan's ultimatum, debated among themselves what—if anything—organized labor as whole should do, and pondered how far members of their own unions would go to support federal workers who earned higher salaries than most union members in an illegal strike against a popular president during an economic downturn. The conflict scared the labor leaders, for they knew that it had the potential to set in place enduring patterns and provide labor's enemies with a victory whose influence might resonate for many years after. Labor's opponents knew this too. At that very moment, within the Reagan administration, an internal debate was finally being settled. For months the administration's moderates had urged concessions to PATCO that would avoid a costly confrontation. The hardliners who had opposed such concessions were relieved that the negotiating was now over. As they rejected further compromise with PATCO and prepared to permanently replace any controllers who refused to heed the president's ultimatum, they were determined that Reagan emerge from the conflict with his image as a decisive leader strengthened.[11]

Yet Jack Maher was not primarily concerned with the political implications or historic significance of the PATCO strike as he drove in to Washington. His thoughts were of his friends and former colleagues.

The procedure when one radar controller replaced another during a shift change called for the incoming controller to plug in his headset, closely study the blizzard of targets moving across the radar screen, and listen to the on-duty controller issuing commands until he was sure that he had absorbed all the details and understood the flow of the sector he was about to take over. Only when the controller coming on duty assured the first controller that he "had the picture" would the first controller unplug and clock out. As he arrived in Washington late in the day on August 3, Maher's first instinct was to "get the picture." He rushed to PATCO's headquarters on North Capitol Street, pumping everyone he saw for information. When Maher learned that PATCO's president, Robert E. Poli, was out of the office, he assumed that Poli was in a secret negotiation with the Reagan people. But no one Maher buttonholed that evening was aware of any negotiations underway. As far as anyone in the PATCO office knew, the White House was refusing to talk while the controllers remained on strike. The one bit of news

Maher did pick up he judged to be insignificant: a rumor that some former cabinet secretaries were offering to mediate the conflict. When the person who shared this with him swore him to secrecy about it, Maher began to worry. If that rumor was the best hope PATCO had, then the situation was worse than he anticipated: there might be no back-channel negotiations undertaken before Reagan's forty-eight-hour deadline passed. Yet, as Maher left PATCO's headquarters he still believed that the union would prevail, as long as the strikers' ranks held firm.

The next morning Maher decided to get the views of his longtime collaborator Mike Rock, who was still ensconced in PATCO's safe house, a mile from the Capitol. As Maher wended his way toward the secret location, he thought about the many jams that he and Rock found themselves in over the years since they helped bring PATCO to birth in 1968. It had never been an easy proposition organizing a strong union in the federal sector under rules that made it illegal not only to strike but also to negotiate over pay or benefits. Maher and Rock had pushed the legal envelope many times before and been threatened repeatedly with firing or worse, but they had never faced a situation quite as serious as this one. If anyone had the nerve to steer the union to victory, Maher thought, it was surely Rock—"Mike Strike," as PATCO members fondly called him.[12]

Yet when Rock opened the door of the safe house, Maher's confidence was not inspired by the sight of his friend. Rock looked worried. This was unlike him. In past battles with the government, Rock had exuded a cocky confidence. On this day, however, Maher found his friend in an uncharacteristically subdued mood. Thinking that Rock might only be tired, and hoping to pick up his pal's spirits, Maher recounted the news he had gleaned at the union's headquarters the night before, including the rumor about potential mediators. "Isn't that the silliest damn thing, this asshole swearing me to secrecy over an offer for a committee?" Maher chuckled. But Rock could not share the laugh. Instead, he sat Maher down and delivered his own grim diagnosis. Reagan was determined to break the strike, Rock said. Once a president takes a stand like that, no union could force him to back down. "Well, Jackie, we got to the end of the road," said Rock to the man who had helped him found PATCO. "It's all over now."

Maher was incredulous. "Mike Strike" ready to throw in the towel only one day into the walkout? He tried to shake Rock from his funk. All was not lost, Maher insisted. PATCO still held high cards. He reminded Rock of the logic behind the union's strategy. The government would be forced to come to terms with the strikers, Maher argued, no matter what the president said. Reagan could not fire three-quarters of the air traffic controller workforce and hope to operate an air transportation system for long. Americans would never tolerate paying many billions more to break the strike than it would cost to meet PATCO's contract demands. Training ten thousand new recruits and reducing flight schedules for years to come would be a price too high for the government to pay. Rock disagreed. Now that PATCO was on strike, he countered, Reagan would welcome the chance to demonstrate that his administration would pay any price rather than yield to pressure from a union. Try as he might, Maher could not convince him otherwise. When their visit came to an end, Maher left the safe house shaken, fervently hoping that Rock was wrong.[13]

The situation could not have been more unnerving for Maher. With a deadline fast approaching in what was already shaping up to be the most momentous American strike of the second half of the twentieth century, the man whose judgment Maher most trusted believed the union they had founded together was about to be destroyed. Making matters worse, Maher realized that it might already be too late for PATCO to change course. It was doubtful that controllers would heed a last-minute back-to-work order from the union's national leaders unless it was accompanied by a new contract offer from the government. The strikers had assumed all along that the government might try to dismiss them before ultimately compromising. Indeed, this assumption was built into the strike plan Maher had helped conceive. Organizers had prepared the union's members in advance for this threat. They had also explained that if the strikers stuck together they would make it impossible for the government to carry through on a mass firing. Thus, as the deadline encroached, PATCO's ranks were holding firm. Like Jim Stakem of northern Virginia, air traffic controllers across the country were standing up for something in which they passionately believed, and they were "not about to fold."

Instantly, the PATCO-Reagan standoff assumed the aspect of a tragedy inexorably unfolding with each tick of the clock. With the president's deadline only twenty-four hours away, a titanic collision now seemed inevitable. Such a collision not only threatened disaster for striking air traffic controllers. It also had the potential to undermine the long-term integrity of the air traffic control system, loosen the moral restraints that had kept private-sector antiunionism in check, and expose the glaring flaws of the American system of labor relations before workers whose incomes and dignity depended upon its presumed protections. The fallout from a collision like this would affect tens of millions of workers who had never boarded an airplane, let alone seen the inside of a control tower.

It was an air traffic controller's worst nightmare, the sickening scenario that had haunted Maher's dreams ever since that grim December morning in 1960. Two targets were converging on a screen. Each sweep of the radar saw them draw closer to a collision. But it was too late to issue any new vectors; too late for course corrections. All Maher could do was watch helplessly as the targets came together, hoping that his friend was mistaken, praying that a disaster could still be averted, and wondering how it had come to this.

What follows is the story of how that moment came about and how it changed America.

THE MAIN BANG

All the guys wanted to do something, and the only thing we
saw is to organize in some fashion.
—AIR TRAFFIC CONTROLLER JACK MAHER

Why the New York midair collision happened was never settled to everyone's satisfaction. Courts wrestled with the resulting lawsuits for more than
ten years. Did the omnidirectional beacons that demarcated the Preston
holding area malfunction? Several pilots later testified that they were not
working properly. Did the receiver on United 826 malfunction and fail to
pick up the Preston signal? Some evidence suggested this possibility. Did
Captain Sawyer fail to slow his jet enough to avoid overshooting the holding
area? Records later recovered from the flight data recorder, or "black box," of
United 826 (the first time such records were ever used in a major U.S.
accident investigation) revealed that the DC-8 entered New York airspace
traveling at over five hundred miles per hour, nearly as fast as a bullet fired
from a .45 caliber pistol (552 miles per hour). Whether excessive speed or
an equipment malfunction was the determining factor in the collision was
never completely resolved.

In busy Hangar 11, word of the accident spread slowly. Air traffic controller
Mike Rock was working the Harrisburg-Philadelphia sector when a Pan
American pilot radioed him, "Do you have the count of how many?" Rock,

a two-year veteran of Hangar 11 was puzzled. "Say again," Rock responded. "There's been a collision," said the pilot. "Do you know how many are dead?" Only then did Rock look across the room to observe several controllers and supervisors clustered around an obviously distraught Ronnie DiGiovanni. Rock noticed that one D-side controller, not even working on DiGiovanni's sector, was so upset he had broken out in hives as big as golf balls.[1]

John Francis "Jack" Maher, also a relative greenhorn in Hangar 11, had no idea that anything had happened until he took a break to refill his coffee cup. He was in a good mood. He had been dreading work that day—not so much because of the weather but because he was scheduled to cover the ocean sector. He despised working the ocean sector because it afforded little direct communication with most traffic. Handoffs did not come from controllers in adjacent sectors. Instead, controllers in the Azores or Bermuda called in position reports on landlines or sent them by teletype. The reports often arrived late, making it difficult to "get the picture" in that sector and to anticipate when a target might suddenly appear. But the day was turning out better than Maher anticipated. When he arrived for his 7 a.m. shift, he learned that Sector 11, the Allentown sector, which handled a large slice of eastbound traffic, was shorthanded. Maher was shifted to cover it. Despite the rotten weather, Allentown had moved like clockwork that morning, and that gave Maher a sense of satisfaction. Yet as he took his break Maher overheard talk about a United DC-8 and a TWA Connie "trading paint." The rumor was that they both went down. He gulped. Twenty minutes earlier he had handed off an eastbound TWA Connie to another controller, who took it into New York airspace. It suddenly dawned on him that he had handled the doomed plane. The thought made him sick.[2]

Although they were both working in Hangar 11 that morning, Rock and Maher knew each other only as familiar faces then. They had never worked the same sector, much less had a chance to get to know each other. Yet, for all they shared in common, they could have been brothers.

Born in the East Bronx in 1936, Michael J. Rock was the son of a New York cop, a second-generation Irish immigrant. His father died of tuberculosis when Rock was eight. His mother, Mildred, the daughter of Ukrainian immigrants, supported Rock and his older brother by working as a waitress and wartime factory hand before settling into steadier work as a telephone operator, where she became a union shop steward. Mike was a handful for Mildred. A rambunctious kid, he loved the streets. He was also big for his age and adept on the basketball courts of the Bronx, which he preferred to the borough's classrooms. He played hooky frequently to perfect his jump shot, and consequently bounced in and out of schools, both public and Catholic. His worried mother was relieved when Mike enlisted in the Navy as soon as he was eligible in 1953. His athletic ability made him a sought-after member of base teams, which in turn helped win him favorable duties, including training as radar operator. When Rock was discharged in September 1957, he considered accepting a college basketball scholarship. But he wanted to get married, and for that he needed a decent job and an income. He intended to become a cop like his brother and father before him. While he waited to gain admission to the police academy, his uncle, a local construction union official, helped get him a job. An unexpected strike disrupted Rock's job as a tile setter's helper and sent him searching for work. At that point, he heard that the FAA was hiring people like him with radar experience. He applied in 1958 and was accepted and assigned to Hangar 11.

Jack Maher shared common roots and a common history with Rock. Maher was also an outer borough boy, born in Flushing, Queens, in 1933. His father died when he was young, his mother also worked as a telephone operator. Like Rock, Maher joined the military out of high school. He enlisted in the Marines in 1952, while the Korean War still raged. Initially assigned to an artillery battalion, he scored well enough on an aptitude test to win assignment to a ground-controlled approach or "GCA" unit, where he learned how to use radar to direct Marine aircraft. When he was discharged in 1957, marriage plans also encouraged him to find steady work quickly. He, too, was hired by the FAA in 1958 and assigned to Hangar 11. There his similarities with Rock ended. Although they shared parallel biographies, the two possessed distinctly different personalities. While Rock was gregarious and outspoken, Maher was quiet and introspective. Rock was a born charmer, Maher a sharp-eyed analyst. Their shared history and complementary personality traits would serve them well once they teamed up.

The life stories that Maher and Rock shared were common among the controllers who "worked the boards," chattered over their headsets, and pushed shrimp boats on the morning of December 16, 1960. Much about their backgrounds and the nature of their work reinforced their commonalities.

First, they were almost all young men (there was only one woman among the more than three hundred controllers in Hangar 11). They had entered a highly technical and fast-evolving profession that had been invented in their lifetimes. Before the 1930s there had been no airport control towers. Ground crews used green or checkered flags to signal permission to land to pilots and red flags to tell them to hold. In bad weather they used "light guns," that aimed beams of red or green at approaching aircraft. As air traffic increased, the disadvantages of the primitive signal system became apparent and airports began experimenting with radio communication between pilots and controllers. The first radio-equipped control tower was built in Cleveland in 1930, but radio-based air traffic control emerged unevenly until the mid-1930s. The country's busiest airports, run by municipalities in Chicago and Newark, handled fifty landings or takeoffs per hour. Traffic patterns and rules were not uniform. Planes sometimes raced to be the first to touch down. It was not until June 1936 that the newly created federal Civil Aeronautics Administration (CAA) took over control centers in Newark, Cleveland, and Chicago, and designated them "airway traffic control centers." These early centers, which served as precursors of facilities like the New York Air Route Traffic Control Center in Idlewild's Hangar 11, were equipped only with a blackboard, a large table map, a teletype machine and telephones.[3]

World War II accelerated the expansion and federalization of air traffic control and provided the impetus for the creation of the controller as an indispensable figure in postwar air transportation. Although there were only 150 airport traffic controllers working for the CAA in 1941, by the end of the war the number had increased more than tenfold, and the CAA operated 115 radio-equipped airport towers. Roughly one-third of the wartime hires were women, but most did not stay on after the war when a hiring surge made the workforce overwhelmingly male. The postwar expansion coincided with the introduction of radar in the terminal radar approach control (TRACON) facilities that guided flights into and out of metropolitan airports and the air route traffic control center (ARTCC) facilities that handled traffic between points of origin and destination. Prior to radar control, the need to space aircraft adequately usually limited airports to as few as five landings per hour in low-visibility instrument weather. The introduction of radar control allowed controllers to shrink the distance between aircraft and more than double the bad-weather capacity of airports. Yet it was not until 1957 that the CAA placed all of the nation's airspace above twenty-four thousand feet under the active supervision of controllers, leading to the expansion of facilities like New York Center. This development came in response to another air disaster: the June 30, 1956, midair collision of two airliners over the Grand Canyon that killed 128 people. That collision in turn led to the creation of the FAA.[4]

The men who worked at Hangar 11 were united by more than their status as first-generation radar controllers. Like Rock and Maher, they shared similar profiles. They were overwhelmingly white (over 95 percent). They were from working-class families, had served in the military, were usually married or hoped to be soon, and had young kids at home or babies on the way. Most were still in their twenties. Few had college educations, although many had taken some coursework courtesy of the GI Bill. As boys, none knew of, let alone aspired to, the work of air traffic control. Typically, they first learned how to separate airplanes while in uniform. After discharge, they went to the only employer who hired people with that skill: the FAA. What the new recruits found in FAA facilities seemed quite familiar to them after their military service: steady employment in a hierarchical bureaucracy; equipment that was too often busted or unreliable; superiors who lorded over them and seemed to delight in breaking green recruits. That President Eisenhower named a former Air Force general and Lockheed Corporation executive Elwood R. "Pete" Quesada as the first FAA administrator in 1958 only reinforced the military culture that predominated in the new agency.

The nature of their entry into employment at the FAA further homogenized these men of similar stock and experience. To a man, they found their introduction to air traffic control reminiscent of boot camp. The first lesson they learned at the FAA was similar to the teaching imparted by Marine drill sergeants on Parris Island: "The trainee was the lowest of the low; he was lower than a pregnant ant," as Mike Rock put it. "Developmental" controllers were barred from eating or drinking coffee at the same table with journeymen controllers. They were compelled to get coffee for senior controllers and even sweep up around the facility. "We were like lackeys. Or you might call us coolies," one remembered. The first day on the job was seared into the memory of another controller. "Hey, asshole!" his supervisor had called as soon as he set foot in the control room. "I want you to get your ass down there, grab that goddamn broom, and start sweepin' from that wall all the way up to the mission supe's desk there up front—right now!" In some cases they were even subject to military-style "white glove" inspections to ensure that they did not miss mopping any spots on the floor.[5]

The training was intense and rigorous, and most of it was on-the-job. New hires began learning the ropes in a facility like Hangar 11, doing menial tasks such as filling out flight strips. Then they were sent to the FAA Aeronautical Training Center, located on the west side of Will Rogers Airport in Oklahoma City, Oklahoma. There the trainees huddled in classrooms, where they learned FAA terminology and procedure and worked out increasingly complex simulated air traffic problems. If they survived their classroom instruction, during which many washed out, they returned to the facility for more intensive training. Often trainees were told to forget what they learned in Oklahoma. They learned that they would be working "the New York way" or the "Chicago way," for each facility had its own idiosyncrasies dictated by its particular traffic patterns. Most of the training was one-on-one. Developmentals were tutored by crewmates as they learned every nuance of the job on individual sectors. At times the training regime could border on sadistic. As young developmentals handled traffic with a senior controller at their side, instructors would sometimes stand behind them, nattering in their ears. "Why're you doing that? What was that for? Look at that guy!" Their purpose was to weed out anyone who could not handle pressure. Trainees were taught to speak in a quick, clear, calm, and confident manner in the most stressful situations so they never distracted or concerned the pilots with whom they communicated, no matter how harried or worried they felt. When developmentals learned a sector well enough, they would take "check rides" with their supervisors, instructors, and senior fellow controllers. If they passed these evaluations, they were "checked out" in one position and could move on to learn another. Once they had checked out in all of the sectors of a facility and mastered each, they were certified as a "full performance level manual controller." More than half of recruits washed out before getting that far. Those who made it, like those who survived the boot camp experience, were bonded together by their harrowing initiation. Having become manual controllers, they were cleared to work radio positions and could begin another intensive round of on-the-job training to become radar controllers. Winning that designation could take more than a year. In many cases, controllers never reached that level.[6]

Controllers tended to share similar personality traits and aspirations. They were generally bright, self-confident, and quick-thinking, but ill-suited to scholarly pursuits. They thought of themselves as problem solvers, people who liked challenges. They sought secure but interesting jobs that would provide salaries on which to raise families. The FAA seemed to offer the perfect fit. FAA trainees were categorized as General Schedule 6 (GS-6) on the federal pay scale. That meant that newly hired controllers could earn $4,080 per year in 1960, or about $127 in take-home pay for each two-week pay period. At a time when the median U.S. family income was $5,620, this was good money for young men recently discharged from the service. If they did not wash out during their rigorous training and their security clearances came through, they were lifted to GS-8. That promotion could bump their pay to almost $6,000 a year, comfortably above the national median.[7]

Generally, they viewed their jobs as tickets to the American Dream then taking shape on the crabgrass frontier of postwar suburbia. They were happy to learn in July 1960 that the FAA would soon move the Hangar 11 facility to the hamlet of Bohemia, New York, forty-five miles to the east and adjacent to Long Island's MacArthur Airport in the Town of Islip. (The FAA decided to move all air route traffic control centers out of densely populated metropolitan areas so that they might still operate in the event of a nuclear attack.) The knowledge that they would soon be relocating to a suburban setting added to the attraction of the work for many controllers. Once they were hired, they began saving to put down $500 on a $15,000 two-bedroom bungalow in a suburban community such as Island Park, on Long Island's south shore. On their FAA salaries, they could make their $142 monthly mortgage payments and still have something left. Their parents might still be living in a Brooklyn apartment—their fathers driving trucks or wrestling shipments on loading docks while their mothers worked a telephone switchboard—but these working-class sons were staking a claim to a middle-class lifestyle, earning enough to allow their wives to leave their retail or service sector jobs and stay home with their young children.[8]

If they could complete their arduous training and avoid washing out, their career prospects seemed excellent. As full performance level radar controllers, they could move up to a GS-11 grade, where they were on a trajectory to earn as much as $10,000 by the mid-1960s. As their families made plans for the future, they envisioned trading in their starter homes in communities like Island Park for bigger models farther out in Long Island's Suffolk County. They could buy homes in communities such as Lake Ronkonkoma with more bedrooms and larger yards, reducing their commutes to the new Islip facility from an hour to fifteen minutes. For these men who lacked a college education, the future seemed bright with promise, and they shared expectations of upward mobility.[9]

Their work, by turns challenging, unnerving, frustrating and rewarding, also drew them together. They worked in teams, instructed each other, handed off aircraft to each other, watched each other's backs, and pitched in to help when a colleague appeared ready to go "down the tubes." They also bore the burdens of the work together. In busy facilities such as Hangar 11, the New York airports, or Chicago's O'Hare International Airport, controllers could expect as a matter of course to eat lunch on position, getting relief only to use the bathroom. They griped to each other about the FAA's dress code regulations. It annoyed them to have to wear white dress shirts and neckties when they worked out of sight of the general public.[10]

They also helped each other cope with the pressure. The level of pressure they encountered in facilities like Hangar 11 was new to them, and at times it could be frightening. In the service, they had never juggled a dozen flights at once, handling targets that might contain a hundred lives apiece. Before coming to the FAA, they had not woken up in a cold sweat terrified that what happened to Ronnie DiGiovanni might happen to them and thinking about poor Stephen Baltz, the fatally injured boy who was found in the Brooklyn snow bank, or Baltz's broken-hearted parents. They all knew how easily it could happen. In training they learned that the "closure speed" of two piston-driven propeller planes headed directly toward each other was greater than six hundred miles per hour. If the aircraft had jet engines, they closed on each other at approximately one thousand miles per hour. They learned that the pilot of a DC-6 jet would have exactly one-tenth of a second to initiate a successful evasive maneuver after spotting a propeller-driven Constellation approaching head on from a distance of two miles. If the pilot did not sight the Constellation until it was one mile away, a collision would be unavoidable. At work they trained themselves not to think about the lives they were handling. They got through the tense periods by invoking the "big sky theory," the notion that the chances of two planes coming together were slim in the vast expanses above. But after the New York collision, it was clear that the sky was no longer big enough. That collective realization was yet another of the ties that bound them together.[11]

Finally, the all-consuming nature of the work forged them into a tight-knit community. By the early 1960s they were regularly working six days a week as the system struggled to keep up with the surging growth in traffic. Their scheduled leaves could be canceled abruptly whenever their supervisors needed another pair of eyes on the scopes. While they looked and dressed just like the office workers, teachers, and other white-collar men they saw on their morning commutes, they occupied the insular world of shift workers. Rotating through day shifts, evening shifts, and midnight shifts in a never-ending cycle that disrupted their circadian rhythms, they found it was difficult to socialize with anyone who was not also an air traffic controller.

Controllers relied upon their leisure pursuits to release them from the pressure and give them an outlet for the resentment they felt at being treated like mere grunts by their supervisors. After work they congregated together in bars like Duffy's tavern in Kew Gardens, where they downed liquid sedation to counteract the adrenaline still pumping through their veins and unloaded to each other about their day, their supervisors, and their grievances. In such places, their neckties and white collars, those ambivalent symbols of both their mobility out of their parents' working-class world and their servility in the hierarchical FAA, were finally loosened. They no longer felt as though they were on a leash—especially after a second beer.

The midnight shift in Hangar 11 occasionally offered the same feeling of freedom. It was on those midnight shifts that controllers first began to push back against the rules they hated. It began with younger controllers insisting that they be allowed to take their damned ties off, especially if as trainees they were also expected to sweep up. "You want me to clean these fucking garbage cans, I'm not going to wear a white shirt and tie," Mike Rock explained. Nobody fired Rock for that. For a couple of glorious hours in the dead of night, ties were optional in Hangar 11. The rules finally relaxed. As Rock's colleague Stan Gordon recalled, when traffic levels fell in the wee hours, idle controllers would take a break. Some might start a game of craps in the corner. Others took orders and set off on food runs as far off as Nathan's Famous Hot Dogs on Coney Island. On special occasions, an intrepid controller might even bring in a movie projector and show a film—the sexier the better—on a blank wall. The problem was that the precious time at Duffy's or on a quiet midnight shift was fleeting. Then it was back to the rules, to the squeeze of rush-hour air traffic, to the bark of an irritated supervisor, to the pressure.[12]

At least they went through it together. In a large center, they might not know the names of everyone on their shift, since ARTCC controllers generally worked with the same team of controllers on their sectors. But they knew that the guys across the room likely had similar experiences, nourished similar aspirations, and shared the same concerns and worries they did. After the New York midair collision they all had concerns about the state of the system. They were all anxious to see how the FAA would respond to the accident.

Organizing in "Some Fashion"

The FAA's response to the collision shocked them. As it happened, FAA Administrator Pete Quesada was in Dayton, Ohio, on the morning of December 16 to attend a luncheon celebrating the fifty-seventh anniversary of the first powered flight, the 120-foot journey of the Wright Flyer I at Kitty Hawk, North Carolina, on December 17, 1903. Moments after laying a wreath at the grave of the Wright brothers, Quesada was informed of the horrendous accident in New York. From that moment on, the FAA seemed determined to avoid blame and deflect whatever concerns the accident raised about the state of the air traffic control system.[13]

On January 4, 1961, hearings on the accident convened before the Civil Aeronautics Board (CAB) in the grand ballroom of the Hotel St. George in Brooklyn. Some believed that the CAB rushed the public hearings in order to give the FAA an opportunity to deflect responsibility for the tragedy. The airline pilots' union tried unsuccessfully to delay the hearings, arguing that never before in the CAB's history had a public hearing "been scheduled with so little time for investigation and preparation." Even so, the FAA suffered what the *New York Daily News* called a "hammering" in the testimony that followed. For ten days, FAA officials, controllers, pilots, engineers, representatives from the airlines and eyewitnesses on the ground testified about what they saw, heard, and did, and commented on the conditions that led to the accident. Because he had handled TWA 266 in the Allentown sector, Jack Maher was one of the seventy witnesses on the list. On paid leave for the duration of the hearings, Maher went to the St. George every day, listened intently, and watched the investigation unfold. He was shaken by what he saw. He and his coworkers knew there were numerous flaws in the FAA's technology and systems. They knew the radar equipment they used in the New York facilities was often older and less reliable than the equipment they had used in the military. They knew handoff procedures for traffic moving between sectors or cleared to land were not clearly defined, let alone consistently applied. They watched as the FAA fought off any blame for the accident, using the data recorded in the DC-8's "black box" to argue that Captain Sawyer, the jet's pilot, was to blame. As the headlines that emerged from the public hearing indicated—"High Speed Laid to Jet in Crash," "Inquiry told Craft Overshot Circle Area at 500 m.p.h."—the agency's strategy worked. It avoided responsibility for the crash.[14]

The FAA might have escaped blame in the eyes of the public, but its approach to the investigation damaged its credibility among its own employees. The agency's public relations campaign confirmed for Maher and many of his coworkers that FAA officials were uninterested in reforming their procedures or upgrading their equipment. Maher had expected that the agency might try to downplay some of the problems in the air traffic control system, but he was not prepared for the whitewashing he witnessed. Even more, he was shocked to learn that the FAA's top officials did not even understand the daily workings of the system over which they presided. The agency's regional officials seemed to know nothing about Hangar 11's operations, controllers' procedures, or equipment. This stunned Maher and many of his coworkers. The system was getting worse, yet the people in charge did not understand it enough to know that anything was wrong, let alone how to fix it. Maher decided then that "the emperor had no clothes."[15]

For weeks afterward, Maher, Rock, and the controllers in Hangar 11 discussed the accident, the testimony at the St. George, and their options over beers after work. In the controllers' view, the nature of the problem was simple to grasp. Scheduled airlines carried fifty-eight million passengers by 1960, which represented a quadrupling of air passenger traffic since 1950. Not only had air traffic grown, but its nature had also changed as high-speed jets replaced piston-engine propeller planes, thus significantly reducing margins of error. By 1960, the nation's twelve thousand air traffic controllers— laboring on inferior equipment and following antiquated rules in 205 airport control towers, 23 terminal radar approach control facilities (TRACONs), and 34 air route traffic control centers (ARTCCs) like Hangar 11's New York Center—were having trouble keeping up, and after December 16, 1960, the "big sky theory" was dead.[16]

Controllers who had been around longer than Rock and Maher argued that the first signs of crisis had surfaced six years earlier on September 15, 1954, a day that became known as "Black Wednesday" in the New York area.

That day controllers were so overwhelmed with instrument traffic that for-ty-five thousand travelers had their flights canceled or delayed for hours, forcing the CAA to put the entire staff of New York Center on an emergency forty-eight-hour work week. Others pointed to the events of June 21, 1956, when rain and fog blanketed much of the Eastern Seaboard on the first day of the busy summer flying season. The air traffic control system experienced the worst airborne traffic snarl it had seen yet. Traffic was backed up all the way to the West Coast, prompting one airline executive to call it "one of the greatest fiascos...that I have ever heard about."[17]

Some senior controllers insisted that the problems facing air traffic con-trollers had been getting only worse since 1956, while Quesada and other federal bureaucrats had done little to help them. Most of the controllers in Hangar 11 agreed that something needed to be done. For many controllers, organizing seemed to be the only solution. Unions were a presence in the blue-collar world from which most of the controllers came. Mike Rock, whose uncle led a local union of tile setters, and Jack Maher, whose uncle was an official in a Michigan plumbers' union local, were not unique in this regard. To men familiar with the labor movement, organizing to get their grievances addressed seemed natural. "All the guys wanted to do something," Maher later recalled, and "the only thing we saw is to organize in some fashion."[18]

To organize in "*some* fashion," yes. But forming a union was not the initial intention of Maher and his colleagues. After all, the government did not rec-ognize or bargain collectively with unions of federal employees. There was another organization that the New York controllers thought could help them get their voices heard, the Air Traffic Control Association (ATCA).

The ATCA's founding on March 31, 1956, coincided propitiously with the onset of the first spasms of the air traffic control crisis. Its impetus came from controllers at Washington National Airport who sent out a call for an organizational meeting. Seventy-five controllers and supervisors who shared the vision of an improved and professionalized air traffic control system responded. The reform impetus behind the ATCA quickly dissipated, how-ever. Within a short time, CAA (later FAA) officials became the dominant voices within the ATCA's governing council. Controllers continued to join the organization, in part because their supervisors urged them to, but they soon found that the ATCA replicated the hierarchical structure of their workplaces. Clifford P. Burton, a former CAA official, served as the ATCA's executive director, and Oswald Ryan, a former chairman of the Civil Aeronautics Board, served as its general counsel. The FAA's deputy administrator, D. D. "Dave" Thomas, became a prominent voice within it. More than half of the ATCA's thirty-person governing council held positions in the FAA hierarchy at the time of the New York midair collision. Rather than providing an engine for reform, the ATCA had become a means for advancing one's career and for "enhancing the stature of the air traffic control profession." Rather than advocating on behalf of controllers, it resembled a social club "like the Lions and the Kiwanis," as one controller put it.[19]

No matter how it was viewed, the ATCA had no trouble recruiting members and growing between 1956 and 1960, in part because it had powerful official backing within the FAA. Many controllers joined the organization while they were still in the military, hoping that ATCA connections would help land them jobs in the FAA after their discharge. Others were recruited when they were sent to the FAA Aeronautical Training Center in Oklahoma City for their classroom instruction. The organization printed and distributed hundreds of copies of a recording by the author of the 1958 Federal Aviation Act, Senator A. S. "Mike" Monroney, an Oklahoma Democrat. Monroney personally touted the advantages of membership and urged young controllers to sign up. If Monroney's voice was not persuasive, the training instructors in FAA facilities could be. The ATCA recruited heavily among that group, and they in turn recruited developmental controllers (many of whom worried that turning down an invitation proffered by their instructor might increase their chances of washing out). By the early 1960s, half of the FAA's controllers had joined the ATCA, including Jack Maher and Mike Rock.[20]

Although the ATCA had obvious limitations, the New York controllers still believed it could become a reform vehicle in the aftermath of the midair collision for two reasons. First, the ATCA promoted a strong ethic of safety and professionalism that provided leverage for controllers who wanted to improve the system. The elements of the ATCA ethic were embodied in the "Controllers' Code," a pledge that the organization disseminated to its members. The code asked controllers to uphold four central obligations of their profession: to their country, which trained them and counted on their competency; to the public they served, whose lives they safeguarded; to their fellow controllers, upon whom they depended; and to themselves, to whom they owed "the personal satisfaction of a professional job well done." These commitments added up to an ethic that the ATCA's Elliott A. McCready proudly called "Controlmanship." As McCready defined it, controlmanship meant placing a premium on safety and resisting the temptation to cut corners in order to "expedite traffic," a constant temptation in a system under ever-increasing pressure. "Let us not forget that if we ignore safety we are betraying the trust that has been vested in us," said one New York controller. This professional ethic, much like the Hippocratic oath of medical doctors, appealed to controllers, who prided themselves on having attained white-collar status in a highly technical and very competitive field without the advantage of a college education. It also gave them a powerful rationale for speaking out in defense of safety and of their profession's integrity.[21]

The second reason to believe the ATCA might help was Francis M. McDermott, a reformer who assumed the position of executive director of the organization in January 1960. Under McDermott's guidance, the ATCA began to speak out more forcefully on behalf of air traffic controllers, even criticizing FAA policies. This must have surprised FAA officials, for McDermott himself was a twenty-two-year veteran administrator in the CAA and FAA. When he worked for the government, McDermott had been known as a technician, not a labor reformer; before joining the ATCA, he last served the FAA as technical adviser to the agency's director of research and development. But once McDermott began to understand the problems that air traffic controllers faced, he took up their cause with zeal. In October 1960, he called for legislation that would allow controllers to retire after twenty years on their high-stress jobs. Just days before the New York accident, he gave a speech in Kansas City in which he alleged that many FAA facilities were using obsolete radar and that the government did not have "the slightest vestige of an overall plan" for its air traffic control system. Unless the FAA acted to improve the situation, he predicted that the country would see traffic jams in the skies as bad as those on city streets.[22]

McDermott refused to pipe down after the New York accident. Prior to the opening of the CAB hearings at the St. George, he spoke out again to say time had almost run out on the "antiquated system" of air traffic control. He called attention to controllers' poor working conditions, which he said would discourage talented people from taking up "such a hazardous and unrewarding occupation." These statements won McDermott an enthusiastic following in Hangar 11 and other overworked FAA facilities. Harried controllers felt that they had finally found their champion. Little did they know that McDermott had numbered his days at the ATCA by speaking out.[23]

The FAA-dominated governing board of the organization was in no mood to tolerate criticism of the agency at the politically sensitive juncture of the worst air disaster in U.S. aviation history and the start of a new presidential administration. John F. Kennedy was sworn in as president days after the hearings at the St. George adjourned. Kennedy's appointee to replace Pete Quesada as FAA administrator, Najeeb E. Halaby, was also anxious to preempt McDermott's efforts to give voice to controllers' discontent. Immediately upon taking the helm of the FAA, Halaby toured the New York area facilities and concluded that they were a "breeding ground" for labor unionism. He feared that McDermott might tap the discontent in these facilities to turn the ATCA into a kind of union, and he resolved to avoid that possibility. During the April 1961 meeting of the ATCA governing council, Halaby requested an unprecedented meeting with the council and also asked that McDermott be excluded from that meeting. Halaby told the ATCA board that he hoped their organization would continue to function as a professional society. If it did, he assured them, the FAA and ATCA would collaborate fruitfully. If not, he warned, then the ATCA and the agency would become antagonists. In the wake of that meeting McDermott resigned, most likely with a strong push from his board, although board members refrained from any public statement. After departing, McDermott remained unapologetic regarding the positions he had taken on behalf of air traffic controllers. The ATCA, meanwhile, moved to erase the McDermott interregnum from the organization's history. Its official publication, the *Journal of Air Traffic Control*, simply excised McDermott's name from its masthead without even mentioning his resignation. To controllers, the message was clear. One concluded that, "They fired him because he was being hardnosed with management."[24]

After McDermott's ouster, it became evident that national ATCA leaders would not allow their organization to lead any internal reform effort within the FAA. The ATCA was so intent on avoiding controversy that its journal did not even comment on the New York midair collision until more than three years had passed. Nationally, the ATCA urged controllers to think twice before criticizing the FAA or its policies. "To qualify for the right of criticism," the *Journal of Air Traffic Control* cautioned members, "a professional is obligated to study and analyze, to test his theories against expected objections, and question even his motivation." Meanwhile, ATCA leaders showered praise on FAA officials for their "character and competency."[25]

As the ATCA became a cheerleader for the FAA, mounting evidence suggested the system was heading for crisis. Within one year of the New York accident, there were three other midair collisions between passenger airliners and smaller general aviation planes. In each case, the larger airliners managed to survive and safely land, but a total of seven people in the smaller aircraft were killed. According to the independent Flight Safety Institute, which studied the industry closely, there were 250 documented "critical incidents" in which two aircraft came within one hundred feet of each other in one four-month period in 1961. Despite the collisions and critical incidents, the ATCA kept quiet. The organization continued to provide a friendly, criticism-free forum for FAA officials.[26]

While the controllers in Hangar 11 rapidly lost faith in the national ATCA after McDermott's ouster, they still hoped that local leaders of the organization might be able to help. In 1962, Bernard M. Raison, a supervisor at New York Center who was sympathetic to controllers' needs, began speaking out on the problems in the system. Raison ran unsuccessfully for national office in the ATCA on a platform advocating relief for air traffic controllers and reform of the FAA. Jack Maher considered Raison "very militant for his day" and yet "very polished" and balanced in his delivery. But FAA officials proved no more tolerant of Raison than they were of McDermott. It was widely known that FAA officials did not appreciate Raison's activism within the ATCA, and New York controllers were convinced that Raison lost his bid for national office only because the ATCA insiders rigged the balloting. Shortly after his unsuccessful campaign, Raison was disciplined for improperly completing paperwork and abruptly transferred from New York Center to Washington Center. Raison would again run for an ATCA office from his new post, and again be defeated. As Mike Rock saw it, the FAA seemed intent on punishing anyone who had the "audacity" to offer "constructive criticism." Many controllers in New York and Washington were inspired by Raison's campaigns, but his fate reinforced controllers' belief that if you "made noise" in the ATCA "your ass was grass."[27]

Unable to count on the ATCA to help improve their lot, the controllers in Hangar 11 were uncertain where to turn. In a twist of fate with profound implications, they were realizing their limited options for organizing at exactly the moment when labor relations in the federal sector were about to undergo a profound transformation.

Towards a New Federal Labor Policy

On the day of the 1960 New York midair collision, newspapers reported President-elect John F. Kennedy's choice of Arthur Goldberg as his secretary of labor. Kennedy's selection of Goldberg, the general counsel of the United Steelworkers of America, was an obvious payback to organized labor for its crucial support in the 1960 election. Goldberg was the prime architect of the 1955 merger that ended the twenty-year rivalry between the American Federation of Labor and the Congress of Industrial Organizations by creating the AFL-CIO. His selection as labor secretary came on the heels of organized labor's heroic get-out-the-vote effort in states such as Illinois, which helped deliver the election to Kennedy. But labor wanted much more from the Kennedy administration than a sympathetic cabinet secretary.[28]

High on the list of the AFL-CIO's priorities was legislation that would allow federal workers to organize unions and bargain collectively.[29] Only ten years earlier, this prospect would have seemed improbable. After the Boston police strike of 1919, there was a widespread backlash against the unionization of workers at any level of government because of the fear that unionization would encourage strikes and paralyze government. That view did not subside much, even during the union upsurge of the New Deal era. Franklin D. Roosevelt rejected the notion that federal workers ought to bargain collectively, linking that possibility to strikes, which he thought would be "unthinkable and intolerable." Opposition to the unionization of government workers carried into the postwar years, and was intensified by a brief postwar strike wave among blue-collar municipal transit, sanitation, and public works employees.[30]

Yet during the 1950s, several developments in private sector labor relations made the unionization of government workers appear less risky to policy makers. The Taft-Hartley Act, passed in 1947, recognized employers' rights to resist unionization, undercutting postwar labor militancy. Communist-influenced unions were ejected from the CIO, opening the door to its ultimate merger with the AFL in a more conservative federation. And private sector labor relations became more routinized, with labor-management conflict contained within the framework of collective bargaining.

These developments made the extension of collective bargaining to government workers seem less threatening.[31]

By the mid-1950s, leading thinkers in the field of public administration began to argue for the introduction of some form of collective bargaining or formalized labor-management conferences to government. In 1955, a special committee of the American Bar Association labelled the labor practices of the federal government "an apparent anachronism," and suggested that a "government which imposes on other employers certain obligations in dealing with their employees may not in good faith refuse to deal with its own public servants on a reasonably favorable basis." When municipal governments in cities like New York and Philadelphia began to bargain collectively with their workers, the federal government seemed increasingly out of step with the times.[32]

Organized labor both seized upon and helped promote this shift in thinking. In the mid-1950s, unions were already beginning to worry about automation sapping their factory-based membership over the long run. Labor leaders were determined to establish a foothold in white-collar jobs. The best opportunity to do that seemed to be in government employment, where labor could exert its political influence to win changes in policy, and where employers were unlikely to resist unions as vigorously as private sector employers. AFL-CIO president George Meany led labor's campaign, arguing that there could be no excuse for continuing to exclude government workers from collective bargaining. Government workers "should not trail along behind the parade of those in private sector employment and private industry," Meany contended. Pointing to what union workers were winning in their contracts, Meany argued that government workers were being left behind. If the federal government wished to avoid destroying the morale of its workers, he argued, it should "recognize without reservation the right of Government employees to maintain a union, and the right to use that union in presenting all sorts of grievances, negotiating on salary and working conditions just the same as the workers in private industry." Meanwhile, Meany and other union leaders deflected one argument against unions in the federal government by assuring policymakers that government workers would "not exercise, or wish to exercise, the right to strike."[33]

With rising calls for a change, the Eisenhower administration considered revising federal policy on recognition of federal workers' unions. The administration's leading advocate for an overhaul was Labor Secretary James

P. Mitchell, a proponent of collective bargaining who had previously directed labor relations for Bloomingdale Brothers. Mitchell did not get far in his effort to change federal policy. He ran into strong opposition from Postmaster General Arthur E. Summerfield, who effectively blocked action on the matter, forcing the Eisenhower administration to limit its efforts to merely cajoling agency heads into pursuing a more collaborative style of management.[34]

With Mitchell's effort blunted, the action shifted to the Democratic Congress, where two veteran legislators took up the cause. Democrat George M. Rhodes of Reading, Pennsylvania, led the way in the House. A Norman Thomas Socialist in his youth, Rhodes had served as president of Reading's Central Labor Union before his election to Congress in 1948. He had introduced his first bill calling for collective bargaining rights for federal workers in 1949. In the Senate, Democrat Olin D. Johnston of Spartanburg, South Carolina, introduced a companion bill. Elected to the Senate in 1944, Johnston was a complex political figure. While he was an ardent New Dealer with a strong labor record, he also defended racial segregation. His segregationist politics did not hinder his defense of federal workers, however. As chairman of the Senate Committee on the Post Office and Civil Service in the 1950s, Johnston made it his personal crusade to extend bargaining rights to them. "*All* government employees should belong to a union," he declaimed. "We in Congress who are their friends need the support of employee organizations to get employee programs and benefits approved, and the stronger the unions are, the easier it is for us to succeed."[35]

The Rhodes-Johnston bill would have recognized the rights of federal workers to organize; mandated that federal agencies "confer" with unions selected by their workers on a wide range of issues, including working conditions and pay scales; and stipulated that unresolved grievances would be placed before an impartial board composed of one management and one labor appointee and chaired by a representative appointed by the secretary of labor. According to one analyst, the bill "stacked the cards so heavily in favor of the organized worker that it was reasonably assumed that its enactment would have led to the large-scale unionization of the federal work force."

The Rhodes-Johnston bill never got to a vote. The Eisenhower administration strongly objected to it provisions. A Pentagon representative warned that it would "undermine management" in the federal government.

With a presidential veto likely, the bill's proponents waited for the day when a Democratic president sat in the White House. That day seemingly arrived on January 20, 1961, when John F. Kennedy took the oath of office, Arthur Goldberg moved into the Labor Department, and the union movement began its push to achieve union rights for federal workers, a push that would soon have a profound impact on air traffic controllers.[36]

PUSHING BACK

The answer has got to be some form of third party intervention.
If we do not grant this [form of dispute resolution] to the unions,
in lieu of the right to strike, it is to be doubted that we will
accomplish much.
— DANIEL PATRICK MOYNIHAN, 1961

A system based on blind faith and obedience must weaken
when faith is shaken by revelation of error or when obedience
no longer can be compelled.
— RUSS SOMMER, 1967

Air traffic controllers and other federal workers did win union rights under
the Kennedy administration. But those rights were far more limited than the
Rhodes-Johnston bill would have offered, and they were not won on Capitol
Hill. Rather, they came from the pen of President John F. Kennedy. Acting
on the advice of those within his administration who feared that Congress
might enact a bill that gave workers too many rights and unions too much
power, Kennedy preempted the legislative process and issued an executive
order intended to placate his labor allies while ensuring that the advent of
collective bargaining in the federal service would alter existing labor relations as little as possible. The result, Executive Order 10988, which was

trumpeted as a huge breakthrough when it was unveiled in 1962, led air traffic controllers and other federal workers to believe that a new era was dawning. No federal workers were quicker than air traffic controllers to seize the opportunity to organize afforded by EO 10988. And none were quicker to discover the order's inadequacies or to realize how much the reality of collective bargaining in the federal sector diverged from its promise. The controllers' disappointed aspirations, combined with continued resistance by the FAA to controller organization, would create a volatile situation by the mid-1960s.

The Shaping of a Weak Executive Order

With a labor-backed president in office, Rhodes, Johnston, and the leaders of organized labor had every reason to believe that their bill would soon become law. In anticipation of the new law, the AFL-CIO's American Federation of Government Employees (AFGE), a union founded in 1932, whose mission of organizing federal workers had yet to be fulfilled on a grand scale, convened a planning meeting in January 1961 to outline an anticipated nationwide organizing effort. "We believe that the sooner organizing campaigns are begun under the new administration the better," explained one union official. The AFL-CIO hoped that the mass organization of federal workers would in turn jump start the movement in sections of the country where union organizing had stalled, such as the South.[1]

Not everyone in the newly seated Democratic administration shared this vision. Some Kennedy officials strenuously opposed the Rhodes-Johnston bill, believing that the introduction of collective bargaining to the federal service would compromise national security. Those who made this argument pointed to the labor agitation underway since the late 1950s at the Florida facilities of the National Aeronautics and Space Administration (NASA). Heavily reliant on skilled machinists, electricians, and construction workers, NASA projects employed a significant percentage of workers from unionized trades. Insisting that union standards be observed on their jobs, these workers staged ninety-two work stoppages between 1956 and 1961 to enforce their demands at Cape Canaveral. Some Kennedy advisers were convinced that a federal collective bargaining law might trigger similar waves of work stoppages elsewhere in government, including agencies charged with defending national security.[2]

Motivated by this fear, Cyrus R. Vance, the general counsel for the Department of Defense, attempted to head off the passage of any federal law. A World War II Navy veteran, product of Yale Law School, Wall Street lawyer, and future secretary of state, Vance was a formidable bureaucratic strategist. Writing to the chairman of the House Post Office and Civil Service Committee, Vance condemned as misguided the effort to "transplant collective bargaining as it is conducted in private industry to the Federal government without giving adequate recognition to the special requirements of the public service." He warned that the Rhodes-Johnston bill would "undermine management" and "create delays and confusion in the operation of the departments and agencies." It was Vance who first urged the president to thwart the legislation by usurping Congress with an executive order. The administration's position would be "strengthened measurably," Vance explained, "if it were possible to state definitively that the President has under consideration and will promulgate at an early date an Executive Order embodying those principles of proposed legislation which are desirable and in the public interest."[3]

Vance even drafted the sort of presidential executive order he had in mind. His draft was designed to extend few new rights to federal workers. It did not mention collective bargaining, mediation of disputes, or arbitration of grievances. It also barred any union from becoming the "exclusive representative for all employees in an activity of the federal government." As one Kennedy adviser explained, Vance's proposal would bring virtually "no significant change in existing regulations."[4]

When labor officials got wind of Vance's activities, they were outraged. They reminded the president that they had sought legislation on federal sector collective bargaining for more than ten years, and they demanded to see any proposed executive order before it was promulgated. Unions also turned to their ally Labor Secretary Goldberg for help.[5]

Labor could not have hoped for a more effective ally in the Kennedy administration than Arthur Goldberg. He was the son of Eastern European Jewish immigrants and a graduate of Northwestern University Law School, who first linked himself to labor during the Depression-era industrial union upsurge in his native Chicago. He had learned the art of political intrigue during his service in World War II, when he helped the Office of Strategic Services organize a network of antifascist labor activists and spies in occupied countries. After the war he rose to become the labor movement's most widely respected legal adviser, before moving on to his position in the Kennedy administration. Once he learned of Vance's plan, Goldberg immediately moved to sidetrack it. If there was to be an executive order drafted on federal union rights, Goldberg wanted to be the one to shape it.[6]

Goldberg pulled in two talented advisers to help him wrest control of the executive order process from Vance. One was Ida Klaus, the labor adviser to New York City Mayor Robert Wagner Jr. A seasoned mediator, and veteran of the World War II–era National War Labor Board, Klaus was the primary architect of the collective bargaining process that Wagner inaugurated through a 1958 executive order that opened the way to bargaining between New York and its municipal unions. She had helped oversee the bargaining relationship that subsequently developed between the city and District 37 of the American Federation of State, County and Municipal Employees (AFSCME), which would become New York's dominant public employee union. On loan from Wagner, Klaus drew on her experience in forging New York's labor relations system to help sketch out a vision for a federal executive order. The second aide to whom Goldberg turned was also a New Yorker, young Daniel Patrick Moynihan, who was already serving on Goldberg's staff. Moynihan was then in the early stages of what would become a storied career that culminated in four terms in the United States Senate. His youth in New York's hardscrabble Hell's Kitchen neighborhood and a stint working as a longshoreman before attending Tufts University on a Navy scholarship made him sympathetic toward labor. Having served as an adviser to New York Governor W. Averell Harriman, Moynihan brought with him an unusual combination of political acumen and analytical brilliance.[7]

In late April, the White House convened a small group, including Goldberg and Vance's boss, Defense Secretary Robert S. McNamara, to discuss how to proceed in response to Vance's memo and draft executive order. Goldberg was ready. He argued forcefully for a thorough study, which he wanted to lead, before the drafting of a presidential order. While Kennedy wanted to preempt the Rhodes-Johnston bill, he had no desire to alienate his union allies, and he knew Goldberg had their trust. So Kennedy took Goldberg's advice. On April 29, he chose Goldberg to chair an "informal study group" that would outline a process for creating an executive order on labor. Members of the study group included John W. Macy Jr., chairman of the Civil Service Commission (CSC); Postmaster General J. Edward Day;

David Bell, director of the Bureau of the Budget; and a representative chosen by Defense Secretary Robert S. McNamara.[8]

Having taken charge of the process, Goldberg convened a series of meetings out of which came a recommendation that the president empower the group as his Task Force on Employee-Management Relations in the Federal Service and give them until the end of the calendar year to hold hearings, collect research, and draft an executive order for his signature.[9] On June 21, 1961, Kennedy accepted these recommendations and named Goldberg to chair the task force. Goldberg in turn named Moynihan as staff director of the initiative.[10]

Five months of difficult wrangling ensued. Agencies ranging from the FAA to the Central Intelligence Agency argued their work was vital to the national security, and therefore ought to be exempt from any order regarding collective bargaining. Meanwhile, conservatives of both parties attacked the task force, warning that its recommendations might force workers to join unions and increase the government's labor costs. Navigating the bureaucratic and political shoals posed no easy task for Moynihan, who devoted most of his time to this project during the last half of 1961.[11]

Throughout the meetings of the task force, organized labor, which was disappointed that the legislative route had been closed, pushed hard for its own vision of federal bargaining rights. The AFL-CIO quickly agreed to three of the task force's prerequisites for any federal executive order: only organizations that did not discriminate on the basis of race would be eligible for government recognition; no federal employee would be required to join a union; and federal employee unions would not be permitted to strike. In return, labor wanted several items. One was a "dues check-off" arrangement, in which the government would automatically deduct union dues from the paychecks of union members, turning over the receipts to the unions. Other demands included the right to bargain over a wide array of issues, such as pay, the right to third-party arbitration of unresolved grievances, the creation of national bargaining units within federal agencies wherever possible, and the constitution of a national board that could rule on labor-management disputes in the federal sector just as the National Labor Relations Board did in the private sector.[12]

There was strong resistance to most of these demands within the administration. While unions wanted workers to pay a representation fee for the unions' service of bargaining on their behalf and handling their grievances, the administration did not want any policy that made it appear that workers were forced to pay dues. While unions wanted a wide scope of bargaining, federal agencies were determined to restrict bargaining as much as possible. While unions wanted national bargaining units, federal agencies wanted to keep bargaining units limited to individual facilities, thereby diluting union bargaining power. Resistance to labor's idea of a "Government Labor-Management Relations Panel" was most intense. Unions wanted a board composed of seven public members appointed by the president, which would be capable of intervening in deadlocked negotiations to "assist the parties in arriving at a settlement through whatever voluntary methods and procedures it may consider appropriate." If mediation failed, the panel would hold public hearings, deliberate on the evidence, and issue a decision that would be "final and binding upon all parties" unless revoked by the president. This demand was simply unacceptable to Chairman Macy of the Civil Service Commission, whose agency would have been marginalized by such a board.[13]

In the end it proved impossible for Goldberg and Moynihan to craft the sort of executive order the labor movement desired within the context of internal administration opposition. Still, Moynihan tried his best. In November 1961, it fell to him to summarize the task force's findings in a way acceptable both to labor and the Kennedy administration. Moynihan did his best to square the circle. His recommendations came close to what labor wanted. He favored a liberal definition of the scope of bargaining. "All matters relating to wages, hours, and working conditions, which are not fixed by law, executive order, or government-wide regulations issued to carry out laws and executive orders, should be subject to negotiation," he suggested. However, in deference to the administration's more conservative voices, he argued that the scope of bargaining would need to be widened gradually and only after the government gained "some experience with labor-management relations within the present spectrum." Moynihan also agreed with labor's position favoring large, agency-wide, or national bargaining units. Most important, he took labor's side on the need for an oversight agency. He suggested that it be called the "Federal Employee-Management Relations Board." It could guide federal agencies in a new way of doing business, which was bound to take "a long period of education and gradual adjustment," he pointed out. In an effort to mollify Macy, Moynihan suggested that the board could be housed within the CSC.

Moynihan believed that the creation of an agency that could resolve labor disputes under the new system was "the central question" before the commission. He feared what might happen if the government recognized workers' rights to organize and negotiate with their employer but provided "no way to get out of an impasse" in negotiations. "The answer has got to be some form of third-party intervention," he wrote. "If we do not grant this to the unions, in lieu of the right to strike, it is to be doubted that we will accomplish much. Indeed, unless we provide some way out of deadlocked negotiations, it would seem rather questionable to start down this road at all."[14]

Moynihan's words were prescient, but they failed to persuade recalcitrants within the task force and the White House. In the end, the ideological dispositions of task force members and the bureaucratic imperatives of the agencies they represented won out over his arguments. The representatives of the CSC, the Defense Department, and the Bureau of the Budget alike were determined to secure a narrowly constructed executive order, and they got their way. The final report, presented to the president on November 30, 1961, did not adopt Moynihan's controversial recommendations.[15]

Labor leaders were disappointed by the draft order the White House drew up in response to the task force report in December 1961. The definition of "employee organization" in the draft order seemed to allow nonunion organizations dominated by management (such as the ATCA) the right to represent workers. It also provided for three confusing levels of recognition. Any legitimate employee organization that petitioned for it could be granted "informal" recognition, which entitled it to present its views to an agency. Organizations that demonstrated support from at least ten percent of workers in a unit would receive "formal" recognition, entitling them to meet and confer with agency officials on labor matters. Finally, organizations that demonstrated majority support in a bargaining unit could receive "exclusive" recognition, allowing them to negotiate agreements with management. A wide range of substantial workplace issues were excluded from negotiation, however, including pay and management's ability to hire, fire, and transfer employees, or to determine the methods, means, and personnel by which operations were to be conducted. Indeed, the words "collective" and "bargaining" never appeared in the order. Finally, the order entrusted to the Civil Service Commission—an agency wedded to the pre–collective bargaining model of labor relations—responsibility for interpreting and implementing the new policy.[16]

Deeply disappointed, unions sent their objections to the White House. They managed to win slight changes in language to prevent management-dominated organizations from representing workers. But they could not fix what they saw as many of the order's deficiencies. The lack of an oversight agency other than the CSC was particularly galling. In words that could have been taken from Moynihan's confidential November memo to the task force, the AFL-CIO's chief negotiator complained, "Some outside forum is essential in such cases if the order is to provide an effective alternative for the right to strike which the employees of a private employer would have under such circumstances but which is denied under the order to Federal employees." But the AFL-CIO was no more successful than Moynihan in getting the administration to accept this position.[17]

Kennedy's team would not budge. Theodore Sorensen, who led the drafting process within the White House, felt that the administration had gone far enough to accommodate organized labor. "We are showing our goodwill toward employee-union leaders by our new recognition, check-off and other policies," he noted. As it was, Kennedy's staff knew that the president would be accused of rewarding his labor backers with access to the dues money of thousands of federal workers. Moreover, they were confident that labor would hail the narrow-gauge executive order as a breakthrough even though it did not give unions many of the things they wanted, because it gave them one crucial thing they sought: an opportunity to organize federal workers. In this, they were right. Thus, on January 17, 1962, President Kennedy issued Executive Order 10988, titled, "Employee-Management Cooperation in the Federal Service."[18]

As Kennedy's aides suspected, labor leaders put aside their private disappointments and showered praise on the order. AFL-CIO president George Meany called it "a Wagner Act for public employees." Meany's enthusiasm was understandable. Union membership among federal workers bloomed after the order. The largest federal employee union, the American Federation of Government Employees, quadrupled within a few years and, by 1969, 843,000 federal workers were covered by collective bargaining agreements. Meanwhile, the order influenced many states to follow with legislation allowing state and local government employees to organize. In 1959, Wisconsin became the first state to pass a public sector collective bargaining law. By 1970, twenty-two states followed Wisconsin's lead, influenced by the trend in the federal sector. As states and municipalities began bargaining with their workers, public sector union membership jumped tenfold bet-ween the mid-1950s and the mid-1970s. This surge was the biggest break-through for labor since the New Deal.[19]

Yet the defects of EO 10988 soon became apparent to the unions. The power given to the Civil Service Commission to interpret and implement the policy was perhaps the largest flaw. While CSC chairman Macy publicly hailed the order as the end of a "papa-knows-best attitude in any level of management," he worked tirelessly to limit the order's influence in pro-moting collective bargaining in the federal civil service. The CSC recom-mended against the recognition of agency-wide negotiating units, consistently interpreted union rights narrowly, and refused to make agency rosters available to unions that wanted to contact workers. The CSC also decided that workers who did not vote in union elections should be assumed to oppose union representation, making it harder for unions to achieve exclusive recognition status. The commission's approach rankled organized labor. "The Executive Order pulled the rug from under the government unions just as they were about to pluck the golden apple," Wilson R. Hart, the foremost expert on federal labor issues explained. "It gave them what they *said* they wanted (recognition), while it deprived them of the windfall they hoped would come with it." As another commentator aptly put it, the order gave unions rights "mid-way between those held by unions in private employment and those of the Soviet Union." It was in this inauspicious con-text that air traffic controllers looked to EO 10988 hoping for relief.[20]

THE BIRTH OF AIR TRAFFIC CONTROLLER UNIONISM

When New York Center, which had been housed in Hangar 11 at Idlewild Airport, moved to an area near MacArthur Airport in Islip, in July 1963, the air traffic controllers of Hangar 11 followed their jobs to the new facility, a windowless building whose exterior bristled with antennae. Like millions of Americans who left urban, working-class neighborhoods for suburbia in the postwar years, Maher, Rock, and their coworkers sought a better life—a middle-class life. Moving out to the middle of Long Island, they left behind Hangar 11's World War II–vintage equipment, but not the stresses of their jobs or the pressures of FAA managers who cared only about how quickly they "pushed tin." As a result, they carried with them the idea that took hold in the aftermath of the 1960 midair collision: they needed an organization that would defend their interests and make their jobs sustainable. Inspired by Kennedy's executive order, and unaware of the degree to which its provisions made it an ineffectual instrument, they came to believe they had a right to organize and negotiate with their employer, the FAA. To men who already shared much in common, including abundant family connections to unions, it nourished a thought that came naturally to them: by organizing, they could improve their lot. In time, the activists among them would find that the order's promises were chimerical, and the organizations it fostered impotent. That discovery would change them.[21]

The Air Traffic Control Association (ATCA) initially benefited from EO 10988, simply because it was the only organization on the ground in FAA facilities. About three hundred controllers joined the ATCA in one day at New York Center in 1964, believing that they could convert their chapter into a vehicle for bargaining collectively with the facility chief. In doing so, controllers hoped to finally address those issues of mandatory overtime, trash cleaning, dress codes, and more. Such aspirations extended far beyond New York Center. At O'Hare International Airport in Chicago, at Atlanta Municipal Airport, and elsewhere, controllers turned hopefully toward their local ATCA chapters. Now that the law allowed federal workers to organize and negotiate with their bosses, the controllers were ready to take advantage of that opportunity.[22]

That ATCA won the right to represent controllers in some facilities revealed the vagaries of EO 10988 as interpreted by the CSC. The presidential order specifically barred organizations that included supervisors in their ranks from negotiating on behalf of federal workers. The ATCA not only included management among its members, but FAA officials dominated its governance. Nevertheless, the CSC let many ATCA chapters apply for recognition as the exclusive representative of air controllers in individual facilities. The ATCA took advantage of these rulings and argued that it, rather than a union, was better equipped to speak for controllers. Unions had "absolutely no understanding of the profession of air traffic control," insisted one ATCA leader, and would simply protect "the weak controller of questionable ability."[23]

The field was wide open for the ATCA for more than a year, for it took that long for any unions to begin organizing controllers. Nor was it initially clear which unions might be best positioned to challenge the ATCA. The American Federation of Government Employees (AFGE) started signing up controllers in the Rocky Mountains as members, and the International Association of Machinists (IAM) developed a following in the Southwest as they parlayed their strength in airport maintenance shops into an organizing effort in control towers. But by 1964 a small Boston-based union not affiliated with the AFL-CIO found the greatest success in the race to organize controllers: the National Association of Government Employees (NAGE).[24]

NAGE was founded in 1961 and led by a wily Bostonian named Kenneth T. Lyons. It originated as the Federal Employees Veterans Association, an association established after the war to lobby on behalf of the employees and veterans of the Charlestown Navy Yard. Its Boston base gave it connections to Democrats with influence in the Kennedy administration. Lyons closely monitored the workings of the Goldberg task force, and in 1961 he changed the name of his organization to position it to take advantage of any opening Goldberg might create. Although NAGE tried organizing in several federal agencies once EO 10988 was promulgated, Lyons soon focused on the FAA as fertile territory largely neglected by other unions. He put a former air traffic controller named Stanley Lyman in charge of organizing controllers.[25]

From the beginning, Lyons and Lyman sought to distinguish NAGE from the ATCA. NAGE announced that it would "not play dummy or 'yes man'" to the FAA. Instead, NAGE delivered harsh critiques of the FAA, pointing out that it was mismanaging the system, understaffing facilities, and causing controllers to handle a punishing workload of takeoffs and landings for five hours at a time without relief. Shrewdly, Lyman campaigned for two reforms with broad appeal among controllers: the opportunity to retire after twenty years on the job, and an expansion of the "familiarization flight" (or FAM) program, which allowed controllers to fly for free in the cockpit jump seats of passenger planes (from that vantage point they would presumably learn how to better direct pilots, having seen things from the pilots' point of view). In the early 1960s, only fully checked-out controllers were allowed to take FAMs. NAGE demanded their extension to developmental controllers as well, reasoning that insights gained on these flights were an essential part of training. NAGE also pointed out that FAMs would train controllers to better do their jobs, whereas airline workers who were granted similar travel privileges in empty coach seats (a widespread industry practice) were merely enjoying a travel benefit.[26]

Armed with these popular proposals, NAGE did well in representation elections held in air traffic control facilities in 1964, establishing strongholds throughout New England, at Washington Center, and Miami Center before the end of the year. Some controllers formed independent associations, such as the John F. Kennedy Air Traffic Controllers Association in New York (the Idlewild airport was renamed for the slain president in December 1963). But by 1965, NAGE constituted the most potent threat to the ATCA.[27]

The representation fight produced a bitter rivalry between the two organizations. It was not just a struggle for access to dues-paying members; it was a "philosophy fight," as Mike Rock aptly termed it. NAGE and ATCA embodied very different visions. The ATCA decried "the threat of organized 'industrial type unionism'" that was "infiltrating many air traffic control facilities." "Beware of the NAGE or any other union coming into a tower," warned one ATCA leader. NAGE, by contrast, emphasized that it was a union, and staked out adversarial positions to show controllers that it would stand up to what it called the "dictatorial atmosphere" in FAA facilities.[28]

The institutional culture of the FAA helped shape the outcome of this rivalry. Few, if any, government agencies proved more resistant to EO 10988 than the FAA. The vast majority of the FAA's air traffic control workforce was made up of military veterans, and the agency was permeated by a hierarchical command-and-control culture from top to bottom. The notion that managers ought to negotiate with controllers about any aspect of their work was anathema to nearly all FAA managers from control tower watch supervisors to top Washington administrators. To Los Angeles Center controller Russ Sommer, it seemed as if the FAA simply wished the executive order "would conveniently 'go away.'" Sommer's view was shared by Edward V. Curran, an experienced labor relations officer hired by the FAA in 1964. Curran, who before joining the government had negotiated with unions on behalf of railroad employers, found that FAA facility supervisors routinely ignored his advice about how to negotiate with unions. They preferred not to negotiate at all.[29]

The harder the FAA fought EO 10988, the more the agency drove controllers toward NAGE. At times, FAA opposition could get petty. At Boston Center in Nashua, New Hampshire, management refused to grant the NAGE local's request for a mailbox in the facility until the union dropped its demand that management guarantee a chair for every controller working the radar room. Such obstructionism convinced many controllers that NAGE's

confrontational approach to the FAA was superior to the ATCA's coopera-
tive posture. Thus, between 1965 and 1967, NAGE pulled ahead of ATCA
in the fight to represent controllers. The FAA worried about the "gradual
withdrawal from the Air Traffic Control Association into a more militant,
rebellious group" as ATCA membership dropped by half between 1961 and
1967. Yet FAA administrators remained oblivious to their own role in
building NAGE.[30]

Two developments contributed to NAGE's growing advantage. The first
was a bungled attempt by the FAA to force controllers to submit to a psychi-
atric examination, a fiasco that provided the biggest single boost to the fortunes of NAGE. On October 15, 1965, the FAA ordered the psychological
testing of the entire air traffic controller workforce as a means of uncovering
"hidden emotional or social tendencies" and "weeding out controllers who
might crack under the strain" of their jobs. The order required controllers to
take a written personality test devised by Dr. Raymond B. Cattell of the
University of Illinois. If they scored poorly, they were scheduled for a psy-
chiatric evaluation. If that went badly, they could be disqualified from
controlling air traffic. Any controller who appealed his disqualification had
to pay the expenses of his case review.[31]

The order outraged controllers. Rather than dealing with the job's major
stressors—such as a growing number of flights, forced overtime, and out-
dated equipment—officials were threatening to remove the victims of the
FAA's poorly managed system. Controllers were further enflamed by the
suspicion that the FAA might use these tests to weed out "troublemakers"
who questioned FAA policies. Then there was the content of the exams
themselves. Controllers could not understand why they were asked to agree
or disagree with statements like, "I admire the beauty of a fairy tale more
than that of a well-made gun." Nor did they understand the need for questions about their views of birth control, their "reaction to the opposite sex,"
or the "nation's involvement in international affairs." Russ Sommer, founder
of the NAGE local at Los Angeles Center, who had emerged as the leading
NAGE activist among controllers in the Los Angeles area, called the exams
"the *coup de grace* to employee faith in management." Nationally, NAGE
leaders denounced the "psycho tests," charging that they were designed to
humiliate controllers and "strip them of their dignity."[32]

The FAA could not have picked a worse time to propose these tests. Not
only were contests for union representation heating up around the country,

but the U.S. Senate had also begun to investigate violations of federal employees' privacy rights. In October 1964, the Senate Subcommittee on Administrative Practice and Procedure sent a questionnaire to federal agencies seeking to determine whether the privacy of employees was "being undermined through misuse of electronic 'bugging' devices and other methods of surveillance." Democratic Senator Russell B. Long of Louisiana did not like what the investigation turned up. "The further we dig," Long reported, "the more disturbing information we uncover." In February 1965, the Executive Council of the AFL-CIO weighed in to condemn the use of surveillance and polygraphs on federal workers. In the context of growing concerns over the abridgement of federal workers' privacy, the FAA "psycho inquisition" ignited a storm of protest.[33]

NAGE locals immediately turned the issue to their advantage. Controllers in Buffalo refused as a group to take the written test. Soon others declined to take the written exams, saying they would only submit to private personal interviews with the "head shrinkers." The FAA tried to crush this resistance with severe penalties. When Duane Leggett, who worked in the tower of Los Angeles International Airport, refused to take the "psycho test," he was reassigned to Los Angeles Center, downgraded to a lower-paid, flight-data position, and saddled with a ninety-mile commute to his new workplace. News of such responses merely infuriated controllers all the more.[34]

At Los Angeles Center, the controversy became especially intense thanks to the leadership of Russ Sommer, a big, blunt-spoken man who had grown up on an Idaho ranch. Sommer had joined the FAA in 1961 after his discharge from the Air Force. His first posting was a small facility in Rawlins, Wyoming, relaying weather reports. He sought a transfer to the new Los Angeles Center when it opened in Palmdale in March 1963, because he wanted a little more excitement in his work. The "psycho test" typified for him the style of FAA management that had led him to found Palmdale's NAGE local: he thought the FAA placed "more value on a worthless piece of paper than upon the dignity of an individual." It was outrageous to be asked about one's feelings about "sex, attitude toward the police, political leanings (conservative/liberal), and whether we could look a man straight in the face while lying," Sommer decided. An employee's right to privacy should be "sacred, as long as he is performing his duties responsibly."[35]

In the summer of 1966, NAGE took its fight to Congress, with the Los Angeles Center local providing crucial evidence. The timing was propitious.

Senator Sam Ervin, the North Carolina Democrat later made famous by his leadership of the Senate committee that investigated the Watergate scandal, had recently introduced a "federal workers' bill of rights" that aimed to end intrusions against federal employees' privacy. Ervin's bill quickly attracted thirty-three cosponsors. As Ervin sought votes for his bill, the FAA proved to be an ideal foil, its psychological exam providing a perfect illustration of the "totalitarian" abuses he sought to end. The bill never became law, but with NAGE locals supplying information to Ervin's staff, and NAGE president Ken Lyons testifying on Capitol Hill, the FAA came under a withering drumbeat of criticism.[36]

Reeling before this political onslaught, the agency had no choice but to modify its policy. At first it allowed controllers to leave test questions blank without penalty. Then it promised to revamp the test and delete intrusive questions. NAGE was having none of it. The union said it would accept no such tests designed by the FAA. "Psychologists agree, *no* testing program can be valid if the assessors do not have the confidence of those being tested," Russ Sommer contended. When Los Angeles Center officials offered to meet privately with Sommer to work out a backroom deal on the program, Sommer refused. "This subject is too vital to be confined to a room or to a few of us," he replied.[37]

As one Newark controller put it, "a rotten employer will create a union every time." The "psycho tests" provided the best illustration yet to thousands of controllers that they needed a union, and NAGE's fortunes improved every day that it fought the exam. By September 1967, NAGE had won recognition for forty-one air traffic control locals and claimed to be the largest federal government union independent of the AFL-CIO. The leaders of the ATCA—who had initially supported the test—were slow to realize how much their position had cost them. In 1967, the ATCA belatedly criticized the "calloused and harsh administration and mismanagement" of the program, and called for it to be dropped. But it was too late by then for the ATCA to recover the ground it had lost to NAGE.[38]

The second opening that NAGE exploited concerned the onset of a deepening crisis in the air traffic control system in the mid-1960s. The system's problems had been simmering since before the New York midair collision of 1960. But some dated the onset of an acute stage in the crisis to June 7, 1963, which became known as "Black Friday" at the FAA. On that day, due to a confluence of high traffic and bad flying weather, New York Center handled thirty-seven hundred instrument operations—four hundred more than its previous record. Between 1963 and 1968, such surges in air traffic became common. The airline industry was bustling and profitable during these years, with airlines boasting a record 11.8 percent profit average on operating revenues in 1965. By 1966, the FAA's 304 control towers were handling forty-five million takeoffs and landings, twice the number handled in 1956. In 1967 there were twenty-three hundred airliners and one hundred thousand private or "general aviation" aircraft crowding American airspace. The bulk of this traffic congested around the 107 U.S. airports that were equipped to handle jets.[39]

It was by far the world's largest system of air transportation, and the FAA simply failed to keep pace with its surging growth. The equipment needs were glaring. As the air travel boom began, some facilities were still using radar equipment inherited from World War II naval vessels. As one controller put it, "We are trying to provide service to six hundred-knot jets with radar equipment designed twenty years ago for ten-knot battleships." The personnel needs were equally evident. Just as traffic began mushrooming in the mid-1960s, the FAA instituted a hiring freeze largely because of the budgetary demands of the Vietnam War. As a result, burdens on controllers relentlessly increased.[40]

The consequences of inadequate equipment and insufficient staffing all too often proved fatal. Between 1962 and 1966, the FAA experienced an average of twelve fatal crashes annually. On December 4, 1965, an Eastern Airlines Constellation heading from Boston to Newark had part of its tail clipped off by the wing of a TWA Boeing 707 en route from San Francisco to New York. The damaged TWA jet made an emergency landing at JFK Airport, but the Eastern flight crashed in Westchester County. Thanks to a heroic feat of piloting, only four passengers died. In July 1967, however, a midair collision between a Piedmont Airlines Boeing 727 and a twin-engine Cessna 310 near Hendersonville, North Carolina, did not end as well. Eighty-two people were lost.[41]

The North Carolina accident contributed to a spike in fatal crashes during 1967. In the first eight months of that year, the FAA tallied ten fatal incidents. Determined to get the spiraling crisis under control, Lyndon Johnson's FAA administrator, Air Force General William "Bozo" McKee, asked director of the FAA Eastern Region Oscar Bakke, who was both an experienced pilot and a veteran FAA administrator, to come to Washington to lead a group charged with devising solutions. Before he could take up his assignment, Bakke nearly fell victim to the problem he was asked to solve. While flying a DC-3 on a training run over Paterson, New Jersey, on September 11, 1967, Bakke saw a jet in the distance coming directly at him. He radioed New York Center controllers to see if they had any traffic to advise him about. They told him all was clear. The jet simply did not show up on their radar scopes. Bakke quickly took evasive action, slowing the climb of his DC-3 and letting the other jet shoot overhead, missing him by a mere five hundred feet.[42]

As the number of such incidents grew, NAGE decided in March 1967 to make safety concerns their top priority for the first time in their organizing. Citing a "hair-raising increase in the number of near-collisions in and around airports," NAGE called for a congressional investigation. FAA facilities were "seriously under-equipped, under-manned, under-compensated and under-administered," facing a "steadily mounting danger of costly air tragedies," Ken Lyons claimed. NAGE further alleged that the FAA was covering up the severity of the problem by underreporting the number of "conflictions" (near midair collisions). NAGE's *FedNews* asserted that there was at least one confliction, and sometimes as many as five, on an average day at New York Center. To deal with the problem, NAGE demanded a 20 percent increase in controller staffing, the purchase of modernized radar equipment, and the creation of an ad hoc committee of journeymen controllers whose members could offer reform recommendations to Congress.[43]

NAGE's criticisms and demands outraged the FAA, but the agency could not ignore them. Deputy Administrator Dave Thomas appointed an unofficial task force to investigate. That initiative led the FAA to promise a series of dramatic reforms in May 1967. It pledged to hire six hundred new controllers, create an annual "Captain's Fund" at each FAA facility for use in improving controllers' morale, and reconfigure watch schedules to "match people to traffic." It also promised to pay overtime to controllers who were forced to put in more than forty hours per week and give controllers two consecutive weeks of scheduled vacation leave at some point during the year. Lyons immediately claimed that NAGE's pressure had won these "humane and sensible" reforms.[44]

The FAA then proceeded to destroy its own credibility by failing to keep these promises. Ultimately, the agency lacked the budgetary authority to follow through on its pledges. Administrator Bozo McKee sympathized with controllers. "If I had my way, they would work five days a week, six hours a day on the radar scopes, and spend the other two hours in training," he privately confided. But McKee's budget could not fund overtime pay. Coming up with that money would require authorizing legislation from Congress, an especially difficult proposition during a year when the costs of the Vietnam War were escalating. With the FAA reneging on its pledges, controllers' morale plummeted. NAGE promptly set up informational picket lines outside airports, leafleting travelers about the problems air traffic controllers were facing, and carrying signs that laid all the blame for those problems on the FAA.[45]

In truth, FAA officials were not entirely to blame. Their ability to alleviate the problems controllers complained about was constrained by the larger politics of the Johnson administration. On October 15, 1967, Congress created the U.S. Department of Transportation. The previously autonomous Federal Aviation Agency was transferred to the new department, where it became the Federal Aviation Administration (and was relegated to equal status with the Federal Highway Administration, the Railroad Administration, and the Coast Guard within the new department). To head the department, Johnson chose Alan Boyd, then undersecretary for transportation in the Commerce Department. No sooner had Boyd taken the reins of the new agency than he realized that Johnson would not support a massive increase in transportation funding while the Vietnam War was straining the nation's finances. Johnson allowed Boyd to request only $7 million to supplement his budget, too little to help the FAA. Johnson also insisted that fees levied on airlines and travelers, not tax revenues, fund any further increases in the FAA budget. Johnson's desire to improve the air traffic system with user fees was little more than a hope. Since Harry S. Truman, every president had sought such fees. Each time, airline lobbyists made sure that the user fee hikes died in the congressional committees that considered them. With no way to pay for the improvements that everyone agreed were necessary, controllers grew restive.[46]

Beyond NAGE

The flaws in EO 10988, which were manifested so clearly by controllers' frustrated efforts to organize to improve the FAA, were also becoming clear to unionists in other parts of the government. By the mid-1960s, EO 10988 was seen as a failure by many in organized labor. As early as January 1964, labor leaders indicated that they were "considerably less than satisfied" with the implementation of the order, and began pressuring President Johnson to correct its flaws. The AFL-CIO formed a committee of public sector union leaders to recommend improvements in the order and recruited sympathetic legislators to introduce bills that would write the reforms into law. Seeking to head off a potentially divisive legislative battle on the issue, Johnson promised to correct the problems with a revised executive order. AFL-CIO leaders reluctantly acquiesced to Johnson's desire to reform the regime through administrative rather than legislative action. But administrative reform proved elusive. After some delay, President Johnson finally established a President's Review Committee on Federal Employee-Management Relations in 1967, naming his labor secretary, W. Willard Wirtz, as its chair. Before Wirtz could bring forward a revised executive order for Johnson's signature, however, Richard Nixon was elected president, thereby nullifying several years of labor's behind-the-scenes efforts to fix EO 10988.[47]

It was in the context of Johnson's failure to repair the flawed executive order that the air traffic controllers' organizing took a militant turn in the summer and fall of 1967. These were volatile months for the country. Racial conflict erupted in Chicago, Detroit, Newark, and other cities as the civil rights movement brought its demands to the North. At the same time, protests against the Vietnam War escalated, leading to a massive march on the Pentagon in October 1967. Another social movement often neglected by historians was also sweeping across American cities that year: state and local government workers were leading the largest surge in unionization since the emergence of industrial unions in the 1930s. By 1967, teachers, social workers, fire fighters, police officers, sanitation workers, and others were organizing and raising a cry for "trade union rights for public employees NOW!" as public sector collective bargaining laws proliferated in the states.[48]

These new public sector unions were not afraid to strike, even though no state had recognized that right. New York City was the epicenter of the new militancy. Since the passage of the Condon-Wadlin Act by New York State in 1947, strikes by government workers were deemed illegal and were punishable by firing. In the 1960s, New York City's workers repeatedly defied the law. Teachers struck in 1960 and 1962 under the leadership of Albert Shanker and the United Federation of Teachers. In 1965, social workers walked out with support from Jerry Wurf, the fiery leader of District 37 of the American

Federation of State, County and Municipal Employees (AFSCME) who had won election as the union's national president in 1964. And transit workers idled buses and subways in January 1966. No one was fired in these strikes, and in each case the unions made gains. The examples coming from New York public unions inspired government employees elsewhere. As other workers followed suit, public sector strikes rose from a mere 15 in 1958 to 254 by 1968.[49]

As the air traffic controllers of metropolitan New York saw teachers, subway drivers, and social workers make gains through militant union action, it was only natural that they would become dissatisfied with the FAA's slow pace of reform. Their impatience had been sharpened by repeated disappointments. That impatience now began to turn against NAGE. Having largely thrust the ATCA aside, NAGE proved unable to successfully channel the growing disenchantment that its campaigns had helped to coalesce.[50]

On paper, NAGE looked strong. By March 1967, it claimed a membership of eight thousand, well more than half of the FAA's controller workforce. But it had little to show for its membership gains. Facility-level negotiations yielded scant gains for the controllers and, thanks to the flaws of EO 10988, there was no agency-wide bargaining in the FAA. No federal workers more urgently needed an agency-wide process to address their fundamental issues than air traffic controllers, who were facing systemic problems. Yet NAGE did nothing to try to engage the FAA on the national level. As a result, controllers were pessimistic about the chances of addressing the main workplace issues on their minds: overtime pay, the hiring of more controllers, and the purchase of new equipment.[51]

NAGE leaders placed the blame on EO 10988. "It is a myth to think for one instant that government employees get a fair shake from management via the executive order," Ken Lyons insisted. Lyons argued that federal workers had "rapidly outgrown the executive order" and, emulating the militant tone of AFSCME's Jerry Wurf, he hinted that controllers would demand immediate action on their problems, even if it took an illegal strike to get that action. "The era of Calvin Coolidge," when government workers did not have the right to strike, "has long vanished," Lyons declared, in a reference to the former U.S. president, who, as governor of Massachusetts, famously broke a strike by Boston police officers in 1919.[52]

Yet Lyons did little more than spout fiery rhetoric, for, in truth, NAGE was part of the problem. From its inception, NAGE was a general union, not a union of air traffic controllers. It aspired to be the largest independent union of federal workers and sought to organize members in multiple agencies, often competing head to head with the AFGE, the federal workers' union affiliated with the AFL-CIO. As a result, Lyons never saw a need to pull NAGE's air traffic controller locals into a cohesive national organization. NAGE never even held a national meeting of air traffic control leaders. In place of an agency-wide plan to improve the lot of air traffic controllers, NAGE simply puffed up its meager accomplishments. When the FAA announced its promised reforms in May 1967, the union's newspaper declared it one of the greatest labor victories in American history and compared Lyons to "a 'young Gompers or Meany' in labor movement stature." (No revised assessment of Lyons's place in labor's pantheon was offered when the FAA reneged on its promises.) NAGE's excessive propaganda only jaundiced controllers' views of the union.[53]

Lacking strong national direction, the most active local organizations of controllers began to assert leadership on their own. The first to do so was the ATCA organization at Chicago's O'Hare International Airport. Directing traffic through the nation's largest hub, O'Hare controllers were arguably the most stressed in the United States. Working under conditions of enormous pressure, they handled 519,430 takeoffs and landings, or "operations," in 1965. The next busiest facility handled eighty thousand fewer operations than O'Hare. Even so, the workload of O'Hare controllers grew heavier over the next two years. On September 9, 1966, O'Hare controllers set a single-day record by handling more than two thousand operations. During long stretches of that day, they averaged one operation every thirty seconds; during the busy dinner hour, the average was one per twenty seconds. Only elite controllers were capable of completing on-the-job training and "checking out" at O'Hare. Yet, as talented as they were, the constant stress of the place took its toll. In the mid-1960s, O'Hare tower could not keep a full complement of journeymen controllers on hand. The pace was simply too punishing. Announcements that the facility was accepting bids on open positions usually attracted few bidders, even though a move to O'Hare would include a significant raise in pay for most controllers. Most of those who did bid for positions there washed out during the training period. Why would someone want to work at O'Hare when they could find work at big facilities in fair-weather cities such as Atlanta, Miami, and Los Angeles that paid just as well and promised less stress?[54]

O'Hare controllers had never warmed to NAGE. In part because they remained outside of it, they did not wait for a national union to come to their aid. They decided that they not only deserved higher pay than controllers elsewhere, but that it was in the FAA's interest that they get it. Unless they managed to raise their pay, they reasoned, the FAA would never attract a full complement of controllers to their facility. The problem was that there was no way within the system for controllers to make this demand of the FAA. According to EO 10988, the FAA was forbidden to bargain with controllers over pay, even if the agency wanted to. But living and working in a union city, the O'Hare controllers were familiar with the power of a job action.[55]

In August 1966, controllers at O'Hare decided to make use of a time-honored union tactic and began a slowdown in protest of their pay and working conditions. It was an independent action, not sanctioned or cleared with national ATCA officials, and it was not difficult to orchestrate. All the controllers had to do was "go by the book"—handle traffic just as the FAA's guidelines mandated. That meant suspending an innovation they had developed that allowed them to handle the surge in traffic they witnessed in the mid-1960s. The innovation was a carefully choreographed dance called the "hold short." FAA regulations provided for a minimum spacing of three miles on jets as they approached an airport for landing, but when traffic got particularly heavy, O'Hare approach controllers could reduce the spacing to two-and-a-half miles, sometimes less. As tower controllers cleared closely-spaced aircraft for landing, they instructed their pilots to "hold short" immediately after touchdown. That meant that as soon as possible after touch down pilots should put their jet engines into reverse, slam on brakes, and turn their planes off the runway at the first available exit, clearing the runway for a jet that was about to touch down right behind them. Pilots appreciated the maneuver. They much preferred it to being "stacked" in long circular holding patterns awaiting a turn to land, or having controllers "spin" them—the process of ordering a jet that was in line to land to circle the airport again because the jet ahead of them had not yet cleared the runway. Spinning a single jet during one of the busiest periods could cause a traffic jam that would extend more than one hundred miles from the airport.[56]

The O'Hare controllers called it "Operation Snowman." Its details were worked out by the tower's most respected controllers and shared with crews during shift meetings. On August 24, 1966, controller Hugh Riddle gave a cryptic warning of its onset to the press. "The rush hours are going to get 'rushier,'" he said. Within days, the O'Hare controllers stopped using the hold short. Instead, they did what the FAA manual instructed. They cleared pilots for landing, watched them touch down, waited until they were under control and then instructed them to take the next left turn off the runway toward their arrival gate. Operating like this, it was impossible to space planes at three miles or less without having to spin some. As traffic backed up, approach controllers would increase the separation between incoming jets in order to re-slot any planes that were being spun. This increased separation cascaded outward in concentric circles that extended hundreds of miles from Chicago: flights were delayed as far away as Los Angeles, Miami, and New York.

The FAA's Washington officials were furious. They immediately dispatched a team to Chicago to observe the controllers in order to identify and correct the problem. Yet the FAA never admitted that a slowdown was in progress. If it had done so, it would have had to concede that under the FAA's own guidelines controllers could not expeditiously handle the level of traffic they normally directed. Only much later, after the controllers suspended their action, did one FAA official admit that, "if a controller went by the book in a high density area, he could not possibly control all of the traffic."[57]

The O'Hare controllers had shown that they could quickly gain the attention of top Washington officials, but they did not gain immediate relief. After several days, they suspended the slowdown and traffic volume at O'Hare again climbed. In August 1967, the tower set a record once more, handling more than sixty thousand operations, an average of one takeoff or landing every forty-four seconds of every hour of every day of the month. During peak hours on peak days, the tower handled one operation every fifteen seconds.[58]

In response, O'Hare controllers reinstituted the slowdown. This time they called it "Operation Snowball." Again, it snarled air traffic into and out of Chicago. Again, the delays affected travelers hundreds of miles from Chicago. And again, Washington officials descended on O'Hare. By the time this second job action was brought to a close, the controllers had won a huge concession. FAA officials worked out an arrangement with the Civil Service Commission through which O'Hare controllers received a three-step "in-grade" pay increase. The top classification for an air traffic controller at O'Hare at that time was GS-12. The in-grade increases put the O'Hare controllers at the top pay range of GS-12 federal employees, regardless of how long they had been in service at that grade level. This amounted to a raise worth roughly $1,100 to the average O'Hare controller. It was the first time air traffic controllers had successfully organized, staged a job action, and won something significant for their efforts.[59]

The O'Hare job actions quickly became the stuff of legend in control towers and radar rooms around the country. Whether they were members of NAGE, ATCA, or independent local groups, air traffic controller activists were electrified by the implications of the O'Hare action. As Russ Sommer put it, they had "the power to strangle a metropolitan area in air traffic simply by following the rules literally." Although NAGE had not convened its air traffic control locals in a national network, the locals had reached out to each other, exchanging newsletters and comparing strategies. This informal network quickly circulated news of the O'Hare breakthrough. "Well, they're doing it," thought the tower controllers at Los Angeles International Airport (LAX). "Why can't we?" Indeed, controllers at LAX felt that if they did not also win upgrades they would be relegated to a "second-class status."[60]

Los Angeles area controllers had already built one of the most successful NAGE strongholds in the country by 1967, leading the fight against the "psycho test" and opposing the practice of forcing developmental controllers to perform janitorial duties. When LAX controllers heard about the O'Hare wage increase, they were "infuriated" to be left out and complained that their cost of living was at least as expensive as Chicago's. The LAX controllers petitioned the FAA's western regional director, citing their own short-staffing problem and demanding upgrades comparable to what Chicago controllers won. With the support of Sommer and the Los Angeles Center local, LAX controllers raised several thousand dollars for a "campaign fund," hired a lawyer and public relations consultant, and took their case to Congress. Regional FAA officials tried to alleviate the short-staffing problem by offering per diem expense payments to supplement salaries of any controllers willing to move to Los Angeles. It was an ill-considered solution. The "tempos" brought in under the plan would end up earning more than resident controllers, further inflaming the LAX activists. After exhausting official channels, the LAX controllers decided to emulate Chicago and inaugurate a slowdown of their own. Only then did the FAA respond to their concerns. The FAA regional office bought new chairs for controllers who lacked them and agreed to an immediate in-grade raise.[61]

News of the LAX controllers' victory in turn ricocheted around the country. "As the lesson of O'Hare had been told at Los Angeles, the story of Los Angeles Tower was burning the wires to New York and Atlanta the next day," reported Russ Sommer. Atlanta and New York controllers began drawing up their own demands and preparing job actions that could help realize them. "We are threatened now with a domino-effect which could pit facility against facility," Sommer worried. "The question is: How do you control the juggernaut once you start it rolling?" The New York controllers had some ideas about that.[62]

Toward a National Controllers' Organization

In the early 1960s, the ATCA developed a strong presence in metropolitan New York's air traffic facilities, including the New York Air Route Traffic Control Center now located outside MacArthur Airport in Islip. Some four hundred controllers worked at New York Center, handling traffic headed into or out of an area extending hundreds of miles beyond New York City, the most heavily traveled airspace in the United States. Since the months following the 1960 midair collision, New York Center controllers had tried to use the ATCA as a vehicle to address their grievances. In the fall of 1964, ATCA Chapter 52 won exclusive recognition at the center under the provisions of EO 10988. The chapter's leadership included chairman John R. Lapine Jr. and program committee chair John F. Leyden (who would go on to play a crucial role in the story of air traffic controller unionism).[63]

As it did in many facilities, the ATCA bungled its early lead at New York Center. In February 1965, ATCA's national leaders decided that rather than bar management personnel from membership in local chapters seeking exclusive recognition in conformance with the requirements of EO 10988, the chapters should suspend pending requests for recognition and surrender it wherever it had been won. This decision crippled Chapter 52 and left the door wide open for NAGE at New York Center. By October 1965, NAGE Local R2–8 won exclusive recognition at New York Center, displacing the ATCA. Mike Rock, Jack Maher, Stan Gordon, and Ed Williams were among the most active NAGE members.[64]

The timing was right for the arrival of NAGE. Air traffic in metropolitan New York rose by 17 percent between 1965 and 1966; at the same time, the number of working controllers remained frozen. New York Center controllers had plenty of grievances. Maher's greatest concerns were the FAA's failure to upgrade equipment and fill staffing quotas; Rock chafed at the agency's rigid managerial style and inadequate pay. Both hoped NAGE would improve the career in which they planned to spend the rest of their working lives.[65]

Fortuitously, shortly after the union was organized at New York Center, Rock received a transfer he had sought to the tower at LaGuardia Airport. Once at LaGuardia, he emerged as leader of its NAGE local. Rock's presence there created a natural axis between union activists at New York Center and LaGuardia, a development that would soon send air traffic controller unionism in a new direction. The possibility for widening that axis emerged when Jack Maher decided to run for the presidency of New York Center's NAGE local in the summer of 1967. Maher's decision did not come easily. He was a generally soft-spoken man who preferred to work behind the scenes. But one year into the existence of Local R2–8 it became apparent that it lacked a leader capable of unifying New York Center controllers. Maher's friend Stan Gordon persuaded him to run. Maher reluctantly agreed on the condition that Gordon stand for election as his secretary-treasurer. Neither man was a stranger to unions: while Maher's uncle was a plumbers' union official, Gordon had grown up in Brooklyn, the son of Russian immigrants with socialist politics. Neither man had firsthand experience with union leadership. Yet that did not concern their coworkers. Disenchantment with Local R2–8 propelled them into office. Almost as soon as they took over the New York Center local, they began to talk with their friend Rock at LaGuardia about building something bigger.[66]

While the American press was focused on the "Summer of Love," reporting on the psychedelic counterculture identified with LSD guru Dr. Timothy Leary or student antiwar protests, a different sort of rebellion was brewing unseen among the suburb-dwelling controllers of Long Island during the summer of 1967. In their cultural styles, politics, and middle-class aspirations, the controllers scarcely resembled 1960s radicals. Yet they shared in common with other disaffected Americans of those years a distaste for hypocritical, inflexible authority structures, and a willingness to challenge them. The straitlaced former Marine Jack Maher was no radical, but he proved as adept at rallying his followers as many of the better known activists of that tumultuous period.

Maher made three decisions that not only revived his local but also began to spread its gospel to other facilities. First, he began a series of weekly meetings at the restaurant above the terminal at MacArthur Airport. Maher knew that controllers' social drinking after a shift was deeply ingrained in the work culture, so he promised free beer to any controllers who attended these meetings. Second, he invited Rock and his LaGuardia contingent, as well as controllers from JFK, to attend. Maher was not known as a great orator. He was given to meandering and mumbling. But in his own way, he would make the same point at meeting after meeting: "We've got to get more control over our jobs. We're getting pushed around." Third, Maher started going directly to the press with controllers' grievances. Information he helped to supply provided the basis for a damning editorial in the *New York Times* on September 23, 1967, which alleged that there were eighty-two near midair collisions over Queens during the previous year. This strategy was risky. After one press conference in which they criticized the FAA, Maher and Gordon were called into their supervisor's office, told that they had violated regulations, and ordered not to speak publicly again. The men refused to comply. They found that the more publicity they generated, the more the FAA paid attention to them.[67]

In the fall of 1967, the weekly meetings at MacArthur Airport incubated an ambitious idea, the creation of a regionwide controllers' organization. New York area controllers handled more than one million flights carrying thirty-four million passengers in 1967. If area controllers could form a regional organization, Maher and Gordon reasoned, they might finally get the leverage they needed in their dealings with the FAA. Rock and the LaGuardia group immediately supported the plan, and the JFK controllers also threw their hats in. An organizing committee from the MacArthur Airport meetings then went to Newark to enlist the support of controllers there. "The more we talked, the more we realized that our problems were exactly the same," Mike Rock recalled. "The working conditions, the retirement, the pay, the lack of a grievance or an appeals procedure, the lack of knowledge that was given to us by management, the doubling up of positions, the overtime problems." At that meeting with the controllers from Newark, the group decided to federate their local organizations in order to act in concert as the Metropolitan Controllers Association (MCA).[68]

The MCA immediately became the locus of controller activism in the Northeast. Under the auspices of the association, the regular meetings that had been held in Islip began to rotate from one facility to another in the New York area so that controllers in each facility could enjoy ownership of the association. It marked the first time controllers in several facilities acted in unison. The association pushed the FAA regional officials for action in a series of meetings, but won no concessions. Management accused the MCA of stirring "unrest and discontent," while the organization's leaders peppered the officials with questions to which "not a decent answer could be contrived." On December 11, 1967, the FAA Eastern Region director sent a memo to Washington warning of rising controller unrest in his district. Inspired by the recent victories in Chicago and Los Angeles, the New York controller contingent put some pressure on the FAA and threatened to launch their own slowdown.[69]

But before initiating a job action, the New Yorkers wanted to first explore a bolder idea: the creation of a national version of the MCA. Jack Maher was convinced that controllers were getting more "united behind the idea of merger or getting all together under one." Forming such an organization would be easier with the approval and support of NAGE's national leaders, Ken Lyons and Stan Lyman. MCA leaders were not optimistic: Lyons and Lyman seemed to care about little more than how to collect money from the union dues check-off. Still, they felt they had to try.[70]

On December 23, 1967, Maher and Gordon flew to Boston to meet Lyons and Lyman for a discussion at a seafood restaurant on Boston Harbor. The New Yorkers made a pitch they thought would appeal to the NAGE leaders. If NAGE set up a national air traffic controllers' division, then the controllers' locals would agree to double their biweekly dues contributions to NAGE to $4 per member. Lyons was completely unreceptive. The NAGE president was skeptical that controllers would agree to a doubling of their per capita dues; he worried that such a plan would drive members out of the union and shrink NAGE's revenue instead of increasing it. Furthermore, Lyons expressed irritation at the job actions controllers had recently staged, noting that these put the national organization in an unfavorable light as it tried to organize federal workers broadly. Lyman reiterated his public position: NAGE would not support a slowdown because it was "like a strike." Deeply disappointed, Maher and Gordon returned from Boston with the realization that if there was to be a national organization of air traffic controllers they would have to create it themselves.[71]

As the New Yorkers reached the end of their rope with NAGE, so did controllers elsewhere. At Jacksonville Center, in northern Florida, the key controller activist Bill South concluded that NAGE had become "another ATCA." In Los Angeles, Russ Sommer got no response to the letters he sent Lyons asking for help. Worried, Sommer drafted a memo for distribution to NAGE locals across the country. Titled "Gathering Storm," the memo predicted a coming crisis. "We stand at a crossroad," Sommer warned. The "father-son relationship" that the FAA had tried to cultivate between management and labor in the past had broken down, and "like many fathers," the FAA had "failed to prepare for the day when its sons would grow up." Now that they had grown up, Sommer wrote, controllers were learning that "there was no future in standing alone." Organizing had required a "considerable reorientation of thought" on the part of controllers; it had been "almost an act of desperation," Sommer observed. But beginning to organize had changed the controllers. "Having taken their stand, fear is gone."[72]

Tellingly, Sommer's memo made no mention at all of NAGE. At that same moment, around the country, air traffic controller activists were reaching the same conclusion: it was time to build a new national organization. An organization of their own.[73]

WHEELS UP

Restlessness and frustration is spotty and scattered among the
three million federal employees, but is beginning to pop up
frequently enough to concern their bosses. Employee activists,
like student demonstrators, are insisting on a voice in making
agency plans and policies.
— *WASHINGTON POST*, 1968[1]

You son-of-a-bitch, you're not my grandfather!
—MIKE ROCK, 1968

808LJ. Mike Rock recognized the call sign of that Learjet immediately, having handled its approach to LaGuardia Airport several times over the previous few months. He couldn't remember when he learned that the jet's pilot was the famous trial lawyer F. Lee Bailey, who flew frequently between New York and his home in Boston. The pilot's identity had not mattered much to Rock before. But a week after Maher and Gordon had returned from their Boston meeting with NAGE leaders empty-handed, hearing the call sign 808LJ suddenly triggered a thought in Rock's mind. He radioed instructions to the lawyer-pilot; then he made a mental note to discuss his idea with his colleagues in the Metropolitan Controllers Association after his shift.[2]

Anticipating that NAGE leaders would disappoint them, the New York controllers had already concluded that they would have to launch a national organization on their own, without the union's help. But they feared taking that step without the backing of someone prominent who could defend them if the FAA tried to threaten them. They had already drawn up a list of famous pilots whose help they sought. In succession, they had contacted Hollywood actor Jimmy Stewart; General Curtis LeMay, the retired former commander of the Strategic Air Command; and television talent show host Arthur Godfrey. Only Godfrey responded. He said he sympathized with their plight, having had run-ins with the FAA himself as a pilot. But he could not help.[3]

What if they could persuade F. Lee Bailey to help them? Rock pitched the idea to his friends. In many ways, Bailey would be a perfect sponsor for their organization, he argued. Bailey would understand them. Born in 1933 in Waltham, Massachusetts, to an ad-salesman father and a schoolteacher mother, he was the same age as Rock and Maher. He also shared the controllers' military background. Bailey had dropped out of Harvard in 1952 to join the Marine Corps and become a fighter pilot. After earning a law degree at Boston University in 1960, he rocketed to prominence by handling a string of notorious cases. His successful defense of Ohio doctor Sam Sheppard in a 1966 retrial reversed Sheppard's 1954 conviction for murdering his wife, and inspired a television series called "The Fugitive." Bailey then defended another accused wife-murderer, Dr. Carl Coppolino. He also represented Albert DeSalvo, the reputed "Boston Strangler," the most prominent American serial killer of the 1960s. As a result of these cases, Bailey was perhaps the best-known trial lawyer in America in December 1967. Rock's colleagues doubted Bailey would divert attention from his booming law practice to help them, but, having nothing to lose, they encouraged Rock to make the call.[4]

The next morning, Rock phoned Bailey's Boston office and left a brief message. "I'm Michael Rock from the FAA. I'm an air-traffic controller, and I would like to talk to you." That afternoon, as Rock handled traffic at LaGuardia, his supervisor tapped him on the shoulder. "Hey Rock, what did you do? Kill your wife?" Rock turned. "What the hell are you talking about?" he asked. "I've got F. Lee Bailey on the phone, he wants to talk to you," the supervisor said.[5]

Rock's overture had been perfectly timed. Having flown in from New York the night before, Bailey assumed that Rock was calling to warn him about an infraction he might have committed. When Rock got on the phone it was Bailey who was a little nervous. Once Rock explained the situation, he found that Bailey was surprisingly receptive. Bailey had purchased his jet after the Sheppard case in 1966. Before that, most of his flying had been under visual flight rules (VFR) and involved minimal contact with air traffic controllers. Flying at higher altitudes in his jet, Bailey found himself communicating more frequently with controllers, getting a sense of how air traffic control operated. He got enough fleeting glimpses into the controllers' world through these interactions to become concerned. Bailey also had a close call in New York only weeks earlier, when he emerged from a cloud bank to find an Eastern Airlines DC-9 passing fifty feet above him—so close he found himself "counting the rivets in its belly." Before his conversation with Rock, Bailey had considered New York controllers "harried and curt." Once Rock described their working conditions, it "all began to make sense" to the attorney. Bailey concluded that Rock was "a very decent and worried young man," and agreed to meet him in New York the following week. So began one of the most unusual collaborations in American labor history.[6]

On the evening of January 4, 1968, Bailey strode into the basement meeting room of a bar near LaGuardia Airport, where he found Rock and the other leaders of the MCA nervously sipping beers. Once Bailey ordered a scotch, the controllers quickly got past the formalities. As one round of drinks followed another, their stories poured out: outdated equipment; forced overtime; an unresponsive bureaucracy; insomnia; ulcers—all the things they felt were destined to shorten their lives. Bailey listened and asked questions. Once he had heard enough, he told the controllers he would help them start an organization. To test the waters for such a group, he asked the New Yorkers to convene a meeting with controller activists from around the country. Bailey's idea electrified them—until he stipulated one condition: that the meeting should take place the following week, on January 11. Swayed equally by alcohol and their desperation for Bailey's help, the New Yorkers agreed, not knowing how they would pull it off. Bailey, in turn, gave them permission to rent a ballroom in his name at the International Hotel near JFK Airport, where several hundred fired-up controllers would hopefully join them.[7]

A week of furious, caffeine-fueled organizing followed. The New York organizers immediately phoned Russ Sommer in Los Angeles. Sommer, in turn, called the West Coast controller leaders he knew. Calls went out to

Miami, Atlanta, Chicago, and other cities where controllers had been organizing in recent years. The fact that many controllers had former military
buddies scattered throughout the FAA aided them in getting the word out.
So, too, did the FAA's own internal communication system. Every night on
the midnight shifts, when nobody was watching, the New York–area activists started calling their friends "here, there, and everywhere," as Stan Gordon
put it. As they called around, the New Yorkers found that Bailey's name
worked like a charm. Controllers on the other end of the line were astonished to hear that a big-shot lawyer was interested in helping them. Many
expressed an interest in meeting him. Bailey's name also worked wonders
with the press and gained the organizers a small advance notice for their
gathering in the *New York Times*.[8]

As they built turnout for the meeting, the New York organizers hastily
considered another question: what should they name their group? After
some debate, they decided to avoid the word "association." They wanted to
demonstrate that the new group would not be another ATCA or NAGE,
each of which used that word. But they also decided (over the objections of
Mike Rock) to avoid the word "union" too. They understood that for many
controllers that word did not fit comfortably with their middle-class aspirations. Bailey's involvement reinforced this thinking. Bailey encouraged the
controllers to think of their group as resembling "the American Bar
Association or something like that." Having discarded union and association,
the organizers settled on two other words: "professional" and "organization."
The first word conveyed controllers' desire to elevate the status of their
work; the second, their wish to build a tough, even militant, expression of
their collective voice. They decided to call their group the Professional Air
Traffic Controllers Organization (PATCO). To Maher these words represented a "compromise between union concept and professional society concept." He thought the name "satisfied to some extent the union people and
the professional society people." They all agreed the important thing was
that they were founding something "that had some clout, some bite, some
real influence," noted Will Burner, the representative from Newark.[9]

Yet the organizers knew that the right name would not guarantee the success of the January 11 meeting; that would depend almost entirely on Bailey.
It was Bailey who fronted the money for the ballroom and arranged for a
fleet of school buses to ferry controllers from across the metropolitan New
York area to the meeting, and it would be Bailey who would pitch the idea of

a national organization at that meeting. Whether he could pull that off was not clear to the New York organizers. "What the hell does he know about air traffic controllers?" Stan Gordon worried. "He's a pilot."[10]

Bailey did not disappoint. He prepared for the meeting as if it was the trial of the century. Every day he phoned Rock and deposed him at length about every facet of the controllers' workday, their vocabulary, and the things they liked and disliked about the job. On the day before the big meeting, Bailey flew to Los Angeles to pick up Russ Sommer in his jet, and as they flew back across the country, Sommer gave him an intensive tutorial on the history of organizing to that point. After landing in New York, Bailey met Rock for his first tour of controllers' workspaces. Rock took him into the LaGuardia radar room and control tower cab, which struck Bailey as "hell on wheels." In the hours before the big meeting, Bailey retired to his hotel room to review what he had learned. When it was time to go downstairs, he pronounced himself ready.[11]

In the ballroom below, the crowd trickled in slowly, causing the organizers considerable anxiety until the buses began arriving with controllers from Newark, LaGuardia, and Islip. By the time the meeting was ready to open, the room was packed with more than seven hundred controllers from twenty-two states. It was "the largest gathering of air traffic controllers that had ever been assembled in one room," according to Rock's reckoning. The key facilities were well represented. From Chicago came some of the organizers of Operation Snowman. From California came LAX Tower and LA Center controllers. Delegations arrived from Minneapolis and Miami, Atlanta and Anchorage. There was even a liberal sprinkling of FAA supervisors and officials, a few of whom flew in from Washington when they heard about the meeting.[12]

The event exceeded the organizers' wildest dreams. By all accounts, Bailey was spellbinding. He spoke without notes, and with what seemed to be an encyclopedic knowledge of the controllers' problems. Listening to him, Stan Gordon could have "sworn that that guy was an air traffic controller." "He had the lingo down, the jargon," said Rock, and "he laid out all the wants and desires of the air traffic controllers." As Bailey spoke, he helped his audience see that the problems controllers faced in New York "were the same problems that existed in Indianapolis and Anchorage and Seattle and Los Angeles and Fort Worth. It was all common," according to Ray Carver of Anchorage. Controllers "had a common cause." Not only did Bailey show that he understood their jobs, he also helped them envision what those jobs could become. "You should be a professional," he told the audience, "you should be like a pilot, you should be treated like a pilot, you should get a salary like a pilot." His words received several standing ovations; even the FAA officials in attendance joined in. When Bailey concluded by asking everyone present to show their commitment to building a national organization by putting ten dollars down, the Professional Air Traffic Controllers Organization was born.[13]

BUILDING A MOVEMENT

The next several months were among the most tumultuous in American history. The Vietnam War, which had escalated since February 1965, took a surprising turn three weeks after PATCO's founding when the North Vietnamese launched the Tet Offensive. That event weakened support for both the war and President Lyndon Johnson. Antiwar Senator Eugene McCarthy soon exposed Johnson's vulnerability in Democratic primaries, forcing the president to end his quest for his party's nomination on March 31. Four days later, Reverend Martin Luther King Jr. was assassinated in Memphis, Tennessee, where he was supporting striking sanitation workers, leading to widespread civil disturbances. In June, Senator Robert F. Kennedy, who had emerged as a frontrunner for the Democratic presidential nomination, was murdered in Los Angeles. As these explosive events were unfolding, few outside the FAA paid attention to a movement that was taking shape among air traffic controllers. But, the spirit of protest that was evident in so many part of America was also finding expression among this unlikely group.

Within days, news of the New York meeting had spread to every air traffic controller in the United States. The New Yorkers had taped Bailey's January 11 speech, and every night for a week, Stan Gordon and his friends on the midnight shift in Islip played it over the FAA's communications system to every facility in the United States. On the other end of the line, controllers taped the speech and circulated it at their facilities. Because some FAA officials first saw PATCO as a potential ally in lobbying Congress for budget increases rather than a union threat, they intentionally ignored the broadcasts. Controllers would later joke, "PATCO was sort of formed on the FAA's nickel." The FAA's benign neglect enraged NAGE officials, who immediately saw PATCO as a rival. When NAGE alleged that the FAA was "promoting this new organization" by allowing its broadcasts, the FAA put an end to the midnight speech transmissions. By then, however, any controller anywhere in the country could readily lay his hands on a copy.[14]

PATCO organizers followed their air barrage with a barnstorming cross-country campaign made possible by Bailey's jet and the controllers' FAM flights. Claiming sick days and vacation time, Maher, Rock, and Gordon took turns flying to big cities with Bailey to address hastily assembled meetings of controllers. After the initial meeting, one of the New York organizers would usually remain behind, then hitch a free FAM trip out "into the boondocks" to speak at smaller facilities before FAMing back to New York for their next shift.[15]

The tour's toughest stop was its first: Chicago. Some of O'Hare's fiercely independent controllers distrusted Bailey, likening him to a "snake oil salesman." Finding an ally there took time, but when a highly respected controller named Jimmy Hays indicated his willingness to join PATCO, other O'Hare controllers followed him. PATCO picked up momentum in Minneapolis, where Bailey attracted two hundred recruits, including a future PATCO leader, Bob Meyer. Then it was on to Miami, where PATCO's pitch went over "very, very well." By the time Bailey and his entourage returned to New York from that initial swing, PATCO had already become a viable national group. Over the next few months, Bailey and the New Yorkers perfected their barnstorming model. In March they flew to Indianapolis, in April to Kansas City. Then it was on to Denver Center in Longmont, Colorado.[16]

In many ways, PATCO's initial growth depended entirely on Bailey. It was his speech that most controllers listened to before they met any PATCO representatives, his name that drew controllers out to the meetings. It was also his movie-star charisma that got controllers' wives to come along, and often they were often the ones who persuaded their husbands to join PATCO. The vision for PATCO that Bailey laid out proved irresistible to listeners. "You had to keep telling yourself I don't believe it, I don't believe it, I don't believe it, because he's going to make it sound damn good," one O'Hare controller explained. Bailey's charm and prodigious memory supplemented his oratorical skills. O'Hare controller Dick Shaftic met Bailey briefly for the first time when the lawyer swept through Chicago on his first barnstorming tour. When Shaftic met Bailey again six months later in

Washington, he was shocked to discover that Bailey not only remembered his name but also where he worked.[17]

Bailey possessed another important advantage as an organizer: he was not a controller. As an outsider, he could transcend the petty rivalries that had historically complicated relations among controllers in major hubs such as New York, Atlanta, Chicago, and Los Angeles, who wanted their respective facilities to take leadership of any national organization. Bailey broke through this parochialism and helped controllers see that their "only real power" would come if they "banded together to strive for the same goal." He conveyed the message effectively. Listening to "a jack-off like Mike Rock and Jack Maher, nobody was going to join," Rock later explained in his typically colorful language. "But F. Lee Bailey laying out the nice words, it attracted the people."[18]

Not all organizing depended on Bailey or the New Yorkers. Many local PATCO organizations sprang up autonomously, while others failed to get off the ground. Ray Carver of Anchorage, Alaska, FAMed to New York for the January 11 meeting. He was so enthused by the gathering that when he returned home he called a meeting of controllers from Fairbanks, Juneau, King Salmon, and Annette Island to form a statewide organizing committee. Each took responsibility for organizing one facility, and within two months Alaska was fully organized. Similarly, at Oakland Center in Fremont, California, controllers did not wait for Bailey. When their facility supervisor refused to allow organizing meetings on the premises, they borrowed a motor home and parked it down the road on the property of a sympathetic church, where it became the staging area for their organizing. Oakland Center soon emerged as a PATCO stronghold.[19]

In other areas, however, even a visit from Bailey failed to jumpstart an organization. The South was particularly difficult territory. A few leaders emerged in the region. One was Bill South, of Jacksonville Center, in Hilliard, Florida. But South found that he had to "pull hen's teeth" to build an organization at the Hilliard facility, where managers clearly discouraged it.[20]

Although it never gained momentum in the South, overall PATCO's growth was so rapid that it outstripped the organization's amorphous structure. Within a month of the founding meeting, PATCO organizers counted four thousand members and $40,000 in initiation fees. Strong PATCO locals emerged in Los Angeles, San Francisco, Pittsburgh, Minneapolis, Miami, and Kansas City, but PATCO still had no constitution or written plan of organization. In the wake of the New York meeting, PATCO's organizers decided that Jack Maher should serve as national coordinator, Russ Sommer as election coordinator, and Stan Gordon as treasurer. Mike Rock was named chairman of PATCO's board of directors, and it was up to him to designate the rest of the board's members. Rock picked strong people from each region. Some had led NAGE or ATCA chapters before joining PATCO. Others were new to controller activism. (It took a bemused Bailey a while to teach board members "that when you're on the board of directors, you're a director, you're not a board of director.") Often Rock also chose local PATCO officers. The first controller in a facility to write to Rock for information about PATCO generally received a packet of membership flyers and a letter designating them the organization's facility representative. PATCO's finances were as haphazardly organized as its governance. Members paid no dues, only a $10 initiation fee. In a tiny office near LaGuardia, a sympathetic nun who knew bookkeeping helped process the initiation income. The costs of organizing soon exceeded income, keeping Stan Gordon, who acted as the organization's treasurer, one step ahead of PATCO's creditors.[21]

PATCO's relationship to F. Lee Bailey was as idiosyncratic as the rest of its structure. Bailey was officially named PATCO's "executive director." He claimed only a token $1 salary for his role. In return, PATCO agreed to pay any expenses he incurred in the course of his work for the organization. Bailey and the PATCO board had an understanding that if PATCO was successful, then the organization would pay him a more substantial fee in its second year.

Having a celebrity lawyer play such a large role in PATCO's early life offered some advantages. For one, Bailey's involvement guaranteed the organization a level of visibility it otherwise could not have attained. Not only did controllers turn out when Bailey came to town; the press did too. Bailey also got other prominent people involved in the controllers' cause. He created an "honorary board of directors" for PATCO and recruited two television personalities, talent show host Arthur Godfrey and *Tonight Show* host Johnny Carson, to serve on it. Press coverage and blessings from prominent names like these in turn attracted more members for the organization.[22]

But Bailey's involvement also carried disadvantages. He had his own strong ideas about how to build the organization and about what sort of group it would be. These did not always dovetail with the thinking of Mike

Rock and other leaders. While Rock hoped to create an organization that could represent controllers under the provisions of Executive Order 10988, Bailey envisioned PATCO as a purely professional organization. The difference created some tensions. While Rock praised Bailey's "golden tongue" he also found him to be "an egomaniac."[23]

One early PATCO venture highlighted some of these differences in vision. Bailey thought that the organization needed a "first class journal," a glossy advertising-laden magazine that could reach multiple constituencies in the aviation community as potential readers or advertisers. Bailey helped finance the journal's launch, inviting a wide range of airline executives, politicians, journalists and aviation enthusiasts to an event at New York's Americana Hotel on February 21, 1968. Speaking to this audience, Bailey jokingly dismissed "rumors" that PATCO was a "Teamster front," or an "attempt by Castro to take over the United States." He made clear that PATCO was not intended to be a union at all. He was proud, he said, that controllers did not approach their grievances "from a rabble-rousing, union point of view wherein they could get what they wanted simply because they wanted it and because everybody else was getting it." And he insisted that PATCO did not endorse the slowdowns staged by controllers in some facilities in previous years. Such methods, he said, were like "Martin Luther King's march into Washington," but they were not "the method of this group."[24]

Mike Rock and some other PATCO leaders chafed at Bailey's words. They did not rule out staging job actions if necessary to win controllers a better future. Nevertheless, they helped Bailey get out the first issues of the journal. Lacking money to circulate it, they packed hundreds of shopping bags with copies of the journal and stacked them in the controllers' ready room at LaGuardia. They handed the bags to departing pilots or flight attendants who, in turn, dropped them off to waiting controllers at the other end of their flight. But controllers never embraced the journal, and it did not last long.[25]

In fact, the differences between Rock and Bailey over the nature of PATCO spoke to an ambivalence that ran deep among air traffic controllers. What sort of "organization" should PATCO be? If it was not a union, should it allow FAA supervisors to join it? Controller opinion often divided along regional lines on such questions. Those who worked in the Midwest, Central States, and South, especially in facilities that once had active ATCA chapters, tended to favor including supervisors. "Let's solve the problems in the air traffic control system and let's do it any way that we can and let's get everybody on board...in a unified process with a common goal," said one advocate of this view. Controllers on the east and west coasts tended to oppose including supervisors. They pointed out that PATCO could not seek exclusive recognition and qualify for a dues checkoff under EO 10988 if managers joined its locals.[26]

The initial lack of clarity concerning PATCO's vision disarmed the FAA. Department of Transportation officials informed the White House that PATCO was attracting controllers "dissatisfied" with NAGE and the ATCA, but assured them that the new organization would not take a "sensational" approach to the issues. After learning that the word union was not mentioned at PATCO's founding meeting, top FAA officials expressed relief that it was not "one of those rotten labor unions," and hoped that it would displace NAGE. Some facility chiefs, like James Boyle of New York Center, allowed PATCO organizers to hold meetings in which they instructed controllers on how to opt out of dues checkoff with NAGE and join PATCO—a fact that enraged NAGE. Even if they did not go that far, many supervisors, particularly younger ones, took a benign view of PATCO. Indeed, some controllers first heard about PATCO from their supervisors. "You do what you need to do," Anchorage facility chief Ray Van Vuren told his controllers when they began organizing. Some low-level managers even viewed PATCO as a potential vehicle to "get their own views 'upstairs.' "[27]

PATCO's ambiguous mission was still unclear when Bailey began seeking recognition from the FAA. In February 1968, he began barraging FAA Administrator Bozo McKee with requests for official recognition of PATCO as a "professional organization." Bailey assured McKee that PATCO's approach would be "professional, in every sense of the word, as distinguished from a unionistic approach." McKee and other agency officials were invited "to make any suggestions they may think appropriate" for PATCO. Bailey even used the threat of union involvement to induce McKee to act. Several "larger unions" had approached PATCO, "anxious to participate" in its work, he explained. Bailey's implication was clear: if PATCO was not recognized, it might turn to one of these union suitors for help.[28]

Recognition was important to PATCO leaders because without it, they could not win dues withholding rights in facilities that might stabilize the organization's finances. But when Rock followed up on Bailey's overtures by asking directly for a dues withholding agreement, the FAA responded that only groups that could qualify as "labor organizations" under the provisions of EO 10988 were eligible for such agreements. To qualify as a labor organization, PATCO leaders would need to formally bar supervisors from joining, even though many had already joined. PATCO would also need to give up the idea of publishing a glossy magazine underwritten by airline industry advertisements: no group could qualify as a labor organization with the FAA if it had commercial relationships with the agency's clients. Pending a decision on what sort of organization PATCO was, the FAA would only allow PATCO to use facility bulletin boards.[29]

As the summer of 1968 approached, it became clear to PATCO leaders that they needed to make important decisions about the future of their organization. Not only did PATCO need a formal constitution and leadership structure, it needed to clarify its status as an organization. To address these questions, PATCO leaders decided to convene a constitutional convention in Chicago on June 30, 1968.[30]

CHICAGO '68

In the summer of 1968, the fault lines that divided America seemed to run straight through Chicago. During the Democratic convention held there in late August, antiwar protestors clashed with Mayor Richard J. Daley's baton-wielding police force in a drama that both riveted the nation and signaled the unraveling of the Democratic coalition. PATCO's convention drew no press coverage and attracted no protests, but it marked as profound a turning point for the FAA as the August convention would be for Democrats.

PATCO organizers booked a few hundred rooms at the Pick-Congress Hotel, but no one knew how many delegates to expect. There was no formal selection mechanism; the convention was open to all comers. Two days before the meeting, only a few dozen controllers had reserved rooms, prompting the hotel to threaten cancellation of PATCO's bloc. "Our guys are funny," Mike Rock assured the hotel's manager. "We never went to hotels. We don't know about this reservation bullshit." Rock understood his people. In the end, 350 controllers, representing every state in the union, showed up.[31]

Over four days of discussion, the delegates made decisions that pointed PATCO decisively toward becoming a union. Three factors ultimately played a role. First, the association model had been discredited in the minds of a slight majority of controllers by the ATCA's ineffectual history. No one wanted PATCO to become "another ATCA." Second, the key activists in PATCO's organizing drive and the ones with the most influence at the Chicago convention, like Rock and Maher, came from blue-collar families with union histories. The Campbell brothers, Charlie (who led PATCO's organizing in Honolulu), and Rex (from Denver Center), were the sons of a union activist in the tire and rubber industry. Ray Carver, PATCO's lead organizer in Alaska, was the son of an Ohio shoe workers' union member. Bill South, who led PATCO in Jacksonville, had grown up the son of a unionized operating engineer in Detroit. And Mike Powderly, secretary of the PATCO local at O'Hare Tower, was the son of a local leader of the Butcher Workmen in Chicago, whose family claimed to be proud descendents of Terence V. Powderly, the nineteenth-century leader of the Knights of Labor. For controllers like these, it seemed natural that PATCO should become a union. Even Bailey understood this, reluctantly concluding that it was "probably unrealistic" for PATCO to remain a professional association: "These kinds of people need a union, respond to a union."[32]

Yet the deciding factor in pushing PATCO toward the union model was EO 10988. Section 6(a)(3) of the order forbade the inclusion of "both supervisors who officially evaluate the performance of employees and the employees whom they supervise" in any organization that sought recognition, the power to negotiate on behalf of employees, and dues checkoff privileges. The New York organizers saw dues checkoff as a matter of life and death. Without it, Rock explained, PATCO could not survive.[33]

Even with this compelling argument, the issue was not decided without a struggle. The question came to a head when controllers from Minneapolis Center introduced a resolution formally welcoming supervisors into PATCO's ranks. This unleashed a final floor battle that the unionists won by a margin of less than three percent. Delegates from the coasts and the Great Lakes region provided just enough votes to prevail. It was a moment of singular importance to the controllers. "For the first time publicly we were telling the FAA, hey, management, you are on one side and we are on the other," observed Rock.[34]

Even as PATCO settled this major question, it adopted a constitution unlike that of most unions. Bailey largely dictated the document. As explained by William Peer, a labor lawyer who later replaced Bailey as PATCO's general counsel, Bailey "created PATCO in the image of the only organization that he was at all familiar with. And that is corporate America." Bailey's constitution created a dual structure, which split authority between controllers and Bailey. On the one hand, it formalized the organization's board of directors, which Rock headed, and created a position of president, to which O'Hare controller Jimmy Hays was elected at PATCO's next convention. On the other hand, the constitution also created the position of "executive director" to run PATCO's day-to-day operations. Bailey envisioned that this person would be someone with "administrative experience," someone from his world. Finally, the constitution provided for a strong general counsel (Bailey), who was in turn empowered to appoint a network of regional counsels. Through the executive director and regional counsels, Bailey would have his own channels through which to influence PATCO's direction. Rock later characterized the arrangement as "a corporation type of constitution" that included "too many lawyers." Indicative of both PATCO's overwhelmingly white membership and how little its leaders understood labor law, the constitution did not include a nondiscrimination clause, which was mandatory for unions seeking recognition under the executive order. When they discovered the omission, PATCO officials had to add the clause after the fact.[35]

On paper, PATCO now qualified as a "labor organization." But that did not make it a union. Its transformation into a union was accomplished not with the stroke of a pen, but rather through the organization's increasingly contentious dealings with the FAA in the months that followed. The contention began even before the convention recessed.

Rock, Maher, and other leaders were determined to leave Chicago with a plan of action that would build the organization. They trained their focus on the issue of mandatory overtime. Total overtime worked by controllers had shot up from an average of some 8,903 hours per week in 1967 to an unprecedented 21,460 hours per week in 1968. PATCO leaders wanted to highlight the problem in order to pressure the government to hire more controllers. Mere petitions had been ineffective, as the experience of recent years had shown. "The time for letter writing is over," said Rock. PATCO's leaders decided to present their reform demands as forcefully as possible.[36]

In a television appearance on the *Tonight Show* hosted by his friend and honorary PATCO board member Johnny Carson, Bailey tipped PATCO's hand prior to the convention. When Bailey described the difficult conditions under which controllers were working, Carson asked, "What would happen if all the controllers finally got to the point where they said they quit?" "The country would shut down," Bailey explained. But, Carson's viewers need not worry, Bailey continued, for the controllers would never strike. Then, he added this: "If they just followed regulations, instead of cutting corners to get more airplanes in—just follow regulations—Kennedy, O'Hare, and L.A. would drop traffic by 50 percent." "Why don't they do it?" Carson asked. "I think they may at some point," said Bailey. So it happened that PATCO's first job action was forecasted on a late-night comedy show.[37]

Prior to 1968, controllers in Chicago, Los Angeles, and New York had engaged in sporadic slowdowns, but these had never been coordinated between facilities, nor planned by a national organization. PATCO was determined to change that. At the convention, a safety committee was organized under the leadership of Maher and Boston controller John F. Meehan. As others hashed out PATCO's constitution, the safety committee crafted what Rock called a "master plan" to put "some pressure on the FAA." They christened it "Operation Air Safety." The idea was to demonstrate that the air traffic control system could not work unless controllers cut corners daily to expedite the traffic flow. Delegates agreed to return to their home facilities and enlist their colleagues in a work-to-rule action that would make clear the need for reform. The Safety Committee urged controllers to give "special consideration" to "fatigue caused by overtime" in determining how many planes they could safely handle at their position. If the FAA tried to penalize any controller who had to slow down to follow regulations, PATCO pledged to defend them. "We must not only stand together," the Safety Committee concluded, "but for the first time we must stand up."[38]

The plan was framed to attract support from a broad range of constituencies inside and outside the FAA. While the Chicago delegates divided over whether to include supervisors in their organization, they united around safety issues. PATCO's more militant members liked the idea of challenging FAA management directly with a job action, making clear that PATCO was a force to be reckoned with. Moderates supported the plan as a way to dramatize the need for improved staffing. The organizers believed that pilots who wanted to see the system improved, travelers who wanted to fly safely, politicians who wanted a well-run FAA, and even some frontline supervisors who felt that Washington neglected their facilities' staffing needs, might support the job action. PATCO hoped to use it to press Congress to increase funding for the FAA.[39]

PATCO announced "Operation Air Safety" as its convention recessed on July 3, in a characteristically unconventional way. Bailey persuaded his friend, television personality Arthur Godfrey, to join him and Rock at the concluding press conference. Godfrey apparently was unaware of what Bailey and Rock were about to announce. As Bailey explained that controllers were going to operate by the book, Rock saw "the blood running out of [Godfrey's] face." When reporters asked if the announcement meant PATCO was calling a slowdown, Bailey denied it. This was not an effort to disrupt air traffic, he explained; rather, an effort to strictly adhere to regulations for the safety of all. Rock added, "The controllers feel, without exception, that their obligation to protect the public against unnecessary air hazards completely outweighs consideration of inconvenience which might arise if minimum separation is observed." The press did not buy it. The *New York Times* headline read: "Air Controllers Order Slowdown."[40]

"We Must Stand Up"

In many ways, PATCO's job action was in sync with the times. Pointing to the rising militancy of state and local government workers in the mid-1960s, many observers expected federal workers to join in before long. Jean J. Couturier, the director of the National Civil Service League, a reform group that had been monitoring government employment since the nineteenth century, predicted that federal workers would be more likely to use "devices such as working by the book," rather than striking. Yet no one foresaw that air traffic controllers would be the first federal workers to launch a nationwide job action.[41]

When the job action came, many relied on a popular novel for an explanation of events. Arthur Hailey's thriller *Airport* was the runaway bestseller of the summer of 1968. The novel focused on the heroic efforts of a harried Chicago controller named Keith Bakersfield, who, haunted by having witnessed a midair collision a year earlier, had come to rely on a stash of sedatives to get through each workday. In the novel's climactic scene, Bakersfield guided a disabled airliner to a safe landing at a fictionalized O'Hare Airport. But after this heroic act Bakersfield could no longer take the pressures of his work. The novel ended with him unplugging his headset, dumping his pills in the trash, and walking out of the control tower never to return. At a time when the strikes of Memphis sanitation workers and New York City teachers spotlighted the problems of more visible government workers, the struggles of the fictional Keith Bakersfield dramatized the plight of controllers who were otherwise invisible to the public.[42]

Delegates returning from the PATCO convention briefed their colleagues on Operation Air Safety. Because PATCO leaders wanted to protect less experienced members in poorly organized facilities, they planned to first slow traffic only in the New York and Chicago hubs. On Monday, July 8, the action began. Rock, Maher, and the others had no idea what to expect, but flight delays soon began to rise. The number of operations per hour on Runway 22L at JFK airport dropped by 25 percent within a week. By the end of the week, controllers in Chicago, New York, Denver, and Kansas City were involved. Less than a week into the action, transatlantic travel was disrupted. "I've never seen delays like this," said one exasperated airline official. "It's ridiculous."[43]

The job action did not require the mass participation of PATCO members to achieve such an effect. This was important, for even PATCO enthusiasts felt ambivalent about slowing down traffic. Expediting flights was so deeply ingrained in the controllers' work ethic that they "felt guilty" about going by the book. However, a minority of strategically positioned controllers was able to cause huge delays in the air traffic system. Controllers were expected to space aircraft five miles apart en route to their destinations and three miles apart during final approach to an airport. In busy periods, they regularly ran a "tight five," which often meant three or four miles en route, and a "tight three," which could mean one or two miles on approach under some conditions. Because a jet traveling at three hundred miles per hour covered one mile in twelve seconds, even slightly delayed directions from controllers resulted in widening spaces between aircraft. If such delays were implemented consistently, a single controller could produce separations of seven miles en route and five miles in final approach, producing a cascade of delays that reverberated through the system. When groups of controllers at multiple facilities did this, they could produce enormous tie-ups.[44]

The case of Jimmy Hays, PATCO's leader at O'Hare, serves to illustrate. Hays was a controller of legendary skill. Coworker Mike Powderly described him as "the most natural controller I ever saw in my life. You could not scare Jimmy Hays." Hays could reportedly "handle any amount of traffic, and he could run any spacing you wanted." But in July 1968, it seemed that Hays suddenly became skittish. He was responsible for handling jets streaming in from two "feeder fixes," spacing them and blending the streams together into the final approach to O'Hare. Normally, Hays easily slotted aircraft five miles apart in stream and could close them to within less than three miles as they neared touchdown. Beginning on July 8, more distance crept in between the jets Hays handled. His supervisors quickly identified the problem, but they could not pinpoint how he was inserting the extra space. Tower supervisor Carl Jortz would stand behind Hays, observing him. As long as Jortz was there, "it was like somebody threw a switch" and Hays "couldn't hit anything but five miles." But when Jortz stepped away, "Jimmy would go and do whatever he wanted to do." In minutes, his aircraft would be spaced at six to seven miles, and delays would mount. Unable to catch Hays breaking rules, O'Hare supervisors nonetheless reprimanded him, arguing that he was "deliberately exceeding requirements." If he did not "obey orders," officials promised further disciplinary action. But Hays refused to buckle, and his example galvanized others.[45]

Meanwhile, controllers at Washington Center had an easier time slowing traffic. They merely had to follow normal procedures. Westbound departure routes out of Washington normally proceeded north toward Baltimore before getting vectored west over Morgantown, West Virginia. But as traffic in the Northeast corridor grew over time, controllers devised shortcuts that took planes out of their prescribed flight paths on busy days. Washington Center controllers would simply ask departure controllers at National or Dulles airports to give them radar handoffs for westbound jets the moment they were airborne. Center controllers would then immediately vector the jets westward to open up more space for northbound flights. During the slowdown, Washington controllers merely suspended this technique, snarling East Coast traffic in the process.[46]

The delays resulting from Operation Air Safety caused significant congestion in the skies above major cities such as New York and Chicago. Typically, when jets entered the airspace more quickly than they could be cleared for landing, controllers would "stack" them, putting aircraft into a circular holding pattern. The larger the jet, the faster its speed, the wider its circling pattern, and the higher its elevation in the stack. Metropolitan New York had eleven basic stacking patterns. After the first week of the job action, these holding areas were jammed, as jets circled and airlines groused about the fuel they were burning. American Airlines estimated that it lost about ten dollars for every minute a plane circled above an airport; Mohawk Airlines claimed losses of $16,500 a day. In an attempt to ease the congestion, officials with the Port Authority of New York and New Jersey, which operated the LaGuardia, JFK, and Newark airports, tried raising fees for private, general aviation aircraft in order to discourage them from flying and thus lightening controllers' workloads. The move had no effect.[47]

As the job action stretched into a second week, its impact deepened. Delays reached their worst levels yet on July 19 in what the *Chicago Tribune* called "the industry's new 'Black Friday.'" Pressure began to build on the FAA as angry fliers began to write to President Johnson. "[T]here is something radically wrong with the entire administration of the system," one writer complained. On July 15, U.S. Rep. Roman Pucinski, a Chicago Democrat, called FAA Deputy Administrator Dave Thomas to complain about a five-hour delay he encountered on a flight from Europe. Pucinski wanted to know why the FAA did not grant the controllers' demands.[48]

The cascading delays produced by Operation Air Safety put great stress on both airlines and PATCO's rivals. Carriers tried to keep passengers happy by laying in extra refreshments or by devising impromptu contests such as "Guess the ATC Delay," in which the passenger who correctly predicted the flight's arrival time won a token redeemable for a free in-flight cocktail. Contracts stipulated that flight crews could not fly more than eighty-five hours per month to ensure they remained well rested and alert. Airlines that serviced cities where the slowdown was strongest soon discovered their crews were using up a substantial number of their allotted service hours in holding patterns. Many Mohawk Airlines pilots had nearly exhausted their monthly quota of flying hours by the end of the third week in July. And on July 23, United Airlines President George E. Keck announced his company might have to begin canceling flights by the end of the month because many of his pilots were nearing their monthly quota.[49] PATCO's rivals were as frustrated as the airlines. NAGE and the ATCA feared that if PATCO's job action succeeded, it would give the new organization a clear advantage in its effort to win air traffic controllers' loyalty. Thus the ATCA attacked Operation Air Safety as a "form of illegal strike" while NAGE tried in vain to get U.S. Attorney General Ramsey Clark to prosecute PATCO for violations of federal law.[50]

Despite the outcries, PATCO's safety-first emphasis won it support from pilots and even some airline officials, while a broader antigovernment mood made the flying public sympathetic. "It's just a shame that they have to do this to get what they want," one anonymous airline official admitted. "Any time they talk safety, they talk right," added a pilot, whose landing in New York was delayed by an hour. "This is not a public be damned thing; you have to educate them somehow," he explained. "This is a two-gallon airport with three gallons of airplanes." A Northeastern Airlines pilot went so far as to explain the job action to his passengers over the cabin intercom and to urge them to write their congressional representatives in support of the controllers as they circled awaiting their clearance. "What can you do, be against safety?" one airline official asked. "It's like being against motherhood."[51]

Controllers also undoubtedly benefited from what Seymour Martin Lipset called "a virtual explosion of anti-government feeling" that spread across the country in the late 1960s. The flying public, it seemed, was ready to believe that the federal government, not the controllers they employed, were to blame for the delays. Even the New York Times, which frequently criticized government workers' unions, took note of the controllers' stress and forced overtime and agreed that the controllers had "major grievances."[52]

FAA leaders decided their best bet was to deny a job action existed. New York Center watch supervisor William Papadeas insisted that any delays were the result of a sudden increase in traffic. Both frontline and senior FAA managers parroted this line. But airline officials disputed the FAA's denials, providing their own statistics to show a 20 percent reduction in the number of landings at JFK during peak hours. Faced with such evidence, the FAA slightly shifted its public stance during the slowdown's second week. Instead of denying the obvious, agency officials said they were investigating but had not been able to "determine yet definitely that there is a slowdown."[53]

In reality, the FAA knew what was happening; the agency simply found it hard to respond. The job action hit the FAA at a vulnerable moment. Administrator Bozo McKee had just announced his resignation, effective at the end of July. With McKee a lame duck, and with President Johnson too preoccupied with Vietnam in the waning months of his presidency to pay attention to the FAA, it fell to FAA Deputy Administrator Dave Thomas to step into the breach. A career FAA man who looked upon controllers as his "boys," Thomas had been surprised by PATCO's swift rise and "offended" that controllers felt they needed such an organization. He was determined to prevent this slowdown from sullying the FAA. Thomas assured members of Congress that the snarling traffic was not the result of a slowdown but, rather, a result of "the complete saturation of the existing workforce." But even as he offered such assurances, Thomas received reports about the extent of the slowdown and the inability of frontline supervisors to stop it. Many supervisors were worried about confronting PATCO. A rumor circulating at O'Hare suggested that any supervisor who tried to discipline a controller for slowing traffic would "have to defend himself at some subsequent time before F. Lee Bailey."[54]

During the first week of the slowdown, Thomas tried to placate PATCO, first by authorizing a notice "conditionally acknowledging the Professional Air Traffic Controllers Organization as a professional society," then by offering extended leaves of absence for Rock and Maher so they could conduct PATCO business if they offered their assurances that "PATCO would act in a responsible and professional manner." But PATCO's leaders would not let up until the agency dealt with their main concerns. Maher announced that PATCO would continue "rescheduling the airlines" into a third week.[55]

By then, Congress took notice. On July 16, the Senate Finance Committee not only exempted the FAA from a congressional mandate for personnel reductions, but added money to the FAA budget to fund the hiring of two thousand more employees than had been sought by the administration. Citing recent congestion in New York, Sen. John C. Stennis, a Mississippi Democrat, argued that the need for FAA funding was "urgent and immediate." As the pressure built, the Transportation Department informed the Johnson White House that it was forming a panel to review the situation. The FAA, in turn, summoned its regional directors to Washington to discuss the delays. The agency was clearly at a loss for how to deal with what one newspaper called "a semi-strike."[56]

Sensing the FAA's weakness, PATCO brought the crisis to a head on July 20, issuing a public call for multisided talks involving the pilots' union, air carriers, the FAA, and PATCO on how to reform the system. The FAA rejected the idea. Instead, it privately offered to meet quietly with PATCO leaders. PATCO leaders accepted the offer. They knew that by doing so, they had already accomplished something unprecedented: this would be the first time federal workers had used a job action to force agency leaders to sit down with their representatives in Washington.[57]

At 9:30 a.m. on July 23, 1968, heat and humidity were already tightening their grip on the capital when three-dozen controllers walked up the marble steps into the FAA's formidable Washington headquarters at 800

Independence Avenue, Southwest. In PATCO's contingent were the New Yorkers Rock, Maher, and Stan Gordon. Others included Russ Sommer from Los Angeles, Safety Committee chair John Meehan of Boston, and Jimmy Hays, who had anchored Operation Air Safety so effectively at O'Hare. The controllers—most of whom had never set foot inside the headquarters of their agency—were ushered into a large conference room, where they were joined by their counsel, Bailey, and an equal number of FAA officials. Before this meeting, the highest-ranking official most air traffic controllers had ever addressed was their facility chief. Suddenly, they were face to face with the agency's top two officials, outgoing administrator Bozo McKee and his deputy, Dave Thomas. If the FAA officials expected the controllers to show deference, they were soon disabused of that notion. According to one official's notes, the controllers "were aggressive and militant to say the least. They came not as petitioners presenting suggestions, but as a militant group laying their demands."[58]

McKee opened the historic meeting by telling the PATCO representatives that the FAA was working to secure the funds necessary to improve the air traffic system and to reform overtime rules. That day, the Senate Finance Committee was expected to report out a bill that would increase the FAA's budget. McKee then warned the controllers of "a general feeling in Congress that its members are being 'Blackmailed' by the FAA and its controllers with a so-called 'Slowdown.'" Rock denied that a slowdown was underway, insisting controllers were only adhering to the FAA's own regulations. Rock then went on the offensive. He presented eight demands. PATCO wanted a comprehensive training program; an overhaul of current rules and regulations; expansion of the FAM program; a commitment to full staffing of all sectors at all times; an end to rules banning controllers from flying planes for hire in their off hours; an agreement to hire trainees at the GS-10 level; the creation of a rule that would allow pilots on short fuel and holding in a stack to notify controllers and get priority clearance; and a guarantee that controllers would be allowed to use their judgment in handling air traffic. "We had it all typed up nice," Rock later explained.[59]

FAA officials were outraged. As they saw it, PATCO's proposals would lead to any controller taking a FAM flight "wherever and whenever he desires" for "any duration of time." Thomas rejected Rock's demands, then added insult to injury by telling the controllers that he considered the FAA one big family. Rock had heard enough. "You son-of-a-bitch, you're not my grandfather," he fumed.[60]

The Washington meeting produced no resolution of the job action, and only increased PATCO's determination to fight. The average delay on flights from Chicago to JFK was longer than ever on the day after the Washington meeting—more than double the average delay a week earlier. The FAA's Midwest regional director privately warned his Washington superiors that the "PATCO situation" was "becoming serious," and that controller organizing was threatening supervisors' efforts to "retain complete control of their facilities." At this point, the air carriers decided to weigh in. On July 24, TWA President Charles C. Tillinghast asked the Civil Aeronautics Board (CAB) for authority to call an industry-wide meeting to discuss the air delays. New York–area congressional representatives also began clamoring for action, as did the major airlines' trade group, the Air Transport Association, and a private aviators' organization, the Airline Owners and Pilots Association. As pressure mounted, PATCO took a moderate public stance. Maher assured reporters that controllers would be "quite willing to break our backs for the next year or two" as long as there was "some indication that there is some relief on the horizon." Media support for PATCO generally held. One typical account claimed that the slowdown had "pushed commercial traffic to the edge of chaos," but admitted that PATCO's demands were "hard to fault." The head of the Air Line Pilots Association's safety committee said he knew of "no other group that merits our support, assistance and cooperation more than those who assist in keeping us from running over one another."[61]

With PATCO more determined than ever, air travel delays increasing, and pressure for a resolution mounting, the FAA could no longer maintain its denials of a slowdown. Moreover, the White House was getting impatient. When CAB Chairman Charles S. Murphy briefed President Johnson on July 26 on the controllers' decision to "follow the book," he emphasized the political costs that would result should Johnson have to "get into the matter at the present time." No one at the FAA wanted to force the president to get involved. Thus FAA Deputy Administrator Thomas began searching for an exit strategy.[62]

On July 30, Thomas phoned Bailey to discuss terms under which PATCO could win dues checkoff from the FAA. If PATCO agreed to publicly disavow a slowdown, Thomas promised supervisors would relax enforcement of the three mile separation rule where warranted. Bailey, in turn, assured Thomas that the controllers "did not wish to quarrel with the agency." By then, PATCO leaders also wanted an end to the conflict. The slowdown was beginning to fatigue controllers, and PATCO was anxious to secure something tangible as a result of Operation Air Safety. Thus, PATCO made several conciliatory gestures. After the Bailey-Thomas conversation, PATCO unveiled a plan to decrease air traffic congestion in New York and offered restrained words regarding FAA officials. Bailey then told a mass meeting of Long Island controllers that PATCO supported Thomas "100 percent."[63]

Over the course of August, PATCO and the FAA held more discussions on the dues checkoff; as talks progressed, the slowdown wound down. When the talks stalled, Bailey warned Thomas that controllers were starting to believe that the FAA thought it "had PATCO by the short hair and intended to squeeze." If an agreement was not forthcoming, Bailey warned, the "volatile" controllers might erupt. Finally, on September 4, an agreement emerged. Rock assured the FAA that PATCO would not "advocate the use of unwarranted sick leave or unnecessary air traffic spacing as methods for the demonstration of controller points of view." In return, the FAA agreed to deduct PATCO dues from the paychecks of the organization's members. The FAA categorized PATCO as a professional association, not a union, which exempted PATCO from the requirement that it demonstrate a showing of interest in each individual facility before gaining the dues checkoff. With this, the slowdown ended.[64]

One month later, an added bonus arrived. On October 11, 1968, President Johnson signed legislation specifically exempting air traffic controllers from restrictions on federal overtime pay, the chief demand that had motivated controllers in Operation Air Safety.[65]

New Vectors

PATCO not only took off in 1968, it created a new dynamic in FAA workplaces. Two things were clear. First, PATCO began to change the relationship between controllers and the FAA. The organization emerged as an independent voice of air traffic controllers unafraid to challenge the FAA, even with militant tactics. When PATCO was founded in January 1968, many FAA supervisors cheered. The agency's top officials hoped it might provide political leverage in battles for increased agency funding. This came to pass: PATCO's slowdown helped wrangle budget increases for the FAA and yielded legislation to compensate controllers for overtime work. But none of this happened in the collaborative way FAA officials envisioned. Operation Air Safety placed the FAA on the defensive and caused agency officials to view PATCO as a threat. An adversarial dynamic began to emerge between PATCO and the FAA as PATCO's militancy drove a wedge between controllers and front line supervisors. As Stan Gordon put it, supervisors "were either with the chief or they were with us. Most of them were with the chief, because they had to be."[66]

Second, PATCO itself was changing. Part of that transformation was organizational. The dues checkoff agreement that PATCO won put it on solid footing. The FAA processed nearly five thousand dues withholding forms for PATCO members in the first two weeks after the agreement. No longer did the organization have to kite checks to survive. On the strength of this funding, PATCO opened a Washington office in September 1968 and outlined an ambitious organizing agenda, setting a recruitment goal of ten thousand members, or more than two-thirds of the controller workforce, by the end of the year. The organization even had enough money to hire a public relations firm. In a matter of months, PATCO leapfrogged over rivals NAGE and the ATCA.[67]

Another part of PATCO's transformation was psychological. Operation Air Safety exposed the FAA's vulnerability and showed PATCO members what they could achieve if they worked together. The results were undeniable: after a long hiring freeze, the FAA was again hiring controllers; after years of congressional neglect, Congress had exempted air traffic controllers from overtime pay restrictions; and the FAA began considering the reclassification of some controllers' positions into higher-paying grades. PATCO even forced air traffic issues into the 1968 presidential campaign when Republican presidential candidate Richard M. Nixon announced that a "first priority" of his administration would be to "strengthen our air controller force, improve their working conditions and provide them with the new equipment they need to keep our airways safe."[68]

This was heady stuff for an organization only months old, and it changed the thinking of many PATCO activists. After its job action, PATCO leaders still boasted that their organization gave "the Air Traffic Controller *profession* the status it has long deserved." But the job action taught PATCO activists that they could advance their professional status through union tactics. That realization helped many overcome their remaining ambivalence about making PATCO a true union.[69]

When the PATCO board met in Kansas City on October 17, 1968, the organization's leaders surveyed a new landscape. "A year ago, for a controller to go against the 'system' would have cost him dearly," one board member observed. But ten months of struggle had produced dramatic change. Controllers now had a national organization capable of defending them. As Jack Maher observed, "It hurt—but we have made it."[70]

CONFLICTION

Theory is that the mailman is a family friend, so
you can't hurt him, but no one knows the air traffic man.
—H.R. HALDEMAN, 1970

The guys are using the word strike. They say the only way
they can get any action out of the FAA is to strike—to
shut this country down.
—NOEL KEANE, 1970

Even after PATCO's 1968 confrontation with the FAA most of its members did not think of their organization as a union. This was not surprising, because PATCO looked nothing like a union. Although PATCO had decided to bar FAA supervisors, it still boasted sixty "corporate members" and seven hundred sympathetic pilot members in November 1968. PATCO's structure resembled that of a corporation, thanks to Bailey's influence.[1]

Its national office was set up on K Street, Washington's lobbyists' row. To run the organization's day-to-day national operations as executive director, Bailey recruited a lawyer and aviation enthusiast named Herman Meyer. Meyer was no trade unionist. An executive with Learjet, he once worked in the office of the FAA's general counsel. He shared Bailey's thinking that PATCO should stay "professional." Meyer believed that controllers could not elevate their status unless they projected the right image. He did not think staging job actions would help. Thus, when controllers complained about their working conditions, he discouraged them from protesting. "Don't let the fact that you are overworked, that your wife is mad at you because you don't make it home for supper, or that you have short weekends, get you down," he urged. "Be professional."[2]

With this kind of structure and leadership, it is unlikely that PATCO would have developed into a full-blown union if not for two developments. The first was a power struggle that emerged from Meyer's effort to take control of the organization in the winter of 1968–1969. In truth, Meyer's tenure as executive director of PATCO was tenuous from the start. He developed no rapport with PATCO's founding leaders, Rock and Maher, both of whom took leaves of absence from the FAA to work full-time for PATCO in this period. The New Yorkers believed controllers should run the organization. They initially tolerated Meyer only because he was Bailey's man. But when Meyer tried to take the lead on matters such as lobbying, they resisted the man they took to calling "Herman the German." Bailey was one thing. At least he helped give PATCO a high profile. But Maher and Rock had no intention of letting Meyer influence PATCO's direction. By February 1969, they were organizing the board against him. They made quick work of it. On March 10, 1969, the board voted 25–2 to fire Meyer. Rock later called it the "first revolt in PATCO." It would not be the last.[3]

Meyer's removal was a turning point for PATCO. It sent the message that it would be a controller-run organization, and that Bailey would not control its destiny. And it solidified a strong team of PATCO leaders. After ousting Meyer, Sommer moved to Washington and shared the work of running PATCO with Rock and Maher. The three soon gained effective control over the operation of the organization and exercised more influence than Bailey. Within a few months, they had revamped the Washington office, paid down PATCO's debt, set up a network of facility representatives, and increased membership to more than seven thousand dues-payers. As veterans of NAGE, all three had come to think of PATCO as a union in the making.[4]

The second development was the deterioration in relations between PATCO and the government in 1969. Once again, the FAA failed to make good on its promises. For budgetary reasons, the FAA resisted implementing the overtime pay bill that President Johnson had signed in October 1968. Controllers saw little change in the overtime situation. Similarly, the FAA's promised reclassification of controllers in some high-density facilities into higher-paying pay grades never happened. FAA officials, determined to nip PATCO militancy in the bud, did not want to be perceived as rewarding PATCO's job action. They also resented the fact that controllers—non–college graduates trained at government expense and earning good salaries—had the audacity to make demands of the agency. Bailey warned that the FAA's attitude "would force PATCO to act like a union," but the agency refused to relent. Relations deteriorated to the point that the FAA warned the lame-duck Johnson White House that another PATCO slowdown might be initiated in December 1968. No renewal of the job action took place, but in January 1969, PATCO spouses began picketing airports, blaming the FAA for their husbands' "high blood pressure, heart disease, nervous breakdowns, [and] the highest rate of ulcers of any occupation in the United States."[5]

The Nixon administration's arrival only worsened matters. PATCO leaders had been encouraged by Nixon's campaign pledge to improve air traffic control and by his nomination of Governor John Volpe of Massachusetts as transportation secretary. Bailey knew Volpe and had even flown the governor in his jet. During these flights, Bailey deliberately left the loudspeakers on so that Volpe could "become acquainted firsthand with the frenetic pace of the communications of air traffic control." As one of the nation's most prominent Italian-Americans, Volpe also represented a constituency that Nixon sought to court, which gave him significant influence in the administration. But Volpe was not keen on negotiating with an aggressive employee group. Moreover, his deputy James Beggs was positively hostile to PATCO. A former official with National Aeronautics and Space Administration (NASA), Beggs began his career at Westinghouse Electric in the 1950s, where he came to despise labor unions. He was convinced they had no place in the FAA. He dismissed out of hand the controllers' contention that they were underpaid and overworked.[6]

Nixon's choice for FAA administrator, John Shaffer, initially held a more benign view of PATCO, but he was unable to reverse the growing animosity between the organization and his agency. A graduate of West Point, World War II combat flyer, and former executive for the nonunion corporation TRW, Shaffer had never before negotiated with unions. Perhaps because of his lack of labor experience, he was open-minded in his first dealings with Rock and Maher. He enjoyed pouring drinks for them and other PATCO activists who visited his office and he relaxed in their presence, indulging a penchant for profanity that occasionally shocked Rock, who was himself proficient in its use. Shaffer was also genuinely interested in improving labor relations at the FAA. After taking office, he urged controllers to express their concerns about agency policies "without fear of reprisal." Yet he was unable to ease relations between PATCO and the government for three reasons. He could not overrule his boss, Secretary Volpe, with whom he got along poorly. (Shaffer occasionally referred to Volpe as "that little Dago down the street" and once spat on his portrait in the presence of PATCO leaders.) He disliked and distrusted Bailey. And he never won the support of the FAA's powerful regional administrators and facility chiefs, who opposed compromising with PATCO.[7]

Despite Shaffer's desire to avoid confrontation, the FAA's independent-minded regional administrators decided to step up resistance against PATCO after Operation Air Safety. They inaugurated what PATCO called a "cold war" in the facilities. Controllers fought back. At New York Center, controllers decided they would no longer sign a logbook each time they used the bathroom, as their facility chief required. When the chief threatened to penalize them, they held their ground and forced him to back down. At Kansas City Center, PATCO controllers began refusing requests to work overtime. And when the chief at Cleveland Center tried to ban controllers with beards from using FAMs because they hurt the "true FAA image," PATCO created such a fuss that Washington officials forced the chief to rescind his order. Bailey might not have been a unionist, but he urged controllers to continue to resist the speedup of their jobs, saying, "If governmental pressure in any form is brought upon you to compromise flight safety by assuming an unrealistic overload, refuse the assignment and report the matter to PATCO at once."[8]

As relations with the FAA soured, PATCO induced friendly legislators to intervene on the organization's behalf, substituting lobbying efforts for their inability of bargain effectively under EO 10988. PATCO found strong allies in Senator Vance Hartke of Indiana and Representative Samuel N. Friedel of Maryland, both Democrats. In 1969 they introduced the New Air Traffic Controller Act, PATCO-endorsed legislation that would provide for early retirement for controllers. Democratic Representative Morris Udall of Arizona also helped, calling for an investigation into the FAA's handling of controllers' overtime following the 1968 law. FAA officials opposed these legislative initiatives and grew angry about what they saw as PATCO's med-dling in agency governance, both on Capitol Hill and in the facilities. Deputy Administrator Thomas alleged that PATCO's activism would create a "state of anarchy" if it continued.[9]

By the time PATCO opened its national convention in Miami on May 23, 1969, conflict between the agency and the organization had escalated. PATCO leaders were convinced they had to pressure the FAA to keep the commitments made after Operation Air Safety. At the convention, delegates elected Jimmy Hays of O'Hare, a hero of the 1968 slowdown, as PATCO's first president. They reconfirmed Rock as chairman of the board and Stan Gordon as treasurer. Delegates then considered how to bring pressure on the FAA. They received little encouragement from Bailey, who opposed another confrontation. "There will be no demonstrations and no slowdown of any kind," he told delegates during his convention speech. But PATCO's leaders were not dissuaded.[10]

When Senator Vance Hartke, the convention's top invited speaker, asked Jack Maher to help him draft his remarks for the event, PATCO leaders saw an opening. Maher seized the opportunity to pen a fiery speech urging controllers to take militant action. Hartke was so horrified by the draft that he deleted vast sections of it, but even in redacted form it retained a militant tone. "Controllers have had enough of vacillation, hesitation, conversation, and procrastination," the senator thundered from the podium. Rock and Maher, in turn, used Hartke's speech to argue that if controllers did stage a job action, they would find a sympathetic audience on Capitol Hill. Speaking to delegates in small clusters before the convention broke up, Rock urged them to "go back to the facilities and relay the message" Hartke had given them. In the meantime, he made plans for a job action, which he called "our first sickout."[11]

The planning for this job action took place amid rising frustration across the country. In an influential April 1969 essay, called "Revolt of the White Lower Middle Class," writer Pete Hamill described the impatience felt by many people who shared the demographic profile of air traffic controllers. Hamill argued that the political disruptions of the 1960s, rising inflation, and the slowing of economic growth produced a rebellious attitude among whites he described as lower middle-class. According to Hamill, they felt a "terrible unfairness in their lives, and an increasing lack of personal control over what happens to them." This phenomenon intersected with the rising tide of public sector unionism in general in the late 1960s to produce increasing militancy among largely white, uniformed government workers who had not been prone to militancy before, such as police officers and fire fighters. These workers did not have the right to strike and rarely attempted outright walkouts because of the risk of a public backlash. But by 1969, they were experimenting with orchestrated efforts to call in sick, the same tactic that gained PATCO's attention. The "sickout" was becoming common enough that cops jokingly called it the "blue flu" and firefighters the "red rash."[12]

"D-Day June 18th!"

PATCO never made a formal decision to conduct a sickout against the FAA. PATCO leaders knew they could not persuade a majority of delegates at the Miami convention to call a sickout, since many still hoped that the organization's differences with the FAA could be worked out amicably. Rock thought that such hopes were naïve, and he worked tirelessly after the convention to organize a job action that could regain PATCO's leverage with the FAA. Just as Operation Air Safety did not require a majority of controllers to participate, the job action Rock had in mind could be effective if he could organize groups of activists in several key facilities to act. He focused on Kansas City, Denver, and Houston as essential nodes and lined up leadership in those locations. Rock's strategy was to put one or two facilities "out on a limb" and then ask others to join in to protect the initial sickout participants from discipline.[13]

How and when to trigger the action was Rock's main problem. A solution presented itself when television host Johnny Carson booked his friend Bailey for an appearance on his *Tonight Show* for June 17, 1969. Earlier that day, Secretary Volpe and FAA Administrator Shaffer were scheduled to testify before the Senate Commerce Committee's aviation subcommittee. In this confluence of events, Rock saw an opportunity to use Bailey's television appearance to signal a strike against the government.

Controversy shrouds this event, and accounts of its origins differ. But these aspects of the story are beyond dispute. In their testimony before the Senate on June 17, Shaffer and Volpe refused to endorse Sen. Hartke's air traffic controller bill and characterized controllers' grievances as overblown. The testimony infuriated PATCO leaders. That night, Bailey spoke of brewing tensions in air traffic control facilities during his appearance on the *Tonight Show*. Unless the FAA addressed controllers' grievances, Bailey warned, the nation was bound to endure a summer of increasing traffic delays. "I'd start walking if I were you—it's going to be tough," PATCO's general counsel told Carson. The next day, air traffic controllers in Kansas City, Houston, and Denver called in sick en masse, and when word of their job action spread, New York controllers followed suit, precipitating nation-wide air traffic tie-ups.[14]

Whether Bailey knowingly participated in this event is unclear. He later denied any direct involvement or foreknowledge. It is possible that Rock instructed facility leaders in chosen locations to listen for phrases that Bailey often used, knowing that Bailey would likely utter the signal. Surviving records indicate that the plans were loose in any event. "If testimony is not favorable, D-Day June 18th!" read a note from Russ Sommer to facility representatives in the Southwest region.[15]

Whether Bailey was directly involved or not, he certainly knew the mood of the PATCO activists. Several days before the *Tonight Show* appearance, he warned Volpe that controllers' ability to "hold it together during what must inevitably be another long, hot summer" would be undermined by "any clear evidence that the Administration does not support their general aims." Bailey cautioned that new leaders were gaining influence in PATCO, whose actions he could not "readily predict."[16]

Whether Bailey intended it or not, when PATCO activists Noel Keane in Kansas City, Rex Campbell in Denver, and Carl Evans in Houston heard Bailey tell Johnny Carson, "I'd start walking if I were you," they believed they had been given a signal. They began calling their members and instructing them to call in sick in the morning. Roughly half of the crews in Kansas City and Denver, and a lesser number in Houston, failed to report for their 7 a.m. shift. The chief at Kansas City was so taken aback over being deserted by his controllers that he reportedly broke down and cried.[17]

The actions at Kansas City, Denver, and Houston caused significant delays. However, Rock and Maher knew they would have a limited impact on the system, and the "sick" controllers would be vulnerable to discipline unless others joined them. Throughout the day on June 18, they spoke to controllers in New York, Chicago, and Washington, hoping to gain support for the sickout. They found an immediate ally in John Leyden, a young New York Center controller who had not played a part in PATCO's early organizing in Islip. An award-winning controller, he was not known as a militant. When Leyden had been involved in an ATCA chapter at New York Center in the early 1960s, Rock had thought of him as a "conservative." But Leyden came from strong union stock. His father was a shop steward in Local 32B of the Service Employees International Union in New York. Leyden had just come off the midnight shift himself when Rock reached him and urged him to "pull all his guys out." When Leyden realized that the Midwest controllers would be vulnerable to discipline if they were out on their own, he did not hesitate. He immediately called in sick himself and spread word among the New York Center controllers that they ought to do the same.[18]

Over the course of June 18, the numbers of sick New Yorkers began to climb and air traffic delays began to mount. By the next morning, more than one-third of New York Center controllers were sick, and another ten percent of the day shift's controllers left during their shift, complaining of illness. Two-thirds of the evening shift called in sick on June 19. In all, about 240 New York controllers were out on June 19. Controllers at Chicago Center followed the example of the New Yorkers; one-third of the evening shift failed to report to the Aurora, Illinois, facility. "Nobody was scared," Rock marveled. Reports reached Washington that one Chicago Center controller who called in sick "was observed at Howard's Bar setting up the 'sick-in' exercise." An assistant chief at Kansas City Tower reported that when he asked one sick controller what ailed him, he was told simply, "Well, Jim, I had to go along with the boys." Within forty-eight hours of Bailey's *Tonight Show* appearance, the *New York Times* reported that, "air travel throughout much of the nation was turned into near chaos."[19]

Delays were worst around New York, where the FAA registered approximately one thousand delayed flights. At one point, sixty jets, their passengers fidgeting, were backed up at JFK in "a double line reminiscent of a rush-hour jam on the Long Island Expressway," as the *New York Times* described it. "It's worse than anything we had last summer," concluded an exasperated airline spokesperson. The FAA estimated that more than two hundred thousand travelers saw flights delayed or canceled.[20]

PATCO came under criticism for the job action. "Calling in 'sick' has become a popular form of lying, especially in government jobs where strikes are prohibited, since teachers in several cities and policemen in New York have shown that they could get away with it," groused the *Chicago Tribune*. Yet PATCO generally received sympathetic press coverage.

Even the *Tribune* placed most of the blame for the sickout on the FAA. "The failure of management in the agency is worse than the behavior of the controllers who employ subterfuge to make their protest," it concluded. The *Dallas Morning News* admitted that PATCO had made an important point about a system in need of reform, "whether their methods were justified or not."[21]

Government officials were livid. Secretary Volpe demanded that Bailey come to Washington on the morning of June 19 to meet with him. When Bailey arrived, he found Shaffer and Beggs waiting with Volpe. The level of animosity in the room was high, and the four argued heatedly. Bailey denied his involvement in the sickout, but offered to do what he could to end it if the FAA agreed to negotiate with him. At that point Bailey and Shaffer retreated to Shaffer's office to commence a daylong negotiation. Bailey wanted the FAA to support the key elements of Hartke's bill: a twenty-year retirement threshold for controllers; an increase in the number of top pay grades controllers could attain; an option that would allow controllers to rotate out of high-density service areas without loss of pay; and no reprisals or harassments of any kind against controllers who participated in the sickout. In the end, Shaffer would only agree to a vague statement saying that the FAA would study early retirement among other options "as ways to make the air traffic control profession more appealing." Believing that this was the best he could get, Bailey said he would call the "sick" controllers back to work.[22]

When Bailey informed Rock and Maher about the results of his negotiation, they were unimpressed and insisted that the sickout continue. While Bailey had been talking with Shaffer, Rock and Maher had initiated their own negotiations with an adviser to President Nixon. Through Helen Bentley, a well-connected labor reporter with the *Baltimore Sun*, they contacted Clark R. Mollenhoff, special counsel to President Nixon. Mollenhoff agreed to speak with them in secret, and the controllers were convinced that the Nixon administration might deliver a better deal through Mollenhoff if PATCO kept up the pressure a little longer.[23]

On the night of June 19, Rock, Maher, Bailey, and Gordon met in a Washington National Airport lounge to discuss their next steps. Rock urged that the sickout go on until all of their demands were met in writing, insisting that the Mollenhoff opening would pan out. PATCO had the FAA "by the short hairs," he said. Maher agreed. But Bailey was adamant that the sickout was making implacable enemies for PATCO and that Volpe could be trusted to help pass PATCO's legislation if the job action ended. It was an emotionally charged exchange, but Bailey prevailed in the end. Later, Rock admitted that he and Maher "broke down crying" after the meeting. Nonetheless, they went to the nearest pay phones and began making calls to end the sickout, believing all the while that it was the wrong decision. Had PATCO kept up the sickout, they were convinced, it would have won for, as Maher put it, "the government did not know what to do—they had never experienced anything of this magnitude before."[24]

As it was, PATCO's leaders soon found that not only had they failed to beat the FAA; they actually lost ground as a result of the sickout. PATCO leaders put the best face they could on their effort, after calling off the action. Organizers made calls over FAA lines from one facility to another announcing, "We won; everything goes back to normal." Maher told the press that controllers "had made their point." More ominously, though, FAA officials not only denied making an agreement with PATCO, they announced an investigation of the sickout. PATCO's nemesis, Kenneth Lyons of NAGE, insisted that his rivals be punished for their illegal job action. Lyons's threats of legal action forced Shaffer to back away from his verbal assurance to Bailey that there would be amnesty for sickout participants.[25]

PATCO leaders felt betrayed. Some returning controllers were threatened with indictment and firing unless they signed statements admitting their culpability. More than 150 ended up claiming their Fifth Amendment rights when asked whether they had been aware of plans for a concerted job action. Outraged at the pressure controllers were receiving from their managers, PATCO leaders threatened to bring air traffic "to a stop" on Monday June 23 if the government did not cease such harassment. The FAA was "sitting on a time bomb and this thing still might go off any moment," Rock warned. But the FAA called PATCO's bluff, and no renewal of the job action took place. Once the sickout had passed, press coverage shifted back in the government's favor. One editorial decided that controllers had "overplayed their hand." Others worried that if PATCO went unpunished, "sudden 'sickness'" might become "the forerunner of federal strikes." Many suggested that the controllers were accruing too much power. "In 48 hours they were threatening the breakdown of the entire continental air safety and separation system," huffed the *Chicago Tribune.*[26]

"We Face Disaster"

With PATCO knocked back on its heels by the failed sickout, the FAA went on the offensive. On July 18, Shaffer announced that PATCO had staged a "concerted work stoppage," and, as a result, the controllers involved would be disciplined by reprimands, suspensions, and "outright removal in a few cases." Additionally, the FAA canceled leaves of absence for Rock, Maher, and Sommer. Most important, the agency terminated PATCO's dues collection agreement. These actions won public support. "If the government let the controllers circumvent the strike ban, the precedent would be fixed and the prohibition throughout the Federal service made meaningless," explained the *New York Times*.[27]

PATCO officials called these actions a declaration of "open war." On July 21, more than one hundred controllers met at the Holiday Inn in Port Jefferson, New York, not far from New York Center, to consider organizing a mass resignation in protest. Maher, Bailey, and Sommer claimed PATCO could marshal up to five thousand resignations if the FAA did not relent. The government was unmoved. "We are hopeful it will not happen, but we are prepared to operate the systems," announced Secretary Volpe. As a precaution, the Defense Department agreed to move military air traffic controllers into FAA facilities if needed.[28]

At the same time, Volpe and Shaffer tried to assuage the controllers' anger. Shaffer invited leaders of PATCO and its rivals, NAGE and the ATCA, to discuss their grievances with him in a joint meeting. Meanwhile, Volpe formed a blue-ribbon commission to study air traffic controllers' problems. The commission would come to be known as the Corson Commission for Dr. John Jay Corson, a consultant from Arlington, Virginia, whom Volpe tapped to chair it. Commission members included experts on labor relations, aviation, and air traffic control. Its executive director was Bert Harding, a widely respected former aide to Sargent Shriver at the Office of Economic Opportunity.[29]

In time, the Corson Commission's work would yield important reforms for air traffic controllers, but as the summer of 1969 drew to a close, its deliberations did PATCO little good. The organization was in a tailspin. When the FAA began suspending controllers who had called in sick, PATCO's mass resignation threat was shown to be a bluff: no one resigned. Rather, members tried to fight suspensions with notes from their physicians attesting to their stress levels.[30]

As PATCO retreated a rift began to open between Bailey and controller-leaders Rock and Maher. In August 1969, the New Yorkers began to consider breaking with Bailey and affiliating PATCO with a union that could provide it support and protection. At the suggestion of *Baltimore Sun* reporter Helen Bentley, who had helped them during the sickout, they began talking with Jesse N. Calhoon, president of the small, but politically potent, Marine Engineers' Beneficial Association (MEBA), an AFL-CIO affiliate that organized the crews of oceangoing vessels. Rock was so impressed by these discussions that he arranged for Calhoon to meet PATCO's executive board without Bailey's knowledge.[31]

Calhoon was in a position to offer PATCO advice, connections, and cash. The advice came first. Avoid outright confrontations with the government, Calhoon counseled. "If they want to beat you, they'll beat you. You do not take on the Congress of the United States and the President of the United States and expect to win." Calhoon next offered his connections. Because MEBA was an active donor to political campaigns, Calhoon could provide access to political actors, such as Senator Warren Magnuson, a Washington state Democrat who chaired the Senate Commerce Committee's aviation subcommittee. At one point, Calhoon helped arrange a meeting between Maher and House Minority Leader Gerald R. Ford of Michigan, in which Ford agreed to approach the FAA about granting a representation election for PATCO as long as his involvement remained secret. Then came the cash. MEBA had a substantial treasury. In September 1969, Calhoon offered a $100,000 loan to help PATCO cover the shortfalls created by its loss of dues withholding. When the FAA tried to block Russ Sommer's return to his old job at Los Angeles Center, Calhoon put Sommer on MEBA's payroll. Over time, PATCO's connection to MEBA would grow stronger.[32]

As Rock and Maher courted Calhoon, the situation at the FAA deteriorated. Around the country, facility chiefs leaned hard on local controller activists. But the toughest blow came when the FAA's Southwest regional director, Henry Newman, who was widely known to oppose controller organization, ordered the mandatory transfer of three PATCO leaders and a sympathetic supervisor from the tower at Baton Rouge, Louisiana, one of the few facilities in the South that was 100 percent organized.[33]

PATCO leaders believed that if they did not resist this effort to break up their Baton Rouge stronghold, they would be "finished in the Southwest Region." And if the FAA could undermine the organization in that region, it would be "the beginning of the end of PATCO," according to Rock. On October 10, 1969, the PATCO board discussed the Baton Rouge case and agreed with Rock that unless they could stop Newman, the FAA might begin transferring controller activists "to Alaska or Guam or wherever the hell they wanted." The board drafted a statement asking the government to rescind the transfers "at once," lest it face "a demonstration on a National basis." Calling the Baton Rouge case "the acid test for controller unity over the country," PATCO announced that it would fight for the Baton Rouge four "no matter what the cost."[34]

Bailey was also ready to fight. He was offended by the FAA's postsickout reprisals and felt that Shaffer had been dishonest with him. The Baton Rouge fight thus unified PATCO, submerging the tensions that had developed between Bailey and the organization's controller-leaders, Rock and Maher. Bailey began touring the FAA's biggest Midwest facilities with Jimmy Hays to rally controllers for the impending struggle. In Indianapolis on October 22, Bailey told controllers that "battle lines" were being drawn. Days later, he warned that a "direct confrontation is looming between FAA and PATCO," and urged President Nixon to "become personally concerned with the problem." He brought his message to a Capitol Hill hearing on November 21, arguing that controllers were suffering "a brutal battering of their morale." He also penned a blistering letter to Shaffer. It savaged the FAA administrator for his "total incompetency," and informed him that unless the FAA fixed the situation PATCO would withdraw "any recognition of you as an administrator of anything and of the FAA as a supervisory force." "If you have any question as to why we must act in this fashion," Bailey closed, "I suggest that you read the Declaration of Independence."[35]

Both PATCO and the FAA sought ways to avoid conflict over the Baton Rouge transfers. The two sides tried and failed to resolve the issue in a November 19 meeting. The FAA twice postponed the transfers, originally set for November 26, in the hopes that tempers would cool. PATCO leaders took advantage of the delay to appeal to President Nixon's labor secretary, George P. Shultz, for help. They asked Shultz to authorize an agency-wide election that could certify PATCO as the collective bargaining agent for controllers under the newly promulgated Executive Order 11491. Nixon had signed that order on October 29 to correct some of the obvious flaws of Kennedy's EO 10988 (including its failure to provide for agency-wide union elections that would give unions the ability to negotiate with agencies on a national level). PATCO leaders believed agency-wide recognition under EO 11491 would protect their members from unfair labor practices like disciplinary transfers. But Shultz would not intervene in PATCO's dispute with the FAA.[36]

As 1969 drew to a close, a conflict seemed unavoidable. The FAA was determined to show that it could not be intimidated. PATCO leaders, in turn, were worried that if they did not fight back soon, they would grow too weak to fight back at all. Losing its dues checkoff arrangement badly injured PATCO's finances. The organization counted only 4,284 members whose dues were current. Three thousand more were months behind on payments. "It is easy to see if this trend is not reversed we face disaster," Rock noted. If the FAA knew how weak the organization was becoming, it would "try to bust us altogether," he predicted.[37]

"Using the Word 'Strike'"

As 1970 began, the conflict brewing between PATCO and the FAA was indicative of a national trend. As union membership grew among state, local, and federal workers, many governments resisted their demands. The unions in turn became increasingly militant. Many followed the example of the fastest-growing union of government workers, the American Federation of State, County and Municipal Employees (AFSCME), which changed its constitution in 1966 to assert the right to strike for all public workers, except law enforcement officers. The number of public sector strikes rose steadily from 15 in 1958 to 411 in 1969. As strikes multiplied, public attitudes became more tolerant. The National Council of Churches, for one, argued that, "public employees should not be denied the right to strike solely by virtue of their public employment."[38]

In 1970, just as PATCO was confronting the FAA, public sector labor militancy was making a quantum leap. While the antiwar protests of 1970 are better remembered, the militancy of government workers was no less evident. New Jersey alone saw twenty-five public sector strikes—up from only one in 1962. During the first three months of 1970, U.S. public workers struck government agencies at a rate of one every thirty-six hours. Over a ten-week period, strikes erupted in twenty-four cities and twenty-eight school systems. Many believed that federal workers would inevitably be affected by this militancy. Indeed, in February 1970, former assistant postmaster general Richard Murphy predicted the federal government would "begin to face much the same sort of strike activity which has so plagued local and state governments in recent years, especially when professional employees become militant and strike." Federal workers would "soon realize," wrote Murphy, that "those who are engaged in the most essential work stand the best chance of winning their objectives quickly through a discontinuance of service." In this context, it is no surprise that PATCO, in describing their options, began using a six-letter word for the first time in public. "The guys are using the word strike," Noel Keane told the *Kansas City Times*. "They say the only way they can get any action out of the FAA is to strike—to shut this country down."[39]

PATCO convened a two-day board meeting at the Jack Tar Hotel in San Francisco on January 23, 1970, to prepare for a confrontation. Before flying to that meeting, Rock and Jimmy Hays met FAA Administrator Shaffer in one last effort to block the transfers. Had it been up to him alone, Shaffer might have agreed with them. But he was under pressure from multiple sources—including regional director Newman, Secretary Volpe, the ATCA, and NAGE—to hold the line. He said there was nothing he could do.[40]

When Rock and Hays shared this news at the Jack Tar the following day, PATCO's course seemed clear. If they did not fight the transfers, the board decided, their organization would be revealed as a paper tiger and its days would be numbered. Thus the board authorized a national job action. To plan the effort, it opened the meeting to PATCO facility representatives and activists from around the country. More than two hundred had already FAMed in to see what the board would decide. The resulting debate concerned not whether PATCO should act, but how. Rock laid out three alternatives: a slowdown, an outright strike, or a strike in the form of a sick-out. Some favored an outright strike, but most judged an open strike to be too risky, since it would be clearly illegal. A slowdown seemed equally unsat-isfactory, since, as happened during Operation Air Safety, it might take weeks before the FAA would even admit that a slowdown existed, let alone attempt to end it through negotiations. A national sickout strike was thus deemed the most appropriate response. After a five-hour discussion, the board voted to call the sickout at noon on Sunday February 15, unless the FAA rescinded the transfers. The plan was to convene sickout participants in locations near their facilities after midnight on the 14th for what was called a "horse count." Attending the meeting meant a controller agreed to call in sick. One after another, they would do so in each other's presence as an expression of solidarity.[41]

Whether PATCO could get enough controllers to participate to make the action effective was never clear. Few activists at the Jack Tar meeting spoke frankly about the levels of support they might get in their facilities. Wanting to avoid being seen as "chicken shit," most facility representatives gave inflated estimates—except for those from the South. "We can't get the guys to go out," said Bill South of Jacksonville. "They're scared." No matter what level of support PATCO could command, its leaders felt they had to act. In PATCO strongholds members were growing impatient. When rank-and-file PATCO members in Oakland learned that they should "expect a strike," they leaped to their feet in a standing ovation.[42]

Before closing the meeting, the board drafted a telegram to John Volpe. It demanded that he halt the transfers and agree to outside arbitration. If PATCO's demands were not met, it said, "all optional air traffic services rendered by our membership above and beyond those that they are required to perform by their contract and by regulations will be withdrawn." The government's response was blunt. The FAA warned PATCO that a "withdrawal of services" would "constitute an illegal strike." As it would do repeatedly in later years, the FAA underestimated the level of discontent among controllers. Its confidential internal memos predicted that, "only at Denver would the controllers possibly be willing to strike" and contended the PATCO board's position did not "really represent the view of the rank and file PATCO members." The FAA was "optimistic" that the threat would dissipate.[43]

The FAA's optimism hinged in part on the promulgation of the Corson Commission's report on January 29, for the report validated many of the controllers' claims and offered the agency an opportunity to embrace reforms not forced on it by employees. The report criticized the FAA. It placed much of the blame for the agency's deteriorating labor relations on "the failure of FAA's management at all levels to truly understand the role of the employee organizations and to accept them as not only legitimate, but hopefully as collaborators in building understanding, satisfaction and an *esprit d' corps.*" Commission members were astonished to learn that Las Vegas blackjack dealers were entitled to more frequent breaks than air traffic controllers. Nor had they ever seen a situation "in which there is as much mutual resentment and antagonism between management and its employees." The FAA pledged to respond to the report's recommendations and hoped this would assuage controllers' anger. But the report backfired, inflaming tensions among controllers instead of reducing them. PATCO was disappointed that Corson said nothing about salary raises, and furious that the FAA announced the creation of employee-management "air traffic advisory committees" to recommend responses to the report. Rock saw these committees as efforts to further displace PATCO.[44]

When it became apparent that the Corson report would not head off the sickout strike, the FAA prepared in earnest for a conflict as PATCO's February 15 deadline neared. It distributed strike contingency plans to all facilities and stepped up its intelligence-gathering efforts. In the months after the June 1969 sickout, many PATCO leaders became convinced that their telephones were tapped. In August 1969, PATCO board member Jerry Miles publicly alleged that the FBI was recording PATCO phone calls. Several PATCO leaders, including Bill South and F. Lee Bailey, reported evidence that seemed to substantiate these allegations. Nonetheless, PATCO had no proof, and an irate FBI Director J. Edgar Hoover forced Bailey to retract the claim. Yet the FBI was not the only agency capable of monitoring controllers. The FAA's Compliance and Security division was staffed by experienced investigators who exercised wide latitude. PATCO leaders called them the "FAA's Gestapo," and went to great lengths to make it difficult for them to spy, using elaborate ruses and codes when they called each other. No record of tapped phones exists, but there is clear evidence that the FAA had informants within PATCO's ranks as the sickout strike neared. One informant in Allentown, Pennsylvania, gave the FAA advance details about how the sickout would be organized. Such surveillance no doubt increased the likelihood of conflict. On the one hand, it exacerbated the animosity of PATCO activists toward the agency; on the other hand, it led FAA officials to believe they had the upper hand and could win any fight with PATCO.[45]

In the last days before the deadline, PATCO leaders pushed hard to boost participation in the scheduled sickout. F. Lee Bailey flew across the country and met with controller activists in areas of PATCO strength, preparing the organization for battle. At meetings like the one held with two hundred controllers in an American Legion hall in Olathe, Kansas, Bailey fired up the membership with talk of an imminent confrontation. On the afternoon of Saturday February 14, Bailey arrived at a Holiday Inn not far from New York Center to caucus with Rock, Maher, and other leaders as the deadline neared.

Those present felt that within the next week PATCO would either "become a solid national organization, or it will have ceased to exist."[46]

The leadership caucus was interrupted at 4 p.m. by a phone call from James Beggs, Volpe's deputy. Beggs offered a meeting between Bailey and Secretary Volpe on Monday February 16, if PATCO called off the pending job action. Sensitive to criticism from PATCO leaders that he had ended the 1969 sickout too soon, Bailey refused. Several hours later, Beggs upped the ante. He offered a meeting with Volpe the next day, said the agency would allow a neutral third party to facilitate negotiations, and promised to address the Baton Rouge transfers with the intention of producing a mutually acceptable outcome. The only catch: Volpe could not meet until 1 p.m. on February 15, one hour after their deadline. Beggs added that Volpe would not meet with them if a job action was underway. The PATCO leaders debated the offer. Some saw it as a ruse, and argued that the organization should "pull the trigger" at noon on the 15th. But this time, Rock, whose militancy had already earned him the sobriquet "Mike Strike" among his colleagues, argued for patience: "No, for a lousy stinking hour we're not going to go on strike." His argument carried the day. At midnight, Bailey informed Beggs that PATCO leaders would come to Washington; the sickout was postponed.[47]

The next morning they flew to Washington, and at 1 p.m., Bailey, Rock, Jimmy Hays, and a few others walked into Volpe's Seventh Street office. There, they found the secretary, Shaffer, Beggs, and their top staff. The sides talked about the Baton Rouge case in general terms, and agreed to invite the Federal Mediation and Conciliation Service (FMCS) to help resolve the dispute.[48]

FMCS director Curt Counts assigned his special assistant, a seasoned mediator named Kenneth E. Moffett, to the case. The son of a United Mine Workers official, Moffett worked for the union before joining the FMCS in 1961. After mediating disputes in the auto, steel, and newspaper industries from its Cleveland office, Moffett came to Washington to work under Counts. PATCO could hardly have gotten a more sympathetic mediator.[49]

Two days after the meeting, Moffett brokered an agreement between the sides to create a fact-finding panel charged with making a recommendation on the transfers. The parties agreed that an FMCS representative would chair the panel, with PATCO and the government each naming one member to it. Until the case was decided, the FAA agreed to postpone any transfers.

Crucially, however, the FAA never agreed in writing to abide by the panel's findings. Despite this omission, PATCO officials viewed the agreement as historic, "the first time in the history of this country that a grievance of federal employees was submitted to arbitration of any sort by an official third party mediator." Rank-and-file controllers were also pleased. "You got them to cry uncle," said one, who noted he was "proud to be a member of an outfit that really has a set."[50]

In reality, the government had not "cried uncle." When the fact-finding panel, chaired by FMCS mediator L. Lawrence Schultz, delivered a 2–1 decision calling upon the FAA to cancel the transfers, Secretary Volpe simply ignored the finding. On March 13, he announced that the Baton Rouge transfers would take effect on March 30. Shaffer informed Bailey that further discussion "would serve no useful purpose."[51]

Feeling that they had no choice now except to resist a blatant effort to override the mediator's findings, the PATCO board set March 25 as the date to commence a national sickout. PATCO leaders believed that if they could get two thousand controllers at key facilities to participate, they could make the system "fold." In order to build support for the sickout, the board drew up a list of demands that went well beyond the issue of the Baton Rouge transfers. They wanted the reclassification of radar controllers to GS-15 and nonradar controllers to GS-14 on the federal salary scale, a six-hour workday, an immediate vote for exclusive representation for PATCO, a twenty-year retirement plan, and amnesty for anyone who participated in the job action. Controllers were advised to assemble in local "horse count" meetings on the night of March 24. They were to call in sick "one hour before time of watch and no sooner" and be prepared to "stay out 10 days or longer." PATCO made no effort to preserve an element of surprise. To the contrary, Rock sent a letter to Defense Secretary Melvin Laird, urging him to take whatever measures were necessary so that the job action would not affect the war effort in Vietnam. PATCO was confident that the FAA would gain no advantage by knowing that a sickout was coming. "There is no individual in this country who can replace the trained air traffic controller," assured PATCO spokesperson Robert Sturgill.[52]

The FAA viewed PATCO's threat as an effort by the organization to "run the FAA," and the agency had no intention of giving in. If PATCO succeeded, one FAA official believed, the organization would be "slowing down traffic whenever something didn't please them." The agency's main concern was to prevent the Labor Department, Civil Service Commission, or other agencies from intervening and trying to mediate the conflict: PATCO had to be defeated. Shaffer's deputy, Alan Dean, drafted a battle plan for the agency that he believed would do the trick in three weeks—just long enough for participating controllers to feel enough of a financial pinch from fines and lost wages to give up their fight. Volpe and Beggs approved Dean's plan and brought it to the White House, where they secured permission to execute it.[53]

Since the first recorded strike against the federal government—an 1835 walkout in the District of Columbia by Washington Navy Yard workers—workers' collective action against the federal government had always been illegal. The 1912 Lloyd-LaFollette Act, which first permitted postal workers to form organizations, specifically prohibited them from joining groups that asserted the right to strike. Federal policy remained consistent on this point from the New Deal through EO 10988. Of course, sporadic strikes had occurred despite the ban. Twenty-five strikes by federal workers were recorded before 1961. But until 1970, federal walkouts tended to be small, isolated, and short, and none significantly disrupted a vital national service. In 1970, the government faced not one but two disruptive job actions. On March 18, postal workers in New York City launched a strike that spread within days to involve over two hundred thousand employees of the Post Office Department. By March 23, President Nixon had asked the National Guard to begin delivering mail in some locations and his administration was promising to address the postal workers' long-festering grievances. The postal strike was winding down just as PATCO's deadline was approaching—and PATCO leaders were confident that they could use their strike and negotiate important reforms, just as their postal counterparts appeared to be doing.[54]

Yet PATCO's threat was unprecedented. The postal strike was a spontaneous, largely uncoordinated uprising that had spread despite the opposition of national postal union leaders. By contrast, under the guise of a sickout, PATCO was poised to carry out the first centrally planned national strike against the federal government. Some controllers clearly were nervous about the prospect. One worried that a national sickout would align PATCO with the "current crop of 'nuts' and 'rabble rousers' who are terrorizing our streets and campuses." But most PATCO supporters believed the time for action had come. "No one really wants this," said Edward Doeble, of New

York Center. "I think it's drastically wrong to do this to the government, but then the government is wrong, too. I don't know what else we can do. We're at a perfect standstill." The "various executive orders hadn't given really much in terms of rights," said another. If PATCO did not stand up now, the organization would collapse, leaders concluded. When the agency refused to rescind the Baton Rouge transfers during a meeting with PATCO on March 23, Rock vowed that the next time he spoke with the FAA, it would be from a jail cell.[55]

The "Easter Uprising"

In the predawn hours on Wednesday, March 25, air traffic controllers began gathering at predetermined sites near their facilities to conduct their "horse count" and initiate their third major job action in twenty months. In bars, banquet houses, and meeting halls from the Suffolk House on Lake Ronkonkoma on Long Island, to the Sportsmen's Club in Fremont, California, approximately thirty-nine hundred controllers congregated to encourage each other. Emotions ran high. "Let's show those motherfuckers we mean business," said one angry Jacksonville controller. But there was also plenty of quiet worry. A good number of the controllers who showed up had qualms about engaging in an action that was bound to be seen as illegal. In some places, "horses" showed up only to change their minds and fail to call in sick. From city to city, and region to region, the level of turnout varied. New York, Chicago, and the West Coast turned out the largest numbers. Except for Miami, turnout in the rest of the South was low. Still, when the word came, PATCO's strongest supporters across the country called in sick. Some did so having just gotten off a shift, even though they were not expected back to work for forty-eight hours. Thus began what Bailey called a "roar of wounded defiance."[56]

Altogether, about one-fourth of the assigned workforce called in sick that first morning, significantly impacting twenty facilities. No one reported to work at the Pittsburgh or South Bend towers. Some 40 percent of controllers called in sick at the Kansas City and Minneapolis centers. Half of the absences came from six air route traffic control centers, with New York, Oakland, and Denver centers leading the way. Even some instructors at the FAA's training facility in Oklahoma City called in sick. The absences had an immediate effect. The airline industry claimed that at least one thousand flights were either canceled or delayed by as much as four hours on that first day, affecting one hundred thousand travelers. Landings at the three New York area airports—LaGuardia, JFK, and Newark—were cut from a normal day's average of roughly fifty per hour to just twelve. The impact of the job action rippled across the globe, canceling flights from as far away as Rome and Tokyo. As the sickout gained momentum through the morning, Rock and Bailey convened a news conference in Washington. While they denied a strike was under way, they warned that controllers would continue to call in sick until the FAA accepted mediation.[57]

The FAA had prepared for this moment. It immediately limited the number of flights to hard-hit areas such as New York and Chicago to half of the normal traffic flow. Every day at 11 a.m., regional directors and their deputies conferred with Washington, updating officials on developments in the field and receiving briefings on the national picture. Throughout the early days, Alan Dean also called in hourly reports to Secretary Volpe. Instead of seeking arrests for violating the statute that outlawed federal strikes, as some PATCO leaders expected, the FAA sought temporary restraining orders in several cities to force PATCO into contempt of court violations that could result in costly fines. However, for all the FAA's preparations, the sickout was larger than it expected, and the agency struggled to keep air traffic moving.[58]

The sickout gained momentum on its second day, as many controllers who had been reluctant to call in sick overcame their fears and joined in. Nearly 90 percent of those scheduled to work at Indianapolis Center failed to show up. Combined with snow in the Midwest, the sickout sent average flight delays up to five hours at some airports. New York airports continued to face the worst delays. At one point, sixty jets were lined up for takeoff on the tarmac at Kennedy, some waiting for as long as three hours; twenty-five aircraft at LaGuardia and thirty-three at Newark were in similar straits. Meanwhile, another fifty jets were stacked up above the metro area, circling in the sky as pilots awaited clearance to land. At 5:30 p.m., the situation had deteriorated so much at LaGuardia that the FAA closed the airport completely to arrivals. Smaller airports were also affected. One hapless jet left LaGuardia for Buffalo after a long delay only to find that it could not land there; after being stacked in the skies over the Buffalo airport for more than two hours, the jet returned to LaGuardia.[59]

PATCO's increased pressure elicited increased government resistance. Shaffer accused PATCO leaders of being motivated by "a thirst for power and an utter disregard for the law." Not only did the government refuse to cancel the Baton Rouge transfers, Shaffer threatened to use transfers more liberally if PATCO did not back down. The FAA sent "sick" controllers telegrams demanding that they report to work or face legal sanctions if they did not furnish medical proof of their illness within twenty-four hours. When Bailey asked for a meeting, he was told that the government would not meet with an organization in the midst of an illegal job action. The FAA also received support from the courts, when U.S. District Court Judge E. G. West of Louisiana upheld the legality of the Baton Rouge transfers.[60]

Even if PATCO leaders had been inclined to end the sickout, it is unlikely that they could have done so after two days. The level of fury and frustration that PATCO members felt toward the FAA ran too high. After years of inadequate responses to their grievances, PATCO's activists wanted to act. "It was just time to do something that we weren't supposed to do," explained Bob Butterworth of Burbank Airport. The FAA's threatened sanctions only strengthened PATCO's resolve. When one Denver activist received a telegram requesting medical proof for his absence, his spouse kicked it into the snow. Bailey, too, was angry. When the FAA sent its telegrams, he urged all working controllers to "walk out of every FAA facility until these orders are countermanded."[61]

Still, "sick" controllers took precautions to protect themselves. When the sickout began, many participants joked that they had the "Flener Flu," in honor of the FAA's director of air traffic, William Flener. Once the FAA threatened discipline, however, controllers hunted for doctors who would vouch for their illness. They were not difficult to find. Controllers in Leesburg, Virginia, spread the word about a certified flight surgeon who would write what one called "get out of jail free cards," for "anybody that walked through the door." In many cases, controllers simply asked for and received Valium prescriptions that made them immediately ineligible to work since FAA regulations prohibited the use of narcotics. Others cited more unusual illnesses, such as the "acute rash, which may have been triggered by contact with a cherry hedge," that afflicted a Miami controller. Participants also banded together for mutual support. Some gathered in rented motel rooms or Moose Lodges. Where it was difficult for controllers to congregate, regional call-in numbers were set up through which controllers received taped status reports. [62]

As the sickout passed into Easter weekend, Bailey announced that PATCO was ready for the "long haul." The FAA's internal figures showed the sickout gaining strength each day during its first week. The strongest participation came from the air route traffic centers. On the day before the job action began, all twenty-one of the FAA air route traffic centers were above 90 percent of normal staffing. On the first day of the sickout, only eleven centers met this level, and by the sixth day only four did. In some PATCO strongholds, sickout participation reached crippling proportions. System-wide, the sickout peaked on the Saturday before Easter, with more than fifteen hundred controllers absent from their shifts. That day only 15 of 143 scheduled controllers reported to the day shift at New York Center; no controllers showed up for work at San Francisco Airport. The Oakland Center workforce was cut in half, as was the number of flights originating in Chicago. With no end to the disruptions in sight, worried business executives pleaded with F. Lee Bailey to restore normal flights.[63]

Travelers had been "remarkably forgiving" during the first days of the sickout, as one airline executive put it, but patience began to fray as the job action affected Easter holiday travel. Passengers on one delayed flight from Chicago to Denver drafted an angry letter to President Nixon. "It's really your fault that we have this situation," they wrote. "You sir, are a weak President." Sometimes letters did not suffice. When a flight from O'Hare to Phoenix was delayed for several hours and then finally canceled, angry passengers stormed the ticket counter in frustration. A few rushed out onto the tarmac, and lay down in front of the wheels of another plane until they were assured they would get to their destination. Even President Nixon experienced the frustrations of the sickout firsthand; the job action delayed the departure of Air Force One from Florida's Homestead Air Force Base after the Easter holiday.[64]

Frustration was not confined to travelers. Spouses of controllers began picketing FAA facilities, shouting "Go Home!" or "Scabs!" at controllers who drove in to work. "I have watched this tension build in this man for three years," said one picketer of her husband. "For us, either the FAA starts solving some of these problems or we have to get out. We can't stand the tension."[65]

TURNING THE TIDE

Anger and frustration could only carry PATCO so far. Its leaders soon found that it was one thing to mount an effective sickout strike against the government for a week. It was another matter to sustain that action against increasing pressure. As the job action neared the end of its second week, the government regained the upper hand, thanks to the FAA's success in fending off potential mediation efforts by the Department of Labor and the recommendation of Nixon's point man on the crisis, adviser Peter Flanigan, that Volpe and Shaffer be given the time necessary to break the sickout. With the support of the White House, Shaffer refused to negotiate with PATCO. "These men are on strike—illegally—against the government," he said. "The only thing to be discussed is punishment." Shaffer reminded the press that like other federal workers, controllers "signed an oath against striking when they took their jobs with the government. They violated that oath, and now they must be punished." "There is no other word to call it but a strike," Volpe agreed. If the sickout was not ended soon, Volpe vowed to dismiss as many as fifteen hundred participants, and promised he would make "no 'deals' on amnesty or mediation."[66]

Despite the public threat to dismiss fifteen hundred controllers, Shaffer and Volpe decided to target only PATCO's known activists, since they believed that a blanket firing threat would only stiffen the spines of participants and cause them to hold out longer. The FAA and transportation officials devised a graduated scale of penalties that would fire known sickout organizers and leaders, but would penalize the majority of participants through suspensions in which they would lose two days' pay for every day of missed work. Secretly, the FAA made plans to dismiss roughly two hundred known PATCO militants.[67]

Nixon's advisers agreed with this approach. In his diary, Nixon's chief of staff H.R. Haldeman wrote approvingly of "the plan...to fire a bunch of them" to "prove government employees can't win by striking." Firing PATCO leaders was all the more necessary, Haldeman believed, because leaders of the recent postal strike were not fired. "Theory is that the mailman is a family friend, so you can't hurt him, but no one knows the air traffic man," hence they "invoke a lot less popular sympathy."[68]

By the second week of the sickout, the government began drawing such distinctions between postal workers and air traffic controllers in public. Whereas the postal strike had been about wages and working conditions, officials suggested the PATCO job action was about nothing less than "whether the government or a union is going to run the nation's airways." As it promoted this view, the FAA also cultivated the loyalty of what it called the "'silent majority' of our controller workforce," borrowing a phrase Nixon had just made popular. Agency officials gave pep talks to working control-lers in teleconferences, prepared commendations for them, and arranged press interviews in which controllers questioned PATCO's motivations and leadership.[69]

The government also succeeded in making F. Lee Bailey a central issue in the strike, thereby deflecting attention from the controllers' complaints. Making references to the imprisoned Teamsters' union leader, government officials accused Bailey of becoming "the Jimmy Hoffa of the airways." The FAA portrayed him as the egotistical and imbalanced mastermind of PATCO's militancy, compared him to "demagogues like Huey Long, Father Coughlin, and Joe McCarthy," and trotted out a staff psychologist who char-acterized him as "a dangerous man." "We must regard Bailey as one who will continually twist the rules because he cannot live within the rules of authority," concluded the psychologist, who had never met Bailey.[70]

As pressure increased, PATCO leaders hunkered down. They discounted the threat of mass dismissals and believed that no penalties would be exacted if the participating controllers hung tough and demanded amnesty as part of any agreement to return to work. Rock ended each daily conference call to sickout leaders by reminding them that "amnesty is spelled H-O-R-S-E-S." As long as PATCO kept at least fifteen hundred "horses" out of work, it would be able to fight firing threats. Over time, though, PATCO found it increasingly difficult to maintain the sickout, for it saw its support dwindle among three groups whose sympathy had been critical to its success in Operation Air Safety: the press, the Congress, and airline pilots.[71]

As the sickout dragged on into a second week, press coverage grew hos-tile. The *New York Times* condemned the "thinly disguised strike" and asked whether "the people of the United States can be held for ransom by any group of civil servants that has a grievance or thinks it has a grievance." The *Times* predicted the direst outcome if the government gave in to PATCO's "Easter Uprising." "If PATCO can strike at Easter and win without penalty to its members, then we need not be surprised if in the future firemen go on strike at the height of a five-alarm fire, public health doctors in the middle of a major epidemic, and policemen at the crest of a crime wave," the *Times* warned. "That way lies anarchy and dissolution of the bonds and restraints that distinguish a civilized community from the jungle." The *Times* expressed relief that "[i]n contrast to the postal strike, there is little public sympathy for this union of a minority of air controllers attempting to bludgeon the

Government into recognizing it as a bargaining agent." But it was not just the *Times'* editorial board who thrashed PATCO. Respected columnists such as Carl T. Rowan and James "Scotty" Reston also piled on, with Rowan calling the sickout "grievously wrong" and Reston deploring the controllers' "public be damned" attitude. Public employee unions in general carry a heavier public relations burden in labor disputes than private sector unions, since opponents can so easily argue that their demands will lead to higher taxes. Despite this handicap, PATCO leaders made little effort to defuse unfavorable coverage. They were more focused on forcing the FAA to come to terms than on explaining their cause to the public.[72]

As the press deserted PATCO, so did Congress. PATCO leaders had hoped that timing the sickout to coincide with a congressional recess would ensure that legislators would experience air traffic delays firsthand and feel moved to intervene to promote a settlement. But the tactic backfired. Instead of investigating controller grievances, members of Congress lashed out at the organization. Even some of PATCO's allies distanced themselves. Rep. Earl F. Landgrebe, an Indiana Republican who considered himself a "friend," told PATCO leaders their timing "was just plain lousy." By calling a job action just before April's federal income tax deadline, Landgrebe explained, PATCO had created the impression in the mind of the average taxpayer that "here was another group of government employees striking for even more of *his* hard-earned coin of the realm." "You blew it," he wrote.[73]

Support from pilots also dissipated. At the outset, some officials of the Air Line Pilots Association supported PATCO. The pilots' union worried that the aviation system was operating under a "reduced margin of safety" and demanded that the union be allowed to inspect conditions in FAA facilities. ALPA did not want to be seen as publicly supporting an illegal job action, however. The union feared feeding public concerns about air safety and discouraging travelers, which would lead to pilot furloughs. The balance between safety and job preservation in the pilots' minds began to shift as furloughs mounted. "Many of our fellow employees are being furloughed without pay because of the power struggle going on among the air traffic controllers," one pilot fumed. "I am opposed to an illegal strike 'sick out,' work stoppage or slow-down by any organization and I want PATCO to know that I am thoroughly disenchanted with their organization," he added. By the end of the second week, such sentiments predominated among pilots.[74]

As support for PATCO diminished among press, politicians, and pilots, the FAA grew more adept at moving traffic under duress after stumbling early in its response to the sickout. To cut down on the massive backups on tarmacs and in the air over major cities, the agency established a "centralized flow control center" in Washington that attempted to coordinate the movement of air traffic nationwide. The idea behind "flow control" was to not allow planes to push back from their gates until it was certain that they could be cleared for takeoff and landing expeditiously. "We learned in twenty-one days what it would have taken us twenty-one months under normal conditions," said William Flener. "We found that we could move a lot more traffic than we thought we could." Thereafter flow control became an effective tool for battling controllers' slowdowns and a way for the agency to assert greater managerial control over air traffic on a daily basis.[75]

Airlines also went on the offensive against PATCO. They had been caught by surprise and financially hurt by the sickout. American Airlines had booked reservations that would have made the 1970 Easter weekend the third highest revenue period in its history, only to see hundreds of its flights canceled. Initially, the airlines' concerned themselves with preventing as many of their own flights from being canceled as possible. But after a week, major carriers came together under the aegis of the Air Transport Association (ATA) to file a lawsuit seeking millions in damages from PATCO.[76]

As support for the sickout plummeted, the courts delivered a deathblow to the sickout. On March 31, the government announced that it was seeking restraining orders against the organization in federal courts in sixteen jurisdictions. Bailey, Rock, and Jimmy Hays were called before Federal District Court Judge George L. Hart Jr. in Washington. PATCO's New York area leaders were summoned before Judge Orrin G. Judd in Brooklyn, in whose court the ATA and its member airlines were seeking both a restraining order and damages. In Cleveland's court, Judge Thomas Lambros threatened to fine controllers $500 for each day they were absent from their jobs. In response to this legal barrage, Bailey held a news conference in Washington's Mayflower Hotel on March 31 and urged controllers to return to work. "There appears to be a deadlock and the public is getting hurt," he said. There is evidence that Bailey's statement was choreographed in advance not as a true back-to-work order, but rather as a decoy that would buy time and provide some degree of protection for the organization's leaders. The notes for one PATCO conference call indicated that Bailey would "go on t.v. and advise to go back" but that his plea was meant to be "completely ignored." Yet some PATCO leaders thought Bailey went too far in the press conference. The lawyer did not issue a pro forma return to work order, as PATCO leaders expected. He disowned the sickout entirely. He conceded that the protest "won the controllers a lot of enemies," and maintained that he had "always been against it." In return for this statement, Judge Hart postponed action against PATCO leaders pending the controllers' return to work. Bailey's statement infuriated many PATCO leaders. Rock later claimed that Bailey had promised him that, "no matter what happened, he would not wilt on us as long as our guys were out."[77]

Still, the great majority of sickout participants held on. While Bailey's statement prompted some controllers to return to work, most refused to go back without an amnesty agreement. This caused Judge Hart to summon PATCO leaders back to court on April 2 and threaten them with contempt of court unless the board endorsed a back-to-work statement. The board continued to resist and refused to attend a meeting to consider drafting such a statement. Unable to get the board to agree to suspend the action, Bailey pleaded with the Nixon administration to sponsor binding mediation. "The postmen got results—money, amnesty—from their strike. The air traffic controller won't understand why he doesn't deserve the same treatment," he explained. The administration was unmoved by that argument.[78]

Day by day, the legal noose tightened. The government compiled a mountain of evidence indicating that PATCO's leaders coordinated a national sickout in violation of the law. Key to the government's case was Mike Rock's letter to Defense Secretary Melvin Laird warning of the impending job action. But the government had other evidence as well, including a conversation recorded over government phone lines outlining sickout plans, and discarded notes recovered from a hotel room in which PATCO leaders had planned the action. Citing this evidence, Hart ruled PATCO in contempt on April 7. However, the judge sympathized with the controllers. Excoriating the FAA for its "extreme provocation" of PATCO, he postponed a penalty hearing until April 11 so PATCO leaders would have time to persuade their members to give up their fight. In the following days, support for the sickout melted. Minneapolis, Cleveland, and Chicago control centers returned to normal staffing conditions. Only New York and Denver Centers were still turning out less than 50 percent of scheduled controllers by April 11. When April 11 came, Hart extended his deadline by one more day but made it clear that he would tolerate no further delay. In New York, striking controllers were set to appear before Judge Judd on the morning of April 13. PATCO had no options left.[79]

As PATCO's board members gathered on Sunday April 12 in the organization's Washington headquarters, they knew they were beaten. They acceded to the inevitable and sent out word to the members: it was time to go back. The next morning FAA Administrator John Shaffer jubilantly informed the White House that PATCO's unprecedented nineteen-day job action against the U.S. government was over. PATCO leaders tried to put the best face they could on the situation. "We hope that some of our message got through to the public," said Ed Williams of New York Center. "We think there are going to be some congressional investigations into some of our complaints." In reality, the organization had won nothing.[80]

Although clearly beaten, the defiant controllers of New York Center refused to return to work like "whipped puppies." Instead, they gathered on the evening of April 13 in the same restaurant at MacArthur Airport where Jack Maher had convened the founding meetings of PATCO's forerunner, the Metropolitan Controllers' Association, three years earlier. As the time came for the midnight shift to report to work, 340 PATCO members fell in line, crew by crew, behind the Glengarry Pipe Band and a color guard furnished by the local firefighters' union. One flag bearer carried an American flag; another bore a yellow Revolutionary War–era flag depicting a rattlesnake over the legend, "Don't Tread on Me." As the bagpipers struck up "Scotland the Brave," they marched up Johnson Avenue to the gates of New York Center. There, the honor guard parted, and the midnight shift reported for duty, each of them wearing a yellow "Don't Tread on Me" pin on their shirts. The moment would live on in PATCO legend. Yet, once the pipes faded and the doors closed behind them, the reality of what had happened became inescapable. Looking at the barbed-wire fence that surrounded the windowless radar facility, Stan Gordon, for one, felt like a prisoner.[81]

COURSE CORRECTION

If the government can do something for the postal workers—
why not air traffic controllers?
—JESSE CALHOON, 1970

I want this done!
—PRESIDENT RICHARD M. NIXON, 1971

By Tuesday, April 14, 1970, staffing patterns were back to normal throughout the FAA. F. Lee Bailey, the man controllers had once viewed as their savior, was already moving on. That day, he took his place beside his next famous client. It was Captain Ernest L. Medina, who was on trial for his role in the infamous My Lai massacre, the Vietnam war atrocity in which U.S. soldiers under Medina's command slaughtered scores of innocent civilians in a South Vietnamese village suspected of enemy sympathies. Bailey proved considerably more adept as a defense attorney than as a labor leader. He ultimately won an acquittal for Medina. PATCO's future seemed less promising.[1]

Indeed, PATCO's very survival was in doubt. Its near destruction changed the organization. A group that did not officially refer to itself as a union, whose members were not certain they wanted a union and whose best known public face had been that of a trial lawyer, had undertaken the sick-outs of 1969 and 1970. The desperate effort to salvage the organization after the failed national sickout finally forced PATCO to resolve its ambivalence about its identity as a labor organization. It became clear to PATCO's members and leaders alike that evolving into a full-fledged union was the best—perhaps the only—option to preserve their organization. Ironically, the government's hostile response to sickout participants completed PATCO's conversion to unionism.

In a few smaller facilities, "sick" controllers were welcomed back warmly by supervisors and coworkers, but this treatment was exceptional. As a rule, the government came down hard on the returnees, determined to teach PATCO activists a lesson. FAA Administrator Shaffer announced that he intended to protect controllers' "professionalism" by removing those who had become a "disruptive influence." He ordered sickout participants placed on administrative duties until the agency investigated their conduct and decided an appropriate punishment. As they waited, some sickout participants were given menial tasks such as transcribing tapes or counting flight strips. Others were simply placed in empty rooms and given no duties at all. The ostracism convinced some sickout participants that the FAA was trying to "reduce them to nothing." Many facility chiefs and supervisors took pains to humiliate those who had had the temerity to sick out. When a returning Pittsburgh tower controller wore a PATCO button on his return to work, his supervisor called him out in front of his colleagues. "I have one of those," he announced, pointing at the button, "but it says 'Kiss My Ass.'"[2]

Some PATCO members talked of resisting the "sledgehammer of punitive action," as one called it. "If the Government is allowed to continue this form of management," warned a Madison, Wisconsin, controller, "the *entire* Governmental work force is liable to walk out." Some Oakland Center controllers compared the FAA's tactics to the actions of a "Viet Cong terrorist squad" executing the leaders of a village who opposed them. "It is now up to each of us to determine the fate of our 'village.' If we roll over and play dead, the FAA will have won." In the end, though, the returnees lacked the power to do much more than express their dissatisfaction through symbolism. At the San Francisco Bay Terminal Radar Approach Control (TRACON) facility controllers began wearing black armbands to work each Friday to protest FAA policies.[3]

The FAA was a hierarchy-bound agency whose managers were determined to restore respect for their authority after the sickout. FAA Deputy Administrator Dave Thomas favored firing hundreds of the union's activists and rebuilding the agency with new recruits. Deputy Transportation Secretary James Beggs agreed. Beggs urged Secretary Volpe to "fire the whole bloody mess." But Volpe and FAA Administrator Shaffer decided on a more targeted approach that would distinguish between sickout leaders and passive participants, firing the former and fining the latter. They hoped that this approach would demonstrate the government's resolve as well as its fairness. They believed that a failure to fire sickout organizers would rob federal antistrike laws of "whatever deterrent effect they still have." But by firing only the organizers, they thought they could retain thousands of other participants who had been trained at great taxpayer expense, while at the same time making clear that the government would not tolerate work stoppages.[4]

FAA deputy Alan Dean was tasked with developing the "table of penalties" that would put this approach into effect. Dean's criteria identified 294 activists who either participated in organizing the sickout or pressured other controllers to participate in it. These offenders were cited for violating the oath pledging to refrain from striking that all federal employees signed when they were hired, and they were given dismissal notices. Dean identified 2,315 others who called in sick, but who had not been active in organizing the protest. They were fined two days' pay for each day absent.[5]

Putting the dismissals into effect took time, allowing PATCO to organize a defense. Some federal judges who had issued injunctions against PATCO during the sickout blocked the FAA from following through on dismissals in their districts. "I can't be in a position of ordering these men to go back to work and when they do they are fired," one judge explained. Even when not restrained by the courts, the FAA could not complete termination until a controller had had a chance to appeal. Thus, three months after the sickout, only thirty-six controllers had been removed. As appeals dragged on, PATCO pointed to the recent liberalization of attitudes toward strikes by government workers. In May 1970, Hawaii became the first state to legalize strikes by some state and local workers. Pennsylvania did so shortly thereafter. In many states that did not actually drop strike bans, enforcement of penalties grew more lax as the public became aware of the grievances of government workers. Prominent politicians also spoke up for PATCO. Democratic Senator Gaylord Nelson of Wisconsin, who as governor had signed the first state law allowing public sector labor collective bargaining in 1959, blamed the sickout on the FAA's intransigence. A bipartisan group of senators, including Democrats Ted Kennedy, George McGovern, and Walter

Mondale, and Republicans James Buckley and Ted Stevens, asked the FAA to reduce its planned penalties. PATCO leaders even reached out to the Nixon administration for help, reminding the president that the vast majority of controllers were military veterans and thus part of the "law and order" constituency to whom he was trying to appeal.[6]

PATCO's campaign put Shaffer and Volpe on the defensive. They disputed the suggestion that controllers were treated more harshly than postal strikers by pointing out that unlike the postal unions, PATCO had conducted three illegal job actions in less than two years. PATCO had "deliberately tried to bring this agency to its knees," Shaffer reminded Congress. Volpe warned that a failure to act "against those who elected to strike will seriously demoralize the employees who elected to honor their oath of office and remain on the job." The FAA had supporters. Civil Service Commission Chairman John W. Macy Jr. applauded the FAA for taking a "strong disciplinary stand against the mass-sickness technique." Assistant Attorney General (and soon-to-be Supreme Court justice) William Rehnquist warned that if the government did not check "insubordination" among its employees, the executive branch would soon "be controlled not by an elected President, but by a number of temporary tenants of government jobs who have no vestige whatever of a popular mandate to operate the branch."[7]

Still, PATCO had managed to raise the political costs of a mass firing high enough to force Shaffer to reduce the number of controllers slated for termination by two-thirds, to around one hundred. To reassure concerned White House officials who wanted the controversy to simply go away, Shaffer promised the dismissals would be kept to "an absolute minimum." Once PATCO's last-ditch efforts to block the firings ended on April 19, 1971, when the U.S. Supreme Court refused to hear an appeal of a lower court decision upholding the FAA's punishments, the number of controllers fired for leading the sickout topped out at eighty.[8]

Although this was the largest number of firings in response to a strike by federal workers, the FAA had fired only 3 percent of the workers it might have removed. Many observers lauded the government for using "a scalpel rather than a club" in response to the sickout. "Rigid enforcement of the law in this case would have had dire consequences," argued labor relations expert Murray Nesbit. "The wholesale firing of scarce trained personnel is not the kind of tactic to be embarked on lightly." Others praised Shaffer for trying to improve channels of communication between the controllers and the FAA after the job action and for moving to implement portions of the Corson Commission report. Shaffer himself promised that sickout participants would not be precluded from future promotions.[9]

For the fired, however, the situation seemed dire. They had lost their jobs and had no hope of regaining them. The agency meant to "destroy, shatter, and send to the four winds one of the most dedicated American servants possible, namely me," one fired controller complained. "No wonder the students riot," wrote the wife of a dismissed controller, referring to recent campus unrest arising from opposition to Nixon's invasion of Cambodia. "We...abhor the violence and destruction, but now understand why." As a group, the fired controllers fared poorly. Working PATCO members were asked to contribute five dollars per pay period to help support them, and many did. But as the months went by, contributions fell off. In October 1970, Jack Maher circulated an angry memo chiding many PATCO members for "*doing absolutely nothing for those dismissed.*" Some fired controllers ended up pumping gas or doing construction labor. Others emigrated to Canada or Australia in search of work controlling air traffic, since the FAA made clear that they would never again work at that job in the United States.[10]

New Leadership

The firings catalyzed PATCO's transformation into a full-fledged union. Just days after the sickout strike collapsed, a battered PATCO board met at the International Hotel in Las Vegas on April 18, 1970, to prepare for the organization's national convention which would follow two days later. The board confronted a grim situation. The firing of sickout leaders and suspension of participants seemed imminent. The organization's treasury was empty. A rift had emerged between F. Lee Bailey and key members of the board, especially its chair Mike Rock. With Jimmy Hays's term as PATCO president coming to an end, leadership tensions were sure to surface around the choice of a successor.

Rock and Maher concluded that PATCO needed a godfather with enough political pull to extricate it from its predicament. In their view, that man was Jesse Calhoon of the Marine Engineers' Beneficial Association (MEBA), who had begun informally advising them in September 1969. Together with Russ Sommer, Bill South, and other board members, they worked on a strategy with Leon Shapiro, MEBA's secretary-treasurer, to ease Bailey out and affiliate PATCO with Calhoon's union. As Rock put it, the time had come to "knock out non-members as policy-making people." At Rock's invitation, Calhoon appeared before the PATCO board on April 19 and made a strong case for affiliation. He stressed MEBA's experience lobbying in Washington, and noted that unlike many AFL-CIO unions, MEBA did not "tie their coat tails to any one party," and thus had many friends in the Nixon administration. "If the government can do something for the postal workers—why not air traffic controllers?" Calhoon asked. It was an offer that the PATCO board was in no position to refuse. Without consulting Bailey, the board voted unanimously to endorse affiliation and put the proposal up for a membership vote.[11]

On April 20, the PATCO convention opened with three hundred "battle scarred but unbowed" delegates in attendance. Dozens of other delegates could not attend because they were subject to federal court orders arising from the sickout that restricted their travel. Both Bailey and Calhoon addressed the convention. Bailey gave a status report on PATCO after the sickout. Calhoon urged delegates to approve affiliation with MEBA. Most delegates reacted warmly to both speeches. Then, in an effort to make the organization compliant with rules for unions seeking to represent federal workers, the convention approved changes in the PATCO constitution that finally eliminated the vacant post of executive director and strengthened the position of president. Having completed this work, the convention turned to the task of electing a president to succeed Jimmy Hays. By choosing thirty-five-year-old John Leyden of New York Center, who supported affiliation with MEBA, the convention confirmed PATCO's new direction.[12]

John Leyden was a union man through and through. Born and raised in Celtic Park in Woodside, Queens, Leyden was the son of an Irish immigrant. His father, Patrick, was an Irish republican from County Clare who had fought in the Easter Rebellion of 1916 before fleeing to the United States, where he eventually became a shop steward in Local 32B of the Service Employees International Union. John attended a seminary high school and considered entering the priesthood before leaving in his senior year to join the Air Force, where he flew combat missions as an airborne radar operator during the Korean War. After his discharge, he was admitted to St. John's University and considered a teaching career. But like so many air traffic controllers of his generation, he did not want to postpone starting a family, so he applied to the FAA and was assigned to Hangar 11 at Idlewild, what Leyden called the "nuthouse." Leyden had not been among PATCO's first boosters. In fact, when New York Center moved to Islip, he had been involved with the ATCA chapter that was then headed by his friend John R. Lapine Jr. When that chapter collapsed, he did not immediately follow Jack Maher and his efforts to build up NAGE in Islip. Not only was Leyden "not considered as militant" in those days, the FAA viewed him as a model controller and nominated him in 1967 for the federal government's top award for civil servants.[13]

It was not until 1969, a year after PATCO was founded, that Leyden became an active member of the organization. Once he became involved, however, he drew on his union heritage and rose quickly in prominence. He had fine political instincts, an agreeable personality, and remarkable skills as an air traffic controller, all of which enabled him to emerge as a leader of the New York Center PATCO local. When Maher asked for his help in getting Islip controllers to call in sick in June 1969, Leyden did not hesitate. During the 1970 sickout, he emerged as a gifted strategist. He developed his own set of political connections independent of PATCO's national leaders, using Long Island lawyer and Republican political operative, James Catterson, as go-between. Through Catterson, Leyden made connections to New York's Gov. Nelson A. Rockefeller and state Assembly Speaker Perry Duryea, which in turn led to a meeting with Assistant U.S. Attorney General William Ruckelshaus during the sickout. Leyden's connections undoubtedly spared him from being targeted for dismissal even though many others whose leadership of the sickout was less identifiable were slated for firing.[14]

In some respects, Leyden's election represented the marginalization of PATCO's founders, Rock and Maher. Although Leyden agreed with their strategy of affiliating PATCO with MEBA, he thought they had run PATCO poorly. He criticized their ad hoc strategizing and lack of political acumen. His criticisms were difficult to ignore, since Leyden himself had proved his mettle during the sickout, staying out for twenty days. Leyden solidified his position by allying with Robert E. Greene, of Denver Center, who was also new to the inner circle of PATCO's leadership. At the convention, Greene joined Leyden's ticket as vice president. Together they carried the votes of delegates who were hungry for organizational stability after two years of frenzied action. Once in office, Leyden presented a more moderate public face for PATCO. "The attitudes of the organization have tempered," he announced. "A lot of us feel a different course must be pursued for future relief of our problems." Nevertheless, he also shrewdly mended fences with Rock and Maher, assuring them that any differences they had had were in the past.[15]

The complex relationship that subsequently developed between Leyden and Rock helped shape PATCO's history for a decade. Rock's reputation for militancy and his personal bond with PATCO activists around the country made him useful to Leyden. In turn, Leyden's obvious ability to unite the union and conduct diplomacy led Rock to acquiesce in the diminution of his own influence, even though doing so rankled him. Although their differences in philosophy and approach were considerable and would never be entirely transcended, Rock and Leyden worked together and built a friendship.[16]

The Rock-Leyden alliance was nurtured at the outset by two shared goals: affiliating with MEBA and ridding PATCO of F. Lee Bailey. The affiliation was accomplished quickly. With the Las Vegas convention on record approving the move, Rock and Leyden successfully appealed to PATCO's membership to ratify it in a mail ballot. On June 12, PATCO announced that the affiliation was official. Through its affiliation with MEBA, PATCO had also joined the AFL-CIO. Thus, the organization whose founders had been afraid to use the word "union" joined the House of Labor.

In many ways, the PATCO-MEBA affiliation was an unlikely partnership. MEBA was one of the nation's oldest unions, founded in 1875 by the engineers who maintained boilers on Mississippi paddlewheel steamers and other ships. In 1970, the union had only eighteen thousand members. More than half of them were officers in the Merchant Marine. But Jesse Calhoon had already been looking for members in such non-maritime fields as banking and securities. With PATCO an affiliate, Calhoon believed MEBA could become a more powerful presence in the transportation sector. PATCO, in turn, hoped that Calhoon and his union might secure PATCO's survival.[17]

The first task after affiliation—ousting Bailey—proved difficult. PATCO's general counsel emerged from the Las Vegas convention with his power curbed by the new constitution. But he had no intention of leaving the organization he had worked so hard to create. Meanwhile, Rock and Leyden, along with most of the PATCO board, believed Bailey had to go, if for no other reason than Calhoon could not abide him. On June 18, 1970, the anniversary of PATCO's *Tonight Show* sickout, the PATCO board convened in Washington for the first time since Leyden's election and the MEBA affiliation to deal with the Bailey issue. In the weeks leading up to the meeting, Leyden and Rock organized the board. Bailey, who was invited to the meeting, had no indication that his future was to be its subject. Once the meeting began, however, its purpose became clear. The normally taciturn Maher introduced the subject, saying it was "time for Lee Bailey to go." Surprised, Bailey quickly defended himself. The ensuing discussion became heated. Bailey's persuasive talents were peerless, but in this case the jury was already decided. After more than an hour of debate, the board voted 11–2 to drop Bailey as counsel. Many board members who voted against Bailey did so with reluctance, as they were grateful for his role in founding PATCO. Rock later called it "one of the most emotional days" of his life. Sitting across from Rock, Bill South could see the toll of the conflict etched on Rock's face. To South, it seemed almost as if Rock was "trying to fire his father."[18]

Once the question was decided, Bailey and PATCO parted amicably. Bailey's lucrative legal practice compensated for whatever slights he felt from his PATCO friends. After his departure, Bailey retained a fondness for the air traffic controllers that came from having "agonized with them, tipped a Scotch with them, and listened to their problems." He later insisted that he would have done it all over again if given the chance. "The men were worth the effort," he said.[19]

With Bailey's ouster, Leyden consolidated power over an organization nearly in shambles. Having lost the privilege of having dues deducted automatically from its members' paychecks by the FAA, PATCO saw its dues-paying membership drop to forty-two hundred. In some facilities the dropoff was 80 percent. The union projected a deficit of $250,000 for 1970. Considering PATCO's precarious situation, FAA officials were convinced that the organization "couldn't possibly survive." By managing to get PATCO through this period, Leyden established a reputation for leadership that would keep him in the union's presidency for a decade.[20]

Leyden began by reorganizing PATCO's national offices in a second floor suite in an office building at 2100 M Street, NW, in the west end of downtown Washington. He brought in Kansas City Center PATCO leader Noel Keane as PATCO's director of labor relations and placed a respected Washington labor lawyer, William Peer, on retainer as PATCO's general counsel. Then he hired a well-known labor consultant, Stanley Ruttenberg, to devise a unionlike organizational structure for PATCO. Ruttenberg's plan called for the dissolution of Bailey's network of regional counsels and the consolidation of the power of the president over the office staff. Leyden used the report to justify his increased control of PATCO's administration.[21]

Leyden then turned to the task of reuniting the organization after the failed sickout. Leyden's job became easier when Rock agreed to step down as chairman of the PATCO board. "Mike Strike" was too closely identified with PATCO's job actions. To replace Rock, the board chose Bill South, of Jacksonville Center, over a feistier candidate, Rex Campbell of Denver Center. With South as chairman and Leyden as president, PATCO was now led by two men who could not be directly blamed for the sickout strategy, making it easier for them to build bridges with both the FAA and controllers who felt burned by the job action.[22]

UNION DIPLOMACY

Leyden turned PATCO around by building three key relationships, beginning with the government. Although the FAA was initially suspicious of Leyden, PATCO's new president reached out with "an attitude of conciliation" and pledged a "new philosophy." Leyden's approach was "to bury the mistakes made by both FAA leadership and PATCO and work together in the future." Leyden also sent messages of peace to the White House, assuring Nixon's assistant Peter M. Flanigan that PATCO was no longer interested in conflict.[23]

The FAA welcomed Leyden's approach, for it, too, was weary of confrontation. Shaffer tried to start anew by commissioning an internal study of his agency's labor relations, which reported that the "paternalistic attitude" of managers had contributed to the pattern of conflict with controllers. Shaffer reciprocated Leyden's overtures by admitting that the FAA was partly to blame for the past problems. "We didn't work hard enough on maintaining good employee relations," he said. The FAA had more resources to apply to its labor force problems after President Nixon signed a bill in May 1970 increasing the tax on aviation fuel and setting aside the new revenue to modernize airports, automate navigation aids, and hire more air traffic controllers. Shaffer asked Bert Harding, staff director for the Corson Commission, to help revamp FAA labor policy. On Harding's recommendation, the FAA introduced new policies designed to win over controllers. One change allowed overworked controllers to bid out of high-density facilities. Another called for the formation of "Air Traffic Advisory Committees," whose members would be elected by controllers and who would have a voice in shaping technical policy regarding air traffic control.[24]

As he reduced tensions with the FAA, Leyden also forged a close relationship with the new president of the Air Line Pilots Association, Captain J. J. O'Donnell. ALPA had been sympathetic to PATCO during Operation Air Safety in 1968, but the pilots were alienated by the 1970 sickout. Leyden was determined to make the pilots' union an ally, though this task would not be easy. Pilots and controllers had a complex relationship, characterized by competition as well as cooperation. They collaborated in the intricate ballet of air traffic control, and they shared much in common. Each walked with a confident swagger born of the knowledge that they had mastered a pressure-packed job and that the safety of air travelers rested on their judgment. It took years of training to learn either craft; washout rates were high; and the survivors considered themselves members of an elite. Yet, in part because of their similarities and interdependence, there were tensions between the groups. It galled controllers that the highly paid pilots in their uniforms seemed to have a monopoly on the romance of aviation, while underpaid and overworked controllers sweated out their workdays in dim radar rooms or behind tinted glass, invisible to the air travelers whose safety they ensured. Pilots in turn were irked by any comparison of men who flew planes to those who monitored radar screens. Some of these animosities could be traced back to their military service, where pilots served as officers, while controllers were enlisted men. Given their differences, it was inevitable that tensions developed between their unions. Since its founding in 1931 by David L. Behncke, ALPA had practiced a form of "elite unionization." While PATCO's members were new to unionism and also viewed themselves as an elite, they came to see pilots as "lace curtain" unionists.[25]

Complicating matters were some fundamental disagreements between pilots and controllers over procedures of air traffic control. Believing that only controllers had the "big picture" on their radar screens, PATCO sought to widen controllers' prerogatives in directing traffic. There was self-interest in this. One of Leyden's fundamental objectives was closing the "financial gap between pilot and controller salaries." "If our profession is to be elevated," he argued, controllers would have to "assume additional responsibilities." This inevitably would mean a "diminishing status role for the pilot profession and an increase in ours." Naturally, the pilots resisted PATCO's push. When PATCO sought increased controller authority during bad weather, ALPA objected. And when PATCO sought a liberalized FAM program, ALPA fought it: pilots wanted to control who could sit in their jump seats. Similarly, when pilots tried to win greater discretion in some situations, Leyden resisted this attempt to "control what the controller does," insisting that it was "none of their goddamn business."[26]

Despite these conflicts, PATCO and ALPA built a mostly supportive relationship in the early 1970s, thanks largely to the friendship that developed between Leyden and O'Donnell. Their bond was grounded both in familiarity and mutual interest. O'Donnell and Leyden came from similar backgrounds. A native New Englander, O'Donnell served in World War II and Korea. He hired on with Eastern Airlines following his discharge in 1956 and quickly became active in the pilots' union, soon emerging as the union's top pension expert. O'Donnell was elected ALPA president in 1971. Like Leyden, he took the helm of a union beset by internal divisions and proved adept at cooling tempers. Although they disagreed—sometimes passionately—on issues that divided their unions, their personal relationship prevented these differences from hardening into full-blown conflict, and they found common ground on many issues. O'Donnell urged the FAA to include controller representatives in planning meetings and supported PATCO's demands for reclassification of controller positions into higher-level salary grades. Leyden, in turn, supported ALPA objectives, such as increased security to prevent "skyjackings," which became a concern after several prominent airline hijackings in the early 1970s.[27]

The third key relationship Leyden developed was with Jesse Calhoon of MEBA. Although he never led a large union or received the kind of attention accorded to someone like Walter Reuther of the United Auto Workers, Calhoon was surely among the more colorful and clever labor leaders of his time. Born in Belhaven, North Carolina, in 1923 to a family that made its living farming, fishing, and oystering, he left home to join the Merchant Marine after the Japanese attack on Pearl Harbor. While at sea during World War II, he joined MEBA. After the war, Calhoon rose in the union's ranks. In the 1950s he developed a close relationship with the union's general counsel, the Harvard-trained lawyer Lee Pressman, himself one of the most interesting figures in the labor movement. Before working for MEBA, Pressman had been one of labor's chief strategists in the 1930s, as general counsel to the Congress of Industrial Organizations under the leadership of John L. Lewis. Pressman had been hounded from that post in 1948 because of his suspected membership in the Communist Party. Shunned by large unions that feared bad publicity, Pressman went to work for the little-known MEBA. Calhoon thought Pressman the smartest lawyer he had ever met; in turn, Pressman recognized Calhoon's considerable talents. In 1965, Calhoon assumed the MEBA presidency through a campaign managed by Pressman.[28]

As soon as he ascended to its leadership, Calhoon sought opportunities to expand his small union. With the aid of his cunning secretary-treasurer, Leon Shapiro (whom PATCO leaders nicknamed "Sharpo"), Calhoon began exploring ways to increase MEBA's leverage at strategic points in the nation's transportation system. Prior to being introduced to Rock and Maher by Helen Bentley in 1969, Calhoon had no interest in the federal sector, where he felt the "only negotiating you could do was over where the water cooler would be." But PATCO was attractive to Calhoon for three reasons. First, air traffic controllers could supplement MEBA's strength in the transportation sector and give it more clout in the congressional transportation committees, where matters central to MEBA's well-being were regularly decided. Second, if PATCO could win recognition as the bargaining agent of controllers, MEBA could add as many as fifteen thousand new members to its ranks, supplementing its political action treasury. Finally, PATCO's straitened circumstances meant that Calhoon could negotiate the affiliation on favorable terms.[29]

Calhoon's terms made MEBA the senior partner in what Leyden called a "marriage of convenience." MEBA would collect monthly per capita dues from PATCO, without giving PATCO members an opportunity to vote for MEBA's officers. In return, MEBA would offer PATCO access to loans from its treasury, political connections that spanned both parties on Capitol Hill, a promise not to interfere in PATCO's internal affairs, and protection from the intrusions of other AFL-CIO unions. The latter point seemed particularly important to Leyden in the summer of 1970, for another AFL-CIO affiliate, the American Federation of Government Employees (AFGE), was considering a campaign to organize controllers after PATCO's sickout debacle. Calhoon's close relationship with two key members of the AFL-CIO Executive Council, Teddy Gleason of the International Longshoremen's Association, and Paul Hall of the Seafarers, helped ensure that the AFL-CIO would grant exclusive jurisdiction over air traffic controllers to PATCO, forcing the AFGE to give up its plans.[30]

In later years, some PATCO activists argued that Leyden gave MEBA too much influence over the air traffic controllers, but in 1970 no one expressed qualms about the arrangement. Rather, MEBA's support seemed like manna from heaven. Calhoon put Rock and Maher on his payroll and sent them and Noel Keane on a cross-country organizing mission. MEBA also cosigned for PATCO's bank loans. Most importantly, Calhoon used his political connections to help PATCO rebuild relations with Congress and the Nixon administration. Although a small union, MEBA possessed considerable political influence thanks to the substantial political action treasury it amassed from its high-paid membership. Under Calhoon, MEBA also acquired a lavish estate in Saint Michaels, Maryland, on the eastern shore of the Chesapeake Bay, to which it could invite favored legislators for a chance to relax. PATCO could not have hoped for a more politically astute tutor than Jesse Calhoon as it learned how to "play the game on Capitol Hill."[31]

Calhoon taught PATCO leaders three key lessons. First, they should pick their politician friends carefully, based upon the leverage they might exert on key committees. Second, they should remember that a well-timed political contribution often mattered more than the size of that contribution. Just before the 1974 mid-term congressional elections, MEBA transferred $20,000 to PATCO so the union could make last-minute contributions that might influence close races and win PATCO some powerful friends. Third, Calhoon explained the importance of seeking friends in both major parties. This was somewhat counter-intuitive for PATCO leaders, since Democrats both controlled Congress and predominated among PATCO members (only 24 percent of whom self-identified as Republicans in a 1978 survey). But PATCO leaders took Calhoon's advice to heart. In time, the union won a diverse array of supporters ranging from liberal Democrats William L. "Bill" Clay of Missouri and Morris K. "Mo" Udall of Arizona to conservative Republicans Newt Gingrich of Georgia and John Rousselot of California (a member of the ultraconservative John Birch Society). "PATCO firmly follows Samuel Gompers' old tradition," explained Leyden. "We reward our friends and punish our enemies."[32]

Members occasionally grumbled about PATCO's political activities. Controllers tended to be politically active—84 percent would later claim to have voted in the 1976 election—and party-line voters objected when the union supported candidates they opposed. But most controllers seemed satisfied that PATCO's influence grew as a result of its political work. By 1980, PATCO and MEBA combined to contribute more than $1 million to congressional campaigns. Over time, the FAA came to appreciate PATCO's political connections: the union's lobbying muscle came in handy when it was time to win budget increases. Members of Congress tended to return phone calls from a campaign contributor like PATCO more quickly than those from the FAA.[33]

Although Calhoon's help was crucial in rebuilding PATCO, the arduous work of reorganizing had to be carried out in the field. Traveling from city to city, Rock and Maher developed a standard approach. They would rent a room, order a keg of beer, and invite controllers in to talk about their problems. A smattering of PATCO diehards usually turned up, but most attendees were skeptics. To win them back, PATCO leaders promised there would be "no more 'showboat' press releases, sick-outs, or slowdowns." They also reminded controllers that the government guaranteed their right to a union. "Uncle Sam says it's OK to organize," said one leaflet. "Not only does Uncle Sam guarantee your right to select a union of your own free choice—he comes in and conducts the election!"[34]

Slowly, the organization began to rebuild. By the time it held its next national convention in Atlanta, a year after the sickout, PATCO boasted a 50 percent rebound in membership and a total of fifty-five hundred dues-payers. Yet this fell far short of a majority of the FAA's nearly fifteen thousand air traffic controllers, and there was scant evidence that PATCO could persuade that majority to support it. The slow progress made it clear that PATCO needed major breakthroughs if it was to become a force once more.[35]

In the search for such breakthroughs, Leyden focused on three objectives: winning clearance from the Labor Department allowing PATCO to seek election as the air traffic controllers' exclusive representative; forcing the FAA to hire back the activists who were fired for leading the 1970 sickout; and persuading Congress to enact "second career" legislation allowing controllers to retire after twenty years on the job. Each of these goals seemed utterly fanciful in the summer of 1971. How could PATCO persuade the government to certify it as an organization that did not assert the right to strike—a prerequisite for any union that aspired to represent federal workers—after it had organized a slowdown and two sickout strikes in the space of twenty months? How could it force the FAA to take back fired controllers after the agency had pledged that it would never do so? Or persuade Congress to enact an early retirement bill that had been fruitlessly debated since ATCA President Francis McDermott first advocated it in 1960? None of these objectives seemed realistic, yet, with MEBA's help, PATCO accomplished all three by the end of 1971.[36]

PATCO's first goal was to obtain Labor Department clearance under the terms of an executive order signed by President Nixon. Responding to the criticisms of Kennedy's Executive Order 10988, Nixon authorized Labor Secretary George P. Shultz to lead a process to revise the government's policy on union recognition and collective bargaining. Nixon issued the outcome of that revision, Executive Order 11491, on October 29, 1969. It corrected several flaws in Kennedy's order that had frustrated unionists. It scrapped the confusing trilevel recognition options in favor of a simple exclusive recognition procedure; put the assistant secretary of labor for labor-management relations in charge of union certifications; allowed for agency-wide bargaining units; authorized the use of the Federal Mediation and Conciliation Service to mediate disputes; and provided for the creation of a Federal Services Impasses Panel, whose help could be invoked when labor-management negotiations deadlocked. Nixon's order left in place the other restrictions, including limitations on the scope of bargaining and prohibitions against striking and the negotiation of contracts that required workers to pay dues or representation fees to the union that represented them.[37]

Prior to the Nixon order, it had been impossible for any organization to win agency-wide recognition as the exclusive representative of all air traffic controllers, a situation that had fostered the chaotic conflict among PATCO and its rivals, NAGE and the ATCA, that had culminated in the 1970 sickout. In order to qualify to be on the ballot for a certification election under the provisions of the new order, a union had to receive clearance attesting to its democratic governance, renunciation of strikes, and repudiation of discriminatory practices. PATCO desperately wanted agency-wide recognition and the dues checkoff that would come with it. In order to win these, it first needed Labor Department certification. Although its record of work stoppages would seem to preclude certification, PATCO hoped that new Labor Secretary James D. Hodgson (who replaced Shultz in July 1970), and Hodgson's deputy, William Usery, would rule in PATCO's favor. Hodgson was a former vice president for industrial relations at Lockheed with a reputation for moderation, which raised the union's hopes. Thus PATCO began pursuing clearance as soon as the dust of the 1970 sickout settled.[38]

Labor Department examiner Louis B. Libbin opened hearings in the summer of 1970 on PATCO's qualifications as an organization to represent air traffic controllers. The FAA strongly opposed PATCO's certification and submitted evidence showing that PATCO advocated strikes and job actions. Rival organizations NAGE and the ATCA also testified against PATCO. With characteristic bluster, Ken Lyons of NAGE warned Libbin that this case would determine "whether the Government will capitulate to those who would deprive the public of essential services in their search for power by means outside the law."[39]

But the rules of evidence aided PATCO. Libbin refused to accept the FAA's documents at face value and told the government that it needed to produce witnesses who could be cross-examined regarding their contents. With MEBA paying PATCO's legal bills, the union presented an effective defense. When Libbin presented his report to William Usery on October 12, 1970, it came out as favorably as PATCO officials could have hoped. Libbin ruled that PATCO had directed an illegal work stoppage, but that the organization could still qualify for national certification if it renounced that sickout and posted a notice in every FAA facility announcing that in the future it would "neither assert the right to strike nor call or engage in strikes, work stoppages or slowdowns." FAA officials fumed but decided against appealing the ruling, believing that would only further alienate controllers.[40]

PATCO was fortunate that the decision on whether to accept Libbin's recommendations rested with Deputy Secretary William Usery. A former official of the International Association of Machinists and an experienced mediator, Usery was a strong advocate of collective bargaining. As a Nixon appointee, he viewed his role as one of maintaining communication lines between unions and the Republican administration while keeping "the confidence of labor" in Nixon's initiatives. On January 29, 1971, Usery approved Libbin's recommendations. Conforming to Usery's order, PATCO posted the required notice renouncing strikes. Sixty days later, Leyden received word that PATCO was officially "cleansed" and able to file for a national representation election.[41]

Although they were cleared to petition for an election, PATCO leaders did not rush ahead. They were mindful of substantial controller skepticism about PATCO resulting from the 1970 sickout, and they did not want to risk losing an election to NAGE. Before going forward, PATCO leaders wanted to secure some wins that demonstrated the union's clout. They knew that no victory could be more symbolically important than forcing the FAA to rehire the activists who had been fired for their leadership of the 1970 sickout.[42]

Bringing Them Back

Calhoon's help on this project was invaluable. On July 7, 1971, Calhoon asked PATCO for a detailed report on the status of discharged controllers and then set to work, using his considerable political connections to try to engineer their rehiring.[43] It was a propitious time for Calhoon to take up this cause, for President Nixon was looking for labor friends. Since his election in 1968, Nixon aspired to build a new majority, peeling away key elements of the Democrats' New Deal coalition, especially blue-collar "white ethnics." Nixon and his advisors believed that a growing rift between liberals and working-class whites over taxes, welfare, affirmative action, and the war in Vietnam was putting the loyalties of many lifelong Democratic voters up for grabs. As Nixon's chief liaison to organized labor, Charles W. Colson, put it, "the labor vote can be ours in 1972."[44]

Although it would later seem incongruous in light of the evolution of party politics since the 1980s, for three decades after World War II mainstream Republicans actively courted a segment of the union vote. Among Republicans Nixon was especially intent on winning over labor allies. He prided himself on his humble origins, avoided confrontations on most hot button labor issues, and believed that he could connect with union rank-and-filers. Nixon was particularly optimistic about winning over members of the building trades, Longshoremen, and Teamsters.

Two developments in the fall of 1971 increased Nixon's desire to court labor. One flowed from his decision to impose wage and price controls to combat inflation in August 1971. The move infuriated AFL-CIO president George Meany, who characterized Nixon's decision to freeze wages but not profits as "Robin Hood in reverse, robbing the poor to pay the rich." The controversy threatened to derail Nixon's effort to win a sizable section of the labor vote in 1972 and gave him an incentive to seek a rapprochement with the unions as his reelection campaign drew nearer. The second development concerned Nixon's decision to sell 150 million bushels of wheat to the Soviet

Union—a decision that itself was influenced by reelection calculations and the knowledge that the sale would send wheat prices, farmers' incomes, and Nixon's farm belt poll numbers soaring. A number of unions objected to the sale on the grounds that it aided a government that was financing and arming North Vietnamese soldiers who at that moment were fighting Americans. Presidents Teddy Gleason of the International Longshoremen's Association, Paul Hall of the Seafarers, and Jesse Calhoon of MEBA announced that their members would refuse to load or ship the grain, threatening to scuttle the deal altogether. At the same time, however, the union leaders privately let the White House know that they were willing to negotiate if Nixon guaranteed that half of the grain would be sent on American ships, served by their members. If Nixon wanted to ship grain, Calhoon made clear, then "one hand has got to wash the other." Like Calhoon, Richard Nixon knew how to cut a deal.[45]

It was in the Oval Office, just before noon on October 29, 1971, that Nixon aide John D. Ehrlichman first told his boss that the unions were threatening to block the grain shipment to the Soviet Union. "Oh, good Godsakes!" Nixon thundered. He immediately summoned his special counsel, Charles Colson, who already had been talking with Teddy Gleason of the Longshoremen's union. "The guy who has the most influence on this staff with Gleason is Colson," said Nixon. A seasoned operative who had come up through Massachusetts politics, Colson had become valuable to Nixon in large part, as Colson himself later put it, because he was "willing to blink at certain ethical standards, to be ruthless in getting things done." Colson was Nixon's fixer. He was also the aide Nixon had designated to court labor leaders like Gleason or Frank Fitzsimmons of the Teamsters. Colson felt comfortable with the labor people, understood Nixon's labor strategy, and liked making deals. Nixon ordered Ehrlichman to "get Colson in on the deal" right away. "I want this done!" he said.[46]

Colson got on the job immediately. That afternoon, he came to the Oval Office to see Nixon, National Security Adviser Henry Kissinger, and Nixon's chief of staff, H. R. Haldeman. Colson told Nixon that he was confident he could "roll some labor unions" to facilitate the wheat shipment. Nixon was glad to hear it and gave Colson free rein to negotiate a deal. "Get something done, or we're going to be in a hell of a spot," he said.[47]

Two days later, Colson informed Nixon the union leaders were "ready to do business." Colson added he would be meeting with Gleason, Hall, and

Calhoon on November 3 to work out the terms of a deal. In the meantime, Calhoon called Leyden to let him know that an avenue toward rehiring the fired activists was opening. "I've got something coming to me from the administration... because of the wheat deal," Calhoon said. Calhoon said he was ready to "get this controller thing moved."[48]

Nixon anxiously awaited the outcome of Colson's negotiations on November 3. When he did not hear back from Colson by noon, he had someone pull Colson from his meeting with the labor leaders for a progress report. Colson assured Nixon he was making "very good progress." Nixon was relieved. "Go in there. Go right back in and say the President wanted to express his, you know, extend his regards and we appreciate their coopera- tion and all that bull." Later that day, Colson reported he had reached an agreement with Calhoon, Hall, and Gleason that only required AFL-CIO president Meany's approval. Nixon never asked for the details. The impor- tant thing was that the deal was done. When Colson called the next day to say that everything was finalized, the president was ecstatic. "Good, good, good.... Well, let me say this, that this is a great triumph for us." Nixon immediately phoned Kissinger to share news of the "tremendous achievement."[49]

The secret deal Colson brokered on Nixon's behalf was complicated. The unions agreed to permit their members to load and ship the grain and waived their demand that at least 50 percent be moved in American ships. In return, the administration promised a ten-year program of subsidies to help American ships compete on a more equitable basis with foreign-flagged ships. The administration also promised a variety of favors to the individual unions, the terms of which were "extremely confidential," according to Colson. All of the parties to the deal "would be embarrassed by its release or disclosure," he explained. When the White House publicly announced on November 5 that labor leaders had agreed to drop their objections to the Soviet grain shipment, one official declared, with a straight face, that "the unions had not asked for anything in return for the grain to be loaded on foreign vessels."[50]

Had it been widely disclosed, one of the items agreed to in the deal would have been particularly embarrassing. Colson agreed to Calhoon's demand that the air traffic controllers fired for leading the 1970 sickout be rehired. The White House instructed the FAA to rehire every fired controller but one, strike leader Mike Rock. Rock did not mind serving as the symbolic sacrificial lamb: he had left the FAA in November 1969 to work full-time for PATCO.[51]

When Transportation Department officials heard that the FAA needed to rehire controllers fired for violating the law, they were incensed. Nixon aide John Ehrlichman broke the news to James Beggs in a phone call. "No, John, we're not going to do that," Beggs responded, adding that Secretary Volpe would "have a fit." But Ehrlichman was adamant. There would be no appeal. The president's decision was final. Beggs, Volpe, and Shaffer "fumed," but they had no choice but to comply. Nixon's desire to move his larger political agenda, which included forging alliances with key unions, overrode the discontent of his subordinates.[52]

The government tried to accomplish the rehiring with as little notice as possible. The FAA let three months pass after the grain deal announcement to ensure that no suspicious observers would draw a linkage. Then, on February 7, 1972, the FAA quietly issued a press release announcing that air traffic controllers "fired for their activist roles in the 1970 strike" could "apply for reemployment." Volpe claimed that this decision was based upon recommendations given him by Shaffer, and that this initiative was being made "solely on the basis of compassion for the fired controllers." The FAA insisted the reemployment offer, "in no way diminished the gravity of striking against the Federal Government." The announcement also implied that not all controllers who reapplied for their jobs would be rehired, and rehiring decisions would be left to local FAA officials in the facilities where the controllers had worked. The FAA fed this same line to Congress. It worked. No immediate connection was made between the grain deal and the rehiring of the controllers as the FAA made good on Colson's promise to Calhoon. All strikers who sought reinstatement were rehired—even those whom regional officials tried to blackball.[53]

The rehiring deal was enormously significant. For more than a year, the FAA had repeatedly vowed it would never rehire strike leaders. Now they were coming back. By waging an illegal fight against the government and returning to their jobs, the sickout organizers seemingly proved that the firing threat was hollow after all. The rehires were scarcely welcomed back with open arms. The FAA insisted on shifting most of them from the facilities where they had worked before their firing. But rank-and-file controllers were amazed that their striking colleagues were rehired at all. The rumors of how the deal had been cut soon circulated to every working air traffic controller. Calhoon's negotiation with Colson became the stuff of legend in FAA facilities. The story did wonders for PATCO's reputation. It demonstrated that PATCO had clout and showed that "when Jesse Calhoon spoke presidents listened." Out in the facilities, Rock reported that organizing started "to roll again" after the deal.[54]

In many ways, the 1970 sickout and its settlement a year later shaped the personality of PATCO and the worldview of its activists. Although it resulted in a putative defeat, the sickout demonstrated that PATCO was a fighting organization, a force to be reckoned with. Not only had the struggle made PATCO "a household name," it helped settle the question of what sort of organization PATCO would be. After the sickout, it "could not be denied any longer that we were actually a labor union. We were no silly professional organization, no benevolent society or anything like that. We were a labor union," as board chairman Bill South put it. The sickout had brought to the surface leaders who were committed to making PATCO a successful union. Rank-and-file controllers viewed those who had "stood tall" and risked their jobs on behalf of their organization and profession as heroes. Their return from exile made a big impression on young controllers. In the returning strike leaders, they saw men who had defied the federal government and lived to tell the tale. "I worked with those gentlemen," said one Chicago Center controller, "and didn't perceive them to be that much different from me or anybody else I knew." If these men could fight the government and win, why couldn't any one of their coworkers do the same?[55]

Cleared for Takeoff

Having secured both Department of Labor clearance and the improbable rehirings, Leyden and Calhoon turned their attention to PATCO's final priority: the passage of early retirement legislation, the Air Traffic Controller Career Act of 1972. As Rock explained, PATCO was looking for "a big win to get the people to rejoin the organization and to get the new controllers to believe in PATCO." The "Second Career" bill, as controllers called it, was indeed big. It would allow controllers to retire with full benefits after twenty years of service if they were at least fifty years old, or to retire at any age after twenty-five years of service. It also provided second career training funds to any controllers who could document that they could no longer direct air traffic because of the stress of their jobs.[56]

Air traffic controllers had called for legislation like this for more than a decade without success. Few observers gave PATCO much of a chance of passing the law after its sickout debacle, but when the FAA decided to support the bill in response to the findings of the Corson Commission a window of opportunity suddenly opened. Knowing that passage of the bill would seal PATCO's claim to the allegiance of the nation's air traffic controllers, John Leyden began actively lobbying for the bill, while Jesse Calhoon made contributions from MEBA's political treasury to key legislators who helped bring it to a successful vote in the House and Senate. Calhoon also helped grease the skids at the other end of Pennsylvania Avenue. In his grain deal negotiations with Colson, he had secured a promise that Nixon would sign the law if it reached his desk.[57]

Nixon signed the bill on May 16, 1972. "Air traffic controllers are Federal professionals who have no counterpart in Government, nor in the civilian side of our economy," Nixon's signing statement explained. "With this legislation we will now be able to train those employees who can no longer work in air traffic control for a second career at Government expense." Nixon sent his counsel, Clark MacGregor, to read his statement at PATCO's national convention the next day in Kansas City. Nixon's words resonated with the broad appeal that his campaign was making to the "silent majority" of working Americans in 1972. "The air traffic controller is a typically proud man; proud of his profession, and proud of his unique service to our country. It is, therefore, with great pride that we recognize him today," said MacGregor.[58]

The bill's enactment was an enormous victory for PATCO. "Every controller in the country that was in the system and paying attention knew that PATCO had worked on it and that it was PATCO's bill," said Rock. Even FAA Administrator Shaffer could not help but be impressed. He understood that without the political muscle of PATCO-MEBA, the bill might never have passed.[59]

In the end, Nixon got what he wanted from his labor strategy. Leyden and Calhoon reciprocated Nixon's aid by joining the Teamsters, Longshoremen, and some building trades unions in endorsing Nixon's reelection in 1972, a year when the AFL-CIO Executive Council decided to remain neutral and withhold support from the liberal antiwar Democratic presidential candidate, Senator George McGovern of South Dakota. Since the AFL-CIO remained neutral, Nixon's endorsement by a handful of individual unions was all the more significant. Nixon won a landslide victory that November, buttressed by the votes of many traditionally Democratic union members. On December 15, after welcoming his labor backers to the White House, Nixon exulted with Colson over the "new majority" they were constructing. "Chuck, we're changing the whole thing. Whoever thought four years ago labor guys would be in this house?"[60]

PATCO leaders also got what they wanted, winning a landslide of their own that fall. Having achieved Labor Department clearance, the rehiring of the fired activists, and the "Second Career" bill, PATCO had shown even the most skeptical controllers that it was an organization with considerable clout. PATCO leaders thus pressed ahead toward a national representation election. Granting PATCO's request, on July 20, 1972, William Usery called for an election to be conducted in more than 350 FAA facilities from Guam to Maine. More than 10,000 controllers cast ballots in that election. Calhoon, Leyden, and PATCO Treasurer Stanley Gordon sat across the table from FAA officials as Labor Department examiners counted the votes on September 20, 1972. The results exceeded the PATCO leaders' grandest expectations: 84 percent voted to make PATCO their exclusive representative. Once the tally was official, Calhoon telephoned Colson with the results. The last part of the deal was now consummated.[61]

It was one of the most remarkable turnabouts in U.S. labor history. In the space of 889 days, PATCO had gone from being a bankrupt organization on the brink of collapse, whose leadership was in turmoil, and whose leading activists were being fired and blacklisted from reemployment in their craft, to recognition as the official representative of air traffic controllers nationwide. Within months of PATCO's certification, 85 percent of the air traffic controller workforce signed up as members and initiated dues checkoff, making air traffic controllers the most densely organized workforce in the federal government, where workers were free to avoid union membership if they chose. (Getting 70 percent of a bargaining unit to pay dues was generally seen as a sign of extremely strong union support before PATCO.)

Indicative of the shift was the new attitude of FAA Administrator Shaffer, who had battled PATCO fiercely in 1970. Following the union's certification, Shaffer said he would be "receptive to any legitimate proposal" in contract negotiations. Shaffer also let his subordinates know that a new day had arrived. "To some FAA managers and supervisors, the need to bargain, consult, and otherwise deal with this emerging third force has represented a drastic change in their earlier-formed concepts of management and in the methods they have used in the past to carry out their managerial and supervisory responsibilities," Shaffer admitted. But it was time for the attitudes of the past to give way, he said, for in the future "more and more management decisions affecting personnel will be made bilaterally with the unions."[62]

Jack Maher, for one, was amazed by the change. "After all that struggle, it seemed too good to be true," he thought. In some ways it was too good to be true. PATCO's astonishing resurrection had been made possible by a fortuitous combination of circumstances and timing. Within a few years some of the union's activists would forget that. The erroneous lessons they later drew from the turnaround of 1970–1972 would contribute directly to PATCO's spectacular destruction less than a decade later.[63]

FLIGHT CEILING

PATCO will not attempt to obtain unrealistic and
unobtainable objectives; but with your support will
pursue legitimate, realistic objectives.
—JOHN LEYDEN, PATCO PRESIDENT, 1973[1]

The time has come for you to resign and call for an
election of more aggressive Union leadership. . . . We
had them "By the Balls" and you let them go.
—DON MCPHAIL, PATCO MEMBER, 1976[2]

Between 1972 and 1977, PATCO emerged as the most militant, most densely
organized union in any bargaining unit of the nation's largest employer, the
U.S. government. During these years, PATCO began to transform the hierarchical, military-like workplace culture of a government agency deeply inhos-
pitable to unionism and collective bargaining. It developed an impressive
infrastructure and produced a talented group of local and national leaders. It
won major new protections for air traffic controllers. It even found a creative
way to pressure the government to raise the salaries of a large portion of the
controller workforce even though it had no right to bargain over pay.

Yet these same years saw PATCO's weaknesses exposed. The mid-1970s
proved to be a challenging time for all public sector unions as the combined

effect of unemployment and inflation produced "stagflation," creating the first economic crisis to grip the country since collective bargaining first came to the public sector in the 1960s. Unions of state and local government workers fought to fend off budget cuts and protect their recent gains from worried politicians who struggled to respond to the fiscal crisis. But the situation was even more difficult in the federal sector, where workers lacked the right to bargain over what mattered most to them, their pay and benefits. The constraints PATCO faced as a federal workers' union became more apparent as inflation eroded the incomes of air traffic controllers while rising unemployment squeezed federal tax revenues, giving the FAA more incentive to resist PATCO's demands. The worsening economic context surfaced deep tensions within the union that were impossible to resolve within the limited framework of federal sector bargaining. By the mid-1970s, these tensions were already threatening PATCO's unity and portending its destruction.

Bringing Unionism to the FAA

A glimmer of the future was visible when PATCO's first contract negotiations with the federal government opened in December 1972. The talks took place in a context of fiscal constraint, for President Nixon had just frozen federal hiring and promotions. Still, PATCO had three advantages going into the talks. First, a leadership transition was under way: FAA Administrator Shaffer and Transportation Secretary Volpe both stepped down after Nixon's reelection. Nixon's trusted aide, Alexander Butterfield, assumed control of the FAA, and Claude S. Brinegar, an oil company executive with little experience in aviation, succeeded Volpe. These men were more intent on moving into their new offices than intervening in the contract talks; they simply wanted a quick settlement. Second, the Civil Service Commission (CSC) was also encouraging an agreement. "Unions have the unenviable task of representing a broad constituency which has numerous, at times conflicting, interests," a CSC negotiating manual explained. The commission urged negotiators to be flexible. "Only on rare occasions should management say 'no' during these initial meetings," it advised. Finally, PATCO's counsel, Bill Peer, had negotiated contracts with the U.S. Postal Service—the reorganized entity that replaced the Post Office Department in 1971—and he was better prepared for a federal sector negotiation than his FAA counterparts, who were new to the process.[3]

Although PATCO, like other federal unions, negotiated within strict parameters that did not include compensation or benefits, the union nonetheless made significant gains in its first contract, winning two improvements that were popular with controllers. The first liberalized the FAM flight program, allowing controllers to take as many as eight FAMs per year. The second was Article 55 of the contract, which detailed a grievance procedure for air traffic controllers. Peer modeled this system on one he had negotiated with the Postal Service on behalf of the Rural Letter Carriers Association. It provided for binding arbitration of grievances when the union and the FAA could not reach agreement on a grievance claim. More than any other feature of the PATCO contract, Article 55 changed the FAA's workplace culture, for it granted controllers the right to an outside-party review that could possibly overturn their supervisors' actions. Controllers overwhelmingly ratified the agreement, which took effect on May 1, 1973. To celebrate, PATCO opened its 1973 convention in New York City with the bagpipers who had led the defeated strikers back to work at New York Center three years earlier, symbolizing just how far the union had come in such a short time.[4]

Adapting to collective bargaining and the constraints of a contract was not easy for the FAA, the culture of which derived from the military backgrounds and inclinations of its managers. Most federal agencies of the early 1970s possessed management cultures that stressed the authority of superiors over subordinates, but the FAA was notoriously hierarchical. One study published in 1983 concluded that its managers "could not tolerate the thought of living and working in a situation in which subordinates were other than deferent, obedient, and compliant."[5]

The FAA was a classic practitioner of what Douglas McGregor, the most prominent management theorist of the era, called "Theory X" management. According to McGregor, Theory X managers assumed that workers disliked and sought to shirk work, gave their maximum effort only when coerced, and preferred being directed to taking responsibility for themselves. The FAA's Theory X approach led controllers to criticize the agency for trying to "vector human beings" as if they were aircraft. Not surprisingly, controllers gave their bosses poor reviews. A survey completed in the mid-1970s found that 85 percent of controllers believed that the FAA did not reward consistently good performance. Most thought the agency was more concerned with hardware than people. Had they been able to design their own workplace culture, controllers might have created something close to McGregor's

"Theory Y" style of management, which saw coercion as self-defeating, assumed that self-directed workers were more productive, and viewed hierarchies as stifling. Throughout the 1970s, the FAA's Theory X practices clashed repeatedly with the controllers' Theory Y desires, producing ongoing discord.[6]

Differences between controllers and supervisors were exacerbated by the fact that all frontline supervisors in the FAA had begun as controllers. The process of moving into management led many new supervisors to lord their power over former colleagues in order to ensure their new subordinates recognized their new authority. When controllers accepted promotions to management, they "would come back like they'd never been on the floor before," as though "they'd forgotten what it was like to be a controller," said their former colleagues. Some controllers joked about new supervisors returning from "lobotomy school," or "having their spines removed to be managers." Many controllers had no desire to make such a transition and passed on the chance to become supervisors because it would have amounted to, as one put it, "turning my back on my own family." Others tried their hand at management, but found the loss of camaraderie it entailed so painful that they returned to controlling aircraft.[7]

Because moving into management required some social distancing, many controllers believed that only the incompetent—"people who couldn't cut the mustard as controllers"—desired to move up. Whether it was true or not, many controllers simply assumed that supervisors could not take the pressure of actually directing traffic. In a workplace where traffic-moving prowess was a measure of manhood, the decision to accept a managerial post was akin to admitting one had "no balls"—or worse. "Who are the 'Prostitutes'?" one union activist asked. "Prostitutes are the brother Controllers who for morally low reasons bid on the staff jobs in your facility." Such views were so deeply ingrained that they undermined efforts to bridge the controller–supervisor divide. When Leyden explored letting controllers who rose to supervisory positions remain as honorary PATCO members, he met such fierce resistance that he immediately dropped the idea.[8]

The introduction of collective bargaining into the FAA's hierarchical workplace culture stirred conflict. Supervisors resisted PATCO's new role, especially those on the front lines who felt that PATCO enabled controllers to set policy more effectively than low-level supervisors could. These supervisors felt that national FAA leaders had "jerked the rug out from under" them and left them like "a man without a country." Their morale plummeted. "You know, I used to be able to just run this tower," one facility chief snapped. "Now I have to ask four controllers if I can wipe my ass." Some supervisors dealt with their loss of unilateral control by becoming all the more aggressive; Chicago Center controllers called this "management by fear." The CSC offered to instruct supervisors on how to adjust their practices to the new world of "bilateralism," but many simply refused to change their ways. Some disregarded the provisions of the 1973 PATCO-FAA contract altogether.[9]

PATCO's facility representatives soon learned that they had to force compliance with the contract. They carried copies of it in their pockets, pulling it out whenever necessary to specify clauses if they found supervisors violating its rules. In general, the facility reps proved to be a tough bunch. When a new supervisor arrived at Indianapolis Center and began to "crack the whip," the rep brought a group of controllers to meet with him to deliver a message. "Here's the deal," the facility rep said. "Don't fuck with us and we won't fuck with you." When the supervisor later tried to pull someone off his position to discipline him, he found that the facility rep "could crack the whip a lot harder than he could." No one would relieve the controller at his position to allow the supervisor to take him aside and berate him. In the end, the supervisor gave up. "There are three things most supervisors need to learn," one PATCO activist advised. "1. You don't wipe your nose on Superman's cape; 2. You don't kiss a rattlesnake; and 3. You don't 'BLANK' with controllers."[10]

Of course, confrontation was not always necessary. Occasionally, the union made its point with humor. Knowing where an obstreperous supervisor purchased his cigarettes, Jacksonville Center controllers stocked the vending machine with books of matches that carried the message, "Smile, PATCO loves you." Denver's PATCO local gave an annual Professional of the Year—"P.O.T.Y."—Award to the facility's worst supervisor.[11]

Ultimately, the grievance procedure embodied in Article 55 of the PATCO-FAA contract provided the best lever for controllers to change the FAA's culture. The arbitration clause PATCO won in 1973 put it at the forefront of a wave of change in the federal workforce. The number of grievances arbitrated under provisions of union contracts in the public sector rose twentyfold between 1968 and 1980. The right to have grievances adjudicated by a third-party arbitrator was a powerful tool in reshaping workplace relations in the FAA, bringing a form of "industrial jurisprudence" to facilities where supervisors had always enjoyed the final word. Jack Maher, who served as PATCO's director of labor relations in these early years, urged controllers to make the most of the system. His mantra was, "Don't debate it, grieve it." Maher's desk was soon piled high with grievance files. By 1977, PATCO was sending about five hundred grievances to arbitration per year.[12]

The decisions rendered in these cases set precedents that expanded controllers' rights and widened PATCO's influence in the facilities. Having represented postal workers before accepting PATCO's retainer, counsel Bill Peer understood arbitration better than his FAA counterparts. He winnowed grievance claims in order to arbitrate only those most likely to win, dropping any that might set damaging precedents. In each case, the FAA tended to base its defense on the same management rights clause in EO 11491, invoking it time after time while paying little heed to the details of the cases. Again and again, the FAA argued in effect that its power to promote, transfer, assign, and direct employees without consulting the union overrode the specific facts of each case. This blanket approach only alienated arbitrators and contributed to PATCO's high percentage of winning cases in the early years of Article 55.[13]

Grievance arbitration expanded the rights of controllers. Through the grievance process, they won the freedom to wear more comfortable clothing, including jeans; the right to wear PATCO buttons in the workplace; the option of using a sick day to care for sick family members; the right to reimbursement for moving costs incurred as a result of forced transfers; and the right to speak more freely in the workplace, including using profanity, without being disciplined. Parking rights were also another oft-grieved issue at airports where close-in parking was scarce. When Des Moines controllers were forced to move their cars from a covered parking lot next to their terminal to an uncovered lot fifteen hundred feet away, they filed a grievance and won the right to return to the covered lot. PATCO brought ten parking cases to arbitration in 1975 alone and won all ten. Winning such fights encouraged controllers to defend their rights all the more strongly. When a facility chief in Hawaii refused to implement an arbitrator's decision granting parking privileges, controllers simply parked in the supervisors' slots until the chief relented.[14]

Interestingly, the FAA's Washington headquarters did not view Article 55 as negatively as did many field supervisors. Prior to the 1973 contract, national FAA officials had been frustrated often by the autonomy of regional officials, who set their own personnel policies. Headstrong regional administrators, like Henry Newman from the Southwest, whose efforts to break PATCO in his region provoked the 1970 sickout, complicated the ability of Washington officials to govern their far-flung agency and deal with its increasingly assertive workforce. Accordingly, Washington officials saw some value in having the agency's labor policies "codified" by the FAA-PATCO contract and arbitration precedents. The contract brought a greater measure of predictability and uniformity to labor relations at the FAA.[15]

Out in the facilities, though, grievance arbitration was, in the end, "a power thing," as one PATCO activist put it. Controllers found that once they had beaten management a few times in arbitration, supervisors "backed off," and the union widened the scope of its influence. Over time, the FAA recovered from its initial blunders and learned how to better contest grievances. By 1980, it was winning nearly as many arbitration cases as it lost. But by then PATCO had effectively used grievances to establish a "right to due process" and made clear that controllers had rights on the job.[16]

Next to winning arbitration, PATCO's second most important victory came with the creation of a national immunity program designed both to protect controllers and improve air safety. Before the 1970s, air traffic controllers had no say in shaping the procedures and policies that governed air traffic. They also had little or no protection when those procedures failed or they made a mistake leading to a "system error" (a violation of procedures). As a result, controllers tended to cover up their mistakes rather than report them. PATCO wanted a way to protect controllers and make it in everyone's interest to report system errors in order to identify and correct the procedures that led to them. Lacking such a system, PATCO encouraged controllers who were accused of errors not to answer a supervisor's questions without a union official present, a stand that led to furious conflict between the union and the FAA.[17]

The standoff between PATCO and the FAA over safety investigations was ultimately resolved by a disaster. On December 1, 1974, a tower controller at Dulles International Airport outside Washington, D.C., cleared a TWA flight for approach. Flying with low visibility, the pilot descended too quickly and crashed into a mountain twenty-three miles west of the airport, killing all ninety-two people aboard. During its investigation of the crash, the National Transportation Safety Board learned that both controllers and pilots previously had alerted the FAA to potential problems associated with the Dulles approach, but the agency had not responded to the warnings.[18]

The disaster also made clear that there was no incentive for pilots and controllers to report safety violations. If either party reported what controllers called "a deal"—an incident in which two planes violated minimum separation standards—they could become embroiled in a lengthy investigation, which could lead to disciplinary sanctions. Thus, both pilots and controllers tended to underreport problems. Furthermore, supervisors abetted this underreporting, for it yielded reports that made their facilities look good.[19]

During the late 1960s, the FAA had experimented with an immunity program in which pilots and controllers were encouraged to report errors, with the promise that if they self-reported they would not be subject to discipline unless they were guilty of gross negligence. The experiment had been popular but short-lived. In the aftermath of the 1974 Dulles crash, PATCO demanded the revival and expansion of the immunity program. The idea was endorsed by the Air Line Pilots Association, members of Congress, consumer groups, and even the General Accounting Office. However, the FAA resisted, suggesting that immunity guarantees would foster laxity in the enforcement of safety procedures.[20]

It was only after Alexander Butterfield resigned as FAA administrator on March 31, 1975, and James E. Dow took on the role of acting administrator that PATCO was able to make headway. Dow, a former air traffic controller, understood the value of immunity. Shortly after taking office he inaugurated the Aviation Safety Reporting System. Under this program, the National Aeronautics and Space Administration (NASA) collected reports on system errors from pilots and controllers; the names of those reporting the incidents were confidential and kept separate from the details of the incidents. Not surprisingly, reports of violations surged, as controllers began reporting incidents they might have previously attempted to cover up. Most pilots, controllers, and supervisors alike soon found the system to be effective at identifying problems and instigating improvements. PATCO expanded on this significant victory in subsequent contract negotiations with the FAA, winning an agreement that controllers and supervisors would jointly revise safety procedures.[21]

Tensions between the union and the FAA over safety issues did not disappear with the immunity program. Some FAA officials believed that immunity only ensured that bad controllers remained on the job; others argued that the self-reporting of safety violations ended up overstating safety problems and made the agency vulnerable to criticism from the Congress. Within a few years, the pendulum would swing again, and FAA leaders would seek to close down the program. But in the mid-1970s, immunity signified to many controllers PATCO's power to reshape the FAA.[22]

STABILIZING AN ORGANIZATION

As PATCO won its first victories, it consolidated itself as an organization. Once the dues checkoff provision kicked in during 1973, PATCO's income rose by 71 percent. This allowed the union to wean itself from MEBA's financial support. In turn, the share of its dues revenues that PATCO turned over to MEBA as part of its affiliation agreement meant that Jesse Calhoon's investment in PATCO began to pay off for MEBA. With a steady revenue stream established, PATCO was able to put its top elected officers on the union's payroll for the first time. By 1974, the regional vice presidents who made up PATCO's executive board were granted leaves of absence from the FAA so they could devote themselves to their offices full time. PATCO could also afford to train its key personnel. In 1973, the union sent Rock to Harvard University's labor education program to learn the art of contract negotiation.[23]

The most significant development in PATCO's organizational stabilization was the emergence of John Leyden as a unifying leader. In a famous passage from his 1948 study of union leaders, *The New Men of Power*, sociologist C. Wright Mills wrote about the many qualities essential for labor leadership. Because unions sometimes needed to behave like armies, the successful labor leader had to be comfortable in the role of "generalissimo," wrote Mills. And because the union also needed to function like a democratic town meeting, the union leader had to be a skillful parliamentary debater. The successful union leader combined the skills of political boss and entrepreneur, and acted as an organizer of discontent—both a "regulator of the workingman's industrial animosity" and "salaried technician of animosity." Leyden perfectly embodied these seemingly contradictory qualities.[24]

Leyden's background and personality were well suited to leading PATCO. He was an award-winning controller, widely respected for his skill—no small point in earning the respect of other air traffic controllers. Like most of his members, he was naturally confident and did not second-guess himself often. He also responded positively to criticism. He accepted from the beginning that that he could never "fulfill the will and desire of every member of PATCO." He was comfortable enough with himself to strike alliances with former or potential rivals as well as any "New York Irish pol," as one observer put it. Having attained the PATCO presidency in 1970 by criticizing the leadership of Rock and Maher, once in office Leyden quickly won over PATCO's founders. Maher often marveled at Leyden's "ability to do a 180 in a matter of minutes." As his courtship of Rock and Maher illustrated, Leyden could be flexible and open-minded when circumstances dictated. "The office I hold leads me to be pragmatic," mindful of "the realities of life," he explained. Yet, Leyden could also stand his ground forcefully. Even his critics allowed that he was honest in letting both friend and foe alike know where he stood on an issue. This quality won him the respect of FAA officials even when they disagreed with him. One FAA administrator characterized him as "a good man to work with," someone "able to make concessions" while at the same time "very supportive of his union and his people."[25]

Leyden's success owed to his ability as a "technician of animosity," as Mills might put it. It was difficult to run a new union in workplaces where, as Rock liked to say, "everybody was smart, everybody was aggressive." Air traffic controllers were a highly independent bunch, more comfortable giving directions than taking direction, and they were as free in their criticism of their leaders as they were of the FAA. PATCO leaders did their best to harness the energy of their members by creating a "rank-and-file democracy" within the union, encouraging controllers to take an active role in running their organization. But local activists inevitably differed from their national leaders on questions of vision, strategy, and tactics. This contributed to a combative relationship between PATCO's leading militants and their president. Leyden accepted this. "It would be nice if…I could make papal announcements and speak 'ex cathedra' and have my membership totally satisfied, unfortunately, my position does not afford me such an opportunity," he told one critic. Still the burdens of office could frustrate Leyden. At times it seemed that that PATCO was made up of twelve thousand critics, and that "Everybody knew better how to do the job."[26]

In the end, Leyden had more difficulty dealing with allies who disappointed him than harsh critics who attacked him. He was not unaware of this flaw. "It is enormously more difficult and it takes greater and far higher courage to face and confront friends who, well-intentioned as they may be, by their actions are only further dividing and undercutting the organization," he confided. However, his self-awareness did not protect him from missteps. He committed a serious one only a year into his presidency. Leyden concluded shortly after his election in 1970 that his running mate, vice president Bob Greene, was ineffectual. In response, he quietly encouraged Noel Keane of Kansas City Center to challenge Greene in 1971. As the election neared, however, Leyden did not have the heart to openly break with Greene. Without Leyden's open support, Keane's challenge collapsed.[27]

Leyden's inability to campaign for Keane in 1971 altered the course of PATCO's subsequent history, for Greene was ultimately unseated in 1972 by a different challenger, Robert Poli of Cleveland Center. After Poli's victory, Leyden and Poli built an effective partnership that defined PATCO's leadership through the rest of the decade. They worked well together, in part because of their different styles and skills. They split key aspects of the union's leadership work between them. Leyden concentrated on PATCO's larger strategy and his public duties. Poli's skills served him well as a problem-solver on organizational matters. Widely acknowledged to be "sharp," possessing a quick analytical mind, Poli was not the type to bluntly confront critics, as Leyden often did. He was more solicitous of and connected better with the union's younger activists. Although they both had considerable egos, Poli and Leyden recognized that their partnership worked. The two men often shared drinks with other PATCO officers at the union's favorite bar, The Embers. On weekends their families socialized, and their wives became friends. But underlying tensions in the Leyden-Poli partnership would surface in time. When that happened and their relationship soured, Leyden proved as reluctant to take on Poli as he had been to dump Greene. Then, the costs of his reluctance would be high indeed.[28]

Recruiting Members

Like all unions in the federal sector, PATCO worked in an "open-shop" environment, meaning that while the union was obligated to represent all air traffic controllers, controllers were not obligated to join PATCO or pay dues in return for that representation. The situation frustrated Leyden, who found nonmembers "neither bashful nor reticent" in invoking the union's aid on grievances, while "enjoying a free ride" on the backs of dues-paying PATCO members. Despite the federal rules that prevented the establishment of a union shop, PATCO achieved the highest union density ratio in the federal sector. In 1976, PATCO claimed 13,681 members, or 85 percent of the controllers who were eligible to join.[29]

PATCO's success in recruiting members owed to the nature of the workforce and the work. Controllers tended to come from similar backgrounds and arrived at the FAA by similar routes. Each of the points of controllers' common work experience served as recruiting grounds for the union. Because most air traffic controllers came from the military until the late 1970s, PATCO began recruiting military controllers even before their discharge. Many military controllers took out auxiliary PATCO memberships knowing that they planned to join the FAA in the near future. Like the ATCA before it, PATCO also recruited at the FAA training school in Oklahoma City. Most instructors at the facility were members. And once controllers began on-the-job training in FAA facilities, the work team became the union's chief recruitment vehicle. Controllers depended heavily on teamwork. No one could learn the job without help, and no one could do the work alone. "If you were a loner, you didn't belong there," one O'Hare controller explained. "You were a team player, or you were nobody."[30]

Developmental controllers often heard about PATCO from their senior team members and trainers. Influenced by the opinions of senior controllers they respected, and whose signoff would be necessary for them to achieve the status of journeymen controllers, many "developmentals" joined within their first months on the job. Those who refused to join could find themselves shunned. "They refer to other nonmembers and myself as 'scabs,'" complained one O'Hare controller. Occasionally, the peer pressure could get out of hand. One nonmember in St. Louis claimed that his coworkers tried to force him into committing a safety infraction in order to blemish his record. His claim was ultimately upheld in arbitration.[31]

The fact that controllers who joined the FAA in the late 1960s and early 1970s hailed from working-class backgrounds also promoted unionization, ensuring a steady stream of recruits who came from blue-collar union families. Many of the activists who emerged to lead PATCO locals by the mid-1970s shared this profile. Gary Eads, of Kansas City Center, had vivid childhood memories of walking picket lines with his father, a St. Louis Teamster. Washington National Airport's John Thornton was the son of a New Jersey Teamster. Ron Taylor, of West Palm Beach, Florida, was the son of a Machinists' union member and the brother of a union activist at the U.S. Bureau of Engraving and Printing. And Indianapolis Center's Terry Bobell, a native of Peoria, Illinois, learned about unions at the dinner table from his father, an operating engineer, and his mother, a public school teacher.[32]

Leaders like these learned how to seize on local issues to build the union in their facilities. Parking rights, more comfortable chairs, a microwave oven in the break room that would free controllers from the need to patronize an expensive cafeteria, the assurance that overtime had to be prescheduled— such demands were the lifeblood of the local union. Fights for more casual dress, such as Miami Center controllers' "take this tie and shove it" movement, were also effective union-building efforts. In such local struggles, the union's organizers received an assist from irritating FAA policies and the agency's hierarchical management culture.[33]

When it began in 1968, PATCO had shied away from embracing a union identity lest the organization put off potential members who believed "professionals" did not need unions. By the mid-1970s, however, Leyden was pleased to note, "The word 'union' no longer sticks in our craw." Rock observed a "tremendous philosophy change" as PATCO activists began "training other controllers to become union guys" and showing them how to exercise their rights under the contract. "We're going to wear our hats and we're going to have our buttons and we're going to support unions locally and get involved with the labor councils around the country and we're going to march in all the parades," Rock told his colleagues. "We're really becoming a union."[34]

This did not mean that PATCO members abandoned the "professional" identity that had been so important to controllers when they began organizing in the 1960s. Rather, like the unionized teachers, nurses, and police officers whose organizations were growing in the 1970s, PATCO activists saw themselves as part of a new wave that was changing the "blue-collar image of the labor movement" and making unions "acceptable and normal" to white-collar workers. The theme of PATCO's 1975 convention—"Pride and Professionalism"—spoke to the idea that unionism and professionalism were not only compatible but also mutually reinforcing. There was "no contradiction in being a 'professional' and being a 'trade unionist,'" Leyden insisted. "We are all Proud Professionals," argued the Oakland Center PATCO newsletter. Indeed, PATCO activists believed that unionism provided the only real defense that they had in the effort to preserve the standards of their profession against low pay, overwork, understaffing, and poor equipment. "Appreciate the complexity of your profession, do not cheapen it," urged Gary Eads.[35]

PATCO members achieved a relative consensus about the relationship between unionism and professionalism in the mid-1970s, but that did not mean that unity prevailed throughout the organization. To the contrary, the union was rife with internal tensions. From the beginning, PATCO wrestled with the differences in outlook and expectations between controllers in larger, high-density facilities, and those in smaller, less busy facilities. The impetus for the formation of PATCO and the leadership of its first job actions came originally from the big facilities such as New York Center, Los Angeles Center, and O'Hare. PATCO's officers—Rock, Maher, Sommer, Hays, and Leyden—came from these facilities. However, the big centers and high-density airports accounted at most for half of PATCO's membership. The other half was dispersed across the nation's smaller and less densely trafficked locations. Differences between the working conditions of controllers at either end of the spectrum could be enormous. While O'Hare handled an average of three operations per minute during peak times, tower controllers in a place like Elmira, New York, might handle three per hour. Differences in pay between controllers in such locations could be considerable. While the top facilities qualified for the GS-13 pay scale, the lowest level facilities were capped at GS-10. Controllers at the top end of the pay scale could earn twice the pay of small-facility controllers.

Leading a union that represented workers in vastly different work environments presented complications for Leyden. From its founding, PATCO's organizers tried to operate with the philosophy that "a controller is a controller is a controller." This philosophy held that all controllers separated aircraft, and what united them was more significant than the differences in their work from facility to facility. In practice, however, all controllers were not equal. Resentment of the higher pay earned by big facility controllers was commonplace among controllers in smaller facilities. Leyden had little patience with this resentment. When small-facility controllers complained to him about pay differences, he wrote back with an offer to help arrange their transfer to O'Hare. That usually ended the discussion, but it did not dispel the bad feelings.[36]

To the contrary, union politics periodically surfaced these resentments. Because the large facilities were easier to organize and communicate with, their concerns tended to carry greater weight within the union. In the late 1970s, southern regional vice president David Siegel was able to triple membership in his region by renting a plane and flying around to each of the ninety locals in his region at least once a year. But, that effort was beyond the means of Leyden or other national officers, who were more likely to visit facilities with concentrated union membership. Because PATCO leaders regularly listened to the big facility controllers, they inevitably prioritized their concerns.[37]

This dynamic fostered a sense of second-class union citizenship among small-facility controllers. A Columbus, Georgia, controller bemoaned "the seeming lack of interest in the lower level facilities by PATCO." Jack Maher often reminded small-facility controllers that PATCO had risked everything for controllers at Baton Rouge's small airport in 1970, but that never dispelled their belief that the union would sacrifice their interests in order to advance those of big-facility controllers. Controllers outside of the union's East Coast strongholds grew tired of playing the "'cow's tail' role," in the words of Charlie Campbell, "always behind and getting crapped on." Smaller facility controllers pointed out that traffic counts could be misleading: where traffic was heavy, staffing levels were higher, and more controllers shared the load. "What makes you think you're working harder because you move ten yards of coal and you got ten controllers to do it, and another facility moves five yards of coal and they got five controllers to do it?" one controller asked.[38]

Regional differences within the union further complicated its political dynamics. The most militant PATCO facilities tended to be on the coasts and in big cities in between, such as Chicago, Pittsburgh, Kansas City, and Denver. Particular areas of PATCO strength could produce extraordinary militancy. Such was the case in the San Francisco Bay area, whose controllers were called the "West Coast Whackos," by some PATCO leaders. But outside of the pockets of militancy, PATCO members could be quite moderate in outlook. This was especially true in the South, where Miami was the only reliable center of militancy (in part because many New Yorkers transferred there).[39]

THE LIMITS OF FEDERAL SECTOR UNIONISM

PATCO never again enjoyed a contract negotiation as easy as its first. Each successive negotiation after 1973 proved more difficult than the last as the expansive economic climate that had nurtured public sector union growth in the late 1960s and early 1970s gave way to oil-crisis induced recession and inflation by 1974. As the economy turned, politicians favored budget cutting and tax rollbacks, and placed all government workers' unions on the defensive. When the FAA and PATCO began negotiating their second contract in 1974, the union focused on two objectives that conformed to the parameters of federal sector bargaining set by the Kennedy and Nixon executive orders, which forbade negotiations over salary. PATCO negotiators decided to fight for further liberalization of the FAM flight program, and for a national job transfer registry that would allow controllers to bid on openings around the country on the basis of seniority. Union negotiators expected a replay of their amicable first negotiation with the FAA, but they were surprised by the government's reaction. The FAA not only rejected PATCO's major proposals, but also the smaller ones the union brought to the table. According to the log kept by PATCO's team, the government negotiator's refrain on item after item was: "NO is my position."[40]

Transportation Secretary Claude Brinegar was responsible for the change in tone in the negotiations. Brinegar, who had not participated in the 1973 talks because he was just assuming office as secretary, assigned his deputy, William S. Heffelfinger, to the 1974 negotiations. Heffelfinger's ability to take over the talks was abetted by the marginalization of FAA Administrator Alexander Butterfield due to the Watergate scandal. After he testified in June 1973 about the existence of a White House tape-recording system, a revelation that ultimately led to Nixon's resignation in August 1974, Butterfield became a pariah to the Nixon administration. With Butterfield isolated and hobbled, Heffelfinger began reviewing the items to which the FAA and PATCO tentatively agreed, vetoing those he disliked. Leyden alleged that Heffelfinger's interference made the negotiations "a charade." But the union lacked a solution. When PATCO's first contract expired on April 3, 1974, there was no agreement in sight. "It was really bullshit going to that table," reported PATCO's Harvard-trained negotiator, Mike Rock.[41]

To make matters worse, the Air Transport Association (ATA), the airlines' trade group, inserted its own views. The airlines had objected to the FAA's use of cockpit jump seats as a bargaining chip in the 1973 PATCO-FAA contract, and it urged the FAA not to include FAMs in the contract talks at all. To reinforce its stance, on August 14, 1974, while the contract talks were stalled, the airlines announced that they would unilaterally cut in half the number of FAMs controllers were allowed annually. Furious PATCO leaders saw this as a deliberate provocation and speculated that the government had colluded with the ATA.[42]

The airlines' action put PATCO leaders in a tough spot. If the union gave up something it had won in its first contract, union officials thought it would signal their weakness and lead to a wholesale rewriting of the first contract on the government's terms. Moreover, controllers regarded FAMs as symbolically important. The FAM program predated PATCO, and controllers had come to view FAMs as an inviolable custom. If PATCO could not defend them, how could it retain controllers' loyalty?[43]

PATCO leaders knew they had limited options. Still smarting from the 1970 job action, members were leery of taking on the government again. An April 1974 survey of members found that while 71 percent supported the principle that federal workers ought to have the right to strike, 54 percent did not think an illegal strike was justifiable. Unless the union took some action, though, PATCO leaders feared the ATA and the government would strip away everything they had won in 1973. They looked for a way to flex their muscles without asking all controllers to support a job action. The union summoned representatives from major facilities to a meeting in Chicago, where Leyden made clear that winning a decent contract was up to them. PATCO would get nothing from the FAA unless it "got some support from the field." He asked the union's "militant minority" to lead a slowdown to defend FAMs.[44]

On October 2, PATCO announced that it would not resume talks with the FAA unless it was permitted to negotiate FAMs. The job action commenced immediately. Rolling delays erupted in the key facilities of New York, Chicago, Washington, Miami, and Los Angeles. At LaGuardia, sixty flights were delayed on October 3. The sporadic nature of the delays made it difficult for the FAA to identify and discipline controllers. "There's never been anything like it," confided one FAA spokesperson. "It's like trying to put out a fire that goes out whenever you send a fire engine to do something about it." The slowdown got the attention of conservative radio broadcaster Paul Harvey, who attacked the "tower boys" for engaging in a "protection racket," the motto of which was "Pay up or we'll sabotage you." But the slowdown worked. After two weeks of rolling delays, ATA officials met with the FAA and PATCO and restored the FAM privileges of the 1973 contract. One airline executive called it "blackmail, pure and simple."[45]

Nonetheless PATCO was unable to consummate a second contract with the FAA until both Brinegar and Butterfield stepped down in the spring of 1975 and were succeeded by William T. Coleman Jr. as secretary of transportation and former air traffic controller James E. Dow as acting administrator of the FAA. With Coleman's support, Dow finally reached an agreement with PATCO on May 4, 1975. The two-year contract inched enough toward PATCO's goals of FAM liberalization and national job bidding to allow Leyden to sell the contract to his members as an improvement over their first.[46]

The kind of celebration that followed the 1973 contract was noticeably lacking in 1975, however, for air traffic controllers, like all federal and many private-sector workers, were beginning to feel the bite of "stagflation." The simultaneous rise in inflation and unemployment ravaged the 1970s U.S. economy in the wake of the 1973–1974 Arab oil embargo. While it hurt most workers, it had a particularly pernicious effect on public employees. Budget deficits and opposition to tax increases led politicians to hold the line on public sector wage increases, even as inflation eroded government workers' earning power. The Ford administration proved particularly resistant to the pleas of squeezed government employees. After assuming office following Nixon's Watergate-induced resignation in August 1974, President Ford made "whipping inflation" his chief economic priority. Ford believed that holding down wage increases was essential in the battle to restrain rising prices. This belief led him to take a hard line with federal workers. Congress set federal salary increases in each budget cycle based on a recommendation delivered by the president after consultation with his director of the Office of Management and Budget (OMB). In the summer of 1975, Ford's OMB director, James T. Lynn, recommended an 8.66 percent pay increase for federal workers. This was slightly less than the inflation rate (at that time above 9 percent). But Ford rejected this recommendation and sent Congress a request for a 5 percent raise instead. Federal workers were outraged. They pointed out that Ford's proposed pay raise amounted to a 4 percent cut in their purchasing power. PATCO joined other federal sector unions in asking Congress to reject Ford's plan. Congress had reversed previous efforts by Ford and Nixon to scale back OMB-recommended pay increases. But with the economy in turmoil in 1975, a coalition of Republicans and fiscally conservative Democrats sustained Ford's recommendation, in effect cutting federal workers' inflation-adjusted salaries.[47]

The vast majority of federal workers could do little more than grumble. They lacked the power to resist the effective pay cut: their unions were weak; they lacked the right to strike; and they had no experience in the use of job actions or other tactics that could get legislators' attention. At most, they could picket the White House and promise to work for the defeat of the salary-cutters in the next election. Air traffic controllers were different, however. As they watched their pay lag inflation, controllers grew restive. Cuts in their real earning power threatened controllers' aspirations to a middle-class lifestyle, and PATCO's more militant members demanded action. "My controllers are angry and they have the 'mad dog' syndrome," Domenic Torchia, a PATCO representative from the San Francisco Bay area, wrote Leyden.[48]

Feeling pressure from below, PATCO leaders considered possible responses to the emerging pay problem. One alternative was for controllers to emulate the postal workers. After their 1970 strike, postal unions helped push an act through Congress that created the U.S. Postal Service as a semi-autonomous corporation and gave unions the right to bargain with the new agency over wages and benefits. In 1975, PATCO commissioned consultant Glen A. Gilbert to design an analogous plan to restructure the FAA. But PATCO leaders concluded that even under the most optimistic scenarios, it would take years to win approval for the plan from Congress. In the meantime, the union needed a short-term strategy to deal with the volatile pay issue.[49]

THE "RECLASS" FIGHT

In the fall of 1975, PATCO decided on a bold plan. The union would attempt to circumvent the prohibitions against bargaining over pay by demanding that the government reclassify controllers to higher grades on the Civil Service's General Schedule (GS) salary scale. The idea of attempting a wholesale reclassification of air traffic controllers had been around for several years; PATCO leaders began talking about it as early as 1968. Before 1975, however, the union had not made "reclass" a priority, in part because the strategy posed some internal political risks. The CSC would conduct any system-wide study of air traffic controllers' jobs; the final results would be out of the union's hands. Such a study might conceivably yield upgrades for some controllers, downgrades for some, and no change at all for others. Yet in 1975, disquiet was prevalent enough in PATCO's ranks to persuade the union's leaders that they ought to push ahead to "get as much as possible for as many as possible," as Rock put it, knowing that they might not be able to help all controllers.[50]

The financial stakes were significant. In the mid-1970s, journeymen air traffic controllers worked in grade levels ranging from GS-10 through GS-13, depending upon the volume and complexity of traffic they handled. At a time when median family income was $14,958, the pay for full performance level controllers ranged from $14,800 to $29,900, depending upon grade level and length of service. PATCO sought to lift job classifications by one grade in each facility, raising GS-13 controllers to GS-14. Winning such upgrades could have a dramatic impact on controllers' incomes. In 1976, the top salary in GS-14 was $37,300, a huge bump for upgraded controllers.[51]

The FAA initially opposed a nationwide study, viewing reclassification as simply a "code word" for "pay increase." The agency feared that controllers would rig the study to make it appear they worked harder than they really did without CSC investigators, neophytes to air traffic control, being any the wiser. But PATCO had a strong argument in 1975. There had been no review of air traffic controllers' job classifications in more than seven years, during which time workloads had increased significantly.[52]

Good arguments alone would not have won a study, however, had a new and more sympathetic administrator not taken over the FAA. John L. McLucas was confirmed on November 24, 1975, and he quickly built a good working relationship with PATCO. Little in McLucas's background would have led one to predict this. He had no labor relations experience. He was descended from Fayetteville, North Carolina farmers, and after serving in the military during World War II, he obtained a doctorate in physics and took a job in the engineering firm Haller, Raymond & Brown. He rose to the top there before taking over leadership of the Boston-based MITRE Corporation, which conducted research for the Pentagon. Nixon brought McLucas to Washington, where he served first as deputy secretary, then secretary, of the Air Force. McLucas had not sought the FAA post, in part because he had no desire to confront labor issues. He had never dealt with unions, and doubted whether they belonged in government. The more he learned about the FAA, though, the more he became convinced that the "anti-union bias" of many of its managers caused the agency problems it "didn't need to have." "Dealing with unions is really like anything else," he concluded. "You just sort of learn to live with them and work with them."

McLucas soon became a favorite of controllers. With his approval, the CSC commenced a system-wide study of air traffic controllers' jobs.[53]

While the CSC conducted its work in the spring of 1976, PATCO leaders grew anxious. The Ford administration was moving in a determinedly anti-union direction as the presidential election year began. The hostility toward labor was part of a strategy designed by Ford's chief of staff, Dick Cheney, and aimed to neutralize the challenge of conservative former California governor Ronald Reagan in the 1976 Republican presidential primaries. Ford's rightward shift led him to veto legislation that would have liberalized picketing rules around construction sites, breaking a personal promise he had made to his labor secretary, John T. Dunlop, that he would sign that law. Dunlop resigned in protest. PATCO leaders worried that members of the CSC, themselves political appointees, would fall in line behind the growing antiunion animus of the Ford administration. "This is turning into a real mess—and mostly because of the very conservative atmosphere in Washington," Leyden confided to a group of controllers. "It may be that we are in for some bad times ahead." PATCO leaders concluded that unless they pressured the CSC, it would bend to prevailing political winds and produce an adverse classification report calling for the preservation of the status quo, or, worse, widespread downgrades—a move that could potentially rupture the union.[54]

As PATCO prepared for its May 1976 convention in San Diego, Leyden asked Jack Maher to design a plan of action for the union's militants. At the convention, Maher called a rump caucus of those members who had been most faithful in past job actions. While most PATCO delegates debated routine revisions to the union's constitution in the hotel's ballroom, Maher's group of forty militants gathered in a smaller meeting room to discuss creating what Rock called "an army of slowdowners" ready to conduct "guerilla warfare." Speaking to the group, Maher outlined a plan to create a national air traffic slowdown to pressure the CSC to produce a favorable reclass report. Maher jokingly dubbed it his "warlock plan." It won the enthusiastic approval of his audience, who in turn dubbed themselves "warlocks." When Maher made his presentation, he was wearing a broad-brimmed, leather Mexican hat he had acquired as a souvenir earlier that day. The warlocks immediately adopted that as their uniform. Before the San Diego convention was gaveled to a close, delegates wearing "warlock hats" were spread across the floor, organizing their colleagues for a confrontation to come. Both in

San Diego and back home in their facilities, the warlocks found a receptive audience. Controllers well knew that the outcome of the reclass report could mean substantial gains or losses in their paychecks.[55]

Leyden still hoped to avoid conflict. He sent word to the White House through McLucas that PATCO would consider endorsing Ford's election in 1976 if the union received a favorable reclass report. But the Ford White House wanted no part of such a deal, which, if leaked, would bring the administration under "intense scrutiny." When Leyden learned on July 21 that not only did the CSC plan to reject PATCO's bid to raise the top controllers' classification to GS-14, but would also call for downgrading controllers at a number of facilities, he decided a fight was unavoidable. If the CSC downgraded controllers, cutting their salaries, Leyden feared it would destroy the union. After conferring with his board on July 27, he gave Maher the go-ahead. The warlocks were instructed to "adhere to strict compliance with work rules," snarling air traffic to protest the CSC's draft report, beginning on July 29, 1976.[56]

As in past job actions, it was not difficult for strategically placed controllers to slow the entire system. The "stagger-by" slowdown used by San Francisco Bay area controllers on July 29 indicated how easily it could be done. From the air, San Francisco International Airport, or SFO, looked like a giant X. It had two parallel north-south runways which were used for departures; these were bisected by two parallel east-west runways used for landings. Using all four runways at full capacity required careful coordination and split-second timing. To manage heavy traffic at SFO, controllers perfected tricks they called the "side-by" and the "squeeze play." The side-by referred to a technique whereby controllers at the Bay Terminal Radar Approach Control (TRACON) facility aligned two jets side by side on parallel paths to land on the parallel east-west runways simultaneously. Three miles behind these two, two others would be aligned to follow in their trails, landing in the same fashion. Meanwhile, two departing jets would be "loaded" by tower controllers side by side on the north-south runways. Once the first pair of landing jets touched down and passed the intersection point of the runways, the two departing jets would be cleared for take off. As soon as the departing jets began accelerating down the parallel north-south runways, tower controllers would run a "squeeze play," sending the next pair of departing jets into the loaded position before the accelerating jets were airborne. Once the departing jets were airborne, the next pair of landing jets would touch down simultaneously on the parallel east-west runways. These techniques moved traffic expeditiously—but they were also easily disrupted.

During the slowdown, Bay TRACON controllers suspended the side-by and instituted a "stagger-by." Instead of synchronizing jets to land simultaneously on the parallel east-west runways, approach controllers staggered them so that one jet landed one minute ahead of the other. Departures were forced to wait until the second jet cleared the runway intersection before they could roll. Meanwhile, tower controllers suspended the squeeze play, strictly adhering to the FAA regulation that two planes should never be on the same runway simultaneously. They waited until the departing jets were actually airborne before loading the next pair. Within minutes, the suspension of the side-by and squeeze play backed up departing flights on the tarmac and slowed the movement of jets hundreds of miles beyond the Bay Area.[57]

As the reclass slowdown began on July 29, tactics like those used at SFO ensured that the FAA experienced its worst traffic since the 1970 sickout. Some 1,467 flights were delayed by at least thirty minutes on the first day. Even Transportation Secretary Coleman fell victim to the slowdown. His Eastern Airlines shuttle to Washington sat on a LaGuardia runway for ninety minutes before takeoff. Coleman was lucky to depart at all: Eastern canceled fifteen shuttle flights that day. "I don't think public employees should use threats to the Civil Service Commission," the irritated secretary declared. His words did not deter the warlocks. On the second day, conditions worsened as delays at LaGuardia hit four hours, and traffic snarled at key airports nationwide. Coleman considered sanctions and ordered supervisors to work overtime to ease delays. The head of the ATA, Paul Ignatius made plans to seek an injunction and penalties against PATCO in the courts, claiming that the slowdown was costing airlines tens of millions. PATCO, in turn, threatened "a holocaust" if authorities tried to discipline controllers.[58]

FAA Administrator McLucas feared the situation might escalate into an even more destructive conflict, and he was determined to avoid this. Although new to labor relations, McLucas knew Leyden needed something tangible before he could suspend the job action. He decided to help Leyden secure what he needed, summoning PATCO leaders and CSC Chairman Robert E. Hampton to a meeting in his office on Saturday morning, July 31. McLucas then persuaded the ATA's Ignatius to give him time to produce an agreement before going to court. The talks in McLucas's office that morning were tense. Periodically the parties took breaks to check on the progress of the slowdown, and McLucas phoned Ignatius on an hourly basis to keep him informed. Finally, at 3 p.m. the parties came to an agreement.[59]

Leyden viewed it as an acceptable compromise. The CSC agreed to release its draft reclass report by August 31. The FAA, in turn, agreed to prepare a response to the draft report within thirty days. McLucas gave his word to PATCO that he would contest unfavorable CSC recommendations and call for classification upgrades at facilities, including raising some heavy-traffic facilities to the GS-14 level. McLucas, in turn, secured a promise from CSC Chair Hampton that he would try to incorporate the FAA's suggestions into final revisions of the reclass report. To seal the bargain, McLucas promised amnesty for any controllers caught slowing traffic during the three-day job action. Word of the agreement went out to FAA facilities less than an hour after the deal was reached, and by that evening flight schedules returned to normal.[60]

Leyden thought he had won the best settlement possible in that situation, but the bruising fight for that deal revealed just how treacherous the reclass strategy was for PATCO. The job action stirred angry reactions from travelers, one of whom accused the union of "playing God and roulette with planeloads of human beings to achieve their aim." It also stoked controversy within the union. A large group of controllers concluded they would not be affected either way by the CSC reclass report and were angry with the union for antagonizing the government, travelers, and airlines. One announced he would not jeopardize his career so Leyden could "stand in front of Mr. McLucas and flex...PATCO muscles." At the same time, union militants accused Leyden of selling out, since he shook hands on a deal without ironclad promises for some GS-14 upgrades. "We had them 'By the Balls' and you let them go," said one critic. Leyden defended himself against such detractors. If PATCO had not acted, he argued, many controllers surely would have been downgraded. By contrast, had the union held out much longer, it would have been saddled with hundreds of thousands of dollars in fines without any guarantee of a better deal. In correspondence with PATCO militants, he was as blunt as he was impatient. They were deluded, he explained, if they thought "the United States government was, at some time in the future, going to capitulate to PATCO."[61]

Leyden's problems multiplied when the CSC issued its draft report on August 31. It was worse than he feared. It recommended no upgrades to the

GS-14 level while downgrading six thousand positions at 155 facilities. Adding insult to injury, the CSC seemingly went out of its way to belittle controllers' claims that they were underpaid, insisting that similar responsibilities and stresses "exist to a strong degree in many other occupations." Leyden called the report "absurd," and predicted that its implementation would trigger a nationwide walkout. "It is as if by design they are looking for a confrontation," he told the press.[62]

McLucas quickly weighed in as promised. He told the CSC its report was "not satisfactory," and vowed to PATCO he would "do everything possible" to rectify it. In the meantime, McLucas urged PATCO to avoid any actions that might trigger conflict. Leyden, however, could not afford to take the job action threat off the table. Therefore, he called his board together on September 8 so that they could prepare to act "with responsible militancy" and do whatever was "necessary to obtain an equitable classification standard."[63]

Board members were aware of rising anger in their regions, especially in facilities that had been recommended for downgrades or passed over for upgrades. "Don't you people give a damn about us?" one local leader wrote. "I have done all I can to keep things cool but it ain't easy," reported another. Prompted by this roiling anger, Leyden and the board engaged in a frank discussion. Leyden reminded his colleagues that the reclass strategy had been risky from the beginning. Even the best-case scenario would not result in across-the-board gains. While he still believed the union could fight off wholesale downgrades, Leyden reiterated that some controllers were bound to be disappointed with the final results: the traffic levels in their facilities simply would not justify an upgrade. He urged the board to stand together against militants who would object to a half-a-loaf settlement. Their pursuit of "unobtainable" demands made such militants dangerous, Leyden argued. "In dealing with the Government," he said, no "organization, union or individual" could afford to make a "winner take all demand." He cited PATCO's 1970 sickout strike as an "example of non-reason, pushing us into a no-win position." The union had to avoid giving in to those who had "suicidal tendencies," he said. "I ask you to continue to share that responsibility and burden with me and not take the easy course of advocating Athenian Democracy with its resultant disaster." Having thus cautioned his board, Leyden asked it to authorize a job action should this become necessary to win modifications in the CSC report. They did so unanimously.[64]

Following the board meeting, PATCO launched an all-out attack against the CSC report. The union criticized the commission for measuring only the volume of traffic from facility to facility, not its complexity. It also unveiled its own study, which proposed upgrading 7,500 positions at 155 facilities and raising 4,250 controllers at the busiest facilities to GS-14. PATCO also brought allies to bear in the fight. Leyden's friend, J. J. O'Donnell of the Air Line Pilots Association chastised the CSC study as "inept." Rep. Mo Udall (D-Ariz.), who was poised to become chair of the House Post Office and Civil Service committee in the next Congress, offered to help persuade the CSC to redo its report. He also promised he would work with PATCO on a long-range legislative fix that would create special job classifications for controllers. The fact that the presidential campaign between Jimmy Carter and Gerald Ford was tightening as it reached its final weeks only heightened the sense of uncertainty.[65]

During these anxious days, McLucas attempted to calm the waters. He knew that many in the Ford administration felt he was not "tough enough." At the FAA, McLucas was surrounded by people who thought he "shouldn't give the goddamn union anything." McLucas also knew many FAA supervisors were staunchly opposed to PATCO's demand for GS-14 status at high-density facilities because many frontline supervisors were also GS-14s. But McLucas himself believed "it wouldn't be the end of the world if we upgraded the larger facilities." He reasoned, "If you want to have people with high morale and so forth and you want them to be outstanding members of the community, you don't want them just struggling along." He also grasped the difficulty of Leyden's position and was determined to give the PATCO president enough to allow Leyden to pacify his membership. In this effort, McLucas found one strong ally, Ray Bellanger, the FAA's director of air traffic. Bellanger had been offended by the CSC's dismissive report. He had controlled traffic himself and he likened the stresses of the work to his experience flying combat missions during World War II. With Bellanger's help, McLucas crafted the FAA's rebuttal to the CSC. The FAA recommended upgrades for about 1,900 positions; raising eight high-density facilities to GS-14; and limiting downgrades to a few facilities totaling about one hundred jobs. Leyden had hoped for more upgrades from McLucas, but in light of the CSC's disastrous report, this was a huge improvement. PATCO immediately turned to the task of pressuring the CSC to accept the FAA's recommendations. It threatened a job action that could disrupt Thanksgiving travel if the CSC's final report was not ready on November 15.[66]

Before that date arrived, Carter defeated Ford in the presidential election. That event suddenly changed the political context within which the CSC operated and gave PATCO more leverage. After the Ford White House had rebuffed PATCO's offer of an endorsement in return for a reclass deal in July, PATCO had endorsed Carter. Now union leaders hoped the incoming administration would come to its rescue. A week after the election, and three days before PATCO's November 15 deadline, the CSC's three members, Chairman Hampton and Commissioners Ludwig J. Andolsek and Georgiana Sheldon, met with PATCO officials. Indicating how much the election had altered relations, the commissioners largely disowned the draft report their staff had prepared in August. They agreed to support upgrading the busiest facilities to GS-14, assured PATCO that only "a few jobs" would be downgraded, and directed their staff to measure the complexity of air traffic as well as volume in a revised report. They also offered to recommend that Congress approve a wholesale reorganization of air traffic controller pay. The commissioners promised a final report by January 15, 1977.[67]

Leyden was pleased with the change in tone, but believed he needed a firmer commitment before the November 15 deadline in order to mollify his union's militants. The CSC had given PATCO no clear indication of the number of facilities to be upgraded. If the final number was low, Leyden feared that the resulting backlash might tear the union apart. Leyden also feared that CSC staff director Raymond Jacobson—"a son of a bitch" in Rock's view—would dictate the content of the final report. So Leyden decided to keep the heat on, and he pressured Jacobson for concessions. Leyden wanted a guarantee that at least eight facilities would be raised to GS-14, with at least twenty-three others upgraded. Jacobson would give no such assurances.[68]

Tension escalated as the November 15 deadline neared. From "Coven Headquarters," Warlock Maher told PATCO's regional vice presidents to prepare to be arrested, and asked them to designate replacements should the job action go forward. Leyden, however, did not believe going to war would enhance PATCO's position. In the final hours before the deadline on the 15th, Leyden convened a conference call with PATCO's board. He urged them to surrender the principle that PATCO would tolerate no downgrades, pointing out that one facility the CSC sought to downgrade was Dallas's

Love Field, which had recently lost most of its traffic to the newly opened Dallas/Fort Worth International Airport. There was no way to save Love, Leyden declared. Leyden then offered assurances that Mo Udall would push legislation liberating the controllers from the civil service structure if the union refrained from a job action and gave the CSC until January to finalize its report. The board accepted Leyden's judgment and decided to wait.[69]

Having put off a job action, Leyden braced for an attack from the union's militants. He entered the reclass struggle knowing he would never "fully satisfy 456 facilities, let alone, 16,000 controllers," but the backlash was more furious than he expected. "Did you sell half of your membership out while planning to tell them that we had our 'foot in the door'?" asked the vice president of the Denver Center local. Controllers in small facilities, who feared being passed over for upgrades, were incensed. "The reclass is nothing but a joke, an obvious sellout," wrote PATCO's Fresno facility rep. "We are not interested in *down the road*."[70]

Leyden spent the two months leading up to the filing of the CSC final report mending fences. "In playing brinksmanship we had to obtain as much as this settlement offers without spilling a single drop of blood," he explained. He dismissed his critics for simply wanting to "'whack the government' or 'show the facility chief who's boss.'" Yet to those he trusted he revealed his own uncertainty: only time and the CSC final report would tell whether it had been right to call off the job action, he admitted.[71]

As he struggled to tamp down the objections of the militants, Leyden used every bit of leverage he could to influence a favorable final report from the CSC. He appealed directly to the lone Democrat on the commission, Kennedy appointee L. J. Andolsek, for help, asking him to press the commission's staff to use volume of traffic, rather than number of air carriers served, as a criterion for determining which facilities would be upgraded to GS-14. Because traffic levels were likely to rise in large facilities, while the numbers of air carriers served were likely to remain stable, this change could mean that facilities that missed the initial GS-14 cut might qualify for a later upgrade if their traffic levels rose. By contrast, the air carrier formula used in the draft report would lock in GS-13 facilities at that level indefinitely. McLucas backed Leyden on this point.[72]

The details of the CSC report were not finally settled until days before the January 15 deadline, when PATCO leaders sat down with the three CSC commissioners and their staff for what Rock called "the final nut-cut." As the meeting began, the CSC was still committed to the air carrier formula. PATCO leaders made clear they would launch a national air traffic slowdown that could potentially disrupt the Carter inauguration, which was one week away, if the formula was not dropped. "We're going to have every airplane in the country holding," Rock threatened. The CSC commissioners found it prudent to surrender the point. They instructed their reluctant staff to accede to PATCO's demand.[73]

The CSC final report approved on January 13, 1977, met Leyden's bottom line. It upgraded eight elite facilities to GS-14. The report also proposed raising thirty-seven other facilities one notch on the GS scale. The upgraded facilities were among the largest in the FAA. Altogether, they represented roughly half the union's membership. Only one facility, Dallas's Love Field, was downgraded. Both McLucas and Leyden were satisfied with the result. Leyden called the final report "a major breakthrough in the effort to bring controllers' compensation into line with their responsibilities." Given how tenuous the situation had seemed six months earlier, the results were extraordinary. They also appeared to demonstrate that PATCO had "achieved something that resembled genuine collective bargaining," as labor scholar Arthur Shostak later contended. "While other federal employees remained subject to the rates set by the Civil Service Commission," Shostak observed, "the controllers were significantly influencing their own salary levels—and their self-esteem."[74]

Many of those passed over for upgrades did not see it that way. Controllers at the GS-13 facilities who did not make GS-14 were among those most angry. An activist from Denver Center warned Leyden that "'special provisions' in our contract for the 'larger facilities'" could "destroy the union." A controller at Honolulu Center, which was also passed over in the upgrade, warned of a similar fate for PATCO: "Whatever is happening within this organization has got to stop. It is becoming like a cancer and in time it will destroy us."[75]

Reverberations from the reclass report soon affected PATCO's internal politics. Kansas City Center, one of the large facilities left out of the elite eight, was home to one of the most outspoken dissidents to emerge from the reclass fight, Gary Eads. When Leyden accepted the promises of CSC Chairman Hampton and decided not to pull the trigger on a national slowdown in November, Eads resigned from a PATCO committee in protest. He told Leyden then that the mood of controllers at his facility ranged from "depression and disappointment to embarrassment and rage," and argued that the "very foundations of PATCO" were "being threatened" by Leyden's inaction. Displeased with the CSC's January report, Eads announced that he would challenge the Central States' regional vice president, Max Winter, for his seat on PATCO's executive board. Eads specifically took issue with Winter's support of Leyden's strategy and promised that, if elected, he would fight for "a more progressive PATCO." Eads went on to defeat Winter in May 1977, giving Leyden's critics a powerful voice on PATCO's board.[76]

The reaction to the reclass fight frustrated Leyden. He believed he had pulled off a remarkable feat, winning significant salary increases for half his membership even though they lacked the right to bargain collectively over pay. He could not understand why his critics did not see it that way; why they could not recognize the impossibility of winning across-the-board increases for all controllers given the existing constraints; why they did not give him credit for making "the best that could be made of a bad situation."[77]

Leyden's problems derived partly from deep tensions within PATCO that were exposed by the reclass fight—tensions that Leyden had finessed to that point but that now threatened to overwhelm him. The driving force in founding PATCO had come from controllers at the elite high-volume facilities. They were the ones who gave the union the power to disrupt air travel and press its demands. Yet, since its inception, PATCO had aspired to the principle that "a controller is a controller is a controller." In many ways, that principle glued the union together. But when it came to the most important issue in the eyes of controllers in the mid-1970s—their pay—the principle gave way to the realities of federal sector bargaining. The reclass strategy, a clever response to the union's inability to address lagging pay through collective bargaining, only heightened the contradictions between the union's aspirations and the realities it faced. It angered Leyden when his critics turned the "a-controller-is-a-controller" principle against him, claiming he had sold out some to benefit others. "I hope that the blood [that] emanates from my heritage can be dispassionate when obligated to respond to various politically motivated allegations," he told a friend. Yet Leyden's anger was as much a response to the impossible situation he faced as a leader of a militant federal employees' union operating under enormous legal constraints during difficult economic times as it was to his critics' charges. As inflation raged, he was unable to protect all his members against its ravages.

Inaction had been unthinkable. Yet his efforts to circumvent the limits of federal sector bargaining had stirred discontent within PATCO's ranks that he found difficult to manage. He steeled himself against the attacks. "I don't give a good shit whether I am called a union boss," he spat. Nevertheless, his defiant words could not entirely mask his true emotions: he felt trapped.[78]

Nor could he see an easy way out. "The only possible solution that I see is complete removal of the air traffic controller from the constraints of the Civil Service Commission GS levels we are presently operating under, and maybe then, and I emphasize, maybe, then can we at least approach some form of equity in the difficult and responsible task performed by *all* controllers represented by PATCO," he concluded. However, Leyden did not foresee the legislative emancipation of controllers from GS grades coming any time soon. In his view, the "political climate and anti-public [employee] sentiment" of the late 1970s did not bode well. Stagflation and budget deficits were stoking voters' fears of high taxes and lost purchasing power. These fears led politicians to resist public employees' demands rather than give in to them.[79]

Significantly, the lessons Rock and many other PATCO militants drew from the reclass fight were starkly different from Leyden's. The key event for Rock and those who shared his viewpoint was the slowdown of July 1976, when PATCO made it clear it would not tolerate wholesale downgrades without a fight. "Not one air traffic controller that was involved ever received any type of discipline," Rock concluded. This showed that militancy worked. "It was a national job action that everybody knew about; we knew we had the clout and everybody stuck together and we pulled it off." The lesson? If PATCO made a significant salary increase its main issue, the union could motivate "an army" of controllers prepared to risk their jobs in order to win tangible benefits. If "we have our shit together and we stick together...we will beat them," said Rock.[80]

The differences expressed in the contending views of Rock and Leyden were submerged for a time after the reclass fight. No one wished to reopen the wounds inflicted by that struggle. But subsequent events would only reinforce the conflicting viewpoints of Leyden and the union's militants, leading them not only to divergent readings of the union's history but to irreconcilable visions of its future. The consequences of their split would be catastrophic.

TURBULENCE

I never felt welcome in PATCO.
—RICK JONES, AIR TRAFFIC CONTROLLER

I don't know whether I even called it sexual harassment
at the time. But I knew it wasn't supposed to be going on.
—CHERYL JENNI, AIR TRAFFIC CONTROLLER

Then you had this surge of the Vietnam kids coming in.
They...just wanted to burn the facilities. They hated the
federal government. They hated any kind of authority.
—MIKE ROCK

For Rick Jones, the night of April 4, 1968, crystallized it. PATCO was in the midst of its inaugural cross-country organizing campaign, not yet three months old. F. Lee Bailey and his entourage had recently swung through the Washington area and ignited enthusiasm among the controllers at Washington Air Route Traffic Control Center in Leesburg, Virginia, thirty-five miles northwest of the nation's capital, where Jones worked. He had been at the center for more than a year, one of only ten African Americans among the roughly three hundred controllers at the facility. Washington Center was already emerging as a PATCO stronghold. Yet Jones had not felt welcome to attend PATCO meetings. They were held at a Leesburg country club that admitted no black members. It was not until he walked into the cafeteria for his coffee break on that April night, though, that Jones finally made up his mind about PATCO. He saw a dozen of his white coworkers huddled around a radio listening to a news bulletin. "The son of a bitch got what he deserved," one said. Then someone turned and noticed Jones. The group silently melted away, leaving him alone by the radio. That was how Rick Jones learned of the assassination of Rev. Martin Luther King Jr. That was when he knew for certain that he could never trust PATCO.[1]

In the early 1960s, when the seeds for PATCO were planted, air traffic control was almost entirely the province of white men. For them, it embodied a vision of manly professionalism and offered the promise of upward mobility from their working-class roots, a house in the suburbs, a wife who did not have to work outside the home, a chance to live a middle-class life-style. Between 1968 and 1978, the air traffic control workforce, like the country, changed in profound ways. The civil rights movement, feminism, and fallout from the Vietnam War altered FAA facilities and the expecta-tions of the people who worked in them. As African Americans, women, and a generation of Vietnam veterans who came of age in the turbulent 1960s entered FAA facilities, homogeneity began to give way to diversity. Like many other institutions in this period, PATCO struggled and often failed to adequately come to terms with the new racial, gender, and generational dynamics unleashed by this transformation. PATCO's inability to forge a greater sense of solidarity among members of differing backgrounds in turn exacerbated the problems the union faced in the aftermath of the reclass fight.

Black Controllers Make Their Way

There were only a few dozen African American air traffic controllers in 1960. The stories of two of the pioneers, Ralph McKnight and Bob Beatty, help illustrate the struggles blacks faced in making their way into the FAA. In many ways, Beatty and McKnight resembled the whites who predominated in FAA workplaces in the 1960s. Both came from urban, working-class families. When Beatty's parents left a North Carolina farm to move to Washington, D.C., his father worked as a chef and his mother as a house-keeper; McKnight, also a Washington native, was the son of a milk truck driver. Both were high school graduates and military veterans. While they shared backgrounds similar to those of white controllers, racial boundaries had demarcated opportunities for McKnight and Beatty. They both attended all-black high schools, graduating before the U.S. Supreme Court's 1954 *Brown v. Board of Education* decision. After stints in the military where they received air traffic control training, both returned to Washington and took courses at Howard University at a time when most air traffic controllers had no college education, yet neither could find a direct route into government employment. In 1953, Beatty was turned away when he first applied for a job controlling air traffic. He made ends meet by driving a cab; McKnight played drums in a jazz quintet.[2]

McKnight was finally hired by the FAA's predecessor, the CAA, in 1956 and assigned to work at Washington Center, which was then housed in Hangar 6 at National Airport along the Potomac. Beatty was hired a year later and worked for a year at Cleveland Center before he could return to Washington, where he, too, was assigned to Hangar 6. By 1958, these two comprised one half of the total number of black controllers in Washington. They found the racism "very dense," and the mood "very chilly" in Hangar 6. There were occasional instances of personal confrontation, but most of the racism they encountered was more subtle. It was most evident during their training and bids for promotion. Blacks found it difficult to get decent training or fair evaluations from white team leaders and supervisors. They had to turn to each other for support, like "children holding hands in a storm," as McKnight later explained. In order to deal with the bias they encountered, senior black controllers met black developmental controllers at McKnight's home and gave them extra training, knowing that blacks would need to be better prepared than whites if they wanted to avoid being washed out by racist instructors.[3]

This fragile support structure nearly collapsed in 1963 when Washington Center was relocated from National Airport to suburban Leesburg, as part of the national civil defense strategy of moving control centers away from cities. Blacks were not enthusiastic about commuting into rural Virginia, where segregation was palpable. They found it impossible to buy homes near Leesburg. Rather than make the long commute, McKnight opted for a leave of absence from the FAA to go to work in Africa, helping the newly independent Republic of the Congo set up an air traffic control service. Beatty gave Leesburg a try, carpooling there with other black controllers, but after two years he transferred back to National Airport to work the tower there.[4]

Those blacks who stayed on at Washington Center proved to be a hardy band. In 1967, Rick Jones joined that group. Also a native Washingtonian, Jones was the son of a baker and a domestic worker. After graduating high school in 1961, Jones joined the Air Force and received air traffic control training at Keesler Air Force Base in Biloxi, Mississippi. Although Keesler was a common reference point for a large segment of the FAA's employees— many of whom were first introduced to air traffic control there—the Keesler experience left a different imprint on Jones than it did on white controllers. Jones was the only African American in a group of seventy-seven air traffic control trainees at Keesler in 1961. He alone among them had to deal with the iron curtain of segregation whenever he left the base. Nonetheless, Jones persevered, received his training and, after five years of service, his honorable discharge. Then he worked on the loading dock of the central post office in Washington, D.C., until a job with the FAA opened up in 1967.[5]

That same year, McKnight returned to the FAA and Washington Center, race-conscious and radicalized after his stint in the Congo. He became active in the Congress of Racial Equality and avidly read the anticolonialist works of Frantz Fanon. He also joined the Revolutionary Action Movement (RAM), a radical Maoist-influenced sect started by supporters of Robert F. Williams, a North Carolina civil rights leader who had advocated armed self-defense for blacks. For a time McKnight even hosted weapons training sessions for fellow RAM members in the basement of his home on Ninth Street in southeast Washington, just blocks from the Marine Corps barracks. McKnight did not recruit his black Leesburg carpool mates into RAM, but his radicalism influenced his friends in indirect ways.[6]

The bias black controllers experienced in training and promotion was exacerbated by the segregation that persisted outside the workplace. Ties forged over beers after work often won a controller sympathetic mentors and eased his progress from one stage to another in his training. But blacks and whites rarely mingled after work. Blacks carpooled back to Washington after a shift change, rather than lingering in the Virginia bars to which whites retired, and where blacks felt unwelcome. The FAA was aware of the problem. Whites' "only association with blacks" took place "during working periods after which they go their own separate ways," a 1970 agency report observed. "They don't meet at the supermarket, don't ride in the same car pool, don't attend social functions together, don't attend the same church, and their wives don't talk over the back fence." But the FAA's awareness of the problem did not lead to a solution.[7]

It was in this context of racial separation and suspicion that PATCO arrived at Washington Center in 1968. Rather than bridging the tensions that existed between black and white controllers, PATCO exacerbated them. The decision of the Leesburg organizers to hold meetings at a whites-only country club naturally alienated black controllers. Although they were invited to the meetings, the blacks knew they would not be welcome to stay afterward to drink with whites at the club's bar. "That's not going to work, we don't want to come to a segregated facility," said Rick Jones. McKnight viewed the situation differently. On the one hand, he thought the FAA was "full of racism." Personally, he frequently felt "unwelcome," and did not expect the majority-white membership of PATCO to make equal employment opportunity a top priority. Yet, on the other hand, as a pragmatic radical McKnight believed the FAA needed an organization that could advocate for better equipment and higher pay for all controllers. So he joined. Most blacks' views of PATCO fell somewhere in between Jones's rejection and McKnight's pragmatic cooperation, one part cautious suspicion and one part guarded hope. Thus PATCO failed to ignite as much enthusiasm among blacks at Washington Center as it did among whites. Nor did PATCO's prospects among black controllers improve much over the next few years. When FBI surveillance of the openly radical McKnight finally made life so difficult for him that he left the FAA in 1970, no senior black controller took his place in defending PATCO's mission in Leesburg.[8]

The initial ambivalence with which blacks greeted PATCO in Leesburg, which boasted more black controllers than any other FAA facility, typified a national pattern that developed in PATCO's first years. Although most African American controllers joined PATCO by the mid-1970s, most never considered the union to be deeply committed to racial justice. PATCO's failure to espouse equal employment opportunity and affirmative action initiatives only furthered this impression among African Americans and led them to rely more on each other than on PATCO. To help ensure that black developmental controllers at Leesburg got a fair shake, senior black controllers expanded their training program for black developmentals, complete with a mock radar setup in the family room of Rick Jones's home in Oxon Hill, Maryland. Developmental controllers showed up almost every day to take instruction from senior black controllers at Jones's home. Using castoff strip holders, clocks, and other equipment, Jones and his colleagues prepared their charges so thoroughly for their "check rides" with white instructors that there would be no possibility of failure, no matter how biased the instructor.[9]

As blacks began to organize themselves, the FAA slowly began to address its race problem. An internal study in June 1968 found that only 2 percent of recently hired controllers were African Americans. That ranked the FAA thirty-third among thirty-nine federal agencies in minority hiring. For the first time, the agency began to consider setting diversity goals for hiring. However, steps to address the problem were not taken until the Nixon administration took office. Finally, under the leadership of John Volpe and John Shaffer, the FAA began aggressively dealing with its race problem in 1969. Volpe directed Shaffer to create a civil rights office at the FAA to develop guidelines and oversee their implementation. Shaffer, in turn, tapped Quentin S. Taylor to lead that office. Taylor and his office soon became a focal point for efforts to reform the agency.[10]

Taylor had grown up in Washington, graduated from the segregated Dunbar High School—the premier black high school in Washington—and received a degree in electrical engineering from Howard University before going to work for the FAA in 1958. He had risen through the ranks of the agency into a junior executive position when Shaffer asked him to direct the civil rights office in 1969. Up to that point, Taylor had always worked in the FAA headquarters and had little contact with air traffic controllers in the field. Soon, though, he began hearing an earful about their problems. Theodore Fagin, one of the few black controllers to work in the elite New York Common IFR Room, known as the "Common Eye," visited Taylor with a black delegation from the New York facilities, including Arthur Varnado of Newark and Luther Quarles of JFK. As Taylor soon realized, this team intended to give him "some instruction and some counsel" in "a very strong way." As they unloaded their complaints on Taylor, the New York area activists found a sympathetic listener. Soon Taylor was hearing similar stories from Rick Jones and Don Taylor of Washington Center and Bob Beatty of National Airport.[11]

Through their meetings with Quentin Taylor, these black controllers became acquainted with each other and began discussing the need for a black controllers' organization. In 1970, they founded the Coalition of Black

Controllers, a group within which Don Taylor of Washington Center played a leading role. Over the next few years, the Coalition worked hand in hand with Quentin Taylor to advance a civil rights agenda within the FAA. It was not easy. Quentin Taylor sponsored a meeting between the Coalition and white controllers in New York in 1970 that exposed deep racial divisions. Blacks said their ability to advance was inhibited because supervisors were groomed and promoted by other supervisors, and there was a clear "inability of the whites to identify with blacks." White supervisors never formed relationships with blacks that would help them envision blacks as potential peers. The Coalition argued that the "scales must be tipped the other way to achieve balance" and demanded the FAA make a concerted effort to promote blacks to supervisory posts. Whites responded that such a move would amount to "unequal opportunity."[12]

With prodding from Quentin Taylor and the Coalition, the FAA, like other federal agencies in these years, did take steps to create more opportunity for black controllers. Shaffer agreed to meet regularly with the Coalition's leaders. He also ordered his regional directors to investigate whether there had been a "a conscious exclusion of Blacks from supervisory ATC positions." The FAA began advertising openings for air traffic controllers in black-owned publications like *Ebony* and *Jet*. It also created its "150 Program," which specifically sought to hire African Americans and other minorities who had no previous experience in air traffic control and aimed to bring them up to speed with intensive training. The trainees were hired at the GS-4 level. After a six-month training course at Oklahoma City they were raised to the GS-7 level that the FAA traditionally used for entry-level controllers. Recruiters for the 150 Program were dispatched to the Postal Service and federal agencies that employed large concentrations of black workers. Shaffer coupled the program with a "1 in 5" policy, which sought to reserve 20 percent of new hires for minorities. "If a minority group person cannot be appointed in each succeeding fifth vacant position, then neither that position nor any further positions should be filled until a minority group person is appointed," he instructed.[13]

The FAA made significant progress in a short time. In 1971, Shaffer named the first black facility chief, promoting Norman Hopkins to run the tower at Erie, Pennsylvania. Some 27 percent of controllers hired in the 1972 fiscal year were minorities. Slowly, these steps began to change the FAA. By 1973, there were more than 800 black air traffic controllers.[14]

Washington Center in Leesburg showed the most rapid change. A group of twenty-one black developmentals started there in 1970. Charles Bolling, a Richmond, Virginia native whose father ran a small roofing business, was typical of this group. Bolling was a postal worker when the FAA recruited him in September 1970. After his six months at Oklahoma City, he was assigned to Leesburg. There, he found a strong support network created by Rick Jones and his colleagues, and he took advantage of the instruction sessions in Jones's family room. There was some resistance to the sudden influx of black controllers at Leesburg. Graffiti materialized on bathroom walls in the facility alleging that the recently hired "niggers" were drug addicts. A note appeared on a facility bulletin board announcing that the FAA was "now hiring monkeys." Despite the resistance they encountered, not a single member of the 1970 class of African American "developmentals" washed out. By 1974, Washington Center had eighty-eight black controllers, the largest contingent in the FAA, where the overall number of blacks approached nine hundred.[15]

There was considerable resistance to the FAA's Equal Employment Opportunity (EEO) program. The agency received a flood of angry complaints from whites. "The bald truth of the matter is, white citizens of this country are not going to be given much, if any, consideration for air controller jobs, but...negro citizens will be given all the consideration in the world," wrote one critic. A white woman whose husband had failed to win a job claimed that "for every white man hired, six blacks have to be hired." "They are not satisfied with equality; they want POWER, and our government is giving it to them," she fumed. While an internal FAA investigation revealed that the woman's husband had simply failed his application test, it was difficult to dispel the myth commonly held by many whites, including some PATCO members, that blacks were simply inferior. The same figures that blacks pointed to as evidence of bias in the training process—a washout rate among black controllers that was up to 24 percent higher than that of their white counterparts—was evidence in the minds of some whites that blacks had less aptitude for the work. This perception was deeply rooted. "For a member of your race, you are fortunate to have this job," a white supervisor told one black controller at Oakland Center.[16]

PATCO leaders, struggling to rebuild their organization in the early 1970s, generally avoided making public statements about the FAA's civil rights program. They knew that many whites opposed it. White controllers in

Memphis called the program "blatantly discriminatory" against whites. "There is virtually no chance of promotion into management under present policies unless EEO is consulted," they claimed. John Leyden was mindful of such sentiment. Although he spoke out against discrimination and defended African Americans against the charge that they had less aptitude for air traffic control work, he did not prioritize equal employment opportunity. Rather, he tried to make the case that the race problem had already been solved. There was "no more democratic profession than air traffic control," he argued, since it did not use "artificial discriminatory barriers of formalized training, such as a college degree, as a means of entry" but instead judged a controller "purely on his real ability and skills." "The result is that controllers come from all walks and conditions of life, from Harlem to Appalachia," he claimed. Although Leyden did not attack the FAA's initiatives, his comments implied that they were unnecessary, much to the chagrin of black activists.[17]

Over time, PATCO became more sensitive to the concerns of black controllers. A change in the Coalition's leadership allowed the two groups to reset their relationship. In 1977 the Coalition of Black Controllers became the National Black Coalition of Federal Aviation Employees and opened its membership to noncontrollers at the FAA. Leyden seized the opportunity to invite the coalition into a dialogue in hopes that the groups could "co-exist in an atmosphere of harmony." The National Black Coalition subsequently named Ervin L. Crenshaw, a controller at the New York "Common Eye" who was a member of both organizations, as a liaison to PATCO. In 1978, Crenshaw convinced PATCO's executive board to establish a committee to work on racial issues. The union began to investigate allegations of racism among instructors in Oklahoma City and to consider ways to use its grievance procedure to combat racial discrimination. Yet the alliance-building work proceeded slowly. A majority of black controllers joined PATCO, and they provided some of the union's best local leaders, like Al Stephens of Bay TRACON, but African Americans never took a proportionate role in running the union. Of the fourteen hundred delegates at PATCO's 1978 convention, only ten were black.[18]

THE PROFESSIONAL WOMEN CONTROLLERS

PATCO also found it difficult to come to terms with issues of gender equality. At its inception in 1968, only twenty-seven women in the entire FAA were certified as full performance level air traffic controllers. Air traffic control was then as male-dominated as any form of civilian government employment in the United States. Challenging that male domination proved even more difficult than erasing the color line.

The powerful linkage between air traffic controllers' work and their manhood made it difficult for women to enter FAA facilities. Controllers considered their work to be manly. "It's ego driven. It's macho," one male controller explained. "It's 'Mine are bigger than yours and I can handle more, I can move more tin than you can move.'" The job required personal qualities that controllers unthinkingly ascribed to men: self-confidence; decisiveness; a knack for mental and emotional compartmentalization; an ability to work under pressure; and an aversion to over-thinking and over-reacting. One observer likened controllers to "matadors and quarterbacks" in their need to make snap decisions: "If you thought too much about it, if you got too analytical, you weren't going to make it." Controllers had begun cultivating these personal qualities during their military service and built their work identities around them at the FAA.[19]

Controllers' sense of manliness was further reinforced by the camaraderie of the work crews. Air traffic control crews functioned like teams. Controllers worked a sector together, got to know each other's strengths and weakness, provided on-the-job training and mentoring to developmentals, and covered for older controllers as they began to lose their skills or stamina. Work crews incorporated new members through an elaborate initiation in which the developmentals first served as errand boys, doing coffee runs and other menial tasks. Senior controllers provided on-the-job training and signed off on a trainee's "check rides," as they worked various jobs in a sector on their way to becoming certified as a full performance level (FPL) controller. Successful trainees quickly learned that their futures depended upon the support of their coworkers. This tended to produce what one called "a ton of camaraderie."[20]

That camaraderie usually held in check the "mine-are-bigger-than-yours" competition that drove the FAAs elite controllers. Occasionally, however, stress overrode the group ethic and competitive spirits became combustible. Fights erupted often enough at Washington Center that controllers who had a beef with each other knew where they could meet to settle it: outside near the generator shack. This, too, reinforced the sense that controlling air traffic was men's work.[21]

If the work was manly, so, too, was leisure, especially the ritual of repairing to a favorite bar after a difficult shift. "After finishing a grueling day the first thing you do is go to a pub and unwind," one controller reported. According to one study, 54 percent of controllers were classified as "heavy drinkers." Even those who did not enjoy drinking felt pressure to "keep up with the boys." The work schedules at the big air route traffic control centers made it difficult for controllers to socialize with non-controllers. Crews rotated through a demanding schedule of shift changes: a week of day shifts followed by a week of night shifts, with a midnight shift every fifth week. Such schedules disrupted controllers' circadian rhythm and made it harder for them to participate in family life. But even this tightened their bonds to each other: everyone on a crew would be out of phase together, reinforcing group cohesion.[22]

The union culture that developed around PATCO further reinforced the manly ethic, for union loyalty was invariably described in male terms. "I was in a hardcore crew. Hardcore union guys. We were pretty ballsy," explained one controller. Another characterized his union buddies as "a motorcycle-riding, gun-toting crew." Mike Rock's praise for the lone PATCO member to participate in the 1970 sickout in Baltimore came down to two words: "Big balls." The way PATCO honored those who participated in the 1970 job action reinforced the idea that union loyalty was a manly characteristic. The union heroes who went out in 1970 were forever known as "horses." Those who stayed at work or who bailed out of the sickout early were called "ponies" or, worse, "geldings." To be known as one of the "horses" of 1970, one controller explained, was akin to being a "made man." It took manly courage to resist the FAA's pressure to cut corners in order to expedite traffic. Resisting that pressure, in the view of many in PATCO, required "balls." "It takes guts to hold up, but we know you will not let us down," assured PATCO's membership newsletter.[23]

The flip side of the controllers' manly work culture was the vision of domesticity that their salaried profession was meant to uphold. Air traffic controllers were overwhelmingly family men. According to one study conducted in the mid-1970s, 89 percent of controllers were married, and 87 percent of them had children living at home, with an average of 2.3 children per family. Most controllers aspired to a life that would allow their wives to stay at home while their children were young. In the mid-1970s, they were more successful in achieving this arrangement than most American working families. Roughly 70 percent of controllers reported that their wives did not work for wages. Of those wives who did work, 84 percent were employed in clerical or sales jobs, many of which were part-time.[24]

Air traffic control facilities were, in short, male-dominated workplaces, and most of the men who inhabited them saw no reason to change that. It was tough for women to enter this world. Not until Lyndon Johnson signed Executive Order 11375 in 1967 did the federal government prohibit employment discrimination against women. It took a few more years before the FAA moved to actively recruit women. In 1971, the agency set its first hiring targets for women controllers, and FAA Administrator Shaffer announced that he sought to make women 16 percent of new hires by 1972. There was no reason why women could not do the work, of course. Many World War II era controllers had been women. FAA officials pointed out that women could "concentrate on details" and "visualize things in three dimensions" just as well as men and suggested that women's voices might be particularly reassuring in high-pressure facilities. As it had done with African Americans, the FAA began recruiting women from across federal agencies.[25]

The women recruited in the early to mid-1970s came from working-class backgrounds similar to male recruits. Deborah Katz worked as a police dispatcher and a secretary at the FAA headquarters. Karen Wessel was a phone company service representative. Cheryl Jenni grew up on a farm in Lewiston, Montana, and taught home economics in Billings. All of them entered the FAA in the 1970s. Whatever the backgrounds of the new recruits, they saw air traffic control as an attractive opportunity to gain an interesting and well-paying federal job. At a time when women were heavily concentrated in the lowest levels of federal employment—80 percent of federal employees working at GS-4 or below were women—they were excited to learn that air traffic controllers could move up to GS-14 in some facilities.[26]

Yet "making it" at the FAA meant entering what former airline stewardess Elizabeth Koch called "a man's world," and navigating an "all-male, ex-military mentality domain." For the most part, men were not welcoming. In some cases women were openly shunned and humiliated. Diane Tyler, a Navy veteran hired at Washington Center, experienced the cold shoulder at her first all-hands meeting. A male controller announced to all assembled that women did not belong in air traffic control because they "take jobs from men who have to support families." Other women got similar receptions.

"You're just here because you're a minority," Deborah Katz was told. If they were lucky, women were merely condescended to and viewed as oddities. The former farm girl Cheryl Jenni felt like a "prize heifer" on display every time her facility chief led touring dignitaries by her post, saying, "This is Cheryl and she's a controller just like all the rest of us." Pilots were also dismissive. Once they got over their surprise at hearing a female voice directing them, all too often they would address the controller as "sweetie." Such terms were used often enough by FAA management that the agency's civil rights office had to remind supervisors in 1975 that, "the women in your office are not 'girls' or 'gals'... 'sweetie,' or 'honey,' or 'dear.' "[27]

Sexual harassment was also rampant. This problem was not unique to the FAA. A 1980 report found that 42 percent of women working for the government reported being harassed during the previous two years. But in this pre-1980 atmosphere of neglect, what one controller described as a "horrendously sexually harassing atmosphere" flourished in FAA facilities. At times, the harassment took the form of seemingly innocuous, but uninvited, workplace flirting. Other times it came anonymously, through obscene phone calls and notes. Sometimes, it took the form of verbal abuse. Occasionally, it could be physical, as in the case of the Denver Center trainee whose coworker stared at her for an entire shift and massaged her back without permission. Sometimes, male controllers intervened when they saw colleagues acting "way out of line." Generally, though, women had to fend for themselves and resist harassment by bringing complaints to the EEO counselors of their facilities.[28]

The case of Washington Center controller Deborah Katz illustrated how hostile the workplace could be. Katz had worked around men before as a police dispatcher, yet she found air traffic controllers far more aggressive than her previous coworkers. She received a steady stream of sexual comments and unwelcome advances, including some from her supervisor. The harassment took such a toll on Katz's health that she filed a successful sexual harassment lawsuit against the FAA.[29]

To successfully negotiate the male work environment and shield themselves from potential harassers, women learned how to become "one of the boys." Drinking with crewmembers was mandatory if a female controller wanted to win their acceptance. So was laughing at their lewd jokes. Humor's function in the workplace illustrated the tightrope that women had to walk. Failing to laugh at an off-color joke might label one a prude and foster isolation; laughing too hard might signal promiscuity and invite unwanted advances. The same caution was required with profanity. Tolerating it and using it on occasion helped women signal their participation in the workplace camaraderie; using it too freely, however, placed women at greater risk of experiencing verbal sexual harassment. Drinking involved careful calibrations, too. When out with the boys, it was important to stay sober and to be very clear that one was not looking for sex or a relationship.[30]

Humor, profanity, and barroom socializing were important signposts, but women won the respect and acceptance of their male coworkers mainly through excellence on the job, although they often had to go to great lengths to prove themselves. When Karen Wessel began her career at Oakland Center, she concluded that the surest way to establish herself was to become the best controller in her cohort. She worked assiduously toward that goal, seeking out experienced controllers as her mentors. In time, she earned a reputation as an outstanding controller, but she refused to rest until she conquered the most difficult assignments available. She campaigned hard for a transfer to the elite Bay TRACON facility, where no women had checked out before. After multiple applications she was finally given a chance and succeeded at Bay. As she met and surmounted each successive obstacle, Wessel found that she "eventually became kind of one of the guys." Similarly, Deborah Katz purposely requested certification in one of Washington Center's most difficult sectors, F Area, which was responsible for intersecting civilian and military jet traffic in a highly complex, densely crowded airspace. She believed that only by checking out in the most difficult sector could she prove her merit, and she succeeded.[31]

As the pioneering generation of women controllers struggled for advancement, they did not find PATCO a particularly useful vehicle for addressing their problems as women. Women held no power within the organization; none served as national-level PATCO officers. The only woman to head a PATCO local, at the small airport in Cheyenne, Wyoming, resigned in 1981 when her members became "mutinous." The union was also slow to address women's issues. Most male controllers and PATCO activists tended to downplay the extent to which women's problems were unique. It "wasn't whether you were male or female that gave you the ability to be a decent air traffic controller," as one man put it. "If the females had a problem, it was oftentimes they would allow their emotions [to] get involved...where the men...seemed to block that out." PATCO was saturated by an ethic of paternalism expressed in the "Message to the Ladies" section of early PATCO newsletters in which the organization stressed how "comforting" it was for the men "to know that we can call on the ladies" for support.[32]

The emerging feminist movement of the early 1970s gave women a language with which to critique both the FAA and PATCO. Most were indirectly affected by the heightened consciousness of sexual harassment and discrimination, but some, like Cheryl Jenni, embraced feminist politics and adapted it directly to their circumstances. Jenni founded a chapter of the National Organization for Women in Billings, Montana. In a similar fashion, the women's rights movement helped encourage women air traffic controllers to follow the example of African Americans and found their own organization, the Professional Women Controllers.[33]

The organization was the brainchild of two women, Sue J. Mostert of the New York "Common Eye," and Jacque Smith of LA Center. Mostert and Smith were a formidable team. Both were military veterans who joined the FAA in 1968. They met during their training in Oklahoma City, where they were two of only three women in a class of more than one hundred trainees. During their early years as controllers, they stayed in touch and compared notes about the struggles they faced working in overwhelmingly male environments where both faced bias. At times the discrimination was flagrant, as when Mostert was denied a FAM flight because airline regulations prohibited women from flying in the cockpit. But even when the bias was less blatant, it was no less infuriating.[34]

After years of frustration, Mostert decided to challenge sexism head-on. She was a motivated and self-confident woman. Raised on a dairy farm in upstate New York, she joined the Army out of high school and reached the staff sergeant rank working as a military air traffic controller. After her discharge, she joined the FAA and was the first woman assigned to work the tower in Albany, New York. She faced a hostile environment there that included outrageous physical harassment. She let her coworkers know that she had zero tolerance for their misbehavior, but some were not deterred. One day when Mostert was leaning over her console, a male coworker grabbed her hips from behind and mimicked a pelvic thrust. Mostert had warned this man before to keep his hands off her. Having already given him fair warning, Mostert did not hesitate to get physical on this occasion. She whipped around, grabbed her assailant by the crotch and squeezed as hard as she could, sending him to the floor writhing in pain. No man touched her again. After Albany, Mostert worked Andrews Air Force Base, and in 1978 she moved to the most elite facility on the East Coast, the "Common Eye," which handled all traffic coming into New York area airports. No woman had ever checked out in the JFK sector of the Common Eye before Mostert. By breaking that barrier, she provided living proof that women could succeed anywhere in the FAA.[35]

After series of discussions over several years with her friend, Jacque Smith, Mostert requested and obtained from the FAA a list of the nearly fifteen hundred women controllers working for the agency in 1978. Dividing the list in two, Mostert and Smith contacted the women and asked them to join a new organization. In January 1979, they convened an organizing committee meeting in Houston with controllers from different regions of the country, and, on April 16, sixty women attended the group's first convention at a Holiday Inn in Bethesda, Maryland. Mostert was elected the first president of the Professional Women Controllers (PWC). They developed a newsletter, the *Women's Air Traffic Control Hotsheet*, or WATCH, and began to organize chapters. By 1980, the PWC was officially recognized by the FAA.[36]

Although many women joined both PATCO and the PWC, relations between the two organizations were never close. Like Rick Jones and the founders of the black controllers' coalition, Mostert distrusted PATCO and felt that women's issues could not get a proper hearing in a male-dominated organization. Mostert herself had quit PATCO after the 1970 sickout and only rejoined it when she was assigned to the Common Eye, a PATCO stronghold, because she did not believe that she could check out there unless she was a member. She quit PATCO once again after checking out. PATCO members in turn generally regarded the PWC as antiunion, and on some occasions when Mostert traveled to speak to women controllers, PATCO activists disrupted her meetings, alleging there was no need for a separate women's group.[37]

However, even PATCO's most loyal women members, like Karen Wessel, decided that they needed their own institution, for without a specific women's voice, PATCO and the FAA would never address women's unique problems, such as access to the best paying controllers' slots. Wessel turned to the PWC, not PATCO, for help after twice being denied an opportunity to transfer to Bay TRACON, a move that would have brought with it a higher salary. A PWC meeting ultimately helped bring enough pressure to bear on the Bay facility chief that he approved Wessel's transfer. The incredulous reaction of some of her male colleagues when she later checked out at Bay confirmed the importance of a group like the PWC to Wessel. "Well, women still can't do this job... except for Karen, she's different," they said.[38]

THE VIETNAM GENERATION

Generational divisions complicated the race and gender dynamics that unfolded within PATCO and the FAA in the 1970s. In some ways, the experience of air traffic controllers was in line with many other post-1960s American workplaces. Contemporary researchers found younger workers to be more rebellious in the 1970s. They were "inclined to take 'less crap' than older workers," not as "automatically loyal" to organizations and hierarchies, and "far more cognizant of their own needs and rights," reported pollster Daniel Yankelovich. In public sector workplaces, where unrest had been uncommon before the late 1960s, this generational shift was often more pronounced. In the FAA, where an increasingly assertive workforce confronted a hierarchical, military-derived management culture, generational dynamics took on heightened importance. The FAA's younger employees were "much more likely than their predecessors to challenge, question, and refuse," concluded the most thorough study of the agency's labor-management relations. FAA supervisors found it difficult to adapt to a new workforce of young, aggressive, intelligent, and increasingly independent-minded controllers—a workforce shaped by the 1960s and the Vietnam War.[39]

The Vietnam experience distinguished controllers who joined the FAA after 1968 from those hired earlier. By 1978, two-thirds of PATCO's membership had joined since the 1970 sickout, and 40 percent had been in the union for less than five years. Despite the FAA's efforts to recruit controllers with different profiles, the vast majority of PATCO members—some 83 percent—still claimed veteran status in 1978. Vietnam-era veterans came to the FAA with experiences very different from those of their predecessors. For those who had experience "in country," the war had left emotional scars, bitterness, and cynicism. Many had volunteered to go to Vietnam. Terry Bobell, of Indianapolis Center, and Jim Stakem, of Washington Center, were typical of this generation. Both joined the Marines after high school rather than pursue college. "I watched too many John Wayne movies, I guess," Bobell explained. Stakem served at Con Tien and Khe Sanh, seeing action in two of the bitterest battles of 1967–1968, and Bobell served at Chu Lai in 1970. Both men returned from Vietnam deeply disillusioned. "The government had made a big mistake," thought Stakem. "The whole Vietnam thing was fake, phony," Bobell concluded. "Everybody died for nothing."[40]

The experiences of Stakem and Bobell were typical. A large percentage of PATCO's most active members in the late 1970s interpreted their Vietnam experience similarly. John Thornton, PATCO leader at Washington National Airport, spent a year in Phan Rang Airbase; Ed Meagher, of Washington Center, worked Saigon's Ton Son Nhut Airport during the Tet Offensive; Carl Kern, of Chicago Center, served at Cam Ranh Bay; and Jim Lundie, who would organize PATCO's field operation before the 1981 strike, served as a forward combat controller in hot zones like Kham Duc. Most of these veterans returned from the war feeling skeptical about "good old Uncle Sam" as a "final arbiter of the truth," as Kern put it. Even many of those who never landed in Vietnam left the service thinking the federal government "was not truthful."[41]

Before the Vietnam War, air traffic control had attracted free-spirited personalities who chafed at boundaries, but this was even truer of the Vietnam-era controllers. Management researcher David Bowers called the controllers who entered the FAA in the 1970s a "counter-authority generation." By their own description, the Vietnam vets were less willing to "blindly follow" orders. "If a bureaucrat gave an improper order, we questioned it," explained Bobell. "We were not going to become a bunch of Nazis blindly following faulty direction." Older controllers noticed the difference. "They were probably from the same cookie cutter as myself," observed George Kerr, who was hired at New York Center in 1961, "only they took their anger and frustration to a different level." Mike Rock, too, was struck by their rebellious attitudes. "They hated the federal government," he concluded. "They hated any kind of authority." At times it seemed to Rock that they wanted to "burn the facilities." Rock's hyperbole pointed to an undeniable truth: controllers hired in the 1970s entered federal employment with an innate suspicion of their employer. A 1981 PATCO survey showed that 75 percent of controllers had very little or no confidence in the FAA.[42]

In many ways, the FAA reciprocated that lack of confidence. One issue that brought mutual distrust to the surface was alleged drug use. The FAA believed Vietnam-era air traffic controllers were more likely to abuse drugs. In July 1971 the agency suspended four trainees from Los Angeles Center for possession of marijuana and amphetamines. Throughout the 1970s, it stepped up its efforts to identify and eliminate drug users, and it began developing a drug-testing program. PATCO sought assurances that the program would be fairly administered and that substance abusers would first be given counseling, rather than shown the door. The FAA interpreted PATCO's stance as nothing more than an effort to shield abusers.[43]

It is difficult to disentangle the facts on this issue, but a few points are clear. First, stress had always been a part of the work of air traffic control, and a temptation toward substance abuse was deeply ingrained in controllers' work culture even before the advent of 1960s-era drug use. Second, alcohol continued to be the main drug of choice among air traffic controllers, and heavy drinking played a central role in air traffic controllers' socializing through the 1970s, as it had in earlier years. A five-year study released by Boston University in 1977 found that controllers were twice as likely to be heavy drinkers as average Americans. Third, drug use increased in the 1970s according to interviews with air traffic controllers, yet drugs were not new to FAA workplaces. Keith Bakersfield, the air traffic controller character in Arthur Hailey's bestselling novel of 1968, *Airport*, relied on his "escape clause," a pillbox he kept in his pocket, to get through stressful days. In the end it is impossible to determine how much drug use might have increased in the 1970s.[44]

Whether more prevalent or not, alleged alcohol or substance abuse provided a flashpoint of conflict between the FAA and air traffic controllers in the 1970s. The Vietnam-era controllers resented the FAA's allegations of their irresponsibility. While they acknowledged that the temptation to abuse substances was inherent in their work, they also pointed to the strong self-policing ethic they practiced in the workplace. The vast majority of controllers respected the same "twelve hours from bottle to throttle" rule that governed pilots. They insisted that what they did in their off hours was their business, as long as it did not affect their ability to control traffic. Moreover, they themselves took measures to keep the workplace clean. On the occasions when someone showed up to work under the influence, it was generally other controllers, not supervisors, who handled them: sober controllers did not want high coworkers making their jobs any harder for them than they already were. At times controllers went to extraordinary lengths to shield a colleague with problems. "We had places we could hide them," where they could "sleep it off," one controller reported. Nevertheless, the FAA never ceased trying to identify and remove controllers found on or in possession of illegal drugs, and tension over drug allegations persisted through the 1970s.[45]

Generational conflict also spilled over into issues of dress and grooming. Hair—that crucial symbol of the 1960s—became the subject of considerable conflict. "I mean some of these people looked like bums, and we were supposed to be professionals," one FAA official charged. The FAA's desire to enforce its vision of professional appearance upon the 1960s generation was met with resentment and resistance. When Bob Butterworth first reported to work at a facility in California, he was told that his hairstyle was "too college." His first thought was, "Oh man, is this going to be a long career.'" At Washington Center controller Ralph McKnight decided to grow a beard. He was ordered to shave, and he refused. "I kept wearing my beard and wearing my beard, and every time I'd come in they would write me up and I would just ignore it," he said. "I would tell them to stick it up their asses." Such defiance became increasingly common.[46]

PATCO attempted to address the sartorial concerns of the younger controllers through Article 61 of the FAA-PATCO contract. In return for the FAA dropping the requirement that male controllers wear ties, the union agreed to language that stipulated that controllers should "groom and attire themselves in a neat, clean manner appropriate to the conduct of government business." The meaning of "neat," "clean," and "appropriate," however, was never really settled. FAA officials came to regret relaxing the necktie requirement, arguing that dropping ties opened facilities to "all kinds of things, old dirty overalls and sandals," women who "showed up with no bra and a t-shirt," and shirts bearing "all kinds of logos, statements," some of them profane or politically radical. On one occasion, the controllers' fight for a freer dress code literally resembled a war for independence. To protest the dress regulations in Kansas City, a controller showed up dressed as Ben Franklin, complete with a powdered wig. When challenged, he claimed to be celebrating the nation's bicentennial.[47]

Friction over alleged drug use, hairstyle, and clothing were symptomatic of the unfolding of generational conflicts in 1970s workplaces. But what made generational conflict particularly salient at the FAA was that these sources of cultural friction converged with deeper structural and technological changes that began transforming the nature of air traffic control as a profession. Automation, deregulation, and inflation began reshaping the profession at precisely the moment when cultural friction peaked.

STRUCTURAL SOURCES OF CONTROLLER MILITANCY

Automation began to transform many American workplaces in the 1970s, but few more so than FAA facilities. The movement to automate air traffic control began with a Kennedy administration initiative called Project Beacon. That program advanced in three stages during the 1970s, spurred on by PATCO's militancy. In 1970, the FAA began deploying an automated air traffic control technology called National Air Space (NAS) Enroute Stage A at twenty centers and sixty-three of the largest airports. Under this system, flight data was entered into a computer in advance. Before a flight was scheduled for takeoff, a program called up its information and printed out a data strip containing the relevant information about the flight's identity, destination, and route. As the flight moved from one sector to another across the country, computers automatically printed out data strips for use by each sector before the flight reached it. NAS Enroute Stage A was operational at all centers by 1975. By then, the second stage of automation, Radar Data Processing (RDP), was already being phased in at centers and TRACONs. RDP radar units displayed alphanumeric identifiers on the screen next to targets as they moved. The information, sent by transponders mounted on each jet, identified the flight, its altitude and speed, and did away with the "shrimp boats" that controllers once moved by hand across radarscopes to track flights. A third innovation, called the Automated Radar Terminal System (ARTS-3), alerted controllers whenever a flight began to descend below a safe level, and it was introduced at terminals in the mid-1970s. With these pieces largely in place by 1979, the FAA began to develop a computer system that could help controllers monitor and direct the traffic flow between major airports, allowing central flow control in Washington to better supervise and manage traffic across the national airspace.[48]

The introduction of these new technologies changed the way controllers did their jobs, often sparking conflict in the process. Jacksonville Center, which was a testing ground for the new systems in the early 1970s, became the locus of repeated clashes between controllers and supervisors, most of which were triggered by flaws in the new systems. Computer failures were frequent early in the deployment of the new technologies. When failures occurred, controllers suddenly found themselves sitting in front of radarscopes filled with unidentified targets. In 1979, the FAA experienced an average of more than one computer outage per day at each of the twenty air route traffic control centers. One computer at Washington Center failed 143 times over a six-month span that year. Controllers could generally sense a computer crash before it occurred: they would notice the system slowing its display of changes in altitude that they knew pilots had already executed. When that happened, a low murmur would spread across the floor as controllers collectively realized what was happening and braced themselves for an inevitable computer crash. One controller likened the sound to "hens getting nervous when the fox comes around."[49]

Controllers did not so much resist automation as criticize its reliability and object to serving as guinea pigs in its introduction. In Jacksonville, Kansas City, and other facilities, they mounted protests against the wobbly new systems. They even invited members of Congress on tours to show them how badly the systems malfunctioned. Yet invariably, when controllers complained about their equipment, they were ignored or told they were "crossing the line" into management's territory.[50]

The advent of airline deregulation added more stress to FAA workplaces in the 1970s. When the decade began, the airline industry was one of the most heavily regulated in the United States; when the decade ended it was at the cutting edge of a wave of deregulation that was reshaping the U.S. economy. The shift against airline regulation came suddenly. In 1938, Congress created the Civil Aeronautics Board (CAB), which governed the airline industry for the following four decades, certifying airlines, approving mergers, granting routes, and approving ticket prices, which were calculated to guarantee a 12 percent annual return on investment to air carriers. By most measures, the CAB's regulations nurtured the growth of U.S. aviation through the boom years of the 1960s. By the early 1970s, however, the CAB came under increasing criticism from proponents of deregulation. The skyrocketing price of aviation fuel, which rose 220 percent between 1969 and 1978 and accounted for one-fifth of airlines' operating costs, led the board to repeatedly raise fares to protect airline profits. By doing so, the CAB angered airline passengers and unintentionally primed Congress for an all-out assault on the regulatory system.[51]

In a bit of irony, that assault was led by Democratic Senator Ted Kennedy of Massachusetts, who was otherwise known as a champion of government regulation. With the help of his aide, Stephen Breyer, a future Supreme Court justice, Kennedy launched an investigation into the CAB's practices in 1975 that eventually showed that the board spent most of its regulatory energy trying to block fare reductions and restrain competition. This consumer-friendly issue never gave Kennedy the edge that he hoped it would for a planned presidential run, but it did help pave the way for the passage of airline deregulation under President Jimmy Carter. With prodding from Cornell economist Alfred Kahn, whom Carter named to chair the CAB, the president signed the Airline Deregulation Act into law in October 1978, beginning a new era in American aviation. Deregulation opened the door to low-cost air carriers with names like People Express and Midway Airlines. They burst into the markets once comfortably controlled by major carriers; in the span of five years, these upstarts doubled the share of the market not controlled by the ten largest airlines.[52]

While deregulation brought new choices and lower fares to consumers, it destabilized conditions for both the major airlines and air traffic controllers. To compete with the discount carriers, major airlines moved away from "point-to-point" air service between cities. Instead, they began to organize their traffic into a "hub and spoke" system, a model pioneered in 1971 by Fred Smith, founder of the airfreight company Federal Express. Smith had perfected methods to move packages from around the country into one central hub airport overnight, and then back out to their destination cities by dawn. Major air carriers now sought to move people the way Smith moved packages. Delta set up a hub in Atlanta; US Air adopted Pittsburgh; Northwest Airlines chose Detroit. As the airlines constructed their networks, traffic levels shot up in the hub airports, many of which were already bearing heavy traffic. The Carter administration insisted that deregulation and the hub-and-spoke system it begat would have no detrimental impact on air traffic control, but controllers who worked hub airports felt like victims of a "speed up." Most hubs had a two-hour window in the morning and in the evening when incoming flights would be crammed in, their passengers transferred to their outbound flights and sent out again. Stress levels inevitably rose during these "rush hours." As one Washington Center controller put it, it was as if the government said "turn the lions loose. Anybody can fly anywhere they want anytime they want to."[53]

As automation and deregulation created new pressures in air traffic control in the second half of the 1970s, controllers' economic prospects were eroded by the inescapable bane of those years, inflation. The average annual inflation rate more than tripled in the 1970s to 7.1 percent (rising from an average of 2.3 percent in the 1960s). Inflation placed a constant downward pressure on the earnings of all federal workers. While many private sector unions, such as the

United Automobile Workers, had won cost of living adjustments (COLAs) that automatically raised wages to match the inflation rate, government workers lacked such protection. Not surprisingly, upticks in the strike rate of state and local government workers in the 1970s tracked inflation. Thus, when the inflation rate jumped by a point to 7.62 percent in 1978, the number of public sector strikes spiked 18 percent as workers pressured their employers for raises. Federal workers were in a unique bind in this period; like most other government employees, they lacked inflation protection. Federal workers depended upon yearly wage adjustments approved by Congress, yet they lacked the ability to pressure their employer with strikes the way municipal workers could. Between 1973 and 1981, federal raises regularly failed to keep up with rising prices. Over this span, federal employees actually saw their inflation-adjusted income cut by an average of 3.1 percent each year.[54]

For air traffic controllers, this erosion of real income seemed especially oppressive. They were highly skilled workers, who trained for years to do jobs that they anticipated would provide a comfortable middle-class lifestyle. Unlike government lawyers, computer programmers, or accountants, they did not have the option of marketing their skills in the private sector or, indeed, to any other employer in the United States. The FAA was their only option. Adding to their anger was the fact that the FAA at times seemed to regard them as serfs. Controllers were incensed that the FAA monitored the personal indebtedness of those whose circumstances forced them to declare bankruptcy, condescendingly instructing controllers to "discharge their private financial obligations" in a manner that avoided creating "an unfavorable image of the Federal Government." Failure to honor "valid debts" was deemed "grounds for disciplinary action against an employee." Such policies only further embittered Vietnam-era controllers. But, unlike other federal workers in the mid- to late 1970s who felt helpless to improve their stagnating incomes, controllers' jobs put them in position to resist what they saw as the government's mistreatment. They stood at a bottleneck in the nation's transit system. They knew they had the power to clog that bottleneck. And they were increasingly of a mind to use that power to defend their interests. [55]

SEEDS OF RESISTANCE

The structural changes that contributed to growing disaffection among air traffic controllers in the 1970s were not unique to the United States. Across the globe, air traffic controllers organized and staged job actions in the 1970s as never before, making it a decade of unprecedented militancy in the labor relations of these workers. Canadian, German, Mexican, French, Australian, and British controllers, among others, staged strikes, slowdowns, or sickouts in the 1970s. During these years, the International Federation of Air Traffic Control Associations, first founded in 1961 to promote information sharing among air traffic controllers in developed countries, took on an advocacy role, calling for better pay and working conditions for controllers worldwide.[56]

The pressures that stirred controllers across the globe in the 1970s were only magnified in the United States, which boasted by far the world's largest and most heavily traveled system of air transportation. In many ways, the American controllers' situation was exceptional. Nowhere else did controllers face the same combination of developments in the late 1970s, including new technologies, a thoroughly reorganized aviation regulatory structure, inflation-eroded salaries, tight restrictions on collective bargaining, and the demoralizing impact of the Vietnam War. In the United States, these factors combined with the tensions associated with the slow diversification of the air traffic control workforce through affirmative action—8.1 percent of all air traffic controllers were racial minorities and 6.3 percent were women in 1981—to make American air traffic control facilities particularly volatile places.[57]

Adding to this volatility was the growing sense among male controllers that the realities they confronted were threatening their most cherished aspirations. In general working-class men had to face new pressures during these years. As the historian Bruce Schulman has observed, in the 1970s conceptions of masculinity in general seemed "up for grabs" and "Americans' most basic notions of manhood needed to be worked out; they could no longer be assumed." The sexual revolution, feminism, and the wave of deindustrialization that took away millions of traditionally male manufacturing jobs altered the terrain upon which American men negotiated the terms of their manhood. This was no less true in the male-dominated world of air traffic control. Air traffic controllers had been attracted to their work in part because it offered a vision of a male-breadwinner-based family life. Controllers generally saw themselves as "middle-class guys with homes in the 'burbs." Like Washington Center controller Sid McGuirk, whose wife left her job as a nurse after their first child was born, they liked the fact that they could "afford to be a one-income family." But the male controllers' aspirations to support one-income families were being challenged during the inflation-ravaged 1970s. The only contemporary surveys with evidence on the question indicate that the number of male controllers whose wives worked for wages outside the home jumped by one-third between 1976 and 1978.[58]

To be sure, controllers generally earned higher incomes, lived in better houses, and enjoyed more job security than their parents had known. Indeed, their objective economic positions were better than that of most American workers. Yet this gave them little consolation. As the 1970s progressed and inflation nipped at their salaries, they felt increasingly undercompensated. According to an internal survey conducted by PATCO in 1977, only 40 percent felt that they earned enough to afford a few luxuries. The majority felt they were just getting by.[59]

In many ways, the issues male air traffic controllers faced in the late 1970s seemed like challenges to their manhood. In an open letter to air traffic controllers, one of their wives put it in just such terms. "All you macho types out there should be ashamed to claim your pride in your profession while allowing the FAA to govern your lifestyle," she scolded. "You have no profession in that case!! You are simply a technician." A "person who sits back and allows a superior (?!?) to degrade his position is a nothing, a no-count," she continued. "Ask your wives—if you still have them—what would they opt for?...I've seen and heard of too many of you turning into cornered, trapped animals; snapping, snarling, sarcastic, and cynical," she concluded. "And you've got to be kidding yourselves to think you'll have a family around to put up with that if you don't have the courage to stand up and fight for yourselves!"[60]

Many American workers struggled with more serious problems during that decade when prices soared, the economy stagnated, and factories closed in bunches. What was exceptional about the air traffic controllers was that, over the course of the 1970s, they became more confident in their belief that their collective power and strategic position in the nation's economy would allow them not only to arrest the forces threatening their aspirations, but to reverse them. Forging a unity of purpose around this effort would be challenging, given the divisions that suffused the air traffic control workforce. But events in the late 1970s would convince a growing number of controllers that the time had come to "stand up and fight."

DOWN THE TUBES

First Officer: Are we clear of that Cessna? . . .
Pilot: Oh, yeah. Before we turned downwind I saw
him about one o'clock, probably behind us now.
—FLIGHT DATA RECORDER, PSA FLIGHT 182

Holy Mackerel. This thing is working.
—MIKE ROCK

The New York midair collision of 1960 remained the nation's worst air
disaster for nearly eighteen years. It was replaced in the record books by
another midair collision that occurred under very different circumstances.
This one took place a continent away on a clear, unusually warm morning in
cloudless skies over San Diego.

Visibility was excellent just before 9 a.m., on Monday, September 25,
1978, when Pacific Southwest Airlines Flight 182, a Boeing 727 carrying
135 people from Sacramento and Los Angeles, was cleared to land at San
Diego's Lindbergh Airport. As he handed off the jet to tower controllers, a
San Diego approach controller warned its pilot about a small single-engine
Cessna on an instructional run three miles ahead. In the Cessna were a flight
instructor and his student, a Marine Corps sergeant practicing instrument
approaches. At the controls of Flight 182, Captain James E. McFeron

acknowledged visual contact with the Cessna. A moment later, as they chatted about other matters, the pilot and first officer lost track of the small plane, and failed to inform air traffic control of this. In the meantime, the approach controller, believing that the pilots had each other in sight, turned his attention to the next inbound flight. Suddenly, McFeron's first officer on Flight 182 remembered the Cessna. "Are we clear of that Cessna?" he asked. "I guess," McFeron replied, adding: "Oh, yeah. Before we turned downwind I saw him about one o'clock, probably behind us now."

But the Cessna was not behind them. It had strayed from the heading that it was given by controllers and had not announced its new heading. The Cessna was now directly ahead of and below the jet, its colors difficult to discern against the rooftops of San Diego by the fact that it was moving in the same direction as the jet, which was quickly overtaking it. As PSA 182 slowed to 165 miles per hour and descended toward two thousand feet in preparation for landing, something instantly caught the first officer's eye. "There is one underneath," he yelled. It was too late. Flight 182's right wing sliced through the Cessna, shattering the small plane and killing its occupants instantly. The jet's right wing was fatally damaged by the impact, its fuel reservoir set aflame. "We are hit, man, we are hit," the first officer yelled. As Captain McFeron struggled to right his craft, it banked uncontrollably. "Tower, we are going down," McFeron radioed. Sixteen seconds after the initial collision, the jet exploded in flames in San Diego's North Park neighborhood, killing everyone on board and seven people on the ground, damaging or destroying twenty-two homes. The last words the cockpit voice recorder collected were, "Ma, I love yah." The final death toll was 144.[1]

As with the accident that shook New York on December 16, 1960, the warning signs were clear in retrospect. The air traffic system came under increasing stress in the late 1970s as air travel rose. In 1977 alone the FAA registered a 13 percent increase in systemwide instrument operations. However, the ranks of controllers were not growing in proportion to this rising workload. While the airlines urged the FAA to fill all vacancies, many facilities continued to operate below staffing quotas. As the workload mounted, the number of system errors rose in 1977 and 1978, and on several occasions prior to September 25 the FAA had dodged bullets. In December 1977, four near-misses were reported: three in the skies around JFK Airport in a two-week span, the last over Maryland when a Washington Center computer failed and two Air Force jets nearly collided. In June 1978, a corporate jet nearly crashed into a commercial flight on a LaGuardia runway.[2]

To cope with the rising traffic levels, the FAA leaned all the more on new technologies that too often proved unreliable. In fact, technological glitches contributed to the San Diego tragedy. Technicians installed a computerized conflict-alert system in the San Diego TRACON six weeks before the accident. The system was programmed to sound an alarm whenever two aircraft were headed toward a confliction. But the alarm went off on average thirteen times a day, usually in what the NTSB investigation later called "nuisance alarms"—situations in which aircraft had each other in sight and were not in danger of colliding. Such a warning sounded nineteen seconds before the San Diego collision, but, given the frequency of nuisance alarms, controllers did not immediately respond. They believed that Captain McFeron had the Cessna in sight.[3]

In the end, the failure of the PSA crew to follow proper rules—keeping potentially conflicting traffic in visual contact and maintaining separation, or immediately informing controllers if they were unable to do so—was cited as the probable cause of the accident. Investigators did not fault the decisions or actions of the San Diego air traffic controllers. Nonetheless, the event contributed to a rupture in an already strained relationship between PATCO and Jimmy Carter's FAA. In the fifteen months that followed the San Diego accident, that rupture would deepen to the point that it destabilized PATCO's leadership and sent the union careening in a new—and ultimately fatal—direction.[4]

Disappointed Hopes, Deepening Dissension

None of this could have been anticipated in January 1977 as the Carter administration took office. Having endorsed Jimmy Carter, Leyden was hopeful that PATCO would recover from the wounds it sustained during the bruising reclass fight and prosper under a more labor-friendly Democratic administration. There was talk that Carter would support congressional legislation to correct the failures of Executive Order 11491, finally putting federal union rights on statutory footing. Federal sector unions hoped Carter would also support widening the scope of bargaining in the federal service, potentially allowing federal workers to bargain over their pay just as postal workers did. If that bid failed, PATCO counted on Rep. Mo Udall to make good on his pledge to separate controllers from the federal salary schedule so as to give them needed raises.[5]

Many of PATCO's hopes came to rest on the shoulders of Carter's FAA administrator, Langhorne McCook Bond, who in a short time proved to be a major disappointment for the union. As the son of William Langhorne Bond, a former Pan American Airways executive who had established the carrier's China routes in the 1930s, Bond was thoroughly familiar with aviation. Educated at the London School of Economics and the University of Virginia Law School, Bond had worked at the Civil Aeronautics Board before becoming an assistant to Secretary of Transportation Alan Boyd in the Johnson administration. After Nixon's election, Bond left government to direct the National Transportation Center, a non-profit research corporation in Pittsburgh. He became secretary of transportation in Illinois before Carter named him to head the FAA.[6]

The thirty-six-year-old Bond was adept in the world of transportation policy, but he knew much less about labor relations. What little experience he had acquired came in his self-described "bare-knuckles" dealings with the Teamsters and AFSCME as Illinois transportation secretary. As he came to Washington in 1977, Bond decided that labor relations within the FAA were in a state of "total chaos" that he blamed mostly on PATCO. Having worked for Boyd when PATCO staged its first job action in 1968, at the outset of his tenure Bond determined to rein in air traffic controller militancy. That determination, combined with an aloof, cerebral manner, made it difficult for Bond to connect with either PATCO's membership or Leyden.[7]

Indeed, Bond passed up a chance to help Leyden early on. More than six months after the CSC reclassification report was approved in January 1977, a large proportion of the controllers designated for upgrades had yet to see their pay increased. This was due to the Whitten Amendment, a rule first adopted during the Korean War and named for its sponsor, Mississippi Democrat Jamie L. Whitten. The amendment required federal civil service employees to serve at least a year in one grade before they could be promoted to a higher grade. Leyden asked Bond to waive the rule for the affected air traffic controllers. Bond had the power to do so, but he refused. As a result the upgrades were delayed and Leyden suffered another barrage from his more militant members.[8]

Off to an unsteady start, relations between Bond and PATCO leaders deteriorated further when they sat down to begin negotiating a new contract in 1977. It was a difficult time for public sector unions at all levels of government. Facing budgetary constraints amid slow growth and inflation, Democratic mayors and governors had already begun to take a harder line in their own negotiations with their employees. The Carter administration was no different.[9]

With no ability to negotiate over salaries, benefits, staffing levels, and technology, PATCO was forced to seek nonbudgetary items, including loosening the dress code, the designation of special bulletin boards in each facility for PATCO's use, and the extension of the FAM program to overseas travel. In an effort to strengthen PATCO's hand heading into the negotiations while simultaneously mollifying controllers who argued that he had sold out during the reclass fight, Leyden supported a bold move at the union's May 1977 convention in Miami: the creation of a strike fund. PATCO was not the first federal employee union to do this. The American Federation of Government Employees had created a similar fund six months earlier. But PATCO's fund represented a much more serious commitment: 15 percent of all dues revenue was placed in a "Controllers Benefit Fund," to be used to pay "members who are disciplined as a result of participation in a nationally sanctioned job action." PATCO's members endorsed the move by a 2–1 margin in a mail ballot. The fund's creation sent tremors through the FAA and increased Bond's determination to rein in PATCO.[10]

After the contract expired in July 1977, the FAA's negotiating position hardened. By September, Leyden was reporting that FAA counterproposals were "appreciably less" than what the agency initially offered. The White House never intervened in the negotiations. Yet the FAA was well aware of the administration's desire to avoid any concessions on staffing or working conditions that would cost the agency money. Negotiations quickly stalemated, and Leyden worried that his union might need "an entirely new approach" if it hoped to make a breakthrough. At the end of September, Leyden suspended negotiations and sent Mike Rock around the country to assess members' readiness for a job action.[11]

PATCO leaders then decided on a two-step strategy designed to force the FAA into concessions. First, the union would launch informational picketing at all of the nation's airports on November 21 to educate the public about its demands. If this did not get the FAA to come to terms, the union would initiate a slowdown before the Christmas holiday, one of the busiest travel periods of the year. Phase one was impressive. PATCO pulled off the "largest organized picketing campaign in the history of federal sector trade unions" on the Monday before Thanksgiving. It had no effect on the FAA's position.[12]

At that point, Leyden decided to implement phase two. He was unsure whether sufficient support existed within the union for a job action, but he felt he had no choice but to threaten one if he wanted an acceptable contract. On the day after the informational picketing, he warned AFL-CIO President George Meany that a major conflict with the FAA was brewing. Then he set a deadline of December 15 with the FAA. If negotiations did not progress by that date, he warned, air travel might be affected. Leyden instructed the PATCO board to assess how many members from their regions would participate in a slowdown if the FAA refused to budge, and how many would endorse "an all-out strike" if the agency tried to retaliate against the slowdown.[13]

As the December 15 deadline neared, a clash seemed inevitable. The FAA presented its "final, best, firm offer" as a "package deal." If PATCO rejected any element of it, the FAA would withdraw the offer. Moreover, the agency would not even put its final positions in writing. Facing a hardline FAA stance, Leyden let the agency know that PATCO was ready for a fight and summoned the union's board and facility representatives to Washington for a war council.[14]

The show of force seemed to work. On December 13, as PATCO activists began arriving at the Capitol Hill Hyatt Regency, the PATCO-FAA negotiations went into around-the-clock mode. The agency eventually offered several concessions: liberalization of the FAM program to include some international flights, access to arbitration for a wider range of disputes, expansion of the controllers' training program, and strong language defining controllers' ability to bid on geographic transfers by seniority. In return, Bond demanded a three-year contract: he wanted to make sure that the next time a president negotiated with the union, it would be early in his administration, when the president's power would be greatest. On balance, PATCO leaders thought it was a good deal. When Leyden described its features to a waiting audience of facility representatives at the Hyatt, they gave him a standing ovation. The PATCO representatives attributed their gains to the union's threatened job action, which in Leyden's view allowed the union to win "some language that was reasonable."[15]

Unfortunately for Leyden, the contract was poorly received in some quarters of the union. As provisions of the agreement were circulated, heated debates broke out in many facilities, re-opening the wounds of the reclass fight. The union's militants thought that, once again, the organization's leaders had settled for too little. Considerable discontent emerged in PATCO strongholds like the New York Common Eye. Militant members there dismissed Leyden's argument that "all-out war" would not have improved the FAA's offer, and rejected his contention that the contract was "the best we could possibly attain without much bloodletting." They believed that a little "bloodletting" might have led the FAA to put more on the table.[16]

Leyden worried that the drumbeat of criticism would lead members to vote down the contract, a phenomenon on the rise among all unions in the 1970s. While he later privately conceded that the contract's language in some areas was "vague, imprecise, and, quite frankly, weak," Leyden felt he had no choice but to campaign aggressively for its ratification. Publicly, he called the contract "the best ever negotiated in the federal sector." He saw no contradiction in his statements: whatever its defects, the PATCO-FAA contract was better than what other federal sector unions were winning. Still, Leyden knew he needed help selling the contract. He decided to make a joint videotape recording with Bond extolling its virtues. As an added enticement, the FAA promised on camera that if Congress passed a law expanding the range of negotiable items, as many believed might happen in 1978, the FAA would "be back at the bargaining table as a result of that law." A copy of the video went to each FAA facility in January 1978.[17]

Ominously, even with the FAA's help, only 62 percent of controllers voted to accept the contract in February 1978, the lowest percentage yet in PATCO's three contract ratification votes. As happened after the reclass fight, different factions drew different lessons from the contract battle. Leyden thought the pact offered proof that "reasonable people can compromise" and showed that PATCO was broadening the rights and privileges of air traffic controllers with each successive contract. To the union's militant members, however, the contract illustrated everything that was wrong with the PATCO-FAA relationship. "They jammed that nothing contract down our throats," said Terry Bobell of Indianapolis. The only reason it was ratified, alleged Jack Seddon of New York Center, was that "the smaller and less militant facilities voted in favor of it" under the influence of "a road show of strong-armed salesmanship by the national office." The union's militants thought the 1978 contract illustrated perfectly why the union would need a credible strike threat for its next negotiation. "We sent our negotiators to Washington D.C. with nothing to back up their demands," explained a Chicago Center activist.[18]

Before the contract debate had a chance to simmer down, Leyden received an unexpected blow. The airlines unilaterally announced that they would not honor controllers' requests for international FAMs. Leyden and Bond had tried to head off this possibility during the negotiations by inviting a representative from the airlines to sit in on the talks. The airlines' association, the ATA, had not accepted that invitation or offered any comments on the FAM clause before the contract was ratified. Still, Leyden had believed that no airline would refuse to cooperate, singling itself out for the ire of controllers who might decide to favor its competitors in prioritizing flights for takeoff and landing. His confidence was misplaced. Once the contract was ratified, the three largest international carriers, TWA, Northwest, and Pan American, announced they would not cooperate on the FAM issue. They refused even to meet with Leyden and Bond to discuss the matter.[19]

The airlines' decision pushed the already weakened Leyden into a corner. He knew that these free flights could be portrayed unflatteringly to the public as an unjustified perk even though most people who worked in the airline industry got similar benefits. But he believed he could not allow a major piece of the contract to be "ruptured" without opening the door to other givebacks. Any perceived weakness on his part would only further erode his authority in the eyes of the union's militants. He sought to head off such a possibility by simultaneously alerting PATCO's activists to the emergence of a "major problem," and appealing to the airlines for their help in preserving the FAA-PATCO contract, which he called the source of "labor stability in the ATC system." Leyden was unable to resolve the issue before PATCO's annual convention opened in Las Vegas in early May. In frustration, he wondered whether the ATA had set him up on the FAM issue simply to lure PATCO into a destructive confrontation.[20]

When the PATCO executive board convened in Las Vegas on May 5, 1978, Leyden laid out the situation to his colleagues. The board agreed unanimously that the union could not let the airlines ignore an aspect of the PATCO-FAA contract, and endorsed a slowdown if the airlines did not rescind their opposition. Only Jack Maher expressed misgivings about whether PATCO members would actually support a job action over FAMs. As it turned out, he was prescient.[21]

Two days later on the floor of the union's convention, PATCO delegates broke into clusters to discuss the proposed job action. A clear majority supported action. Significantly, however, leaders from nine of the FAA's largest facilities, whose members had either opposed or weakly supported the 1978 contract, spoke against Leyden's plan. Militant leaders of the "Big Nine" did not want the union to go to war over an issue tangential to the real needs of controllers. "In good conscience, I could not endorse a job action over an issue which my members had voted against," said Jack Seddon. Delegates from smaller facilities, who had long felt that the Big Nine controllers only looked out for their self-interest, dismissed Seddon's stance. They helped give Leyden the majority he needed to endorse a job action beginning on May 25 if the airlines refused to relent. Nonetheless, the dissension cast a pall over delegates as they dispersed to their home facilities. Even supporters of the job action were less than enthused about the prospects of this fight. Being able to take a FAM to Europe had some training value for those controllers who handled international traffic; but many PATCO leaders understood that a job action over international FAMs would give the union bad publicity. Moreover, they did not believe that many controllers would even utilize such flights. The FAMs were "a bullshit thing," said Domenic Torchia, PATCO's West Coast board member.[22]

The situation could hardly have been more dangerous for PATCO. Still recovering from the bruises sustained during the reclass struggle and the recently concluded contract negotiation, the union was about to launch a fight over an issue that would be hard to justify to the flying public. Support for the FAM job action was tenuous; leaders of key facilities were on record against it; and the union's most influential ally, Capt. J. J. O'Donnell of the Air Line Pilots Association (ALPA) strongly opposed international FAMs. It was a recipe for disaster, but PATCO leaders plunged ahead, convinced that they had to defend their contract.[23]

On May 23, Leyden warned airline executives that a "spontaneous" slowdown might erupt if they failed to honor international FAMs. "They can allow us a free seat or spend money burning fuel," he told the press. "We've implored our people to be patient, but I think they're about at the end of their rope." The airlines stood pat. They knew that in the event of a job action, they could return to federal court in Brooklyn to secure a contempt citation against PATCO for violating the permanent restraining order left in place by Judge Orrin Judd at the conclusion of the 1970 sickout strike.[24]

Having made the threat, PATCO now had to follow through on it. The slowdown began on May 25 in a few select facilities. Within a day, it began producing significant delays. The airlines immediately went to court and secured an injunction, but PATCO pressed on. As the slowdown moved into its second week, it spread to more facilities in the East. On June 7, delays averaged thirty minutes at Washington National Airport, where controllers were clocked handling ten operations per hour fewer than normal. Delays neared one hour at New York area airports. As traffic backed up, PATCO publicly denied that it was engaging in a job action in an effort to avoid fines under the restraining order's terms.[25]

While the slowdown continued, the FAA pursued a hands-off approach. Bond was miffed with the airlines for their refusal to abide by the PATCO-FAA contract. As far as he was concerned, the airlines had asked for this fight. Publicly, the FAA suggested that delays might be due to inclement weather. Privately, it gave PATCO a green light to force the airlines into compliance, or, as Mike Rock put it, "carte blanche to knock their jocks off." But even with the threat of FAA discipline removed, PATCO leaders struggled to enlist rank-and-file support for the action. Delays never compared with those created during the union's July 1976 reclass slowdown.[26]

Sensing PATCO's weakness, the airlines held firm. By the end of the first week in June, Leyden realized PATCO was losing. Had the union been able to count on "total participation" in the slowdown, he believed the issue could have been resolved "in two or three days," but participation by controllers at key facilities had been "tepid at best." Indeed, members flooded Leyden's office with complaints. Some viewed the slowdown as a poor strategic decision, squandering the "mighty weapon" of a job action on a demand that was "irresponsible and ridiculous." They called it "misguided" and "stupid," and said it had "no merit to it whatsoever." Others objected as a matter of principle. "On this issue, I believe we are wrong," one controller told Leyden. Even the union's attorney, Bill Peer, privately thought the slowdown "indefensible." Given collapsing support for the action, Leyden sued for peace. ATA officials agreed to discuss FAMs with him if he called off the slowdown. On June 8, Leyden issued the order, but once he suspended the job action he had lost his leverage. The ATA yielded nothing.[27]

In the end, the slowdown had won PATCO nothing but internal dissension, bad press, frayed alliances, and a whopping court fine. A job action that much of the public perceived as an example of union power run amok was in actuality the product of PATCO's weakness, its inability to widen the terms of collective bargaining or even enforce aspects of the contract its members had approved. This irony escaped public note. Instead, angry travelers showered Leyden with screeds. Writing from a jet that circled New York, one likened his fate to "those falsely imprisoned or sky-jacked." "I am thoroughly fed up with the arrogant, self-serving 'don't give a damn attitude' of the air controllers in this country," fumed a Denver businessman. Letter writers urged Congress to curb runaway union power. "The unions can shut down this country right now with the powers Congress has granted them," declared one irate citizen. "The tail has been wagging the dog long enough!!" added another. "Since only 20% of the working people belong to labor organizations, please explain to me why the other 80% must put up with, and be an involuntary partner to this coercion!!!" Pilots were no more sympathetic. Even had he been inclined to, J.J. O'Donnell was in no position to defend PATCO's demand over his members' objections; O'Donnell himself was in the midst of a tough reelection battle in 1978.[28]

Then there was federal judge Thomas C. Platt. In Platt's Brooklyn courtroom, PATCO faced the prospect of $1 million in fines for violating the 1970 injunction against job actions. Platt reminded the union's leaders that as federal employees they had taken an oath not to engage in job actions. Were the government to fail to enforce this oath, he intoned, "chaos would inevitably result." PATCO was lucky to cut a deal with Platt. In exchange for admitting that the union had violated the restraining order, Platt reduced the fine to $100,000. Platt's fine won praise from the nation's newspapers. It was high time that someone started "controlling the air controllers," observed the *Washington Post*.[29]

Season of Discontent

Coming swiftly on the heels of the reclass fight and the disappointing 1978 contract, the international FAM debacle left PATCO reeling in the late summer of 1978. It was exactly at this vulnerable moment that hopes evaporated for the passage of congressional legislation that might have improved the bargaining power of PATCO and other federal sector unions.

Federal sector unionists such as John Leyden had viewed the election of Jimmy Carter with great hope. During his first months in office, Carter encouraged those hopes with a series of actions labor favored. He named a union representative to the Federal Employee Pay Council, which advised him on salaries. He pledged to reform the 1939 Hatch Act, which barred federal workers from participating in most partisan political activity. And, most importantly, he said he would sign legislation to put federal sector union rights on statutory footing for the first time.[30]

However, Carter soon disappointed labor supporters. By 1978 his administration was focused on fighting inflation, doing little to aid labor's cause. Indeed, economists Alfred Kahn and Barry Bosworth and U.S. Trade Representative Robert Strauss, leaders of the administration's inflation-fighting team, urged Carter to hold the line with unions, whose contracts they argued, promoted inflation. After proposing a federal salary increase that kept pace with inflation in 1977 (the first time a president had done so in five years), Carter reversed course the next year and offered an increase that trailed the inflation rate. In each subsequent year of his administration, the gap between federal salary increases and inflation widened. His record on other labor priorities was equally disappointing. When Hatch Act reform encountered opposition from a coalition of Republicans and conservative Democrats, he let it die in a Senate committee without lifting a finger. During negotiations with postal unions in 1978, he encouraged negotiators to hold the line. Finally, most labor leaders believed that Carter did not exert himself enough to end a Senate filibuster that doomed passage of labor's top priority, a labor law reform bill that would correct glaring weaknesses in the National Labor Relations Act.[31]

It did not bode well that the effort to finally legislate the union rights of federal workers, hitherto spelled out only in executive orders, came to fruition just as Carter's alliance with organized labor began to unravel. At the outset, federal sector unions had great hopes that Carter would endorse legislation expanding their bargaining rights. "Until federal employees are statutorily granted the right to negotiate on wages, they will never be assured of comparability in pay with their private sector counterparts," explained Vincent L. Connery, president of the National Treasury Employees Union (NTEU). At the very least, federal unions needed the ability to bargain over "fringe benefits, work procedures, automation, job classification, job security, contracting out, training, union security, and travel and per diem," added Leyden. When Carter took office it was not unreasonable to believe that federal workers could win such rights. Some federal workers already had them: printers in the Government Printing Office had been able to bargain over wages since the passage of the Kiess Act in 1924; employees of the Tennessee Valley Authority had had that right since the 1930s. Legislators introduced a number of bills in 1977 that would have accomplished what the federal unions sought. Some bills even offered limited strike rights to federal employees.[32]

However, like Kennedy in 1961, Carter wanted the White House rather than the Congress to control the federal government's collective bargaining policy. Like Kennedy, Carter preempted Congress with a move of his own. On May 27, 1977, Carter created the Federal Personnel Management Project to study the civil service system and recommend reforms. The move effectively put all related legislation on hold. In January 1978, Carter's project delivered its findings, which recommended a sweeping reform of the federal civil service but ignored labor's demands for a significant restructuring of federal collective bargaining policy. Using that report as their template, Carter's staff drafted the outlines of the Civil Service Reform Act (CSRA), which the president introduced at a news conference on March 2, 1978. Tellingly, Carter framed his bill as a cost-cutting and efficiency-promoting measure, not a plan to strengthen the rights of federal workers. "There is not enough merit in the merit system," he said. He promised the bill would streamline a government "mired in its own red tape," offer "less job security for incompetent Federal employees," and give "conscientious civil servants" rewards for good performance. He said nothing about union rights.[33]

Carter's announcement triggered months of tense negotiations among White House officials, legislators, and labor leaders over the contents of Title VII, the labor-management relations section of the CSRA. Carter's negotiators made clear that not only would they oppose the extension of any strike rights or union-security provisions to federal workers, but they also opposed widening bargaining rights to cover compensation and benefits. When labor's allies, Democratic Reps. William D. Ford of Michigan and William L. Clay of Missouri, balked, the administration threatened to simply transfer Nixon's Executive Order 11491 wholesale into Title VII of the act, perpetuating what labor considered an unacceptable status quo.[34]

Labor's negotiating position weakened over the summer of 1978 when a political earthquake rocked California. On June 6, voters overwhelmingly approved Proposition 13, a radical tax-cutting measure spearheaded by conservatives Howard A. Jarvis and Paul Gann. The initiative slashed taxes, froze property tax assessments at 1975 levels, and limited future property tax increases to 2 percent per year. Immediately, iterations of the tax limitation movement erupted in dozens of other states. The "tax revolt" was on.[35]

As opposition to taxes grew, public sector unions found themselves in the crosshairs. This was no coincidence. Since 1973, a conservative organization with an innocuous name, the Public Service Research Council (PSRC), had been working tirelessly to blame them for fomenting strikes and winning wage increases that raised taxes. The group took its inspiration from the work of Sylvester Petro, a libertarian law professor at Wake Forest University, who described the growing power of government unions in the 1970s as the gravest threat to the nation's liberty. Unions intended nothing less than to take over government, Petro argued, using their power to elect politicians who would raise taxes, increase government workers' pay, and feed a cycle that would lead inevitably to socialism. If the unions could not be stopped, Petro warned, "the time will have arrived for us to take to the hills and the fields and the caves once more, as our ancestors have frequently had to do when integral—sovereign—government has broken down."[36]

The movement Petro inspired was growing and well funded by 1978, thanks to a new breed of conservative direct-mail fundraisers like Richard Viguerie. The PSRC itself was led by a skilled propagandist named David Y. Denholm, who had worked for California's chapter of the antiunion National Right to Work Committee before coming to Washington to fight government unions full time. Denholm was a tireless advocate. In 1974, he began circulating a popular pamphlet called *Public Sector Bargaining and Strikes*, which argued that collective bargaining laws only increased the likelihood of government workers' strikes. In 1975, he played a significant role in blocking congressional legislation that would have extended collective bargaining rights to all state and local government workers. In 1978, he launched an academic journal, a biweekly newsletter, and a lobbying arm called Americans Against Union Control of Government. He also attracted a list of prominent supporters, including Sen. Jesse Helms, Republican from North Carolina, the conservative thinker Russell Kirk, and the publisher Henry Regnery. In the latter years of the 1970s, Denholm's PSRC fueled the fears that public sector unions were out to create a form of socialism or even a "new feudalism." (Such visions struck a chord with Anthony Burgess, author of the classic dystopian novel, *A Clockwork Orange*: his 1978 novella *1985* evoked a frightening future in which unions controlled government and freedom was but a memory.) When the tax revolt erupted, Denholm's organization was thus well positioned to link the concerns of tax-weary, inflation-battered voters to the threat of government workers' unions. It was a link that Proposition 13 architect Howard Jarvis himself embraced. Jarvis alleged that public sector unions were "trying hard to run the country" and pledged he was "not going to let them do it."[37]

The tax revolt was dangerous for labor in part because it threatened to drive a wedge between public and private sector union members. "There are individuals out there, and interestingly many are unionists in private industry, who believe that public sector bargaining, not inflation or the growth of government, has been the chief contributor to the high cost of government," one labor analyst observed. Private sector unionists who sympathized with government employees in the 1960s, were less inclined to do so in 1978. The government worker was perceived as "having caught up with, and in some cases surpassed his private industry cousins." Noting that union members were "taxpayers too," the *Wall Street Journal* happily predicted a coming "schism between private and public employee unionism." Labor mediator Benjamin Aaron was stunned by the sudden decline of support for public sector unions. "The term 'government employee' has now joined 'politician' and 'bureaucrat' in the lexicon of opprobrium of many members of the general public," he wrote.[38]

Government unions tried to deflect the criticism. Attacking "demagogic politicians" who scapegoated them and offered "simplistic solutions to complex problems," they pointed to studies that showed government workers trailed their private sector counterparts in winning wage increases to offset inflation. PATCO too worked to debunk the "Proposition 13 mentality," which saw air traffic controllers as "lazy, incompetent public servants who are biding their times in order to rip off the system," as one Boston activist put it. "We can no longer tolerate being branded by the public as civil servants supping at the public trough," agreed a West Coast controller. Leyden repeatedly addressed the issue. "We are not the overpaid, underworked, Proposition 13, federal employee that the normal person in this country, who looks at federal employees, thinks," he objected. "We are the most productive group of federal employees in this country." Yet the fact that the "normal person" now regarded federal workers as "overpaid and underworked" illustrated the difficulty of Leyden's task. The truth was that neither PATCO, nor the labor movement as a whole, could stop the unions-raise-taxes argument from tightening its grip on public consciousness in

1978. Too many Americans were feeling the pinch of inflation and the stagnation of their incomes.[39]

In this atmosphere, there was little chance for unionists to win expanded union rights from Congress. With labor's allies on Capitol Hill in retreat during the summer and early fall of 1978, the White House made sure that Title VII of the CSRA did not widen federal workers' bargaining rights. The final version of the act included significant reforms. It abolished the Civil Service Commission, dividing its former functions among new agencies, the Office of Personnel Management (to handle job classifications and other personnel policies) and the Merit Systems Protection Board (which provided a court of appeals for federal personnel cases). It also created the Federal Labor Relations Authority, and gave it the power to rule on bargaining impasses. But Title VII of the act gravely disappointed federal unionists. It did not allow collective bargaining on wages or benefits, gave no strike rights to federal workers, and disallowed agency shop contracts that would permit unions to collect a fee from non-members whom they were required to represent in contract negotiations and grievance procedures. Rep. William Clay pronounced Title VII "a rape in broad daylight," and delegates at the 1978 AFGE convention denounced Carter for his "blatant lies to federal workers." The protests failed to move the president. He signed the CSRA into law on October 13, 1978.[40]

Unfortunately for PATCO, the CSRA fight was not the last in its string of disappointments. Relations between Langhorne Bond and PATCO deteriorated radically in 1978 even as Congress debated the contents of the act. Bond had sympathized with PATCO's plight in the spring, when the air carriers refused to honor international FAM requests. However, after PATCO's slowdown, he got tough with the union in response to criticism from his legendary predecessor, former FAA Administrator E. R. Quesada, who excoriated PATCO for using the "tools of the Mafia," extortion and blackmail, to advance its demands. Bond had great respect for Quesada, and he concluded, "The son-of-a-bitch is right." Bond resolved not to let PATCO pressure the FAA again. This was welcome news for many local and regional FAA officials, who themselves had been anxious to take on the union.[41]

Bond's actions on three issues that arose in quick succession put PATCO on the defensive. The first came in August 1978, when the FAA released a report on the health of air traffic controllers, prepared by Dr. Robert M. Rose of Boston University. The report documented that controllers had higher than normal rates of hypertension and insomnia, felt deep dissatisfaction with their treatment by the FAA, and were more prone to drinking problems than people of similar demographics. Nevertheless, the FAA decided to stress the report's best features, arguing that it showed that controllers were "as healthy as men of similar ages in the general population, except for a higher than normal rate of hypertension." This decision infuriated PATCO activists, who saw it as a bid to undermine their demands for workplace reforms.[42]

A second blow was delivered on October 1, 1978, when the Second Career Program PATCO won after the 1970 sickout was terminated. The program, which PATCO won in 1972, had allowed controllers to retire early if they could demonstrate work-related medical disabilities. After only six years, the program became embroiled in controversy. Investigative journalists found evidence of fraud in the administration of the program in the Southeast region. There, dozens of controllers were granted early retirement on what appeared to be dubious medical grounds. These revelations led Congress to terminate its funding. PATCO asked Bond to defend the program, but he would not. Many controllers subsequently blamed Bond for its termination.[43]

The horrific accident that took place over San Diego on September 25, 1978, set the context for the third blow. The San Diego disaster shocked Bond and sharpened his opposition to the immunity program PATCO had won during the Ford administration. Bond had long believed that the system wrongly offered immunity for "gross mistakes" and thus protected "deficient pilots and controllers," and he pointed to a December 1976 study that found little evidence that the program improved safety. The San Diego accident galvanized Bond's determination to change the program. Pilot error was found to be the primary cause of the collision, yet after the accident Bond notified PATCO that the FAA would make unilateral changes in the immunity program, effectively removing protections from controllers. Leyden felt blindsided by the move.[44]

As 1978 came to a close, PATCO was reeling. A cascade of events had pummeled the union in the space of a year: a disappointing contract, a disastrous job action, legislative disappointment, and termination of the retirement and immunity programs. "The last few months would best be characterized as time to be deleted from our short history," Leyden remarked.[45]

THE FIFTH COLUMN, THE CHOIRBOYS, AND THE 1981 PLAN

But there was no delete button that could undo the events of 1978. Leyden had tried his best to wipe the slate clean after the FAM debacle. Like his political hero John F. Kennedy after the Bay of Pigs episode, he took full responsibility for the failure. "When you fuck up…the best thing you can do is go out and acknowledge that you made a mistake," he said. Knowing that he had "much fence-mending to do," Leyden rented a small plane and toured the country. He received a mixed reception. Bill Taylor of Tucson, who had emerged as an outspoken militant in his region, was grateful that Leyden "didn't bullshit us." But not everyone was so generous. Leyden met with Indianapolis controllers on June 27, and he described the meeting as "a shouting match." The Indianapolis crowd was representative of one segment of the union that had begun to doubt his leadership. "Had the cause been right, had the execution and communications been right, then the general membership would have come through," insisted members such as Jack Watson of Houston. Leyden's failure to pick a fight worth winning had led to the disaster, Watson insisted. Now it was time that "heads roll from the *top*."[46]

As criticism of his actions grew, Leyden at times lashed back at his foes, reminding them that the entire board had supported the FAM slowdown. He attributed the post-slowdown criticism to "political opportunists" who were "using this issue to further divide PATCO." It was time for the union's militants to wake up to reality, Leyden told one critic. "As long as some perceive that PATCO is the cure-all for whatever problem either an individual or a facility has, and turn to us expecting their wildest aspirations to become a reality, we will stay divided," he warned. He urged militants to remember that PATCO represented "a very diverse group with differing philosophical and psychological motivations—the extreme conservative on the one and the ultra-militant on the other." He explained that it was his "responsibility to coalesce these two forces and walk the middle and not be all things to all people and promise to deliver the aspirations of both forces." But the critics were no longer listening. For the first time, Leyden wondered whether he could hold the union together. "Too often I am the recipient of unreasonable demands that are not now attainable and never will be," he said.[47]

Whether Leyden could survive PATCO's string of disappointments became an open question in the fall of 1978 as a "Fifth Column" movement arose in the western states and spread through a series of informal regional meetings. Larry Courtroul and Jeff Whittaker, two outspoken Leyden critics, convened the first of these meetings in Denver after the FAM slow-down. Courtroul explained that the meetings would "get together some of the people in PATCO that are concerned for this organization," insisting that they were "in no way intended to undermine our elected officers." The Denver militants invited "PATCO notables" from around the country, such as Bill Taylor of Tucson and Bob Butterworth of Bay TRACON, but they pointedly excluded the union's national or regional officers. Free from the oversight of national officers, the meetings undertook a searching discussion of PATCO's situation. "Nothing was happening through the 'collective begging' process," Carl Kern of Chicago Center explained. "Sickouts weren't doing it, slowdowns weren't doing it. Changes were occurring, but they were so infinitesimally measurable that it wasn't worth the effort." Therefore the meetings began to consider "the ultimate job action," a strike. Once that subject arose, the meetings inevitably raised questions about the union's leaders, Butterworth recalled. "Did they have the cajones to do it? Were they going to be radical enough?"[48]

The Fifth Column meetings resonated especially well among the younger, Vietnam-era veterans in PATCO's ranks. By the late 1970s, they were beginning to redefine PATCO's culture in the FAA's facilities. Dozens of local PATCO newsletters with names like *Tower Power* sprang up in this period and became their mouthpieces. These sheets showed no patience for controllers who did not support a militant organization. The Phoenix local's newsletter excoriated the boss's pet who "dances like a puppy on a leash." A Seattle newsletter columnist condemned go-along, get-along controllers for "what they are doing to my family, my profession, and my facility."[49]

The Fifth Column movement found some sympathy on PATCO's national board from two recently elected regional vice presidents, Gary Eads of Kansas City Center and Dominic Torchia of Oakland Center. Both men were sons of labor—Eads's father had been a Teamster, Torchia's an electrical worker. Both had been touched by the seminal experiences of the 1960s. Torchia grew up in the San Francisco Bay area, and as a high school student he hung out at the University of California at Berkeley, where he witnessed the famous "Free Speech Movement" protests. Eads had been present at similarly important Sixties moment. As an Air Force controller on Guam, he dispatched the first B-52s for their bombing runs in "Operation Rolling

Thunder," the event that marked the sudden escalation of the Vietnam War. Both the idealism and the disillusions of the 1960s left their marks on these men. They believed passionately in PATCO, and neither had much trust in the government. Both grew critical of Leyden's leadership.[50]

They were not alone in their concern over PATCO's direction. George Brandon from the Southwest regional vice president voiced concerns after the FAM debacle. Most importantly, the union's founders, Mike Rock and Jack Maher, never condemned the Fifth Column movement. Rock, for one, applauded its willingness to talk about striking. "We have abused the slow-down method," he argued. "If we're going to go, let's call it a strike and go out. Shut the entire country down." This would be the only way to win "a substantial amount of money and benefits," he contended. "Not what you can negotiate under the present law, but money and benefits such as a shorter workday or workweek."[51]

Leyden understood the frustrations of the Fifth Columnists. Federal collective bargaining policy left "little room for movement in areas most important to the controller workforce, specifically wages and hours of employment," he admitted. He agreed that until PATCO could negotiate such issues it would "continue to be placed in an almost untenable position." Where Leyden parted from his critics was in his assessment of the member-ship's willingness and ability to break out of the confines of federal sector collective bargaining through a strike. Leyden doubted that enough PATCO members would risk their jobs to force the government to change the bargaining rules for air traffic controllers. Even if members could be induced to support an all-out strike, he doubted they could win. The government could not be forced by a job action into making such a significant conces-sion, he believed.[52]

By the time the PATCO executive board met in Chicago on September 5, 1978, it was clear that Leyden's argument was losing ground. When he asked the board to join him in condemning the Fifth Column meetings, he was rebuffed. Torchia and Eads argued that the meetings provided a needed forum for activists; other board members agreed. When it became clear that Leyden could not unite the board against the Fifth Column movement, he backed off. This marked a turning point for PATCO: the militants were beginning to affect the union's policy.[53]

Lacking the strength to oppose the militants outright, Leyden looked for ways to co-opt them. The task did not require a major shift. He had always been careful in his discussion of the feasibility of a strike: while he privately believed that an all-out strike could be disastrous, he would "never say never," since keeping the possibility of a strike alive simultaneously gave the union some leverage with the FAA and mollified the union's militant members. In the fall of 1978, Leyden simply adjusted his rhetoric and expressed a willingness to talk about strike planning. Doing so made sense to him not only because of union politics, but also because relations with the FAA were deteriorating and the possibility that the union could win anything significant in its 1981 negotiations without a threatened job action was fast evaporating. "I'm just not going to put the organization or the people at risk any longer with a slowdown when the consequences are going to almost be the same as if you go for a direct strike," Leyden explained.[54]

This line of thinking led Leyden to authorize Maher, Rock, and Vice President Robert Poli to begin exploring a strike plan for 1981. At Leyden's request, Maher reached out to dissidents like Jack Seddon, inviting them to join him in creating the 1981 plan—a plan Leyden hoped he would never have to use, but which he now felt was necessary to construct.[55]

Maher identified key activists from each region and invited them to a meeting at the O'Hare Inn in Chicago to begin working out details of the plan. At that first meeting, Maher coined a name for the committee that would plan the "future S _ _ _ _ E," as one memo termed it. He called his strike coordinators, "The Choirboys." That name was meant to convey a sense of harmony around the message they would convey, "everybody singing the same song." But Maher also associated the name with Joseph Wambaugh's 1975 novel *Choirboys*, which was made into a popular 1977 movie. Wambaugh's story concerned a tight-knit group of rowdy Los Angeles cops and their shady, extralegal, after-hour pursuits, which they ironically called "choir practice." Since PATCO's Choirboys would be engaging in their own extralegal activities—planning an illegal strike against the government—Maher thought the name fit. The others agreed. Soon Maher's coordinators were known throughout the union as the Choirboys. But, as soon as the name stuck, Maher had second thoughts about it. At the end of the novel, he remembered, Wambaugh's characters "basically destroy themselves." By then it was too late to pull the name back, so Maher kept the thought to himself.[56]

By the spring of 1979, the Choirboys began fleshing out their strike plan. They were especially influenced by a fifty-six-day teachers' strike that erupted in St. Louis in mid-January 1979, closing 140 schools. Like federal workers, the St. Louis teachers had no right to strike or bargain collectively with their school board. Nonetheless, they hung together, withstood court orders and a firing threat, and won raises of over $1,000. The key to their victory was their ability to stay united: only 11 percent of teachers crossed picket lines when the board attempted to reopen the schools. School officials simply could not replace their entire teaching force, so after weeks of threats, they decided to settle. Applying this principle to the FAA, Maher's strategists worked out a formula that they believed could achieve similar results. If they could get 80 percent of controllers to strike, Maher and the Choirboys believed, they could effectively shut down the nation's air system. As happened in St. Louis, the government might threaten to dismiss them, but when it became clear that air travel could not work without them, the government would have to come to the bargaining table. At that point, PATCO and the FAA would bargain like any employer and union in the private sector, federal prohibitions notwithstanding.[57]

No federal sector union except PATCO could have dreamed of executing such a plan. None could ever hope to pull 80 percent of an agency's workforce out on a strike. Nor would a strike by any other group of federal workers have such an immediate impact on the nation as a walkout of air traffic controllers. PATCO was in a unique position. If it could simply get 93 percent of its own members to strike, that would account for 80 percent of all air traffic controllers. Hitting that figure was possible, the Choirboys believed, if PATCO framed contract demands attractive enough to get members to risk their jobs for them, and if the union's leaders gave the rank-and-file a strike plan that inspired confidence.[58]

Mike Rock outlined the thinking to a group of facility representatives in January 1979. "The key to the program is it will be for money, a substantial amount of money," he explained. "If the membership authorizes the national to call a strike, we go into negotiations in 1981 with money as part of our package, and other things, shorter workweek, health benefits, the whole nine yards." It would not be an easy struggle, Rock warned. PATCO members could "expect the injunctions once again, the threats of going to jail, the fines, the dismissals, the suspensions, and everything else that goes along with a nice strike." But, if the Choirboys did their work well and the membership maintained solidarity, Rock believed, the plan could work.[59]

Although he continued to doubt the wisdom of an all-out strike against the federal government, Leyden approved the plan. He had always argued on principle that controllers should have a right to strike; it was the prospect of an *actual* strike that worried him. He was relieved, however, that 80 percent of controllers would have to agree to strike before the Choirboys' plan could be actuated. Privately, Leyden doubted that the Choirboys could ever persuade the requisite share of the union's "multiphilosophical" membership to support an illegal strike. Still, Leyden believed that by working toward this goal the Choirboys would strengthen his hand going in to the 1981 negotiations and make it possible for him to win a much better contract. As Leyden explained to his colleagues, "the threat is often the more important weapon than the act itself." Leyden immediately brandished the threat, telling *Aviation Daily* in May 1979 that if the FAA continued to ignore controllers' demands, "the basic principle that 'no contract, no work' may be coming for us in 1981."[60]

Once the strike plan was hashed out in the spring of 1979, Maher began expanding the Choirboy network. By the summer, he had recruited sixty Choirboys. Crucially, it was agreed that Choirboys should not be elected union officials. The motivation behind that was twofold. First, union officers would be the likely targets of arrest during an illegal strike. The Choirboys' identity would not be publicized, so they could keep a walkout going even if the union's elected leaders were jailed. At the same time, because national union leaders chose them, Choirboys could remain loyal to the national plan and would not need to worry about representing the membership in their facilities. Their job was to learn the plan, educate members about it, and build support for it. Many of the Choirboys had participated in the Fifth Column meetings. Most had no previous experience in elected union leadership. They were chosen on the basis of their organizing skills and leadership qualities. Most were young. Some were women, like Nancy Sittig from the Tamiami, Florida, tower, who referred to herself as a "Choirperson." They hailed from diverse backgrounds, but shared a single belief: the union could win if it organized well. As the program gathered momentum, Leyden asked Vice President Bob Poli to take over its administration.[61]

In preparing members for a strike, the Choirboys had their work cut out for them, according to a series of internal union polls carried out by labor educator Art Shostak in 1979. Shostak found that 90 percent of PATCO's membership had never participated in a strike before. Only 40 percent indicated that they would be willing to strike to win their most cherished demands, and only 53 percent said they would honor a picket line if a majority of their colleagues struck. Many who opposed striking cited the oath that they signed when they became federal employees: "I am not participating in any strike against the Government of the United States or any agency thereof, and I will not so participate while an employee of the Government of the United States or any agency thereof."[62]

Choirboys worked hard to change these numbers. They devoted their off days and took unpaid leave to travel through their regions educating members about the plan. A meeting organized by Fort Worth Center Choirboy Lee Grant on November 15, 1979, was representative of such sessions. Grant invited Poli to address an audience of seventy-five controllers. In his remarks Poli explained why the union needed to be ready to strike. "In the past slowdowns and sickouts was the only tool we had to show displeasure," Poli noted. But these tools had "caused division...among the controllers." PATCO's past failures had led the union's leaders to rethink their strategy, Poli explained. Only the strike weapon could change the equation. Other public workers had used strikes to great effect, Poli pointed out, even when they were illegal. "Our studies show that the only ILLEGAL strike is an unsuccessful one," he said. The audience warmly applauded.[63]

As Poli had done in Fort Worth, the Choirboys repeatedly pointed to the example set by other government workers in the late 1970s. That example was powerful. The strike rate jumped among state and local government workers by 18 percent in 1978. In 1979, a record 545 strikes disrupted the public sector, with teachers leading the way. During the 1979–1980 school year, there were some 242 teachers' strikes. The example of unionized teachers was especially encouraging to controllers. If college-educated professional teachers could strike and win, why not air traffic controllers? On September 6, 1979, Poli sent each Choirboy a copy of the American Federation of Teachers' *Strike Preparedness Booklet* and urged them to quote it in meetings "to demonstrate that this group of *professionals* (like any other) must, at times, resort to the ultimate weapon."[64]

To supplement the Choirboys' organizing, PATCO set up a two-week training program for Choirboys and local activists at the AFL-CIO's George Meany Labor Studies Center in Silver Spring, Maryland. Maher and PATCO veteran Bud Long served as instructors in the program. Rock taught PATCO history to each group of activists that attended. The curriculum immersed controllers in American labor history, labor law, and the history of strikes. Trainees watched a film about striking coal miners in Harlan County, Kentucky, and read a book about the Industrial Workers of the World, the radical union movement of the early twentieth century that had advocated a "general strike" of all workers. By the end of 1979, some three hundred activists had gone through the program.[65]

By the fall of 1979, the Choirboys were achieving discernable results. Local PATCO newsletters began circulating the arguments in favor of a strike. "Well brothers and sisters, how long are you going to take it on the chin before you fight back? Carter and company have been spear-heading a drive to strip away your benefits and, at times, your dignity," read one column. "STRIKE IS NOT A DIRTY WORD," read another. "Give us a chance, okay guys?" wrote a Seattle Center correspondent. "Let us tell you we have grown up, and are ready to go for all the marbles." A Great Lakes region newsletter reminded readers, "Politicians will react only to one concept—CLOUT." The arguments helped. By the end of 1979, PATCO raised the share of those who said they would respect a picket line of their coworkers to 69 percent. Younger controllers led the way. Some 90 percent of those under thirty indicated a willingness to strike. The union still had a long way to go to meet its goal. Strike support lagged in the South. But the Choirboys were making progress. "Holy Mackerel," Rock thought. "This thing is working." Board member David Siegel, from the union's southern region, concluded that once the Choirboy program got going PATCO leaders could not have shut it down even if they tried. It was channeling the stifled aspirations and pent-up grievances of too many controllers.[66]

PILOT ERROR

Some have said that our demands are unrealistic—pie in the
sky pipe dreams! I don't believe that and neither should you.
—ROBERT POLI

I pledge to you that my administration will work very closely
with you to bring about a spirit of cooperation between the
President and the air traffic controllers.
—RONALD REAGAN

John Leyden should not have been surprised when his vice president, Bob
Poli, walked into his office on January 2, 1980, to make an abrupt announcement a few days before Leyden and Poli were to meet the PATCO board in
Chicago. Poli explained that he planned to challenge Leyden for the union's
presidency at PATCO's convention in Las Vegas in April. That Leyden did
not anticipate this moment was a measure of how little affinity he had for the
militant spirit animating the Choirboy program that Poli was overseeing,
for, in many ways, Poli's announcement was a natural outgrowth of the
program. Feeling betrayed, Leyden picked up the gauntlet. "Let's have at it!"
he said. Yet soon after Poli left his office, Leyden realized how tough a battle
it would be. Leyden discovered that Poli had secretly organized a majority of
the PATCO board to back his candidacy.[1]

Poli's challenge had been in the making for months. As strike planning gathered momentum in the autumn of 1979, Poli outlined plans to put one Choirboy in each facility by the end of 1980. The Choirboys had become Poli's network within the union. Most of them proved more loyal to him than Leyden, thinking that PATCO's longtime president "would never turn the card" in 1981, no matter how well they organized or how inadequate the FAA's contract offer. Bill Taylor of Phoenix was among those who questioned Leyden's militancy. "Who speaks for our outrage?" he asked. "Where is the militancy that this organization was founded upon?" Others claimed Leyden was "building a tenured union bureaucracy for PATCO" rather than preparing to fight the FAA. Such sentiments were so widely shared at the union's 1979 convention that a near majority sought to strip Leyden of the power to appoint the national negotiating committee for 1981.[2]

Leyden took the criticism in stride. "Unfortunately, politics is a very real part of any organization," he said. He called his critics "extreme militants" who would "not hesitate to use gelignite on a tower." He also lectured them about the burdens of leadership. "I do not have the luxury of making an incorrect judgment and after calling for an open job action or strike, having to pick up the pieces, if the battle turns into another Dunkirk," he scolded. Leyden remained confident that he was in touch with the thinking of the average air traffic controller, who was more interested in security and incremental improvements than in risking everything to achieve a wholesale breakout from the rules of federal-sector bargaining. Indeed, for all the criticism he had taken over the previous two years, Leyden remained popular among a majority of members. Yet, as he belatedly realized on January 2, he had lost the support of the Choirboy network.[3]

The key defector was likely Mike Rock. "Mike Strike" strongly supported the Choirboys. Rock doubted Leyden's commitment to the 1981 plan and resented Leyden for not giving him a bigger role in the union. Rock talked with Poli about challenging Leyden, and he secretly helped test the waters for Poli. Poli then quietly won over a majority of the seven-person board one by one. George Brandon of the Southwest region, Dave Siegel of the South, and Gary Eads from the Midwest were the first to back him. The deciding vote, Bob Meyer of the Great Lakes region, was harder to pick up. Meyer agonized for days before supporting Poli. Once he did, Jack Maher also came over. It was a painful decision for Maher. While he liked and respected

Leyden, Maher concluded that his friend was not fully committed to the Choirboy program.[4]

All of this happened unbeknown to Leyden. Perhaps to salve his wounded pride, he later attributed Poli's act to a rift between the men stemming from a romantic affair Poli conducted with a secretary. Leyden disapproved of that affair: his wife and Poli's wife were friends. That episode, which generated considerable gossip in the union, did harm the relationship between Poli and Leyden, but it was not responsible for Poli's challenge. That challenge would not have happened without the differences that developed between PATCO's top two leaders over the preparations for 1981—differences that also widened a breach between Leyden and former backers like Maher. When he learned Maher had decided to back Poli, Leyden called it "the biggest disappointment" in his life.[5]

As Leyden arrived in Chicago for the January 7 PATCO board meeting, he believed he could still defeat Poli at the union's convention in April, no matter where the board stood. He still had a strong base nationally, if not among the Choirboys. And he still had a mind to fight when he entered the conference room at the O'Hare Airport Hilton and came face to face with Poli, Poli's four backers on the board, two undecided board members— Dominic Torchia and Charlie Campbell—and Leyden's lone supporter, George Kerr, from New York Center. In the hotel's corridors and lobby, hundreds of controllers who had flown in after hearing rumors of a leadership fight milled about, adding to the drama.[6]

The meeting quickly degenerated into a fusillade of mutual recriminations as the buried grievances of a long partnership gone awry erupted. After hours of argument, it became clear that Poli and Leyden would be unable to work together in the months before the election. Poli announced that he was resigning the vice presidency to campaign from the outside. He scrawled a resignation letter effective immediately and walked out. By then, Leyden, too, decided he had had enough. His rejection by the majority of the board hurt, all the more because it followed three punishing years in the union's presidency. He did not relish the prospect of leading a divided union into 1981. On the spot, he decided that Bob Meyer would be the best candidate to unify the organization. So after leading PATCO for ten tumultuous years, Leyden wrote his own brief resignation letter, effective February 1. Then he rose and left the meeting, hoping that Meyer would be elected interim president.[7]

PATCO's board members were stunned. "What the fuck do we do now?" Torchia asked. A vigorous discussion ensued, but it did not lead to Meyer's elevation, as Leyden had hoped. Instead, Poli's backers argued that the board should reject his resignation and accept Leyden's so that, on February 1, Poli would become the union's president. Kerr objected. He was convinced that his colleagues wanted to install Poli at any cost to "show the world that they were big union guys who knew how to take on Uncle [Sam]." When they grasped what the majority intended, Kerr and PATCO counsel Bill Peer went to Leyden's room to ask him to withdraw his resignation. Leyden refused. "I'm going home," he said. Thus, at 7 a.m., after an all-night meeting, the board voted 6–1, with Kerr dissenting, to accept Leyden's resignation and reject Poli's.[8]

Leyden left PATCO on February 1, 1980, and was eventually recruited to serve as executive director of the AFL-CIO's Public Employees Department. Poli ascended to the union's presidency. The board voted Bob Meyer in as interim vice president. In its first act, the new leadership team expanded the Choirboy network.[9]

As word of what transpired in Chicago spread through PATCO, it inspired mixed reactions. Ardent supporters of the 1981 program expressed relief. "Leyden wasn't aggressive enough," observed one Choirboy. Yet Leyden's many supporters, who had no inkling that a fight was brewing, were confused. "We really couldn't figure out what was going on," recalled one. The news alarmed those who had the most qualms about the Choirboy program. They likened Poli's ascension to a coup d'état and alleged that the board "took away our rights as PATCO members to decide who shall be the President of PATCO." Leyden's farewell letter scarcely poured oil on the troubled waters. "I do not believe Mr. Poli is competent to lead PATCO or that he possesses any characteristic, personal or professional, which is needed to head the Organization," he wrote.[10]

Anthony Skirlick Jr., who edited the PATCO newsletter at Los Angeles Center, was typical of those angered by Poli's sudden ascension. He blamed "Godfather Rock" and the "sword wavers" who were determined to strike in 1981. PATCO "cannot expect to change the world by not allowing airplanes to fly," Skirlick warned. "The moderates among us know what the FAA has in store for us this time." Skirlick feared that PATCO's moderates no longer had a voice in the union's leadership. "If this Union becomes so monolithic that the meekest among us are not allowed to object to the lions among us," he

Jack Maher, ca. 1960, when he worked in Hangar 11 at New York International (Idlewild) Airport. (Courtesy of Ursula Bethmann.)

Mike Rock, in 1958, the year he was hired as an air traffic controller and assigned to Hangar 11. (Courtesy of Joan Rock.)

New York air traffic controllers huddle over a radar screen with flight strips in the background and "shrimp boats" on their screen, March 1960. (Photo by Joseph Scherschel; permission of Time Life Pictures/Getty Images.)

The wreckage of United Flight 826 at 7th Avenue and Sterling Place, Park Slope, Brooklyn, December 16, 1960, after it collided with TWA Flight 266 over Staten Island. The disaster, which took 134 lives, triggered controllers' efforts to organize. (Photo by Hal Mathewson; permission of *N.Y. Daily News* Archive via Getty Images.)

The FAA's faulty equipment was lampooned in this editorial cartoon for the *Journal of Air Traffic Control* just months before the fatal New York midair collision in 1960. (Courtesy of the *Journal of Air Traffic Control*.)

Both the domestic ideal of the breadwinning air traffic controller and the stress of the job are depicted in this editorial cartoon by a Fort Worth, Texas, controller, 1960. (Courtesy of the *Journal of Air Traffic Control*.)

A bas-relief by artist Margaret Grigor for the Air Traffic Control Association's Award of Merit depicts the manly ideal of "controlmanship," 1961. (Courtesy of the *Journal of Air Traffic Control*.)

Famed criminal lawyer and skilled pilot F. Lee Bailey relaxes at home in 1967, months before Mike Rock asked him to help organize the nation's air traffic controllers. (Photo by Robert Peterson; permission of Time Life Pictures/ Getty Images.)

LIFE STACK-UP
Danger and confusion
of the air traffic jam

AUGUST 9 · 1968 · 35¢

The August 9, 1968,
issue of *Life* depicts the
results of "Operation Air
Safety," an unprecedented
national air traffic slowdown
that marked PATCO's arrival.
(Photo by Bob Gomel;
permission of Getty Images.)

Mike Rock (left) and Jack Maher (right) make PATCO's case in a meeting with Senator
Peter H. Dominick (R-Colo.), 1969. (Courtesy of Ursula Bethmann.)

PATCO's patron, President Jesse Calhoon (right) of the Marine Engineers' Beneficial Association, with President Richard M. Nixon, during the period when Calhoon engineered the rehiring of controllers fired for their participation in the organization's 1970 sickout. (PATCO Collection, Southern Labor Archives, Georgia State University.)

John Leyden, who served as president of PATCO from 1970 to 1980, and built it into one of the most successful—and militant—unions in the federal service. (Courtesy of John Leyden.)

Leyden endorsed President Nixon's reelection in 1972, giving the union crucial political leverage in its effort to gain official recognition in its own election that year. (Courtesy of John Leyden.)

PATCO's national leaders celebrate its election as the exclusive representative of the nation's air traffic controllers, September 20, 1972. From left to right, Robert Sturgill, John Leyden, Mike Rock, John Lapine, Robert Poli, and Stanley Gordon. All but Poli, the recently elected vice president of the union, were veterans of Hangar 11. (Courtesy of Joan Rock.)

PATCO's first negotiating committee. Seated (left to right): PATCO's counsel William B. Peer, John Leyden, Robert Poli, and Leyden's secretary, Carol Padgett. Standing behind Poli is Mike Rock and to Rock's left is Charlie Campbell. (Courtesy of Joan Rock.)

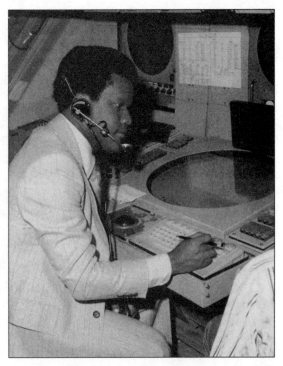

Rick Jones, cofounder of the Coalition of Black Controllers, at work in the Washington Air Route Traffic Control Center in Leesburg, Virginia. (Courtesy of Rick Jones.)

Sue Mostert (seated) and Jacque Smith in January 1979, with the logo of the Professional Women Controllers shortly after they founded that organization in an effort to give women controllers a voice. (Courtesy of Sue Mostert Townsend.)

Over the course of the 1970s, new computer-based technologies began to transform the work of air traffic controllers. Here controllers work on updated equipment, ca. 1977. (Courtesy of the Federal Aviation Administration.)

In preparation for the union's expected contract battle in 1981, PATCO's activists—the Choirboys—circulated buttons like these (including one celebrating the "Horses" who led the union's 1970 sickout). (Author's collection.)

PATCO executive board following Robert Poli's ascension, 1980. Seated (left to right), Vice President Robert Meyer, Poli, and David Siegel (Southern region); standing, John Palino (Great Lakes), Domenic Torchia (West), Charlie Campbell (Pacific), Gary Eads (Central), George Brandon (Southwest), and George Kerr (East), who was John Leyden's only supporter among this group. (Courtesy of Domenic Torchia.)

Reagan's men, Federal Aviation Administrator J. Lynn Helms (left) and Secretary of Transportation Drew Lewis, in 1981. Helms prepared his agency to break a controllers' strike while Lewis hoped to avert one at the bargaining table. (Photo by J. Scott Applewhite; permission of the AP Photo Archive.)

Attorney General William French Smith (left) and Drew Lewis flank President Reagan during a press conference in the White House Rose Garden on August 3, 1981, at which the president laid down his 48-hour ultimatum. (Photo by Jeff Taylor; permission of the AP Photo Archive.)

New York controllers and their families at Eisenhower Park on Long Island on August 5, 1981, the morning they were to be fired. They are holding the same "Don't Tread on Me" flag that was carried by sickout strikers in 1970. (Photo by Yvonne Hemsey; permission of Getty Images.)

PATCO board member Domenic Torchia, shown picketing in August 1981, typified the younger generation of controllers who had been influenced by the cultural and political upheavals of the 1960s. (Courtesy of Domenic Torchia.)

Military air traffic controllers deployed to the control tower of Chicago's O'Hare International Airport in the first days of the strike. (Photo by Lee Balgemann; permission of the AP Photo Archive.)

AFL-CIO President Lane Kirkland (left) and PATCO's Robert Poli at the 1981 Labor Day Parade in New York City, September 8, 1981. While they appeared friendly in public, their relationship was distant before the strike and strained after it. (Photo by Carlos Rene Perez; permission of AP Photo Archive.)

Comparing striking air traffic controllers to Poland's heroic Solidarnos̀c̀ (Solidarity) movement, workers rally in support of PATCO, Houston's Hobby Airport, August 1981. (PATCO Collection, Southern Labor Archives, Georgia State University; permission of photographer Scott Van Osdol.)

The PATCO strike legitimized strikebreaking in the private sector, a development that contributed to the near disappearance of strikes from U.S. labor relations over the subsequent thirty years. This 1997 cartoon by Ted Rall indicates how futile strikes seemed to most American workers by the end of the twentieth century. (Permission of Universal Uclick.)

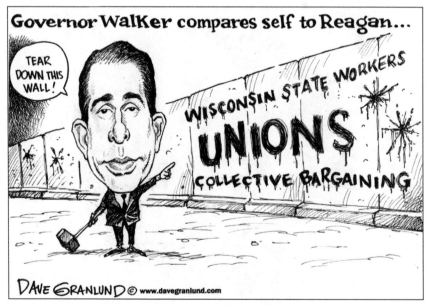

Almost 30 years after the PATCO strike, in February 2011, Gov. Scott Walker invoked Reagan's confrontation with PATCO in passing a law to strip Wisconsin public workers of their bargaining rights. (Permission of cartoonist Dave Granlund and Cagle Cartoons, Inc.)

In 1996, Jack Maher (left) launched a new organization called PATCO Local 6881. Here Maher is pictured with two former strikers who joined the new group, the original PATCO's first president, Jimmy Hays (center), and Ron Taylor, who succeed Maher in leading the reborn PATCO. (Courtesy of Ron Taylor.)

This button worn by fired air traffic controllers signified their determination to stick together. Thirty years later its words speak to the enduring impact of their failed 1981 walkout on American labor relations. (Author's collection.)

concluded, "then this Union is not worth a tinker." When the local president at Los Angeles Center refused to distribute his editorial criticizing Poli's ascension, Skirlick resigned from his editorial post.[11]

Before he could focus on the 1981 program, Bob Poli first needed to beat back a challenge to his presidency that was supported by PATCO's moderates. George Kerr, the Eastern region representative on PATCO's board and Leyden's sole supporter at the Chicago meeting, announced that he would challenge Poli at the union's April 1980 Las Vegas convention. Kerr was a formidable challenger. He had grown up in Bridgeport, Connecticut, the son of a union machinist. He joined the FAA in 1961, actively participated in the job actions of 1968–1970, and won his first local union office in 1971 before rising to PATCO's executive board in 1978. Kerr had his differences with Leyden in the past—he had opposed the 1978 FAM slowdown, for example—but he was offended by the way Poli had organized secretly against Leyden. "It wasn't aboveboard," he said. Kerr recruited Tom Galloway, a PATCO stalwart at Washington Center, as his running mate.[12]

Kerr waged a tough campaign, alleging that Poli engaged in financial improprieties as he worked to undermine Leyden. He demanded that Poli open PATCO's books and phone records, in an effort to uncover the "dark particulars" of the "conspiracy." Poli refused. Kerr cited this as evidence of Poli's malfeasance. Poli, in turn, charged Kerr's supporters with suppressing his campaign literature in the Eastern region and dispensed Mike Rock to campaign for him in the region, where Rock's influence was still strong.[13]

For several reasons, the outcome of the election was never truly in doubt. Foremost was the desire of most voting delegates to avoid further divisions a year away from the expiration of the PATCO-FAA contract. Facing the 1981 negotiations as a divided union would invite disaster, these delegates thought. "We still want to believe in 1981," as one put it. The desire to achieve unity worked to Poli's advantage. Kerr and Galloway took pains to avoid being seen as spoilers of the 1981 program, although both had their doubts about it. Thus, while they attacked Poli for malfeasance, they never criticized the Choirboy program. They reasoned that doing so would backfire on them and weaken the union going into 1981, no matter which side won the election. That position was understandable, but it left them unable to tap the latent doubts of moderate members who worried about the growing strike talk. By forfeiting such an appeal, Kerr, in effect, allowed the central issue to become which candidate was best positioned to unify the union around the

1981 program. Since he already enjoyed the support of six of seven board members, Poli had the strongest claim to that mantle. The fierce desire for unity furthered Poli's cause. As one former Leyden supporter who was "appalled" by the way Poli came to power put it, "We all know that we need PATCO, and we want a strong president."[14]

When the vote was taken at Caesars Palace on April 21, 1980, Poli won a decisive victory, outpolling Kerr by 64–36 percent. In a gesture of unity, Kerr then moved that Poli's election be made unanimous. Poli's supporters were elated, believing that they now had "the planning, potential, and most important of all, the national leadership to make 1981 a success." They never looked beyond the aggregate results to notice a disturbing omen: Kerr won six of the biggest facilities in the nation, the air route traffic control centers at New York, Boston, Washington, Miami, Dallas-Fort Worth, and Chicago, meaning that Poli had not yet earned the trust of controllers in strategically crucial facilities whose cooperation would be indispensable to the success of any walkout.[15]

Confirmed to the PATCO presidency, Robert Edmond Poli bore some similarities to his predecessor. Like Leyden, he was reared in a union culture. He was born in Pittsburgh on February 27, 1937, just days before the Steel Workers Organizing Committee won its breakthrough contract with U.S. Steel, marking the ascension of industrial unionism. He grew up within sight of the massive steel mills of Braddock and Homestead, in one of the nation's strongest union towns. His career resembled Leyden's as well. After graduating from high school, he joined the Air Force, was trained as an air traffic controller, and rose to the rank of staff sergeant. Following his discharge, he was hired by the FAA, worked at facilities in Pittsburgh and Cleveland, got involved in PATCO early, and rose quickly to its vice presidency.[16]

There Poli's similarities with Leyden ended. The differences in appearance were most obvious. Leyden was a man of average build; Poli was a larger man, with prematurely gray hair, glasses, and (by 1981) a beard. Differences in style were also apparent. Whereas Leyden considered himself independent, took pride in being a pragmatist about PATCO's capabilities, and did not shrink from jousting with his critics, Poli was more adept at and devoted to building consensus. While Leyden saw his ability to withstand baseless criticism as one of his chief assets, Poli sought to deflect disapproval and charm potential critics. He inspired and demanded a higher degree of loyalty in those close to him than Leyden had sought. Loyalty was a key determinant in

Poli's choice of Richard Leighton to replace Bill Peer as PATCO's counsel. Leighton was not prominent in the Washington labor bar, and was less experienced in labor law than Peer, but he offered one crucial asset: loyalty to Poli. The circumstances under which Poli became president reinforced his natural tendency to cultivate loyalty. His relationships with the Choirboys and the PATCO board members who had stood with him against Leyden were crucial to his ascension. Poli did not forget that.[17]

Outside of PATCO's ranks, opinions regarding Poli's sudden rise were generally unfavorable. Jesse Calhoon, who had paid scant attention to PATCO's internal affairs in the late 1970s, was troubled by the sudden switch, which caught him by surprise, and J. J. O'Donnell of ALPA, who had repeatedly beaten back challenges from dissidents in his own union, sympathized with his ousted friend and regarded Poli as an interloper and a "con artist." But it was among FAA officials that Poli's elevation raised the most concern. Langhorne Bond regarded the "January 1980 revolution" as evidence of "the hardcore taking over PATCO." He was convinced that Poli's rise meant PATCO would try to "bring America to its knees" in 1981.[18]

Everywhere Bond looked in the spring of 1980, he saw reason for concern. Atlanta Center controllers began refusing call-in overtime assignments in order to pressure their facility to schedule overtime in advance. Acting as "responsible and patriotic Americans," New York controllers threatened not to handle aircraft from the Soviet Union or Iran, citing as their reasons the Soviet invasion of Afghanistan and the U.S. hostages being held by Iranian revolutionaries. In Miami, the FAA concluded that controller Ron Palmer directed a Braniff International Airways jet into a thunderstorm in retaliation for the airline's refusal to honor controllers' FAM flight requests. According to an FAA tape, after giving the pilot a heading that would ensure a bumpy ride, Palmer said, "I want you to, ah, make sure ya get this information back to your Vice President... ya know what I mean?" Palmer was ultimately reinstated when an arbitrator concluded that the meaning of his statement was ambiguous. But all of this added up to one thing in Bond's mind: the militants had taken over PATCO, and a 1981 strike was now a probability.[19]

THE FAA PREPARES

Bond had in fact begun preparing for a PATCO strike in the fall of 1978. At that point, he filed a complaint against PATCO before the Federal Labor

Relations Authority, alleging that PATCO's "benefits fund" was in reality a strike fund. The FLRA ruled against Bond, finding that the benefits fund by itself did not prove that PATCO was bent on an illegal strike. Convinced that PATCO was preparing a 1981 walkout, Bond pressed on. He opted for what the National Public Employer Labor Relations Association called the "prophylactic approach," the theory that the best way to avert a strike was to prepare so well and so openly for one that a union would lose its nerve. "Once public employees realize that management is prepared for a strike and can deliver a satisfactory level of service to the citizenry during a strike the strike technique may be obviated," one strike preparation manual of the time explained. In the fall of 1978, Bond pushed his team to draft a detailed strike contingency plan that could ensure a "satisfactory level of service." The FAA flew front-line supervisors from several key facilities to Washington to help devise that plan under the guidance of two veteran administrators, Vince Malone and Jack Ryan. The plan anticipated significant losses of personnel in the large air route traffic centers, and redistributed most en route control duties to the TRACONs in what planners called a "tower to tower" system. On the theory that the contingency plan itself could have a deterrent effect, Bond had sent Leyden a copy of it in May 1979.[20]

Poli's ascension convinced Bond that he had better step up his preparations for 1981. He decided to replace air traffic director Dick Failor, whom he saw as insufficiently hard-nosed, with Failor's deputy, Ray Van Vuren, a Korean War veteran who had joined the FAA in 1955. Van Vuren was well prepared for the job. He had been promoted to crew chief at O'Hare in 1961, and moved steadily up the ladder since then, serving a stint as director of air traffic for the Eastern region in New York in the mid-1970s, where he dealt with some of PATCO's most militant facilities. Bond believed Van Vuren was a fighter who could "rally the troops with strong words."[21]

Under Van Vuren's leadership, FAA strike planning accelerated. In 1980, there were roughly seven hundred sectors across the airspace governed by the FAA. Van Vuren's plan called for trimming these sectors by 30 percent, consolidating them wherever possible. His planners looked closely at the traffic loads and configurations in each sector, modifying flows and transferring space and altitude from one facility to another to reduce potential bottlenecks where the absence of controllers might have the greatest impact. His plan also perfected the "flow control" principle the FAA used in past PATCO job actions, whereby planes were held on the ground until their passage to their destinations could be guaranteed without threat of "stacking" over destination airports. Fewer planes in the air at any given time meant controllers would not need to separate aircraft by altitude as much as usual, thus reducing stress on the system.[22]

Van Vuren's plan was modeled on the presumption that roughly half of the controllers might participate in a walkout. Bond and Van Vuren believed that if they could keep two thirds of flights in the air for a month during a walkout of that magnitude, they could break it, forcing the controllers to abandon their demands and return to work. The plan relied heavily on supervisory personnel stepping in to take the place of strikers. There were roughly twenty-five hundred supervisors in the nation's air traffic control facilities, spread across roughly twenty-one centers and nearly five hundred towers. They had all begun as controllers, and with retraining they could be ready to plug in and direct traffic again. Van Vuren found that, as a rule, supervisors were highly motivated to help out because "They'd had it up to their chins with the union." Another three thousand people worked as flight service personnel, who could not control air traffic but could help in other ways. Van Vuren reached out to the airlines to include them in the planning, conferring with ATA president Paul Ignatius. By October 1980, Bond distributed Van Vuren's revised plan, confident that it could break any walkout PATCO organized.[23]

Meanwhile, Bond tried to "talk the strike to death." After Poli's ascension Bond began warning about a coming strike. The more he talked about it, the less chance the union would try it, he reasoned. He presented a copy of PATCO's strike plan in testimony before a congressional committee; he spoke about it on television news programs. He raised the alarm everywhere he went. His warnings got the attention of other federal agencies. When he approached the Justice Department for help in 1980, U.S. attorneys pitched in, issuing statements warning that a strike against the U.S. government was illegal and punishable by fines and jail terms. Such help made Bond optimistic that he could thwart PATCO. Moreover, he believed that the times favored him. He thought that the public tolerance for government workers' strikes was fast evaporating, and if controllers did strike, he was sure they "were not going to be viewed as poor, put-upon, abused people."[24]

Yet Bond's public campaign did not achieve the deterrent effect he anticipated. Rather, it seems it exacerbated the situation. Poli condemned Bond's "provocative adversarial tactics," and the Choirboys pointed to Bond's contingency plan and apparent belligerence as clear evidence that the FAA wanted to weaken PATCO going into the 1981 negotiations. The only way to strengthen the union's hand, PATCO leaders argued, was to pull together behind the strike plan. That argument helped push many undecided controllers toward the Choirboys.[25]

PATCO Prepares

Unfortunately for PATCO, Poli stumbled badly just as he tried to accelerate his own preparations for 1981. The cause was, ironically, a union problem. In the spring of 1980, twenty members of PATCO's national staff, led by research director James E. Lyons, formed the PATCO Employees Union in an effort to bargain collectively with PATCO, their employer. Jack Maher supported their effort, confident that Poli would also support it. In an initial meeting with Lyons and Maher on May 23, 1980, Poli seemed receptive. That did not last long. Days later, Poli posted a notice indicating that four employees, including Lyons, were ineligible for union representation due to their managerial responsibilities. The employees saw this as an effort to undercut their union and filed an unfair labor practice charge with the National Labor Relations Board (NLRB). Tensions escalated. Finally, on July 28, Poli announced the layoff of four employees, including Lyons, due to a budgetary shortfall. Because all four had been involved in the staff union effort, they naturally saw the layoff as a union-busting move and circulated an open letter to PATCO members, detailing the "bloodbath at PATCO's national office," and asking, "Which Side Are You On, Brother?"[26]

PATCO clearly faced financial problems in 1980, as it ran up expenses in preparation for 1981. Poli decided to economize in several areas, including suspending the union's training program at the AFL-CIO's George Meany Center. But the timing and targets of the staff layoffs were suspicious enough to cause the NLRB to rule that PATCO had committed an unfair labor practice. It took more than a year for that decision to be handed down, but Maher did not wait for it. When the layoffs were announced, he quietly resigned from PATCO in protest. Not wishing to weaken the union he had helped found, he said he was leaving for health reasons, to seek treatment for alcoholism (which was also true). Maher's departure in the summer of 1980 was a blow to PATCO. It was Maher who began the Choirboy program, and he who would have been field director for the strike. Before he left, he handpicked a successor, Jim Lundie, a highly decorated Vietnam War veteran. Lundie proved to be a gifted organizer, but he never enjoyed the level of trust among members that Maher had earned after twelve years as the union's top strategist.[27]

The fallout from the staff organizing effort reverberated for months afterward. Controllers in the field were confused by it. "We just don't need any problems and especially now," huffed a member from Texas. To tamp down concerns, Poli circulated a letter giving his version of events. Most members gave Poli the benefit of the doubt in the interest of unity. But Maher's departure introduced tensions between Rock and Poli just as the union prepared its negotiating strategy.[28]

When Poli announced PATCO's negotiating team for 1981 days after firing Lyons, he included some veterans of past contract negotiations, such as Carl Vaughan of Pittsburgh Tower. However, Rock, who had participated in each PATCO negotiation to that point, was not on the list. Poli gave a larger role to the union's emerging younger leaders, whom he considered his base, replacing Rock with Dennis Reardon, a young militant who had not participated in past negotiations. The PATCO Employees Union claimed Rock was left off the negotiating committee in retaliation for his support of Maher and Lyons. Whether that was true was not clear. But one thing was undeniable: PATCO began serious preparations for its biggest negotiation yet without the benefit of the three people who were most responsible for leading the organization since its founding. Maher and Leyden had departed, and Rock was marginalized.[29]

As the negotiating team set to work, it pored over data collected in repeated surveys of the union's membership conducted by consultant Art Shostak. There was no ambiguity in that data regarding what air traffic controllers saw as their top priority: their salaries. When asked to choose between higher pay, a shorter workweek, or improved benefits, 69 percent of controllers named higher pay as their top priority. Nor was this result anomalous. In every internal poll conducted by the union between 1979 and 1981, pay was the top issue.[30]

This was not surprising. While federal workers in general saw their pay fall behind inflation in the late 1970s, the problem was more pronounced for higher-paid federal workers such as air traffic controllers. A 1981 study showed that the higher one moved up the ladder in federal employment, the greater the gap that developed between federal pay and the pay for comparable work in the private sector. At the GS-13 level, a common grade for full performance level controllers at radar facilities, the study found that federal employees earned an average of $36,613, which was 18 percent less than their private sector counterparts of comparable skill and experience. It was also unsurprising that controllers believed that collective bargaining could help them close that gap: they need only look at the Postal Service. A 1979 study by the U.S. General Accounting Office found that the postal workers, who could bargain over their pay, fared much better than federal workers, who could not. Postal workers' compensation rose by 94 percent between 1970 and 1977, a period when the consumer price index rose by 65 percent; in comparison, federal workers saw their compensation rise by only 47 percent over these years, which meant that the purchasing power of their pay declined.[31]

Framing a salary demand for their negotiations was a tricky proposition for the negotiating team. They realized that if they set the demand too high, it would "create an image of controllers as prima donnas with salaries and benefits above the average." If the economy worsened, a high wage demand would be "labelled outrageous and inflationary." The negotiators were also mindful of the political shift that would reach fruition in the 1980 election. "We must recognize that times are changing," a Choirboy's memo warned. "Conservative economic and political theories are becoming more popular. 'Take away from the federal employee' is becoming a favorite rallying cry."[32]

Still, PATCO negotiators favored an aggressive demand on salaries despite these concerns. Foremost was the knowledge that if significant raises were not included in the demands, it would be harder to motivate controllers to support the union's 1981 effort. Ancillary issues like FAM flights would no longer do. Indeed, Pensacola controllers demanded that the union drop the FAM issue entirely. "In 1981 I want more money and better benefits," read a petition signed by the Floridians. "I don't want or need a free ride on any air carrier." Taking such views to heart, one local PATCO leader recommended that negotiators demand "at least twice the pay."[33]

Negotiators also worried that if they did not set salary demands high enough, controllers who felt underpaid might lose patience and wage their own campaigns, facility by facility, as happened in the days before PATCO was formed. Washington National controllers had staged slowdowns in 1978 to win an upgrade after being left out of the reclass upgrade of 1977. In 1980, O'Hare controllers tried the same tactic. The problems of excessive workloads that had dogged O'Hare in the late 1960s persisted; O'Hare controllers logged twelve thousand hours of overtime in the first nine months of 1980. When a lawsuit filed by Local 316 alleging that the stress-laden O'Hare workplace violated occupation health and safety rules was thrown out by the courts, the controllers decided to act. In early August 1980, Local 316 controllers began "withdrawing enthusiasm" from their work, demanding a salary increase. When the FAA failed to respond, they initiated a full-scale slowdown on August 15, delaying more than six hundred flights.[34]

The O'Hare protest caught both the FAA and PATCO's national leaders by surprise. The FAA filed an unfair labor practice allegation against PATCO with the FLRA, and secured a temporary restraining order demanding an immediate return to normal operation. Bond also went on a public relations offensive, alleging that salaries of O'Hare's radar room controllers already averaged $43,000. In this case, Poli sided with Bond. By acting on their own, the Chicagoans were threatening PATCO's 1981 plan, he believed. "If an illegal wildcat slowdown did occur in Chicago, it was exclusively the product of O'Hare, and not in any way associated with the Organization as a whole," Poli announced. Facing a united front from the FAA and PATCO's national leaders, O'Hare controllers called off their action and avoided monetary penalties—but not public ire. "It is absolutely criminal when those individuals who have the public at their mercy attempt such maneuvers," declaimed one delayed traveler.[35]

The O'Hare episode encouraged PATCO negotiators to stake out an aggressive position so that no group would go off on its own, but other considerations reinforced this same leaning. One was the tension between large and small facilities that had proven so explosive during the reclassification fight of 1976. Rex Campbell began circulating an open letter months before PATCO drew up its demands for 1981. It argued that the union could not stage a successful strike "unless everybody gets an equal share." Small-facility controllers would not jeopardize their jobs "so New York and Chicago can get the lion's share and then they get the crumbs," Campbell warned. The union needed to offer everyone a big slice of the pie. The same logic held when it came to inducing African Americans and women—who had not seen PATCO as a particularly welcoming organization—to throw their enthusiastic support behind the 1981 program. Finally, rising animosity toward the FAA influenced the shape of PATCO's demands. Since 1978, the conflict-ridden relationship between controllers and their employer had plumbed new depths. A later study commissioned by the FAA concluded that rank-and-file resentment of the agency influenced PATCO's negotiating posture: anger that was difficult to channel in any other way was simply "projected onto 'harder' economic issues" like salary demands.[36]

All of these factors led PATCO's negotiating team to endorse the most far-reaching set of demands ever made by a union of federal workers. These included an immediate $10,000 across-the-board pay increase for all controllers, an additional 10 percent increase after one year; a cost-of-living allowance that would raise controllers' wages 1.5 percent for every one percent increase in the consumer price index; a 30 percent bonus for time controllers spent conducting on-the-job training; and a four-day workweek with three consecutive days off. These demands were unprecedented and went far beyond what the law allowed federal workers to negotiate. Taken together, the demands illustrated how far PATCO had traveled from its formative days, when Rock had argued, "air safety can't be bought with salary increases."[37]

On October 1, 1980, Poli mailed these negotiating demands to the union's membership, urged members to read them, and noted that what PATCO could ultimately win at the bargaining table would depend on their "degree of commitment." Gary Eads cautioned controllers not to regard the demands as "pie-in-the-sky." Controllers had been "very carefully conditioned to understand that they should be *damn grateful* they get what they get and should not expect more," Eads explained. Such thinking would no longer do.[38]

In the field, the demands were generally well received, especially among younger members. Most accepted the logic that an aggressive opening position would help the union win more in the end. Ominously, however, a significant number of controllers were not ready to "drink the Kool-Aid," as one put it, comparing the union's demands to the November 18, 1978, mass suicide of more than nine hundred followers of cult leader Reverend Jim Jones in Jonestown, Guyana. One Florida controller regarded the $10,000 demand as "almost an embarrassment" in a time of economic trouble. Most controllers kept their qualms to themselves, but some openly prophesied that these demands would come back to haunt the union. "Our greed should not exceed that of our fellow federal workers. If it does, then are we willing to go it alone on the suicide mission of all time?" asked Anthony Skirlick of Los Angeles Center. Skirlick warned that private sector workers were feeling increasingly insecure and fearful of higher taxes. "Unrealistic demands in the face of this change is suicide," he warned.[39]

PATCO leaders dismissed as disloyal cranks Skirlick and the few others who publicly questioned the demands. The planners believed they had done their jobs well. They had constructed a set of demands that would motivate controllers to risk their jobs in order to push the FAA out of the restrictive boundaries of federal sector collective bargaining. Ironically, the failure of the Civil Service Reform Act to let federal workers bargain over wages had contributed to the inflation of PATCO's demands: the union's leaders felt that offering a huge potential payoff was necessary if the union was to forge enough unity to pressure the FAA to move negotiations beyond what the statute permitted. Almost a year would pass before PATCO leaders realized how badly their demands damaged their cause with potential allies and the public. By then, it was too late to change course.

REAGAN'S PROMISE

As his team perfected a contingency plan tight enough to defeat a national strike in 1981, one thought haunted Langhorne Bond: would President Jimmy Carter have the nerve to see it through? Carter "didn't have a lot of sympathy with illegal strikes," Bond knew. Still, Carter was a Democrat, and labor was a major constituency of his party. Would he feel pressured to compromise with strikers rather than let the contingency plan force them to relent? Carter's likely reaction to a strike was the one thing Bond "couldn't figure out."[40]

PATCO had figured out Carter enough to know that his administration had been disastrous for air traffic controllers. The loss of the early retirement and immunity programs and the steady erosion of real earnings left little enthusiasm for Carter in PATCO's ranks, even though Democrats outnumbered Republicans by a significant margin in the union. Members complained that he made federal workers "the expendable lamb at the altar of fiscal sacrifice" and argued that the treatment of federal workers was "worse under this so-called Democratic administration than it was with the Republicans." During his presidency, Leyden had counseled patience, arguing that Carter was struggling with a poor economy and a conservative resurgence. By the time Poli took over the union, patience was gone. It did not take "a political science major to figure out where the present administration is coming from and where it is headed," noted Gary Eads. Under Carter, Eads predicted, federal employees would be "hit quicker, more decisively, and harder than any other segment of our society."[41]

PATCO was scarcely alone in its disenchantment. Across the labor movement, leaders were furious with Carter for a long list of failures and broken promises. Carter promised to support labor law reform, then he sabotaged its chances by insisting that the Senate first deal with the controversial Panama Canal treaty. By the time the bloodied Democratic majority ratified the treaty it lacked the cohesion to overcome a Republican-led filibuster of the labor bill. Carter promised Hatch Act reform, which would loosen restrictions on federal workers' ability to engage in political activity, and then stood by idly while the reform bill died in committee. He promised a robust economic stimulus, yet delivered measures that the AFL-CIO found anemic. He promised to place federal workers' rights on statutory footing, and then opted for a restrictive approach to federal union rights.[42]

But it was public employee unions like PATCO that were most disappointed with Carter. Jerry Wurf, leader of the largest public sector union, AFSCME, had been among Carter's first labor backers in 1976. By 1979, Wurf had given up on Carter. Ken Blaylock, president of the AFGE, the largest union of federal workers, tried to warn the president that he had a labor problem. "Mr. President, you've made everybody out there, every employee out there mad," he told Carter at a private political lunch, "you're pissing off every federal worker out there." Unless something changed, Blaylock warned, Carter would lose the federal workers' vote. Blaylock was more blunt in the assessment he gave the AFL-CIO Executive Council: "I can't guarantee my wife will vote for him," he said. Labor's disenchantment provided an opening for Sen. Ted Kennedy's spirited primary challenge to Carter for the Democratic nomination. Had Kennedy been successful in his quest, it is likely that PATCO would have endorsed him. Carter's victory in the nomination fight foreclosed that possibility and put PATCO in a bind.[43]

Endorsing Carter was impossible when his FAA was doing everything it could to weaken PATCO's negotiating position in advance of the anticipated 1981 contract talks. PATCO could have followed the lead of the AFGE, which declined to endorse any candidate when no one received 50 percent of the votes in the union's straw poll. But when the campaign of Republican nominee Ronald Reagan came looking for unions to join its electoral coalition,

PATCO leaders found it difficult to resist the temptation of endorsing what by mid-October 1980 appeared to be a winning campaign.[44]

In retrospect, it seems stranger that a union of federal workers would consider endorsing Reagan in 1980 than it did at the time. Reagan was clearly a conservative, but that did not mean he was reflexively antiunion. He was, after all, a former labor leader. As president of the Screen Actors Guild from 1947 to 1952, Reagan had led Hollywood actors in their first strike against the film studios. As his politics arced from liberal to conservative in the years between his SAG presidency and his election as governor of California in 1966, Reagan had not embraced the shrill antiunionism of some conservatives. To be sure, he was no friend of the farm worker movement that swept California's Central Valley under the leadership of César Chávez in the 1960s: his policies consistently favored growers' interests over those of Chávez's laborers. In other respects, however, Reagan took care not to alienate unions. He spoke proudly of his days at SAG, and as governor he disappointed the right-to-work movement, which felt "no connection, no communication, no sympathy" from him.[45]

The distance between Reagan and antiunion activists was particularly evident in the way Reagan had handled public sector employment relations in California. Governor Reagan's labor policy did not differ substantially from that of most elected officials, Republican or Democratic, in the late 1960s and early 1970s. As the movement to organize and extend union rights to public employees gathered momentum, Reagan's California responded in ways similar to the rest of the nation. As governor, Reagan signed the Meyers-Milias-Brown Act in 1968, which cleared the way for local governments in California to bargain collectively with their employees. Like almost all the state laws adopted in that period, the act banned public employee strikes. Still, most observers saw it as a progressive piece of legislation. As public sector labor militancy rose in California, Reagan did not react more harshly than the other figures of his time. More than one hundred illegal strikes by public workers erupted in California between 1970 and 1974. Local officials tended to react moderately to these strikes. Court orders were obtained in one-third of the conflicts, but only six strikes were apparently ended by such orders. Nearly all strike settlements included amnesty clauses, and in only sixteen cases were any punitive actions taken against strikers. Reagan never campaigned against public sector unions or specifically encouraged tougher sanctions against their strikes.[46]

Reagan's moderation was evident in his response to controversial strikes during his tenure as governor. On July 17, 1969, California saw its first full-scale strike by police officers and firefighters when these workers struck the community of Vallejo, northeast of San Francisco, seeking pay increases. The *San Francisco Examiner* called the strike "unforgivably irresponsible as well as illegal," and warned that if it succeeded, police officers and firefighters elsewhere in the state would "strike at will and with impunity; the jungle will soon lie just beyond every citizen's door." In his response to the walkout, Reagan adopted a firm but measured tone that stopped short of the *Examiner*'s overheated rhetoric. Paraphrasing a remark made by the governor of Massachusetts, Calvin Coolidge, during the 1919 Boston police strike, Reagan announced that "no one has the right to strike against the public safety." But rather than raising the specter of jungle law in the manner of some editorialists, Reagan merely called the walkout "extremely unfortunate." The governor promised state public safety personnel to Vallejo so that no one would lose police or fire protection, but he did not meddle in the Vallejo negotiations or vilify the strikers. The five-day strike ended when the city approved a 9 percent salary increase. Reagan did not criticize the settlement, and his moderate stance won him the opprobrium of the leaders of California's right-to-work movement.[47]

Reagan also demonstrated restraint when he confronted the first strike ever conducted by California state employees. On May 22, 1972, five hundred employees of the State Water Resources Department struck, endangering the operations of a 685-mile network of pipelines and tunnels that brought water to Southern California. These employees, members of the California State Employees Association, demanded pay increases of 21 percent in order to bring their wages in line with federal water project employees. The strike threatened to become bitter: state authorities alleged that strikers sabotaged some equipment before they walked out. Newspaper editorials condemned the walkout, giving the governor plenty of room to come down hard on the strikers. Instead, Reagan showed forbearance. "State law is very explicit such a strike is illegal," the governor pointed out. Yet he treated the walkout as a case of unauthorized absence from work rather than an illegal concerted action against the state. Under California law, state employees were subject to termination after five consecutive days of unauthorized absence. Reagan made clear that the state would invoke this provision if the strikers did not return to work, but he refrained from saber rattling. When asked what would become of the strikers at the end of five unexcused work-days, Reagan responded, "We hope that won't happen." Nor did Reagan forbid his administration from negotiating with the union in the midst of this illegal strike. While state officials publicly said they "would not and could not legally bargain with CSEA," officials held talks with the union behind the scenes. Reagan offered to send the legislature a request for a 12.5 percent raise for the strikers in 1972, to be followed by a similar raise in 1973. At the same time, his director of water resources promised the union that the state would seek no punitive actions against the strikers if they returned to work. The water workers accepted the offer and the strike ended before the five-day window closed. In the first strike ever waged by California state workers, Reagan thus left the impression that a union could not only strike without incurring penalties, but it also could make gains.[48]

Reagan's 1980 presidential campaign sought to woo unions disaffected with Carter by leveraging these moderate aspects of Reagan's labor record in California and his position as the first former union president to mount a serious campaign for the White House since Socialist Eugene V. Debs. In searching for labor backers, the Reagan campaign turned to the same unions Nixon had pursued in 1972, including the Teamsters and PATCO's parent, MEBA. Both unions endorsed Reagan. MEBA's Jesse Calhoon, who had come to despise Carter, was quick to sign up. After raising half a million dollars for the Democrat in 1976, Calhoon found that he could barely get the Carter White House to return his phone calls. By 1980 he told associates he wanted nothing to do with "that person" in the White House. When Reagan adviser Ed Meese assured Calhoon that Reagan would be "very sympathetic" to MEBA's concerns, Calhoon was sold. MEBA's move in turn made it easier for PATCO to consider endorsing Reagan.[49]

Having observed Reagan up close during his years as a right-to-work activist in California, Public Service Research Council director David Denholm, a leading opponent of public sector unions, was particularly worried about the Reagan campaign's pursuit of PATCO's endorsement. Denholm closely followed PATCO's preparations for 1981, and he feared that in its efforts to pick up some token labor support, the Reagan campaign might make promises that would end up rewarding PATCO for its militancy. As it happened, Denholm had good reason to worry.[50]

As talks opened with the Reagan campaign, PATCO did not automatically offer its endorsement. Rather, PATCO officials conducted quiet, but detailed discussions with the campaign, set forth specific conditions, and elicited a set of promises from Reagan himself before it made its endorsement. The negotiations took place between PATCO's counsel, Richard Leighton, and Michael P. Balzano Jr., who was working out of the Reagan campaign's Rosslyn, Virginia, headquarters as its labor liaison. Balzano was an experienced hand, having helped coordinate outreach to blue-collar workers for the Nixon administration. As a result of the Balzano-Leighton discussions, Poli agreed to endorse the Republican in a televised press conference in Florida on October 23, in return for a letter from Reagan spelling out the details of the campaign's commitments to PATCO.[51]

This agreement nearly unraveled. As the endorsement date neared, the Reagan letter did not arrive. Poli had no intention of endorsing Reagan without some commitment on paper. So, three days before the scheduled press conference, Leighton dictated six specific points that PATCO wanted Reagan to commit to, and that he believed he was being promised by the campaign through Balzano and other Reagan emissaries. Two dealt directly with the FAA: First, PATCO demanded that Langhorne Bond be replaced by "a competent administrator"; second, it demanded an opportunity to nominate candidates to succeed Bond, to comment on finalists for the job, and to veto anyone it deemed "totally objectionable." Three of the other four points addressed work conditions. In these, PATCO sought the replacement of outdated air traffic control equipment; reduction of work hours for controllers; and full staffing of all air traffic control positions. The final point addressed an issue the Civil Service Reform Act failed to correct for PATCO. The union wanted an opportunity to advocate for increased pay for controllers, and for negotiating rights in collective bargaining equal to, or greater than, those enjoyed by postal workers, including the right to strike in some circumstances. Leighton sent these points to Balzano, writing, "If you or anyone else in the governor's campaign has second thoughts about any of the agreements set forth in this letter, please respond immediately by certified mail or telegram to me, so that the PATCO endorsement can be aborted before anyone suffers any embarrassment." No objections were sent back to PATCO. Rather, Balzano secured a signed letter from Reagan to PATCO pledging his good will toward the union.[52]

Reagan's letter, also dated October 20, was in many ways a remarkable document. "I have been thoroughly briefed by members of my staff as to the deplorable state of our nation's air traffic control system," wrote Reagan. The candidate's letter did not specifically agree to the six demands Leighton had communicated to the campaign, but neither did it specifically reject them. Instead, the letter mentioned PATCO's concerns and promised that Reagan would address them. Reagan wrote that he deplored controllers' "working unreasonable hours," promised to "take whatever steps are necessary to provide our air traffic controllers with the most modern equipment available," and pledged to "adjust staff levels and work days so that they are commensurate with achieving a maximum degree of public safety." Reagan also promised to "appoint highly qualified individuals who can work harmoniously with the Congress and the employees of the government agencies they oversee" and said that he would work with PATCO to "bring about a spirit of cooperation between the President and the air traffic controllers." To outside observers, the Reagan letter appeared to contain the standard fare campaigns dished out to targeted constituencies. But in the context of the communications that preceded it, it is understandable why some PATCO leaders might have believed that Reagan gave a wink and a nod to their six basic demands.[53]

The letter was certainly far more than PATCO had gotten from the Carter administration. With Reagan's letter in hand, Poli polled his board members. They quickly assented to the endorsement: to them it appeared to be the union's best bet for avoiding a costly strike in 1981. Poli met privately with Reagan for thirty minutes prior to the press conference on October 23 in Tampa at which the endorsement was announced. Poli was impressed by Reagan's "warmth and fairness." Why not? At the press conference Reagan offered the union another bone: he said he was considering exempting air traffic control from the across-the-board federal hiring freeze he would institute if elected. Thus PATCO joined the Reagan coalition.[54]

PATCO members knew nothing about the political maneuvering behind the Reagan endorsement. Most heard of it after it was announced in the media. In an October 22 memo to PATCO local presidents, Poli explained the endorsement in simple terms: while the Carter administration "consistently denigrated Federal employees," Reagan promised to address "the legitimate needs of the controller workforce." Still, reaction to the move among the union's rank and file was decidedly mixed. The union's Republicans and conservative Democrats generally approved. So did many involved in the planning for 1981, like Choirboy Jim Stakem of Washington Center, who had never before voted for a Republican. But there was a significant backlash among a large portion of PATCO's members and activists who could not understand why their union was breaking ranks with the AFL-CIO in order to support a conservative, budget-cutting Republican. One PATCO spouse was so outraged that her husband's union had endorsed what she called "a conservative, lying, anti-labor, anti-Union, anti-minimum wage,...and anti-training programs candidate" that she resigned from a PATCO spouses group in protest.[55]

Poli became defensive about the endorsement in the face of such criticism. It was "a very difficult one for the Board members and myself," he assured critics. To mollify members who were angry about the endorsement, some PATCO leaders mischaracterized the extent and specificity of Reagan's private promises to PATCO. "We leaked the word that he had promised us a six-hour day," Mike Rock later explained.[56]

Because PATCO's endorsement process unfolded at a high level and behind closed doors, rumors like the promised six-hour workday flourished wherever PATCO's members discussed the election. Copies of Reagan's letter to Poli circulated freely among PATCO members, and most read between its lines to speculate about the specific promises alluded to by Reagan's generalities. Controllers were not sure exactly what had been pledged, but most believed that Reagan promised significant gains to the union. The result was that when Reagan cruised to a smashing victory over Jimmy Carter on November 4, 1980, controllers' expectations of what they might be able to get from his administration rose to levels profoundly out of sync with the political realities of the moment.

In time, PATCO leaders would come to regret the Reagan endorsement, and many commentators would note the obvious irony in the story of a union destroyed by a president whose election it had endorsed. But few understood the true depths of that irony. PATCO's leaders endorsed Reagan in the belief that his election provided the only plausible scenario for gaining an acceptable contract without a strike in 1981, the only available avenue for achieving goals they had long sought but were unable to achieve on their own. Yet the way that endorsement was proffered and secured actually increased the likelihood of a disastrous strike. Because each side saw the other as an instrumentality that could help it attain something it desperately desired—for the Reagan campaign it was a symbolically important labor ally and for PATCO it was a president who could help it make a breakthrough at the bargaining table—each side had an interest in believing what it wanted to believe about the nature of their bargain. Without realizing it, the Reagan campaign gave PATCO leaders both implicit permission and an incentive to foster soaring expectations among rank-and-file controllers and activists— expectations that would ultimately prove impossible to satisfy at the bargaining table. By colluding in each other's fantasies, the two sides together had created a dangerous situation that would soon alter the course of American labor relations.

DEAD RECKONING

The solution probably lies in providing additional benefits in at
least two areas: direct pay increases and shorter hours.
—REAGAN AIDE CRAIG FULLER

They didn't give us anything.
—CONTROLLER RON TAYLOR

"I believe a strike will happen," Langhorne Bond announced on November 8, 1980, in his most unequivocal prediction to date. PATCO was determined to walk out in 1981, he told the press. To his frustration, his words were little noted, buried in a back section of the *Washington Post*, unmentioned by the *New York Times* and other leading newspapers. The focus of news coverage that week was not PATCO, but rather Ronald Reagan's stunning defeat of President Jimmy Carter. No one then could foresee how Bond's prediction and Reagan's election would soon intersect.[1]

The 1980 election fundamentally reshaped the American political landscape. Riding Reagan's coattails, Republicans took control of the Senate and gained thirty-five seats in the House, giving them and their allies, the fiscally conservative "Boll Weevil" Democrats, enough leverage to enact Reagan's broad program of tax cuts, social program reductions, and deregulation over the opposition of Democratic House Speaker Tip O'Neill. The

"Reagan Revolution" moved American politics in a new direction, breaking decisively from New Deal–Great Society liberalism, and inaugurating a conservative ascendancy that would define American politics for the rest of the century.

While Reagan had not specifically campaigned against unions during the election, focusing instead on the ways in which his policies would spur economic growth, most union leaders greeted his election as an unmitigated disaster, and with good reasons. His administration rolled back enforcement of occupational safety and health laws and opposed increases in the minimum wage. His appointees to the National Labor Relations Board tilted its orientation sharply in favor of employers. And he nominated construction company executive Raymond J. Donovan as secretary of labor without consulting the AFL-CIO, as his predecessors had done before filling that seat. Public sector unions were especially alarmed at the incoming president's policies. Even before he left the Capitol grounds after taking the oath of office, Reagan signed a federal hiring freeze; his cuts in aid to state and local governments made collective bargaining more difficult for unions at that level; and to oversee the federal workforce as director of the Office of Personnel Management Reagan appointed Donald Devine, a hardline conservative.[2]

Reagan's Labor Strategy

Despite their dangerous implications for the larger labor movement, there was no indication in these first months that Reagan's policies boded ill for air traffic controllers. Nor was it clear after the administration's first months that the White House would find itself in a conflict with PATCO that would prove more damaging to labor in the long run than any of Reagan's legislative initiatives. To the contrary, PATCO officials believed that the spirit of the October 1980 Reagan-Poli entente held strong. While the leaders of other federal employee unions anticipated "rough sledding" under Reagan, PATCO leaders thought they would be exempt from the ill effects of Reagan's policy agenda, citing "assurances" given by the president-elect himself. The optimism of PATCO leaders was not baseless, nor did it rely only on the blandishments offered in Reagan's October 20 letter to Poli. The incoming administration was in fact fleshing out a labor strategy in which an envisioned alliance with PATCO and a few other select unions was intended to play a symbolically important role.[3]

Robert W. Searby, whom Reagan later named the U.S. representative to the International Labor Organization, outlined a labor strategy for the president-elect in a secret memo drafted after the election titled, "Organized Workers and the Potential for a Republican-Conservative Governing Majority." Searby grounded his analysis in one surprising finding of post-election voter analysis: despite the all-out opposition of the AFL-CIO and a get-out-the-vote operation called by its director "the best labor effort we ever fielded," Reagan won nearly as many votes from union households (44 percent) as Carter (47 percent). To Searby these figures indicated that "patriotic and socially conservative union-members" were ripe to be picked from their "unholy alliance" with the Democratic Party. "It is now within our power to break, once and for all, the virtual monopoly of the union/liberal alliance while, simultaneously, defining a respectable place for organized labor in our national commonwealth—a place compatible with an era of conservative Republican dominance," he wrote. How to fold "Reagan Democrats," Searby's "patriotic and socially conservative" union members, into a permanent Republican majority became a central concern for White House political director Lyn Nofziger in 1981.[4]

The White House liaison to organized labor, Robert Bonitati, formerly of the Air Line Pilots Association, argued that the four unions that had endorsed Reagan's election could provide a springboard for the larger labor strategy the White House contemplated. "In trying to expand the group of labor unions supporting the President, our first priority must be to see that our friends... are treated well and that their good treatment is communicated to the rest of the labor community," Bonitati advised. "Taking care of your friends is a well-established concept among labor politicians, and most are currently watching to see if the Teamsters, MEBA, the Professional Air Traffic Controllers and the National Maritime Union receive special treatment from the Administration," he added. "If other labor leaders see it is worthwhile to align with the Administration they will begin to follow suit."[5]

Reagan himself was well equipped to carry out the strategy. His personal charm and his history as a union leader proved valuable assets. He relished telling stories of his years with the Screen Actors Guild, attributed his negotiating skills to his union experience, and professed great admiration for labor's past accomplishments even as he criticized its present political agenda. He brought his message straight to union audiences. Indeed, the president was pursuing his labor courtship at the Washington Hilton on March 30, 1981, when he was shot and wounded by John Hinckley while heading to his limousine after speaking to representatives of the nation's building trades unions. Reagan's heroic recovery earned him the admiration of many more trade unionists, who applauded his good-humored bravery.[6]

The timing seemed right for a Republican bid to divide the labor movement and win over a share of its members. The AFL-CIO was then under the leadership of Lane Kirkland, a competent administrator and union diplomat but one who lacked Reagan's charisma or ability to move a larger political agenda. A cerebral, sardonic, slow-talking son of a South Carolina businessman, Kirkland had become a union man more by accident than political commitment, joining the International Organization of Masters, Mates, and Pilots when he went to sea as a merchant marine officer during World War II. Following the war, he obtained a Master's degree in foreign relations at Georgetown University and began a promising career as a union staff researcher and speechwriter until he was hired as special assistant to AFL-CIO President George Meany in 1960. He proved his loyalty at Meany's side during the tumultuous 1960s, when labor's support for the Vietnam War isolated it from other progressive forces. This paved the way for his election as secretary-treasurer of the AFL-CIO in 1969. Ten years later he succeeded labor's cigar-chomping octogenarian chieftain, but by then it was clear labor was in decline. Kirkland had barely initiated his plan to revive labor's fortunes—luring the United Automobile Workers back into the AFL-CIO, offering support to new organizing drives in the open-shop South, and reaching out to cement alliances with civil rights and feminist organizations—when Reagan's election put labor on the defensive.[7]

Reagan's bid for the affections of rank-and-file union members offended Kirkland. "We have to pick up that challenge and we have to fling it back," he told aides. Shortly after the election, Kirkland invited two of Reagan's closest advisers, counselor Ed Meese and CIA director William Casey, to the AFL-CIO's offices on 16th Street. After exchanging pleasantries, Kirkland invited his guests over to his window, from which they could see the president's mansion on the other side of LaFayette Park. "You ought to come to the window for a minute. I have quite a view," said Kirkland. "That's a wonderful view Lane, a really nice view," Reagan's men agreed. "Yes, and you know the great part about it?" Kirkland continued. "After you guys are long gone, we'll still be right here." Kirkland made his point more forcefully the following

May, when he asked the AFL-CIO Executive Council to approve a plan for a massive march of union members and allies on Washington in September 1981 to protest the Reagan agenda. Labor would call that event Solidarity Day.[8]

Reagan's advisers interpreted Kirkland's raised hackles as an indication of his insecurity. They knew that the president's ability to attract union voters to a program promising deregulation, budget cuts, and tax reductions in order to spur growth and create jobs was no mere Election Day fluke. They also possessed a copy of a confidential internal poll that the AFL-CIO itself had commissioned among its members just prior to the 1980 election. The poll revealed a deep resonance for aspects of Reagan's message among union voters: a majority of them favored a constitutional amendment to balance the federal budget and blamed government more than business for the economy's plight. Reagan's advisers also knew that there were limits to how far Kirkland would press his attacks. Even as Kirkland fought Reagan's economic policies, he sought an alliance with the president on foreign policy based on their shared anticommunism. Kirkland's friend and Reagan's national security adviser Richard V. Allen helped facilitate cooperation between the administration and the AFL-CIO on one top priority for Kirkland: aid to *Solidarność*, the union movement led by Lech Walesa that was then challenging Poland's Communist government.[9]

Making major inroads among labor voters even as it implemented economic policies that the union movement opposed, it seemed that the Reagan administration might have its cake and eat it too. It therefore had no interest in provoking confrontations with unions that might upset the balance, allowing labor leaders to circle the wagons and characterize the president as antiunion. Reagan could more effectively pursue his aims if he avoided that label.[10]

PATCO leaders understood Reagan's political stance. It resembled Richard Nixon's 1972 strategy. They recalled that Nixon's desire to court labor votes in the service of his dreams of party realignment during his reelection campaign had helped salvage PATCO after the 1970 sickout and win it recognition and a first contract with the FAA. They thought it was possible for Reagan's political ambitions to play a similar role in 1981, providing the leverage that PATCO needed to break free of the constraints of federal sector collective bargaining and win wage increases, a shorter workweek, and other "non-negotiable" items. After all, as Reagan's adviser

Bonitati said and PATCO leaders knew, other unions would be "watching to see" if it was "worthwhile to align with the Administration." The larger political context that so alarmed Kirkland thus did not dampen the optimism of PATCO leaders that 1981 might bring the breakthrough they had long hoped for.

Reagan's Men

Indeed, nothing discouraged PATCO leaders from believing that the stars were aligning in their favor. Reagan's appointment of a forty-nine-year-old native of Philadelphia, Andrew L. "Drew" Lewis, as secretary of transportation seemed to be one good omen. Lewis was close to Reagan and, unlike some others in Reagan's inner circle, he was a pragmatist, not an antiunion ideologue. A graduate of the Harvard Business School, Lewis was experienced in both the transportation business and politics. In the 1970s, he led the reorganization of the bankrupt Reading Railroad. In 1974, he ran unsuccessfully for Pennsylvania governor against incumbent Democrat Milton J. Shapp, but he performed well enough to become one of the Keystone State's leading Republicans. Lewis first impressed Reagan by helping deny him the Republican nomination in 1976. After falling short in his spirited challenge to Gerald R. Ford in the Republican primaries, Reagan had attempted a bold preconvention maneuver to try to steal the nomination. He announced that if nominated, he would name moderate Republican Sen. Richard S. Schweiker of Pennsylvania as his vice presidential running mate. By doing so, Reagan hoped to both ease the fears of moderates, and pluck the Pennsylvania delegation from Ford's column. Had the gambit worked, Reagan would have displaced Ford as the 1976 Republican nominee. Lewis headed the Pennsylvania delegation, however, and held it for Ford in the face of tremendous pressure, earning Reagan's grudging respect. When Reagan began assembling his 1980 campaign team, one of his first calls was to Lewis.[11]

Lewis assumed his post knowing that he would face a contract negotiation with PATCO during his first year. The prospect did not worry him. He had a record as a tough negotiator. Yet his years in the railroad industry had taught him that labor agreements provided stability in the workplace. He prided himself on having learned to game out negotiations. "I know what you have to get…to get re-elected and I know what I can afford to give you," he would tell his labor counterparts. "What we've got to do is work it out." Lewis thought PATCO's demands and its claims of overwork and underpay were grossly inflated, but he believed that an agreement would be reached if pragmatism prevailed on both sides of the bargaining table during the 1981 negotiations. He was the best negotiating partner PATCO could have hoped for from the Reagan administration.[12]

Lewis's moderate presence helped offset that of the man Reagan appointed to run the FAA. J. Lynn Helms was a hard-charging fighter pilot by nature, very different in temperament and experience from Lewis. Born in rural Arkansas in 1925 and raised in Norman, Oklahoma, he was the son of a railroad brakeman. He attended college on an ROTC scholarship, joined a Marine Corps jet fighter squadron and saw action during the Korean War. After Korea he worked as an instructor at the Patuxent River Naval Air Station on the Chesapeake Bay, where he trained test pilots, including future astronaut Neil Armstrong. In 1956 he left for the defense industry and moved up the corporate ladder at North American Aviation, Bendix, and the Norden Division of the United Air Craft Corporation, before he took the reins of Piper Aircraft, a leading manufacturer of general aviation planes. Helms grew increasingly hostile toward unions as his career progressed. In the aerospace industry, where government contracts defrayed the costs of collective bargaining, he tolerated it. When he took over Piper, however, he believed that union contracts were preventing the company from competing effectively with rival plane manufacturers. Shifting manufacturing from a unionized Pennsylvania plant to a nonunion Florida plant became one of his key objectives at Piper.[13]

Surviving records suggest that, in keeping with the October 1980 Balzano-Leighton agreement, the Reagan team shared Helms's name with PATCO before naming him FAA administrator. It would have been understandable if PATCO had objected to Helms. Helms subscribed to the approach toward the 1981 negotiations suggested in *Mandate for Leadership*, the policy recommendations compiled for the Reagan administration by Edwin Feulner, founder of the conservative Heritage Foundation. Feulner's volume made recommendations on every conceivable policy issue. When it came to PATCO, the volume specifically warned against taking a "wishy-washy" approach. Helms heartily concurred. He ridiculed PATCO's claims that controllers were overworked, believed that the FAA was overstaffed by at least twenty-five hundred controllers, and characterized PATCO's salary demands as ludicrous. "Go and get yourself a guitar and be a rock and roll singer, and then you can make that kind of money," he said. Yet there is no record that PATCO objected to the appointment. PATCO leaders correctly believed that Helms would not control the upcoming negotiation, while his presence at the helm of the FAA reassured conservatives that the administration would not cave in to PATCO.[14]

Indeed, Helms did not play a significant role in the contract negotiations. After conferring with the White House, Drew Lewis decided to depart from the precedent set in past PATCO-FAA talks. He, rather than Helms, would oversee the process, and personally enter the negotiations at their critical hour. Helms would concentrate on preparing the agency to weather a strike if the negotiations failed, a role that he himself preferred in any event. As soon as he settled into his job, Helms pressed Ray Van Vuren to further refine the FAA's contingency plan so that it would be ready.[15]

NEGOTIATING

No one in the administration believed that PATCO would hold out for the full range of demands it drew up in the fall of 1980. That package would have cost the government between $300 million and $1 billion annually, according to one White House estimate, and it was a nonstarter in the administration's view. But PATCO's actual bottom line was not clear. Reagan's Office of Management and Budget believed the administration should take a tough line in the negotiation. One OMB memo called controllers "perhaps the most overpaid, pampered employees in the Nation," and argued that agreeing "to even a portion" of PATCO's demands could be "characterized as bad management." Yet, the administration feared that a strike could easily cost more than a negotiated contract—bleeding $150 million a day from the national economy, according to one White House estimate. The administration hoped to avoid a blow of that magnitude when the economy was already weak, so the White House set no bottom line before the talks opened limiting how far Lewis should go to avoid a strike.[16]

Talks formally opened on February 12, 1981, when Poli and the PATCO negotiating committee sat across the table from a team of FAA and Transportation Department officials. From the beginning, the process unfolded differently from other federal sector contract talks. For one thing, the government retained top-flight private legal counsel from Morgan, Lewis

& Bockius, a law firm known for aggressively representing employer clients in labor negotiations. Drew Lewis retained William J. Curtin, the firm's leading labor lawyer, and George A. Stohner, an emerging star of the firm, even before Reagan was sworn in. Curtin and Stohner had reputations as "heavy hitters," tough lawyers experienced in high-pressure parlays. They advised government negotiators from the beginning, with Stohner personally sitting in on every negotiating session.[17]

The talks also attracted high-level attention from the Federal Mediation and Conciliation Service. Director Ken Moffett was familiar with PATCO, having been involved in the 1970 PATCO-FAA conflict. Moffett had his hands full in 1981. Postal unions and the Major League Baseball Players Association were both also heading into negotiations in the summer (the baseball players ended up striking on June 12 and forcing the cancellation of one-third of the season). But Moffett gave the PATCO-FAA talks top priority. He closely monitored the PATCO talks, and assigned a trusted mediator, Brian Flores, to oversee them on a daily basis. PATCO could not have hoped for a more sympathetic mediator. Flores was a union veteran, having led the Newspaper Guild at the *Washington Post* during a series of conflicts with publisher Katharine Graham in the early 1970s before leaving the labor movement to join the FMCS.[18]

During March and April the talks proceeded slowly as the sides began discussing the least controversial issues. As they progressed over the following two months, Flores was surprised by what he observed. In the other federal sector negotiations he had handled, lawyers on each side of the bargaining table spent much of their time "quoting federal regulations back and forth to each other." This did not happen in the PATCO-FAA talks. It appeared to Flores as if both sides were treating these talks differently. This was evident when PATCO first put its pay demands on the table in the late spring. When the federal negotiators explained that these items were nonnegotiable, PATCO negotiators responded by saying, "We'll work it out on the picket line." Flores had never seen another federal union make such a statement.[19]

By May rumors that the sides were going to bargain over pay began swirling around the contract negotiations. "The crux of this thing is what the Administration is going to do in light of the endorsement," one anonymous government official observed. No one on either side had a definitive reading on how far the administration would go, but it was clear that PATCO expected a big breakthrough. Knowing that any contract language involving pay or benefits would require the approval of Congress, PATCO began lining up support in the body. At the union's behest, Representative William L. Clay of Missouri introduced a bill that embodied PATCO's wish list and rounded up thirty cosponsors for it in the House.[20]

The buzz around the contract talks began to worry conservatives, including some members of the administration. "I have to ask myself why an air traffic controller should be paid as much as the Cabinet Secretaries," said one official who refused to be named. Concerned conservatives did their best to pressure the administration to hold the line in the talks. David Denholm of the Public Service Research Council was particularly alarmed. Recalling what he had seen during Reagan's term as governor of California, Denholm worried that the administration would sacrifice principle for pragmatism in its efforts to pay PATCO back for its endorsement. To preempt that possibility, Denholm circulated a position paper on Capitol Hill outlining the dangers inherent in meeting any of PATCO's demands. He warned legislators that PATCO was preparing an illegal strike intended to "bring the government to its knees," if it did not get its way. It would be better to take a strike, no matter how costly, and defeat it, than make concessions that could create a dangerous precedent for all federal workers, he argued. The efforts of Denholm and others to stir up opposition to the talks began to pay off as critical letters arrived at the White House. "If you don't come down hard on these bums, the union organizers will try to unionize the Army, Navy, and Air Force," one correspondent warned. "Half-hearted attempts to mediate the outrageous demands of PATCO will lend legitimacy to their wants," said another, who urged Reagan to show he could not be "used as a foil for the lust for power of these unions."[21]

By mid-May the government had still not decided how far it might go to meet PATCO's demands, and federal negotiators fended off all efforts to talk about salary increases, the length of the workweek, and other key demands. This came as no surprise to PATCO. From the beginning its leaders believed that the government would only cross the line into the "nonnegotiable" territory when it understood that PATCO's strike threat was serious. That threat, they believed, would provide the leverage necessary to overcome whatever internal opposition might exist within the administration to breaking precedents with this contract. On more than one occasion, Poli reminded his Reagan administration interlocutors that "The only illegal strike is an unsuccessful strike."[22]

When PATCO's national convention met in New Orleans on May 22, 1981, the union was prepared to execute the next phase of its plan. Three days before the delegates arrived, the PATCO executive board met to discuss the state of the negotiations and set a strike deadline. They chose June 22. On May 23, Poli made it official—and public. In a fiery speech to PATCO delegates in the ballroom at the Fairmont Hotel in the French Quarter, he announced that the union would stage a nationwide strike, shutting down air traffic from Key West to Anchorage, Puerto Rico to Guam, if it did not get an acceptable contract. Unless the Reagan administration altered its bargaining position, Poli announced, the controllers would walk. "I vow to you that the skies will be silent," he thundered. His speech elicited wild cheers and a standing ovation that lasted for several minutes. Although some delegates harbored private misgivings about PATCO's actual readiness to strike, none shared their views publicly. The strike plan was overwhelmingly approved. After the vote, many delegates marched down Bourbon Street to their favorite bar, chanting, "Deuce, Deuce! Deuce, Deuce!" in excited anticipation of June 22, when the credible strike threat that so many had worked so hard to build over the previous two years would finally pay off, liberating them from the constraints of federal sector bargaining once and for all, rectifying years of mistreatment and neglect. To mediator Flores, who was attending the convention as an observer, it seemed that the expectations of the PATCO delegates were detached from reality. "This is going to be bad, bad, bad, bad," he told Moffett.[23]

In the short run, though, PATCO's strike deadline accomplished its purpose. When it reached Washington, the news changed the nature of the negotiations. Up to that point, White House officials did not follow the talks daily and delayed deciding how far to go in order to avoid a strike. Once the deadline was set, that approach changed. Craig Fuller, the secretary to Reagan's cabinet, began monitoring the talks and sharing details with White House counselor Ed Meese, while Drew Lewis got personally involved in the talks for the first time.[24]

Meese occupied a unique position in the Reagan White House in 1981. Along with the president's chief of staff, James A. Baker III, and communications director Michael Deaver, he was a member of the "troika" that effectively ran the Reagan administration, directed its policy apparatus, and crafted its message. Each day these three met for breakfast at 7:30 a.m. to review the major issues of the day. At 8:30 they convened senior staff, made assignments, and listened to reports before they met with the president at 9. Meese's role in the group was twofold. He acted as Reagan's chief liaison to executive departments, and also as "keeper of the conservative vigil," as one insider put it. If anyone on the president's staff was predisposed to blocking concessions to PATCO, it was Meese. But he trusted Lewis's judgment and saw the negotiations less as a fight over principle than "a problem that had to be dealt with."[25]

Following the PATCO convention, White House officials began to move toward a consensus on their final offer, with Lewis pressing for flexibility in the interest of avoiding a strike. Specifically, Lewis asked for authority to address a portion of the controllers' salary demand. His request was controversial. When the White House asked the OMB to evaluate it, the agency strongly opposed the idea, arguing that the government never had bargained before on salary issues. Doing so would be a mistake that would "establish a dramatic precedent," the OMB report concluded. On June 5, domestic policy adviser T. Kenneth Cribb was dispatched to Lewis's office to share the OMB objections. Lewis refused to budge. In his judgment, if the contract offer failed to address the salary issue at all, PATCO would certainly stage a costly strike. He told Cribb that he believed he needed "a 5 percent across the board add-on" to avoid a strike, and he asked for a high-level meeting at the White House to discuss the idea. The meeting was set for June 11.[26]

Lewis went to the meeting determined to win approval for his proposed package. Prior to the meeting, he circulated a memo to Reagan's top advisers impressing upon them the staggering costs a strike would exact on the economy. Lewis predicted that eight thousand of the nation's seventeen-thousand-controller workforce would strike and the walkout might be honored by 85 percent of controllers in some major facilities. To avoid this, Lewis sought approval for a precedent-setting package at the meeting. It included an unprecedented 5 percent addition to base salaries and a string of other sweeteners: an exemption for controllers from federal caps on premium and overtime pay; an increase in the night shift differential from 10 percent to 20 percent of salary; a guaranteed paid one-half-hour lunch period; a stipulation that controllers in high density facilities would no longer spend more than 6.5 hours per day on position; and severance pay that would give any controller medically disqualified after at least five years on the job a one-year salary in lump sum payment.[27]

Never before had the government offered so much in a negotiation with a federal employees' union. Lewis's proposed terms clearly crossed into the territory of items previously considered nonnegotiable, according to the terms of the 1978 CSRA and previous presidential orders. "Adoption of this package should avoid a strike," one internal administration assessment concluded. "However, the concepts outlined in this paper represent a significant departure." Some worried that the proposal would conflict with the administration's efforts to slow government spending and reduce inflation and create a precedent that would encourage other federal unions "to adopt militant PATCO tactics." With negotiations between the U.S. Postal Service and its unions commencing, some Reagan advisers thought the Lewis offer would encourage the postal unions to hold out for more. In short, then, there were many reasons why Meese, OMB Director David Stockman, and others present at the June 11 meeting could have decided to reject Lewis's proposal. But they approved it. Meese concluded that Lewis struck the right balance for a president who was "trying to be helpful" to an ally while at the same time trying to rein in federal spending. The group recommended that the president endorse Lewis's approach. Lewis was confident that Reagan would concur. From his conversations with the president, he believed Reagan "knew exactly what we needed" in order not to "put them on strike." On June 12, he received the word he anticipated: his proposal was approved.[28]

"Nut-Cracking Time"

PATCO leaders had no way of knowing in mid-June that they had already crossed into uncharted territory, winning approval from a conservative president for a contract that far exceeded anything the federal government had offered a union before. PATCO leaders were focused instead on executing the next part of their plan, building support for the strike vote they would hold at midnight on June 22, in order to gain the final bit of leverage they believed they needed to get the best possible offer from the administration. FAA officials in the field were similarly unaware of the proposal that had been approved by the White House. As they saw PATCO ratcheting up its strike preparations, their focus was on preparing the agency for a strike that seemed increasingly likely. Consequently, tension levels in the FAA's facilities reached unprecedented levels in the final two weeks before "Deuce, Deuce."

In June 1981, Alex Hendriks, a European official with the International Federation of Air Traffic Controllers' Associations, toured New York Center and was astonished by the level of labor-management animosity that pervaded the facility. His tour guide stopped at the threshold of the control room explaining that as a supervisor he could not step inside without inciting a torrent of verbal abuse. When Hendriks himself went in, he was immediately questioned: "Are you a controller, or are you management?" Hendriks had seen labor disputes in visits to air traffic control facilities in many countries over the years, but he never saw a more polarized environment.[29]

The situation in Islip was typical. Conflicts erupted over matters large and small in the weeks before the deadline, as management and the union both geared up for a conflict. The struggle that erupted over a tee shirt at Oakland Center symbolized the rising tension. African American controller Dwayne A. Theadford defied an order by facility chief Erwin Buschauer banning any public statement supporting a strike. Ignoring the order, Theadford donned a tee shirt that was widely distributed among PATCO activists in preparation for 1981. It depicted the U.S. government as a bald eagle swooping down, its talons extended, about to attack a mouse labeled PATCO. The mouse was depicted as unfazed, standing on its hind legs, disdainfully raising the middle finger of its right paw to the eagle in an obscene gesture. Beneath the tableau was emblazoned, "PATCO, the Last Act of Defiance." When Theadford refused to remove the shirt, he was suspended for five days.[30]

A later study commissioned by the FAA found that many agency supervisors took actions that seemed intentionally provocative in this period. Even some controllers who did not intend to strike wondered whether officials wanted to provoke a walkout as a means of getting rid of PATCO's most troublesome activists. As supervisors exerted their authority more robustly, PATCO pushed back harder. When an O'Hare supervisor asked a PATCO member coming off break to relieve an on-duty controller who was not a PATCO member, he was told, "I don't relieve scabs." FAA facilities became tension-filled tinderboxes as June 22 drew near.[31]

In the final days, Choirboys made their closing arguments, and "fence-sitters" felt pressure to declare which side they were on. Unless they stood up in 1981, a Corpus Christi activist argued, controllers would have to "blow the dust off the white shirt, brush the lint from the black slacks, and invest in several narrow black ties." Controllers were, by nature, decision makers. They were trained from the first to size up problems and make choices quickly, to be decisive when faced with high-pressure situations. "Even if it was a wrong decision, make a damn decision, because you can fix it," one instructor liked to tell trainees. "What you can't fix is doing nothing." So they made their choices.[32]

As they did, new divisions and new solidarities emerged. Strike supporters and opponents ceased mixing in the cafeterias and break rooms, or over after-hours drinks. Friendships were recemented or eroded, depending on how one answered the question: "are you prepared to strike?" Even family ties could be strained. In Chicago, Bob Mischke, an O'Hare supervisor and his son, a PATCO supporter at Midway Airport, ended up on different sides of the widening divide. The act of declaring before their coworkers that they would put their jobs on the line, by striking if need be, created powerful ties of unity among those who took this step. Long-simmering grievances and resentments reconfirmed strike supporters in their decisions and redoubled the resolve of many. Denver PATCO leader John Haggerty detected a powerful momentum building behind this solidarity. "It was almost like no matter what they offer in the way of a contract this is what we're going to do." The force of it worried even some local PATCO leaders. The president of one Massachusetts local wrote Reagan that PATCO had "NO OPTIONS" left in its dealings with the FAA. "I plea that with your help cooler heads might prevail and that sanity might enter the negotiation process," he added.[33]

As battle lines were drawn in the facilities, the contract talks moved to the FMCS headquarters on K Street, where Moffett hosted the negotiations in his conference room. Drew Lewis joined the talks at this point. Moffett and Flores were impressed. Never before had a cabinet officer represented the government in a negotiation like this. Watching Lewis and his outside counsel work, Flores thought, was like watching a symphony. The lawyers knew when to let Lewis take the lead and when to take it themselves. During breaks, the government side called the White House to give Craig Fuller updates, which he in turn passed on to Meese.[34]

During these final sessions, the government began to unveil the dimensions of its offer. Moffett and Flores were surprised to see how far the Reagan administration was prepared to go to satisfy PATCO. As Lewis laid out aspects of the proposal, Moffett watched Poli's reaction closely, thinking PATCO "came out a big winner." But Poli did not seem impressed. Lewis tried to sell Poli with the argument that a half a loaf is better than none, adding "we're doing something here that no one else is about to do in government, which is to negotiate with you over wages, hours, and working conditions." Poli was unmoved. He believed that PATCO deserved, had been promised, and could get more. On June 17, he walked out of the talks.[35]

It seemed clear to Moffett and Flores at that point that PATCO leaders intended to push the negotiations to the brink in order to maximize their leverage. The unprecedented concessions the Reagan administration had already made in the talks only solidified a belief in the minds of PATCO leaders that their plan was working. They now knew the administration *was* prepared to negotiate with them over their salaries. How far they could get the administration to go in granting them concessions they would only learn on the night of June 22, when they showed the FAA that 80 percent of air traffic controllers were prepared to walk out and shut down air traffic. Gary Eads wrote the president directly with a warning. "Unless some higher authority becomes involved soon, a nationwide controllers strike will take place on June 22, 1981. This is not a threat. It is instead a statement of what I believe the unfortunate facts to be."[36]

On Thursday morning, June 18, Craig Fuller reported to President Reagan and the troika of Meese, Baker, and Deaver that an air traffic control strike appeared likely on June 22 unless a breakthrough occurred over the weekend. Fuller outlined in detail what the government had offered to date. Combined with a scheduled pay increase to all federal workers that would take effect in October, Fuller explained that controllers would receive an 11.4 percent total salary increase under the government's proposal. This did not seem to be enough, Fuller explained. He then observed that the government might "need to consider an additional increase for the controllers" to prevent a strike. "The solution probably lies in providing additional benefits in at least two areas: direct pay increases and shorter hours," he wrote. But improving the offer posed risks, he noted. "The question remaining is how much can we afford to offer in terms of the direct dollar cost to satisfy the controllers and in terms of the precedent we set that must be considered when we deal with other federal employees."[37]

There was no consensus on whether the administration should sweeten its offer. OPM director Donald Devine was among those who opposed negotiating over salary as a matter of principle, fearing that its effects would ripple through the entire federal workforce and encourage other unions to demand similar privileges. Lewis, however, argued for flexibility and believed a few minor concessions might do the trick. The White House entrusted Lewis to make the judgment. According to notes taken by Reagan aide David Gergen at a June 20 White House meeting, the goal was to avoid a conflict with Poli and not "back him into a corner."[38]

With the strike deadline hours away, the two sides reconvened at 2 p.m. on Sunday June 21. They made no progress before breaking for dinner at 6:30. By the time the sides reconvened at 9, it was already apparent that whatever marginal sweeteners Lewis might make in the final hours would not avert a strike vote. "The strike is on," Poli told a television news reporter on his way into the final round of talks that night. Asked again whether a strike was now a certainty, Poli answered, "Absolutely," before correcting himself to say, "there's still a question." As the talks entered their final hours, Lewis suggested different ways Poli could apply the government's money offer to increase controllers' salaries, or lengthen the thirty-minute paid lunch break each day, effectively reducing their workweek. According to PATCO negotiator Dennis Reardon's notes, around midnight, Lewis and Poli began discussing the possibility of trimming another ninety minutes more from controllers' weekly work schedules.[39]

As midnight passed, it was clear to the mediators that a ninety-minute reduction would not be enough to get Poli to call off the vote. Instead, Poli kept talking while he awaited a report from the field on the strike vote that was being taken at that moment around the country. During a break, Flores and Moffett took Poli aside, asked him if he was sure he knew what he was doing, and warned him that FAA officials seemed ready to handle a strike. "Are you sure, Bob, that they don't have a fucking black box to run this thing?" asked Flores. Poli assured the mediators that the FAA could not operate for long if PATCO struck. It was clear to them that he was determined to come back to the table with his ultimate weapon, an announcement that the controllers were walking out unless the government substantially improved its offer. The skies would be silent. Only then would the union know exactly how far the government was prepared to go.[40]

WILD HORSES

Around the country, controllers began converging on their local strike headquarters for the long-anticipated "horse count" early that Sunday evening. At a labor temple in Billings, Montana, the ballroom of a Holiday Inn in

Aurora, Illinois, an electrical workers union hall in West Palm Beach, Florida, an auto workers local in Indianapolis, and in more than one hundred other locations, they began gathering after dinner. They did not plan to return home until after the first shift began in facilities the next morning. By then, they knew they would either have won an unprecedented contract redressing what they believed were years of underpay, overwork, and mistreatment, or they would be embarked on an unprecedented strike for such a contract. The "horse counts" were not secret ballots. Simply by showing up to these meetings, controllers indicated that they were prepared to stand together and were ready to strike if necessary. As they streamed in, feelings of anxiety, dread, excitement, and relief comingled. The day for which the union had long prepared had finally arrived. They sat, talked, smoked, listened to speeches... and waited. As the Choirboys took their headcounts, they were surprised to see some "fence-sitters" had shown up and disappointed to discover that some controllers who seemed like reliable strike supporters had developed cold feet. At midnight Eastern Time, the count began. Leaders at each location counted heads and phoned in the results to regional representatives who aggregated them and relayed them to strike coordinators working in PATCO's nondescript "safe house" on Capitol Hill, a location that Jack Maher had picked out a year earlier before leaving PATCO.[41]

Everyone knew the count would not be 100 percent accurate. In Hawaii, the evening shift was working during the count and PATCO leaders had to guess which controllers would show up once the shift let out. Still, none of the strike leaders was prepared for the results that were being tabulated in the Washington safe house. Midway through the count, it began to appear for the first time that the union might not hit the 80 percent goal that planners had set for strike participation, the number they thought they needed to successfully shut down the system. This trend defied the careful estimates the union had made in preceding weeks. Choirboys never thought they would exceed the 80 percent mark by a wide margin, but they were convinced they would hit it. They had worked for so many months on reaching that threshold that failing seemed inconceivable. The final results of the strike vote shocked them: the union fell short by about 5 percent.[42]

A little after 3 a.m., Poli took a call from field coordinator Jim Lundie in the office of the FMCS deputy director, which PATCO used as its caucus room. It was at that moment that Poli learned the "disheartening news concerning our field support," according to the notes kept by Dennis

Reardon. "At 3:30 a.m. we knew we did not have the 80%," Reardon wrote. Poli immediately conferred with his board members. At least one suggested calling the strike anyway. But that idea was rejected. In shock, they agreed that Poli should go back in and finalize the best contract he could get. When the negotiations reconvened after that phone call, the mediators detected an immediate shift in mood. They guessed that PATCO would not strike after all because Poli suddenly seemed willing to accept items he had previously rejected. Lewis and the government negotiators also understood what had happened. PATCO leaders later speculated that the government had bugged the phone lines and heard the news as soon as Poli did. It is impossible to either verify or disprove this allegation. But, in the end, it did not matter. The fact that Poli did not return to the bargaining table with word that a strike was on told the government negotiators all they needed to know. "Suddenly they became very hardnosed," Reardon's notes reported.[43]

At that point, only half of the ninety-six bargaining points had been settled. Over the next few hours the negotiators went through the remaining items, settling them one by one, agreeing to carry forward language from the 1978 PATCO-FAA contract on all but four items. As this process unfolded, it was unclear if the government would leave on the table the offer the White House had approved on June 12 and that PATCO had rejected earlier in the evening. According to both mediators and Reardon's notes, Lewis restrained his negotiators from taking back items previously offered. "Only through Lewis' intervention were we able to regain any of our losses," Reardon noted. Lewis's help was little comfort to Poli and his team at that point: they were forced to accept a contract that they had previously characterized as unacceptable. "At 10:30 a.m. we finally left FMCS with a less than satisfactory agreement," wrote Reardon. As they departed, Poli and Lewis each stepped before a bank of television cameras to comment on their tentative agreement. "I'm pleased with the settlement," Poli lied. "We felt that, with the present economic conditions, it is a good package for us."[44]

When news reached the individual cluster meetings that the union had not hit its national target, the Choirboys were devastated. After so much hard work, they had failed to meet their goals. Some shed tears of frustration, but the reaction throughout PATCO's ranks was less uniform. In Longmont, Colorado, one member recalled that emotions ran the gamut. Many were relieved that the union would not strike. In the Bay Area strike hall, a member reported a combination of emotions somewhere between "disappointment and 'thank God.'" So it was at the Quality Inn in Leesburg, Virginia, where Washington Center controllers gathered. At the union hall in West Palm Beach, Florida, relief, confusion, and disappointment intermingled. But the union's most committed activists tended not to grasp the full range of emotions their colleagues were feeling. At the Holiday Inn on Route 31 in Aurora, Illinois, where Chicago Center controllers gathered, Carl Kern was sure that "all the people that were there were ready to go. Absolutely ready to go" on strike. But just feet away from Kern, Rich Andrews was feeling relieved at not having to walk out.[45]

Over the next few days, PATCO members' emotions continued to swirl as they learned details of the tentative contract. It fell far short of their opening demands, yet it had brought them far more than any previous FAA-PATCO contract, more than any other contract offer ever proffered by the federal government. After the fact, scholars agreed that it was a precedent-setting document that drew the government "beyond the outer limits of bargaining" under federal law, and seemed to "have altered all labor relations in the federal service." Union leaders with experience in government bargaining also saw it that way. When Jesse Calhoon learned the details, he pronounced it "the best civil service contract ever negotiated." Reaction to the contract by those who had hoped the Reagan administration would hold the line provided another measure of how much PATCO had won. Langhorne Bond was dumbfounded. "The union won," he thought. The administration had conceded the union's right to bargain over compensation. "You can't concede it," he said. "And they conceded it anyway." Many in the administration made a similar assessment. OPM Director Devine believed the administration had given away too much and thus would encourage other federal unions to match PATCO's gains. At the FAA, Ray Van Vuren, who believed he had his agency poised to break a strike, was furious. "They won," he decided, concluding that the contract would only encourage PATCO to continue being "obnoxious and insubordinate."[46]

Opposition to the tentative contract was loudest among conservatives. The National Right to Work Committee concluded that it "bodes evil for American taxpayers" and warned that "strike scenarios" of "other hungry public sector union officials" would become commonplace. "What we effectively did is bargain for wages and benefits with federal employees for the first time," argued the PSRC. "Government officials now anticipate that all other federal government unions will attempt to bargain for wages and benefits." PSRC Director David Denholm believed that Reagan's policy of fiscal restraint was "doomed to failure" in light of the PATCO agreement. Denholm contemplated a federal lawsuit to block the agreement from taking effect.[47]

Although such critiques worried administration officials, they believed they had the ability to marshal the congressional support necessary to fund the commitments they had made to PATCO. Lewis was confident that Senate Majority Leader Howard Baker, a Tennessee Republican, would help round up GOP votes despite the grumbling of conservatives like Senator Bob Dole of Kansas. Lewis also believed he could rely on the votes of liberal Democrats. One of the first calls Lewis placed was to Senator Ted Kennedy. "I'm going to have trouble with this thing in my own party," he explained. Kennedy promised to help if Lewis pledged to deliver a large bloc of Republican votes. With Kennedy and Baker both behind the tentative contract, Lewis was sure he could get it through.[48]

Lewis was so intent on defending the contract offer from right-wing critics who claimed it was too generous that he barely considered the possibility that controllers, who had sought much more, would reject the package as inadequate. Initially, rejection seemed a remote possibility. Many controllers, including activists who had helped build support for a strike, reacted positively to the first reports of the contract's contents, seeing it as a significant "step in the right direction." John Haggerty, president of the Denver Center local, was representative. He recalled feeling "a little bit of an elation" when he heard the terms. "Wow, we got something done here," he thought. "This isn't bad."[49]

Within forty-eight hours, however, a negative reaction began to crystallize. The more controllers compared the tentative contract to their opening demands, the less satisfied they were. Most had realized that they would not gain everything contained in PATCO's original demands, but the tentative contract fell so far short of the union's ambitious opening bid that it became difficult for union activists to see it as the sort of breakthrough labor relations experts believed it to be. Edwin Wintermeyer, president of PATCO's Pittsburgh local, described the June 22 agreement as "a Band-Aid for a cancer." Mike Gulbranson of Spokane thought it "an insult to every air traffic controller." Ray Carver of Minneapolis Center simply called it "a piece of shit." "There was no thirty-two-hour work week," Ron Taylor explained. His conclusion: "They didn't give us anything." Ed Meagher called the tentative agreement "insulting." It would have taken some work for PATCO's leaders to get their members to see the contract as a significant victory. It soon became apparent that they had no stomach for that task. The apparatus they would have needed to use to sell the contract, the Choirboy network, was distinctly unenthused by its terms. In some ways, the administration's willingness to break precedent by negotiating over compensation made it harder for Choirboys to settle. By setting a new precedent, the administration had validated the Choirboys' assumption that controller militancy could push the government into uncharted territory. That logic in turn raised a tantalizing corollary. If PATCO had gotten this much by only rattling its saber, it would undoubtedly get more if it unsheathed the weapon. Had the union demonstrated that its members were ready to walk, the Choirboys were convinced, Lewis would have offered more. How much more would never be known until the union took that step.[50]

By the time PATCO locals held meetings to review the contents of the tentative contract, momentum was building against it. Choirboys played key roles in helping members understand what had been offered and how far short it was from meeting the union's goals. It became hard for those who viewed the contract favorably to hold their ground in arguments with critics. Jim Morin of LaGuardia arrived at a meeting of his local intending to support ratification of the contract. When he found only one other person willing to speak for ratification, he changed his mind. Passions shaped by many years of perceived neglect and mistreatment began to stir. One PATCO spouse from Vermont implored Poli to "help our men attain a better contract and not settle for what has been offered, for if they do, then the term 'loser' will come with it."[51]

Poli and PATCO's Washington officials conferred by phone with PATCO's board, Choirboys, and key regional leaders during the forty-eight hours after negotiators reached agreement on the tentative contract. As they shared information among themselves regarding the reaction, the board reached a turning point. Had they stood together as one and resolved to support the contract in the face of internal critics, the board would have stood a good chance of selling the agreement to members who were still absorbing its details and who generally did not recognize the precedent PATCO had won at the bargaining table. The board, however, proved unwilling to take on the critics of the contract. "If we'd have said 'yes,' they would have voted 'no,'" David Siegel later explained. This would have divided the union and "made the board look very foolish," Siegel concluded. So rather than standing up for the tentative agreement, board members gave a green light to the contract's critics. On June 24, PATCO revealed to the press that the union was being inundated with "hundreds of letters, telegrams, mailgrams, and phone calls expressing dissatisfaction with the settlement." Siegel predicted to reporters that the membership would reject the contract by a 3–1 margin. That same day, rather than issuing a statement supporting the tentative contract in an effort to shape members' views of its terms, Poli and the PATCO board announced that they would convene a special meeting in Chicago on July 1–2 at which the board would hear from activists and consider whether to recommend ratification. Thus signaling their own unwillingness to campaign for the contract, the board opened the door to a wave of anticontract sentiment that swept through the union like an irresistible juggernaut over the following week.[52]

As the impulse in favor of rejection gathered steam, a situation unfolded in Washington that would make further concessions to PATCO a virtual political impossibility even if the Reagan administration had been inclined to offer more. During the runup to the June 22 negotiations, someone (perhaps someone in the administration who wanted to halt any further negotiations with PATCO) leaked to members of Congress a copy of the October 20, 1980, letter from PATCO's counsel Richard Leighton to Reagan's campaign aide Michael Balzano detailing the union's specific demands, including the replacement of FAA Administrator Bond. Several House Democrats, including Rep. Geraldine Ferraro of New York, got copies of that letter and immediately saw in it a chance to attack the president, whose popularity to that point had confounded them. Even as PATCO members were debating whether to accept the June 22 offer, Ferraro and three of her Democratic colleagues sent a copy of Leighton's letter to Attorney General William French Smith, charging that the letter constituted possible evidence that the Reagan campaign had violated the law by agreeing to fire a government official in return for a campaign endorsement. Ferraro and her colleagues demanded that Smith appoint an independent prosecutor to investigate. The allegations were reported in the *Washington Post* on June 28, and Leighton responded two days later with a lengthy letter to Smith rebutting the charges. Smith did not grant Ferraro's request for an investigation, but her letter effectively foreclosed any possibility that the administration could offer PATCO more in a second round of negotiations. Any further concessions to PATCO would have invited further scrutiny of the Leighton-

Balzano negotiation and allowed Reagan's critics to claim he was cutting a sweetheart deal as payback for PATCO's endorsement.[53]

To defend the president from accusations that he had made a shady back-room deal with PATCO, Reagan supporters who had been silent initially on the tentative contract began to characterize it as a shining example of presidential fortitude. Reagan had not made unprecedented concessions to a union that had endorsed him, the president's defenders insisted. Instead, he had clearly gotten the better of the union. On June 30, Reagan loyalist Lindley H. Clark Jr. peddled this view in the *Wall Street Journal*. "The administration hung Mr. Poli out to dry" and won "a great victory for the government," Clark wrote, in a column that seemed intent on putting to rest the charges Ferraro and her colleagues had raised. Clark completely elided the precedent-setting nature of the tentative FAA-PATCO contract and sug-gested with a straight face that it was "what the government offered from the start." Reagan was a tough negotiator, Clark explained. "Mr. Poli endorsed Mr. Reagan and what did it get him? He settled for a tiny fraction of what he asked." Moreover, by taking Poli to the brink of a strike and offering him so little, Reagan showed Poli he was prepared to "bomb him into rubble." Clark predicted that Poli would have a hard time selling the contract to his mem-bers. Inevitably, Clark's prediction had a self-fulfilling quality. The union's activists photocopied and circulated the column as evidence that PATCO had been snookered.[54]

Within the union, support for the contract was rapidly evaporating. Unbeknown to PATCO leaders, within the administration any remaining political will to negotiate further with PATCO was disappearing just as quickly. In this charged context, PATCO's board members headed to their special meeting in Chicago, where the union had announced its first job action only thirteen years earlier.

All day on July 1 in a conference room at the O'Hare Hilton, and over dinner at Nick's Fishmarket, the board debated the merits of the contract, their chances of securing ratification, and their prospects of getting a better offer if they called a strike. In that discussion, Poli listened to his board more than he tried to shape their views. Charlie Campbell was the lone board member who entered the debate favoring approval of the contract. Most board members favored outright rejection and the setting of another strike date. Michael Fermon of Boston, who had succeeded George Kerr as Eastern region vice president, took a middle position. He favored rejection, but cautioned against a strike. Fermon argued that PATCO did "*not* have an army of sufficient size to wage a *successful* war at *this* time." Instead of striking, PATCO should go to the media and lobby Congress, expressing the "absolute frustration, dissatisfaction and disillusion [*sic*] that the membership has for the 'system,'" he argued. As the discussion unfolded, one issue helped seal the debate. If the union did not reject the contract and set another strike date, "internal fighting" would erupt throughout the ranks. Some facilities would stage their own work stoppages, and the union would lose its unity. By the time they left Nick's Fishmarket after midnight, the group had reached a consensus.[55]

The next day, July 2, 1981, in the ballroom of the airport hotel, the PATCO board heard from hundreds of activists, local union officials, and Choirboys. When Poli opened the floor to comments and questions, controllers leaped to their feet and lined up ten-deep at microphones on the floor, where one by one they poured forth a torrent of anger and dissatisfaction. Supporters of ratification in the room were quickly marginalized into silence by the size and vehemence of the antiratification group. Critics of the contract alleged that the FAA had negotiated in bad faith, had spied on PATCO, and had pulled items off the table once it was clear that the union would not strike. Most had made up their minds in favor of a new strike date. Ominously, some controllers threatened to strike with or without the union.[56]

Having elicited these views, the board briefly recessed and formally voted on a resolution. By a vote of 8–0, the board recommended rejection of the tentative contract. Having shaken hands with Lewis on the agreement, Poli abstained in that vote. Vice President Bob Meyer read the resolution to the hundreds gathered in the ballroom. Pandemonium ensued. Cheers, screams, and stomping feet soon morphed into a chant of "Strike! Strike! Strike!" that gripped the room for more than two minutes.[57]

"We Had to Strike"

Outside observers had difficulty understanding what had happened in Chicago and why. Many blamed Poli for the board's decision. To Drew Lewis, the Chicago resolution was evidence that Poli did not have the authority to speak for his membership and could no longer be trusted as a negotiating partner. Many other union leaders, including J. J. O'Donnell of the Air Line Pilots, concluded that Poli did not have the fortitude to stand up to his union's militants and make them understand the limits of the possible. Mediator Ken Moffett decided that Poli was simply too inexperienced for such a high-stakes negotiation. But most PATCO activists believed Poli could not have held back the tide even if he tried. As one Choirboy explained, the "consensus of opinion was if Bob wasn't going to lead us out, then Bob was going to go." After thirteen years of FAA-PATCO conflict and three contracts, each of which was more disappointing than the last, the pent-up fury that had built up among a critical mass of controllers could not be defused by the details of the June 22 offer. Too many PATCO members wanted to take on the FAA "because they were just sick of them."[58]

Once the PATCO board recommended rejection of the tentative contract, a strike became all but inevitable. The allegations of Rep. Ferraro and her colleagues that the Reagan administration had been engaged in improper dealings with PATCO and threats by David Denholm and other conservatives to challenge the PATCO-FAA negotiation in court ensured that the administration would not risk offering PATCO any more contract sweeteners. At the same time, once it had recommended against the contract, the PATCO board felt that it had no choice but to secure an overwhelming rejection and a successful strike vote if it hoped to budge government negotiators. Failing to do so would show the union to be a paper tiger.[59]

As members voted on the contract in July by mail ballots, PATCO's leaders prepared the union for the conflict that now seemed necessary. On July 16, a meeting of Choirboys and PATCO national officials in Washington debated a revision of the union's strike plan. There was a general agreement that the 80 percent threshold might have been set too high. "How would the membership react to a major change in the strike plan?" an outline for this meeting asked. At the meeting, officials were asked to consider an explosive question: "Could we change the numbers required and still be successful?" According to one calculation offered at the meeting, PATCO fell 811 controllers short of hitting its strike vote in the early morning hours of June 22. By eliminating data system specialists from the calculation, the union could lower the threshold by 260. Others suggested excluding developmental controllers from the count to further lower the threshold. A variety of revisions of the 80 percent formula were discussed.[60]

There is no written record of the strike plan revisions that were made that day. Subsequently, PATCO strikers and scholars alike tended to believe that a new formula was adopted that made it easier for the union to reach its strike target. But these ex post facto analyses missed a larger point: by July 16, formulas and specific numbers no longer mattered. Having decided to reject the government's last offer, PATCO leaders knew they had to strike. If they brought a second round of negotiations to the brink and again failed to call a strike, the union would lose any remaining leverage. "We'd be dead!" PATCO militant Bill Taylor of Arizona later explained. According to Taylor, PATCO "had no choice after June 22; we *had* to strike, regardless of the vote!" If the union did not strike, the FAA would "tell the world we didn't have the support of our people and they'd move on us like never before!" PATCO "had to tell everybody we had gotten the numbers this time around," said Taylor. The union "couldn't let a number we had set ourselves, a number that we could have set 5 or 10% higher or lower, get in our way," he added.[61]

To persuade the members to reject the tentative contract and to prepare them for a second strike vote, Choirboys and PATCO leaders fanned out across the country. When Poli took to the hustings he told the story of how the government negotiators had pulled items off the table once they realized the union was not prepared to strike. He suggested that, if PATCO went to the brink again and this time stood united, it could wrest a fair offer from the government. As that argument spread through the union, the group solidarity forged by their shared histories, reinforced by the nature of their work, and galvanized by years of conflict between their union and the FAA took hold among the controllers. Even before the ratification ballots were counted, the next step was clear.

TRADING PAINT

It's going to be like flying the Enola Gay. You're going to
drop something on August 3rd and you're going to turn
around and you're going to know that it's something big
and huge and you're going to see it and it's going to
shake the airplane and it's going to shake the world. But
you don't know what you've got until you drop it.
—DOMENIC TORCHIA, PATCO LEADER

On Wednesday, July 29, Poli called Drew Lewis to say that 95.3 percent of
PATCO members had voted to reject the tentative contract. Lewis had been
anticipating the call since PATCO's July 2 Chicago meeting. He immediately issued a statement to the press alleging that Poli broke the promise he
made on June 22 to work for contract ratification. Lewis then told Craig
Fuller that PATCO would likely not accept any incremental offer before
calling a strike to increase its bargaining leverage. As if to confirm Lewis's
analysis, PATCO released a press statement of its own saying that it would
give the government only five days to come up with an acceptable contract
offer. If such an offer was not forthcoming, the union would strike on
Monday morning, August 3.[1]

On July 31, Lewis visited the White House to discuss with Meese, Fuller,
and other top officials how to approach the final negotiations. For many

reasons, Lewis and the others never seriously considered adding anything to their package. Doing so would serve only to reawaken the Leighton-Balzano endorsement controversy, which could be damaging to the president. Additionally, many administration officials believed that too much had been conceded in the earlier contract. OPM Director Devine, among others, was relieved that PATCO had rejected the precedent-setting tentative contract, and hoped PATCO's folly would allow the administration to wipe the slate clean. Furthermore, White House officials worried about the impact any further concessions to PATCO would have on postal workers who were at that moment preparing to vote by mail on a contract their leaders had just negotiated. If the administration budged on PATCO it would invite the postal workers to reject their pact in hopes of getting a better one as well. Most importantly, though, the character of Reagan's presidency was on the line. Administration officials were determined not to give in to the threat of an illegal strike. If a union could force the U.S. government into concessions, they believed, it would call Reagan's resolve into question and send the message to foreign powers that the American president lacked toughness.[2]

For all of these reasons, it was agreed that the government would add no money to its proposal. Wanting an olive branch, at least for symbolic purposes, Lewis sought White House support for an approach that would add no money to the June 22 proposal but would give PATCO complete flexibility on how to allocate the funds that had been offered. If the union wanted to devote the entire package to salary increases, it would be free to do so. Meese strongly backed this approach. Lewis also told the White House he would stay at the bargaining table until the end, so that it would be clear that it was Poli who walked out.[3]

DRAWING THE LINE

PATCO leaders knew that they were about to launch something unprecedented, but they believed they were ready. In April 1980 PATCO had distributed a fifty-five-page strike-planning booklet to members. In the months that followed, the union prepared as though it was going to war. Strike planners developed "clusters" of locals that could coordinate their activity during the anticipated strike independent of national direction should PATCO's leaders be arrested. Clusters had established secret "safe houses" from which local strike efforts could be directed in the event that union headquarters were raided. Strike planners urged local clusters to set up decentralized calling trees to pass information and recommended that members use phone booths or friends' phones when communicating vital strike information. Planners also advised members to employ codes to transmit important messages; "enciphering systems can keep computers busy for 99 years trying to figure them out," one memo explained.[4]

The planning also extended to personal finances. For months, Choirboys urged their members to prepare for a prolonged and difficult fight. Controllers were counseled to line up part-time jobs, eliminate credit card debt, and stock up on essentials. Some went so far as to take out second mortgages on their homes to build up a short-term financial cushion. Planners also warned that some strike leaders would be arrested for defying injunctions. Some or all would be threatened with firing. And some of the union's leaders might even be singled out to lose their jobs permanently in a poststrike settlement, even if the union held out for amnesty for all strikers. Such warnings were sobering, especially for most PATCO members who had not been through PATCO's 1970 sickout.[5]

Yet, despite the warnings, most members were not as prepared for a long struggle as their leaders believed. Most thought that an air traffic controllers' strike would be short if it took 80 percent off the job. One survey of PATCO members found that two-thirds believed that a strike would be settled within fifteen days. With that in mind, few controllers prepared financially for a much longer struggle. Fewer still considered the possibility that mass firings and the permanent replacement of ten thousand or more controllers could result from a strike. They did not believe the FAA could lose that many controllers and continue to function.[6]

Many members were also latecomers to the idea of striking. In May 1979, when the union first polled its membership on this issue, only 53 percent said they would support a national strike. By March 1981, after nearly two years of work by the Choirboys, that number rose to 84 percent—but this likely overstated the true support level, since only 78 percent of the union's membership returned the survey and strike supporters were more likely to do so. At most, only two-thirds of PATCO's membership ever clearly indicated in an anonymous survey that they would support a strike. A later study showed that the typical strike supporter felt a higher degree of alienation from the FAA; experienced more job-related stress; worked in a high-density facility; and tended to be younger and better educated. Others who did not fit this profile decided to support the walkout for a variety of reasons, including their loyalty to their coworkers, their belief in the basic justice of PATCO's cause, and their perception that the union was on the verge of making a major breakthrough that would upgrade their profession. Still others decided to support the strike due to simple peer pressure rather than a deep commitment to PATCO's goals or strategy.[7]

No matter their motivations, PATCO members and their families did not take the decision to strike lightly. "It's frightening to take on the federal government," admitted a Raleigh-Durham Airport controller. "I'm scared stiff." For most, deciding to break the oath against striking that they were required to take as federal employees was difficult. But they reasoned that they had done all they could to redress their grievances through lawful means. "I know I'm breaking the law, but I don't feel like a criminal," one controller explained. They saw striking as a form of civil disobedience forced upon them by federal laws that denied them their full collective bargaining rights. Yet this argument did not make the decision easier. As the clock ticked down toward the strike vote, many tearful conversations took place in controllers' families. "Daddy may even have to go to jail," the wife of one Vermont controller told her children. If he did, they should not "be ashamed," she said. Instead, they should "be very proud of him," because if that happened it would be "for a great cause." In most cases, families pulled together to support the strike. Nearly one hundred spouses' support groups formed in anticipation of the walkout. "I support him regardless of the hardships that might be imposed on our family, because he has the courage and conviction to fight for what is right," one PATCO wife wrote.[8]

As they made their decisions, controllers developed personal rationales for their actions. Although money was at the heart of the union's demands, few saw their decision in monetary terms. For most, the impending conflict was primarily a battle over principles: ensuring that they and their coworkers could reach retirement age in their jobs without burning out from stress; guaranteeing that their jobs would survive as sustainable portals into the middle class; and above all, winning dignity and respect from the FAA. Each of them found their own ways to manage their anxiety as the hour neared. Some turned to sardonic humor. Not a few made references to the infamous 1978 People's Temple mass suicide, involving the followers of Rev. Jim Jones in Jonestown, Guyana, and spoke proudly of "drinking the Kool-Aid." But, like Don Kopsic, the president of PATCO's Miami local who called himself "a Kool-Aid type at heart," such references spoke of their resolution to see their cause through to the end. As they saw it, the FAA forced them to drink from the cup of conflict, and they were not going to shrink from it.[9]

The FAA was no less ready for a fight. The agency had been preparing for it since 1979. Under Helms, the FAA continuously updated and revised Langhorne Bond's strike contingency plan. No one had been more pleased by the news that PATCO had rejected the June 22 tentative agreement than Helms. He had been outraged by the concessions made in that pact and thought they would only encourage ongoing militancy from PATCO. He was determined to stand up to the union. "I'm a retired Marine Corps colonel, and I don't give in," he said.[10]

As the deadline neared, director of air traffic Ray Van Vuren reviewed the FAA's three-part plan. The first part relied on "flow control," limiting the number of flights that were allowed to take off to ensure that any plane aloft could be guided expeditiously to its destination with exaggerated degrees of separation. To manage flow across the nation, the FAA had constructed a special facility at its Independence Avenue office. The Central Flow Control Facility, known as "Central Flow" or "CF-Squared," could keep tabs on the entire system with direct phone lines to each of the nation's centers and towers. By monitoring twenty-two "pacing airports"—hubs that handled 70 percent of all passenger traffic—and the twenty air route traffic control centers, the Washington facility could keep its finger on the pulse of air traffic around the nation. They would adjust traffic flow accordingly by relying on computer programs that spat out models of varying capacity, depending upon the number of controllers who remained on the job. While controllers handled an average of thirty-three thousand departures on a typical summer day, the system was capped at ninety-five hundred departures for the first day of a strike with an ability to adjust the numbers as warranted. With flow control in place, the FAA could redeploy controllers as needed to areas of greater traffic density. The plan also secured the cooperation of Canadian and European governments, whose aviation agencies agreed to modulate flow into the United States to avoid overloading the U.S. system.[11]

The second part of the FAA's plan addressed the recruitment of replacement workers. The key group of replacements was to be furnished by the FAA's own frontline management. All FAA supervisors had once worked air traffic. In 1980, the FAA initiated a plan for supervisors to receive recertification and retraining that would allow them to go back to directing traffic.

Most were ready to go on August 3. Military air traffic controllers constituted a second source of replacement workers. Defense Secretary Caspar
Weinberger offered to deploy up to eight hundred military controllers to
FAA facilities if PATCO struck. The FAA also reached out to retired air
traffic controllers and pilots, training them to undertake support work for
replacement controllers in the event of a strike. Finally, the agency's training
facility at Oklahoma City geared up to receive an unprecedented wave of
new trainees. Officials ordered hundreds of new desks, printed manuals and
course syllabi, and even reserved rooms in area motels to house trainees
who could not find space in the Oklahoma City facility's dormitories.[12]

PATCO officials were aware of and tended to dismiss the importance of
these two aspects of the FAA's preparations. Union strategists believed that
the system could not operate for long under the reduced capacities that
would be forced on it by a walkout, and flow control and replacement
workers would be unable to pick up the slack of thirteen thousand strikers,
each of whom had trained for years for their positions. But PATCO's leaders
did not anticipate or understand the significance of the third aspect of the
FAA's strike preparations: the cooperation that the agency elicited from the
Air Transport Association, the trade group of the nation's airlines.[13]

Like other aspects of the contingency plan, the negotiations with the airlines began under Bond but did not reach fruition until Helms and Lewis
took over strike planning. The Reagan officials knew that winning the cooperation of the airlines was essential if they were to withstand the pressure of
a strike. For the airlines, an air traffic control strike presented a host of challenges. Even talk of a possible strike caused many travelers to make other
transportation plans or cancel trips altogether, thereby cutting ticket sales.
A full-scale strike presented a great many unknowns to airline executives,
who were already struggling with a spike in fuel prices and a deepening
recession, in addition to the ongoing turbulence in their industry unleashed
by the 1978 airline deregulation act. Yet it was this turbulence that provided
the context for an entente that was struck between the airlines and the FAA
over how to respond to a PATCO strike.[14]

Simply put, with the FAA's help, the major airlines came to see a PATCO
strike as an opportunity to temporarily resurrect a semblance of airline regulation. The strike-imposed regulatory framework would offer them a spell of
relief from intense competition during which they could complete their tran-
sitions to the deregulatory era. Helms understood the problems the industry

was facing, and he presented an effective argument to airline officials. As revenues eroded in 1981 under the pressure of the economic slowdown and high fuel prices, he knew that many of the nation's major airlines continued to carry unprofitable routes that sent planes aloft less than half full, simply because they feared that if they dropped such routes their competitors would snap them up and use them to enhance their own strategic positions. Helms presented the FAA strike contingency plan as a way for airlines to shed their least profitable routes without fear of aiding their competitors.[15]

Helms laid out the argument to the ATA with characteristic bravado. "You got so damn much excess capacity now that you're going broke flying airplanes with only 35 to 40 percent loading factor. And I'm going to give you an excuse to put some of those airplanes on the ground, and cut down your staff. And you're going to blame me. And you're going to come through it," he said. "And you're going to be stronger and better and better off." The cutback in overall flights would allow the airlines to consolidate their systems without losing market share, and by the time the system came back up to prestrike levels, the airlines would have developed a better footing for the era of deregulation. "I'm going to wear that black hat and I'm going to save your ass," Helms told the airlines. It was a logic with which airline executives could not quarrel, and it won over longtime critics of deregulation like Bob Crandall, who led American Airlines.[16]

With the airlines ready to support the administration during a strike, the three key pieces of the FAA plan were in place. The agency also had plenty of lead time. Since hearing reports of PATCO's July 2 meeting in Chicago, FAA officials had been certain that a strike was coming and used the following month to tweak and perfect aspects of their plan. The final computer models were being churned out on Sunday, August 2, just as PATCO members were heading off to their "horse count," unaware of how far the airlines were prepared to go to help the government defeat them. At that point Helms had a final question for air traffic director Van Vuren. "Tell me something, can you truly operate this system?" he asked. "Yes," Van Vuren replied. "That's good enough for me," said Helms.[17]

Final Hours

When it became clear on July 31 that a strike was imminent, the leaders of the AFL-CIO and leading Democrats on Capitol Hill, who had paid little attention to the PATCO situation over previous weeks, unaware of how serious PATCO's intentions were, suddenly realized that they had a destabilizing crisis on their hands. Before departing for Chicago for a meeting of the AFL-CIO Executive Council that was to begin on August 3, Lane Kirkland and his second-in-command, Secretary-Treasurer Tom Donahue, began making calls. Donahue asked Jesse Calhoon to intercede with Poli, in order to get him to put off his deadline. "You cannot win this strike," Calhoon told Poli. His warning did not deter PATCO. Nor did pleas from Speaker of the House Tip O'Neill and other leading Democrats who also asked the union to postpone the strike deadline.[18]

From his weekend retreat, Camp David, President Reagan conferred by phone with his top advisers as they debated how to respond to a strike that now seemed inevitable. Two questions were paramount in the advisers' minds: When should the president address the situation? And what should he say? Some advisers advocated having the president issue a statement on Sunday August 2, warning controllers in advance that if they struck, the administration would cease negotiations with PATCO and would terminate strikers for staging an illegal job action. Issuing a clear warning would provide cover to controllers who felt pressured to strike but were not personally committed to the strategy, advocates of this view held. Others countered that if Reagan spoke and the strike occurred in spite of his statement, it would make him look weak. After consulting with Reagan by phone, the latter point of view prevailed. From this point forward, a chief concern of Reagan's advisers became ensuring that the president appear strong in the face of PATCO's challenge.[19]

Had Reagan's advisers been more aware of history, they might have understood the value of having the president issue a clear warning in his own words prior to the walkout, especially if the administration intended to take quick and drastic action to end the strike. Such a warning would have signaled unambiguously that the administration intended to handle this strike in a way that differed from past labor conflicts. There were thirty-nine work stoppages recorded against the federal government between 1962 and 1981. Most of these actions were small-scale and brief. But in only eight of those instances were any strikers discharged, and in those cases firings were targeted, not imposed in a blanket fashion. The most common penalty levied for these illegal job actions was loss of pay. In anticipating how the Reagan administration would respond to a strike, PATCO officials looked to that twenty-year pattern as well as to their own history—especially their success in winning back jobs for the controllers fired for their role in the 1970 sickout-strike. They anticipated that known strike leaders might indeed lose their jobs—at least for a while. They did not understand that the Reagan administration was finalizing a decision to break dramatically with precedent in handling a walkout by issuing blanket and permanent terminations. Indeed, PATCO leaders interpreted the administration's groundbreaking June 22 proposal, as inadequate as it was in their eyes, as evidence that Reagan would strike a deal in the end.[20]

The ultimate resolution of the second item debated by Reagan's advisers—what the president would say—ensured that the strike that was about to unfold would become a turning point in the nation's labor history. When Langhorne Bond commissioned the FAA's first strike contingency plan, he did not intend to permanently replace an entire striking workforce. Rather, the plan was meant to defeat a strike by showing that a walkout could not shut down the air traffic system. If the plan worked well, it would demonstrate the futility of a strike, lead to its rapid dissolution, and effectively remove the strike threat thereafter as a viable PATCO weapon. The decision on how to penalize the strikers, Bond knew, would be made by the White House, not the FAA. How Jimmy Carter would have responded, "what the president would do under pressure," Bond did not know. In contrast, Reagan's likely approach was never in doubt among his advisers. He would not tolerate an illegal strike.[21]

For Reagan it was not a question of whether to invoke the law and dismiss striking controllers from their jobs but, rather, how much time to give them to reconsider their position before terminating them. According to some of his advisers and an early draft of his August 3 statement, Reagan's initial inclination was to speak out in the first hours of the strike, and announce that "controllers who do not return to work immediately will be terminated." But Lewis, Helms, and Devine all counseled against "immediate" dismissals and argued for extending a deadline. Giving strikers time to consider their situation would encourage those marginally committed to the strike to break ranks and return to work, minimizing losses to the FAA. How long should the deadline be? Lewis believed that a longer deadline would ensure that more controllers returned to work, keeping costs down. Helms argued that forty-eight hours was sufficient. In the end, Reagan opted for the forty-eight-hour timeline, finalizing his decision on the morning of August 3.[22]

By the time the final round of negotiations began at 2:30 p.m. on Sunday August 2, at the headquarters of the Federal Mediation and Conciliation Service, each side had girded for battle. The sense of tension and uncertainty that marked the June 21 talks was gone. To the mediators, Moffett and Flores, the bargaining session took on the air of an empty ritual. Lewis tendered the offer that the White House had cleared: PATCO could do whatever it wanted with the $40 million package, but its value would not be increased, he announced. Poli rejected the offer and put PATCO's original demands back on the table. Lewis warned Poli that the president would dismiss strikers rather than negotiate with them and announced that military controllers would begin arriving at FAA facilities at 4:00 p.m. in preparation for the strike. Poli was unfazed. After breaking for dinner, the two sides resumed talks at 9 p.m. When they took a break at 10:30, Moffett went to his office to call AFL-CIO Secretary-Treasurer Donahue with the news that a strike would undoubtedly begin within hours.[23]

At that hour controllers were assembling in their cluster meetings in locations across the country, as they had done on June 21. To many, the gatherings evoked feelings of déjà vu. "Same people, same emotions, same everything," as one strike supporter remembered. But, in general, the mood was more determined and less anxious than before. In some locations, Choirboys locked the doors to dramatize the fact that no one was to leave until after their scheduled shifts began in the morning. In the Electrical Workers' hall in Mineola, New York, where LaGuardia controllers gathered, it seemed to Jim Morin that his co-workers were so ready to strike at that point that "the FAA could have capitulated on everything and they would have still wanted to flex their muscles." The uncertainties of June had given way to the clear realization that they would be on strike in the morning. Domenic Torchia was so certain that he wore his suit to his cluster meeting so that he would be ready to be interviewed for the morning shows on the East Coast.[24]

As the count began in the cluster meetings, Mike Rock joined longtime PATCO activist Bud Long at the union's Capitol Hill safe house, where the results would be tabulated. Poli asked Rock, who had been marginalized since the dustup over PATCO's staff organizing effort during the previous summer, to take on this role, and Rock had agreed. As the union's cofounder and its longtime guiding spirit, Rock was in a unique position to deflect any challenge to the strike count that would be given that night. Full records of the final strike vote do not survive. Only a tally of the turnout in the big "Level I" facilities exists among PATCO's records. That tally showed mixed results. The strike turnout was highest at PATCO's historically militant facilities: at least 90 percent of controllers at New York Center, LaGuardia, JFK, the New York TRACON (formerly the Common Eye), O'Hare, Denver, Los Angeles International, Pittsburgh, Miami, and Bay TRACON supported the strike. However, key air route traffic control centers at Washington, Kansas City, Oakland, and St. Louis did not hit 75 percent, nor did the key hub airports at Dallas/Fort Worth, Atlanta, and Philadelphia. According to this tally, the union turned out 79.8 percent of controllers at the Level I facilities, just short of the 80 percent overall goal. Whether PATCO was able to match or exceed this turnout level at smaller facilities is uncertain, but unlikely. Therefore, while there is no doubt that more than 70 percent of controllers turned out in the strike vote, it is probable that the union fell somewhat short of the 80 percent threshold envisioned in its initial plan. Yet the final numbers did not matter. By the early morning hours of August 3, PATCO had come too far to turn back.[25]

Reflecting the union's determination was the fact that PATCO negotiator Dennis Reardon's notes, in contrast to those of June 22, make no mention of a strike vote being phoned in to PATCO's negotiating team. Nor were the mediators aware that any word came in from the field to Poli. To the contrary, mediator Flores concluded, "They knew they were going." At 2:30 a.m., according to Reardon's notes, Poli advised Lewis that their differences "appeared unresolvable," and he rose to leave. "You're making a mistake for the country by doing this, you're making a mistake for the union by doing this, and you're making a mistake for yourself," said Lewis.[26]

When word was passed back to the cluster meetings around the country that PATCO was on strike, cheers went up. The reaction of striker Carl Kern was typical. He felt a "kind of elation." Finally, he thought, "the suspense is over, a decision has been taken, now we're going to go forward one way or the other. We're going to win or lose this thing, but we're moving, we're not Mickey Mouse-ing around here with these guys anymore." The cheers unloosed by Kern and his colleagues vocalized animosities that had built up over more than a decade. A pent-up store of resentments accumulated over narrow-tie-and-white-shirt dress codes, "psycho tests," abusive supervisors, humiliating fights over FAM privileges, workplace stress, the inability to bargain over the things that really mattered, and salaries that lagged inflation year after year finally had an outlet. Air traffic controllers were standing up. They were on strike.[27]

TURNING THE CARD

At 7 a.m., the hour when the day shift normally would be plugging in, picket lines went up at airports and control centers up and down the Eastern Seaboard. For workers who spent their days in windowless radar rooms or behind the tinted glass of control towers, simply standing together in the sunlight, making themselves visible to the flying public they served, felt liberating. A sense of determination and optimism pervaded their ranks. Controllers were showing themselves, demanding recognition, demonstrating that the system could not operate without them. In most locations, as the cars carrying supervisors and nonstrikers passed through the pickets, they were greeted with jeers that were more mocking than angry. Those who crossed the line had placed themselves outside of the circle of solidarity: that was their loss. In some places, the picketing became raucous as the day went on. Outside Chicago Center, in Aurora, Illinois, hundreds of picketers created a huge traffic jam and elicited an aggressive response from the police. To be sure, some who crossed the line complained of enduring a "barrage of profanity and name calling." In some locations nonstrikers used back gates and service tunnels to get into their facilities. But there was no stone throwing or other acts of violence.[28]

Rick Jones was grateful for that. The cofounder of the Coalition of Black Controllers had long since given up on PATCO, and had been urging black controllers not to risk their careers for a union that had done nothing to advance equal employment opportunity. He was determined to report to work on August 3. Yet he worried about how his red Cadillac El Dorado would fare passing through the picket line. As he drove up to the gate into Washington Center, in Leesburg, Virginia, he was comforted to see that there were as many Virginia State Police officers on hand as there were picketers. Driving past familiar faces that were kept well back by the police, including the faces of many friends, black and white, whom he believed had been duped into supporting a suicidal strike, he was thankful that Virginia was a right-to-work state.[29]

At 7 a.m., Lewis, Helms, their negotiator George Stohner, and others gathered at windows on the top floor of the FAA building, from which they could see National Airport in the distance. As they watched the first flight take off, they could not be sure whether the government's contingency plan would actually work. Within the hour, they would learn that the strike was worse than they anticipated. Helms received a call reporting that attendance was way off. Ninety percent were absent in New York and Boston. Only six controllers showed up for duty at O'Hare. Helms gave the order to implement the highest-level response in the contingency plan, cutting the number of flights that would take off that day by more than half. Every supervisor, regardless of shift, was called in to work. Ironically, one of PATCO's founders, Russ Sommer, was one of those who got a call that morning. He had long since moved up to the supervisory ranks. On August 3 he plugged in and began directing traffic for the first time in years.[30]

President Reagan began his day as usual with his 9 a.m. meeting with the Baker-Deaver-Meese troika. After receiving his national security briefing, Reagan called in Lewis, Attorney General William French Smith, and other advisers to review the status of the strike and finalize the statement he would make that morning. Lewis told the president that the air traffic system was running at half its capacity, but working "better than anticipated." He added that while the strike numbers were high, he believed that only half of the strikers would stay out.[31]

At that point, Reagan finalized his decision giving the strikers forty-eight hours to return to their jobs. If they refused to heed the deadline, they would be dismissed. According to the notes of the meeting taken by communications adviser David Gergen and the accounts of those present, Reagan was adamant about this. "Dammit, the law is the law and the law says they cannot strike," Gergen's notes quoted the president. "Having struck, they have quit their jobs, and they will not be rehired." Reagan said he did not "see any other way." A "very convicted" Ed Meese chimed in: "If the law says they can't strike and they go on strike then they've quit. Period." The only reason to wait 48 hours, Reagan noted, was to give enough time "for this message to reach everyone." Meese then outlined what White House officials should stress in public: the controllers were engaged in an illegal action demanding a settlement several times larger than the one Poli had shaken hands on in June. When Attorney General Smith added that the Justice Department would begin arresting two strikers per day in each of seventeen preselected jurisdictions, doubling the number after a few days, Reagan became irritated. Smith's plan seemed to suggest that after the forty-eight hours strikers would still be considered federal employees who had violated the law by striking. Reagan wanted everyone to understand that they would no longer be government employees if they did not heed his deadline. "They have terminated," he said. "They're in defiance of the law." Smith agreed. "If not back in 48 hours then they will have been deemed to have quit," he said.[32]

Reagan then reviewed the text of the statement he would read to the press at 11 a.m. in the Rose Garden. He expressed dissatisfaction with the draft his staff had prepared and he pulled out some notes that he had written.[33] He drew from those notes in shaping the final version of the statement. One addition concerned the difference between strikes in the public and private sectors. "Let me make one thing plain; I respect the right of workers in the private sector to strike," his insertion read. "Indeed as president of my own union I led the first strike ever called by that union.... But we cannot compare labor management relations in the private sector with government," it continued. "Government cannot close down the assembly line." The second addition referred to the oath against striking taken by all federal employees, which Reagan decided to quote verbatim.[34]

Presidents had intervened repeatedly in labor disputes in the nineteenth and early twentieth centuries, but never as quickly and forcefully as Reagan planned to do that morning. In the past, presidents had usually broken strikes only after it could be credibly claimed that public opinion demanded their actions. "By reserving his influence to be used as a last resort," a president "adds greatly to the effectiveness of his efforts when action is finally taken," wrote one historian of such interventions. An exception to this rule occurred in 1946, when President Harry S. Truman headed off a railroad strike by threatening to draft strikers into the military if they walked out. But even Truman's threat did not convey the air of finality with which Reagan closed his statement that morning: "I must tell those who failed to report for duty this morning they are in violation of the law and if they do not report for work within 48 hours they have forfeited their jobs and will be terminated."[35]

As Reagan finalized his statement in the White House, the summer meeting of the AFL-CIO Executive Council, which included the presidents of the federation's largest unions, was being gaveled to order at the Hyatt Regency hotel in Chicago. It was supposed to have been an upbeat meeting. Lane Kirkland had been looking forward to welcoming auto union president Doug Fraser to his first council meeting since the UAW had rejoined the

AFL-CIO. Kirkland was also intending to finalize plans with his fellow union leaders for a massive September 19 "Solidarity Day" march on Washington in protest of Reagan's social and economic policies and program cuts. Moreover the council was set to discuss the upcoming AFL-CIO national convention, scheduled for New York in November, where they would celebrate the one-hundredth anniversary of the founding of the Federation of Organized Trades and Labor Unions, the forerunner to the AFL. But there would be no time to plan on this morning. As the assembled union presidents gave Kirkland their attention, he announced that PATCO had led the nation's air traffic controllers out on strike. The meeting's original agenda was immediately put aside.[36]

News of the walkout made no one in the room happy, least of all Kirkland. He explained that PATCO had not warned or consulted the AFL-CIO about this strike. The assembled union chiefs were baffled. Few had paid PATCO much heed before then. Some only dimly realized that PATCO was an affiliate of the AFL-CIO through MEBA. Many others knew only that PATCO had broken ranks with the labor federation to support Reagan's election. The first reaction of the Executive Council was disbelief that any union would launch a strike of such magnitude, placing itself in open defiance of both the law and a popular president, without at least having lined up support from other unions. Doug Fraser summed up the second reaction. "This could do massive damage to the labor movement," he said. Many union leaders were angry with Reagan. "This man has gone not only back on a campaign pledge and a direct pledge to these people," remarked Glenn Watts of the Communications Workers, "but he's on the verge of destroying the lives of a lot of people." Most of the leaders agreed that air traffic controllers, like all workers, ought to have the right to strike. In practical terms, however, they viewed the PATCO strike as an impending disaster, a no-win situation. They could not fail to speak up for striking workers, but they knew how damaging it could be for their movement to support an illegal strike against a popular president waged by taxpayer-funded workers who already earned what the general public considered good salaries. They knew that many of their own members, let alone nonunion workers, would oppose such a strike.[37]

Whether it was possible for the AFL-CIO to do more than speak out on PATCO's behalf hinged largely on the views of two union leaders, J. J. O'Donnell of the Air Line Pilots and William Winpisinger, of the International Association of Machinists (IAM), whose members maintained aircraft.

If their unions refused to fly planes or repair engines, then air traffic would grind to a halt no matter how well the FAA contingency plan was working. Some Reagan aides feared this scenario. "Had the machinists gone out, we couldn't have withstood it," a transportation official later said. "It would have closed every single airport." "Wimpy" Winpisinger was an avowed socialist, known for his fiery rhetoric. He did not disappoint on this occasion, lecturing the Executive Council on the need to stand up to Reagan. But Wimpy stopped noticeably short of saying he was ready to pull machinists off their jobs. He wanted to hear what other unions, especially the pilots, were prepared to do. No doubt Wimpy knew what the pilots would say. O'Donnell explained to the council that pilots would not support PATCO, even if he tried to order them to honor controllers' picket lines. The pilots' relationship with PATCO had deteriorated in recent years, O'Donnell explained, and many pilots viewed the strike as a threat to their jobs and incomes. O'Donnell no doubt vocalized the fears of many in the room, explaining, "If I call my people out and they don't go, I'm dead." When the two unions best positioned to support PATCO failed to step forward with more than words, no other union leaders present were willing to do so. Thus, AFL-CIO leaders never seriously considered staging mass walkouts or sympathy strikes to support PATCO. Knowing and sharing his constituents' reservations, Kirkland never pressed them to do more than they felt comfortable doing.[38]

At 11 a.m. Reagan walked into the Rose Garden, flanked by Lewis and Smith. Facing television cameras and members of the press, he read his statement giving the strikers their forty-eight-hour notice. "I believe that there are a great many of those people, and they're fine people, who have been swept up in this and probably have not really considered the result, the fact that they have taken an oath," he said in an answer to a reporter's question. He hoped they would "remove themselves from the lawbreaker situation by returning to their posts," he said. Pressed as to why he did not choose a less extreme penalty, Reagan bristled. "What lesser action can there be? The law is very explicit. They are violating the law," he snapped. "You can't sit and negotiate with a union that's in violation of the law." Drew Lewis added that the FAA was prepared to let the strikers go. "There's a waiting list in terms of people that want to be controllers and we'll start retraining and reorganizing the entire FAA traffic controller group," he said.[39]

Reagan's Rose Garden speech transformed the PATCO strike only a few hours after it began. It was no longer merely a labor dispute between a federal agency and its workers. It was now a challenge to the power of the federal government and the legitimacy of its laws. In that confrontation, public opinion rallied strongly behind the president. Reagan's aides were pleased to learn that calls to the White House switchboard supported the president by a 13–1 margin. Much to the administration's delight, some messages of encouragement came from union rank-and-filers. "Hold firm in your actions!" urged a Colorado union member, who complained that PATCO had turned down a contract worth twice what his own union had recently negotiated. "When labor leaders condemn you for your actions, stand firm," he said. "Don't for a minute let yourself believe they speak for all of their rank & file members." To preserve the good will of union supporters, Reagan's advisors urged the Justice Department to slow the planned arrests of strikers. "We do not want to make martyrs out of the union leaders," one aide noted.[40]

When word reached the AFL-CIO meeting in Chicago that Reagan had offered an ultimatum, Kirkland called a recess and went to a telephone. He called Drew Lewis to urge that both sides sit down to talk. Others, including John Leyden, who was at the Chicago meeting representing the Public Employees Department, also furiously dialed calls to Washington. But calls to Bob Poli, Ken Moffett, Donald Devine, and others produced no movement. The Reagan administration would not negotiate during an illegal walkout, and PATCO would not end its strike without an improved contract offer. By then, most of the labor leaders were furious with Poli, believing he had botched the negotiations and launched a potentially suicidal strike. Since Reagan had spoken, however, the union leaders also had to go on the record.[41]

Reconvening their meeting, the union heads hammered out a public statement that hid their private anger at Poli and unequivocally supported the strikers. Most of the members of the Executive Council knew what it was like to lead an unpopular walkout, and they did not want to add to PATCO's burden by putting a sliver of daylight between the labor federation and the striking controllers. Thus, their statement placed the blame for the conflict squarely on the FAA's history of "subterfuge, evasion, and delay," and warned that efforts to hire replacement workers would endanger safety. The statement demanded that the government "call off its punitive measures against PATCO and engage in frank and open negotiations designed to alleviate the clearly justifiable grievances of the air traffic controllers." It was the right thing to do, Kirkland's assistant, Ken Young, later explained. "Who are we to say to any given group of workers, 'You're crazy'? They've got plenty of other people to tell them they are crazy. What they need from us is some help and maybe some guidance and support and a hand that will get them to where they want to be," said Young. "The bottom line is you have to help your sisters and brothers." To show their support, Kirkland and the other union leaders picketed alongside PATCO members at O'Hare, then chartered a bus back to Washington, stopping to speak to PATCO strike rallies outside Cleveland and Pittsburgh.[42]

In union halls and strike headquarters around the country, thousands of controllers watched Reagan's Rose Garden speech live on television. Most were not surprised to hear him present an ultimatum. Choirboys had prepared them for this. They knew that threats were also leveled during the 1970 sickout. Many read Reagan's statement as a necessary piece of posturing that would provide political cover for the deal that would eventually be cut to end the strike. "Well, okay. Now what's the quid pro quo?" thought Jack Maher, PATCO's ex-leader. Maher, who had helped draw up the strike plan, did not believe the system could operate without 80 percent of its controllers, so there had to be a deal in the end. Most strikers thought this way. "Anybody can fire anybody, but you are going to have to resolve the problem," said Ron Taylor of West Palm Beach.[43]

Thus, rather than intimidating strikers or breaking their ranks, Reagan's speech galvanized them. The short window Reagan gave them meant that they would have to make their final decisions before seeing how well the system could function without them and before feeling the squeeze of a lost paycheck or two—the factors that Langhorne Bond had felt would guarantee the success of his contingency plan no matter who the president was or how he dealt with the strikers. Reagan made the confrontation a matter of principle, and the strikers were happy to oblige him. For them, principles were also at stake, and none was more important than solidarity. They would not be broken. They would stand together as one. When strikers in the Tampa Bay cluster, who listened to Reagan's speech on the radio, heard him announce the forty-eight-hour deadline, they drowned out the remainder of the speech with an impromptu version of Johnny Paycheck's popular country music anthem, "Take This Job and Shove It." "Fuck the president," said Minneapolis controller Ray Carver. "We've done it. Let's stand by it. Let's see what the outcome is. If they can make her float, let her float." The PATCO strikers were not giving in.[44]

Beneath the veneer of bravado, there was considerable worry among many strikers. They understood the significance of the fact that Reagan himself, rather than one of his cabinet officers, delivered the ultimatum. That made it impossible for anyone else to step in to mediate. Now, in order for PATCO to win, the president of the United States had to lose. Ed Meagher of Washington Center understood what that meant. "This is over," he thought. "I've got to look for a new job." Anna Mosely, the wife of an Atlanta Center striker, also grasped it, and, as she later recalled, became "just plain hysterical."[45]

Even PATCO leaders had qualms. They knew the forty-eight-hour deadline would not give the government enough time to see that the system would buckle without the twelve thousand strikers. They understood that staying out was a gamble. But, after years of frustration with the FAA, after coming so far down the road they believed would liberate them from the restrictions that made federal sector collective bargaining seem like an exercise in futility, they were ready to take a final step into the unknown. Board member Domenic Torchia likened it to the dropping of the first atomic bomb. "It's going to be like flying the Enola Gay," he said. "You're going to drop something on August 3rd and you're going to turn around and you're going to know that it's something big and huge and you're going to see it and it's going to shake the airplane and its going to shake the world. But you don't know what you've got until you drop it." When Torchia saw Reagan deliver his ultimatum, he knew that the odds were against PATCO. But he likened himself to Reagan in one respect. "Once I make my decisions," Torchia said, "it's over."[46]

CROSSING THE LINE

Over the next forty-eight hours, facility chiefs and supervisors made calls to strikers and tried to use the president's threat to cajole some back to work. Such calls rarely changed minds; going back meant crossing a picket line, which was out of the question for the vast majority of PATCO strikers. Ed Meagher had already concluded that the strike was lost, but this son of an electrician would not cross over. "You have to sometimes choose in life and you have to choose who you want to be with," he said. "I knew I couldn't be a scab." A few senior controllers were able to avoid termination without crossing the picket line. Will Burner, PATCO's charter member at Newark

Airport, was one of those. After Reagan spoke, he went straight to the FAA building in New York to file his retirement papers before the deadline. He found himself waiting in line with dozens of people who were there to apply for the strikers' jobs.[47]

Some union members later questioned why Poli did not order strikers back to work before the deadline passed, continuing the struggle through a slowdown or other pressure tactics. At one point in PATCO's planning, that had been an option. When Mike Rock outlined the original plan to a group of facility representatives in January 1979, he explained that strikers "might have to be called back to work first," because "the government... don't negotiate while you're on the streets." But as PATCO's leaders perfected a strike plan they believed would eventually force the FAA to capitulate, that option was discarded along the way. Slowdowns and work-to-rule actions had never succeeded in producing a huge breakthrough in the past, planners reasoned, and there was no reason to think they would produce an agreement better than the one the union had just rejected. Added to this were the emotions of the strikers themselves. Even had the PATCO board joined with Poli to issue a back-to-work order on the night of August 4, the board feared that a large number of angry controllers would disregard it and stay out anyway. If that happened, PATCO's unity would be broken, those who stayed out would be dismissed, and those who returned to work would lack the leverage to protect themselves or those whom the government wanted to fire. The union's best hope was for the strikers to stick together.[48]

There were some last-minute defections. About five hundred strikers returned to work with the morning shift on August 5. An equal number went back before the deadline elapsed later that day. Overall, PATCO estimated that at least 10 percent of strikers returned to work at ten key facilities, including the key air route traffic control centers in Houston, Miami, and Indianapolis. Washington Center saw the highest return rate, with 22 percent of those who walked out on August 3 returning to work. Most of those defections did not surprise strikers, for they were known to be marginal strike supporters. But a few defectors were previously vocal strike advocates. Their lot was not easy. As they slipped past picketers they severed most of their closest friendships. Inside, they were not welcomed with open arms, but rather often regarded with contempt by non-strikers for having helped bring on the conflict whose consequences they now sought to escape. One defector drove through an angry picket line only to have his supervisor tell him, "People inside don't want to work with you. You go sit in the trailer out back until we decide what to do."[49]

In retrospect it is remarkable that there were so few defections, considering that the strikers had been warned directly by the president of the United States that if they did not return to work, they would be fired by the only employer in America who hired people with their specialized training. If fired they would lose not only their jobs but also the careers that once guaranteed them a middle-class lifestyle. Even PATCO leaders later expressed surprise that roughly 90 percent of those who walked out on August 3 stayed out.[50]

On the morning of August 5, when it became clear that no mass defections would occur, Reagan's advisers felt considerable anxiety. A day earlier, Drew Lewis had predicted that 50 to 80 percent of strikers would return. Now he and other top officials watched the clock, hoping for a major movement that never came. They had already extended Reagan's deadline slightly by offering controllers the chance to return with their scheduled shift at any time on August 5. But, as the day wore on, Craig Fuller gloomily reported to Meese that there was "no improvement in the number of controllers on the job." Reagan himself was serene, preparing to host a state visit from Egyptian leader Anwar Sadat, his confidence bolstered by the knowledge that phone calls and telegrams to the White House continued to support him by a 10–1 margin. He also believed he had adopted a course from which there could be no turning back.[51]

On August 5, in locations across the country, PATCO strikers and their families gathered to mark the passing of forty-eight hours since Reagan issued his ultimatum. In many places the demonstrations were boisterous. Daytona Beach controllers gathered in a high school parking lot and led a rousing countdown to the deadline before heading to the shore for a family picnic. New York area controllers gathered at Eisenhower Park in Nassau County, on Long Island, equidistant from MacArthur Airport to the east, where Jack Maher had hosted the first meetings of the Metropolitan Controllers Association, and JFK Airport to the west, where Hangar 11 had once housed the earliest advocates of air traffic controller organizing. The New Yorkers were also in high spirits that morning. When a federal marshal appeared and began handing out copies of an injunction ordering them back to work, they shooed him away, chanting "We want a contract." At 11 a.m., the controllers and their families formed a large circle, held hands, and observed a moment of silence. The incongruities of the scene attracted the attention of New York's colorful newspaper columnist, Jimmy Breslin. To all appearances, the people gathered that morning were middle-class Long Islanders, "members of suburban white America," Breslin noted. Almost all of the men were military veterans; many had voted Republican in the last election. And yet, here they were defying both the law and an American president. Breslin could scarcely believe his eyes when, at "the moment they were supposed to be fired on order of the President of the country," the controllers and their families became silent and then suddenly "their right fists shot up into the air" in what the columnist called, in a reference to a famous black radical of the 1960s, a "Stokely Carmichael salute." Breslin thought he might be witnessing the last dying embers of the 1960s. Considering that the history of unresolved conflict that led to this moment stretched back to the Kennedy era, his thought was closer to the mark than he could have realized.[52]

Once the fateful hours had passed, though, the resolve that had kept strikers together quickly gave way to worry. As he stood in that circle at Eisenhower Park, James Morin of LaGuardia Tower was thinking, "Jeez, what happens next?" After sending their kids to play on the beach following their rollicking countdown to the deadline, Daytona Beach controllers huddled around a portable television hoping for news of a settlement. When no news came, several left visibly shaken. "We've been through a lot together, including Vietnam," said the wife of one striker. "But this is different.... We're so law abiding we've never even gotten a traffic ticket. Yet here we are defying the federal government."[53]

Jack Maher and Mike Rock, the two men whose partnership had founded PATCO, also struggled to make sense of the moment. Although Maher had left PATCO a year earlier, he drove up to Washington from South Carolina to be with his union friends in the hours before Reagan's deadline lapsed. Maher had been shocked to learn that no back-channel negotiations were underway in those final hours. Still, he was certain that there had to be a negotiated resolution to the walkout. There was no way the system could function without the strikers. Maybe there would be some sacrificial lambs, as there had been in 1970, but in the end there had to be a deal. It was only after he tracked down Rock at PATCO's safe house on August 4, with the deadline ticking down to its final twenty-four hours, that Maher entertained doubts. As PATCO's cofounders started comparing notes on the strike, it was as though they had traveled back in time to the tense strategy sessions of 1968 or 1970. But this time there was a difference: Rock, the confident militant of previous conflicts, predicted that the strike would end badly. "It's all over now," he said. Maher argued with him, but Rock would not change his mind. "You can back down the secretary of transportation, the FAA, or an individual congressman or senator," he explained, as Maher was preparing to leave. "But you put the president of the United States publicly in a corner, he can't back down."[54]

ALUMINUM RAIN

We all seem so helpless, so fast, as if an ax had
cut us off from the rest of human life to die.
—PATCO STRIKER ALBERT R. RUBINOSKI

Very importantly . . . governments internationally have been
very impressed with the President's strong position on this issue.
—OPM DIRECTOR DONALD DEVINE

The strike unfolded in every state and territory and stretched across the Atlantic to affect European air travel. Its impact was visible in hundreds of localities, any city large enough to have an airport. Every local television news show in the country could film its picket lines; all but the smallest of small town newspapers could cover its local angles. The imposition of a presidential deadline shone an intense spotlight on it and elevated the sense of drama that enveloped it. No strike in American history unfolded more visibly before the eyes of the American people or impressed itself more quickly and more deeply into the public consciousness of its time than the PATCO strike. No strike proved more costly to break. And no strike since the advent of the New Deal damaged the U.S. labor movement more.

Breaking the PATCO strike was not easy, nor was the government's victory assured. As the forty-eight-hour deadline passed, the FAA had many thousands fewer controllers on the job than anticipated. Air traffic was nearly halved during the first week of the walkout, and so many travelers worried about safety that flights were only 30 percent full. Delays ranged up to four hours in some locations on August 6, the day after Reagan's deadline. Bus companies reported a 40 percent increase in business. Rental cars were in short supply.[1]

The first week put the FAA's contingency plan to the test. As dismissal notices went out to some 11,345 strikers, it fell to 4,669 nonstriking controllers, 3,291 supervisors, 800 military controllers, and about 1,000 newly hired personnel to control the nation's air traffic. At the outset, these controllers were scheduled for sixty-hour workweeks, usually six ten-hour days per week. At Cleveland Center in Oberlin, Ohio, and other hard-pressed facilities, the FAA brought in cots and bedrolls and set up spare rooms as makeshift dormitories to save tired controllers from having to commute (and encounter angry picketers). Controllers often stayed in their facilities for 36 hours at a time. "It was a hard life," said one. The wife of a Philadelphia controller who stayed on the job complained that she had never seen her husband "so *exhausted.*" "Actually, it seems as if the staff who stayed are being 'held hostage,'" she wrote. "How long can these people be expected to hold on?" The long workdays persisted. It took a month before the agency was able to reduce "scheduled" workweeks to forty-eight hours for 70 percent of the controller workforce. In reality, most of those controllers worked many hours above those scheduled. And for nearly a third of the workforce who labored in the high-volume facilities, workweeks of close to sixty hours continued for many months.[2]

With working controllers pressed to the limit, it is doubtful that the FAA's plan would have succeeded without the help of those who had never worked in FAA facilities before. The eight hundred military controllers who arrived for strike duty encountered a steep learning curve. The wide range of aircraft that they now had to direct and the complexity of the civilian airspace created challenges for them. Some adapted well to the work; most were not equipped to handle any but the most minimally challenging positions. But even the least effectual of their number helped free up skilled controllers and supervisors to help out in more challenging sectors. By September, the FAA was also able to count on help from nearly fifteen hundred pilots who had been furloughed as their airlines cut back flight schedules. Although they had never directed traffic, their familiarity with the system allowed them to take up support tasks within the facilities that lightened the load on working controllers.[3]

The FAA also hired and trained hundreds of new controllers in short order. Occurring as it did on the cusp of a major recession, the PATCO strike created thousands of desirable job openings. Within a month of the firings, more than one hundred thousand applications poured in. The FAA wasted no time in hiring replacements. Some 230 trainees were brought on within forty-eight hours of the deadline. The FAA academy in Oklahoma City geared up quickly to receive the successful applicants. Prior to the strike, the academy had trained cohorts of seventy controllers at a time. In the fall of 1981, it was handling classes twenty times that size, and hiring three hundred retired controllers as temporary instructors. Before going through the Oklahoma City program, many new hires were sent to small airports to handle support tasks. Typical of these, unemployed steel mill worker Mary Wunder of Pennsylvania was assigned to the small airport at Wilkes-Barre to handle flight data entry. As unemployment rose in the "Reagan recession" of 1981–1982, there was no shortage of workers like Wunder who saw a stable government job as a godsend.[4]

Yet supervisors were undoubtedly the most effective replacement workers. Few supervisory groups in any industry were better equipped to take the place of a striking workforce than those in the FAA. The entire front-line supervisory workforce had once controlled air traffic. They understood the work, and they were experienced in it. For months prior to the walkout, they had trained and recertified in case of a walkout. In some ways, it was ironic that they would play such a large role in defeating PATCO. At its inception, PATCO had flirted with taking supervisors in as members, and might well have done so had Executive Order 10988 not forbidden it. Moreover, many of PATCO's supervisors in 1981 were former PATCO members and veterans of its past job actions. When PATCO activists would assure him in the months before the strike that they could shut the system down, supervisor Russ Sommer, who helped lead the union during 1968–1970, would shake his head. "If you don't take the first line supervisors with you they're going to kill you," he would respond. While PATCO planners had hoped that the rusty skills of former controllers like Sommer would snarl the system, they underestimated the extent to which the Automated Radar Tracking Screen (ARTS-3), introduced in the years before the strike, made it easier for those whose skills had diminished to step in and direct traffic, especially when traffic levels were cut back as much as 50 percent.[5]

Yet it would have been impossible to break the strike with replacement workers alone. The cooperation of nearly five thousand air traffic controllers who either stayed on the job or returned to work before the deadline passed ultimately allowed the FAA's contingency plan to succeed. On average, these working controllers tended to be slightly older and more experienced than strikers. Those closer to retirement proved more cautious about losing their jobs. But others stayed on the job because they simply did not want to break their oaths or because they distrusted PATCO. Included in this number were many of the activists prominently associated with the National Black Coalition of Federal Aviation Employees or with Professional Women Controllers. Sue Mostert and Rick Jones, who had been instrumental in organizing women and black controllers, prevailed upon their colleagues not to strike. Quentin Taylor, the founding director of the FAA's civil rights office, who was retained by Lynn Helms as a special adviser, also urged blacks not to follow PATCO out. Although it appears that African Americans and women struck in proportions roughly equal to those of white men across the FAA facilities, the influence of Jones, Taylor, and their colleagues was especially evident at Washington Center, which had one of the lowest strike rates of any large FAA facility. Indeed, Washington Center retained enough controllers to allow for some to be used to alleviate shortages in hard-hit locations such as New York and Chicago, where their tours of duty lasted as long as eighteen months.[6]

Government officials did their best to keep the spirits of working control-lers high despite the hardships and long hours. No morale-booster was more effective than money, and after years of allowing the pay of air traffic control-lers to lag inflation, the government suddenly sprang into action to address controllers' pay concerns. Weeks into the strike, Lewis offered an 11.4 percent increase in salary and benefits, not including overtime, to supervisors and working controllers alike. By offering paid lunch breaks, the FAA also short-ened the effective workweek of controllers to 37.5 hours (as offered in the June 22 tentative agreement), guaranteeing more hours of overtime pay to nonstrikers. In 1982, the FAA boosted controllers' pay another 6 percent above the raise granted to all federal employees. These were the largest raises conferred on air traffic controllers since they began organizing in the 1960s. Ironically, then, the PATCO strike achieved its primary goal: it raised the income of air traffic controllers significantly above both the prevailing GS schedule and what the government had offered at the bargaining table.[7]

The government also offered the working controllers thanks and praise. Whenever he traveled, Lewis visited the local control tower or center in order to congratulate those who were working. Each Friday, Helms would address the entire workforce over the FAA's communications frequency, delivering a status report and pep talk. He used these weekly talks to outline coming innovations that would improve the controllers' working conditions, such as the soon-to-be introduced Traffic Collision Avoidance System (TCAS), which would alert pilots when another aircraft encroached dangerously on their airspace. In one address, Helms likened the working controllers to the Royal Air Force pilots who won the Battle of Britain against the Nazis in 1940.[8]

No matter how dedicated the replacement workers, and no matter how fully articulated the FAA's contingency plan, the success of the government's contingency plan still depended on the cooperation of the airline industry. In the weeks and months after August 3, the basic logic that Helms had outlined to the airlines before the strike held up. The strike provided the airlines with what one economist called "a respite from intense competitive pressure." Without doubt, airlines suffered what one industry executive called a "short-term penalty" from the strike. By one account, TWA lost $10 million the first day of the strike alone. One estimate concluded that the strike cost the airline industry overall $35 million per day, or more than $1 billion per month at the outset.[9]

PATCO leaders had believed that such staggering losses would cause the airlines to pressure the administration to settle. That never happened. To the contrary, airline executives strongly supported President Reagan. "As long as they feel they can strike and win, they would continue to use this type of tactic in the future," wrote the president of Republican Airlines, which claimed losses of $15 million in the first days of the strike. "I believe it is better to settle this matter once and for all." The chairman of American Airlines thanked the president for "reestablishing respect for law and controlling inflation," and thereby creating "a business environment in which the temporary losses we suffer now can be more than fully recouped." To show their good will, several airlines provided free meals to working controllers until it was pointed out that these could be construed as bribes offered to a regulatory agency. But free food was the least of the airlines' gifts to the FAA. Throughout the early months of the strike the Air Transport Association worked closely with Helms, coordinating the support of its member airlines for the FAA's strikebreaking plan.[10]

The airlines' unity did not fray until the summer of 1982, when it became clear that the FAA would be unable to restore its pre-strike levels of traffic any time soon. By then, the large legacy carriers began to realize that the respite they had hoped for from the pressures of deregulation was stretching into an ominous multiyear revenue squeeze. A year into the strike, Pan Am had yet to recover 31 percent of its prestrike departures; TWA was off by 17 percent. The anxieties of airline executives were sharpened by the shuttering of Braniff International in May 1982 and by the robust expansion of the upstart Southwest Airlines, which used the strike to greater strategic advantage than any other, extending beyond its regional base by picking up routes the FAA approved at the low-volume airports ignored by larger airlines. But even when they privately griped about the FAA, airline executives never publicly broke with Reagan. Their staunch support was a crucial component of PATCO's defeat.[11]

While the contingency plan held up under the strains of the first month of the strike, PATCO was subjected to an unprecedented government-led legal offensive. Despite the warnings from some Reagan advisers that the administration should avoid turning strike leaders into martyrs, the Justice Department sought the arrest of dozens of strikers for breaking the federal government's no-strike law or defying court orders to return to work. Federal marshals were dispatched to picket lines, union halls, and homes to deliver summonses. A photograph of Norfolk, Virginia, controller Steve Wallaert being led to jail in handcuffs and manacles made newspapers across the country. In the end, seventy-eight PATCO strikers were charged in connection with the strike. Their cases reached a variety of outcomes. Some struck plea deals to avoid jail. Others were convicted, with sentences ranging from one year on probation to fines and jail time of a few days or months. A handful successfully fought conviction on the grounds that they were selectively prosecuted. Charges were dropped against others. The union, too, was penalized. PATCO was ordered to pay $28.8 million in damages to the airlines, a sum that far exceeded its assets. Fines against the union would have been even more catastrophic had several judges not revised their penalties downward when it became clear that the government would not let strikers return to work, even if they wanted to, once the deadline passed.[12]

Finally, the strikers' inability to gain significant support from the general public for their walkout made it impossible for them to alter the strike's dynamic. Defending a strike whose signature demand was a $10,000 across-the-board salary increase would have been difficult in the best of times. But rather than developing a strategy around this problem, PATCO strike planners for the most part ignored it, believing that their ability to shut down air travel would be their key weapon, not public opinion. When the union discovered that the strike did not force the government to negotiate, it was too late to try to appeal to the public. In truth, even had the union tried to court public support, it could not have chosen a less auspicious moment to undertake that task. A deepening recession was beginning to send unemployment rates toward double digits in August 1981; an unpopular baseball strike had already resulted in the cancellation of more than seven hundred games and stirred animosity against anyone who could be portrayed as a "pampered" union worker; talk of a possible postal strike still loomed; and, having recovered from John Hinckley's assassination attempt, President Reagan was still enjoying great personal popularity.[13]

The Reagan administration, by contrast, realized its public relations advantages and aggressively exploited them. Under the tutelage of his public relations officer Linda Gosden (whose father, Freeman Gosden, was an originator of the 1930s radio show *Amos 'n' Andy*), Drew Lewis assiduously courted the press. He appeared daily on news programs and held frequent press briefings, assuring the public that the skies were safe and sticking unswervingly to the administration's line that the strikers would not be rehired. The administration's line was picked up and amplified by many sympathetic media outlets and commentators. None was more passionate than the popular radio broadcaster and longtime PATCO antagonist, Paul Harvey, whose analysis was syndicated nationally on the ABC Radio network. Harvey relentlessly flogged PATCO's wage demand as greedy, blamed PATCO for past midair collisions, and called strikers unpatriotic. He applauded Reagan for giving labor its comeuppance. "As industry's tycoons of the Thirties got their wings clipped, labor's leaders in the Eighties are getting their wings clipped," he chirped. "Not because of any class-related antagonism, but because any excess, ultimately, inevitably is its own undoing."[14]

Fighting PATCO proved beneficial for President Reagan's poll numbers. They shot up in August 1981. Like the rogue states of Libya and North

Korea, PATCO provided a perfect foil for the president, observed the *Washington Post*. Seeing the president's poll numbers soar, in turn, discouraged any members of Congress from defending PATCO. Although House Speaker Tip O'Neill urged the administration to rehire the fired controllers, he quietly told PATCO's officials not to get their hopes up.[15]

Faced with this public relations debacle, PATCO primarily relied on one message: a failure to bring back the strikers would inevitably bring on a disaster, a midair collision or "aluminum shower." To substantiate this claim, PATCO members monitored and recorded radio communications between controllers and pilots in many places, filed Freedom of Information Act requests in search of incriminating documents, and even sorted through the trash dumpsters outside some facilities. None of these efforts produced a "smoking gun" capable of convincing the public that the air traffic control system was in chaos. A report by the Aviation Safety Institute that found twice as many hazard reports as usual during the first month of the strike received little public attention. In the end, forecasts of aluminum rain put the union in an unfortunate light, allowing critics to contend that controllers were rooting for a disaster in order to win their jobs back. The union never overcame these negative perceptions. [16]

CONFLICTIONS AVERTED

As well constructed as the FAA's contingency plan was, it could not control for two factors, the actions of U.S. airline pilots and foreign air traffic controllers. Either group could have thwarted the FAA's careful plans. If pilots decided that the skies were unsafe and refused to fly, they could have frozen air travel and placed enormous pressure on the administration to negotiate with PATCO. Had air traffic controllers from other nations refused to clear aircraft bound for the United States, it would have been equally devastating. In the tense early weeks of the strike both of these threats loomed large.[17]

There was never a chance that the Air Line Pilots Association would instruct its members to honor PATCO picket lines as a matter of union principle. ALPA's members were too angry with PATCO to consider such action. Pilots were furious that the controllers' strike cut back flights during the peak summer travel season, giving the airlines an excuse to demand concessions from them. ALPA tried to protect its members from the adverse impacts of a strike by concluding agreements before the walkout with the major carriers that guaranteed pilots a minimum of seventy-six hours of flying-time pay during the first month of a walkout and seventy-two hours in subsequent months, unless the airlines were forced to implement furloughs. However, pilots understood that a strike that was not settled quickly would produce thousands of furloughs, and thus they generally viewed PATCO's walkout as a threat to their livelihoods.[18]

But ALPA could have aided PATCO's cause, and potentially forced the government to come to terms with the controllers, without ever criticizing the president, or taking a stand on union principles. ALPA members only needed to exercise their discretion as pilots. According to Federal Aviation Regulation (FAR) 91.3, pilots had the final authority to determine whether conditions were unsafe for flying. If pilots concluded that the system was unsafe, they could have invoked FAR 91.3 and refused to fly, effectively shutting down air traffic without fear of penalty. ALPA conducted its own independent monitoring of the system's safety during the strike. ALPA's Air Traffic Control Committee, chaired by Captain Tom Sheppard, had the task of collecting reports daily from pilots and analyzing the system's performance. Had ALPA president J. J. O'Donnell concluded on the basis of Sheppard's reports that the system was unsafe and publicized Sheppard's findings, the union need not have ordered pilots not to fly. Pilots could have reached their decisions individually.[19]

In fact, what Sheppard's committee found was troubling. Each day after August 3, the confidential status reports Sheppard sent to O'Donnell raised more concerns. By the strike's third day, Sheppard began to worry about the exhaustion of replacement controllers and told O'Donnell that, "if the system continues at present staffing levels, fatigue of the people working will have a safety impact." On day four he warned of "a higher potential of danger." Captain Louis McNair, of Delta Air Lines, underlined these worries in his report to Sheppard's committee that day. "In the current operating environment," he wrote, "the possibility of a controller detecting a pilot deviation in time to prevent a safety hazard is remote." On the sixth day, Sheppard reported eleven system errors—more than in the first four days of the strike combined—and concluded that the system was "beginning to weaken." Sheppard warned O'Donnell of the "possibility that safety will continue to deteriorate as the strike continues." His concerns intensified when the FAA refused to allow ALPA observers into FAA facilities to verify conditions.[20]

The situation did not improve during the strike's second week. ALPA safety monitors began to describe a "situation that deviates from previous standards," and worried that the understaffed system could not hold up much longer under the stress of lengthened workdays. Many pilots told Sheppard's committee that, while they opposed the strike, they wanted the system restored to its pre–August 3 state. Some working air traffic controllers were so worried that they began passing information to Sheppard as well. One controller who stayed on the job at Houston Center reported that safety had been "set back 10 years minimum." "I worked this past week with a data systems specialist who hasn't talked to an airplane in over 4 years. He had been certified as safe and qualified in less than an hour," the controller wrote. "We have supervisors working who couldn't separate two flies with a screen door, yet they work traffic." These reports were not made public. Yet, on August 11, two pilots invoked FAR 91.3 and refused to fly.[21]

Had ALPA circulated Sheppard's reports among its members, the number of pilots citing 91.3 certainly would have risen, leading to plummeting numbers of passengers willing to fly. But O'Donnell kept those reports confidential even while he publicly downplayed concerns about compromised air safety. Any chance that ALPA would change course evaporated on August 18, when the union's executive board met to discuss the state of the system. The union's leaders knew of the concerns of Sheppard's committee, but did not judge them serious enough to recommend a systemwide grounding of flights. The board unanimously concluded that the skies were safe. Speaking to the press on August 19, O'Donnell said, "I can say without equivocation the air traffic control system in this country is safe. If it were not safe, we would be the first to speak out."[22]

Many PATCO strikers saw the pilots' decision to keep flying as "the kiss of death" for their walkout. PATCO disputed O'Donnell's characterization in its own press conference on August 19, claiming that there had been fifteen near midair collisions in fifteen days. That very afternoon two general aviation planes collided south of San Jose, California, killing the pilot of one of the aircraft, and seemingly underlining PATCO's point. Strikers blamed the collision on controller fatigue, but FAA officials denied the charge. The fact that it involved two single-engine planes and produced only one fatality kept it from becoming a major story.[23]

ALPA never considered changing its position on the safety of the system for two reasons. First, O'Donnell believed that the government would go to any length to defeat PATCO once the union had defied the president's ulti-matum. "I cannot conceive of the government backing down from its posi-tion," he told the press. If ALPA complained about safety or made Sheppard's concerns public, O'Donnell believed the government would be more likely to "size the air transportation system down" than to negotiate with PATCO. This would have only meant more endangered airlines and more furloughed pilots. The second reason was the degree of anti-PATCO animus within ALPA. Most pilots had little sympathy for PATCO. O'Donnell himself dis-covered the depths of anti-PATCO feeling when he concluded his August 19 news conference by saying it would be "in the country's best interest" if Reagan declared victory and rehired any strikers who were willing to admit their mistake. The comment elicited a storm of outrage in ALPA's ranks. Pilots at Delta and Eastern Airlines approved resolutions denouncing O'Donnell's call for rehiring; others showered him with angry telegrams. ALPA's president was forced to defend himself in an open letter to his mem-bership by arguing that he called for leniency for strikers in order to defend pilots from layoffs that would result from a long walkout. The controversy subsided, but O'Donnell never recovered the confidence of his members. He was voted out of office in November 1982, a blow that was cushioned, fittingly enough, when President Reagan appointed him deputy undersecre-tary of labor in 1983.[24]

Had they acted in concert, the air traffic controllers of other nations also could have crippled the FAA's contingency plan. None were better posi-tioned to accomplish this than Canadian controllers. Having staged a national strike themselves in 1972, members of the Canadian Air Traffic Controllers Association (CATCA) supported PATCO's walkout, and were outraged by the U.S. government's apparent determination to break it. Once dismissal notifications began going out to PATCO strikers, CATCA resolved to take action. On Monday August 10, CATCA authorized its members to refuse clearance to flights headed into or from U.S. airspace on the grounds that the American system had become unsafe. The Canadian job action immediately disrupted transatlantic flights, which used the "Great Circle Route" that took them over Canada's Maritime Provinces, where they were directed by controllers at Gander, Newfoundland. It was possible to reroute some transatlantic flights straight across the Atlantic to pass over Portugal and the Azores. However, most could not be rerouted, and thousands of travelers on both sides of the ocean were stranded. Canadian authorities swiftly suspended twenty-nine controllers and sought an injunction against the job action from the Canadian Supreme Court, but this only seemed to worsen matters. Portuguese controllers announced that they would join the boycott at midnight on August 15, effectively closing off all transatlantic flights.[25]

The U.S. government mobilized quickly to defuse the threat. Lewis and Lynn Helms immediately pressured their Canadian counterparts to rein in CATCA. Helms went so far as to secure an Airborne Warning and Control System (AWACS) jet from the Air Force and an Aegis missile cruiser from the Navy that could serve as control communications centers guiding transatlantic flights from off the Canadian coast if the Canadians refused to handle them. Canadian officials, in turn, threatened CATCA with legal action. The tactics worked. On the morning of August 12, the Canadian union called off its boycott. Portuguese controllers began a forty-eight-hour boycott of U.S. flights on August 16, but without Canadian support, their action had little impact.[26]

PATCO's last chance to elicit meaningful international support rested with the International Federation of Air Traffic Controllers' Associations (IFATCA), an organization PATCO had left years earlier when the Americans objected to the high dues assessment on their organization. Although PATCO's relations with IFATCA were not close, many air traffic controller organizations believed that they could not stand idly by while the U.S. government broke a sister organization. Prodded by French and Portuguese members, the IFATCA board convened an emergency session on August 13 to discuss the PATCO situation. At that meeting they decided to summon IFATCA representatives from sixty-one nations to an emergency meeting of the organization on August 22 in Amsterdam to decide what action to take on PATCO's behalf.[27]

The news alarmed Reagan's advisers. White House counsel Fred Fielding worried that IFATCA was "uncontrollable and could force the president into an untenable position." The administration sought whatever leverage it could find to persuade foreign governments to keep their controllers working U.S. flights. One particular measure proved quite effective. In 1980, as airline deregulation was transforming U.S. aviation, the Civil Aeronautics Board ordered U.S. airlines to cease participating in the ticket-price-setting mechanism operated by the International Air Transport Association, a device that restrained competition and kept transatlantic fares high. Fearing that their national airlines would be harmed by U.S. carriers offering cheaper fares, foreign governments strongly objected to the order, which was set to take effect on September 15, 1981. The White House decided to use the CAB order as a bargaining chip. In order to garner good will from the governments whose help he sought in defeating PATCO, President Reagan agreed to delay the implementation of the CAB order, allowing the practice of collusive price setting to persist. The gesture was effective. Foreign governments remained united in their desire to keep air travel to the United States open.[28]

Under the best of circumstances, it would have been difficult to get IFATCA's member associations to declare a worldwide sympathy action on PATCO's behalf. After all, a significant number of IFATCA's affiliates were not unions at all, but rather associations that included both controllers and their supervisors. The Reagan administration's behind-the-scenes lobbying of key governments made it even harder for IFATCA to take meaningful action when its representatives convened at the Ibis Hotel at Amsterdam's Schiphol Airport on August 22. PATCO vice president Bob Meyer pleaded for their help, and delegates from several European controllers' associations called for united action. But no majority could be marshaled behind a boycott of American flights. In the end, IFATCA agreed only to send a team to the United States to see if it could mediate a settlement. When that team arrived in Washington several days later, its members were rebuffed by U.S. officials. That effectively ended IFATCA's involvement.[29]

BACK CHANNELS

When it became clear that no outside forces would intervene to save them, PATCO strikers began to pin their hopes on rumored back-channel negotiations. There were, indeed, members of the Reagan administration who wanted to see some of the fired strikers rehired: Drew Lewis worried about the long-term stability of the air traffic system; Donald Devine was concerned about the enormous cost of training a new generation of controllers; Labor Secretary Ray Donovan fretted that the blanket firing of the strikers would antagonize organized labor and make it harder to work with unions that otherwise supported the president, such as the Teamsters. Such sentiments were discussed openly within the administration and occasionally even uttered in public. At a meeting with an employers' group on August 13,

Reagan adviser Martin Anderson implied that the administration might consider rehiring those who had not actively supported the strike.[30]

Labor leaders were desperately interested in exploring whatever openings existed. Lane Kirkland himself passed a proposal to the White House through a moderate Republican, Senate Majority Leader Howard Baker of Tennessee, on August 14. It provided that, in return for the resignation of Poli and other top PATCO officers and their admission that the strike was illegal and that they had misled rank-and-file controllers, the administration would rehire strikers with the exception of Poli, PATCO's national officers, and some prominent strike proponents. Under Kirkland's plan, rehired strikers would pay a fine, reaffirm their no-strike oath, and vow not to harass nonstriking controllers, in return for the administration's creation of a fact-finding investigation to examine their grievances and deliver non-binding recommendations. If the administration agreed to these conditions, Kirkland would endorse the solution, affirming that the strike was illegal and that the president had acted properly. Kirkland's offer represented a huge concession and would have amounted to a humiliating renunciation of the position that the AFL-CIO took at its 1975 convention, in which it endorsed the right to strike for all government workers as a matter of principle. Labor leaders were willing to swallow their pride in this case, however, in an effort to avoid the horrific spectacle of an entire workforce of strikers permanently replaced. Kirkland wanted "a civilized way of resolving this strike." As he explained to Ed Meese, the prospect of the strikers' permanent replacement made the struggle a question of simple humanity more than union rights. "We're not talking about five-letter words like PATCO and union; we're talking about going on the battlefield and shooting the wounded."[31]

As Kirkland's offer was circulated in the White House, Ken Blaylock, president of the largest union of federal workers, the American Federation of Government Employees (AFGE), searched with Kirkland's blessing for someone inside the administration with whom to negotiate. Opening channels came naturally for Blaylock, a plumber by trade. Elected national president of the AFGE in 1975 at the age of forty-one, he had established himself as a shrewd political operative who had dealt effectively with both Republican and Democratic administrations. With a reputation for pragmatic militancy, he served in the president's post for longer than any of his predecessors. Because his union represented federal employees, Blaylock had a strong interest in trying to rescue PATCO strikers. He feared the mass firing of controllers would weaken all federal unions. Blaylock found a potential negotiating partner in Donald Devine, director of the Office of Personnel Management, with whom he had frequent dealings.[32]

Although Devine and Blaylock were poles apart politically, neither man wanted to see relations poisoned between the administration and federal workers. In the days following the Rose Garden deadline, they talked about the outlines of a potential settlement that might allow for the rehiring of a large number of strikers. Devine made clear from the outset that the administration could not be placed in the position of negotiating with workers on strike illegally. In mid-August, Blaylock outlined a deal that responded to Devine's condition. He proposed that Poli order strikers back to work for ten days while negotiations took place, when, in reality, a settlement between the union and the administration would have been worked out secretly in advance. The show of public negotiations while the controllers were back at work would shield the administration from accusations that it negotiated with strikers. Devine listened to the proposal, and on August 19, he met with Blaylock in Drew Lewis's office.[33]

Whether the administration would have approved Blaylock's proposal is doubtful, but this became a moot question when PATCO leaders learned of its provisions. They feared that if strikers went back under what George Brandon called "a clandestine offer of a job with no contract and no union," strike leaders would be singled out and fired, the union broken, and the FAA free to hire back only the most compliant controllers. In mid-August, with avenues of outside support for their strike drying up, PATCO leaders still believed that the FAA needed at least six thousand strikers to return to work if the system was to continue operating over the long term. The only question to be settled in their minds was, "Can they get this quantity back without the rest?" They were determined to protect all the strikers. "If we all hang together, we'll still win," argued field coordinator Jim Lundie.[34]

The prospects of securing a back-channel agreement, never propitious, dimmed further on August 21 after a public misstep by Labor Secretary Donovan. Speaking to a contractors' convention in Biloxi, Mississippi, Donovan said the administration was looking for "a way out of what I can only describe as the most difficult legal situation as it applies to government-union relationships that anyone can remember." The White House immediately disowned Donovan's statement and insisted that he had been misinterpreted. Reagan was not seeking "a way out." Drew Lewis reiterated the point. "We are not going to take them back," he said. Thereafter, Ed Meese informed Donald Devine and others that he wanted no more discussions, no matter how informal, about rehiring, and Craig Fuller underlined the point for all White House staffers: "no strikers will be rehired."[35]

Over the next few months, rumors of renewed back-channel talks arose periodically, but there was never any credible evidence that a member of Reagan's inner circle condoned such talks, and in any case no breakthroughs occurred. After the fact, various theories were advanced for why back-channel negotiations failed. Some, including Blaylock, placed a good deal of the blame on PATCO leaders for being inflexible in their demands. Others held that premature leaks snuffed out the talks. But these theories overlooked a more important reason: President Reagan himself. According to his closest advisers, Reagan never considered revising his position. As Ed Meese put it, Reagan "didn't want to do anything that would look like we were backing down and not enforcing the law." He worried that allowing strikers to return to work would take away "whatever preventative effect that [firing them] would have on people doing the same thing again." Although PATCO leaders held out hope through October for a behind-the-scenes resolution, they never came close to one.[36]

Solidarity's Limits

Unaware of these secret machinations, rank-and-file members of the AFL-CIO received little direction from their leaders in Washington regarding how to respond to the very public breaking of a nationwide strike. "Member unions will have to decide for themselves what to do," Kirkland advised. "I am not going to make that appraisal." For most union activists, the appraisal was not difficult. It made little difference to them that the strikers had never fully embraced the rest of organized labor, that PATCO had broken with the AFL-CIO to endorse Reagan's election, or that its walkout was illegal. What they saw were brothers and sisters in trouble, and they were determined to help. While union members flooded the White House with protests, other public sector unionists voiced their support to PATCO. "You are fighting the good fight for all of us who are organized to bargain in the public sector," one Colorado teacher wrote Poli. "Your union has embarked on a new battlefront that will set the tone of labor relations for years to come. Please maintain the struggle!" added a municipal worker from Kalamazoo.[37]

Meanwhile, in cities across the country, unions of all sorts lent PATCO strikers a hand. When Honolulu and Tucson strikers could no longer afford to rent headquarters, carpenters and firefighters unions gave them space. New York City electrical workers sent PATCO $25,000. Citing the help that mine workers gave them during a difficult strike in 1947, the Communications Workers of America promised $1 million. Unions from Europe, Japan, and Australia also sent money. Nearly a year after the walkout began, PATCO was still receiving donations.[38]

In the eyes of many union members the PATCO fight concerned a fundamental human right: the freedom all workers should have to strike in protest of their conditions. Union activists knew that in the early nineteenth century, courts once treated all strikes as illegal conspiracies. The strike only gained legal legitimacy after decades of struggle. The "only way employees gained the right to strike was by exercising that right," as one teacher put it. PATCO's supporters generally believed bans on public sector strikes were fast becoming anachronistic, and hoped that the PATCO walkout would end such bans altogether. Kansas City firefighters thanked PATCO leaders for attempting to "attain for public employees the ingredients basic to free trade unionism." In defending the controllers' right to strike, unionists often compared PATCO to Lech Walesa's *Solidarność* (Solidarity) movement, which had been battling Poland's Communist government since its formation in the Lenin Shipyards of Gdansk in September 1980. Reagan had repeatedly championed the right of the Poles to strike against their government, the argument went. How could he deny American workers "the same basic right"?[39]

Many activists were angry with their national leaders for failing to do more for PATCO. "It's a shame that our international union doesn't have enough intestinal fortitude to come out in support of your cause," wrote one steelworker. "This strike could have been won already, but the labor bureaucrats haven't done anything but issue paper resolutions," argued West Coast longshoremen. "Nationally, the labor unions have sold PATCO out," concluded a Philadelphia teacher. In some settings, activists took militant actions in defense of PATCO. Union marches briefly blocked access to the Oakland and San Francisco airports. Machinists' union locals staged sporadic slowdowns. And some individual trade unionists paid a heavy price to take a stand for the controllers. When bus driver James West refused to cross a picket line to pick up passengers at Cleveland's airport, he was fired on the spot. The only thing PATCO members could offer him in return was their gratitude and a ride home to Pittsburgh.[40]

Although the controllers' walkout galvanized many union activists, less committed rank-and-file unionists never mustered much sympathy for controllers as the "Reagan recession" increased their anxieties about their own situations. Angry letters from workers arrived daily in PATCO's offices. "Your problem is you have no idea of the temper of the people in the U.S. today. You had better learn for your future welfare and the welfare of unionism in the U.S.," read one. "Hey Mac: Anyone who defies the U.S. gov't and the President of the USA Stinks," said another. "You guys are getting too big for your britches." Some union members urged Reagan to hold his ground. "Before they went out I was all for them. Then, I found out how much pay they are now receiving for the job and how much they want in wage raises alone," wrote a member of the Communications Workers of America. "We don't like our pay situation any more than they do, but you don't see us out on strike," added a firefighter. "Let them run into burning buildings for a living and see how their nerves stand up."[41]

The prevalence of such sentiments solidified the perception that AFL-CIO leaders began forming on the strike's first morning that any militant direct action on behalf of the controllers' would divide their unions. As it was, labor found it difficult to remain united even in its symbolic support for PATCO. An effort by some in the Screen Actors Guild to expel Reagan from the union, in which he held a lifetime membership, fizzled as the organization's pride in claiming a president of the United States as a member outweighed anger at his treatment of other unionists. Meanwhile, building trades unions pursued closer ties to Reagan, undaunted by his status as the nation's leading union-buster.[42]

The Reagan White House lost no opportunity to press its advantage with more sympathetic unions. Thus on September 3, 1981, exactly one month into the strike, President Reagan spoke to a national convention of the United Brotherhood of Carpenters. To celebrate the centennial anniversary of the founding of their union, the Carpenters had invited Reagan to address them months earlier. Even before the strike began, his speech was bound to be an historic event, the first time a former union president addressed a national union convention as president of the United States. The Carpenters decided not to cancel the engagement despite the controversy that swirled around PATCO, but Reagan's staff worried that the event could lead to an unseemly confrontation. Thus, in an early draft of the president's remarks, Reagan's speechwriters decided not to mention PATCO in the text they prepared, hoping to avoid boos from the union audience. But Reagan insisted that the issue be addressed head-on, and personally drafted part of the speech that publicly rebuked labor for tolerating the PATCO strike. When the Wagner Act was ratified in 1935, Reagan told the Carpenters, even John L. Lewis said labor "had no intention of allowing any segment of government to be organized with the right to strike." Reagan went on to note that Franklin Roosevelt viewed government strikes as "unthinkable and intolerable." There could be no retreat from this position, Reagan insisted. "We cannot, as citizens, pick and choose the laws we will or will not obey. And I hope that organized labor today, and its leadership, will recognize that you, the rank and file they represent, are the supreme authority in our land; that you are the employers of all who serve in government, elected or appointed, and none of us in government can strike against you and the interests of you, the sovereign people." Reagan's hard-hitting lecture elicited no boos. Carpenters sat respectfully if uncomfortably through the remarks.[43]

Labor leaders continued to support striking controllers publicly throughout the fall of 1981, making a defense of PATCO a central theme of the massive "Solidarity Day" march on Washington that took place in protest of Reagan's policies on September 19, 1981. Steve Wallaert, the Virginia controller whose photograph in handcuffs symbolized the government's crackdown on PATCO, was a featured speaker at the event, the largest U.S. labor march ever held. But militant calls for union members to blockade Potomac River bridges and close down National Airport went unheeded; Reagan himself ignored the protest, departing for Camp David before the marchers arrived. Once the crowds of protestors dissipated, labor's practical efforts on PATCO's behalf rapidly diminished.[44]

On October 22, 1981, PATCO's struggle came one step closer to its end when the three-member Federal Labor Relations Authority, created by the 1978 Civil Service Reform Act to oversee federal labor law, decertified PATCO as the official representative of air traffic controllers. The board ruled that PATCO's violation of the no-strike rule had disqualified it from representing federal workers. "There is no PATCO," Drew Lewis said, when he learned of the decision. PATCO appealed the ruling, but the appeal itself floundered. During the course of it, some evidence came to light suggesting that Albert Shanker, the president of the American Federation of Teachers, had improperly lobbied a member of the FLRA to oppose PATCO's decertification. Although the appeal was not officially denied until June 1982, by November 1981 the outcome of the strike was beyond doubt. PATCO was broken. Its striking members were banned for life from the highly technical work for which they had spent years training.[45]

The breaking of PATCO cast an ominous shadow over the AFL-CIO national convention that opened in New York City on November 16, 1981. The event was to have been a grand affair marking the centenary of the founding of the Federation of Organized Trades and Labor Unions, the organization once headed by Samuel Gompers. In the aftermath of PATCO's decertification, the convention felt more like a wake than a celebration. Poli addressed the delegates, sharing details of his members' suffering: threatened felony convictions, impounded cars, blocked adoptions, shattered family finances, blacklisting not only by the FAA but other employers as well. He pleaded for help and apologized for PATCO's missteps. "We will learn from our mistakes," he said. In response, some delegates eloquently defended the right to strike as inalienable. Others called for militant action. "There's no question that this is the first union they're going to break or try to break, but not the last if they succeed to break this union," said a San Francisco hotel worker. In the end, though, the convention merely approved an Executive Council resolution condemning the "brutal punishment" of the strikers, asking affiliated unions to assist them, and demanding that Reagan "return these workers to their jobs."[46]

By the end of November, local PATCO offices were closed, picket lines had dwindled, and fired controllers who had not yet done so began searching for work. Some local leaders kept in touch with their clusters from their homes. Others, exhausted from the dispiriting fight, gave up. Realizing they had been defeated, many wrote letters pleading for their jobs. "I have never been a trouble-maker. I never broke the law before," wrote one. "I want another chance." Some others were simply despondent. "I look around this PATCO headquarters and see the men, women, and children whose lives and their future are seemingly destroyed. We all seem so helpless, so fast, as if an ax had cut us off from the rest of human life to die," observed a Cleveland Center striker. It was as if they had been "lined up like lambs and slaughtered," said another.[47]

The realization of defeat exacted a high emotional toll. Some strikers turned on PATCO. "It would appear that our whole plan of attack was to go on strike and then wait and see," fumed an angry Choirboy from El Paso, who found himself facing "the reality of no job, or a low-paying job." Financial stress and poststrike recriminations divided many PATCO families; separations and divorces mounted. The first suicide came ten days into the strike when an Indianapolis striker was found dead in his garage with his car running. By the end of November there were three more suicides, including one of a PATCO spouse who hanged herself in her kitchen with unpaid bills strewn on a nearby table.[48]

Closing the Door

Ironically, the crushing nature of PATCO's defeat created one last opportunity for strikers to salvage their jobs. As it became clear that Reagan had prevailed, public opinion began to shift: the majority had supported the firing of the strikers in August, but began to favor their rehiring by November. Editorials in the *Los Angeles Times*, the *Washington Post*, and other leading papers urged the president to take back those who had not instigated the walkout. Columnist William Raspberry, who applauded Reagan for proving that no-strike oaths "were more than words on paper," urged the president to show leniency, continuing "a long American tradition of being uncompromising in war and generous in victory." Many strong Reagan supporters agreed. Jude Wanniski, a leading proponent of Reagan's supply-side economics, urged "forgiveness." Former Nixon speechwriter turned conservative columnist William Safire advised Reagan to "demonstrate that American justice is not only swift and certain but that it can be tempered by a willingness to offer a second chance." Republican Rep. Jack Kemp of New York announced his support for rehiring. "The president has made his point," he said; "now for the safety of travelers we must get them back to work."[49]

As such sentiments spread, some of the same Reagan advisers, who only months earlier were working on a labor strategy that they hoped would gain the administration the support of a significant slice of union members, began urging the president to defuse the animosities that had inflamed relations between the administration and the unions over PATCO. In response to these concerns, the White House invited the AFL-CIO Executive Council to meet with the president on December 2. With only two members dissenting—Glenn Watts of the Communications Workers and William Winpisinger of the Machinists—the council accepted his invitation.[50]

Prior to the meeting, Kirkland made clear to Vice President George H. W. Bush that a resolution to the PATCO strike would be "the major topic of discussion" when labor leaders met with the president, and they would view the meeting as a failure unless Reagan expressed "some indication of flexibility." On the day before the big meeting, it appeared that the president might show flexibility after all. On December 1, in a separate meeting with Teamsters union leader Frank Fitzsimmons (who was not a member of the AFL-CIO), Reagan hinted that he would allow the fired strikers to apply for other federal jobs, although not for work with the FAA. The *Washington Post* viewed this as a possible "first step toward allowing some of the 11,000 fired controllers to regain jobs in the nation's undermanned airport control towers." Rehiring suddenly seemed like a possibility. "I'm optimistic. It's obviously the first major break," said the president of PATCO's local at Baltimore-Washington International Airport. It was not just PATCO strikers who jumped to such conclusions. Panicked conservatives promptly begged Reagan to hold his ground. How the last chapter of the strike would play out suddenly appeared to be up for grabs.[51]

When Kirkland and a dozen members of the Executive Council arrived at the northwest gate of the White House at 10:30 a.m. on December 2, they were looking for a breakthrough. Their mood darkened when they found themselves waiting for the president, making small talk with Vice President Bush for twenty minutes in the Cabinet Room, under the watchful gaze of a portrait of Calvin Coolidge, whose breaking of the 1919 Boston police strike had seemingly inspired Reagan's handling of PATCO. When Reagan finally entered the room in a characteristically jovial mood, took his seat in the center of the long table, and propped his note cards up against his coffee cup, all they could do was hope for the best.[52]

It was a most unusual meeting. Never before had union leaders sat in the Cabinet Room with a president who had once been in their shoes. Yet no president had ever delivered a more painful blow to the union movement than Reagan. Understandably, the exchange began awkwardly. Reagan welcomed the labor leaders and stressed the common ground they shared in an anticommunist foreign policy and a growing economy, but everyone in the room knew that it was not what they shared in common that brought them together on this morning. As soon as Reagan finished his welcoming remarks, Kirkland brought up PATCO. Labor had a "very large bone in our throat" over the president's handling of the strike, said Kirkland, for the president was treating strikers as if they had committed an unpardonable act, a "monstrous sin." The strikers had been punished enough, Kirkland continued. Unemployed for four months, their families were in crisis. It was time for Reagan to show mercy, help the economy, and rescue the beleaguered air transportation system by rehiring the strikers.

Reagan's first response was disheartening. He strongly defended his actions. "We are not trying to punish people who went out on strike," he chided. Not only had they taken a personal oath not to strike, Reagan said, they had been warned in advance that if they struck "they would simply be quitting their jobs." Strikes were fine in the private sector, the president argued, but "government cannot shut down the assembly line." Having made his point, Reagan tried to mollify the unionists by reiterating the statement he had made on the previous day: he was considering a waiver that would allow controllers to apply for jobs elsewhere in the government, but not at the FAA.

Kirkland wanted more. The AFL-CIO leader contrasted Reagan's handling of the PATCO strikers with Nixon's handling of the 1970 postal strike and urged Reagan to show restraint as Nixon had done. Reagan responded that his administration had offered PATCO a good contract but that the union had rejected it. Then he tried to put Kirkland on the defensive, reminding him that the strikers had broken the law. "Are some laws okay to break and others not?" he asked. "We are not trying to punish—but the law is the law." For good measure, he asked Kirkland, "Should the military be allowed to strike?"

The meeting threatened to break down at that point. Then J. J. O'Donnell, the union leader whose stance had most aided the FAA's contingency plan, spoke up. O'Donnell shifted the tone of the conversation, saying that labor was not there to question Reagan's handling of the strike. "The strike is over. You have won," he said. The question now was how to handle its aftermath. Having won, O'Donnell argued, it was possible for Reagan to show mercy without compromising his principles. He reminded Reagan that thousands of innocent workers had been furloughed as a result of the strike, including machinists and pilots, and that the entire economy was suffering. He urged Reagan to sit down with Drew Lewis and Kirkland to find a way to rehire some controllers. Teachers' union leader Albert Shanker chimed in to support this approach.

Reagan seemed pained. He told the group he didn't want to fire anyone, even for "justifiable cause." Then he seemingly cracked open a door. "One of our first steps is the waiver we are asking for," he said. "I can't go beyond that since Drew isn't here." It was not exactly the breakthrough that labor leaders wanted, but it was significant. If Reagan saw the waiver allowing controllers to apply for other federal jobs as "one of our first steps," and if he intended to consult with Lewis about other steps, then it would seem that the rehiring of some fired strikers at the FAA might be possible later. Whether this was a dodge, the labor leaders could not tell. Reagan's last words did not clarify matters. He closed by saying that the final authority in the case of public employees must be "the people themselves." "They are the employers of all of us." With that, the president departed, leaving the labor leaders uncertain as to whether he would take any other steps.[53]

It was only in the days after the meeting with labor leaders that the president arrived at a final, irrevocable decision on whether to hire back any PATCO strikers to their old jobs. Unquestionably, he had the power to authorize rehiring if he chose to. He also had qualms about permanently banning those who were not avid strike supporters from vital jobs that they had been trained to do at taxpayer expense. In the end, though, his top aides argued that holding the line against any rehiring was vital to his presidency, and Reagan concurred.[54]

The key arguments were set forth in a December 7 memorandum outlining Reagan's alternatives that OPM director Donald Devine drew up for Ed Meese. Devine suggested three possible approaches. Reagan could maintain the status quo, with strikers banned from ever returning to the FAA, and barred from applying for other federal jobs for three years as the law stipulated. He could accede to those who were asking him to show mercy, and allow strikers to apply for air traffic control jobs at the FAA, provided that they were not strike leaders. Or he could take a middle road and waive the three-year ban on strikers applying for other federal jobs while continuing to bar them from ever returning to the FAA.

Devine's cost-benefit analysis of these alternatives was revealing. Rehiring PATCO strikers at the FAA would help rebuild the system and spare the government enormous expenses, he noted, but would also risk creating the perception that the president was retreating from his August 3 ultimatum.

At the same time, simply preserving the status quo would illustrate the president's consistency, but feed a growing perception that he lacked compassion. The best course, Devine argued, was the middle way. Allowing controllers to apply for jobs at other federal agencies but banning them for life from the FAA would allow Reagan to "appear magnanimous and Presidential, without changing his fundamental position."

Devine's memo also made clear the domestic and international political calculations that informed the president's decision. Rehiring strikers to their old jobs would "not be understood by a critical mass of the President's constituency," Devine warned. Such a move would dismay both conservatives and the business community. Rehiring the strikers to their old jobs would also send mixed signals to "governments internationally" that had been "very impressed with the President's strong position on this issue," he wrote. Although it went unmentioned in the memo, the government that Reagan advisers were most intent on impressing was that of the Soviet Union. By showing that he would carry through on his threats and defend his principles no matter the cost and despite critics who called for a softer approach, Reagan could reinforce his image of toughness. According to this thinking, the more costly the strike, and the more his refusal to rehire strikers was perceived as stubborn or even risky, the more his image as a strong world leader would benefit from it. Thus the third option—refusing to rehire any strikers to their former jobs, but allowing them to apply for other federal openings— made the most sense. "It will not be seen as 'backing down,'" Devine assured.[55]

With Devine's memo in hand, Reagan's top advisers—Vice President Bush, Drew Lewis, Craig Fuller, Fred Fielding, and the troika of Ed Meese, James Baker, and Michael Deaver—met with their boss on December 9 to finalize his decision. With all of the rationales now laid out, Reagan decided in favor of the plan his advisers placed before him. It removed the three-year debarment and allowed strikers to apply for jobs elsewhere in the federal government, instructed OPM to use traditional standards to evaluate their applications for other federal jobs, and confirmed that they would not be allowed back at the FAA.[56]

The confirmation of the strikers' permanent exile from air traffic control facilities hardly came as a surprise to PATCO's leaders. By December, the union's national staff had dwindled and disbanded. To pick up the slack, several PATCO activists moved to Washington and worked as volunteers trying to hold the union together. Domenic Torchia came from California, Bill Taylor from Arizona, Gary Eads from Kansas City, and Cheryl Jenni from Billings. Meeting with AFL-CIO leaders, lobbying on Capitol Hill, they fought on through the end of the year, their spirits bolstered by gallows humor. "We got them right where we want them," Taylor joked. But good humor could not hide the harsh realities. As PATCO's leaders debated what to do, Gary Eads scribbled a revealing one-word doodle in his notes: "Waterloo."[57]

As the year came to an end, Poli decided that his continued presence would hinder PATCO's efforts to salvage controllers' jobs. He and Vice President Bob Meyer resigned on New Year's Eve. "I will never, as long as I have a breath left in me, say that the issues for which we struck were incorrect, that we did not have good reason to go on strike," Poli wrote. The next day, PATCO's executive board elected Eads and Torchia as president and vice president of the broken union.[58]

Snowed Under

Since an air disaster over the skies of New York on a wintry day in 1960 had sown the seeds for PATCO's creation, perhaps it was eerily fitting that another wintertime air disaster marked the end of the union's hopes. The final chapter in the breaking of the PATCO strike began to unfold in a snowstorm on January 13, 1982. The light flurries that began that morning in Washington, D.C., became a steady snowfall after noon. Flights were held at their gates for more than an hour at National Airport in mid-afternoon to allow snowplows onto the runways. One of the delayed departures was Air Florida's Flight 90, a Boeing 737 bound for Tampa, originally scheduled to leave at 2 p.m. Passengers and crew sat aboard the plane, watched the snow fall, and waited. At 3:10, a deicing truck arrived and sprayed down the plane to prevent ice from building up on the wings and fuselage. At 3:40, the ground controller in charge finally gave the all-clear to push back, and the jet rolled out to take its place, seventh in a line of aircraft awaiting departure. At 3:59, Flight 90 finally reached the head of the line and was cleared for takeoff. As it gathered speed down the runway, its crew became worried. Although the jet had reached takeoff speed, its nose did not lift off the ground until it used up another quarter-mile of runway. Once airborne, the jet shook violently. At an altitude of 340 feet, it began to lose lift. The pilot frantically pulled back on his stick, his engines at full throttle. Still the jet dropped. Shearing the tops off several vehicles on Washington's Fourteenth Street Bridge, it plunged into the icy Potomac River, killing seventy-four people aboard the jet and four on the bridge. Miraculously, five survivors were plucked from the water.[59]

Multiple factors contributed to the Air Florida tragedy. An investigation showed that too much time elapsed between Flight 90's deicing and its clearance for takeoff, allowing fatal amounts of ice to accumulate on the wings. The Boeing 737's tendency to pitch upward in icy conditions and the crew's relative inexperience in such weather were also ruled contributing factors. PATCO strikers insisted that another cause also played a role: air traffic control error. The press initially dismissed that contention. But the NTSB hearings that opened on March 1 exposed the fact that the air traffic controller who cleared the doomed jet for takeoff, a supervisor who had resumed controlling traffic on August 3, had also cleared an Eastern Airlines jet to land behind Flight 90 on the same runway before the flight was airborne. Indeed, the tower controller informed Flight 90 of this as he cleared the jet for takeoff. "No delay on departure if you will. Traffic is two and a half [miles] out for the runway," he radioed. Whether this information might have influenced the Air Florida pilot's actions and contributed to any reluctance to abort his ill-fated takeoff suddenly became an issue. Raising further concerns was the revelation that the Air Florida and Eastern jets closed to within less than one mile, according to radar data. FAA regulations mandated that aircraft should not come within two miles of each other when landing or departing. If they were separated by less than one mile, the jets would have been on the same runway at the same time—a clear violation of FAA regulations, the strikers contended. The FAA denied that the controller's instructions were a factor in the crash. In the end, the NTSB supported the FAA's interpretation.[60]

To PATCO strikers, the NTSB finding amounted to yet another coverup. It galled them even more that President Reagan not only paid no price for the disaster, he profited politically from it, making it the basis for a precedent-setting piece of political theater during his State of the Union address on January 26, 1982, less than two weeks after the disaster. With the economy in a deepening recession and his poll numbers slipping, Reagan gave a stirring speech and closed by summoning Americans to a heroic rendezvous with destiny. To remind his audience of "the spirit of American heroism at its finest" he turned to the Air Florida tragedy. Pointing to a young federal worker named Lenny Skutnik, who sat beside First Lady Nancy Reagan in the gallery of the House chamber, the president told his story. Skutnik was on the banks of the Potomac when Flight 90 crashed into the river. He saw one of its few survivors, Priscilla Tirado, flailing in the water, unable to grasp a line dropped by a rescue helicopter. Without regard for his own safety, Skutnik jumped into the river and saved her. The entire Congress rose to give this American everyman a hero's standing ovation. "Don't let anyone tell you that America's best days are behind her, that the American spirit has been vanquished," Reagan continued. "We've seen it triumph too often in our lives to stop believing in it now."[61]

That speech marked a beginning and an end. A new tradition was born that night. Thereafter, other presidents would emulate Reagan in using their State of the Union speeches to highlight the triumphs of everyday Americans, basking in the reflected glow of their heroism. But, for all intents and purposes, a union also died that night. Although PATCO's legal appeals would drag on for months, its marginalization was now complete. The aluminum rain that the union predicted had fallen. But rather than rescuing PATCO, that storm confirmed its destruction.

DEBRIS FIELD

If the withdrawal of the right to coerce by the threat to strike is
to become politically acceptable, a truly great leader—of
exceptional eloquence, and intellectual pertinacity—will have
to arise. I expect to be told, however, that I am hoping in vain
for a Messiah, that only the intervention of heaven could break
through the barrier of 'political impossibility,' which excludes
any effective curbing of strike-threat power.
—UNION OPPONENT W. H. HUTT, 1973

The PATCO strike helped make Ronald Reagan's presidency. Even before its outcome was certain, observers considered it a defining event—not only for the man, but also for his office. Reagan's resolute response to the walkout, his admirers argued, was a bracing tonic that revived a weakened presidency after the nation saw the previous five administrations end in tragedy, frustration, defeat, or resignation. The PATCO strike tested Reagan's mettle and set the tone for an age "when character was king," as one acolyte put it. It was not only Reagan's followers who adopted these views. They became matters of conventional wisdom. Pulitzer Prize–winning columnist and *Washington Post* editorial page editor, Meg Greenfield, a consummate Washington insider, represented the consensus. Reagan's handling of PATCO accomplished "a huge infusion of presidential credibility, even among some people who deplored the act itself," Greenfield argued. It showed that the president stood by his threats and was "willing to take the political consequences" of governing from "a set of unshakable basic beliefs."[1]

The image of the stern law-and-order president that emerged in the popular imagination after August 3, 1981, did not square with the Reagan whose advisers did not denounce PATCO's aggressive and explicitly stated demands when seeking the union's endorsement in 1980, or the Reagan who authorized his aides to go beyond what the law allowed in negotiating with the union in June 1981, thus inadvertently encouraging PATCO's militants to believe they could push him for more. But inconvenient or contradictory facts were soon swept aside as the irresistible storyline of a president who stood his ground, no matter the cost, took hold. This powerful narrative erased contradictory nuances from the public memory so effectively because it seemed to connect and explain two defining developments of the Reagan era: the end of the Cold War and the rise of conservatism.

Many observers saw the PATCO strike primarily through the prism of the Cold War. National Security Adviser Richard V. Allen called it "Reagan's first foreign policy decision." Partisans of this view held that the strike played the same role for Reagan that the Cuban Missile Crisis had played for John F. Kennedy, providing an opportunity for the president to demonstrate to the Soviet Union his strength under pressure. Two weeks after PATCO walked out, the conservative *New York Times* columnist William Safire predicted that Reagan's "display of law and order macho" would give him "a reputation for strength that enables him never to have to put it to the test." Reagan's official biographer, Edmund Morris, contended that the PATCO confrontation allowed Reagan to demonstrate to foreign leaders that he was "a sheriff capable of swift hard action." This image, many have argued, helped shape the closing chapter of the conflict with the Soviet Union. Later in the decade, when Soviet leader Mikhail Gorbachev pursued diplomacy with Reagan that led ultimately to the Soviet Union's peaceful dissolution ten years after the PATCO strike, some suggested that the breakthrough was made possible by what one foreign policy analyst called Reagan's "PATCO style of negotiating."[2]

Indeed, the world did take note of Reagan's handling of PATCO. When House Speaker Tip O'Neill visited Moscow not long after the PATCO strike, he learned that the Soviet leaders had been deeply impressed by Reagan's actions. So too were Reagan's admirers in the United Kingdom. The *London Times* celebrated "Mr. Reagan's Short Way with Strikes," and expressed the hope that Conservative Prime Minister Margaret Thatcher would follow Reagan's example. In repeated confrontations with British unions in the early 1980s, Thatcher did just that. "One begins to get the impression that the two countries could just swap leaders without anyone really noticing any difference in the policies pursued in either," one British journalist observed of Thatcher's and Reagan's labor policies.[3]

Reagan's breaking of the PATCO strike, more than any other act of his presidency, also announced the dawn of a conservative era. In one typical reading, author John C. Armor argued that Reagan's decisive response represented nothing less than a repudiation of America's recent political history, the end of a liberal era. "Would the air traffic controllers...fear the no-strike law if an ideological child of Franklin Roosevelt were in the White House, rather than a child of Calvin Coolidge? John Kennedy, perhaps, instead of Ronald Reagan?" he asked. That the question seemed to answer itself indicated how much Americans perceived the strike as a pivot point. Conservatives such as George F. Will celebrated it as marking the end of liberal permissiveness and a runaway rights revolution, a welcome reassertion of conservatism and authority. "In a sense, the '60s ended in August 1981," crowed Will.[4]

The Death of PATCO

As grand interpretations of the strike's significance gained credence, the remaining hopes of some strikers that Reagan would reconsider and take them back evaporated. Still, the remnants of PATCO struggled on into 1982 with such hopes. "I believe PATCO will survive and, in the future, we will be much wiser for the experience," said its new president, Gary Eads. PATCO leaders issued a series of public *mea culpas* in hopes that they would open the way to a resolution. In a *New York Times* piece, Poli accepted responsibility for the strike and allowed that he had unwittingly helped make himself into a caricature, a "bearded Jim Jones and an Ayatollah who was holding the flying public hostage." In a letter to the members of PATCO's Southwest region, board member George Brandon admitted that the union had struck for "an unrealistic goal." By threatening to silence the skies, PATCO had become an aggressor, and "Americans don't really like aggressors," Brandon wrote, adding, "We should hope we will never see the day anyone defeats the U.S., when it doesn't want to lose."[5]

While admitting their mistakes, the union's leaders fought through the spring of 1982 to win support for the strikers' rehiring. With PATCO finances wiped out by massive fines and its paid staff gone, the task was daunting. The fierce loyalty that the union still commanded among many members kept the volunteer staff going into the summer of 1982. Some strikers continued sending whatever contributions they could. "I just received my tiny fed tax refund for 1982 and thought I'd pass part of it on to assist you," one wrote. "Hang in there; we ain't dead yet."[6]

But such devotion could not save PATCO. On June 11, 1982, the U.S. Court of Appeals upheld the union's decertification. Two weeks later, on June 25, the remnants of PATCO's executive board gathered for their final meeting at a Holiday Inn in Lenexa, Kansas, where they voted not to appeal PATCO's decertification to the U.S. Supreme Court. They also approved a statement urging PATCO members to seek their jobs back by filing individual appeals through the Merit Systems Protection Board, the quasi-judicial agency created by the 1978 Civil Service Reform Act to rule on appeals from disciplinary actions. "No member should have any guilt feeling about return-ing to work at the earliest opportunity," the resolution read. Then, with sixty activists in attendance, the board voted to declare bankruptcy and dissolve the organization that had been launched with such enthusiasm on a January night in New York fourteen years earlier. "It is over for PATCO," Eads announced. "President Reagan has proven his point to everyone." "Labor has responded," he added bitterly, "and we have witnessed that response." PATCO's demise was not enough to satisfy the Air Transport Association, however. Years later the group was still trying to collect $32.5 million in fines from the defunct union.[7]

The dissolution of PATCO did not end strikers' efforts to achieve rehir-ing. Eads immediately founded a new organization, the United States Air Traffic Controllers Organization (USATCO), a nonprofit group dedicated to that project. USATCO took possession of PATCO's mailing list, established a newsletter, and continued the telephone hotlines that PATCO had maintained for strikers. Free of PATCO's name and debts, Eads hoped for a lobbying breakthrough. He roamed the halls of Congress for more than two years, pushing legislation that would return strikers to work. He sol-diered on until Reagan's landslide victory over Walter Mondale in the 1984 presidential election. A week after the votes were counted, with Reagan set to occupy the White House for four more years, Eads gave up and folded USATCO.[8]

Without an organization, PATCO strikers struggled on through the 1980s, forming what anthropologist Katherine Newman called a "brotherhood of the downwardly mobile." The long-term economic costs of the walkout for PATCO families was staggering. According to a 1986 study by the Government Accounting Office, 70 percent of fired controllers had yet to find jobs that matched their prestrike income. One-third earned incomes so low their families qualified for food stamps. Thirteen percent lost their homes. One fifth still worked in entry-level jobs in clerical, sales, service, or unskilled manual labor five years after they struck. Twenty-five years later, Antoinette Pole, a striker's daughter, still remembered the humiliation she felt when her classmates learned that she qualified for free school lunches because her father was jobless. Like many PATCO families, Pole's unraveled under the stress. Her parents divorced.[9]

IDEOLOGY AND AIR SAFETY

It cost more to break the PATCO walkout than any other labor conflict in American history. The FAA paid the law firm of Morgan, Lewis & Bockius $376,000 for the services of Bill Curtin, George Stohner, and their colleagues: the AFL-CIO called it "the highest fee ever paid to an anti-union consultant to bust a union." But this was a tiny fraction of the overall price of the conflict. According to a conservative estimate, the cost to taxpayers of retraining replacement controllers alone came to $2 billion. The losses to airlines, difficult to measure precisely, were estimated at one billion per month during the early months. The ripple effects of the decline in airline travel and loss of jobs in related industries are even harder to calculate, but likely also ran to many billions.[10]

It took years for the FAA to recover. The agency's worst-case scenario had envisioned that air traffic would return to prestrike levels by the end of 1983. That proved completely unrealistic. By the end of 1982, the agency was forced to implement a new national spacing program to deal with an ongoing shortage of controllers that was still years from being rectified. The problems the FAA faced in staffing Chicago Center were typical. Prior to the walkout, 330 fully certified controllers and 108 trainees worked at that

facility. Eighteen months after that strike, the number of fully certified controllers was down 65 percent while traffic was down only 28 percent.
Developmental controllers outnumbered fully certified controllers, 137 to
116. Controllers were handling more flights per person and spending more
time training developmentals in 1983 than they had before the strike. Even
so, Chicago Center was in better shape than many facilities; forty-three of its
controllers were on loan to other facilities worse off.[11]

The FAA's efforts to train new controllers were soon enveloped in controversy. As early as December 1981, members of Congress began receiving
reports that instructors in the Oklahoma City facility falsified test scores in
order to push more developmental controllers through training. In 1982,
the NTSB uncovered evidence that developmentals hired since the strike
were being used to train other developmentals. On May 19, 1983, the NTSB
urged the FAA to postpone planned increases in air traffic until it could raise
the number of fully certified controllers. "In my sector, it's a struggle every
day. We're not seeing the light at the end of the tunnel," said one senior
controller. "The experience level is as low as I've seen it in 25 years," admitted
another. "We've got controllers who have never held traffic in a thunderstorm before."[12]

Another factor that complicated the FAA's recovery was the airlines'
increased use of the hub-and-spoke model, replacing the point-to-point service that predominated before deregulation. After 1981, airlines decreased
service in smaller airports to focus on building hubs. By 1983, commercial
air carriers had pulled completely out of 106 small airports in 31 states and
cut the number of scheduled flights they offered in more than half of the 668
communities then offering commercial passenger service. As smaller airports lost service, hub traffic grew. In 1983, Continental Airlines was landing
and departing twenty-four jets within a 106-minute window each morning
at its Houston hub. Because keeping layover times down helped attract fliers,
Continental sought to keep its jets on the ground for no more than eighty
minutes each. The result was an intense concentration of traffic every day in
Houston that was replicated at other hubs. These rush hours required large
numbers of highly skilled and experienced senior controllers, a demand the
FAA struggled to meet for the remainder of the decade.[13]

As the FAA's recovery efforts sputtered, Drew Lewis and Lynn Helms
moved on. Lewis departed the Reagan Cabinet at the end of 1982 to become
chief executive of Warner Amex Cable Communications. Helms left his

FAA post a year later. His resignation followed two embarrassing stories in the *Wall Street Journal*. One reported seemingly shady business dealings that produced substantial profits for Helms, but plunged several ventures into bankruptcy. The other found some evidence that while it was under his leadership in the mid-1970s, Piper Aircraft had knowingly kept from the FAA information concerning a safety defect in one of its aircraft models.[14]

The departure of Lewis and Helms created an opening for some in Congress to push for rehiring controllers. In the House, Democrats William D. Ford of Michigan and Ron Dellums of California, and Republicans Jack Kemp of New York and Jim Jeffords of Vermont, were among those who took up that cause. Helms had opposed any rehiring on the grounds that returning strikers would undermine the morale of working controllers. After his departure this argument carried less weight. Many working controllers, like Anthony Skirlick Jr. of Los Angeles Center, a vocal critic of PATCO leadership and an opponent of the strike, thought the lifetime ban was wrong and wanted most of their fired colleagues back. "This is a labor dispute, not a Holy War," Skirlick wrote President Reagan, urging him to stop the "genocide of a skilled workforce." Many supervisors also shared this view. "I know my men, how they feel and think," said one. "Sure they are apprehensive with talk of rehiring and the unknown, but they know the experience level is drastically low and…quality is lacking." Rehiring, he said, was "long overdue." Even Lewis, who consistently defended the ban in public, conceded before he left the administration that "life would be easier" if the FAA rehired "a couple of thousand strikers."[15]

Not only did Reagan administration officials oppose all talk of rehiring, they seemed determined to punish the strikers. "They made their bed and they can sleep in it," said FAA director of air traffic, Ray Van Vuren. That attitude was widely held within the administration, whereas evidence of mercy was scant. U.S. attorneys continued prosecutions of some local leaders long after the strike was broken, sending two Texas strikers to jail in 1983. The Department of Housing and Urban Development instructed its regional officials to refuse relief to PATCO strikers who applied for federal aid to families in danger of home foreclosure. Officials also tried to blunt the effect of Reagan's December 1981 order allowing strikers to apply for federal jobs outside the FAA by limiting their ability to get hired at the only two agencies not subject to a hiring freeze in 1982, the Defense Department and the Postal Service. The White House contended that because the Postal Service was a semi-independent entity, the Reagan order did not apply to it. Postal officials would not hire PATCO applicants until Rep. Ford, who chaired the House Post Office and Civil Service Committee, interceded in August 1982. The Defense Department refused to hire strikers into any office that "interfaced" with the FAA, putting much of the department off limits to former strikers. Some strikers were even dismissed from the National Guard.[16]

The apparent blacklist extended beyond U.S. government agencies. Private companies that contracted to provide training and services to the FAA, or air traffic control services to very small airports that the FAA was unable to staff with its personnel in the poststrike era, were required to sign contracts in which they agreed not to recruit controllers fired for striking in 1981. Many fired controllers looked for jobs abroad, taking advantage of the fact that English was the international language of air traffic control. Still, the governments of some U.S. allies were reluctant to risk antagonizing the Reagan administration by hiring PATCO veterans.[17]

Nothing better demonstrated the extraordinary lengths to which the administration went in its effort to punish the strikers than its handling of the appeals they filed before the Merit Systems Protection Board. The MSPB heard appeals in the cases of 10,284 fired strikers. Privately, federal officials predicted that they might lose as many as seven hundred appeals in cases in which appellants could convince the MSPB that they had been coerced into striking. But the government was determined not to let that happen. They fought every case vigorously, refusing to accept any striker's claim that they were coerced. Despite the enormous investment of government legal resources in fighting these appeals, the MSPB still ruled in favor of 350 strikers and ordered the FAA to rehire them. In the vast majority of those cases, the FAA simply refused to comply. The agency appealed some adverse MSPB rulings to the courts and said it was "studying" others. Nearly two years after the strike the FAA had taken back only one-third of those ordered rehired by the MSPB. Years later, Congress learned that the FAA had falsified documents in order to subvert the MSPB appeals of many fired controllers. At Chicago Center, a "war room" was set up where, according to one lawyer, "the largest and most systematic evidence alteration scheme in the history of American jurisprudence" took place. Sign-in sheets were back-dated, initials forged, and documents showing that some controllers were on approved vacations during the walkout were altered to suggest that they were absent without leave.[18]

Nor would the administration consider clemency for a single PATCO member convicted of strike-related charges. When the possibility was raised among Reagan's advisers, White House counsel Fred Fielding vetoed it as "out of sync with what has obviously been a broad, vigorous and consistent pattern of Federal enforcement of the anti-strike laws." It was not that Reagan's advisers eschewed appeals for clemency as a general rule. While blocking pardons for PATCO strikers, they approved one for Eugenio Martinez, who had been convicted of participating in the infamous break-in at offices of the Democratic National Committee at the Watergate complex in 1972. Indeed, that pardon was rushed through in advance of Reagan's vote-courting visit to Martinez's Cuban exile community in Miami in 1983. "It is very disheartening to see thousands of postal workers in the early 1970s go on 'strike' and get amnesty. See thousands of draft resisters return to the country after the Vietnam conflict, and get amnesty. Then see a convicted Watergate personality be granted a Presidential Pardon," one bitter PATCO striker wrote Reagan. To striker Ray Carver, it seemed that Reagan was "doing things with a vengeance. He was going to teach us what poverty was."[19]

The administration would not moderate its stance during Reagan's second term, as Republican Rep. Guy Molinari of New York found. Elected to Congress in the Reagan landslide of 1980, Molinari supported Reagan's firing of the strikers in 1981. But in his role as the ranking member on the investigation oversight subcommittee of the House Committee on Public Works and Transportation, Molinari began to worry by 1985 about the long-term effects of the strike on air safety. In April that year, a near-collision occurred at Minneapolis–Saint Paul International Airport when a controller erroneously cleared one jet to taxi across the path of another that was accelerating down the runway toward takeoff. A collision that could have cost five hundred lives was narrowly averted only because the departing jet's pilot was able to lift off over the top of the taxiing jet. Touring FAA facilities, Molinari discovered that safety levels in the system were worse than he thought. Because he found working controllers reluctant to speak in the open about problems, fearing the wrath of their supervisors, he began to hold private meetings with them at which he invariably heard "horror stories" that confirmed his view that "the system was at risk."[20]

Molinari proposed a simple, and in his mind, sensible measure to improve safety. He introduced a bill that would provide for the rehiring of one thousand elite, award-winning controllers who had struck but who could demonstrate that they had not been among the strike's organizers or vocal supporters. The White House furiously opposed the effort. Reagan aides even went so far as to threaten to deny White House visitors' passes to Molinari's constituents if he persisted. Molinari would not give up. Cooperating with Democratic Reps. Richard Durbin of Illinois and Elliot Levitas of Georgia, he looked for ways to package his bill so the administration could not block it. In October 1986, he succeeded, attaching his amendment to a supplemental spending bill that Reagan needed to sign to keep the federal government operating.[21]

The fate of that initiative illustrated the president's determination to safeguard the symbolism associated with the PATCO strike. The spending bill was passed just prior to the president's departure for a summit meeting with Soviet leader Gorbachev in Reykjavík, Iceland. Reagan had no intention of softening his reputation before that meeting. He delayed his departure in order to sign a veto of the bill. "Score one on the diplomatic front for the tough guy" fumed the fired striker Bill Taylor. "Departure to Iceland was only minutes away, but time was taken to threaten the Congress with shutting down the government if the 'PATCO provision' was not removed from the two-day funding Bill."[22]

Molinari kept up his fight for two more years, amassing more evidence of a system stretched to its limits. He and his colleagues found that seven years after the PATCO strike, the vital New York TRACON still had only 199 of its complement of 243 authorized staff, and most of its controllers were still working six days per week. But no amount of evidence was capable of changing Reagan's mind about the strikers. Nor would Reagan's successor, George H. W. Bush, consider undoing the lifetime ban. When it became clear that Bush would carry on Reagan's policy, Molinari gave up the fight, mystified by the apparent triumph of ideology over common sense. By then, most PATCO controllers also had given up on the idea that they would ever work for the FAA again. In 1989, Bill Taylor, who edited a newsletter called *PATCO Lives: The Lifeline* for fellow strike veterans, reported the lack of progress in the rehiring fight. He counseled his readers that it was time to accept that "there's 'life after the FAA.' "[23]

Molinari's experience illustrated one of the most important yet underappreciated political consequences of the PATCO strike. As Reagan's confrontation with controllers emerged as a defining event of his presidency, unqualified support for his firing of controllers became a litmus test of Republican loyalty. The effect of this was to marginalize the voices of moderate Republicans like Molinari, Kemp, and Jeffords, who considered themselves friends of organized labor on many issues. This in turn accelerated the rise of avowedly antiunion conservatives within the party then headed by a former union president. When conservative Newt Gingrich ascended to the position of Speaker of the House in 1995 and advocated destroying key union protections embodied in the Wagner Act, he would not advertise the fact that early in his career he had sought and received PATCO's electoral support or that the union planned a reception for him after his first election to the House in 1978. The post-PATCO Republican mainstream had moved too far by then in the direction of unambiguous antiunionism, a considerable distance from where Reagan had stood in 1980 when he appealed to unionized air traffic controllers and other "Reagan Democrats."[24]

Public Workers on the Defensive

Fired air traffic controllers and pro-labor Republicans were scarcely the only casualties of the 1981 conflict between PATCO and Ronald Reagan. Just as a janitor, a sanitation worker, and a butcher were among those killed when the wreckage of United Airlines Flight 826 rained down on Brooklyn on December 16, 1960, so, too, did many workers who had never set foot in an air traffic control facility suffer from the deadly fallout of PATCO's collision with Reagan. Among the first to feel the effects of the broken strike were other public sector workers. Since the signing of John F. Kennedy's Executive Order 10988 in 1962, membership in unions had surged at every level of government, as had public workers' willingness to strike. As private sector unions faltered in the 1970s, the growth of public sector union membership had given a welcome lift to organized labor. The fiscal crisis of the mid-1970s had created challenges for public sector unions, but did not dampen their militancy. A successful strike by municipal workers in San Jose, California, in July 1981, which won "comparable worth" pay for women, a pathbreaking demand that promised to erase long-standing gender disparities, led some to predict that the 1980s would bring huge advances for public sector labor. The PATCO strike one month later helped explode those hopes and ensured that public sector unions would spend much of the 1980s on the defensive.[25]

Federal sector unions and their members were the most obviously affected. Ken Blaylock called the destruction of PATCO "a disaster for collective bargaining in the federal sector." Postal union leader Moe Biller bemoaned its "chilling effect on federal labor relations." Unions found it more difficult to organize and retain members in the open-shop federal sector once Reagan demonstrated PATCO's vulnerability. In the two years following the strike, the number of federal workers covered by union contracts suffered its biggest drop since the government began keeping track in 1963. Agencies also became noticeably tougher in negotiations. When the Postal Service took a hard line during negotiations in 1984, observers attributed it to the precedent set by Reagan in 1981. Faced with increased resistance, most unions scaled back their demands rather than risk a damaging confrontation. "If Reagan can destroy PATCO, he can destroy us too," reasoned James M. Pierce, president of the National Federation of Federal Employees. "Right or wrong, a lot of unions became less aggressive," Pierce conceded. As unions lost bargaining leverage, they saw their ability to attract and retain members erode. The AFGE, the largest federal sector union, saw its membership drop by 30 percent between 1980 and 1987.[26]

The fallout also hit state and local government workers. Union opponents hoped Reagan's example would "strengthen the hand of local governments everywhere," and, judging by the mail the president received from mayors, such hopes were not unfounded. "Too often in the past we have 'negotiated' away what is right, because it was easier," confessed the mayor of Romulus, Michigan. Reagan's firing of the controllers would "make the work of municipal administrators easier in dealing with the public sector labor groups," predicted the mayor of Garland, Texas. "Stick by your guns," came the word from Waterville, Wisconsin; "I am behind you," read a cable from Dyersburg, Tennessee; "remain firm in your resolve," urged the chief executive of Snyder, Texas. A gathering of 50 Oregon mayors praised the firing of the controllers as "just great." This groundswell led municipal union leaders to fear the emergence of "thousands of little Ronald Reagans across the country in every town saying 'Fire them,' whenever public employees confronted them in a labor dispute."[27]

The president's success in replacing the striking air traffic controllers was taken by many as a sign that unionized government services were bloated and could stand serious cutbacks. Not only conservatives read it that way. "The strike provides proof—that's right *proof*—that the government is as badly featherbedded as we've feared," huffed liberal journalist Jonathan Alter. "If overstaffing occurs in an area where we didn't really expect it, where the union had convinced a lot of people the workplace was *under-staffed*—then imagine how bad the featherbedding is in government offices where we *do* expect it." As such views ascended to the status of conventional wisdom, elected officials took note: antiunion politicians pressed their attacks, and former union allies sought to distance themselves from anything that could be portrayed as giving too much to public employee unions. In the fall of 1981, teachers, the leading edge of government employee unionism in the 1970s, complained that school boards were demanding an unprecedented number of concessions in contract talks. A clear indicator of the worsening climate for government workers was the sagging curve of union density, the percentage of eligible workers who joined unions. Through the 1970s, public sector union membership continuously rose on a trajectory that would have seen half of all government workers becoming union members in the 1980s. But membership growth rates stagnated in the post-PATCO years, and public sector union density never crested 40 percent.[28]

Yet one should not overstate the impact of the PATCO strike on public sector unions. They survived the post-PATCO-strike era and remained the most vibrant part of the labor movement in the late twentieth century. Their difficulties in expanding after 1981 were attributable to multiple factors, including the increased privatization of public services. But there was one area in which the PATCO strike's influence seems indisputable: it made government workers much less willing to strike.[29]

Indeed, public sector union militancy pivoted abruptly around the PATCO strike. Throughout the 1970s, the number of state and local government workers' strikes grew, setting a new record in 1979. In the aftermath of the PATCO strike, such walkouts fell precipitously. It is difficult to measure the dimensions of the decline in militancy with precision because the Reagan administration ceased publishing annual data on government workers' strikes after 1981. But fragmentary evidence indicates a stunning drop off. Scholar David Lewin found a 40 percent decline between 1980 and 1982 in state and local government strikes and a 50 percent decline in the number of days public service workers were idled by strikes. The Public Service Research Council found a 42 percent drop in teachers' strikes during the 1981–1982 school year alone. Some observers at the time believed that the dip in strike activity would be brief. But evidence from New York, the most densely organized state, indicates that there was no rebound. The number of government workers' strikes recorded in New York during the seven years after 1981 was 90 percent less than the number recorded during the seven years before.[30]

It is difficult to accurately measure the impact of the PATCO strike alone on public sector labor militancy in the United States, because government workers' strikes declined elsewhere in the industrialized world after 1980, although less precipitously. Yet anecdotal evidence suggests a strong causal relationship between Reagan's busting of PATCO and the change in U.S. strike patterns: employers, workers, and neutral observers alike credited Reagan's action with the shift. Reagan's firing of the controllers was "blessed by all elected officials from every level of government in the United States who have been faced with public employee strikes," as one Fort Lauderdale official explained. In the 1970s, municipal officials had been reading manuals that urged them to make peace with their striking employees, even if their walkouts were illegal. After PATCO, this was no longer the case. "Breathes there a city manager with a soul so dead that they will not want to look like a hero when he sees the President of the United States being applauded for being tough and closing every door to a settlement in defiance of all the civilized rules of collective bargaining?" wondered AFL-CIO Secretary-Treasurer Tom Donahue. Donahue accurately predicted the response of public officials. Their desire to emulate Reagan changed the calculus for workers. A year after the PATCO strike, the director of the Federal Mediation and Conciliation Service attributed the steep drop in government strikes to the "chilling effect" of Reagan's actions. Unionized teachers, among others, admitted feeling "intimidated" by the PATCO firings. Fear of waging strikes, in turn, changed the nature of public sector collective bargaining. After 1981, government employee unions substituted increased political action and campaign contributions for strikes as they looked for the best way to influence their employers.[31]

THE REBIRTH OF STRIKEBREAKING

By adjusting their goals and tactics, public sector unions survived the PATCO strike relatively intact. It was among private sector union workers that the influence of the controllers' strike proved enduringly devastating,

for PATCO's destruction marked the beginning of the end of one of organized labor's most reliable weapons: the strike. Occurring at a vulnerable
moment in U.S. working-class history, the PATCO debacle catalyzed a
revival of strikebreaking that helped marginalize the strike as a feature of
American labor relations by the end of the twentieth century.

The marginalization of the strike was a remarkable and unanticipated
development. Strikes had been an indispensable weapon in the arsenal of
U.S. unions since workers staged the first "turnouts" in the early nineteenth
century. Withholding their labor provided workers the leverage they needed
to win better wages and working conditions, and indeed the right to collectively bargain at all. As unions won legal protections in the years after the
1935 Wagner Act, workers' right to strike was widely accepted as necessary
to the proper function of labor markets. The strike "must be accepted as a
commonplace on the economic scene wherever collective bargaining is to
take place within a free market system," economist Allan M. Cartter observed
in 1959. Strikes imposed costs on both sides—lost wages for workers, lost
profits for employers—that prevented either side from exploiting the other,
helping maintain a rough equilibrium in labor-management relations,
Cartter's generation believed. Throughout the 1960s and 1970s, that view
held, and the strike remained a crucial element of private-sector labor relations. In the post-PATCO era, however, the strike weapon swiftly disappeared from the American labor scene, a development that held staggering
consequences for private sector workers.[32]

A few saw it coming within days of Reagan's firing of controllers. "Union
busting on this scale hasn't been seen in the last forty years," warned one
longshoremen's union leaflet. "If PATCO loses this strike, no union is safe."
The National Journal agreed: "By taking a rough stance, the Administration
has obviously sent a signal to others in management positions; if the
government can break the unions, then private employers can too." Hoping
that Reagan's treatment of PATCO would discipline unions and stiffen the
spines of employers in the private sector, the Wall Street Journal became a
cheerleader of the president's policy toward PATCO, reprinting an account
of Calvin Coolidge's breaking of the 1919 Boston police strike to show how
bold action had tamed disruptive unions in the pre–New Deal era. The
Journal's business readers hoped that Reagan's defiant stand, like Coolidge's,
would help usher in a more employer-friendly age. The key to this shift was
the legitimization of a tactic that had become uncommon in post–New Deal

labor relations: the breaking of strikes through the use of permanent replacement workers.[33]

Private sector employers had long enjoyed the right to replace strikers. Shortly after the Wagner Act became law, the U.S. Supreme Court in the 1938 case *NLRB v. Mackay Radio and Telegraph* indicated that nothing in the act prevented employers from hiring replacement workers during an economic strike when wages and working conditions, rather than union recognition or unfair labor practices, were at issue. Even though the decision confirmed the employer's right to hire replacements, relatively few employers exercised this right in the post–World War II era. Even in cases where employers did hire replacement workers, they tended to discharge replacements and welcome strikers back to their old jobs at the conclusion of a walkout.[34]

The seeds were planted for a change in the use of replacement workers in the 1970s when an aggressive new union-avoidance industry sprang up in the United States. The rise of a global economy in which container ships, computers, and satellite communication made it possible to produce goods for the American market in low-wage, offshore environments created new opportunities for U.S. employers, and new incentives for them to free themselves from union contracts. The stagflation and plant closings of the mid-1970s provided an opportunity for employers to press their advantage over workers who were put on the defensive by the emerging global economy. In this context, new organizations arose to combat union influence, like the Business Roundtable, founded in 1972. These were accompanied by a sudden proliferation of antiunion labor consultants, such as James L. Dougherty, whose volume *Union-Free Management—And How to Keep it Free* became a popular handbook for business executives.[35]

The new antiunionists believed that taking the strike weapon away from workers was a prerequisite for weakening the "union menace." In their 1973 treatise, *Labor Unions—How To: Avert Them, Beat Them, Out-Negotiate Them, Live With Them, Unload Them*, Herbert Rothenberg and Steven B. Silverman argued that the strike was the "very keystone" of the labor movement. If employers learned how to break strikes effectively, they wrote, then "the whole of the labor movement would instantly become as ineffectual and sterile as would its picket-lines." But, to successfully undermine labor's power to strike, employers needed more than the backing of the law or favorable economic conditions. They also required a compelling moral argument. Conservative economist W. H. Hutt took up that point in his 1973 book, *The Strike-Threat System: The Economic Consequences of Collective Bargaining*. To defeat labor's "strike threat," Hutt argued, employers needed to characterize strikes as "a type of warfare under which privileged groups can gain at the expense of the unprivileged." Hutt argued that the strike-won wage gains of union workers were simply passed along in the form of higher prices, which ultimately exploited nonunion workers. Hutt's argument gained traction in the mid-1970s, as average American wage earners saw their real earnings decline while the cost-of-living adjustments (COLAs) won in many collective bargaining agreements offered union members some protection from the worst effects of inflation.[36]

The public sector militancy that spread in the 1970s provided test cases for Hutt's thesis that strikes could be portrayed as victimizing the unprivileged. Union opponents argued persuasively that each gain won by government employees through strikes was passed on to other workers in the form of higher taxes and fees. Such arguments helped make the public sector an ideal arena for the relegitimization of strikebreaking. In 1974 the school board in Hortonville, Wisconsin, permanently replaced striking teachers, winning strong community support for the action. In 1977, Atlanta Mayor Maynard Jackson, a former civil rights leader and union ally, fired striking sanitation workers 48 hours into a walkout and hired replacements. He was rewarded later that year with a smashing reelection victory. Although Jackson, unlike Reagan, would later rehire most of the fired workers, the political boost he gained from the confrontation worried unionists. While the Hortonville and Atlanta episodes were harbingers, neither was prominent enough to change the dynamics of strikes nationally. There was a slight increase in private employers' willingness to break strikes by hiring replacements in the second half of the 1970s, but a large shift in employers' behavior would not occur until Ronald Reagan showed the way in dramatic fashion on the national stage.[37]

It took Reagan's breaking of PATCO to thoroughly legitimize striker replacement in the eyes of most employers. By conferring legitimacy on strikebreaking Reagan decisively altered the course of U.S. labor relations. Not only did Reagan's handling of PATCO dramatize the effectiveness of the replacement tactic on the grandest scale and in the most visible way possible, it demonstrated that even the most skilled workers were replaceable. No other employer but the federal government could have made this point so effectively, for no other employer could spend so freely for so long to demonstrate it. By the same token, with its widely publicized demand for $10,000 across-the-board salary increases funded by federal taxes and fees, no union could have provided a clearer illustration of Hutt's argument that strikes ultimately exacted costs not from employers but from other workers.[38]

The larger context within which the PATCO strike occurred magnified its influence as a catalyst. A "perfect storm" of economic developments made the years 1979–1983 the most vulnerable moment for American workers since the Great Depression. Crucial in shaping this moment were the conscious policy decisions made in Washington by the man whom Jimmy Carter appointed to head the Federal Reserve Bank of the United States, Paul Volcker. To arrest the inflation rate that dogged the U.S. economy in the late 1970s, Volcker instituted a form of monetary shock therapy, raising interest rates to a postwar high in an effort to trigger an inflation-killing recession. The first stage in Volcker's plan produced tremendous economic pain, as inflation hit 13.5 percent and unemployment 7.2 percent in 1980. Ironically, the strategy undermined support for the president who had appointed Volcker, and eased the way for Reagan's election. In the long run, though, Volcker achieved his desired effect. Unemployment hit a post–World War II high of 9.7 percent in 1982, and inflation fell, reaching 1.9 percent by 1984. But the high unemployment took a heavy toll on working-class families. During 1981–1983, 12.3 percent of the U.S. workforce experienced at least one involuntary job loss. Not until 1987 did unemployment finally recede below 7 percent.[39]

Reagan's trade policy exacerbated working-class insecurity during these years. Treasury Secretary Donald Regan teamed up with Volcker to strengthen the U.S. dollar in the early 1980s by increasing its value by 35 percent against a broad mix of international currencies between January 1981 and November 1982. This dollar-strengthening effort made U.S. exports more expensive to potential foreign buyers, exaggerating the effects of the economic recession in manufacturing cities. Overall, 2.4 million manufacturing jobs disappeared between 1979 and 1983. The hemorrhaging of manufacturing jobs, in turn, created a pool of downwardly mobile unemployed workers whose presence in the job market helped depress the wages of still-employed workers. As workers' fears of unemployment grew, employers found it easier to extract wage concessions that reduced manufacturing wages by 5 percent between 1979 and 1982.[40]

The ascendancy of a conservative Republican administration provided a final bit of context. The Reagan administration's targeted outreach to socially conservative unions notwithstanding, public policy tilted decisively against unions and worker protections once Reagan took office. The minimum wage was allowed to languish and its purchasing power fell to its lowest level since World War II. The Occupational Safety and Health Administration (OSHA) experienced severe cutbacks. And the ideological orientation of the agency that enforced workers' Wagner Act rights to organize and bargain collectively, the National Labor Relations Board, underwent the most profound change since the board's inception in the 1930s. Under the leadership of Donald Dotson, the man whom Reagan appointed to chair the board, the NLRB issued a string of decisions that weakened union rights—including strike rights. In one such decision the Dotson Board ruled in 1984 that verbal abuse of replacement workers by picketing strikers was an unfair labor practice that could invalidate the claim of an offending striker to reinstatement at the conclusion of a strike.[41]

This confluence of economic and political factors ensured that Reagan's replacement of the PATCO strikers would resonate more deeply than any strikebreaking episode over the previous half-century. Reagan and his advisers did not intentionally set out to use the confrontation with PATCO to change the course of U.S. labor relations, as their efforts to settle with the union in June 1981 show. But having confronted and broken PATCO in August 1981, they were determined to take no action that would limit the impact or influence of that act. Reagan's decision to annihilate the union and prevent any strikers from regaining their jobs turned a reluctant confrontation into a game-changing event in American industrial relations.

Martin Jay Levitt, a professional union-buster, immediately grasped the importance of Reagan's action. In August 1981, he was working on an assignment for John Sheridan and Associates, a leading union-avoidance firm. Levitt's job was to subvert a local union negotiating its first contract after winning the right to represent nursing home workers in Sebring, Ohio, midway between Cleveland and Pittsburgh. He was stringing along the contract negotiations to the point that the frustrated union leaders began considering a strike just at the moment that Reagan fired the air traffic controllers. Levitt could hardly believe his luck. Each night on the evening news, nursing home workers were treated to stories about what Levitt called "the biggest union bust in history," one that "recast the crimes of union busting as acts of patriotism." Given this fortuitous coincidence, Levitt decided that the best way to undermine the Sebring union was to dare its members to strike and "scare them into believing strikers would lose their jobs." The strategy worked. After many weeks of stalemated talks, the union prepared to strike to try to jump-start the bargaining process. Levitt immediately ran ads for replacement workers in the local newspaper and spread word that there was a backlog of job applicants. As the strike date neared, the union's members grew anxious. When the deadline arrived, the workers lost their nerve. "Nothing happened. No one walked out," Levitt recalled. "No one showed up with picket signs. No one." Its strike threat exposed as a bluff, the union lost all bargaining leverage and soon folded. In short order, Levitt's services were in high demand through the Midwest. Everywhere he went, he used the threat of permanent replacement workers "to fill the laborers of industry with dread."[42]

The influence of the PATCO strike was also visible far from the shadowy world of union-busters behind the ivy-covered walls of America's finest and most respected business schools. In 1982, three professors from the University of Pennsylvania's Wharton School of Business brought out a volume titled *Operating During Strikes: Company Experience, NLRB Policies, and Government Regulations*. Charles R. Perry, Andrew Kramer, and Thomas J. Schneider opened their book by touting Reagan's "dramatic handling" of PATCO as the best illustration of "a relatively new phenomenon in United States industrial relations—the determination of management to operate facilities when employees strike." They went on to argue that replacing strikers could be a beneficial business move for any employer and urged executives to shed "the fear of failure and the fear of confrontation." If they only summoned the will to break strikes, employers would acquire "enhanced power and control in union-management relations," the professors promised. The tactic of replacing striking workers could then become what Perry called a new "management power asset."[43]

Management's embrace of strikebreaking fundamentally altered the calculus of U.S. labor-management relations. Since the Great Depression, strikes had become such a routine feature of the industrial scene that economists such as Sir John Hicks described their function with mathematical precision. In the 1930s, Hicks invented a way to graph strike dynamics. He depicted two intersecting lines: a downward-sloping "resistance curve," which illustrated the degree to which union resistance diminished over time as the economic hardship of a walkout took its toll; and an upward-sloping "concession curve," which illustrated employers' increasing willingness to settle a strike as the economic costs of a prolonged shutdown escalated. When a strike began, and neither strikers nor their employer had paid a price for the shutdown, the curves were farthest apart. But as a walkout lengthened, they would begin to converge, Hicks argued. The costs endured by each side would push them toward settlement. Eventually the curves would intersect at point P, where each side would agree on wage W after a strike of S days. The value of W or S would naturally vary, depending on the circumstances of a strike, the workers who waged it, and the marketplace, but the basic structure of the intersecting resistance and concession curves would hold. The task for negotiators was to properly assess both their opponent's curve and their own. In the best of all worlds, both sides could find wage W, "the highest wages which skillful negotiation can extract from the employer," without having to reach a strike of S days—or ideally without striking at all. The Hicks model was not without flaws. Over the years, economists tweaked and refined it. But all revisions assumed that there was a point P to be found in any labor conflict. After 1981, that assumption crumbled.[44]

In the 1980s, prominent employers saw strikes not as conflicts to be avoided, but as opportunities to break or tame unions. The mutual search for point P that had characterized past labor-capital conflicts gave way to a new era in which employers were determined to set wages unilaterally. By 1983, the new approach was visible. That year, the copper mining giant Phelps Dodge demanded that its Arizona workers agree to a wage freeze and give up the automatic cost-of-living adjustment that protected them against inflation. The union accepted the freeze but resisted the COLA give-back. When their contract expired on July 1, the miners struck over this demand. Copper strikes had occurred like clockwork after the expiration of each three-year contract over the two previous decades. In the past, each side eventually agreed on a wage W after strikes of varying lengths. But 1983 was different. Phelps Dodge hired replacements and refused to modify its demands. Violent confrontations erupted in Morenci and other Arizona mining communities when strikers tried to keep strikebreakers from their jobs. Democratic Governor Bruce Babbitt mobilized the National Guard to protect the strikebreakers. The mines continued to operate. Finally, in January 1985, the replacement workers were given the chance to decertify the union in an NLRB-supervised election, completing the destruction of collective bargaining in the copper mines. In November 1983, seven thousand bus drivers struck Greyhound after the company demanded that they accept wage and benefit cuts. Inundated with thirty-five thousand applications for the strikers' jobs, the company put its buses back on their routes with replacement drivers, and the strike collapsed. The union accepted an 8 percent wage cut and an agreement that newly hired drivers would be paid even less.[45]

By the mid-1980s, similar conflicts began unfolding with monotonous regularity. In its August 1985 contract negotiations, George A. Hormel & Company demanded a wage cut of 23 percent from workers in its Austin, Minnesota, meatpacking plant. When the union refused and went on strike, the company reopened its plant with replacement workers. After many months of bitter struggle, national leaders of the United Food and Commercial Workers forced the Austin workers to accept a huge wage cut as the only way the union could survive in the plant. At Continental Airlines in 1984, the *Chicago Tribune* in 1985, and TWA in 1986, the stories were the same: employers' demands for concessions triggered strikes; replacements were recruited; unions were routed.[46]

No union was hit harder by the strikebreaking tsunami than the United Paperworkers' International Union. In 1985, the union struck the Georgia-Pacific paper mill in Crossett, Arkansas, when the company insisted on taking away workers' paid Christmas and Fourth of July holidays. When the company brought in replacements, the strike crumbled and the holidays were surrendered. In 1986, Boise Cascade broke a Paperworkers' strike in their Rumsford, Maine, paper mill with the help of replacements. On the basis of that experience, the company compiled a booklet called the "Worker Replacement Plan" for use in its other plants. In 1987, International Paper broke strikes in Jay, Maine, Lockport, Pennsylvania, and DePere, Wisconsin. Wayne Glenn, the frustrated president of the Paperworkers, laid the blame for his union's decimation directly at President Reagan's feet. Reagan had given employers a clear mandate, he said. "If it's all right for the President of the United States to do it, well it's all right for us CEOs to order it done."[47]

That refrain became common during the 1980s. Back in his private sector labor law practice after the PATCO strike, George Stohner of Morgan Lewis was confronted by sophisticated executives who asked, "Well, if the president of the United States can fire strikers, why can't I?" Stohner found himself having to explain that it was legal for private sector workers to strike. But he did not have to explain that it was also legal to replace strikers. Businessmen readily grasped that truth, and it contributed to what Stohner saw as a general "toughening" of employer attitudes. Nothing better illustrated the attitudinal shift than the burgeoning business that arose around strikebreaking. There were about one hundred union avoidance consultants active in the United States in the mid-1970s. Their number grew tenfold by the mid-1980s. Many specialized in strikebreaking services. Companies such as Worldwide Labor Support promised to deliver skilled replacement workers and kept databases with the names of thousands of workers who were willing to cross picket lines. Others, such as Vance International, provided security to struck plants. With the aid of such companies, employers permanently replaced three hundred thousand striking workers in the 1980s by one estimate. But this number does not begin to measure the impact of the new strikebreaking phenomenon. According to one sample, replacements were employed in roughly 20 percent of strikes. But even when they were not hired, the mere possibility of their hiring caused workers and unions to back down from confrontations and soften their demands. Unions still won some strikes in the 1980s, as walkouts by miners against the Pittston Coal Company and telephone workers against NYNEX showed in 1989. But such big wins became rare.[48]

Finding it difficult to win walkouts, unions scrambled for alternatives to what one activist called "the old-fashioned strike." In 1986, the AFL-CIO produced *The Inside Game: Winning with Workplace Strategies*, a manual that encouraged workers to avoid strikes that could lead to their replacement. It counseled, "When an employer begins trying to play by the new rules and actually force a strike, *staying on the job and working from the inside* may be more appropriate." Increasingly, unions advocated such "inside campaigns" or corporate campaigns aimed at mobilizing shareholders or public opinion against employers in preference to strikes. While they occasionally proved effective, such campaigns never replaced the potency and immediate impact that strikes once held for workers.[49]

The destruction of the strike as a viable means of leverage for workers could not have been predicted in the late 1970s. The number of major work stoppages reported by the Bureau of Labor Statistics held remarkably steady between 1960 and 1980, even though the overall share of U.S. workers represented by unions declined. During those twenty years, the United States averaged 286 major work stoppages annually (events involving at least one thousand workers). After 1981, the pattern changed. The United States never again saw the annual number of major work stoppages reach even one-third of pre-PATCO levels. During the 1980s, the annual average plummeted to eighty-three; during the 1990s it sank to thirty-four; during the 2000s it was twenty. Each year the evidence mounted: strikes had become too risky for most American workers to undertake.[50]

As the number of strikes diminished sharply after 1981, a budgetary decision by the Reagan administration further removed them from public consciousness. From 1947 through 1980, the Bureau of Labor Statistics meticulously catalogued every strike that involved at least six workers in the United States. In 1981, the Reagan administration announced that it would dramatically curtail the collection of strike data to save the taxpayers' money. Thereafter only the statistics concerning work stoppages involving at least one thousand workers were recorded. The publication of federal data on state and local government workers' strikes was suspended altogether. Not only were strikes diminishing after 1981, they were becoming statistically invisible, erased from popular consciousness, and lost to historical record.[51]

As the ability of workers to stage successful job actions plummeted after 1981, so too did unions' bargaining leverage. This in turn made it easier for employers to discourage private sector workers from choosing union representation. An average of 221,212 workers won union representation annually through elections conducted by the National Labor Relations Board during the ten years before the PATCO strike. The number was halved between 1980 and 1982, and never recovered in subsequent years. During the ten years after the PATCO strike, the annual average was 97,123.[52]

BITTER VINDICATION

Paradoxically, one of the few bright spots for the troubled labor movement of the 1980s was to be found in the FAA, where union agitation began again a mere two years after the PATCO strike. There had been a half-hearted attempt to reform the agency's personnel practices following the strike, when Drew Lewis appointed Lawrence Jones, president of the Coleman Company, an outdoor equipment manufacturer, Bruce Fuller of Harvard Business School, and David G. Bowers of the University of Michigan, to investigate the FAA's practices and recommend reforms. In 1982, the group presented Lewis with an unflattering report that placed a large share of the blame on management for the breakdown in labor relations at the FAA. The task force recommended a thorough revision of the agency's management policies. Lewis expressed gratitude for the findings, but the recommendations gathered dust. The same problems that PATCO had complained about in the 1970s began to plague the nonstrikers, replacement workers, and new hires that staffed facilities after the strike. As happened in the 1960s, the FAA's poor managerial practices spurred controllers to organize.[53]

Within two months of the strike, a group of working controllers at Washington Center formed a group called the National Controllers' Advisory Committee. Its purpose was "not to act as a negotiating team," one proponent explained, "but as a representative group to advise the FAA of our wishes." The FAA expressed no interest in meeting with the group. By 1983, spontaneous job actions occurred in some locations. That summer at New York Center, in an action that recalled PATCO's 1968 Operation Air Safety, controllers began implementing "a very soft 'slow down,'" spacing flights by twice the required distance in order to protest overwork and other grievances.[54]

By the spring of 1984, scattered instances of resistance began to coalesce into organizing efforts at Washington Center and across several New England facilities. The movement at Washington Center drew the support of a number of activists who had been PATCO members but who had left the union prior to the strike. The Leesburg facility soon became a hub of FAA organizing. The Washington Center controllers called their organization the National Air Traffic Controllers Association (NATCA) and they asked for help from the American Federation of Government Employees. AFGE president Ken Blaylock assigned a uniquely qualified organizer to aid them: John Thornton, who had previously led PATCO at National Airport. It was not an assignment that Thornton relished. "I didn't want to do it," he later recalled. "These were people who had replaced me." But, reasoning that the government would never rehire PATCO strikers until a union returned to the FAA, Thornton accepted the work. By May 1984, more than two hundred NATCA supporters at Washington Center petitioned for a union election. Soon, efforts to organize NATCA chapters spread to New York, Atlanta, and Indianapolis.[55]

AFGE's strategy was to try to organize separate drives in each FAA district and then combine the resulting organizations into a national air traffic controllers union. The first district targeted was New England, where controllers held their first organizing meeting in May 1984. They formed an AFGE district called the American Air Traffic Controllers Council (AATCC) and filed for a regionwide election.[56]

The government tried to deflect the AFGE-sponsored regional organizing drives by arguing before the Federal Labor Relations Authority that the FAA could only recognize unions that represented a national, rather than a local or regional bargaining unit. The FLRA sided with the agency, forcing organizers to round up signatures from 30 percent of the FAA's entire controller workforce before they could win the right to an election. The stalling tactic worked for a time. The AFGE did not have the financial resources for a national union campaign. Other unions briefly flirted with the idea of sponsoring the organizing drive, only to back away.[57]

At that point, fate intervened. Once again, a midair collision shook air traffic controllers. On November 11, 1985, in fading light just after sunset, a Falcon 50 Executive Jet collided with a single-engine Piper Cherokee over northern New Jersey. All those aboard both planes were killed. The wreckage of the jet plunged to the ground in the crowded community of Cliffside Park, demolishing two buildings instantly and igniting a fire that destroyed four more. The accident took six lives in all, including one on the ground. Eerily, it took place only ten miles northwest of the spot where a DC-8 had crashed to the streets of Brooklyn on December 16, 1960. Controllers were not judged at fault in the accident. The tower controller at Teterboro Airport had warned both pilots of each other's presence, and before turning to other duties he had ascertained that the jet, which was on a landing approach, had visual contact with the Cherokee. But the accident demonstrated to controllers how much they needed an organization to speak out on their behalf. Just as the 1960 accident had stirred organizing interest among the controllers of Hangar 11, the Teterboro midair collision galvanized New York area controllers behind the NATCA movement. (One of them, Barry Krasner, would go on to become president of the union.) A few weeks later, in December 1985, PATCO's old patron stepped into the breach. C. E. "Gene" DeFries, who succeeded Jesse Calhoon as president of MEBA, announced that his union would take on NATCA as an affiliate and once again would fund a nationwide organizing drive to win a union for air traffic controllers. Thornton signed on as lead organizer.[58]

Over the next eighteen months, NATCA's campaign gathered steam, following in PATCO's early footsteps. On September 23, 1986, eighteen years after PATCO held its constitutional convention in Chicago, two hundred air traffic controller delegates returned to that city to ratify NATCA's constitution. Significantly, the NATCA constitution included a no-strike clause, but this scarcely placated the FAA. Admiral Donald D. Engen, who succeeded Lynn Helms as FAA administrator, opposed NATCA, and made clear that he preferred to "deal directly with . . . people rather than through a bargaining agent." He claimed there was little support for NATCA among controllers. Evidence soon belied his claims. "We need a union, we really do," said one Cleveland Center controller who had been hired as a strike-breaker in 1981.[59]

NATCA's organizing took off following the Chicago convention. By January 1987, almost half of the controller workforce had signed its petition demanding a union election. The FLRA responded by setting up a mail ballot a few months later. The results of that ballot were announced on June 11, 1987. Nearly 70 percent of the FAA's controllers endorsed NATCA as their representative. Air traffic controllers were once again unionized. Although NATCA officials made clear that they would "obey and respect the law," the return of an air traffic controllers' union to the FAA so soon after PATCO's destruction stunned the Reagan administration. For AFL-CIO leaders, the NATCA election amounted to a vindication of sorts. They had desperately wanted to see controllers organized before Reagan left office. Lane Kirkland welcomed the controllers into the AFL-CIO with a special reception. "The election is a turning point and the start of a new trend," crowed MEBA's president. NATCA agreed to its first tentative three-year contract with the FAA on January 13, 1989—seven days before the end of Reagan's presidency—and ratified it three months later. Many elements of the PATCO-FAA contracts of the 1970s were embodied in the seventy-seven-article agreement.[60]

Most PATCO strikers found it difficult to relish NATCA's victory. The fact that men and women who took the jobs created by their firing now had a union was cold comfort to many who still entertained the hope that they might be allowed to return to the FAA once Reagan left office. Strike veteran Bill Taylor expressed their feelings in the pages of *PATCO Lives: The Lifeline,* the quarterly strike-alumni newsletter that he edited. "Not that we didn't expect reorganizing to occur, nor even self-serving individuals to use it for their own gain," he wrote, "but to embrace those who during the past six years have taken the jobs of professional controllers, worked hard to keep them locked out, and overwhelmingly told congressional investigators that they should never be reinstated, is well beyond the level of hypocrisy we've become accustomed to in Washington, D.C." Hearing union leaders describe NATCA as "a symbol of labor's resurgence" made Taylor feel scorned and forgotten.[61]

ELUSIVE REDEMPTION

In the late 1980s, Taylor emerged as a leader of an indefatigable group of PATCO veterans who refused to give up fighting to get their jobs back. After being fired, Taylor had moved to Washington to volunteer in the PATCO office. He intended to stay for a few months at most, but he never left. He took over the duty of posting recorded updates on a call-in number to keep strikers abreast of the union's efforts on their behalf. After PATCO was decertified and USATCO flamed out, Taylor began editing *PATCO Lives: The Lifeline,* in which he regularly exhorted his colleagues to keep the faith. NATCA's triumph only caused Taylor to redouble his efforts. If the FAA could transform strikebreakers into unionists so quickly, he contended, then it was obviously wrong to blame PATCO alone for the 1981 strike and unfair to ban strikers from the FAA for the rest of their lives. One person who accepted this argument was 1988 Democratic presidential nominee Michael Dukakis. While holding a substantial lead over George H. W. Bush in opinion polls early in the campaign, Dukakis promised that as president he would authorize the rehiring of PATCO strikers by the FAA. "Perhaps by this time next year ... all of us will be into another whole phase of our recovery," Taylor exulted in *PATCO Lives: The Lifeline.* But those hopes evaporated along with Dukakis's early lead. During the Bush presidency, some Democrats continued to speak out against the "cruel life sentence unprecedented in the history of this government" that Reagan had imposed on the strikers. NATCA also spoke up increasingly on the strikers' behalf. Tensions between NATCA and the Bush FAA led many NATCA activists to identify with PATCO, and in 1990 the union endorsed a removal of the strikers' lifetime ban from the FAA. But when it became clear that Bush had no intention of undoing Reagan's policy, even Taylor considered giving up.[62]

Bill Clinton's victory over Bush in 1992 did not immediately raise the hopes of the oft-disappointed strike veterans. The new president reminded Taylor of Jimmy Carter, a president "second only to Ronald Reagan himself when it came to hostile treatment of air traffic controllers." Taylor's suspicions were understandable. As a moderate governor of Arkansas, a charter member of the fiscally conservative Democratic Leadership Council, and an advocate of the North American Free Trade Agreement (NAFTA), a treaty strongly opposed by organized labor, Clinton was not seen as a "labor Democrat." Yet Clinton had good reason to want to hand unions an important symbolic victory by reversing Reagan's ban, especially since he was intent on ratifying NAFTA over their objections. He could also point to an ongoing controller shortage: there were nearly two thousand fewer controllers in 1993 than there had been in 1981, while the volume of air traffic had risen 28 percent.[63]

As the inauguration neared, expectations rose. Taylor marshaled his network into action to push Clinton for an executive order removing the ban. "For almost twelve years they've thrown everything they had at us," he wrote. "We're still here," and "most importantly, we still have *the ability to affect our own destiny.*" His hotline, which normally received eight hundred calls a week, got four times that number during the month of Clinton's inauguration. Meanwhile, a second group of more moderate strike veterans called Controllers United sprang up and added their voices to those asking Clinton for relief. Newspaper editorials and public opinion polls alike indicated support for a removal of the ban.[64]

Despite this groundswell, six months passed with no word from the White House. President Clinton issued several executive orders favorable to labor during that time, but conspicuously ignored the former controllers. Only after he signed the Omnibus Budget Reconciliation Act of 1993, the budget-balancing bill on which he staked so much of his presidency, did Clinton finally act, and then the manner of his action seemed designed to minimize controversy. On August 12, 1993, with Congress in recess, much of the press corps on vacation, and the president in Colorado, the White House issued a statement signed by the secretaries of transportation and labor and the director of the Office of Personnel Management, rather than the president. "While the administration does not condone illegal job actions in the federal government, reasonable people would agree that after 12 years former air traffic controllers should be able to apply for employment," it read. "The President believes that it is time to put this chapter of labor management relations behind us."[65]

No matter how muted its delivery, the news triggered celebrations among PATCO veterans and their defenders. The announcement put "a tombstone on a terrible era in our nation's history," said labor's ally, Rep. William D. Ford. It meant "the era of the all-powerful boss is over," concurred John Leyden, who had moved on to direct the AFL-CIO Public Employee Department. Although twelve years had passed since they had been fired, and they had necessarily gone on to other careers, within a year, an astonishing 40 percent of the strikers fired in 1981 applied to return to the FAA. Among them was Domenic Torchia, who had become a successful stockbroker since being fired in 1981. Like many of his colleagues, he could not resist the chance to resume work he had loved. Those who did come back were welcomed into the union by young NATCA activists such as Paul Rinaldi of Dulles International, who respected them for having "paid the ultimate sacrifice" in defense of the controllers' profession.[66]

Yet excitement soon gave way to renewed bitterness among many former strikers, as they learned that their applications would be processed without preference. To regain employment at the FAA they had to compete against much younger recruits. The FAA estimated that it would have room to hire back only fifty former strikers each year. But even that estimate was scaled down when the agency instituted a systemwide hiring freeze in February 1994, only six months after Clinton lifted the ban. PATCO strikers and their allies complained, but to no avail: by the second anniversary of the Clinton directive, only thirty-seven former strikers were actually working again at the FAA. Those who were in their forties at the time they were fired knew the long waiting lists meant they had little chance of sitting before a radar screen again.[67]

Subsequent reforms implemented by the Clinton administration only increased PATCO strikers' feelings of being left behind. In 1996, Clinton signed an FAA Reauthorization Act, whose Senate sponsor was Arizona Republican John McCain. The act enabled the FAA to abandon the standard federal GS pay scale for controllers and allowed the agency greater latitude to negotiate with NATCA over pay, the very goals PATCO had once sought. In 1998, NATCA and the FAA signed a new $10.6 billion contract which provided a revamped classification system for controllers that would result in substantial pay increases. Relatively few PATCO strikers would ever have the chance to work under the new rules they had sacrificed their careers to win.[68]

Bill Taylor was one of those who never had a chance to celebrate. He died on July 16, 1994, knowing that the vast majority of PATCO strikers who had applied for their old jobs would never return to air traffic control. "So here we are, twelve years later and, in some ways, back at the beginning," he concluded in one of his last newsletter columns. "It appears that if we still want a chance to work in our profession, we're going to have to fight for it, as much or more than ever." In the end, Clinton's removal of the ban that had kept strikers from being rehired by the FAA and his liberalization of air traffic controller pay amounted to nothing more than a tantalizing mirage for most PATCO veterans. Their exclusion from the fruits of these victories represented for them one final indignity—one more punishment inflicted on workers whose disastrous strike had marked the onset of an ominous new era in American labor relations.[69]

BLACK BOX

Our past is prologue.
—JACK MAHER

And let me tell you something partner: it's hard to
unplow the ground.
—STRIKER RAY CARVER[1]

The investigation of the New York midair collision of 1960 was the first in the United States to utilize a "black box." The device—actually painted bright red to facilitate its identification amid charred wreckage—had been perfected only a few years earlier by an Australian researcher named David Warren. It recorded flight data, providing evidence that could help determine the causes of fatal events. The recovery of the device from the wreckage of United Flight 826 in Brooklyn allowed investigators to determine that pilot error was the primary cause of the accident that took 134 lives on a gray December morning. In many ways, the black box left behind by the 1981 collision between PATCO and Ronald Reagan has proven more difficult to decipher.

Debates about the causes of the PATCO strike commenced almost as soon as termination notices went out to striking air traffic controllers; debates about its consequences followed soon after. Initial interpretations of the cause varied. Some contended that the strike was the inevitable product of greedy union overreach, the logical outcome of the mistaken experiment of public sector unionization. Others argued that PATCO had been "led into a trap," lured by Reagan campaign promises into a strike that was intended to destroy organized labor. The facts did not fit well with either interpretation. Proponents of the first thesis overlooked the deep flaws in federal labor policies, the poor management, the long-simmering grievances, the inability of vital workers to be able to bargain collectively over the things that mattered most to them, and the twenty-year history of conflict and neglect that set the stage for the air traffic controllers' strike. Proponents of the second thesis ignored the Reagan administration's early political outreach to segments of organized labor and the precedent-setting nature of its June 1981 offer to PATCO. These flawed interpretations lived on nonetheless for they reinforced the worldviews of their adherents, allowing them to avoid the messy reality of this watershed conflict, for which many actors on both sides bore some measure of responsibility.[2]

Ultimately, there has been little disagreement that the strike changed the presidency of Ronald Reagan and delivered a huge blow to organized labor. Yet, assessing the true extent of its impact on either Reagan or labor has been more difficult, for history has often become entangled with myth and legend.[3]

Without doubt, the strike elevated Ronald Reagan's stature, strengthened his hand as president, and was "crucial in forming a lasting image of the president's toughness," as political scientist James W. Ceasar put it. According to journalist Haynes Johnson, it helped make Reagan a "mythic figure in American life." But, as with all legends, what was remembered and passed on diverged from what actually happened. Reagan's dramatic breaking of the strike obliterated from historical memory those missteps of his campaign and administration that had increased the likelihood of a strike, leaving in their place only the image of a president's mythic "toughness" under pressure. Thus twenty-five years after the PATCO strike, the *Wall Street Journal* applauded "Ronald Reagan's refusal to allow the union to bargain over pay," willfully oblivious to the fact that Reagan *did* allow PATCO to bargain over pay. During his presidency Reagan's critics marveled at his ability to avoid blame for his mistakes—a talent that led Congresswoman Patricia Schroeder to dub him famously as the "Teflon President." That quality adhered to him in death. His public image as the stern sheriff who taught lawbreaking strikers a lesson continued to overshadow any inconvenient facts in the PATCO affair. Celebrations of the centennial of Reagan's birth on February 6, 2011, inevitably cast the PATCO strike only as evidence of Reagan's firm presidential leadership.[4]

While the PATCO strike became a key element of the Reagan legend, its impact on American labor also took on mythical proportions that occasionally obscured reality. An abundance of commentators asserted that the PATCO strike had "served notice that a new day in government-labor-management relations had dawned," and that it marked a turning point in the history of American labor relations. Often such pronouncements perpetuated a "simplistic analysis of union decline" in which too much causal weight for labor's problems in the years since 1981 was ascribed to this single event. To be sure, had the PATCO strike never occurred, the U.S. labor movement still would have faced enormous struggles over the subsequent three decades. A host of trends were already beginning to transform U.S. labor relations when the strike erupted: the decline of industrial and the rise of service employment; globalization; the reduction of job-protecting tariffs; the introduction of new technologies that made business more flexible and mobile; and the increasing tendency of American corporations to resist collective bargaining. These factors would have challenged labor whether or not Reagan had broken PATCO.[5]

Yet while the PATCO strike did not *cause* American labor's decline, it acted as a powerful catalyst that magnified the effects of the multiple problems that beset American unions. It did so in part because it had such a dispiriting psychological impact on workers. In 1981, Americans witnessed the dramatic destruction of a union on the largest public stage imaginable. They saw technologically sophisticated, seemingly indispensable workers permanently replaced by their employer. And they watched public opinion uphold this action while the AFL-CIO stood by helpless to prevent the most widely watched strikebreaking act to that point in world history.[6]

It is impossible to know exactly how U.S. labor history would have unfolded had PATCO not been broken. But one thing is beyond dispute: the memory of PATCO's destruction long haunted American workers. More than a decade later, PATCO's ghost still had the capacity to instill fear, as Chicago teachers discovered in 1993. That year leaders of their union, like many union officers in that period, agreed to a concessionary contract that included a pay freeze. Angry rank-and-file teachers threatened to vote that contract down. But their minds were easily changed by union officials. The teachers' union leaders only needed to summon PATCO's ghost to tamp down the incipient rebellion within their ranks. "Remember PATCO?" asked a leaflet circulated by the union's leaders. "Their union was destroyed and they all lost their jobs. Don't let that happen to us." The leaflet worked. When the contract votes were tallied, the dissidents saw their support melt away. The teachers accepted their pay freeze by a wide margin.[7]

Efforts to exorcise the fearful memory of PATCO's destruction proved futile in the 1990s. Organized labor and its political allies rallied behind legislation to curb the use of replacement workers in strikes, and Congress held nine sets of hearings on the issue. These hearings generated the Striker Replacement Act, a bill that would have banned the use of permanent replacements in most strikes. It was introduced in 1993 with fanfare and pledges of support from the Clinton White House. The bill quickly passed the House of Representatives, but was blocked in the Senate by a Republican-led filibuster. In a last-ditch effort to counter arguments that the bill would instigate a wave of economically disruptive strikes, Senate sponsors renamed it the "Worker Fairness Act." But that did not secure the sixty senators necessary to overcome the filibuster and make the bill law. The Republican takeover of the Congress in the 1994 elections ensured that no similar legislative initiative would be resurrected.[8]

An attempt to limit the use of replacement workers through executive action was no more successful. On March 8, 1995, President Clinton issued Executive Order 12954, instructing federal agencies to cease contracting with employers who permanently replaced lawfully striking workers. The order never took effect. The Republican-controlled Congress blocked its implementation until the U.S. Court of Appeals for the District of Columbia overturned it in 1996. The court held that because the order preempted the National Labor Relations Act as interpreted by the *Mackay* decision, it exceeded the bounds of presidential authority.[9]

Labor activists looked hopefully to the few prominent union successes of the 1990s for evidence that PATCO's ghost had finally been banished. When members of the United Steel Workers union outlasted the Ravenswood Aluminum Company in 1992 and won back their jobs after a twenty-month lockout, labor scholars Kate Bronfenbrenner and Tom Juravich suggested that the struggle had finally snapped "the pattern that emerged out of the 1980s of broken unions and divided communities." But the Ravenswood victory was not widely repeated, and no resurgence of labor militancy followed it. Similarly, when the Teamsters staged a success-ful nationwide strike against United Parcel Service (UPS) in 1997, the union's president Ron Carey claimed the victory would turn the page on the PATCO era. "It ends the PATCO syndrome. A 16-year period in which a strike was synonymous with defeat and demoralization is over," agreed historian Nelson Lichtenstein.[10]

Yet the "PATCO syndrome" lived on. Labor's brief euphoria after the UPS victory wore off and the number of strikes continued to dwindle year by year. By the twenty-first century, American strikes had declined by stag-gering proportions. The Bureau of Labor Statistics reported that only forty-six thousand workers participated in major work stoppages in 2002, less than 2 percent of the comparable figure for 1952. But even those anemic numbers seemed high by 2009 when the government reported only five major work stoppages involving a mere thirteen thousand workers—ironi-cally, a tally that roughly equaled the number of workers who had walked off the job in a single, momentous strike on August 3, 1981.[11]

The near disappearance of strikes led some in labor to worry about the long-term implications of the shrinking "pool of union activists with any strike background whatsoever," and to fear that the experience of waging—let alone winning—a strike might disappear from the collective memory of U.S. workers. Would workers ever again risk their jobs by walking out in support of each other when so few of them had ever seen a strike firsthand, let alone participated in one? Could workers ever hope to defend their inter-ests effectively if striking was simply no longer an option, no matter how unfairly employers behaved?[12]

For PATCO veteran Tom Gaffney, these questions were deeply personal. A native of the Twin Cities and a Vietnam veteran, Gaffney had joined the FAA in 1974 and was serving as a facility representative when the PATCO strike took place. He was thirty-two years old when he was fired in 1981. His marriage dissolved, and he went on to work at a series of jobs over the next few years, including a stint as a chimney sweep, before he finally obtained high-paying work as an airline mechanic for Northwest Airlines in Minneapolis in the mid-1980s. As he watched striking meatpackers get replaced at the Hormel plant in nearby Austin, Minnesota, in 1986, he felt like he was watching a replay of his PATCO experience. He began to worry that what had happened to him was simply the beginning of a much larger process in which American workers were losing the power to defend themselves through collective action. Gaffney saw strikes as a weapon of last resort. "You don't want to [strike]," he explained. "It hurts all around." But he thought the strike was "the only bargaining chip" workers had in the end. He never dreamed he would have to ante up his last chip not once, but twice. On August 19, 2005, Gaffney joined other machinists at Northwest and walked out rather than accept the 25 percent wage cut the company demanded. The Northwest walkout ended nearly as disastrously as PATCO's strike. Northwest hired replacements and, after fourteen months of struggle, forced the union to accept terms even harsher than it first proposed. When the strike was called off, Northwest kept the replacements on the job and made strikers wait for openings before they could reclaim jobs as mechanics. Gaffney had only participated in two strikes in his entire working life. He and his coworkers were routed each time. "I'm afraid it'll take nothing short of a small revolution in order to wake people up," he concluded. "But I don't know if it'll happen in our lifetime. Or mine anyway."[13]

Gaffney's despair was understandable in light of the trends that defined working-class life in the early twenty-first century. The share of private sector workers represented by unions declined to less than 7 percent in 2010, the lowest level in a century. As workers' leverage diminished, the wealth created by rising labor productivity was increasingly translated into larger profits and ballooning executive salaries, rather than wage increases and improved benefits. In turn, as the incomes of a broad swath of workers' stagnated while those at the top saw their incomes bulge, the extent of economic inequality reached levels unseen in the United States since the 1920s.

Most government workers were shielded from the full force of this storm through the early years of the twenty-first century. Although their compensation rates differed little from those of private sector workers possessing similar skills, experience, and education, public sector workers' jobs and benefits tended to remain more secure. More importantly, government workers avoided the antiunion pressures that built up in the private sector, as their unionization rate remained above 35 percent. The resiliency of government workers' unions and the continuous decline of private sector unionization combined to make government workers a majority of the shrinking U.S. labor movement by 2009. But while public sector unions often exerted enough influence to effectively defend their members' interests, they were not strong enough to push through reforms in federal labor law that would make it easier for private sector workers to unionize in an environment that had been transformed by globalization and increased employer resistance to unions. As unionization further declined in the private sector, public sector unions in turn were more isolated and vulnerable. And, since government workers furnished an ever-greater share of organized labor's political contributions and get-out-the-vote operations, they came under sharper attacks from their political opponents.[14]

The "Great Recession" that began in 2008 set the stage for the escalation of those attacks. The worst economic crisis since the 1930s consumed the first two years of Barack Obama's presidency and overwhelmed the limited stimulus program he was able to get through Congress, sending unemployment over 10 percent and pushing federal, state, and local governments into the red. During the midterm elections of 2010, discontent with government deficits and the slow pace of recovery helped propel a Republican takeover of the U.S. House of Representatives and twenty state legislatures. Antiunion forces were determined to capitalize on these circumstances to weaken public sector unions. "The fiscal crises facing state and local governments and school boards makes [sic] these unions and their political clout vulnerable, potentially at the mercy of a Republican controlled House of Representatives," observed conservative commentator Dick Morris after the election. "We may, at long last, have a way to liberate our nation from the domination of those who should be our public servants but instead are frequently our union masters," he concluded. Following the election, antiunion forces advanced initiatives to weaken organized labor in a half dozen states, fueled by charges that an "elite" of unionized government workers was exploiting hardworking taxpayers.[15]

The most inflammatory of those state battles took place in Wisconsin, when Republican governor Scott Walker introduced a bill to strip most public workers of collective bargaining rights, insisting that Wisconsin jurisdictions could no longer afford to bargain with their unions. That episode revealed how powerful the ghost of PATCO remained thirty years after the controllers' strike. By his own account, on Monday, February 7, 2011, just before he went forward with his bill to scuttle bargaining rights, Walker gathered his staff together for what he called a "kind of the last hurrah before we dropped the bomb." Pulling out a picture of President Reagan, Walker urged his advisers to gird for battle. "You know this may seem melodramatic," he said, "but thirty years ago, Ronald Reagan . . . had one of the most defining moments of his political career, not just of his presidency, when he fired the air traffic controllers." Reagan's stand had changed the course of history, Walker explained. Now it was time to follow Reagan's example. Walker made clear that he would not accept the unions' offers of monetary concessions to meet Wisconsin's budget shortfall. He wanted to roll back their bargaining rights. "I'm not negotiating," he said. "This is our moment, this our time to change the course of history."[16]

The Wisconsin battle showed how effectively the PATCO strike had been mythologized in the thirty years since it occurred. Governor Walker himself clearly knew little about Reagan's actual handling of PATCO. Reagan had not set out to "drop a bomb" on PATCO. Unlike Walker, he had negotiated with the union and only drew the line at condoning an illegal strike. Not only had Reagan never challenged the controllers' bargaining rights, he had authorized his aides to exceed what the law had allowed in trying to reach an accord with the controllers during a budget season when he was seeking cutbacks elsewhere. But none of that seemed to matter thirty years later. The only significant fact for Walker and his allies (as for most commentators who analyzed Walker's evocations of Reagan) was that Reagan broke PATCO and by doing so changed the course of history.

Both the differences in approach taken by Walker and Reagan and the nation's diminished capacity to grasp or appreciate those differences said much about the transformation of American politics since 1981. By 2011 it was becoming difficult to remember that there was once a time when the right to organize and bargain collectively had enjoyed a significant measure of bipartisan support in the United States. There was a deep irony here, for the actions of Ronald Reagan, the only president ever to have led a labor union, a man who as governor had presided over the extension of collective bargaining rights to California's public workers, who as president had been prepared to break new ground in negotiating with federal workers, ultimately did more to catalyze this antiunion shift than any other.

The fate of the PATCO veterans in many ways symbolized the plight of millions of American workers in this harsh new era. Their downward mobility was a harbinger of what awaited many in a time characterized by massive economic reorganization and declining union power. Yet, when anthropologist Katherine Newman studied PATCO strike veterans, she found that they coped better with their misfortune than most other workers who had suddenly "fallen from grace" and lost high-paying jobs. The key to their resiliency, Newman found, was the sense of community that bound them together. Whether they thought their 1981 demands had been justified or overreaching, whether they approved of the Choirboys' strike strategy or criticized it, whether they had been able to rebuild their lives or continued to struggle years after the strike, PATCO veterans drew comfort from the ties that bound them to each other and the sense that they risked all for a shared cause, however unpopular. "When I meet a controller for the first time, I feel like I know him," one veteran said. "Even if he worked two thousand miles away from me, I know what he's been through." The feeling was widely shared among PATCO's alumni. "No matter what your situation might be, the one true thing that has kept all of us together over the years is what WE ALL did in 1981," said one. "We will be brothers and sisters forever." Domenic Torchia agreed. "No person or group will ever take the memory of the PATCO brotherhood from us," he said. "The bond is as strong as that of Pearl Harbor survivors."[17]

Over the years, strike veterans commemorated their bonds to each other in reunions large and small. On August 3, 1982, the first anniversary of the walkout, strikers from the Rocky Mountain region gathered for a "PATCO Solidarity Party" at Whiskey Bill's, a Denver controllers' bar. Such reunions popped up spontaneously in many other cities. In time, they coalesced into larger gatherings. In 1990, veterans of the 1970 sickout gathered in Orlando, Florida, for a reunion. A year later, on the tenth anniversary of the PATCO strike, the first national reunion of strikers convened in Washington. On the twentieth anniversary of the strike, they met in Las Vegas. Those who could not attend such events often kept private vigils like the one observed by Bill Fauth, the former president of PATCO's Chattanooga local. For ten years straight, Fauth would meet two or three friends on August 3 and together they would picket the tower where they had once worked.[18]

Preserving the memory of their experience—the evidence from their personal black boxes—became an abiding cause for many PATCO veterans. "We are an important facet of American history and it needs to be preserved no matter if we were seen as right or wrong," one wrote in 1985. They went to great lengths to document their experience. One veteran helped track down a huge cache of PATCO's central office records that ended up in a Virginia warehouse after the union's decertification. He helped arrange for their deposit in archives at Georgia State University. Others donated collections of their personal papers to a PATCO collection at the University of

Texas at Arlington. And many simply held on to their own private collections of clippings and memorabilia, sharing them with friends and family.[19]

More than a few chose to write about what they had been through. Striker David Skocik collaborated with sociologist Arthur Shostak on the first book written about the strike. Several other veterans or spouses penned memoirs, historical accounts, novels, graduate theses, and even screenplays based on their experiences. In their nonfiction efforts, they shared stories of their sufferings and personal triumphs over adversity. In their fictional accounts, they invented happy endings that had eluded them in life. Thus an unproduced screenplay by Bill South chronicled how controllers' union leaders named Mike Maher and Jack Rock used a sickout to force the dismissal of a hated FAA administrator. Striker Terry Paddack's self-published novel told how controllers' solidarity caused a U.S. president to have a change of heart. After pledging to fire striking controllers Paddack's president reversed himself, brought the controllers back, and dismissed his ornery FAA administrator instead.[20]

So strong were the bonds that united former strikers, so powerful was their desire to find a happy ending that these impulses led eventually to a resurrection of sorts for PATCO. Once again, Jack Maher was the instigator. After the death of Bill Taylor and the suspension of Taylor's newsletter *PATCO Lives: The Lifeline,* Maher emerged as the center of the PATCO controllers' network. Since his departure from PATCO in 1980, Maher had gone on to work as a teachers' union organizer, but he never ceased thinking about the fired air traffic controllers. When it became clear that most PATCO veterans would never have a chance to return to the FAA after Clinton lifted the ban, Maher decided once again "to organize in some fashion." On December 6, 1995, he sent a letter to the PATCO strikers' mailing list with the news.

Maher's letter was a call to arms. "Since 1981, the landscape has been predictably littered with the bodies of increasing numbers of 'displaced' workers of our stripe as [AFL-CIO] mucky mucks publicly or privately acknowledge that 'it' all began with the PATCO strike," he wrote. It was time to stop mourning about the past, Maher argued. It was time to focus on the future, time to organize. "Our past is prologue," he wrote. Maher announced that he would reestablish PATCO as an AFL-CIO union, affiliated with the Federation of Physicians & Dentists, itself a branch of the largest public sector union, the American Federation of State, County, and Municipal Employees (AFSCME). The organization would be called PATCO Local

6881, its numbers marking the 1968–1981 lifespan of its namesake. "Establishing a PATCO in the AFL-CIO will by its very existence make one hell of an historic statement," Maher proclaimed.[21]

Maher's invitation attracted responses from a few hundred strike veterans, and PATCO Local 6881 was launched on January 11, 1996, the twenty-eighth anniversary of the original PATCO's founding. While pressing the FAA to rehire more former strikers, the new PATCO managed to successfully organize controllers at several small facilities where air traffic control duties had been contracted out to private for-profit firms. When Maher's health deteriorated, Ron Taylor, who had headed PATCO's West Palm Beach local in 1981, took over the organization, and ultimately established it as an independent union. Fifteen years after its founding, the new PATCO soldiered on, representing several dozen working controllers, and advocating for aging strike veterans, a poignant reminder of the organization whose memory it kept alive.[22]

For Jack Maher and Mike Rock, the story came full circle. The friendship they had formed in Hangar 11 in the aftermath of the 1960 collision had provided the bedrock upon which PATCO had been founded. Like so many bonds forged through PATCO, their connection lasted to the end of their lives. Maher paid a final visit to his friend in April 2004. The two had seen each other less frequently as time went on. Health problems had kept Maher from meeting Rock in Las Vegas at the twentieth reunion of PATCO strikers. But now it was Rock's health that was failing; he was dying of cancer. Their last visit took place in a hospital room in West Islip, just a few miles from New York Center, where in 1967 they had cohosted the first meetings of PATCO's predecessor, the Metropolitan Controllers Association. Maher knew it was a farewell visit, and braced himself to say goodbye. Although they had gone their separate ways after 1981, the two men had remained close. "It was a funny friendship, because we were so different in so many ways," Maher observed. "Even when we never did agree, we agreed to continue on." The warmth of their friendship was rekindled as they reminisced during this last visit. But it was what Rock said when it was time for Maher to go that stuck with his friend. "Well, it's the end of the road, Jackie," Rock said. "It's all over." Maher realized then that Rock had spoken these same words when the two had met on that tense morning in PATCO's safe house on August 4, 1981, as the union they had founded was locked in struggle with a president, with so much hanging in the balance.[23]

Maher himself died four years later at the age of seventy-five. During the years between Rock's death and his own, he stayed in touch with PATCO veterans. He followed NATCA's contract negotiations and watched as the FAA struggled with a personnel crunch, as thousands of controllers hired after the strike began to reach retirement en masse. With growing concern, he also followed the labor movement's continuing struggles—its declining membership rates, diminished capacity to strike, inability to reform out-dated labor laws. He also saw the storm clouds gathering, portending a deluge that might wash away the gains public sector workers had fought so hard for since the 1960s. As more and more private sector workers lost strong union protection, saw their incomes stagnate, their health care costs soar, and their retirements grow more precarious, Maher knew it would become easier for labor's opponents to isolate unionized government workers and characterize their salaries and pensions as inflated. He realized that an assault was coming against public sector unionism, the passionate cause to which he had devoted so much of his life. All of this convinced Maher that his good friend Mike Rock had been wrong about one thing after all: It was *not* over. PATCO's past was prologue—prologue to a story still unfolding.

ACKNOWLEDGMENTS

★

It would not have been possible to write this book without the assistance of many people and organizations. I must begin by acknowledging a debt to all of those who agreed to be interviewed for the book. I was fortunate to be able to talk to more than one hundred people who participated in the events described herein. They ranged from PATCO officers and strikers, to air traffic controllers who refused to strike, officials from six presidential administrations, airline pilots and executives, union presidents, air traffic controllers' spouses and children, and politicians. For many PATCO members, these interviews were emotionally difficult, and I am especially grateful to those who were willing to recount what was for them a traumatic event in their lives. Unfortunately, a number of those to whom I am most indebted have died in the years since I spoke with them, including Mike Rock and Jack Maher. I hope this book has adequately preserved their experience. I also want to thank John Thornton and John Leyden, my first interviewees, whose willingness to share their personal stories persuaded me to write this book, and who helped connect me to many others whose stories helped shape it. I am particularly grateful to the following people for helping connect me to others whom I interviewed for the book: Andy Anderson; Langhorne Bond; Doug Church; Tony Dresden, who first suggested that I pursue this project; Brian Flores; Cheryl Jenni; Rick Jones; Mark Knauss; Bob Lambrecht; John Leyden; Jack Maher; Chuck Miller; Ken Moffett; Mike Rock; Bill South; Ron Taylor; John Thornton; Domenic Torchia; and Sue Mostert Townsend. I especially want to acknowledge Jack Maher, who shared documents and memories as well as analysis and encouragement. His passion for this story helped light my way.

Others kindly loaned me files, scrapbooks, photos, and other memorabilia from their own collections. I am indebted to Arthur Shostak, an accomplished sociologist, who worked as a consultant to PATCO in the years just before the strike and went on to become (along with David Skocik) the first chronicler of the strike and its impact. Over the years, Art continued to study and write about PATCO, collecting boxes of research materials that he generously shared with me. Art's help was indispensable. I am also grateful to Mike Rock's widow, Joan Rock, and Jack Maher's daughter, Ursula Bethmann, for loaning me pictures and sharing recollections of their loved ones. The following people were kind enough to share important personal material with me: Charlie Campbell, Ed Curran, Rick Jones, Gabe Gabrielsky, Noel Keane, Bob Lambrecht, John Leyden, Jack Maher, Sue Mostert Townsend, Russ Sommer, Bill South, John Thornton, and Domenic Torchia.

Archivists at several institutions were enormously helpful. I am most indebted to Julia Young, who headed the special collections department that housed the Southern Labor Archives at Georgia State University when I began working in the PATCO records there. Julia and her staff allowed me to work in the records when they were still an unprocessed collection. Without their help at a critical early point in my research, I could not have undertaken this book. I am also indebted to Traci JoLeigh Drummond, the current archivist of the Southern Labor Archives, and her colleague Harold Hansen for their indispensable help as I readied this book for publication. I am grateful to Gary Spurr, George N. Green, and Claire Galloway for helping me access relevant PATCO records stored at the University of Texas at Arlington. At the Ronald Reagan Presidential Library, archivist Cate Sewell was unfailingly helpful.

I was fortunate to be able to lean on the help of top-notch research assistants, most of whom I also was privileged to have as my students. They helped me transcribe interview tapes, track down articles, and retrieve materials from distant libraries or archives. I am grateful to Paul Adler, Tina Braxton, Caitlin Connelly, Patrick Dixon, Edmund Donnelly, Catherine Guzman, Nicole Manopol, Adam McKean, John Molluzzo, Marc Palen, Kevin Powers, Adam Smith, Stephanie Swain, Nick Zeleniuch, and Maya Zwerdling. Other students passed on relevant citations and evidence to me from their own work, including Evan A. North, Tula Connell, Jennifer Pish Harrison, and Joseph Hower. Lt. Col. Tracy

Szczepaniak, USAF, was helpful in arranging for me to tour FAA facilities to observe controllers at work. Mike Feinsilber, a former reporter and an exemplary writer, read early drafts of my first chapters and offered a number of helpful suggestions. Christopher England proofread portions of an early version of the manuscript. James Benton carefully combed the penultimate version, offered on-point suggestions, and saved me from a number of errors. Molly Rubenstein's keen eye helped me clarify several key passages. And Andy Hazelton proved to be a reliable and sharp-eyed editor, researcher, and photo wrangler, who read over the manuscript several times and pushed me to be clearer about what I was writing. Together they immeasurably enriched this book.

A number of institutions supported my research and writing. For providing grants and fellowships that gave me necessary time away from teaching, I am grateful to the American Philosophical Society, the Charles Warren Center for Studies in American History at Harvard University, the Graduate School of Georgetown University, the National Endowment for the Humanities, and the Woodrow Wilson International Center for Scholars.

A number of individuals at Georgetown University were supportive at critical junctures. These include my colleagues at the Kalmanovitz Initiative for Labor and the Working Poor—Jennifer Luff, Katie Corrigan, Sarah David Heydemann, and John Tremblay—who lightened my load in innumerable ways as I finished the book. I am fortunate to be a member of a wonderfully collegial department, and I would like to thank my History Department colleagues for their support over the years since I first presented the idea for this book to them as a job talk. I am especially grateful to Daniel Ernst, Katie Benton-Cohen, Maurice Jackson, and Michael Kazin, who helped in direct ways; History Department chairs JoAnn Moran Cruz, James Collins, John Tutino, and Aviel Roshwald; and History staff assistants Djuana Shields and Kathy Buc Gallager. The support of others at Georgetown was also critical, including deans Jane McAuliffe and Chet Gillis, provosts Dorothy Brown and James O'Donnell, and presidents Leo O'Donovan, S.J., and John J. DeGioia.

Many scholars listened to or read portions of this book as it was taking shape and generously shared their comments, criticism, and encouragement. Among them were Dorothy Sue Cobble, Jeff Cowie, Nelson Lichtenstein, Adolph Reed Jr., Bob Zieger; my colleagues during my fellowship year at the Charles Warren Center, especially Alice O'Connor,

Meg Jacobs, Ron Schatz, and Rob Steinfeld; my colleagues at the Woodrow Wilson International Center for Scholars, especially Sonja Michel, Kathleen Frydl, Alan Kuperman, Flagg Miller, Marty Sherwin, Asher Kaufman, and Karsten Paerregaard; participants in the Americas Initiative Seminar at Georgetown University, especially Denise Brennan, Melissa Fisher, Doug Reed, and John Tutino. I would also thank Bob Shogan for sharing sage advice about writing, Meghan Winchell for tips on doing oral history, and my friend and collaborator Jean-Christian Vinel for helping me sharpen my thinking.

Michael Kazin, Mel Dubofsky, and Bob Zieger read a penultimate version of the manuscript and shared comments with me that significantly improved this book. All three have been enormously supportive of my work and unfailingly generous with their help over many years. Judith Stein and Jeff Cowie, my colaborers in the vineyards of 1970s-era labor history, from whose work I've learned a great deal, as the foregoing pages should make clear, also offered insightful comments and suggestions. Dubofsky, Kazin, Zieger, Eric Arnesen, and Alice Kessler-Harris supported my grant and fellowship proposals. My friends David Tamarin and Colin J. Davis encouraged this project in its earliest phase, and Phil Boroughs, S.J. helped me see it in a fuller context. Vicky Bijur offered useful publishing advice. And Nick Salvatore, who first got me interested in labor history as an undergraduate student, was a good friend to me, and this book, providing warm encouragement from beginning to end.

I am grateful to my agent Sandra Dijkstra for believing in this book, and to her staff, Elise Capron and Elisabeth James for their expert help. Niko Pfund and the staff of the Oxford University Press, including Alexandra Dauler, Purdy, Jaimee Biggins, and Marc Schneider have been a pleasure to work with, as were copy editor Laura Lawrie and reader William Stott. I am especially indebted to my editor, Dave McBride. I was fortunate to find in Dave exactly the right editor for this book. He immediately grasped its significance, and by doing so helped me convey this story more effectively.

Finally, I would like to thank my friends and family, without whom I would not have finished this long and consuming project. My siblings, Anne, Marybeth, Michael, and Jude offered love and support, as did my brother and fellow historian Jim, whose passion for our shared craft inspires me. My parents, Joe and Marybeth and my wife's parents, Muriel and Arthur Reis, cheered me on as I began work on this book. Sadly, none of the four lived to see it completed. I feel their loss keenly, but I am grateful to catch glimpses of them in the eyes of my lovely daughters, Mara and Elisa, who entered this world while I worked on this book and who bring so much joy into my life. Finally, I thank their mother, my love, Diane, who stood by my side through it all and believed in me. She made it possible for me to believe, too.

ABBREVIATIONS USED IN THE NOTES

★

AFL-CIO DLR   AFL-CIO Department of Legislation Records, Record Group 21, George Meany Memorial Archives, Silver Spring, Md.

ALPA   Air Line Pilots Association Records, Walter P. Reuther Library of Labor and Urban Affairs, Wayne State University, Detroit, Mich.

ChiTr   *Chicago Tribune*

ChiST   *Chicago Sun-Times*

CPD   *Cleveland Plain Dealer*

DDEPL   Dwight D. Eisenhower Presidential Library, Abilene, Kans.

DPM   Daniel Patrick Moynihan Papers, Library of Congress Manuscript Division, Washington, D.C.

FAA   Records of the Federal Aviation Administration, Record Group 237, National Archives II, College Park, Md.

GERR   *Government Employee Relations Report*

GUC   *Government Union Critique*

GUR   *Government Union Review*

IAM   International Association of Machinists Records, Southern Labor Archives, Special Collections and Archives, Georgia State University Library, Atlanta, Ga.

JATC   *Journal of Air Traffic Control*

JCPL   Jimmy Carter Presidential Library, Atlanta, Ga.

JFKPL   John F. Kennedy Presidential Library, Boston, Mass.

LAT   *Los Angeles Times*

LBJPL   Lyndon B. Johnson Presidential Library, Austin, Tex.

NYDN   *New York Daily News*

NYP   *New York Post*

NYT	*New York Times*
PATCO	Records of the Professional Air Traffic Controllers Organization, Southern Labor Archives, Special Collections and Archives, Georgia State University Library, Atlanta, Ga.
PATCO/UTA	PATCO Collection, Southwest Labor History Archives, Special Collections, University of Texas at Arlington, Arlington, Tex.
PL	*PATCO Lives: The Lifeline*
PMN	*PATCO Membership Newsletter*
RMNPM	Richard M. Nixon Presidential Materials, National Archives II, College Park, Md.
RRPL	Ronald Reagan Presidential Library, Simi Valley, Calif.
SacU	*Sacramento Union*
SDU	*San Diego Union*
SFC	*San Francisco Chronicle*
SFEx	*San Francisco Examiner*
StLPD	*Saint Louis Post-Dispatch*
WJU	William J. Usery Papers, Southern Labor Archives, Special Collections and Archives, Georgia State University Library, Atlanta, Ga.
WHORM	White House Office of Records Management
WP	*Washington Post*
WSJ	*Wall Street Journal*

NOTES

★

GETTING THE PICTURE

1. *NYT*, December 22, 1960, 14; *NYT*, January 14, 1961, 16, 46; *NYDN*, January 5, 1961, 6; *NYP*, January 5, 1961, 14; *NYT*, December 17, 1960, 1, 8; Patricia *Sawyer, Administratrix of the Estate of Robert H. Sawyer, Deceased, Plaintiff-appellant, v. United States of America, Defendant-appellee*, United States Court of Appeals, Second Circuit, 436 F.2d 640 (1971); argued November 20, 1970; decided January 4, 1971.
2. For background, see Arthur B. Shostak, and David Skocik, *The Air Controllers' Controversy: Lessons from the PATCO Strike* (New York: Human Sciences Press, 1986); Willis J. Nordlund, *Silent Skies: The Air Traffic Controllers' Strike* (Westport, Conn.: Praeger, 1998); Michael Round, *Grounded: Reagan and the PATCO Crash* (New York: Garland Publishers, 1999).
3. Interviews with Mike Rock, August 4, 2001, Las Vegas, Nev., and August 13, 2001, Islip, N.Y.; interviews with Jack Maher, August 7, and August 8, 2006, by telephone. Unless otherwise noted, the author conducted all the interviews cited in this book and possesses transcripts of the interviews.
4. Statement Before the Press, August 3, 1981, 10:45 a.m., OA 10520, David Gergen Files, RRPL.
5. Stakem quoted in *WP*, August 5, 1981, B1, B8; interview with Jim Stakem, Auburn, Va., August 7, 2002. On the siege of Con Thien, see James P. Coan, *Con Thien: Hill of Angels* (Tuscaloosa: University of Alabama Press, 2004). On Ronald Reagan and the SAG, see Garry Wills, *Reagan's America: Innocents at Home* (New York: Doubleday and Company, 1987), 255–309.
6. Quoted in W. J. Rorabaugh, *Kennedy and the Promise of the Sixties* (New York: Cambridge University Press, 2002), 16.
7. Wilson R. Hart, "The U.S. Civil Service Learns to Live With Executive Order 10988: An Interim Appraisal," *Industrial and Labor Relations Review* 17 (January 1964): 203–222.
8. On the shifts of the 1970s, see Jefferson Cowie, *Stayin' Alive: The 1970s and the Last Days of the Working Class* (New York: The New Press, 2010); Judith Stein, *The Pivotal Decade: How America Traded Factories for Finance in the 1970s* (New Haven, Conn.: Yale University Press, 2010); *Rightward Bound: Making America Conservative*

in the 1970s, Bruce Schulman and Julian Zelizer, ed. (Cambridge, Mass.: Harvard University Press, 2008); Bruce Schulman, *The Seventies: The Great Shift in American Culture, Society, and Politics* (New York: The Free Press, 2001).

9. Michael H. LeRoy, "The Changing Character of Strikes Involving Permanent Strike Replacements, 1935–1990," *Journal of Labor Research* 16:4 (Fall 1995): 423–438; and "Regulating Employer Use of Permanent Striker Replacements: Empirical Analysis of NLRA and RLA Strikes 1935–1991," *Berkeley Journal of Employment and Labor Law* 16 (1995): 169–207; Bureau of Labor Statistics, Annual Report on Major Work Stoppages, *http://www.bls.gov/news.release/wkstp.t01.htm* (accessed on March 4, 2011).

10. Richard Freeman, "Unionism Comes to the Public Sector," *Journal of Economic Literature* 24:1 (March 1986): 41–86; Michael Goldfield, "Public Sector Union Growth and Public Policy," *Policy Studies Journal* 18 (Winter 1988–1989): 404–420; Joseph A. McCartin, "Bringing the State's Workers In: Time to Rectify an Imbalanced U.S. Labor Historiography," *Labor History* 47:1 (February 2006): 73–94.

11. Interview with Ken Young, November 30, 2001, Silver Spring, Md.; interviews with John Leyden, July 14, and July 21, 1998, Washington, D.C., and August 4, 2001, Las Vegas, Nev.; interview with Paul Hallisay, August 28, 2001, Washington, D.C.; interview with Kenneth Moffett, August 28, 2001, Washington, D.C.; "Minutes of Meeting of the Executive Council of the American Federation of Labor and Congress of Industrial Organizations," August 3–5, 1981, pp. 1–7, Box 18, IAM; interview with J. Lynn Helms, May 3, 2002, Westport, Conn.; interview with Drew Lewis, June 22, 2004, Schwenksville, Pa.; interview with Edwin Meese III, February 1, 2005, Washington, D.C.

12. Maher (August 8, 2006) interview.

13. Maher (August 8, 2006) and Rock (August 13, 2001) interviews.

CHAPTER 1

1. Interview with Mike Rock, August 13, 2001, Islip, N.Y.

2. Interview with Jack Maher, June 2, 2003, by telephone.

3. Nick A. Komons, *Bonfires to Beacons: Federal Aviation Policy under the Air Commerce Act, 1926–1938* (Washington, D.C.: U.S. Department of Transportation, 1978), 299–300, 308–309.

4. John R. M. Wilson, *Turbulence Aloft: The Civil Aeronautics Administration Amid Wars and Rumors of Wars* (Washington, D.C.: U.S. Department of Transportation, 1979), 113–116; Stuart I. Rochester, *Take-Off at Mid-Century: Federal Aviation Policy in the Eisenhower Years, 1953–1961* (Washington, D.C.: U.S. Department of Transportation, 1976), 189–219.

5. Mike Rock, "PATCO History," January 10, 1979 (tape and transcript in the author's possession); interview with Bill South, June 28, 2003, by telephone; interview with Robert Lambrecht, July 24, 2003, by telephone; interview with John Leyden, August 4, 2001, Las Vegas, Nev.

6. Clifford D. Slack, "University of ATC," *Journal of Air Traffic Control* 1:4 (April 1959): 29–30, 32; interview with Bob Beatty, August 1, 2002, Fort Washington, Md.

7. Interview with Stan Gordon, Washington, D.C., November 15, 2001; U.S. Census Bureau, Historical Income Tables—Families, *http://www.census.gov/hhes/www/income/histinc/f07ar.html* (accessed March 17, 2010).

8. Kenneth T. Jackson, *Crabgrass Frontier: The Suburbanization of the United States* (New York: Oxford University Press, 1987), 231–245; Gordon interview, November 15, 2001.

9. Gordon (November 15, 2001) and Rock (August 13, 2001) interviews; interview with John Leyden, Washington, D.C., July 14, 1998.

10. Rock (August 13, 2001) and Maher (June 2, 2003) interviews; interview with Dick Shaftic, June 18, 2004, by telephone.

11. Stuart I. Rochester, *Take-Off at Mid-Century: Federal Aviation Policy in the Eisenhower Years, 1953–1961* (Washington, D.C.: U.S. Department of Transportation, 1976), 60.

12. *NYT*, September 14, 1969, Sec. 6, p. 112; Rock interview, August 13, 2001; Gordon interview, November 15, 2001.

13. Rochester, *Take-Off at Mid-Century*, 285.

14. *NYT*, December 30, 1960, 41; *NYDN*, January 6, 1961, 6; *NYT*, January 10, 1961, 1.

15. *NYP*, January 4, 1960, 5; *NYP*, January 5, 1961, 14.

16. Glenn D. Tigner, "Air Traffic Control: What It Is and How It Grew," *JATC* 1:1 (July 1958): 11.

17. Rochester, *Take-Off at Mid-Century*, 60; *NYT*, August 5, 1956, 66.

18. Interview with Jack Maher, June 2, 2003, and August 7, 2006, by telephone; Rock interview August 13, 2001.

19. Interview with Ray Van Vuren, March 11, 2002, by telephone; interview with Will Burner, June 26, 2003, by telephone; *JATC* 1:4 (April 1959): 37; *NYT*, April 19, 1961, 77; *NYT*, April 1, 1956, 168; quotation from interview with Bill Harding, June 29, 2002, by telephone.

20. Interview with Carl Kern, July 22, 2003, by telephone; interview with Ray Carver, July 27, 2003, by telephone; Mike Rock, "PATCO History," January 10, 1979; "1963 Directory," *JATC* 5:4 (Mar. 1963): 26–27.

21. "Controllers Code" *JATC* 3:4 (April 1961): 2; Elliott A. McCready, "Controlmanship," *JATC* 1:2 (October 1958): 19; Herbert C. Spiselman, "Woe, the Weary Controller!" *JATC* 1:3 (January 1959): 7.

22. Frank McDermott, "International Air Traffic Control," *JATC* 3:2 (October 1960): 2; *NYT*, December 13, 1960, 62.

23. *NYDN*, January 4, 1961, 8; *NYT*, January 4, 1961, 67.

24. Richard J. Kent, *Safe, Separated and Soaring: A History of Federal Aviation Policy, 1961–1972* (Washington, D.C.: U.S. Department of Transportation, 1980), 73–74; *NYT*, April 17, 1961, 77; *JATC* 3:4 (April 1961): 2; interview with Rex Campbell, February 15, 2002, by telephone.

25. "Editorial: New York Mid-Air," *JATC* 6:3 (November 1963): 3; quotation from "Obligations of Criticism," *JATC* 4:5 (May 1962): 2; Oswald Ryan, "FAA Justice," *JATC* 5:4 (January 1963): 24.

26. *NYT*, December 16, 1961, 51; *NYT*, May 26, 1962, 50; *NYT*, September 11, 1961, 48; *NYT*, September 10, 1962, 58; *NYT*, August 11, 1963, 27; "The Loaded Pistol," *JATC* 4:4 (March 1962): 2.

27. Maher (June 2, 2003), Leyden (August 4, 2001), and Rock (August 4, 2001) interviews; Rock, "PATCO History," January 10, 1979. His transfer did not silence Raison. He ran unsuccessfully for the ATCA presidency, in 1964 and 1968. *WP*, June 5, 1964, C1; *WP*, July 10, 1968, A20.

28. *NYT*, December 16, 1960, 26.

29. R. Alton Lee, *Truman and Taft-Hartley: A Question of Mandate* (Lexington: University of Kentucky Press, 1966); Clyde W. Summers, et al., *Union Democracy and Landrum-Griffin* (Brooklyn, N.Y.: Association for Union Democracy, 1986).

30. Joseph Slater, "Labor and the Boston Police Strike of 1919," in *The Encyclopedia of Strikes in American History*, ed. Aaron Brenner, Benjamin Day, and Immanuel Ness (Armonk, N.Y.: M.E. Sharpe, 2009), 239–251; Sterling D. Spero, *Government as Employer* (1948; repr., Carbondale, Ill.: Southern Illinois University Press, 1972), 9, 219. One exception to federal collective bargaining was the Tennessee Valley Authority. See also Michael L. Brookshire and Michael D. Rogers, *Collective Bargaining in Public Employment: The TVA Experience* (Lexington, Mass.: Lexington Books, D.C. Heath, 1977).

31. Nelson Lichtenstein, *State of the Union: A Century of American Labor* (Princeton: Princeton University Press, 2003), 98–140; Robert H. Zieger and Gilbert J. Gall, *American Workers, American Unions* (Baltimore: Johns Hopkins University Press, 2002), 182–213.

32. William Seal Carpenter, *The Unfinished Business of Civil Service Reform* (Princeton: Princeton University Press, 1952), 68–70; O. Glenn Stahl, *Public Personnel Administration* (New York: Harper & Brothers, 1956), 281–282; Bar Association quoted in Wilson R. Hart, *Collective Bargaining in the Federal Service: A Study of Labor-Management Relations in United States Government Employment* (New York: Harper & Brothers, 1961), 3; Charles O. Gregory, *Labor and the Law*, rev. 2nd ed. (New York: Norton, 1958), 521.

33. Remarks of George Meany to Joint G.E.C. Legislative Conference, May 14, 1957, file 50, Government Employees Council, 1956-/01–1959/12, Box 22, AFL-CIO Department of Legislation Records, Record Group 21, George Meany Memorial Archives, Silver Spring, Maryland [hereafter AFL-CIO DLR]; William C. Doherty, "Government Workers and Organization," *American Federationist* (June 1956): 9.

34. "White-Collar Lag," *Fortune* 51 (April 1955): 79; Revised Draft on Executive Order on Recognition of Federal Employees Organizations, 1955, Box 22, file 19, Government Employees, 1955/02–03, AFL-CIO DLR; Robert J. Donovan, *Eisenhower: The Inside Story* (New York: Harper & Brothers Publishers, 1956), 383–384; Hart, *Collective Bargaining in the Federal Service*, 7; Minutes of Cabinet Meeting, October 28, 1955, Cabinet Meeting of October 28, 1955 file, Cabinet Series, Box 6, DDEPL; Rocco Siciliano to the Heads of Executive Departments and Agencies, June 3, 1958, Cabinet Meeting of June 6, 1958 file, Cabinet Series, Box 11, DDEPL.

35. John Ervin Huss, *Senator for the South: A Biography of Olin D. Johnston* (Garden City, N.Y.: Doubleday, 1961); Johnston quoted in Wilson R. Hart, "The Impasse in Labor Relations in the Federal Civil Service," *Industrial and Labor Relations Review* 19 (January 1966): 187.

36. Hart, *Collective Bargaining in the Federal Civil Service*, 141; quotation from Wilson R. Hart, "The U.S. Civil Service Learns to Live With Executive Order 10988: An Interim Appraisal," *Industrial and Labor Relations Review* 17 (January 1964): 205; *WP*, May 15, 1956, 17; Edward B. Powell Jr., quoted in U.S. Senate, Committee on Post Office and Civil Service, *Union Recognition Hearings Before the Committee on S. 3593* (84th Congress, 2nd session; May 15, 24, June 14, 1956), p. 141.

CHAPTER 2

1. "Comparison of Union-Management Bills, 87th Congress," Folder 4, Box I: 75, Daniel Patrick Moynihan Papers, Library of Congress Manuscript Division [hereafter cited as DPM]; Franz E. Daniel to Department Heads, January 12, 1961, file 28, Government Employees, 1961/01–08, Box 22, AFL-CIO DLR.
2. U.S. Senate, Permanent Subcommittee on Investigations of the Committee on Government Operations, *Work Stoppage at Missile Bases*, 87th Cong., 2nd Sess. (Washington, D.C.: Government Printing Office, 1962), 3, 11. Right-to-work advocates fumed about union influence on NASA projects. "Closed Shop Unions Again Stall Missile Program," *National Right to Work Newsletter*, September 22, 1961, 4.
3. Cyrus R. Vance to the Chairman of the House Committee on Post Office and Civil Service, March 22, 1961, and Cyrus Vance to David E. Bell, March 22, 1961, Government Service file, Box 11, Myer Feldman Papers, John F. Kennedy Presidential Library, Boston, Mass. [hereafter cited as Feldman Papers, JFKPL].
4. "ExecutiveOrder_____ProvidingfortheRecognitionofFederalEmployeeOrganizations and Procedures for Adjustment of Grievances," n.d. [March 1961], and "Major Issues Presented by H.R. 12 and Related Bills Providing for the Recognition of Federal Employee Unions and Establishing Procedures for the Adjustment of Grievances," April 27, 1961, Government Service file, Box 11, Feldman Papers, JFKPL.
5. James K. Langan to the President, March 17, 1961, LA 7 Unions file, Box 465, White House Central Subject file, JFKPL; Frederick G. Dutton to Goldberg, March 21, 1961, FG Department of Labor file, Box 160, and Arthur Goldberg to James K. Langan, March 25, 1961, LA 7 Unions file, Box 465, both in White House Central Subject file, JFKPL.
6. David Stebenne, *Arthur J. Goldberg: New Deal Liberal* (New York: Oxford University Press, 1996), 3–44; E. C. Hallbeck to Andrew J. Biemiller, April 6, 1961, and Biemiller to Goldberg, April 19, 1961, both in File 51, Government Employees Council, 1960/02–1961/12, Box 22, AFL-CIO DLR.
7. Godfrey Hodgson, *Gentleman From New York: Daniel Patrick Moynihan, A Biography* (Boston: Houghton Mifflin, 2000), 1–72.
8. Frederick G. Dutton, Memorandum for Mr. William Carey, April 21, 1961, LA 7 Unions file, Box 465, White House Central Subject file, JFKPL; Memorandum, Fred Dutton to Arthur Goldberg, April 29, 1961, Government Service file, Box 11, Feldman Papers, JFKPL.
9. Goldberg to Myer Feldman, June 7, 1961, and Goldberg to Myer Feldman, June 14, 1961, Secretary's Reading File, Reel 7, Department of Labor Records, JFKPL; James K. Langan to John F. Kennedy, June 16, 1961, file 42, John F. Kennedy, 1961/01–1961/11, Box 29, RG21, AFL-CIO DLR; Donald E. Schulz to National

Council of Government Employees, AFL-CIO, August 24, 1961, and Andrew J. Biemiller to Donald E. Schulz, August 29, 1961, file 28, Government employees, 1961/01–08, Box 22, AFL-CIO DLR.

10. John F. Kennedy to Heads of Departments and Agencies, Re: Employee-Management Relations in the Federal Service, June 22, 1961, Folder 2, Box I: 75, DPM; Hart, "The U.S. Civil Service Learns to Live With Executive Order 10988," 206.

11. Allen W. Dulles to Arthur J. Goldberg, August 19, 1961, Folder 2, Box I: 75, DPM; John McLucas, "Crossing the River: My Life at the FAA," unpublished ms., n.d. (in the author's possession), p. 20; Moynihan to The Secretary, July 27, 1961, Folder 3, Box I: 75, DPM; Rep. Basil Whitener to John F. Kennedy, October 26, 1961, PE 1 Employment Relations Activities, November 1961 file, and Rep. J. Ernest Wharton to President of the United States, November 30, 1961, PE 1 Employment Relations Activities, December 1–15, 1961 file, both in Box 673, White House Center Subject file, JFKPL, and Goldberg to Sen. Prescott Bush, November 29, 1961, Departmental Reading Files, Reel 10, Department of Labor Papers, JFKPL; "Hearings Set by President's Group on Federal Employee Relations," August 25, 1961, Folder 4, Box I: 75, DPM.

12. Goldberg to John O'Connor, August 11, 1961; Goldberg to John W. McKay, August 11, 1961; and Goldberg to Joseph Amman, et al., August 3, 1961; all on Reel 8, Secretary's Reading Files, Department of Labor Papers, JFKPL.

13. AFL-CIO Draft Executive Order, August 1961, and "Notes, AFL-CIO Proposed Executive Order Recognition of Federal Employee Unions," n.d. [1961], both in Folder 4, Box I: 75, DPM.

14. Daniel P. Moynihan, "An Impression of the Possible Course of Employee Management Relations in the Federal Service in the Light of Proposals Presented at the Public Hearing and in the Employee Organization Questionnaires," n.d. [November 1961], Folder 8, Box I: 74, DPM.

15. A Policy for Employee Management Cooperation in the Federal Service: Report of the President's Task Force on Employee-Management Relations in the Federal Service, November 30, 1961, Folder 4, Box I: 75, DPM.

16. "Memorandum: Proposed Executive Order on Employee-Management Cooperation in the Federal Service," December 27, 1961, file 44, Government Employees, L-M Task Force, Box 22, RG21, AFL-CIO DLR.

17. "Memorandum: Proposed Executive Order on Employee-Management Cooperation in the Federal Service," n.d. [December 1961], File 51, Government Employees Council, 1960/02–1961/12, Box 22, RG21, AFL-CIO DLR.

18. Theodore C. Sorensen, Memorandum for the President, December 1, 1961, Sorensen file, Box 63a, President's Office Files, JFKPL; Ralph De Toledano, Let Our Cities Burn (New Rochelle, N.Y.: Arlington House Publishers, 1975), 22; "Memorandum: Proposed Executive Order on Employee-Management Cooperation in the Federal Service," n.d. [December 1961], File 51, Government Employees Council, 1960/02–1961/12, Box 22, RG21, AFL-CIO DLR; L. David Korb to the Files, Re: Meeting at the Bureau of the Budget on Proposed Employee Management and Appeals Orders, January 15, 1962, Folder 9, Box I: 74, DPM; James P. Bradley, Memorandum to the Special Counsel to the President, January 8, 1962, and JFK to Goldberg, January 17, 1962, both in FE 6 Executive file, Box 100, White House Central Subject File, JFKPL.

19. Kenneth O. Warner, ed. *Management Relations with Organized Public Employees: Theory, Policies, and Programs* (Chicago: Public Personnel Association, 1963), 221; Meany quoted in Joseph C. Goulden, *Meany* (New York: Atheneum, 1972), 327; Bob Repas, *Collective Bargaining in Federal Employment,* 2nd ed. (Industrial Relations Center, University of Hawaii, 1973), 11; Sar A. Levitan and Alexandra B. Noden, *Working for the Sovereign: Employee Relations in the Federal Government* (Baltimore: Johns Hopkins University Baltimore: Johns Hopkins University Press, 1983), 15; Joseph Slater, *Public Workers: Government Employee Unions, the Law, and the State, 1900–1962* (Ithaca, N.Y.: Cornell University Press, 2004); Michael Goldfield, "Public Sector Union Growth and Public Policy," *Policy Studies Journal* 18 (Winter 1988–1989): 404–420.

20. Macy quoted in Wilson R. Hart, "The U.S. Civil Service Learns to Live With Executive Order 10988: An Interim Appraisal," *Industrial and Labor Relations Review* 17 (January 1964):176; Repas, *Collective Bargaining in Federal Employment,* 94; Hart, "The U.S. Civil Service Learns to Live With Executive Order 10988," 205; quotation from Bob Repas, "Collective Bargaining Problems in Federal Employment," in Eugene C. Hagburg, ed., *Problems Confronting Union Organizations in Public Employment* (Columbus: Ohio State University, 1966), 7, 21.

21. *NYT*, September 1, 1963, 58.

22. Interview with Stan Gordon interview, November 15, 2001, Washington, D.C.; *JATC* 6:6 (May 1964): 33.

23. *NYT*, September 30, 1962, Sec. 5, 19.

24. Interview with Rex Campbell, February 15, 2002, by telephone; interview with Mike Rock, August 13, 2001, Islip, N.Y.

25. Interview with Edward V. Curran, Washington, D.C., August 23, 2001; interview with Mike Rock, August 4, 2001, Las Vegas, Nev.

26. *FedNews*, May 26, 1965, 2; *FedNews*, November 1, 1965, 1; *FedNews*, July 8, 1965, 1; *FedNews*, August 8, 1965, 3; *FedNews*, September 16, 1966, 9.

27. *GERR*, 24, February 24, 1964, A2; *GERR*, 67, December 21, 1964, A7.

28. Rock, "PATCO History," January 10, 1979; "ATCA's Ninth National Meeting: Convention Report," *JATC* 7:3 (November 1964): 13–14; *FedNews*, May 5, 1967, 9.

29. *GERR*, 67, December 21, 1964, A7; *NYT*, July 17, 1964, 54; Russ Sommer, "Gathering Storm: A Study of the Impending Crisis in Federal Aviation Employee/ Management Relations," NAGE Local R12–15, September 20, 1967 (copy in the author's possession); Curran interview.

30. *FedNews*, November 1, 1965, 2; quotation from interview with Alan Dean, August 6, 2003, Washington, D.C.; *NYT*, April 19, 1961, 77; *NYT*, April 30, 1967, 88.

31. *NYT*, January 30, 1966, Sec. 5, 13.

32. "Personality Problem: A Study of the FAA Psychological Testing Program," Contract Committee, Local R12–15, NAGE, May 16, 1966 (copy in the author's possession); *GERR*, 160, October 3, 1966, A14; "Million Dollar Mistake: Another Look at the FAA Psychological Program," NAGE Local R12–5, January 22, 1968 (copy in the author's possession); Sommer, "Gathering Storm"; *FedNews*, January 25, 1966, 1.

33. Long quoted in *GERR*, 58, October 19, 1964, A6–7; *GERR*, 77, March 1, 1965, A11; *FedNews*, July 18, 1966, 1, 6.

34. *FedNews*, July 18, 1966, 1, 6; letter from Russell J. Sommer to Ken Lyons, October 30, 1967 (copy in the author's possession).

35. Interview with Russ Sommer, June 22, 2004, by telephone; Contract Committee, Local R12–15, NAGE, "Personality Problem: A Study of the FAA Psychological Testing Program," May 16, 1966 (copy in the author's possession).

36. *WP*, August 11, 1966, A25; *GERR*, 156, September 5, 1966, A5; *GERR*, 160, October 3, 1966, A7, A14; *GERR*, 192, May 15, 1967, A8; *GERR*, 153, August 15, 1966, A3, A5.

37. Contract Committee, Local R12–15, NAGE, "Personality Problem"; letter Russell J. Sommer to P. V. Siegel, MD, October 10, 1967 (copy in possession of the author); quotations from Russell J. Sommer to P. V. Siegel, MD, December 11, 1967, and Russell J. Sommer to P. V. Siegel, MD, January 16, 1968 (copies in the author's possession).

38. Interview with Will Burner, June 26, 2003, by telephone; Office of Labor-Management Relations, U.S. Civil Service, *Union Recognition in the Federal Government: Listings by Agency, November 1967* (Washington, D.C.: U.S. Civil Service Commission, 1967), 255–276; *FedNews*, January 18, 1967, 4, 6; ATCA quoted in *NYT*, April 30, 1967, 88.

39. *NYT*, August 24, 1966, 48; *NYT*, September 10, 1967, 209; *NYT*, September 21, 1967, 1; *NYT*, November 20, 1966, A16.

40. Anonymous controller quoted in *NYT*, November 20, 1962, 54; *NYT*, February 6, 1966, Sec. 5, 21.

41. *NYT*, September 18, 1967, 1; *NYT*, December 4, 1965, 1; *NYT*, July 20, 1967.

42. *NYT*, September 18, 1967, 1; *NYT*, September 17, 1967, 28.

43. *GERR*, 185, March 27, 1967, A14–15; *FedNews*, March 28, 1967, 1, 6.

44. Curran interview; Lyons quoted in *GERR*, 193, May 22, 1967, A2.

45. McKee quotation from Oral History of William F. McKee, November 18, 1970, p. 24, Presidential Papers, LBJPL; Curran interview; *NYT*, July 28, 1967, 63.

46. *WP*, March 4, 1966, A16; *WP*, November 7, 1966, A1; interview with Alan Boyd, June 26, 2003, by telephone; Dean interview, August 6, 2003; *WP*, September 21, 1967, A1, A7; *NYT*, September 21, 1967, 1; *NYT*, September 22, 1967, 25; *NYT*, September 28, 1967, 31.

47. Statement of the AFL-CIO Government Employees Council quoted in *Government Employee Relations Report*, January 27, 1964, A-4. George Meany to President Lyndon B. Johnson, February 12, 1964, file 45, Government Employees, L-M Task Force, 1964–02–1964–08, Box 22, RG21, AFL-CIO DLR; Wilson R. Hart, "The Impasse in Labor Relations in the Federal Civil Service," *Industrial and Labor Relations Review* 19 (January 1966): 187; George Meany to John F. Griner, March 6, 1967, File 46, Government Employees, L-M Task Force, 1966–09–1967/11, and AFL-CIO Program to Improve Collective Bargaining in the Federal Service, September 28, 1967, File 54, Government Employees Council, 1967/03–1967/09, both in Box 22, AFL-CIO DLR; interview with W. Willard Wirtz, Washington, D.C., June 5, 2002, notes in the author's possession.

48. Quotation from Al Bilik, "The Other Fourteen Percent," in *Problems Confronting Union Organizations in Public Employment*, ed. Eugene C. Hagburg (Columbus: Ohio State University, 1966), 33.

49. Dennis Gaffney, *Teachers United: The Rise of New York State United Teachers* (Albany: State University of New York Press, 2007), 29–47; Joseph C. Goulden, *Jerry Wurf: Labor's Last Angry Man* (New York: Atheneum, 1982), 132–133; Joshua B.

Freeman, *In Transit: The Transport Workers Union in New York City, 1933–1966* (Philadelphia: Temple University Press, 2001), 334–335; *GERR*, 123, January 17, 1966, B-1; Richard J. Murphy, "Public Employee Strikes," in *The Crisis in Public Employee Relations in the Decade of the 1970s*, ed. Richard J. Murphy and Morris Sackman (Washington, D.C.: Bureau of National Affairs, 1970), 73–74.

50. Sommer, "Gathering Storm."

51. *FedNews*, October 20, 1966, 13–14; Sommer interview; *GERR*, 185, March 27, 1967, A14.

52. Lyons quoted in *FedNews*, May 5, 1967, 20, 19; *FedNews*, May 5, 1967, 20, 19.

53. *FedNews*, June 12, 1967, 1, 16.

54. *NYT*, March 13, 1966, 88; *NYT*, October 3, 1966, 18; interview with Dick Shaftic, June 18, 2004, by telephone.

55. Shaftic interview.

56. Shaftic interview.

57. Shaftic interview; Riddle quoted in *NYT*, August 24, 1966, 48; anonymous FAA official quoted in *WP*, January 27, 1968, A15.

58. *NYT*, September 23, 1967, 32.

59. Shaftic interview; "Gathering Storm: A Study of the Impending Crisis in Federal Aviation Employee/Management Relations," NAGE Local R12–15, September 20, 1967 (copy in the author's possession).

60. Sommer quotations from Sommer, "Gathering Storm," and Sommer interview.

61. *FedNews*, January 25, 1966, 17; memo quoted in Sommer, "Gathering Storm."

62. Quotations from Sommer, "Gathering Storm."

63. *NYT*, July 21, 1963, 67; *JATC* 6:6 (May 1964): 33; *GERR*, 67, December 21, 1964, A8; *JATC* 7:2 (September 1964): 31.

64. *GERR*, 76, February 22, 1965, A6; Rock interview, August 4, 2001; Rock interview, August 13, 2001; Gordon interview, November 15, 2001; *FedNews*, November 1, 1965, 18.

65. *NYT*, August 24, 1966, 48; interview with George Kerr, August 17, 2001, by telephone.

66. Gordon interview, November 15, 2001; interview with Jack Maher interview, June 2, 2003, by telephone.

67. Gordon interview, November 15, 2001; *NYT*, September 23, 1967, 25.

68. *NYT*, July 11, 1968, 39; Rock, "PATCO History," January 10, 1979.

69. Rock, "PATCO History," January 10, 1979; *FedNews*, December 26, 1967, 7; D. D. Thomas to Director of Eastern Region, Re: Controller Unrest Problem, February 16, 1968, Performance Evaluation file, Box 286, FAA; Rock interview, August 13, 2001; *NYT*, December 16, 1967, 6.

70. Maher interview, June 2, 2003; Rock, "PATCO History," January 10, 1979.

71. Stan Gordon interview with Don R. Kienzle, February 2, 2000, Paul A. Wagner Oral History Project (copy in the author's possession); Lyman quoted in *WP*, January 27, 1968, A15; Gordon interview, November 15, 2001; Maher interview, June 2, 2003.

72. Interview with Bill South, June 28, 2003, by telephone; letter from Russell J. Sommer to Ken Lyons, October 30, 1967 (copy in the author's possession); interview with Russ Sommer, June 22, 2004; Sommer, "Gathering Storm."

73. Interview with John Leyden, August 4, 2001, Las Vegas, Nev.

CHAPTER 3

1. *WP,* July 7, 1968, A22.
2. Mike Rock, "PATCO History," January 10, 1979 (tape and transcript in the author's possession); interview with Mike Rock, August 13, 2001, Islip, N.Y.
3. Rock, "PATCO History," January 10, 1979.
4. Rock, "PATCO History," January 10, 1979; *NYT,* September 20, 1970, 246; F. Lee Bailey with John Greenya, *Cleared for the Approach: F. Lee Bailey in Defense of Flying* (Englewood Cliffs, N.J.: Prentice Hall, Inc., 1977), 87; *WP,* April 11, 1970, A1.
5. Rock interview, August 13, 2001; interview with Jack Maher, June 2, 2003, by telephone.
6. Bailey, *Cleared for the Approach,* 81, 83; interview with F. Lee Bailey, October 28, 2002, by telephone.
7. Rock, "PATCO History," January 10, 1979; Gordon interview, November 15, 2001; Maher interview, June 2, 2003; Rock interview, August 13, 2001; interview with Will Burner, June 26, 2003, by telephone.
8. Stan Gordon interview with Don R. Kienzle, February 2, 2000, Paul A. Wagner Oral History Project (copy in the author's possession); *NYT,* January 11, 1968, 74.
9. Rock interview, August 13, 2001; Bailey interview; Bailey, *Cleared for the Approach,* 87; Maher (June 2, 2003) and Burner interviews.
10. Gordon interview, November 15, 2001.
11. Rock, "PATCO History," January 10, 1979; interview with Russ Sommer, June 26, 2003, by telephone; Rock interview, August 13, 2001; Rock, "PATCO History," February 14, 1978, unmarked file, Box 373, PATCO. Note: the author was granted access to the PATCO records at a time when most of the collection was unprocessed. Box numbers, and in some cases titles of folders within which documents are located, might have been changed since then. Archivists and the finding aid available at the Southern Labor Archives, Georgia State University Library, should aid readers in locating the documents cited. The author would be pleased to assist archivists and researchers wherever possible in tracking down originals.
12. Rock, "PATCO History," January 10, 1979; Arthur B. Shostak and David Skocik, *The Air Controllers' Controversy: Lessons from the PATCO Strike* (New York: Human Sciences Press, 1986), 48; interview with Dick Shaftic, June 18, 2004, by telephone; Maher interview, June 2, 2003; Interview with Alan Dean, August 6, 2003, Washington, D.C.
13. Stan Gordon interview with Don R. Kienzle, February 2, 2000 (copy in the author's possession); Rock, "PATCO History," January 10, 1979; interview with Ray Carver, July 27, 2003, by telephone; Maher interview, June 2, 2003; Rock, "PATCO History," January 10, 1979.
14. Interview with Stan Gordon, November 15, 2001, Washington, D.C.; interview with Bill Harding, June 29, 2002, by telephone; Kenneth T. Lyons to Allen Boyd, January 22, 1968, Employee Relations file, Box 289, Records of the Federal Aviation Administration, Record Group 237, National Archives II, College Park, Md. (hereafter cited as FAA); Maher interview, June 2, 2003; William F. McKee to Secretary of Transportation, February 16, 1968, Employee Relations file, Box 289, FAA.
15. Rock, "PATCO History," January 10, 1979.

16. Interview with Mike Powderly, July 29, 2003, by telephone; Maher interview, June 2, 2003; Gordon interview with Don R. Kienzle, February 2, 2000; *Kansas City Star*, April 26, 1968, Noel Keane Scrapbook (copy in author's possession); interview with Rex Campbell, February 24, 2002, by telephone.

17. Interview with Charlie Campbell, February 11, 2002, by telephone; interview with Mike Powderly, July 29, 2003; Shaftic interview.

18. Shaftic interview; Rock, "PATCO History," January 10, 1979.

19. Carver interview; interview with Dominic Torchia, May 23, 2003, by telephone.

20. Interview with Bill South, June 28, 2003, by telephone.

21. Maher (June 2, 2003), Gordon (November 15, 2001), and Sommer interviews; Rock, "PATCO History," January 10, 1979; Bailey interview; interview with Bob Butterworth, February 1, 2002, by telephone.

22. Bailey interview; Rock, "PATCO History," January 10, 2002; "Transcription of F. Lee Bailey's Conversation with Johnny Carson on the 'Tonight Show,' Channel 4, About Air Traffic Controllers, June 10, 1968," PATCO file, Box 289, FAA.

23. Rock, "PATCO History," January 10, 1979.

24. Rock, "PATCO History," January 10, 1979; "Meeting of Professional Air Traffic Controllers Held at the Americana Hotel, New York City, on Wednesday, February 21, 1968," PATCO file, Box 289, FAA.

25. Rock, "PATCO History," January 10, 1979; Rock interview, August 13, 2001.

26. Carver, Rock (August 13, 2001), and Gordon (November 15, 2001) interviews.

27. White House Report, January 10, 1968, DOT file, Entry 14, Box 272, FAA; Curran interview; Joseph H. Tippets to Kenneth T. Lyons, March 21, 1968, Employee Relations file, Box 289, FAA; Maher (June 2, 2003) and Butterworth interviews; interview with Ray Van Vuren, March 11, 2002, by telephone; quotation from Sommer, "Gathering Storm" (copy in the author's possession); an example of this can be found in D. D. Thomas to Director of Eastern Region, Re: Controller Unrest Problem, February 16, 1968, Performance Evaluation file, Box 286, FAA.

28. William F. McKee to Bailey, April 2, 1968, Professional Air Traffic Controllers Organization file, Box 277, FAA; Bailey to McKee, March 25, 1968, PATCO file, Box 289, FAA; Record of a Telephone Conversation with Wayne Smith, May 27, 1968, Memorandum for the Record file, Entry 14, Box 272, FAA; Alan L. Dean to Rock, n.d. [1968], PATCO file, Box 289, FAA.

29. Rock to Joseph H. Tippets, June 21, 1968, PATCO file, Box 289, FAA; McKee to Bailey, June 12, 1968, PATCO file, Box 277, FAA.

30. McKee to Bailey, June 12, 1968, PATCO file, Box 277, FAA.

31. John J. Seddon, "PATCO, A Perspective" (M.A. thesis, State University of New York Empire College, 1990), 44; Rock, "PATCO History," January 10, 1979; Gordon interview, November 15, 2001.

32. Carver, South, Powderly, and Bailey interviews.

33. Rock interview, August 13, 2001.

34. Rock, "PATCO History," January 10, 1979.

35. Gordon interviews, November 15 and November 29, 2001, Washington, D.C.; Rock, "PATCO History," January 10, 1979; interview with Bill Peer, July 1, 2004, Bethany Beach, Del.; Rock interview, August 13, 2001; Report to the General Assembly from PATCO Sub-committee on Executive Director's Duties and Salary, n.d. [1968],

Correspondence file, Box 343, PATCO; Rock, "PATCO History," January 10, 1979; Michael J. Rock to E. J. Anderson, July 5, 1968, PATCO file, Box 289, FAA.

36. Rock interview, August 13, 2001; Memorandum for Secretary Volpe, April 1, 1970, Employee Strikes Jan.–Apr. file, Box 321, Entry 14, FAA; Rock, "PATCO History," January 10, 1979.

37. "Transcription of F. Lee Bailey's Conversation with Johnny Carson on the 'Tonight Show,' Channel 4, About Air Traffic Controllers, June 10, 1968," PATCO file, Box 289, FAA.

38. Rock, "PATCO History," January 10, 1979; Maher interview, June 2, 2003; Safety Committee Recommendations, n.d. [1968], Unfair Labor Practices file, Box 343, PATCO.

39. Maher interview, June 2, 2003; Joe Califano to the President, May 17, 1968, Safety-Traffic Control File, Box 5, CA 5 General Aviation, White House Central Files, Presidential Papers, LBJPL.

40. Rock, "PATCO History," January 10, 1979; NYT, July 4, 1968, 40; NYT, July 4, 1968, 40.

41. WP, July 7, 1968, A22; Couturier quoted in WP, April 8, 1968, D4.

42. Arthur Hailey, Airport (Garden City, N.Y.: Doubleday & Company, 1968).

43. Rock, "PATCO History," January 10, 1979; D. D. Thomas to John Maher, August 30, 1968, Professional Air Traffic Controllers Organization file, Box 277, FAA; NYT, July 13, 1968, 17.

44. Shaftic, Maher (June 2, 2003), and Carver interviews.

45. Quotations from Powderly interview; NYT, July 18, 1968, 66; "Confirmation of Discussion," July 23, 1968, Employee Grievances file, Box 290, FAA.

46. Interview with Ralph McKnight, June 29, 2002, by telephone.

47. NYT, July 24, 1968, 1; NYT, July 20, 1968, 1; NYT, July 21, 1968, 32; NYT, July 13, 1968, 17.

48. ChiTr, July 23, 1968, 1; Sanford Solender to Lyndon B. Johnson, July 19, 1968, and John Santucci to Lyndon B. Johnson, July 19, 1968, Safety-Traffic Control File, Box 5, CA 5 General Aviation, White House Central Files, Presidential Papers, LBJPL; D. D. Thomas, Record of Congressional Inquiry from Congressman Pucinski, July 15, 1968, Air Traffic Control file, Box 296, Entry 14, FAA.

49. NYT, July 22, 1968, 70; NYT, September 12, 1968, 93; NYT, July 21, 1968, 32; NYT, July 23, 1968, 1.

50. ATCA quoted in NYT, July 6, 1968, 41; Kenneth T. Lyons to Ramsey Clark, July 8, 1968, PATCO file, Box 289, FAA.

51. Airline personnel quoted in NYT, July 13, 1968, 17; "motherhood" quotation from NYT, July 16, 1968, 78.

52. Seymour Martin Lipset and William Schneider, The Confidence Gap: Business, Labor, and Government in the Public Mind (New York: The Free Press, 1983), 16; NYT, July 25, 1968, 45.

53. NYT, July 4, 1968, 40; NYT, July 14, 1968, 66; NYT, July 13, 1968, 1; interview with Alan Dean, August 6, 2003, Washington, D.C.; NYT, July 18, 1968, 66; NYT, July 14, 1968, 66.

54. Interview with Gene Weithoner, November 16, 2001, Alexandria, Va.; Record of Congressional Inquiry, Congressman Pucinski, July 15, 1968, Memorandum for

the Record file, Entry 14, Box 272, FAA; quotation regarding Bailey from William B. Flener, Record of Telephone Call with D. Barrow, July 16, 1968, PATCO file, Box 289, FAA.

55. Joseph H. Tippets to Michael J. Rock, July 9, 1968, PATCO file, Box 289, FAA; D. D. Thomas, Record of Telephone Conversation with George Gary, July 12, 1968, Air Traffic Control file, Box 296, Entry 14, FAA; *NYT*, July 22, 1968, 37.

56. *NYT*, July 17, 1968, 1; Jim Gaither to Larry Levinson, July 22, 1968, Safety-Traffic Control File, Box 5, CA 5 General Aviation, White House Central Files, Presidential Papers, LBJPL; *LAT*, July 28, 1968; Editorial, "Air Traffic Crisis," *Burlington* (Vt.) *Free Press*, July 26, 1968, Scrapbook, Box 512, PATCO.

57. *NYT*, July 21, 1968, 32; Rock, "PATCO History," January 10, 1979; "Highlights of [PATCO] Board of Directors Meeting Held July 21 through 23, 1968, in Washington, D.C.," Atlanta Office, Box 49, PATCO File, ALPA.

58. Rock interview, August 4, 2001, Las Vegas, Nev.; Raymond G. Belanger, Random Notes from PATCO FAA Meeting of July 23, n. d. [July 1968], PATCO file, Box 289, FAA.

59. *NYT*, July 23, 1968, 1; *NYT*, July 24, 1968, 1; "Results of Meeting with FAA Officials in Washington, D.C., on Tuesday July 23, 1968, Atlanta Office, Box 49, PATCO File, ALPA; Rock, "PATCO History," January 10, 1979.

60. Raymond G. Belanger, Random Notes from PATCO FAA Meeting of July 23, n. d. [July 1968], PATCO file, Box 289, FAA; William V. Vitale, FAA/PATCO Meeting, July 23, 1968, PATCO file, Box 289, FAA; Rock interview, August 4, 2001.

61. *NYT*, July 26, 1968, 2; Regional director quotation from Duane Freer to Mr. Walker, August 13, 1968, PATCO file, Box 289, FAA; *NYT*, July 25, 1968, 45; *Kansas City Star*, August 28, 1968; *NYT*, July 26, 1968, 1; *NYT*, July 26, 1968, 2; clipping, James Holahan, "The Quartet and the Four Thousand," *Business & Commercial Aviation*, [July 1968], Scrapbook, Box 512, PATCO; Maher quoted in *NYT*, July 26, 1968, 1; Editorial, "Air Traffic Mess," *Michigan City* (Ind.) *News Dispatch*, July 26, 1968, Scrapbook, Box 512, PATCO; ALPA quotation from S. W. Hopkins, August 16, 1968, PATCO file, Box 46, Atlanta Field Office Collection, ALPA.

62. *NYT*, July 27, 1968, 53; Charles S. Murphy to the President, Re: Air Traffic Delays, July 26, 1968, Safety-Traffic Control File, Box 5, CA 5 General Aviation, White House Central Files, Presidential Papers, LBJPL.

63. Record of Telephone Conversation with F. Lee Bailey, July 30, 1968, Memorandum for the Record file, Entry 14, Box 272, FAA; *NYT*, July 31, 1968, 27; Record of Telephone Conversation with George Gary, July 31, 1968, Memorandum for the Record file, Entry 14, Box 272, FAA; D. D. Thomas, Record of Telephone Conversation with George Gary, July 31, 1968, PATCO file, Box 289, FAA.

64. Record of Telephone Conversation with F. Lee Bailey, July 31, 1968, Memorandum for the Record file, Entry 14, Box 272, FAA; Correspondence in PATCO file, Box 289, FAA; D. D. Thomas to Assistant Secretary of Transportation, August 19, 1968, and Thomas to Secretary of Transportation, September 5, 1968, DOT file, Entry 14, Box 271, FAA; Nathaniel H. Goodrich to TGC-1, March 11, 1970, NAGE file, Box 322, Entry 14, FAA; Rock, "PATCO History," January 10, 1979.

65. D. D. Thomas to Secretary of Transportation, October 10, 1968, DOT File, Box 271, FAA; *NYT*, October 12, 1968, 73; *NYT*, October 12, 1968, 73; Notice to the

Press, October 11, 1968, Safety-Traffic Control File, Box 5, CA 5 General Aviation, White House Central Files, Presidential Papers, LBJPL.

66. Alan Boyd to the President, Re: Air Traffic Congestion, August 16, 1968, Safety-Traffic Control File, Box 5, CA 5 General Aviation, White House Central Files, Presidential Papers, LBJPL; *NYT*, December 3, 1968, 1; interview with Ed Curran, August 23, 2001, Washington, D.C.; interview with Cecil Mackey, November 1, 2002, by telephone; Weithoner interview; Gordon interview, November 15, 2001.

67. PATCO Newsletter typescript, September 20, 1968, PATCO file, Box 289, FAA; Gordon interview, November 15, 2001; Rock, "PATCO History," January 10, 1979; *PMN*, September 25, 1968, 2; Harshe-Rotman & Druck was the firm. John Britton to Michael J. Rock, n.d. 1968, Scrapbook, Box 512, PATCO; Alan L. Dean to Federal Aviation Administrator, Re: Meeting with Kenneth T. Lyons, October 22, 1968, NAGE file, Box 289, FAA.

68. John W. Macy Jr., *Public Service: The Human Side of Government* (New York: Harper & Row, 1971), 132–133; Gordon interview with Don R. Kienzle, February 2, 2000; Rock, "PATCO History," January 10, 1979; *PMN*, September 25, 1968, 3; *PMN*, September 25, 1968, 4; Nixon quoted in *Kansas City Star*, October 4, 1968.

69. PATCO Newsletter typescript, September 20, 1968, PATCO file, Box 289, FAA.

70. *PMN*, October 30, 1968, 13; Minutes of Board of Directors Meeting, October 17–18, 1968, Box 457, PATCO; *PATCO Newsletter*, November 14, 1968, 20; Maher quotation from *PMN*, January 14, 1969, 32.

CHAPTER 4

1. Interview with Mike Rock, August 13, 2001, Islip, N.Y.; interview with Russ Sommer, June 22, 2004, by telephone; Rock to Board of Directors, November 20, 1968, Board of Directors file, Box 499, PATCO; *PMN*, October 30, 1968, 15.

2. F. Lee Bailey with John Greenya, *Cleared for the Approach: F. Lee Bailey in Defense of Flying* (Englewood Cliffs, N.J.: Prentice Hall, 1977), 92; D. D. Thomas to All Regional Directors, November 27, 1968, PATCO file, Box 289, FAA; Meyer quoted in *Longmont* (Col.) *Times-Call*, August 22, 1968, Scrapbook, Box 512, PATCO.

3. *PMN*, December 24, 1968, 30; Anonymous controller quoted in *PMN*, August 13, 1969, 4; Mike Rock, "PATCO History," January 10, 1979 (tape and transcript in the author's possession); Minutes of the Board of Directors Meeting, March 10, 1969, Box 457, PATCO; interview with Russ Sommer, June 22, 2004, by telephone.

4. *PMN*, May 16, 1969, 72; Sommer interview; *Special Report to PATCO Members*, March 12, 1969; Facility Representatives file, Box 330, PATCO; *PMN*, August 13, 1969, 1.

5. *NYT*, January 4, 1969, 54; *PMN*, December 3, 1968, p. 21, and October 16, 1968, p. 9; quotation from interview with Alan Dean, August 6, 2003, Washington, D.C.; interview with F. Lee Bailey, October 28, 2002, by telephone; summary of OST/FAA Conference with Professional Societies, November 20, 1968, Employee Relations file, Box 289, FAA; White House Report, November 27, 1968, DOT file, Entry 14, Box 271, FAA; *NYT*, January 6, 1969, 28.

6. Quotation from Bailey, *Cleared for the Approach*, 92; interview with James Beggs, August 14, 2003, Bethesda, Md.

7. *NYT*, March 28, 1970, 19; interview with Noel Keane, June 3, 2003, by telephone; Rock interview, August 13, 2001; Shaffer quoted in interview with Ed Curran, August 23, 2001, Washington, D.C.; John H. Shaffer to Regional Directors, et al., Re: FAA's Communications/Work Environment, February 9, 1970, Regional-Multiple file, Entry 14, Box 305, FAA; Bailey interview; interview with James Beggs, August 14, 2003, Bethesda, Md.; *NYT*, February 20, 1969, 93; Bailey, *Cleared for the Approach*, 92.

8. "Cold war" quote in *PMN*, May 16, 1969, 75; Stan Gordon interview with Kienzle, February 2, 2000 (in the author's possession); interview with Gary Eads, November 7, 2002, Fairfax Station, Va.; *PMN*, October 30, 1968, 16; D. D. Thomas, "Denial of FAM Trip Privileges to Bearded Controllers," November 5, 1968, PATCO file, Box 289, FAA; Bailey quote from *PMN*, March 21, 1969, 53.

9. *PMN*, March 7, 1969, p. 47; April 11, 1969, p. 56; Beggs interview; Thomas quoted in *PMN*, April 30, 1969, 62.

10. Gordon interview with Kienzle, February 2, 2000; Rock, "PATCO History," January 10, 1979; *PMN*, June 3, 1969, 1; Bailey quoted in *NYT*, May 28, 1969, 93.

11. *Airport/Airways Development Hearings Before the Subcommittee on Aviation of the Committee on Commerce*, 91 Cong., 1st sess., June 25, 1969, p. 394; Rock, "PATCO History," January 10, 1979.

12. Pete Hamill, "The Revolt of the White Lower Middle Class," *New York*, April 14, 1969, 29; A. James Reichley, "The Way to Cool the Police Rebellion," *Fortune* 78:7 (December 1968): 109–113, 150–152; John H. Burpo, *The Police Labor Movement: Problems and Perspectives* (Springfield, Ill.: Charles C. Thomas, 1971), 31; Richard J. Murphy, "Public Employee Strikes," in *The Crisis in Public Employee Relations in the Decade of the 1970s*, ed. Richard J. Murphy and Morris Sackman (Washington, D.C.: Bureau of National Affairs, 1970), 76–77.

13. Interview with Rex Campbell, February 24, 2002, by telephone.

14. *Airport/Airways Development Hearings Before the Subcommittee on Aviation of the Committee on Commerce* 91 Cong., 1st sess., June 17, 1969, p. 24; Bailey quoted in "Summary of Evidence of Concerted Action on Part of PATCO to Effect ATC Absenteeism," n.d. [1969], PATCO file, Box 387, Entry 14, FAA.

15. Bailey, *Cleared for the Approach*, 94; Rock, "PATCO History," February 14, 1978, pp. 30–31, unmarked file, Box 373, PATCO; Keane interview; Rock, "PATCO History," January 10, 1979; Maher interview, June 2, 2003; Russell J. Sommer to All Southwest Facility Delegates, Re: F. Lee Bailey, June 11, 1969, PATCO file, Box 387, Entry 14, FAA.

16. Bailey to John Volpe, June 12, 1969, Correspondence file, Box 343, PATCO.

17. Mike Rock, "PATCO History," January 10, 1979; interview with Noel Keane, June 10, 2003, by telephone.

18. Rock, "PATCO History," February 14, 1978, p. 31, unmarked file, Box 373, PATCO.

19. Rock interview, August 13, 2001; *NYT*, June 20, 1969, 1; *ChiTr*, June 20, 1969, 1; Rock quote from Rock, "PATCO History," January 10, 1979; Chicago and Kansas City quotes in "Summary of Evidence of Concerted Action on Part of PATCO to Effect ATC Absenteeism," n.d. [1969], PATCO file, Box 387, Entry 14, FAA; *NYT*, June 20, 1969, 1.

20. Quotation from *NYT*, June 20, 1969, 1; *NYT*, June 21, 1969, 1.

21. *ChiTr*, June 20, 1969, 16; *Dallas Morning News*, June 25, 1969, June 1969 folder, Box 512, PATCO.

22. Minutes of the Board of Directors Meeting, July 27, 1969, Box 457, PATCO; Bailey, *Cleared for the Approach*, 94–95; *NYT*, June 20, 1969, 1.

23. Rock, "PATCO History," February 14, 1978, p. 32.

24. Rock, "PATCO History," January 10, 1979; Rock, "PATCO History," February 14, 1978, p. 34; interview with Jack Maher, June 2, 2003, by telephone.

25. Rock interview, August 13, 2001; "Summary of Evidence of Concerted Action on Part of PATCO to Effect ATC Absenteeism," n.d. [1969], PATCO file, Box 387, Entry 14, FAA; *PMN*, September 26, 1969; Maher quotation in *NYT*, June 21, 1969, 1; Kenneth T. Lyons to John Shaffer, June 21, 1969, PATCO file, Box 387, Entry 14, FAA; Rock, "PATCO History," January 10, 1979.

26. Minutes of the Board of Directors Meeting, July 27, 1969, Box 457, PATCO; *NYT*, June 22, 1969, 58; PATCO Meeting Minutes, November 19, 1969, Libel Bailey v. Anderson file, Box 530, PATCO; *NYT*, June 23, 1969, 78; *NYT*, June 24, 1969, 45; J. H. Shaffer, GENOT, June 23, 1969, PATCO file, Box 387, Entry 14, FAA; *Terre Haute (Ind.) Tribune*, June 24, 1969, June 1969 folder, Box 512, PATCO; *Schenectady Gazette*, July 1, 1969, July 1969 file, Box 512, PATCO; *Watertown (N.Y.) Times*, June 26, 1969, June 1969 folder, Box 512, PATCO; *ChiTr*, June 21, 1969, 5; *NYT*, June 26, 1969, 81.

27. *NYT*, July 2, 1969, 86; *NYT*, July 1, 1969, 82; *NYT*, July 19, 1969, 50; E. J. Anderson to James Hayes, July 28, 1969, Correspondence file, Box 343, and E. J. Anderson to James E. Hays, October 3, 1969, Leaves of Absence file, Box 343, PATCO; *NYT*, August 8, 1969, 32.

28. *NYT*, July 19, 1969, 50; Volpe quoted in *NYT*, July 22, 1969, 78; Ferris Howland, Record of Conference with Major General Beyerly, Director of Operations, USAF, July 17, 1969, Air Traffic Service Contingency Plan, Employee Strikes Jan.–Apr. file, Box 321, Entry 14, FAA.

29. *NYT*, July 25, 1969, 93; *NYT*, July 22, 1969, 78; *Kansas City Star*, July 22, 1969, Noel Keane Scrapbook. Corson was chairman of Fry Consultants. *ATCA Bulletin*, August 12, 1969; *PMN*, August 27, 1969, 2; Curran interview.

30. *NYT*, July 30, 1969, 78; Leyden to James J. Boyle, September 17, 1969, [this letter is loose, in no folder], Box 436, PATCO; Rock interview, August 13, 2001.

31. Rock, "PATCO History," February 14, 1978, unmarked file, Box 373, PATCO; Maher interview, June 2, 2003; Rock, "PATCO History," January 10, 1979; interview with Jesse Calhoon, August 24, 2001, by telephone.

32. Calhoon quoted by Rock, "PATCO History," January 10, 1979; Maher interviews, June 2, 2003, and August 7, 2006; *WP*, October 15, 1976, C2; Maher to Jesse Calhoon, August 29, 1969, and Calhoon to Maher, September 4, 1969, MEBA file, Box 499, PATCO; Sommer interview.

33. Lonnie D. Parrish to Claude J. Schuldt, October 31, 1969, Indianapolis file, Box 470, PATCO; Walter B. Beuchler to Robert Sturgill, September 11, 1969, Correspondence file, Box 343, PATCO. The controllers in question were James A. Henson, Shelby F. McCurnin, and James R. Sparks. Rock, "PATCO History," January 10, 1979; Southeast Regional Newsletter #4, October 21, 1969, Baton

Rouge file I, Box 470, PATCO; Maher interview, June 2, 2003; James A. Henson to Whom it May Concern, October 16, 1969, Baton Rouge file I, Box 470, PATCO.

34. Curran and Rock (Aug. 13, 2001) interviews; quotation from Rock, "PATCO History," February 14, 1978, p. 35–36, unmarked file, Box 373, PATCO; "PATCO History," January 10, 1979; Minutes of the Board of Directors Meeting, October 10–12, 1969, Box 457, PATCO; Rock to Shaffer, October 13, 1969, PATCO file, Box 322, Entry 14, FAA; *NYT*, October 13, 1969, 91; *PMN*, October 20, 1969, 1.

35. *PMN*, October 28, 1969, 4; Bailey quoted in Lonnie D. Parrish to All Personnel, November 3, 1969, Unfair Labor Practices file, Box 343, PATCO; *PMN*, November 4, 1969, 3, 5, 6; *PMN*, December 3, 1969, 2; Bailey to Shaffer, October 30, 1969, PATCO file, Box 322, Entry 14, FAA.

36. PATCO Meeting Minutes, November 19, 1969, Libel Bailey v. Anderson file, Box 530, PATCO; Action Plan for Use in Future Air Traffic Controller Absenteeism, n. d. [1969], Injunction-Overtime file, Box 470, PATCO; *PMN*, November 18, 1969, 6; *PMN*, December 14, 1969, 3; *PMN*, January 15, 1970, 3; *PMN*, November 4, 1969, 1; Bailey to George P. Schulz, October 30, 1969, PATCO file, Box 322, Entry 14, FAA; E. J. Anderson to James E. Hayes, December 5, 1969, National Exclusive Recog. file, Box 343, PATCO.

37. Financial Report, December 31, 1969, Financial Report 1969 file, Box 257, PATCO; Rock to Board of Directors, December 23, 1969, Correspondence file, Box 343, PATCO.

38. "Policy Statement on Public Employee Unions: Rights and Responsibilities Adopted by International Executive Board, AFSCME, AFL-CIO, July 26, 1966" in *Sorry…No Government Today: Unions vs. City Hall*, ed. Robert E. Walsh (Boston: Beacon Press, 1969), 67–70; *WP*, March 1, 1970, 27; "Major Faiths Sound Themes of Racial Justice, Right to Strike," in *Sorry…No Government Today*, 232–234.

39. Benjamin Aaron, et al., *Final Report and Proposed Statute of the California Assembly Advisory Council on Public Employee Relations, March 15, 1973* (Sacramento: California State Assembly, 1973), 198; *Work Stoppages in New Jersey, 1962* (New Brunswick, N.J.: Institute of Management and Labor Relations, Rutgers University, 1963), 14; *Work Stoppages in New Jersey, 1970* (New Brunswick, N.J.: Institute of Management and Labor Relations, Rutgers University, 1971), 9; Carmen D. Saso, *Coping with Public Employee Strikes: A Guide for Public Officials* (Chicago: Public Personnel Association, 1970); Murphy, "Public Employee Strikes," 77; clipping, *Kansas City Times*, January 1, 1970, Noel Keane Scrapbook (copy in author's possession).

40. Maher interview, June 2, 2003; Rock interview, August 13, 2001.

41. Carver and Rock (August 13, 2001) interviews; Rock, "PATCO History," January 10, 1979.

42. Rock, "PATCO History," February 14, 1978, p. 38; Rock, "PATCO History," January 10, 1979; interview with Bill South, June 28, 2003, by telephone.

43. National Directors of PATCO to John A. Volpe, January 25, 1970, PATCO file, Box 322, Entry 14, FAA; Shaffer to Michael J. Rock, January 30, 1970, PATCO file, Entry 14, Box 301, FAA; Quotation from "PATCO—Issues and Problems," February 3, 1970, PATCO file, Box 322, Entry 14, FAA; "Situation Report on PATCO Strike Threat," February 6, 1970, PATCO file, Box 322, Entry 14, FAA.

44. Corson report quoted in U.S. Senate Committee on Post Office and Civil Service, *Air Traffic Controllers: Report to Accompany S. 3959* (Washington, D.C.: Government Printing Office, 1970), 132, 5; *U.S. News & World Report*, April 13, 1970, 24; *PMN*, January 15, 1970, 2; Volpe to Rock, February 10, 1970, PATCO file, Entry 14, Box 301, FAA.

45. "Strike Contingency Plans—Personnel Action," February 5, 1970, PATCO file, Box 322, Entry 14, FAA; *NYP*, August 8, 1969, 5; South interview; Bailey to J. Edgar Hoover, August 29, 1969, FBI PATCO file, FOIPA Number 927360, File Number 62–113,065; interview with Ken Moffett, August 28, 2001, Washington, D.C.; Director to SAC Los Angeles, August 12, 1969, FBI PATCO file, FOIPA Number 927,360, File Number 62–113,065; Bailey to J. Edgar Hoover, August 29, 1969, FBI PATCO file, FOIPA Number 927,360, File Number 62–113,065; Dean interview, August 6, 2003; Gestapo quotation from interview with Bill Harding, June 29, 2002, by telephone; Maher interview, August 8, 2006; James Grambart to John H. Shaffer, February 10, 1970, PATCO file, Box 322, Entry 14, FAA.

46. *Olathe* (Kan.) *Daily News*, February 15, 1970, Noel Keane Scrapbook; *Kansas City Star*, February 14, 1970; *NYT*, February 15, 1970, 78; Grambart to Shaffer, February 10, 1970, PATCO file, Box 322, Entry 14, FAA.

47. *PMN*, March 2, 1970, 1–2; *NYT*, February 15, 1970, 78; *NYT*, February 16, 1970, 73; Rock, "PATCO History," February 14, 1978, unmarked file, Box 373, PATCO; Rock, "PATCO History," January 10, 1979.

48. *PMN*, March 2, 1970, 2; *WP*, February 16, 1970, A5; February 17, 1970, A8; John H. Shaffer to All Regional Directors, February 17, 1970, Regional: Regions and Staff file, Entry 14, Box 305, FAA; Gordon interview, November 15, 2001.

49. Moffett interview.

50. Shaffer to All Regional Directors, February 17, 1970, Regional: Regions and Staff file, Entry 14, Box 305, FAA; *NYT*, February 18, 1970, 28; Gordon interview, November 15, 2001; Rock, "PATCO History," January 10, 1979; Rock interview, August 13, 2001; PATCO quotation from *PMN*, March 2, 1970, 1; controller quotation from Brian to Messrs Rock, Hays, Maher, February 20, 1970, Telegrams: FAA, Facility Chiefs, Citizens, and Peeved PATCO Members file, Box 531, PATCO.

51. *PMN*, March 2, 1970, 2; Moffett interview; James A. Washington to L. Lawrence Schultz, March 11, 1970, BTR Crisis III file, Box 470, PATCO; Shaffer to All Regional Directors, March 13, 1970, Regional-Multiple file, Entry 14, Box 305, FAA; *NYT*, March 18, 1970, 93; Shaffer to Bailey, March 13, 1970, PATCO file, Entry 14, Box 301, FAA.

52. Rock, "PATCO History," February 14, 1978, p. 41–42, unmarked file, Box 373, PATCO; Handwritten notes, [March 1970], all in FBI PATCO file, FOIPA Number 927,360, File Number 95–160,487; Rock to Melvin Laird, March 23, 1970, PATCO file, Box 322, Entry 14, FAA; Rock interview, August 13, 2001; Sturgill quoted in *NYT*, March 24, 1970, 26.

53. Beggs and Dean (August 6 [quotation], and August 8, 2003, Alexandria, Va.) interviews.

54. Eugene H. Becker, "Analysis of Work Stoppages in the Federal Sector, 1962–1981," *Monthly Labor Review* (August 1982): 51; Aaron Brenner, "Striking Against the State: The Postal Wildcat of 1970," *Labor's Heritage* 7:4 (1996): 4–27.

55. Quotation from Patrick A. Tillery to Bailey, November 19, 1969, Thailand Center file, Box 320, PATCO; Harry E. Robinson to PATCO Board of Directors, February 26, 1970, Telegrams: FAA, Facility Chiefs, Citizens, and Peeved PATCO Members file, Box 531, PATCO; Doeble quoted in *Newsday*, March 25, 1970, 4; quotation from interview with George Kerr, August 17, 2001, by telephone; Curran interview; John Leyden and Ed Curran, unpublished book manuscript, p. 24 (in the author's possession).

56. Interview with Dick Shaftic, June 18, 2004, by telephone; South (quotation), and Gordon (November 15, 2001) interviews; interview with Domenic Torchia, May 23, 2003, by telephone; Rock, "PATCO History," January 10, 1979; interview with Gary Eads, November 7, 2002, Fairfax Station, Va.; Bailey, *Cleared for the Approach*, 98.

57. *NYT*, March 26, 1970, 1; interview with Robert E. Lambrecht, July 24, 2003, by telephone; *NYT*, March 26, 1970, 1; *NYT*, March 26, 1970, 1; *NYT*, March 26, 1970, 1.

58. Van Vuren interview; *NYT*, April 16, 1970, 82; *NYT*, March 26, 1970, 1; Dean interview, August 8, 2003; Rock, "PATCO History," February 14, 1978, p. 43, unmarked file, Box 373, PATCO; Shaffer to All Air Traffic Control Facilities, March 25, 1970, Regional-Multiple file, Entry 14, Box 305, FAA; Curran interview.

59. *NYT*, March 27, 1970, 1.

60. Shaffer quoted in *NYT*, March 27, 1970, 14; Shaffer to All Air Traffic Controllers, March 27, 1970, Regional-Multiple file, Entry 14, Box 305, FAA; *NYT*, March 28, 1970, 19; *NYT*, March 27, 1970, 14; Shaffer to Chiefs of All Air Traffic Facilities, March 26, 1970, Controller Strike Outgoing Correspondence file, Box 401, Entry 14, FAA; *NYT*, April 1, 1970, 1; *NYT*, March 28, 1970, 19.

61. Quotation from interview with Bob Butterworth, February 1, 2002, by telephone; Rex Campbell interview; interview with George Kerr, August 17, 2001, by telephone; *WP*, March 27, 1970, A2; *NYT*, March 27, 1970, 14.

62. Quotation from South interview; quotation from interview with Ed Meagher, May 31, 2002, Washington, D.C.; interview with Donna Taylor, Washington, D.C., April 22, 2003; rash example in Re: Vernon R. Webber, n.d. [1970], Florida March 23–April 17, 1970 II file, Box 205, PATCO; Butterworth interview; Gordon interview, November 15, 2001; *WP*, March 29, 1970, 17; Rex Campbell interview.

63. Bailey quoted in *NYT*, March 28, 1970, 1; Center Staffing—Daily Average Percent of Normal, n.d. [1970], Employee Strikes May–July file, Box 321, Entry 14, FAA; Center Staffing—Daily Average Percent of Normal, n.d. [1970], Employee Strikes May–July file, Box 321, Entry 14, FAA; Flener, GENOT 0/78, March 30, 1970, Controller Strike Outgoing Correspondence file, Box 401, Entry 14, FAA; *NYT*, March 29, 1970, 50; *ChiTr*, March 29, 1970; *ChiST*, March 28, 1970; *NYT*, April 7, 1970, 1; Dick Boyle to F. Lee Bailey, April 2, 1970, Telegrams: FAA, Facility Chiefs, Citizens, and Peeved PATCO Members file, Box 531, PATCO.

64. *NYT*, March 28, 1970, 19; Passengers of Flight 915 United to the President, March 29, 1970, White House Central File, LA6–4, Box 16, Richard M. Nixon Presidential Materials, National Archives (hereafter cited as RMNPM); *Chicago Today*, March 28, 1970; *NYT*, March 31, 1970, 26.

65. Clipping, n.d. [April 1970], Noel Keane Scrapbook; *WP*, March 29, 1970, 17; picketers quoted in C. D. DeLoach to Mr. Tolson, March 30, 1970, FBI PATCO file, FOIPA Number 927,360, File Number 62–113,403, Section 1; *WP*, April 11, 1970, A7; spouse quoted in *WP*, April 7, 1970, A7.

66. Shaffer to Virgil J. Wolfe, April 1, 1970, Labor Department file, Entry 14, Box 303, FAA; Beggs interview; Dean interview, August 8, 2003; *WP*, April 11, 1970, A7; Shaffer quoted in *WP*, April 2, 1970, A2; Volpe quoted in *WP*, March 31, 1970, A1 and GENOT 0/96, April 5, 1970, Controller Strike Outgoing Correspondence file, Box 401, Entry 14, FAA.

67. Dean interview, August 8, 2003; Shaffer to Regional Directors, et al., March 30, 1970, Regional-Multiple file, Entry 14, Box 305, FAA.

68. H. R. Haldeman, *The Haldeman Diaries: Inside the Nixon White House* (New York: G. P. Putnam's Sons, 1994), 145–146.

69. Quotation from *WP*, April 1, 1970, B9; "silent majority" from Draft Press Release, May 8, 1970, Employee Strikes May–July file, Box 321, Entry 14, FAA; William V. Vitale to Edward Curran, April 3, 1970, Office of Labor Relations file, Entry 14, Box 306, FAA; GENOT 0/96, April 5, 1970, Controller Strike Outgoing Correspondence file, Box 401, Entry 14, FAA; *NYT*, April 7, 1970, 88.

70. Hoffa quotation from *NYT*, April 12, 1970, Section 4, 3; *NYT*, April 3, 1970, 20; *NYT*, April 17, 1970, 1; *WP*, April 18, 1970, B9.

71. *WP*, March 28, 1970, A1; Bill South to Joseph McCartin, August 31, 2006 (letter in the author's possession).

72. Quotation from *NYT*, March 28, 1970, 26; *NYT*, March 31, 1970, 40; Rowan quoted in Carl T. Rowan syndicated column, n.d. [April 1970], Noel Keane Scrapbook (in author's possession); Reston quoted in *Kansas City Star*, April 1, 1970.

73. Dean (August 8, 2003) and Beggs interviews; Shaffer to Senator Stennis, April 1, 1970, PATCO file, Box 322, Entry 14, FAA; Earl F. Landgrebe to PATCO, April 27, 1970, General Correspondence file, Box 531, PATCO.

74. John B. D'Albora to Charles H. Ruby, March 30, 1970, Box 8, PATCO File, Pres. Part II, ALPA; Clyde Muirheid to All Members, April 10, 1970, Atlanta Office, Box 49, Air Traffic Control Committee File, ALPA; Dean L. Phillips to Charles H. Ruby, April 13, 1970, Box 8, PATCO File, Pres. Part II, ALPA.

75. *NYT*, May 2, 1970, 65; *NYT*, March 29, 1970, 1; *NYT*, April 2, 1970, 1; Flener quoted in the *NYT*, May 10, 1970, 86.

76. *NYT*, March 29, 1970, 1.

77. *NYT*, March 31, 1970, 1; Bailey quoted in *NYT*, April 1, 1970, 1; *WP*, April 1, 1970, A1; handwritten notes, n.d. [March 1970], FBI PATCO file, FOIPA Number 927,360, File Number 95–160,487; *WP*, April 1, 1970, A1; Rock, "PATCO History," January 10, 1979.

78. *NYT*, April 5, 1970, 1; *NYT*, April 2, 1970, 1; *NYT*, April 3, 1970, 1; *WP*, April 3, 1970, A10; Shaffer, GENOT 0/91, April 2, 1970, Controller Strike Outgoing Correspondence file, Box 401, Entry 14, FAA; Bailey quoted in *NYT*, April 4, 1970, 1.

79. *NYT*, April 7, 1970, 44; *NYT*, April 7, 1970, 1; Shaffer to All Regional Directors, Re: Interim Report on Facts Gained in Investigation of Current Strike, April 8, 1970, Regional-Multiple file, Entry 14, Box 305, FAA; *NYT*, April 8, 1970, 1; Hart quotation from *WP*, April 8, 1970, A16; *NYT*, April 7, 1970, 88; PATCO Air Traffic

Controller Strike Status Report, April 10, 1970, Employee Strikes Jan.-April file, Box 321, Entry 14, FAA; *NYT*, April 13, 1970, 17; Rock, "PATCO History," February 14, 1978, pp. 44–45, unmarked file, Box 373, PATCO; Center Staffing—Daily Average Percent of Normal, n.d. [1970], Employee Strikes May-July file, Box 321, Entry 14, FAA; *NYT*, April 12, 1970, 68.

80. Minutes of the Board of Directors Meeting, April 12, 1970, Box 457, PATCO; Rock, "PATCO History," February 14, 1978, pp. 44–45, unmarked file, Box 373, PATCO; John H. Shaffer, Bi-Weekly Report for the Vice President, April 13, 1970, DOT file, Entry 14, Box 304, FAA; Williams quotation in *NYT*, April 14, 1970, 1.

81. Quotation from Rock, "PATCO History," January 10, 1979; *NYT*, April 15, 1970, 85; interview with John Leyden, July 14, 1998, Washington, D.C.; *Newsday*, April 14, 1970, 9; Gordon interview, November 15, 2001.

CHAPTER 5

1. *NYT*, April 15, 1970, 85.

2. Interview with Bob Butterworth, February 1, 2002, by telephone; Shaffer to Associate Administrators, et al., Re: "Labor Management Relations," April 17, 1970, Regional: Regions and Staff file, and Shaffer to Regional Directors, Re: Supplemental Guidance for Air Traffic Control Strike, Regional-Multiple file, both Entry 14, Box 305, FAA; Shaffer to All Regional Directors, April 13, 1970, Controller Strike Outgoing Correspondence file, Box 401, Entry 14, FAA; interview with Dick Shaftic, June 18, 2004, by telephone; interview with Rex Campbell, February, 24, 2002, by telephone; interview with Ray Carver, July 27, 2003, by telephone; interview with Stan Gordon, November 15, 2001, Washington, D.C.; Statement by Richard Martin, n. d. [1970], 1970 Harassment file, Box 1, Pittsburgh Tower PATCO Records, UTA.

3. *PMN*, May 13, 1970, 1; Carl E. Vaughan to Senator Hugh Scott, June 16, 1970, 1970 Congressional Letters file, Box 1, Pittsburgh Tower PATCO, PATCO/UTA; Air Traffic Controllers of Madison Tower to All Unions and Persons Concerned with Unfair Labor Practices, May 14, 1970, Controller Dismissals Through August 1971 file, Box 265, PATCO; correspondence in PATCO file, Box 322, Entry 14, FAA; Thomas M. Foster to Charlotte Reid, May 30, 1971, Employee Grievances file, Box 354, and "Proposed Action: Greater Pittsburgh Airport," December 19, 1970, Air Traffic Service file, Entry 14, Box 305, Entry 14, FAA.

4. Quotation from interview with James Beggs, August 14, 2003, Bethesda, Md.; *NYT*, April 17, 1970, 74; *NYT*, May 10, 1970, 86; Charles Culhane, "Labor Report: Federal Unions Watch PATCO case for Clues to the Future Policy on Federal Strikes," *National Journal*, October 3, 1970, p. 2162.

5. Interview with Alan Dean interview, August 8, 2003, Alexandria, Va.; Richard J. Murphy, "Public Employee Strikes," in *The Crisis in Public Employee Relations in the Decade of the 1970s*, ed. Richard J. Murphy and Morris Sackman (Washington, D.C.: Bureau of National Affairs, 1970), 71; interview with Ed Curran, August 23, 2001, Washington, D.C.; Shaffer to the Secretary, Re: Implementation of the Corson Committee Report (Report #3), June 12, 1970, DOT file, Entry 14, Box 304, FAA; Culhane, "Labor Report," 2166.

6. *NYT*, April 22, 1970, 89; *NYT*, May 2, 1970, 65; anonymous judge quoted in *NYT*, April 30, 1970, 70; John F. Maher Greetings, July 24, 1970, National Correspondence file, Box 10, George Brandon Collection, PATCO/UTA; *United States of America v. Professional Air Traffic Controllers Organization ("PATCO")* et al., No. 34,968, United States Court of Appeals for the Second Circuit, 438 F.2d 79; 1970 U.S. App. LEXIS 6007; 75 L.R.R.M. 2834; 64 Lab. Cas. (CCH) P11, 342; July 15, 1970, Argued; December 10, 1970, Decided; Gaylord Nelson et al. to John A. Volpe, June 11, 1970, PATCO file, Box 322, Entry 14, FAA; *Federal Times*, July 1, 1970; Sen. James W. Symington to John Volpe, July 20, 1970, Unmarked folder, Box 330, PATCO; Sen. James L. Buckley to John A. Volpe, April 26, 1971, Strikes file, Entry 14, Box 354, FAA; John F. Leyden to Richard Nixon, September 22, 1970, White House Central File, LA6–4, Box 16, RMNPM.

7. K. M. Smith to the Under Secretary, September 3, 1970, DOT file, Entry 14, Box 304, FAA; Shaffer to Ted Stevens, August 14, 1970, Employee Strikes Aug. file, Entry 14, Box 321, FAA; Volpe quoted in Culhane, "Labor Report/Federal Unions Watch PATCO Case for Clues to the Future Policy on Federal Strikes," 2162; John W. Macy Jr., *Public Service: The Human Side of Government* (New York: Harper & Row, 1971), 132; William H. Rehnquist, "Public Dissent and the Public Employee," *Civil Service Journal* 11:3 (January–March 1971): 10.

8. Shaffer to Under Secretary, July 14, 1970, DOT file, Entry 14, Box 304, FAA; John H. Shaffer, "Constructive Discipline," November 3, 1970, Regional: Regions and Staff file, Entry 14, Box 305, FAA; *WP*, November 7, 1970, F13; List of Proposed Disciplinary Actions by Region and Facility, July 7, 1970, Employee Strikes May-July file, Box 321, Entry 14, FAA; Shaffer quote from Shaffer to Peter M. Flanigan, October 8, 1970, White House Central File, LA6–4, Box 16, RMNPM; *NYT*, April 20, 1971, 86; Shaffer, "Constructive Discipline," November 3, 1970, Regional: Regions and Staff file, Entry 14, Box 305, FAA; *WP*, November 7, 1970, F13; *NYT*, December 13, 1970, 75; Shaffer, Status of Court Injunctions Restraining FAA Disciplinary Actions, January 27, 1971, DOT file, Entry 14, Box 337, FAA; NYT, November 22, 1970, 84.

9. *WP*, February 2, 1971, B9; Murray B. Nesbitt, *Labor Relations in the Federal Government Service* (Washington, D.C.: Bureau of National Affairs, 1976), 381; Shaffer to the Secretary, Re: Implementation of the Corson Committee Report (Report #3), June 12, 1970, DOT file, Entry 14, Box 304, FAA; Shaffer, "Constructive Discipline," November 3, 1970," Regional: Regions and Staff file, Entry 14, Box 305, FAA.

10. John B. Saxman Jr. to William B. Spong Jr., April 21, 1971, Controller Dismissals Through August 1971 file, Box 265, PATCO; Mrs. Larry K. Jones to Senator, June 24, 1970, PATCO file, Box 322, Entry 14, FAA; interview with Domenic Torchia, May 23, 2002, by telephone; Rock, "PATCO History," January 10, 1979; Leyden to Board of Directors, September 18, 1970, Memorandum Re: Board and National Officers file, Box 498, PATCO; Maher quotation from National News Memorandum #16, October 20, 1970, Box 1, Houston ARTCC PATCO Collection, PATCO/UTA; Carver interview; *NYT*, November 22, 1970, 84; Dean interview, August 8, 2003.

11. Interview with Bill Peer, July 1, 2004, Bethany Beach, Md.; quotation from Rock, "PATCO History," January 10, 1979; Minutes of the Board of Directors Meeting, April 18–19, 1970, Box 457, PATCO; *PMN*, May 13, 1970, 1.

12. *PMN*, May 5, 1970, 1; Report on PATCO convention, H. Ray Lahr to Charles J. Ruby, April 24, 1970, Box 8, PATCO File, Pres. Part II, ALPA.

13. Interview with John Leyden, July 21, 1998, Washington, D.C.; *Journal of Air Traffic Control* 7:2 (September 1964): 31; interview with George Kerr, August 17, 2001, by telephone; Curran interviews.

14. Interview with John Leyden, July 14, 1998, Washington, D.C.; John Leyden and Ed Curran, unpublished book manuscript, pp. 34–35 (in the author's possession); List of Proposed Disciplinary Actions by Region and Facility, July 7, 1970, Employee Strikes May–July file, Box 321, Entry 14, FAA.

15. Leyden (July 14, 1998) and Gordon (November 15 and 29, 2001) interviews; *PMN*, May 5, 1970, 1; Leyden quoted in *WP*, April 24, 1970, A8.

16. Peer interview.

17. *Federal Times*, July 1, 1970; *Federal Times*, May 20, 1970; *NYT*, June 12, 1970, 77.

18. Rock, "PATCO History," January 10, 1979; Peer, Gordon (November 29, 2001), and Leyden (July 14, 1998) interviews; Minutes of the Board of Directors Meeting, July 1, 1970, Box 457, PATCO; interview with Bill South, June 28, 2003, by telephone.

19. *NYT*, June 20, 1970, 58; *NYT*, April 17, 1970, 74; Rex Campbell interview; F. Lee Bailey with John Greenya, *Cleared for the Approach: F. Lee Bailey in Defense of Flying* (Englewood Cliffs, N.J.: Prentice Hall, 1977), 113, 109; quotation from pp. 113–114.

20. Peer interview; interview with Jack Maher, June 2, 2003, by telephone; Maher to Board of Directors, National Officers, Regional Vice Presidents, May 21, 1970, National Correspondence file, Box 10, George Brandon Collection, PATCO/UTA;. Leyden to Board of Directors, September 18, 1970, Memorandum Re: Board and National Officers file, Box 498, PATCO; interview with David Siegel, June 27, 2003, by telephone; Report, Year Ended December 31, 1970, Financial Report 1970 file, Box 257, PATCO; Curran interview.

21. Interview with Noel Keane, by telephone; South interview, June 10, 2003; Stanley A. Ruttenberg to Leyden, June 15, 1970, Board Meeting June 16–17, 1970, file, Box 218, PATCO; Leyden to Board of Directors, September 10, 1970, Memorandum Re: Board and National Officers file, Box 498, PATCO.

22. *NYT*, May 10, 1970, 86; Maher (August 7, 2006), Rock (August 13, 2001), South, and Leyden (July 14, 1998) interviews.

23. William E. Broadwater, Record of Telephone Call with John Leyden, July 1, 1970, PATCO file, Box 322, Entry 14, FAA; spokesperson Robert C. Sturgill to William Vitale, July 6, 1970, PATCO file, Box 322, Entry 14, FAA; Peter M. Flanigan to John F. Leyden, December 22, 1970, White House Central File, LA6–4, Box 16, RMNPM.

24. "Personnel Administration in the Federal Aviation Administration, Department of Transportation," September 1970, Personnel Management file, Box 317, Entry 14, FAA; Shaffer quoted in *NYT*, May 10, 1970, 86; Shaffer to Associate Administrators, et al., Re: Labor Relations Responsibilities, May 4, 1970, Washington Offices file,

Entry 14, Box 305, FAA; Bertrand M. Harding to Shaffer, Re: Status of John Leyden, PATCO President, June 25, 1970, Office of Labor Relations file, Entry 14, Box 306, FAA; *NYT*, May 22, 1970, 62; Volpe to Robert L. Tully, July 30, 1970, Box 8, PATCO File, Pres. Part II, ALPA; Shaffer to the Secretary, Re: Implementation of the Corson Committee Report (Report #2), May 7, 1970, DOT file, Entry 14, Box 304, FAA; Shaffer, "Establishment of Air Traffic Advisory Committees," June 18, 1970, Assoc. Administrator for Personnel and Training file, Box 305, Entry 14, FAA.

25. Leyden interview, July 21, 1998; interview with Andy Anderson, June 3, 2004, by telephone; Butterworth interview; George E. Hopkins, *The Airline Pilots: A Study in Elite Unionization* (Cambridge, Mass.: Harvard University Press, 1971).

26. Leyden quotations from Leyden to Ken Baker, December 1, 1975, Series 100, Box 2, PATCO; Leyden interview, July 21, 1998; *WP*, May 31, 1974, A6; Butterworth interview; Leyden quoted in *GERR*, May 29, 1978, 5.

27. Interview with Paul Hallisay, Washington, D.C., August 28, 2001; interview with J. J. O'Donnell, September 7, 2001, by telephone; Leyden interview, July 21, 1998; O'Donnell to Shaffer, April 27, 1972, ALPA file, Box 375, Entry 14, RG 237; Leyden to O'Donnell, October 21, 1976, Series 100, Box 4, PATCO; Leyden to O'Donnell, November 16, 1972, PATCO File, Box 8, Pres. Part II, ALPA.

28. Interview with Jesse Calhoon, August 24, 2001, by telephone.

29. South, Calhoon, and Leyden (July 14, 1998) interviews.

30. Gordon interview with Kienzle; Keane interview; *WP*, July 29, 1971, F9.

31. Charlie Campbell and Leyden (July 14, 1998) interviews; Rock, "PATCO History," January 10, 1979; *WP*, November 2, 1974, A2; Rock (August 13, 2001), Gordon (November 29, 2001), and South interviews.

32. Gordon interview, November 29, 2001; *WP*, November 2, 1974, A2; Leyden (July 14, 1998) and South interviews; Memo, Robert E. Poli to All Regional Vice Presidents, July 12, 1976, Series 100, Box 2, PATCO; Siegel interview; quotation from Leyden to Les Hall Jr., June 16, 1977, Series 100, Box 6, PATCO.

33. Leyden to Robert E. Morris, January 25, 1974, Series 100, Box 4, PATCO; Leyden to Harrel D. Spangler, July 15, 1974, Series 100, Box 2, PATCO; Leyden to David G. Benson, Jack Karr, and Freddy Whitt, September 30, 1974, Series 100, Box 2, PATCO; PATCO Questionnaire Number 1, n.d. [1978], January 1979 Board Meeting file, Box 218, PATCO; "What PATCO Is All About," by John F. Leyden, n.d. [February 1974], Series 100, Box 4, PATCO; Frank A. Laurito to Heidi Shippee, November 3, 1980, National MEBA Political Action Committee's Master List file, Box 199, PATCO; Gordon interview, November 29, 2001.

34. Martin Wein to Robert E. Greene, March 6, 1971, Miami Tower file, Box 320, PATCO; Keane interview; Rock, "PATCO History," January 10, 1979; Robert E. Greene to Hershel I. Maurer, July 30, 1970, New York Center file, Box 498, PATCO; "Uncle Sam Says … It's OK to Organize," leaflet, n.d., Folder 14, Box 4, James Wright Collection, PATCO/UTA.

35. *WP*, April 29, 1971, G9; Rock, "PATCO History," January 10, 1979.

36. Leyden interview, July 14, 1998.

37. Milden J. Fox Jr. and Huntly E. Shelton Jr., "The Impact of Executive Order 11491 on The Federal Labor Management Relations Program," *Journal of Collective Negotiations in the Public Sector* 1:2 (May 1972): 113–124; Bob Repas, *Collective*

Bargaining in Federal Employment, 2nd ed. (Honolulu: Industrial Relations Center, University of Hawaii, 1973), 54–74.

38. Leyden to Richard Moushegian, December 12, 1972, Series 100, Box 2, PATCO; Charles Culhane, "White House Report: Nixon Eyes Blue-Collar Workers as Potential Source of Votes in '72," *National Journal* (January 3, 1971), 234.

39. John H. Shaffer to Secretary of Transportation, June 15, 1970, DOT file, Entry 14, Box 304, FAA; *NYT,* May 27, 1970, 93.

40. *NYT,* May 27, 1970, 93; PATCO Recognition Question (Hearing Examiner's Recommendations), October 16, 1970, PATCO file, Box 322, Entry 14, FAA; *Federal Times,* October 31, 1970; PATCO Recognition Question (Hearing Examiner's Recommendations), October 16, 1970, PATCO file, Box 322, Entry 14, FAA; J. H. Shaffer to the Secretary [of Transportation], October 14, 1970, and Shaffer to the Secretary [of Transportation], October 23, 1970, both in PATCO file, Box 322, Entry 14, FAA.

41. Culhane, "White House Report: Nixon Eyes," 234; *WP,* January 30, 1971, A14; Leyden interview, July 14, 1998.

42. *WP,* November 17, 1970, B11; Rock interview, August 13, 2001.

43. Memorandum for Mr. Calhoon, July 7, 1971, Controller Dismissals Through Aug. 1971 file, Box 265, PATCO.

44. Jefferson Cowie, "Nixon's Class Struggle: Romancing the New Right Worker, 1969–1973," *Labor History* 43 (Summer 2002): 257–283; Edmund F. Wehrle, "Partisan for the Hard Hats: Charles Colson, George Meany, and the Failed Blue-Collar Strategy," *Labor: Studies in Working-Class History of the Americas* 5:3 (2008): 45–66; H. R. Haldeman, *The Haldeman Diaries: Inside the Nixon White House* (New York: G. P. Putnam's Sons, 1994), 370; Colson quotation from Memorandum for H. R. Haldeman, September 14, 1970, Nixon Labor Politics file, Box 96, Colson Papers, RMNPM.

45. Allen J. Matusow, *Nixon's Economy: Booms, Busts, Dollars, and Votes* (Lawrence: University Press of Kansas, 1998), 154–162; Meany quoted in *Newsweek,* September 6, 1971, 4; Calhoon interview.

46. Charles W. Colson, *Born Again* (Old Tappan, N.J.: Chosen Books, 1976), 57; Conversation 607–614, Oval Office, 11:33 a.m., Cassette 1333–1335/1334–1, Nixon White House Tapes, RMNPM.

47. Conversation 608–1, Oval Office, October 29, 1971, 5:20 p.m., Cassette 1336–1, Nixon White House Tapes, RMNPM.

48. Conversation 13–60, White House Telephone, November 1, 1971, 7:42 p.m., Nixon White House Tapes, RMNPM; Leyden interview, July 14, 1998.

49. Conversation 13–83, White House Telephone, November 3, 1971, 9:00 a.m.; Conversation 13–99, White House Telephone, November 3, 1971, 12:22 p.m.; Conversation 301–325, Executive Office Building, November 3, 1971, 3:01 p.m., cassette 1399–5/1400–1401; Conversation Number 300–316, Executive Office Building, November 4, 1971, 3:47 p.m.; Conversation Number 300–317, Executive Office Building, November 4, 1971, Cassette 1391–17, Nixon White House Tapes, RMNPM.

50. Colson to Peter Flanigan et al., November 4, 1971, Nixon Labor Politics file, Box 96, Colson Papers, RMNPM; *NYT,* November 6, 1971, 5.

51. Calhoon interview; Rock to Shaffer, November 26, 1969, Correspondence file, Box 343, PATCO; Rock interview, August 13, 2001.
52. Beggs interview.
53. FAA News Release, February 7, 1972, Employee Strikes file, Box 387, Entry 14, FAA; *WP*, February 8, 1972, A4; Shaffer to William L. Hungate, March 2, 1972, Employee Strikes file, Box 387, Entry 14, FAA; *WP*, February 8, 1972, A4; Keane interview, June 3, 2003; E. V. Curran to Shaffer, Re: Re-Employment of Robert C. Sturgill, September 5, 1972, Office of Labor Relations file, Box 369, Entry 14, FAA.
54. Rock, "PATCO History," January 10, 1979; Leyden to Keith Lilak and Tracy Perry, December 4, 1972, Series 100, Box 2, PATCO; interview with Russ Sommer, June 22, 2004, by telephone; Carver, Rex Campbell, Leyden (July 14, 1998), South, and Rock (August 13, 2001) interviews.
55. *PMN*, May 13, 1970, 2; South interview (quotation); interview with Ed Meagher, May 31, 2002, Washington, D.C.; "gentlemen" quotation from interview with Rich Andrews, August 11, 2003, by telephone.
56. Rock, "PATCO History," January 10, 1979.
57. Leyden interview, July 14, 1998; *WP*, March 13, 1974, A4; Rock, "PATCO History," January 10, 1979.
58. Quotation in *PMN*, May 1972, 3.
59. Leyden interview, July 14, 1998; Rock, "PATCO History," January 10, 1979; Shaffer to Leyden, August 14, 1972, PATCO file, Box 369, Entry 14, FAA.
60. Leyden interview, July 14, 1998; *NYT*, October 25, 1972, 32; Conversation 34–92, White House Telephone recording, December 15, 1972, RMNPM.
61. *WP*, September 22, 1972, A4; Maher interview, August 7, 2006; Gordon interview, November 29, 2001.
62. Leyden interview, July 14, 1998; Bob Repas, *Collective Bargaining in Federal Employment*, 2nd ed. 11; Shaffer to Leyden, October 20, 1972, PATCO file, Entry 14, Box 369, FAA; Shaffer to Regional and Center Directors, et al., Re: Labor-Management Relations, October 6, 1972, Regions and Staff 1972 file, Entry 14, Box 367, FAA.
63. Maher interview, August 7, 2006.

CHAPTER 6

1. Leyden to Brother Controller, November 27, 1973, Series 100, Box 4, PATCO.
2. Don McPhail to Leyden, July 30, 1976, JFL Press Conferences file, Box 398, PATCO.
3. Shaffer to All FAA Employees, December 12, 1972, Personnel Management file, Box 383, Entry 14, FAA; Leyden to National Negotiating Committee, December 13, 1972, Series 100, Box 2, PATCO; Edmund Preston, *Troubled Passage: The Federal Aviation Administration During the Nixon-Ford Term, 1973–77* (Washington, D.C.: U.S. Department of Transportation, 1987), 15; Office of Labor-Management Relations, U.S. Civil Service Commission, *Management Practices Manual: No. V, Negotiations* (Washington, D.C.: OLMR, U.S. Civil Service Commission, 1975), 34, 23.
4. Preston, *Troubled Passage*, 120–121; interview with Bill Peer, July 1, 2004, Bethany Beach, Del.; Mike Rock, "PATCO History," January 10, 1979 (tape and transcript in the author's possession).

5. Robert G. Vaughan, *The Spoiled System: A Call for Civil Service Reform* (New York: Charterhouse, 1975), 13; quotation from David G. Bowers, "What Would Make 11,500 People Quit Their Jobs?" *Organizational Dynamics* (Winter 1983): 18.

6. Douglas McGregor, *The Human Side of Enterprise* (New York: McGraw-Hill, 1960), 33–47; anonymous controller quoted in Robert M. Rose, C. David Jenkins, and Michael W. Hurst, *Air Traffic Controller Health Change Study: A Prospective Investigation of Physical, Psychological and Work-Related Changes* (A Report to the FAA on Research Performed Under Contract No. FA73WA-3211, Awarded to Boston University, August 1978), 121.

7. Interview with Bob Mischke, June 23, 2004, by telephone; interview with Mike Rock, August 13, 2001, Islip, N.Y.; quotations from interview with John Thornton, Washington, D.C. August 6, 1998; interview with Ron Taylor, February 12, 2002, Stewart, Florida; interview with Bruce Meachum, July 28, 2003, by telephone; interview with Robert Lambrecht, July 24, 2003, by telephone.

8. Lambrecht interview (quotation); interview with Carl Kern, July 22, 2003, by telephone; FLRA Charge Against Labor Organization or its Agents, March 13, 1980, 6-CO-18, Box 296, PATCO; FLRA Charge Against Labor Organization or its Agents, November 28, 1980, 2-CO-46 file, Box 296, PATCO; "no balls" quotation from Anonymous questionnaire, Box 158, PATCO; "Definition of a Prostitute," n.d. [1980], May–June 1980 Correspondence, Box 401, PATCO; Minutes of Board of Directors Meetings, May 9–11, 1974, May 1974 Executive Board Meeting file, Box 218, PATCO.

9. Quotation from interview with Ray Van Vuren, March 11, 2002, by telephone; "wipe" quotation from interview with Bill Harding, June 29, 2002, by telephone; *Chicago Center PATCO News*, n.d. [1976], 2, Regional Newsletters, Box 379, PATCO; Office of Labor-Management Relations, U.S. Civil Service Commission, *Management Practices Manual: No. VI, Managing Under Bilateralism, A Supervisor's Guide* (Washington, D.C.: OLMR, U.S. Civil Service Commission, 1976), 3.

10. Interview with Gary Eads, November 7, 2003, Fairfax Station, Va.; Ron Taylor interview; and Ed Curran, August 23, 2001, Washington, D.C.; Rock, "PATCO History," January 10, 1979; "whip" quotation from interview with Terry Bobell, August 5, 2003, by telephone; "BLANK" quotation from Gary Greene, "View from the Top," *Crowded Skies*, June 1981, p. 2, Newsletters file, Box 221, PATCO.

11. Interview with David Siegel, June 26, 2003, by telephone; *Denver PATCO Planet*, July 1978, Box 378, PATCO.

12. Grievance statistics in Levitan and Noden, *Working for the Sovereign*, 62. On the notion of "industrial jurisprudence," see Sumner Slichter, *Union Policies and Industrial Management* (Washington, D.C.: Brookings Institution, 1941); David Brody, "Workplace Contractualism in Comparative Perspective," in *Industrial Democracy in America: The Ambiguous Promise*, ed. Nelson Lichtenstein and Howell John Harris (New York: Cambridge University Press, 1993), 176–205; Maher quoted in Rock, "PATCO History," January 10, 1979; arbitration numbers in M. J. Fox Jr. and Danny R. Potter, "Arbitration of Grievances Between PATCO and FAA: The Agency's Approach," *Journal of Collective Negotiations in the Public Sector* 6:1 (1977): 53.

13. Rock to Regional Vice Presidents, July 22, 1975, Series 100, Box 2, PATCO; Rock to E. V. Curran, July 21, 1975, Series 100, Box 2, PATCO; Peer, Charlie Campbell, Siegel, and Keane interviews; Fox and Potter, "Arbitration of Grievances Between PATCO and FAA," 54, 60.

14. Grievances reported in National News Memorandum, September 16, 1974, Newsletter folder, Series 100, Box 4, PATCO; interview with Bruce Meachum, July 28, 2003, by telephone; *GERR*, March 27, 1978, 4; *GERR*, March 10, 1975, A1; Benjamin H. Wolf Papers, Accession #5539, Box 132, File 17, Catherwood Library, Cornell University; *GERR*, November 11, 1974, A5; *GERR*, June 16, 1975, A1; *GERR*, September 1, 1975, A4; interview with Rex Campbell, June 24, 2002, by telephone.

15. Curran interview.

16. Meachum interview; Paul Hadley to Dennis Reardon, July 24, 1980, unmarked file, Box 1, Dennis Reardon/PATCO Records, PATCO/UTA (this document shows PATCO won 20 decisions in 1980, while losing 17 and splitting nine); quotations from Grievance Record, Robert C. Fox, December 22, 1980, file AGL-80–918-ZMP-3, Series 440, Box 161, PATCO; and Michael B. Kline to Charlie [Charles R. Campbell], August 19, 1979, file APC-79-33-Mkk-3, Series 440, Box 161, PATCO.

17. Interview with Carl Kern, July 22, 2003, by telephone; Leyden to E. V. Curran, January 16, 1974, Series 100, Box 4, PATCO; Curran to Leyden, December 26, 1974, FAA 1974 file, Box 200, PATCO.

18. *WP*, February 22, 1975, A3.

19. Interview with John Leyden, July 21, 1998, Washington, D.C.

20. *WP*, December 24, 1975, A1; *WP*, April 5, 1975, B1; *NYT*, April 5, 1975, 58; Leyden interview, July 21, 1998; Leyden to Benjamin O. Davis, February 25, 1975, Series 100, Box 2, PATCO; Leyden to William T. Coleman Jr., May 21, 1975, Series 100, Box 2, PATCO.

21. *NYT*, April 5, 1975, 58; interview with Ray Van Vuren, March 11, 2002, by telephone; Peer interview; interview with John Thornton, Washington, D.C.; Leyden interview July 21, 1998; interview with Steve Elliott, June 10, 2003, Leesburg, Va.

22. Leyden to John L. McLucas, January 20, 1976, Series 100, Box 4, PATCO; interview with John McLucas, November 16, 2001, Alexandria, Va.

23. Report, Year Ended December 31, 1973, Financial Report December 31, 1973 file, Box 257, PATCO; Rock, "PATCO History," January 10, 1979; *GERR*, November 12, 1973, A9; interview with Bill South, June 28, 2003, by telephone.

24. C. Wright Mills, *The New Men of Power: America's Labor Leaders* (1948, repr., Urbana: University of Illinois Press, 2001), 3–4.

25. Leyden to Richard E. Robitaille, October 11, 1973, Series 100, Box 4, PATCO; "pol" quotation from interview with Kenneth Moffett, August 28, 2001, Washington, D.C.; Maher to Leyden, February 9, 1972, Box 525, PATCO; Rock interview, August 13, 2001; "180" quotation from Maher interview, August 8, 2006; "pragmatic" quotation from Leyden to Richard E. Robitaille, October 11, 1973, Series 100, Box 4, PATCO; FAA quotation from Van Vuren interview.

26. Quotation from interview with Mike Rock, August 4, 2001, Las Vegas, Nev.; Leyden quotations from Leyden to Michael S. Elliott, January 21, 1977, Series 100, Box 4, PATCO. On PATCO union democracy, see Richard Hurd, "Professional

Employees and Union Democracy: From Control to Chaos," *Journal of Labor Research* 21:1 (Winter 2000): 103–115.

27. Leyden quotation from Informal Notes for N.Y. Meeting, March 11, 1976, Chicago and New York Meetings folder, Box 436, PATCO; interview with Stan Gordon, November 29, 2001, Washington, D.C.; interview with Noel Keane, June 10, 2003, by telephone.

28. Gordon interview, November 29, 2001; Rock, "PATCO History," January 10, 1979; South, Keane, and Thornton interviews; interview with Bill Robertson, June 10, 2002, by telephone.

29. Leyden to Raymond C. Losornio, August 22, 1974, Series 100, Box 2, PATCO; Memo, Glenda to John Leyden, August 31, 1976, Series 100, Box 2, PATCO.

30. Interview with Terry Bobell, August 5, 2003, by telephone; interview with Sid McGuirk, June 19, 2002, Washington, D.C.; interview with Karen Koch, August 8, 2003, by telephone; quotation from Lambrecht interview.

31. Maher to Leyden, February 9, 1972, Box 525, PATCO; interview with Charles Bolling, July 23, 2002, Bowie, Md.; quotation from William K. Burns to Richard Scholz, December 12, 1977, unmarked file, Box 221, PATCO; Taso P. Anthan Case file, St. Louis, Box 142, PATCO; *WP*, November 6, 1976, D2.

32. Eads, Thornton, Ron Taylor, and Bobell interviews.

33. Siegel, Bobell, Curran, and Ron Taylor interviews.

34. Leyden to Gilbert Lujan, March 24, 1975, Series 100, Box 2, PATCO; Rock interview, August 13, 2001.

35. "Blue collar image" quotation from Charles M. Rehmus, "Labor Relations in the Public Sector in the United States," in *Public Employment Labor Relations: An Overview of Eleven Nations*, ed. Charles M. Rehmus (Ann Arbor: Institute of Labor and Industrial Relations, University of Michigan and Wayne State University, 1975), 39; Address by John F. Leyden, May 31, 1975, 1975 Convention Guests, Invitations, Responses, Awards file, Box 382, PATCO; Leyden to David P. McArdle, February 28, 1978, Series 100, Box 2, PATCO; *Oakland Center Advisor*, Aug. 1975, 1, Regional Newsletters, Box 379, PATCO; Gary W. Eads to All Controllers, September 4, 1975, Box 1, Kansas City ARTCC PATCO Records, UTA.

36. Rex Campbell, and Leyden (August 4, 2001) interviews.

37. Siegel, Rock (August 13, 2001), and Shaftic interviews.

38. Columbus controller James N. Osment to Leyden, September 24, 1974, PATCO Reclassification Committee file, Series 100, Box 222, PATCO; Maher interview, August 7, 2006; "cow's tail" quotation from Charles R. Campbell to Leyden, October 17, 1974, November 1974 Executive Board Meeting file, Box 218, PATCO; Rex Campbell interview.

39. Rex Campbell, Siegel (quotation), Maher (August 7, 2006), Rock (August 13, 2001), and South interviews.

40. Leyden to E. V. Curran, January 2, 1974, Series 100, Box 4, PATCO; quotation from Leyden to Brother Controller, November 27, 1973, Series 100, Box 4, PATCO; Daily Record of Negotiations, February 27, 1974, 4–5, 1974–75 Negotiations Daily Record file, Box 200, PATCO; Rock, "PATCO History," January 10, 1979.

41. John McLucas, "Crossing the River: My Life at the FAA," unpublished ms., n.d. (in the author's possession), 19; Leyden and Curran, unpublished book manuscript,

50; *GERR*, November 12, 1973, A8–A9; *GERR*, April 1, 1974, A12; Leyden quoted in Preston, *Troubled Passage*, 124; Daily Record of Negotiations, February 27, 1974, 4–5, 1974–74 Negotiations Daily Record file, Box 200, PATCO; *GERR*, April 1, 1974, A12; Memorandum, Leyden to Members of the Negotiating Committee, April 18, 1974, Series 100, Box 4, PATCO; Memorandum, Leyden to National Negotiating Committee, June 27, 1974, Series 100, Box 4, PATCO; quotation from Rock, "PATCO History," January 10, 1979.

42. Preston, *Troubled Passage*, 120–121; Leyden to Albert V. Casey, August 30, 1974, Series 100, Box 2, PATCO; *WP*, September 28, 1974, D1; Curran to Leyden, September 30, 1974, FAA 1974 file, Box 200, PATCO; *WP*, September 28, 1974, D1; Leyden to Albert V. Casey, September 25, 1974, Series 100, Box 2, PATCO; Press release, "PATCO Files ULPs Against DOT, FAA," September 4, 1974, Series 100, Box 2, PATCO.

43. Interview with Andy Anderson, June 3, 2004, by telephone; interview with Ed Meagher, May 31, 2002, Washington, D.C.; Ron Taylor interview; Robert E. Poli to J. J. O'Donnell, July 19, 1974, Series 100, Box 2, PATCO; Robert Poli to Regional Vice President, April 26, 1976, Series 100, Box 4, PATCO; O'Donnell interview; Rock interview, August 13, 2001; G. S. Moore, "SF-160 Program Revision," October 26, 1970, Air Traffic Service file, Box 305, Entry 14, FAA.

44. Anonymous questionnaires, n.d. [April 1974], Box 158, PATCO; Rock, "PATCO History," January 10, 1979.

45. *GERR*, October 28, 1974, A3; FAA spokesperson quotation in *NYT*, October 5, 1974, 14; Paul Harvey, "Commentary on Work Slowdown," October 3, 1974, 1974 Slowdown Publicity file, Box 331, PATCO; Gary W. Eads to Paul Harvey, October 24, 1974, Box 1, Kansas City ARTCC PATCO Records, PATCO/UTA; Noel Keane to Paul Harvey, October 8, 1974, Series 100, Box 2, PATCO; Anonymous executive quoted in Preston, *Troubled Passage*, 125.

46. *GERR*, October 28, 1974, A3; Leyden to William T. Coleman, March 17, 1975, Series 100, Box 2, PATCO; *GERR*, May 15, 1975, A10; *NYT*, May 8, 1975, 42; *GERR*, May 15, 1975, A10; 1975 FAA-PATCO Agreement, Box 39, PATCO; Rock, "PATCO History," January 10, 1979.

47. *GERR*, October 6, 1975, A4–A6, Z1–Z5.

48. Domenic Torchia to Leyden, n. d. [July 1976], and Leyden to Torchia, n. d. [July 1976], Executive Board Meeting July 1976 folder, Box 436, PATCO.

49. *WP*, May 31, 1975, E45; K.C. ARTCC 1975 PATCO Convention Report, Box 1, Kansas City ARTCC PATCO Records, UTA; Address by John F. Leyden, May 31, 1975, 1975 Convention Guests, Invitations, Responses file, Box 382, PATCO; Burner interview; *WP*, April 30, 1975, A4; *GERR*, May 5, 1975, A8.

50. Peer interview; Rock, "PATCO History," January 10, 1979.

51. *WP*, July 31, 1976, A1; U.S. Census, "Historical Income Tables: Families," http://www.census.gov/hhes/www/income/histinc/f07ar.html (accessed April 26, 2010); *NYT*, November 13, 1976, 8.

52. Curran interview; J. H. Shaffer to James B. Pearson, March 15, 1972, Security of Control of Air Traffic file, Box 397, Entry 14, FAA; Leyden to Robert B. Parke, October 14, 1975, Series 100, Box 2, PATCO.

53. McLucas interview; quotations from McLucas, "Crossing the River," 19, 21; Torchia interview, and Leyden (July 21, 1998) interviews; Memo for the Record,

Leyden, October 17, 1975, Series 100, Box 2, PATCO; Poli to William T. Coleman Jr., October 24, 1975, Series 100, Box 2, PATCO.

54. "Seminar Report," Local 302, Great Falls, Mont., April 3, 1976, Series 100, Box 5, PATCO.

55. Rock, "PATCO History," January 10, 1979; Maher (August 7, 2006) and Moffett interviews.

56. Preston, *Troubled Passage*, 244; Leyden to James A. Jurjevich, August 6, 1976, Series 100, Box 2, PATCO; *WP*, July 29, 1976, A27.

57. Interview with Bob Butterworth, June 26, 2003, by telephone.

58. Preston, *Troubled Passage*, 245; *WP*, July 29, 1976, A27; McLucas, "Crossing the River," 23; *WP*, July 31, 1976, A1; *NYT*, July 30, 1976, A9; July 31, 1976, 9; *GERR*, August 2, 1976, A9; *NYT*, July 31, 1976, 9.

59. Preston, *Troubled Passage*, 246; McLucas, "Crossing the River," 22; Rock, "PATCO History," January 10, 1979.

60. *NYT*, August 1, 1976, 31; *GERR*, August 2, 1976, A9; Preston, *Troubled Passage*, 250.

61. Leyden to William B. Lombardi, August 6, 1976, Series 100, Box 2, PATCO; "playing God" quotation from *WP*, August 12, 1976, A14; dissident quotation from James A. Jurjevich to Leyden, July 30, 1976, JFL Press Conferences file, Box 398, PATCO; "by the balls" quotation from Don McPhail to Leyden, July 30, 1976, JFL Press Conferences file, Box 398, PATCO; Leyden quotation from Leyden to Don McPhail, August 6, 1976, Series 100, Box 4, PATCO.

62. "Minutes of Proceedings of the U.S. Civil Service Commission," November 12, 1976, By the Book Nov. 1976 file, Box 290, PATCO; *GERR*, September 6, 1976, A5.

63. *WP*, September 2, 1976, D9; *GERR*, September 6, 1976, A6; Memorandum, Leyden to the Files, September 2, 1976, Series 100, Box 4, PATCO; Mailgram, Leyden to All Facilities, September 2, 1976, Series 100, Box 4, PATCO.

64. Minutes of the Board of Directors Meeting, September 8–9, 1976, Box 457, PATCO; quotations from Robert E. Olsen to Leyden, September 8, 1976, General Responses to Job Action file, Series 100, Box 222, PATCO and Dom [Torchia] to Leyden, September 6, 1976, General Responses to Job Action, Series 100, Box 222, PATCO; Leyden quotations from "President Leyden's Report," September 8, 1976, Series 100, Box 4, PATCO.

65. "PATCO Reply to the Tentative Standards for Proposed Position Classification Standard for Air Traffic Control Series, GS-2152," n.d. [ca. 1976]; "Minutes of Proceedings of the U.S. Civil Service Commission," November 12, 1976, By the Book November 1976 file, Box 290, PATCO; O'Donnell to Robert E. Hampton, October 12, 1976, Series 100, Box 4, PATCO; Leyden to Morris K. Udall, November 12, 1976, Series 100, Box 4, PATCO; Mo Udall to John Leyden, November 12, 1976, By the Book Nov. 1976 file, Box 290, PATCO; Leyden to Quentin N. Burdick, November 12, 1976, Series 100, Box 4, PATCO; *GERR*, October 25, 1976, A12.

66. Rock, "PATCO History," January 10, 1979; *Chicago Center PATCO News*, October 7, 1976, 2, Regional Newsletters, Box 379, PATCO; McLucas quotations from McLucas interview; Curran interview; "Minutes of Proceedings of the U.S. Civil Service Commission," November 12, 1976, By the Book Nov. 1976 file, Box 290, PATCO; *GERR*, November 15, 1976, A6.

67. "Minutes of Proceedings of the U.S. Civil Service Commission," November 12, 1976, By the Book Nov. 1976 file, Box 290, PATCO; *GERR*, November 15, 1976, A6; *WP*, November 16, 1976, B3.

68. Leyden to Ray Jacobson, November 13, 1976, Classifiscation file, Series 100, Box 222, PATCO; *NYT*, November 13, 1976, 8; Leyden to Ray Jacobson, November 13, 1976, By the Book November 1976 file, Box 290, PATCO; Leyden to Ray Jacobson, November 13, 1976, By the Book November 1976 file, Box 290, PATCO.

69. Coven Headquarters to Regional Vice Presidents, November 15, 1976, Re: War/Peace, By the Book November 1976 file, Box 290, PATCO; Leyden to David Morton, December 2, 1976, Series 100, Box 2, PATCO; Statement by PATCO, November 15, 1976, By the Book November 1976 file, Box 290, PATCO; *WP*, November 16, 1976, B3; *NYT*, November 16, 1976, 33; *GERR*, November 22, 1976, A10.

70. Leyden to Bob Mehling, December 22, 1976, Series 100, Box 4, PATCO; "Vice President's Report," *Rocky Mountain Hi*, January 1977, 2, Regional Newsletters, Box 379, PATCO; Marlton Burks to John Leyden, December 8, 1976, Series 100, Box 4, PATCO.

71. Leyden to Thomas Ferring, December 2, 1976, Series 100, Box 4, PATCO; Leyden to Domenic V. Torchia, December 2, 1976, Series 100, Box 2, PATCO.

72. Leyden to Robert E. Hampton, December 14, 1976, Series 100, Box 4, PATCO; Leyden to Lud Andolsek, January 3, 1977, Series 100, Box 4, PATCO; "Classification Break Points," n.d. [1976], Series 100, Box 4, PATCO; Rock, "PATCO History," January 10, 1979; Leyden to Jack Watson, December 10, 1976, Leyb files, WHF Name File, JCPL.

73. Leyden to Morris K. Udall, January 12, 1977, Series 100, Box 4, PATCO; Rock, "PATCO History," January 10, 1979; Rock (August 13, 2001) and McLucas interviews.

74. "Classification Break Points," n.d. [1977], Series 100, Box 4, PATCO; McLucas, "Crossing the River," 23; Leyden quoted in *GERR*, January 24, 1977, 3; Arthur B. Shostak and David Skocik, *The Air Controllers' Controversy: Lessons from the PATCO Strike* (New York: Human Sciences Press, 1986), 65–66.

75. "A Message to President John F. Leyden from a PATCO Member," *Rocky Mountain Hi*, February 1977, 6, Regional Newsletters, Box 379, PATCO; Norbert Cordiero to Brother Controllers, February 6, 1977, Regional Newsletters, Box 379, PATCO.

76. Gary W. Eads to Leyden, November 18, 1976, and Eads to Fellow PATCO Members, November 15, 1977, Box 1, Kansas City ARTCC PATCO Records, UTA; Maher interview, August 7, 2006.

77. Maher interview, August 7, 2006; Leyden to John C. Lovelace, July 11, 1978, Series 100, Box 2, PATCO.

78. Leyden to John C. Lovelace, July 11, 1978, Series 100, Box 2, PATCO; Leyden to Gary M. Fitzgerald, March 21, 1977, Series 100, Box 2, PATCO; Leyden to Domenic V. Torchia, March 8, 1977, Series 100, Box 2, PATCO.

79. Leyden to Michael S. Elliott, January 21, 1977, Series 100, Box 4, PATCO.

80. Rock, "PATCO History," January 10, 1979.

CHAPTER 7

1. Interview with Rick Jones, June 24, 2002, Fort Washington, Md.
2. Interview with Bob Beatty, August 1, 2002, Fort Washington, Md.; interview with Ralph McKnight, June 29, 2002, by telephone.
3. Beatty and McKnight interviews.
4. Beatty and McKnight interviews.
5. Jones interview.
6. McKnight interview; Timothy B. Tyson, *Radio Free Dixie: Robert F. Williams & The Roots of Black Power* (Chapel Hill: University of North Carolina Press, 1999).
7. "Black/White Air Traffic Control Operational Personnel Meeting—New York Facilities," December 11, 1970, New York Center file, Box 498, PATCO.
8. Jones and McKnight interviews; interview with Charles Bolling, July 23, 2002, Bowie, Md.
9. Jones interview.
10. "June 30, 1968, Minority Group and Female Employment Report," September 24, 1968, Equal Opportunity file, Box 289, FAA; Oscar Bakke to the Secretary of Transportation, November 21, 1968, DOT file, Entry 14, Box 271, FAA; Bertrand M. Harding, Extension of 20% Minority Hiring Policy, June 29, 1971, Equal Opportunity file, Entry 14, Box 353, FAA; interview with Quentin S. Taylor, April 21, 2010, Vienna, Va.
11. Quentin Taylor interview.
12. Beatty and Jones interviews; quotations from "Black/White Air Traffic Control Operational Personnel Meeting—New York Facilities," December 11, 1970, New York Center file, Box 498, PATCO.
13. Beatty and Jones interviews; quotation from Shaffer to EA-1 et al., Re: Survey of Black Air Traffic Controllers, November 20, 1970, Regional-Multiple file, Entry 14, Box 305, FAA; Shaffer to the Secretary, Re: Implementation of the Corson Committee Report (Report #3), June 12, 1970, DOT file, Entry 14, Box 304, FAA "Wanted: Black Air Traffic Controllers," *Ebony* (April 1970): 55; Shaffer to Secretary of Transportation, February 20, 1970, DOT file, Entry 14, Box 303, FAA; and last quotation from Shaffer to All Regions, March 3, 1971, Equal Opportunity file, Entry 14, Box 353, FAA.
14. Shaffer to Secretary of Transportation, May 17, 1971, Equal Opportunity file, Entry 14, Box 353, FAA; Shaffer to Secretary of Transportation, February 9, 1971, DOT file, Box 337, Entry 14, FAA; Shaffer to Secretary of Transportation, August 14, 1972, DOT file, Box 370, Entry 14, FAA; McGuirk interview; "Control Tower Boss at Kennedy," *Ebony* (March 1973): 78.
15. Bolling and Jones interviews; "Control Tower Boss at Kennedy," 78.
16. Quotations from Milton Karchin to Shaffer, n.d. [June 1971], and Mrs. Eddie T. Vanada to Sen. Howard Baker, June 15, 1971, both in Equal Opportunity file, Entry 14, Box 353, FAA; Shaffer to Howard Baker, July 6, 1971, Equal Opportunity file, Entry 14, Box 353, FAA; Leon C. Watkins to ADA-1, June 19, 1978, Equal Opportunity file, Entry 14, Box 446, FAA; last quotation from Frederick Benedict to Henry Cashen, June 15, 1971, Employee Grievance file, Entry 14, Box 354, FAA.
17. Quotation from Concerned Controllers to Bob Poli, n.d. [October 1980], Equal Employment Opportunity Committee file, Box 445, PATCO; Leyden interview,

July 21, 1998; *PMN*, January 1969, 36; *GERR*, November 12, 1973, A10; Leyden quoted in Press Release, November 2, 1973, FAA's EEO Sham file, Box 36, PATCO; Leyden to Robert C. Bateman, November 19, 1973, Series 100, Box 4, PATCO.

18. "Update: 1978 Convention," Black Coalition of Federal Aviation Employees file, Box 421, PATCO.

19. "June 30, 1968, Minority Group and Female Employment Report, September 24, 1968," Equal Opportunity file, Box 289, FAA; quotations from Leyden interview, July 21, 1998; interview with Ed Meagher, May 31, 2002, Washington, D.C.; quarterback quotation from *WP*, November 25, 1965, K3.

20. Interview with Terry Bobell, August 5, 2003, by telephone; interview (quotation) with Steve Elliott, June 10, 2003, Leesburg, Va.

21. Interview with Ed Meagher, May 31, 2003, Washington, D.C.; Jones interview.

22. Quotation from "Air Controllers' Agony," *Newsday*, June 20, 1969, June 1969 folder, Box 512, PATCO; Robert M. Rose, C. David Jenkins, and Michael W. Hurst, *Air Traffic Controller Health Change Study: A Prospective Investigation of Physical, Psychological and Work-Related Changes*, A Report to the FAA on Research Performed Under Contract No. FA73WA-3211 Awarded to Boston University, August 1978, p. 444; Meagher interview; interview with John Haggerty, October 11, 2002, by telephone.

23. Quotations from interview with George Kerr, August 17, 2001, by telephone; interview with Jim Stakem, August 7, 2002, Ashburn, Va.; Mike Rock, "PATCO History," February 14, 1978, p. 42, unmarked file, Box 373, PATCO; Rock (August 13, 1981, and August 4, 1981) and Kerr interviews; *PMN*, November 14, 1968, p. 20.

24. Rose, et al., *Air Traffic Controller Health Change Study*, 37–38.

25. William V. Vitale to All Regions, June 7, 1971, Regions—Multiple 1972 file, Box 367, Entry 14, FAA; Quotations from *NYT*, May 31, 1970, 58; interview with Diane Tyler, November 6, 2002, Reston, Va.

26. Interview with Deborah Katz Pueschel, October 31, 2002, by telephone; interview with Karen (Wessel) Koch, August 8, 2003, by telephone; interview with Cheryl Jenni, October 29, 2002, by telephone; *GERR*, August 25, 1980, 5.

27. Koch quoted in *NYT*, May 31, 1970, 58; Tyler, Pueschel, and Jenni interviews; Leon Watkins to All Headquarters Employees, April 10, 1975 (document in the author's possession).

28. *GERR*, September 29, 1980, 8, January 28, 1980, 10, February 4, 1980, 13; Meachum (quotation), Koch, Jenni, Bobell (quotation) and Jones interviews.

29. Pueschel interview; Affidavit, Deborah A. Katz, August 18, 1981, File 81–34, Entry 14, Box 163, FAA.

30. Jenni, Pueschel, Bobell, and Koch interviews.

31. Koch and Pueschel interviews.

32. Pueschel, Koch, and Jenni interviews; resignation letter, Janice Boyte to Brothers and Sisters, March 10, 1981, Central Region Incoming file, Box 396, PATCO; Grievance Record, Thomas Farrell, June 21, 1980, file AGL-80-623-AMP-3, Series 440, Box 161, PATCO; Tyler interview; quotations from Elliott interview, June 10, 2003; Message to the Ladies quoted in Minutes of the Board of Directors Meeting, October 10–12, 1969, Box 457, PATCO.

33. Jenni interview. See: Nancy MacLean, *Freedom Is Not Enough: The Opening of the American Workplace* (Cambridge, Mass.: Harvard University Press, 2006); Dorothy Sue Cobble, *The Other Women's Movement: Workplace Justice and Social Rights in Modern America* (Princeton: Princeton University Press, 2004).

34. Mostert was later known by her married name, Sue Mostert Townsend. Jacque Smith's married named during part of this period was Jacque Wilson. W. A. Reedholm to A. C. Hall, September 23, 1969 (document in the author's possession).

35. Interview with Sue Mostert Townsend, November 20, 2009, by telephone.

36. Sue Mostert Townsend, "A Historical Walk Through Professional Women Controllers, Inc." http://pwcinc.org/dmdocuments/PWC%20History.pdf (accessed June 10, 2008); *WP*, May 21, 1979, C2; Professional Women Controllers Timeline (document in the author's possession).

37. Townsend interview.

38. Koch interview.

39. Daniel Yankelovich, "The Meaning of Work," in *The Worker and the Job: Coping with Change* (Englewood Cliffs, N.J.: Prentice Hall, 1974), 30, 42; Arnold M. Zack, "Impasses Strikes, and Resolutions," in *Public Workers and Public Unions*, ed. Sam Zagoria (Englewood Cliffs, N.J.: Prentice Hall, 1972), 101; Cary Hershey, *Protest in the Public Service* (Lexington, Mass.: Lexington Books/D.C. Heath, 1973), 1; Lawrence M. Jones, David G. Bowers, and Stephen H. Fuller, "Management and Employee Relationships within the Federal Aviation Administration," 41; Weithoner interview.

40. Statistics from PATCO Questionnaire Number 1, n.d. [1978], January 1979 Board Meeting file, Box 218, PATCO; John L. Cirafici, "CCT at Khe Sanh," *Air Power History* 37:1 (1990): 47–52; Bobell interview; Stakem interview.

41. Interview with John Thornton, August 6, 1998, Washington, D.C.; Meagher interview; interview with Robert Lambrecht, July 24, 2003, by telephone; interview with Carl Kern, July 22, 2003, by telephone.

42. Katherine Newman, "PATCO Lives! Stigma, Heroism, and Symbolic Transformations," *Cultural Anthropology*, 2:3 (August 1987): 322; David G. Bowers, "What Would Make 11,500 People Quit Their Jobs?" *Organizational Dynamics* (Winter 1983): 11; Bobell interview; Terry E. Bobell, "PATCO: An Insider's View," typescript, n.d. [1996] (copy in the author's possession); interview with Rex Campbell, February 24, 2002, by telephone; interview with George Kerr, August 17, 2001, by telephone; interview with Mike Rock interview, August 4, 2001, Las Vegas, Nev.; Arthur B. Shostak, Analysis of PATCO Questionnaire Data, Questionnaire 5, March 1981, box 400, PATCO; interview with Ron Taylor, February 12, 2003, Stewart, Fla.

43. *Federal Times*, July 14, 1971, clipping in Noel Keane Scrapbook (copy in possession of the author); Leyden to E. V. Curran, October 12, 1977, Series 100, Box 2, PATCO; Rock to Terry Snyder, June 28, 1976, Series 100, Box 2, PATCO.

44. Rose et al, *Air Traffic Controller Health Change Study*; Meagher interview; Jenni interview; interview with Carl Kern, July 22, 2003, by telephone; Arthur Hailey, *Airport* (Garden City, N.J.: Doubleday, 1968), 435; interview with Terry Bobell, August 5, 2003, by telephone.

45. Quotation from Meagher interview; interview with Domenic Torchia, May 23, 2002, by telephone; interview with Bill Harding, July 29, 2002, by telephone; interview with Carl Kern, July 22, 2003, by telephone; reports on FAA efforts to police drug use in *WP*, September 19, 1980, B2; *GERR*, October 6, 1980, 6; *GERR*, October 13, 1980, 7.

46. McKnight interview; interview with Ray Van Vuren, March 11, 2002, by telephone; interview with Bob Butterworth, February 1, 2002, by telephone.

47. Meagher interview; July 31, 1974 agreement on Article 61, in Negotiation Binder, Box 198, PATCO.

48. On automation in the white-collar workplace, see Mark McColloch, *White Collar Workers in Transition* (Westport, Conn.: Greenwood Press, 1983), 175; John McLucas, "Crossing the River: My Life at the FAA," unpublished ms., n.d. (in the author's possession), 20; Raymond G. Belanger, "The Electronic Air Force: Automating the Crowded Sky," *Air Force Magazine* 58:7 (1975): 62–63; *NYT*, February 17, 1979, 61.

49. *WP*, November 21, 1979, C3; *WP*, November 7, 1979, C7; quotation from Haggerty interview.

50. Interviews with Bill South, June 28, 2003, and David Siegel, March 27, 2003, by telephone.

51. Paul Stephen Dempsey and Andrew R. Goetz, *Airline Deregulation and Laissez-Faire Mythology* (Westport, Conn.: Quorum Books, 1992), 169–174; Richard H. K. Vietor, "Contrived Competition: Airline Regulation and Deregulation, 1925–1988," *Business History Review* 64:1 (Spring 1990): 74–75; Anthony E. Brown, *The Politics of Airline Deregulation* (Knoxville: The University of Tennessee Press, 1987), 97–98, 101. For an example of such a critique, see Robert Poole Jr., "The Frenzied Skies," *The Freeman* (May 1970): 273–286.

52. *NYT*, February 20, 1975, 66; Stephen Breyer, "Reforming Regulation," *Tulane Law Review* 59 (1984): 19; Anthony E. Brown and Joseph Stewart Jr., "Competing Advocacy Coalitions, Policy Evolution, and Airline Deregulation," in *Policy Change and Learning: An Advocacy Coalition Approach,* ed. Paul A. Sabatier and Hank C. Jenkins-Smith (Boulder, Colo.: Westview Press, 1993), 85–86; Andrew R. Goetz and Christopher J. Sutton, "The Geography of Deregulation in the U.S. Airline Industry," *Annals of the Association of American Geographers* 87:2 (June 1997): 239.

53. Interview with Paul Hallisay, August 28, 2001, Washington, D.C.; interview with J. J. O'Donnell, September 7, 2001, by telephone; Vance H. Trimble, *Overnight Success: Federal Express and Frederick Smith, Its Renegade Creator* (New York: Crown, 1993); interview with Langhorne Bond, November 2, 2002, by telephone; quotation from Meagher interview.

54. "The Public Strikes Back," *Newsweek,* September 18, 1978, 71; "Why So Many Strikes By Public Workers," *U.S. News & World Report,* August 7, 1978, 65; McCartin, "Fire the Hell Out of Them," 78–81. Real income cuts are based on figures in Patrick Purcell, "Federal Employees: Pay and Pension Increases since 1969," *Congressional Research Service* 94–971 (January 20, 2010), 7, and Bureau of Labor Statistics Consumer Price Index, ftp://ftp.bls.gov/pub/special.requests/cpi/cpiai.txt (accessed May 5, 2010); Advisory Committee on Federal Pay, Bureau of Labor Statistics, *A Decade of Federal White-Collar Pay Comparability* (Washington, D.C.,

Advisory Committee on Federal Pay, 1981); Levitan and Noden, *Working for the Sovereign*, 81.

55. Wayne J. Barlow to Richard Nolan, September 20, 1978, Conduct and Discipline file, Box 447, Entry 14, FAA.

56. Neil Vidler, *Under Control: The Story of the International Federation of Air Traffic Controllers' Associations* (Montreal: The Federation, 2001); interview with Harri Henschler, November 6, 2003, by telephone.

57. Statistics from Dennis S. Feldman to David A. Trick, January 21, 1981, Statistics file, Box 204, PATCO.

58. Bruce J. Schulman, *The Seventies: The Great Shift in American Culture, Society, and Politics* (New York: Free Press, 2001), 177; "burbs" quotation from Jonathan King, "One Strike and You're Out," *Sunshine: The Magazine of South Florida* 409 (August 4, 1991): 14; Jenni interview; McGuirk interview; Rose, et al., *Air Traffic Controller Health Change Study*, 38; PATCO Questionnaire Number 1, n.d. [1978], January 1979 Board Meeting file, Box 218, PATCO.

59. Meagher interview; Charles R. Clark, "Unofficial Research Paper," n.d. [1977], FAA Project Professionalism file, Box 220, PATCO.

60. "An Open Letter to Controllers by LAX TRACON Controller's Wife and Family," *Mountain Wave*, n.d. [late 1980] (copy in the author's possession).

CHAPTER 8

1. National Transportation Safety Board, *Aircraft Accident Report: Pacific Southwest Airlines, Inc., Boeing 727–214, N533PPS, and Gibbs Flight Center, Inc., Cessna 172, N7711G, San Diego, California, September 25, 1978*, Report No. NTSB-AAR-79–5 (Washington, D.C.: NTSB, April 20, 1979), 62–65 (copy in the author's possession).

2. Langhorne Bond to Paul Ignatius, January 25, 1978, ATA file, Box 437, Entry 14, FAA; Walter A. Jensen to Quentin S. Taylor, March 27, 1978, ATA file, Box 437, Entry 14, FAA; *NYT*, December 14, 1977, II, 13; *WP*, January 6, 1978, B1; *NYT*, June 24, 1978, 1; *WP*, February 23, 1978, C1.

3. *NYT*, November 21, 1978, 18; NTSB, *Aircraft Accident Report*, 18–20.

4. NTSB, *Aircraft Accident Report*, 1.

5. Leyden to Jesse M. Calhoon, August 9, 1976, Series 100, Box 222, PATCO.

6. W. Langhorne Bond with James E. Ellis, ed., *Wings for an Embattled China* (Bethlehem, Penn.: Lehigh University Press, 2001); McLucas interview, November 16, 2001; *WP*, March 31, 1977, 11; Langhorne McCook Bond resume, Langhorne Bond folder, Box 232, PATCO.

7. Interview with Langhorne Bond, November 2, 2001, by telephone; interview with Ed Curran interview, August 23, 2001, Washington, D.C.

8. *WP*, May 5, 1977, 5; Leyden to Langhorne Bond, June 23, 1977, Series 100, Box 2, PATCO; Leyden to Langhorne Bond, July 5, 1977, Series 100, Box 6, PATCO.

9. Joseph A. McCartin, "Fire the Hell Out of Them: Sanitation Workers' Struggles and the Normalization of Striker Replacement in the 1970s ," *Labor: Studies in the Working-Class History of the Americas* 2:3 (Fall 2005): 79–80.

10. Notes on Article 9, June 20, 1977, Master Copy 1977 Contract Negotiations, Box 554, PATCO; Notes on Article 61, June 28, 1977, Master Copy 1977 Contract Negotiations, Box 554, PATCO; Rock, "PATCO History," January 10, 1979; Office

Memo from Diana Smith August 11, 1975, FAM Trip Correspondence, 1975 file, Box 158, PATCO; FAM Trip Request August–December Departure, 1975 file, Box 158, PATCO; *GERR*, October 4, 1976, A9; *GERR*, June 6, 1977, 6; Robert E. Poli to Matthew E. McGanaghan, October 31, 1977, Series 100, Box 2, PATCO; Dues Resolution file, Box 399, PATCO.

11. Leyden to All Regional Vice Presidents, July 6, 1977, Series 100, Box 2 and Leyden to all Regional VPs, September 22, 1977, Series 100, Box 6, PATCO; *GERR*, July 18, 1977, 8; Bond interview; *GERR*, October 3, 1977, 9; "Western Region Seminar [Minutes]," October 2, 1977, Series 100, Box 5, PATCO.

12. *NYT*, November 19, 1977, 8; Leyden to Meany, November 22, 1977, Series 100, Box 6, PATCO.

13. Rock, "PATCO History," January 10, 1979; Leyden to Meany, November 22, 1977, Series 100, Box 6, PATCO; John F. Leyden to All Regional Vice Presidents, November 30, 1977, and Bill Peer to Dear Sir, December 7, 1977, 1977 Negotiations file, Box 262, PATCO.

14. "Contract Negotiations, Final Agency Position," n.d. [December 12, 1977], 1977 Negotiations file, Box 262, PATCO; Leyden to All Regional Vice Presidents, Re: Proposed Meeting of the Facility Reps on Dec. 15, November 30, 1977, Leyden December 1977 Chronological File, Box 6, PATCO.

15. *WSJ*, December 16, 1977, 13; Leyden to the Files, Re: SF-160 Overseas FAM Program, June 12, 1978, Overseas FAM Trips file, Box 439, PATCO; Rock, "PATCO History," January 10, 1979; *WP*, December 16, 1977, A2.

16. Leyden to Raymond F. Duffield, January 10, 1978, Leyden January 1977 Chronological File, Box 6, PATCO.

17. Sandor M. Polster, "Insubordinate Rank and File," *The Nation*, June 21, 1971, 782–784; Leyden to Bernard Hoffman, May 4, 1979, Series 100, Box 6, PATCO; Leyden quoted in *GERR*, January 2, 1978, 5; "Transcript of Video Tape," 1978, Transcript 1978 Contract file, Box 204, PATCO.

18. *NYT*, February 20, 1978, IV, 7; *GERR*, March 20, 1978, 9; Leyden to Brock Adams, December 27, 1977, Series 100, Box 6, PATCO; Bobell interview; John J. Seddon, "PATCO, A Perspective" (M.A. Thesis, State University of New York Empire State College, 1990), 84; Colin Smith quoted in *Chicago Center PATCO News*, March 24, 1978, Box 378, PATCO.

19. Bond interview; interview with John Leyden, July 21, 1998, Washington, D.C.; Leyden to David J. Crombie, March 30, 1978, Series 100, Box 2, PATCO; Leyden to Francisco A. Lorenzo, March 31, 1978, Series 100, Box 2, PATCO; Memo, Leyden to the Files, March 29, 1978, Series 100, Box 2, PATCO; Leyden to Edwin J. Colodny, Pres. Allegheny Airlines, March 31, 1978, Series 100, Box 6, PATCO.

20. Mike Rock, "PATCO History," January 10, 1979 (tape and transcript in the author's possession); Leyden to Jack Seddon, April 3, 1976, Series 100, Box 6, Leyden to Edward I. Colodny, April 26, 1978, Series 100, Box 2, Leyden to William T. Sewell, April 26, 1978, Series 100, Box 6, and Leyden to G. Brian Smith, July 5, 1978, Series 100, Box 2, PATCO.

21. Interview with Gary Eads, November 7, 2002, Fairfax Station, Va.; interview with Jack Maher, August 7, 2006, by telephone; interview with John Thornton, August 6, 1998, Washington, D.C.

22. The "Big Nine" were: New York Center, New York Common IFR Room, JFK Tower, LaGuardia Tower, Cleveland Center, Chicago Center, O'Hare Tower, Atlanta Tower, and Atlanta Center. Rock, "PATCO History," January 10, 1979; Seddon, "PATCO, A Perspective," 87; interview with Rex Campbell, February 24, 2003, by telephone; interview with Domenic Torchia, May 23, 2002, by telephone.

23. *NYT*, May 27, 1978, 34.

24. Leyden quoted in *WP*, May 24, 1978, B2; *GERR*, May 29, 1978, 5.

25. *WP*, May 27, 1978, A5; *GERR*, June 12, 1978, 7; *WP*, June 7, 1978, C1; *NYT*, June 8, 1978, 24, C1.

26. *NYT*, June 24, 1978, 1; Rock, "PATCO History," January 10, 1979.

27. Leyden to the Files, Re: SF-160 Overseas FAM Program, June 12, 1978, Overseas FAM Trips file, Box 439, PATCO; Leyden interview, July 14, 1998; G. Brian Smith to Leyden, June 20, 1978, Series 100, Box 6, PATCO; interview with James Morin, June 19, 2002, Washington, D.C.; MaryAnne Borick Smith to Leyden, June 21, 1978, and Robert Devery to Leyden, July 5, 1978, Series 100, Box 6, PATCO; Peer interview; *WP*, June 9, 1978, C11.

28. Leyden to Robert Devery, July 5, 1978, Series 100, Box 2, PATCO; Peter L. Brandeis to Patrick D. Moynihan [*sic*], June 30, 1978, Lawrence C. Stern to Langhorne M. Bond, June 23, 1978, R. E. Bennett to Sen. Floyd K. Haskell, July 7, 1978, David H. Sullivan to Senator Schweicker, July 17, 1978, and Donald J. Renner to Congressman Samuel L. Devine, July 5, 1978, all in PATCO file, Box 446, Entry 14, FAA; Leyden to J. J. O'Donnell, June 13, 1978, Series 100, Box 6, PATCO; Capt. L. F. Sullivan to Leyden, July 10, 1978, 1978 Slowdown General file, Box 331, PATCO; interview with Paul Hallisay, August 28, 2001, Washington, D.C.; interview with Andy Anderson, June 3, 2004, by telephone; interview with J. J. O'Donnell, September 7, 2001.

29. *WP*, July 18, 1978, A6; *NYT*, July 18, 1978, Sec. II, 17; Platt quoted in *GERR*, July 24, 1978, 3; Torchia interview, May 23, 2003; *NYT*, June 24, 1978, 1; *GERR*, July 3, 1978, 5; Leyden to Forrest West, July 5, 1978, Series 100, Box 6, PATCO; *WP*, July 20, 1978, A20.

30. Gary M. Fink, "Fragile Alliance: Jimmy Carter and the American Labor Movement," in *The Presidency and Domestic Policies of Jimmy Carter*, ed. Herbert D. Rosenbaum and Alexej Ugrinsky (Westport, Conn.: Greenwood Press, 1994), 783–803; *GERR*, May 30, 1977, 5; *GERR*, August 8, 1977, 8; *GERR*, July 18, 1977, 7.

31. Judith Stein, *Pivotal Decade: How the United States Traded Factories for Finance in the 1970s* (New Haven, Conn.: Yale University Press, 2010), chs. 10–11; *GERR*, October 16, 1978, 6.

32. David Rubinstein to Stu Eizenstat, February 15, 1977, Labor Correspondence file, Box 110 Chief of Staff files, JCPL; Connery quoted in *GERR*, May 30, 1977, 5; Leyden to Lloyd A. Johnson, February 9, 1977, Series 100, Box 4, PATCO; Thomas R. Donahue to Landon Butler, February 22, 1977, AFL-CIO file, Box 85, Chief of Staff Files, JCPL; *GERR*, February 28, 1977, 16; *GERR*, April 25, 1977, 3; *GERR*, April 25, 1977, 3; *GERR*, May 16, 1977, 7.

33. Henry H. Robinson, *Negotiability in the Federal Sector* (Ithaca, N.Y.: New York State School of Industrial and Labor Relations, 1981), 3; Levitan and Noden, *Working*

for the Sovereign, 34; Carter quoted in *GERR*, March 6, 1978, 38–39, and *NYT*, March 3, 1978, 1.

34. *GERR*, April 24, 1978, 6, 8; *GERR*, May 1, 1978, 6.

35. *NYT*, June 8, 1978, A25; *GERR*, June 12, 1978, 16; *GERR*, September 18, 1978, 18; *The Great American Tax Revolt*, Lester A. Sobel, ed. (New York: Facts on File, 1979).

36. Interview with David Denholm, January 28, 2004, Vienna, Va.; "Public Employee Union Bosses Mount New Drive for Federal Law Legalizing Forced Unionism," *National Right to Work Newsletter*, April 29, 1974, 5; Sylvester Petro, *The Labor Policy of a Free Society* (New York, 1957); Petro, "Sovereignty and Compulsory Public-Sector Bargaining" *Wake Forest Law Review*, 10 (March 1974): 25–165 (quotations from pp. 165, 28).

37. Joseph A. McCartin, "A Wagner Act for Public Employees: Labor's Deferred Dream and the Rise of Conservatism, 1970–76," *Journal of American History* 95:1 (June 2008): 123–148; Public Service Research Council, *Public Sector Bargaining and Strikes*, 2nd ed. (Vienna, Va.: The Council, 1976); "The Union Strikes, the Government Capitulates," *Government Union Critique*, November 24, 1978, 7; Eliot Marshall, "The New Feudalism," *The New Republic*, January 20, 1979, 13–16; Anthony Burgess, *1985* (Boston: Little, Brown and Company, 1978). The PSRC's journal was called the *Government Union Review*; its newsletter was called *The Government Union Critique*. Jarvis quoted in *GERR*, October 30, 1978, 9.

38. *GERR*, April 16, 1979, 10; *WSJ*, June 27, 1978, 22; Benjamin Aaron, "Future of Collective Bargaining in the Public Sector," in *Public Sector Bargaining: Industrial Relations Research Association Series*, ed. Benjamin Aaron, Joseph R. Grodin, and James L. Stern (Washington: Bureau of National Affairs, 1979), 294.

39. *GERR*, October 2, 1978, 13; Marla Taylor, *Cost-of-Living Escalators in the Public Sector* (Berkeley, Calif.: Institute of Industrial Relations, 1978), 3; *Junkyard Press* [Local PATCO newsletter], October 1, 1979; *ZBW PATCO Newsletter*, December 1978, Box 378, PATCO; *Western PATCO News*, July 17, 1979, Box 378, PATCO; Statements of Mr. John F. Leyden at Spokane Area Summer Aviation Seminar, August 23, 1979, Papers, Addresses Leyden file, Box 34, PATCO.

40. Sar A. Levitan and Alexandra B. Noden, *Working for the Sovereign: Employee Relations in the Federal Government* (Baltimore: Johns Hopkins University Press, 1983), 35–36; Clay quoted in *GERR*, August 14, 1978, 9; AFGE quoted in *GERR*, August 14, 1978, 8; *GERR*, October 16, 1978, 7.

41. Quesada quoted from *Washington Star*, June 26, 1978, A-9, clipping in Quesada file, Box 238, PATCO; Bond interview; interview with Ray Van Vuren, March 11, 2002, by telephone.

42. Robert M. Rose, C. David Jenkins, and Michael W. Hurst, *Air Traffic Controller Health Change Study: A Prospective Investigation of Physical, Psychological and Work-Related Changes*, A Report to the FAA on Research Performed Under Contract No. FA73WA-3211 Awarded to Boston University, August 1978; FAA Press Release, August 10, 1978, Rose Report file, Box 203, PATCO; Dr. John C. LaRosa to Robert E. Poli, August 15, 1978, Rose Report file, Box 203, PATCO; Leyden to Dr. Phillip L. Polakoff, January 24, 1979, Series 100, Box 4, PATCO.

43. *Rocky Mountain Hi*, February 1977, 2, Regional Newsletters, Box 379, PATCO; *NYT*, November 28, 1976, 26; Philip M. Swatek to AOA-1, December 22, 1976, Personnel Relations and Service file, Box 428, Entry 14, FAA; "Report to Congress on the FAA Reevaluation of Second Career Training," 1979, Reports file, Box 467, Entry 14, FAA; Pat Schroeder to Members of Subcommittee, July 31, 1979, Schroeder file, Box 200, PATCO; Leyden to Pat Schroeder, August 1, 1979, Schroeder file, Box 200, PATCO.

44. Quotations from Bond interview; Bond to Leyden, March 15, 1979, Memos to Facility Reps file, Box 347, PATCO; Leyden to Brock Adams, March 2, 1979, Series 100, Box 4, PATCO; Adams to Leyden, April 3, 1979, Aviation Safety Reporting System file 1, Box 232, PATCO; *WP*, March 27, 1979, A18; *NYT*, April 1, 1979, Sec. 4, 18; Amendment to the Minutes of the Executive Board Meeting of May 12–14, 1979, Leyden 1979 Chronological File, Box 6, PATCO; *GERR*, September 17, 1979, 6.

45. Leyden to Paul Cannon, August 21, 1978, Series 100, Box 6, PATCO.

46. Quotations from Leyden interview, July 14, 1998, and Leyden to Robert Devery, July 5, 1978, Series 100, Box 2, PATCO; Bill Taylor quote from *Newsletter*, September 10, 1978, Box 5, PATCO; Larry Phillips to Leyden, June 29, 1978, Series 100, Box 6, PATCO; *The Black Pit*, July 12, 1978, Box 378, PATCO. This discussion of PATCO factionalism has been enriched by Geoff Johnson and his paper "Democratizing PATCO: A History of Minneapolis Local 305" (in the author's possession).

47. Leyden to Larry Phillips, July 6, 1978, Series 100, Box 6, PATCO; Leyden to Sam Riddles, July 6, 1978, Series 100, Box 2, PATCO; Leyden to Russell J. Verney, July 11, 1978, Series 100, Box 6, PATCO.

48. Courtroul quoted from "Fifth Column Meeting," *Denver PATCO Planet*, August 1978, Box 378, PATCO; interview with Carl Kern, July 22, 2003, by telephone; interview with Bob Butterworth, February 1, 2002, by telephone; Seddon, "PATCO, A Perspective," 92.

49. Quotations from *Skhab Sheet*, July 1980, Box 142, PATCO; "Your Battle, Our Blood," *Seattle Needle*, October 1979, Box 379, PATCO.

50. Torchia and Eads interviews.

51. Minutes of the Board of Directors Meeting, January 12–15, 1979, Box 457, PATCO; Rock, "PATCO History," January 10, 1979.

52. Leyden to the Editor, *ZBW Newsletter*, July 6, 1978, Series 100, Box 6, PATCO.

53. Minutes of the Board of Directors Meeting, September 5–8, 1978, Box 457, PATCO; Eads interview, November 7, 2002; Maher interview, August 7, 2006.

54. Leyden interview, July 21, 1998.

55. Seddon, "PATCO, A Perspective," 92–93.

56. Paul D. Amato to Membership, Local 160, October 31, 1980, PATCO East Regional Correspondence file, Box 347, PATCO; Joseph Wambaugh, *Choirboys* (New York: Delacorte Press, 1975); *The Choirboys*, dir. Robert Aldrich (Universal Films, 1977); Maher (August 7, 2006) interview.

57. *St. Louis Globe-Democrat*, January 15, 1979, 1A, January 16, 1A, March 13, 1A; *WP*, March 13, 1979, A5.

58. Text-2, January 1, 1980, Strike File #1, Box 397, PATCO; interview with Ken Blaylock, June 30, 2003, by telephone.

59. Rock, "PATCO History," January 10, 1979.

60. Leyden to Mike Moss, September 23, 1977, Leyden September–October 1977 Chronological file, Box 6, PATCO; Leyden interview, July 21, 1998; Leyden quotation attached to D. M. Reardon to Richard J. Leighton, May 30, 1980, May Chron file, Box 265, PATCO.

61. Text-2, January 1, 1980, Strike File #1, Box 397, PATCO; Eads interview, November 7, 2002; Stakem interview, August 7, 2002; Thornton interview, August 6, 1998; Ron Taylor interview, February 12, 2002; Nancy Sittig to Membership Services, March 10, 1982, Box 256, PATCO; Leyden interview, July 14, 1998.

62. Arthur B. Shostak and David Skocik, *The Air Controllers' Controversy: Lessons from the PATCO Strike* (New York: Human Sciences Press, 1986), 82; interview with Arthur B. Shostak, April 27, 2008, Washington, D.C.; PATCO Questionnaire Number 1, n.d. [1978], January 1979 Board Meeting file, Box 218, PATCO; Minutes of the Board of Directors Meeting, May 12–14, 1979, Box 457, PATCO; oath quoted in Willis J. Nordlund, *Silent Skies: The Air Traffic Controllers' Strike* (Westport, Conn.: Praeger, 1998), 6. The outlook of PATCO members on strikes did not differ significantly from that of other federal workers. See Louis V. Imundo, *Why Federal Government Employees Join Unions: A Study of AFGE Local 91, at Tinker Air Force Base* (Norman, Okla.: Bureau for Business and Economic Research, University of Oklahoma, 1972), 30.

63. Kern interview; Poli quoted in "Minutes of the PATCO General Membership, November 15, 1979," Meeting Minutes file, Box 3, DFW Tower PATCO Records, PATCO/UTA.

64. "The Public Strikes Back," *Newsweek*, September 18, 1978, 71; "Why So Many Strikes By Public Workers," *U.S. News & World Report*, August 7, 1978, 65; Barry Crickmer, "Strike: Halting Public Worker Walkouts," *Nation's Business*, September 1980, 33; Poli to Committee Members, Re: American Federation of Teachers Strike Plan, September 6, 1979, Box 264, PATCO.

65. 1977 Rep School Contracts file, Box 21, PATCO; Leyden to All Instructors, July 20, 1978, Rep School Correspondence file, Box 21, PATCO; Maher to Leyden et al., July 21, 1977, Rep School Correspondence file, Box 21, PATCO; Minutes of the National Finance Committee Meeting, Apr. 20–21, 1980, Financial Report file, Box 1, AR 397 PATCO Local 332 Records, PATCO/UTA; Harding interview. The IWW book was Joyce L. Kornbluh, *Rebel Voices: An I.W.W. Anthology* (Ann Arbor: University of Michigan Press, 1964).

66. "Editorial," *PATCO Progressive*, August 22, 1979; "From the President," *The Apple Source*, August–September 1979; "Analysis of Questionnaire Number 3," *Seattle Needle*, November 1979; "Postal Settlement," *Great Lakes PATCO News*, September 26, 1978, all Box 378, PATCO; Arthur B. Shostak, Analysis of PATCO Questionnaire Data, Report 1: National and Builder Data, Questionnaires 2 and 3, January 1980, and Arthur B. Shostak, "Analysis of PATCO Questionnaire Data, Report 2: Regional and 'Builder' Data," February 1980, Shostak Report #2 file, Box 400, PATCO; interview with Mike Rock, August 13, 2001, Islip, N.Y.; interview with David Siegel, June 27, 2003, by telephone.

CHAPTER 9

1. Interview with John Leyden, July 14, 1998, Washington, D.C.; Poli to Leyden, January 3, 1980, 1980 and Leyden to Poli, January 3, 1980, 1980 Elections file, Box 382, PATCO.
2. Poli to the Committee, Re: Board Meeting, October 11, 1979, Chron file, Box 264, PATCO; Leyden interview, August 4, 2001; interview with Domenic Torchia, May 23, 2002, by telephone; Bill Taylor, *Newsletter*, March 20, 1979, box 5, PATCO; "Editorial," *ZBW PATCO Newsletter*, March 1978, Box 378, PATCO; Resolution 7, 1979 PATCO Convention, 1979 Convention Resolutions file, Box 383, PATCO.
3. Leyden to Michael V. Krause, June 16, 1977, Series 100, Box 2, PATCO; Leyden to Kenny G. King, February 1, 1979, Series 100, Box 4, PATCO.
4. Interviews with Mike Rock, August 4, 2001, Las Vegas, Nev., and August 13, 2001, Islip, N.Y.; interview with John Leyden, August 4, 2001, Las Vegas, Nev.; interview with David Siegel, June 27, 2003, by telephone; interview with Jack Maher, August 7, 2006, by telephone; interview with Gary Eads, November 7, 2002, Fairfax Station, Va.; Torchia interview.
5. Leyden interview, July 14, 1998.
6. Leyden interview, July 14, 1998; interview with George Kerr, August 17, 2001, by telephone; interview with John Thornton, August 6, 1998, Washington, D.C.; interview with John J. Haggerty, October 11, 2002, by telephone.
7. Leyden (July 14, 1998), Kerr, and Torchia interviews; National Executive Board to Bill Lombardi, January 12, 1980, John F. Leyden (resignation) file, Box 399, PATCO.
8. Notes signed by Torchia and Campbell, January 8, 1980, John F. Leyden (resignation) file, Box 399, PATCO; Resolution, January 8, 1980, Executive Board Resolutions, Box 457, PATCO; Torchia, Kerr, Leyden (July 14, 1998, and August 4, 2001), Peer, Charlie Campbell, Eads, and Maher (August 7, 2006) interviews; Addendum to the Minutes of the Board of Directors Meeting, January 7–8, 1980, Box 457, PATCO.
9. Interview with John Leyden, July 21, 1998, Washington, D.C.; Resolution, February 1, 1980, Executive Board Resolutions, Box 457, PATCO; Minutes of Conference Call, February 1, 1980, Conference Calls file, Box 347, PATCO; Memorandum from Robert E. Poli to Choirboys, January 10, 1980, Re: Proposed Expansion of the Choirboy Program, "Mon." file, Box 1, Dennis Reardon/PATCO Records, PATCO/UTA.
10. Interview with Bill Harding, June 29, 2002, by telephone; Dirk J. P. Visser IV to Dick Swauger, n. d. [February 1, 1980], Arthur J. Brooks to PATCO National Board, February 7, 1980, Leyden to All Facility Reps, January 9, 1980, Leyden Resignation file, Box 399, PATCO.
11. Anthony J. Skirlick Jr. to Dominic Torchia, February 29, 1980, Regional Correspondence PATCO West 1980 file, Box 290, PATCO; Anthony J. Skirlick Jr. to Editor, *Flying Magazine*, July 21, 1984, ALPA Scab Case file, Box 28, WJU.
12. Kerr to Poli, January 28, 1980, Robert E. Meyer to Poli, February 1, 1980, and Galloway to Poli, February 4, 1980, 1980 Elections file, Box 382, PATCO; Poli to Galloway, January 30, 1980, Chron file, Box 264, PATCO; Kerr interview.

13. Campaign Update, n.d. [1980] and Controllers for Kerr and Galloway to All PATCO Members, Re: Chicago, n.d. [March 1980], Blue File, Box 1, KCARTCC, PATCO/UTA; quotations from Kerr interview; Poli to Kerr and Thomas G. Galloway, March 13, 1980, Regional Correspondence file, Box 396, PATCO; Eads to Dear Brothers and Sisters, April 3, 1980, Box 1, Kansas City ARTCC PATCO Records, PATCO/UTA.

14. Quotation from Bruce W. Campbell to Poli, n.d. [January 1980], Eastern Region Incoming file, Box 347, PATCO; Elliott and Kerr interviews; quotation from *Open Mike*, April 1980, Box 380, PATCO; quotation from Elliot M. Simons to Poli, August 21, 1980, MacNeill/Lehrer file, Box 209, PATCO.

15. Minutes of the National Finance Committee Meeting, April 20–21, 1980, Financial Report file, Box 1, PATCO Local 332 Records, PATCO/UTA; *Boston Terminal Crier*, Summer 1980, Box 380, PATCO; quotation from Larry Phillips to Poli, April 28, 1980, 1980 Convention Invitations and Responses file, Box 382, PATCO; *The Roll Call*, 1980 News File, Box 380, PATCO.

16. *NYT*, August 4, 1981, B8; *WP*, August 7, 1981, A5.

17. Siegel and Torchia interviews; interview with Terry Bobell, August 5, 2003, by telephone; interview with Rex Campbell, February 24, 2002, by telephone; interview with Charlie Campbell, February 11, 2002, by telephone; interview with Bill Peer, July 1, 2004, Bethany Beach, Del.; interview with Kenneth Moffett, Washington, D.C.; Leyden and Curran, unpublished book manuscript, p. 91.

18. Interview with Langhorne Bond, November 2, 2001, by telephone; interview with Jesse Calhoon, August 24, 2001, by telephone; interview with J. J. O'Donnell, September 7, 2001, by telephone.

19. FLRA Charge Against Labor Organization or its Agents, January 31, 1980, 4-CO-15, Box 296, PATCO; Anthony J. Maimone to President Carter, January 21, 1980, PATCO FBI Investigation file, Box 400, PATCO; Press Release, September 24, 1980, Aeroflot Incident file, Box 142, PATCO; Thomas R. Jones to Ronald Palmer, May 1, 1980, Ronald Palmer file 1, Box 142, PATCO; Ronald Palmer files, 1–2, Box 142, PATCO; *GERR*, December 1, 1980, 7; "Angry Air Controllers Prepare Tough Tactics in Fight on FAA Pact," *WSJ*, July 2, 1980, 1; *GERR*, December 1, 1980, 7.

20. Bond interview; Philip B. Heymann to Bond, September 22, 1978, PATCO file, Box 446, Entry 14, RG 237, NA; Bruce D. Rosenstein to Edward V. Curran, November 20, 1980, Strike file, Box 42, PATCO; *GERR*, December 1, 1980, 9; *GERR*, March 20, 1978, 18; quotation from Lee T. Patterson and John Liebert, *Management Strike Handbook: A Guide to Handling Public Employee Strikes* (Chicago: International Personnel Management Association, 1974), 5–6; Leyden to Bond, May 9, 1979, Series 100, Box 6, PATCO; *GERR*, November 24, 1980, 6.

21. Bond interview; interview with Ray Van Vuren, March 11, 2002, by telephone.

22. Van Vuren interview.

23. Bond and Van Vuren (quotation) interviews; Langhorne Bond to Regional and Center Directors, Re: Job Action Contingency Plan, October 9, 1980, Alleged Strike 1981 File, Box 221, PATCO.

24. Interview with Ed Curran, August 23, 2001, Washington, D.C.; D. M. Reardon to Richard J. Leighton, May 30, 1980, May Chron file, Box 265, PATCO; *NYT*, August

26, 1980, 14; *WP*, October 5, 1980, B2; Van Vuren interview; *GERR*, October 6, 1980, 11–12; quotations from Bond interview.

25. Quotations from Poli to Curran, October 3, 1980, Chron file, Box 330, PATCO; interview with Brian Flores, July 29, 2002, Washington, D.C.

26. Maher interview, August 7, 2006; Poli to Facility Representatives, August 14, 1980, Memos to Facility Reps file, Box 347, PATCO; William C. Humphrey to James E. Lyons, August 7, 1980, Correspondence with PATCO file, Box 1, James D. Wright Papers, PATCO/UTA; Jack Maher to David E. Pentz, September 23, 1980, Benefits Committee Correspondence 1980 #2, Box 400, PATCO; Leyden and Curran, unpublished book manuscript, p. 95; quotations from Paul Hadley et al. to Brothers and Sisters, August 4, 1980, Folder 14, Box 1, James Wright Collection, PATCO/UTA.

27. Minutes of Conference Call, July 8, 1980, Conference Calls file, Box 347, PATCO; Robert E. Meyer to Michael Ryan, October 29, 1980, Finance Committee file, Box 311, PATCO; Poli to Facility Representatives, July 30, 1980, Memos to Facility Reps file, Box 347, PATCO; William C. Humphrey to PATCO Employees Union, August 7, 1980, PEU file, Box 172, PATCO; *WP*, January 4, 1982, A10; Maher interviews, August 7, and 8, 2006.

28. Elliot M. Simons to Poli, August 21, 1980, MacNeill/Lehrer file, Box 209, PATCO; "PATCO Moves Warily Toward Contract Talks," *Federal Times*, September 8, 1980; quotation from Michael Bern to Jim Miller, September 4, 1980, PEU file, Box 172, PATCO; Poli to Member, August 28, 1980, Internal PATCO file, Box 42, PATCO.

29. Robert E. Meyer to All Facility Representatives, July 30, 1980, Memos to Facility Reps file, Box 347, PATCO; Paul Hadley et al. to Dear Brothers and Sisters, August 4, 1980, Folder 14, Box 1, James Wright Collection, PATCO/UTA. The NLRB found PATCO guilty of committing an unfair labor practice, although the decision did not come until after the decertification of the union. *WP*, January 4, 1982, A10; Rock interview, August 13, 2001.

30. PATCO Questionnaire Number 1, n.d. [1978], January 1979 Board Meeting file, Box 218, PATCO; Arthur B. Shostak, Analysis of PATCO Questionnaire Data, Questionnaire 5, March 1981, Box 400, PATCO.

31. Sar A. Levitan and Alexandra B. Noden, *Working for the Sovereign: Employee Relations in the Federal Government* (Baltimore: Johns Hopkins University Press, 1983), 78–79; *Comparative growth in compensation for postal and other Federal employees since 1970: Report to the Congress by the Comptroller General of the United States* (Washington, D.C.: General Accounting Office, 1979), as cited in *GUC*, March 2, 1979, 4; consumer price index calculations based on BLS statistics published in the Consumer Price Index for All Urban Consumers (CPI-U), ftp://ftp.bls.gov/pub/special.requests/cpi/cpiai.txt (accessed November 8, 2010).

32. Text-2, January 1, 1980, Strike File #1, Box 397, PATCO; "Text #1," n.d. [ca. 1980]; "Mon." file, Box 1, Dennis Reardon/PATCO Records, PATCO/UTA.

33. Maher interview, August 7, 2006; quotations from Karl F. Aeppli to Fellow Controllers, July 23, 1980, Negotiations 1980–81 file, Dennis Reardon/PATCO Records, PATCO/UTA; quotation from Robert L. Cotte to George Brandon, May 23, 1980, Contract Negotiations General Correspondence 1 file, Box 209, PATCO.

34. *GERR*, October 6, 1980, 12; *GERR*, May 2, 1977, 7; *ChiTr*, August 16, 1980, S1; interview with Dick Shaftic, June 18, 2004, by telephone.

35. *ChiTr*, August 17, 1980, 2; Curran to Poli, August 17, 1980, 1980 Slowdown O'Hare file, Box 331, PATCO; *NYT*, August 18, 1980, 12:6; *ChiTr*, August 18, 1980, 12; *ChiTr*, August 19, 1980, 3; Poli quotation from Presidential Update, August 22, 1980, Memos to Facility Reps file, Box 347, PATCO; Minutes of Conference Call, August 18, 1980, Conference Calls file, Box 347, PATCO; traveler quoted in *ChiTr*, August 24, 1980, A4.

36. Rex Campbell interview; PATCO's leaders in Syracuse made arguments similar to Campbell's in Information Letter, Jeff Hall, n.d. [October 1980], PATCO East Regional Correspondence file, Box 347, PATCO; Bowers, "What Would Make 11,500 People Quit Their Jobs," 9.

37. Memo, George Kerr to Facility Representatives, November 7, 1980, Contract 1981 file, Box 221, PATCO; Rock quoted in *WP*, November 25, 1968, A14.

38. Poli to Dear Member, October 1, 1980, unmarked file, Box 311, PATCO; Eads quotation from *The Sentinel*, October 1980, Box 1, Kansas City ARTCC PATCO Records, PATCO/UTA.

39. D. M. Reardon to George W. Kerr, October 17, 1980, Contract 1981 file, Box 221, PATCO; D. M. Reardon to Charles Campbell, October 17, 1980, Benefits Committee Correspondence 1980 #2, Box 400, PATCO; Flores interview, July 29, 2002; Gaffney interview, August 9, 2006; "Kool-Aid" quotation from Powderly interview; John R. Hall, *Gone from the Promised Land: Jonestown in American Cultural History* (New Brunswick, N.J.: Transaction Books, 1987); "embarrassment" quotation from interview with Pete Kellum, August 10, 2006, by telephone; Anthony J. Skirlick Jr. to Dominic Torchia, February 29, 1980, Regional Correspondence, PATCO West 1980 file, Box 290, PATCO.

40. Bond interview.

41. Robert E. Meyer, *Great Lakes PATCO News*, April 26, 1978, Box 378; *ZBW Newsletter*, February 1978, Box 378, PATCO; Leyden to Tom Scanlan, December 2, 1977, Series 100, Box 6, PATCO; Eads quotation from *The Sentinel*, March 1980, Newsletters file, Box 1, Kansas City ARTCC PATCO Records, PATCO/UTA.

42. Interview with Ken Young, November 30, 2001, Silver Spring, Md.

43. Interview with Ken Blaylock, June 30, 2003, by telephone.

44. Joseph C. Goulden, *Jerry Wurf: Labor's Last Angry Man* (New York: Atheneum, 1982); Blaylock interview.

45. Todd Holmes, "The Economic Roots of Reaganism: Corporate Conservatives, Political Economy, and the United Farm Workers Movement," *Western Historical Quarterly* 41:1 (Spring 2010): 55–80; interview with David Denholm, January 28, 2004, Vienna, Va.

46. California Public Employment Relations Board, *2000–2001 Annual Report* (Sacramento: October 15, 2001), 10; Jack Blackburn and Gloria Busman, *Understanding Unions in the Public Sector: A Policy and Practice Publication* (Los Angeles: Institute of Industrial Relations, University of California at Los Angeles, 1977), 145.

47. *SacU*, July 18, 1969, 1; *SFEx*, July 18, 1969, 1; *SFEx*, July 22, 1969, 3; *SacU*, July 22, 1969, C8; Winston W. Crouch, *Organized Civil Servants: Public Employer-Employee*

Relations in California (Berkeley: University of California Press, 1978), 89, 234; editorial quoted, *SFEx,* July 22, 1969, 34; Reagan quoted in Allen Z. Gammage and Stanley L. Sachs, *Police Unions* (Springfield, Ill.: Charles C. Thomas Publisher, 1972), 64, and *SFEx,* July 21, 1969, 7; *SFC,* July 14, 1969, 1; *LAT,* July 19, 1969, 18; Denholm interview.

48. *LAT,* May 23, 1972, 3; *SFC,* May 24, 1972, 9; *SDU,* May 26, 1972, B16; Reagan quoted in *SacU,* May 24, 1972, A1, and *LAT,* May 24, 1972, 3; *LAT,* May 26, 1972, 3; *SacU,* May 25, 1972, A3; *SFEx,* May 23, 1972, 3; *SFEx,* May 26, 1972, 11; *SFC,* May 27, 1972, 8; *SacU,* May 27, 1972, A1; *NYT,* May 27, 1972, 12; Crouch, *Organized Civil Servants,* 41, 236; Ronnie G. Cebulski and Clara Stern, "A Five-Year Study of California Public Employee Strikes," *California Public Employment Review* No. 25 (August 1975).

49. Interview with Robert Bonitati, August 23, 2001, Alexandria, Va.; Calhoon interview; interview with Edwin Meese III, February 1, 2005, Washington, D.C.

50. Denholm interview.

51. On Balzano and Nixon, see *WSJ,* June 21, 1972, 1. Mr. Balzano would not consent to an on-the-record interview for this book.

52. Richard Leighton to Michael Balzano, October 20, 1980, Box 34F, Fred Fielding Files, RRPL; Richard Leighton to William French Smith, June 30, 1981, Box 34F, Fred Fielding Files, RRPL.

53. Ronald Reagan to Robert E. Poli, October 20, 1980, Reagan Endorsement file, Box 203, PATCO.

54. Torchia and Siegel interviews; Richard Leighton to William French Smith, June 30, 1981, Box 34F, Fred Fielding Files, RRPL; "warmth" quotation from Poli to Editors of all national newspapers, August 9, 1981, Media Contacts file, Box 221, PATCO; *WP,* October 24, 1980, C3; *NYT,* October 24, 1980, A16.

55. Memo, Poli to All Local Presidents, October 22, 1980, Chron file, Box 330, PATCO; *WP,* October 24, 1980, C2; Stakem, Carver, Harding, Ron Taylor, and South interviews; Mary Senecal to Poli, November 3, 1980, Support Groups file, Box 438, PATCO.

56. Poli to Mary H. Senecal, November 18, 1980, Chron file, Box 330, PATCO; Rock interview, August 13, 2001.

CHAPTER 10

1. *WP,* November 8, 1980, F1.

2. Arch Puddington, *Lane Kirkland: Champion of American Labor* (Hoboken, N.J.: John Wiley & Sons, 2005), 117; interview with Thomas Donahue, October 11, 2001, Washington, D.C.; Robert Bonitati to Ed Meese and Jim Baker, May 19, 1981, AFL-CIO File, Robert Bonitati Files, RRPL; Donald J. Devine, *Reagan's Terrible Swift Sword: Reforming & Controlling the Federal Bureaucracy* (Ottawa, Ill.: Jameson Books, Inc., 1991), 5.

3. *GERR,* November 17, 1980, 8; *GERR,* November 24, 1980, 7.

4. AFL-CIO political director Al Barkan quoted in *NYT,* November 9, 1980, 30; Robert W. Searby, "Organized Workers and the Potential for a Republican-Conservative Governing Majority," n.d. [November 1980], Labor Strategy 6 file, OA 6845, Robert Bonitati Files, RRPL; Bob Bonitati to Elizabeth Dole, Re: Meeting

with Lyn Nofziger on June 12, June 11, 1981, Labor Strategy 1 file, OA 6845, Robert Bonitati Files, RRPL.

5. "A Suggested Labor Strategy," n.d. [1981], Labor Strategy 1 file, OA 6845, Robert Bonitati Files, RRPL.

6. Interview with Robert Bonitati, August 23, 2001, Alexandria, Va.

7. A. H. Raskin, "Lane Kirkland: New Style for Labor," *New York Times Magazine* (October 29, 1979): 4–5; Paul Buhle, *Taking Care of Business: Samuel Gompers, George Meany, Lane Kirkland and the Tragedy of American Labor* (New York: Monthly Review Press, 1999), 205; Puddington, *Lane Kirkland*, 116–135.

8. Kirkland quotations from interview with Ken Young, November 30, 2001, Silver Spring, Md.; "Minutes of Meeting of the Executive Council of the American Federation of Labor and Congress of Industrial Organizations," May 7–8, 1981, Box 18, IAM; Bonitati interview.

9. Interview with Ken Young, November 30, 2001, Silver Spring, Md.; interview with Edwin Meese III, February 1, 2005, Washington, D.C.; Opinion Research Survey Inc., "National Survey of AFL-CIO Union Members," August 1980, AFL-CIO file, i-iii, Robert Bonitati Files, RRPL; Richard V. Allen to Bob Bonitati, September 28, 1981, AFL-CIO file, Robert Bonitati Files, RRPL.

10. "A Suggested Labor Strategy," n.d. [1981], Labor Strategy 1 file, OA 6845, Robert Bonitati Files, RRPL.

11. Interview with Drew Lewis, June 22, 2004, Schwenksville, Pa.; *WP*, August 9, 1981, A10; interview with Mark Knause, June 27, 2003, Washington, D.C..

12. Lewis interview; *LAT*, August 7, 1981, p. 1; interview with J. Lynn Helms, May 3, 2002, Westport, Conn.; Knause interview.

13. Helms interview; *NYT*, August 11, 1981, B9; Meese interview.

14. "Transcript of Personal Interview with FAA Administrator J. Lynn Helms, conducted by Nick A. Komons and Edmund Preston, Jan. 23, 25, 26, 1984," FAA Historian's Office (copy in the author's possession), p. 78; Helms interview; Charles Heatherly, ed., *Mandate for Leadership: Policy Management in a Conservative Administration* (Washington, D.C.: The Heritage Foundation, 1981), 630–631. In a handwritten note to David Gergen, written in the margins of a copy of Reagan's October 20, 1980, letter to Poli, Craig Fuller wrote: "PATCO reviewed Helms—no objection." See Ronald Reagan to Robert E. Poli, October 20, 1980, OA 10520, David Gergen Files, RRPL.

15. Lewis and Knause interviews; interview with Lee Verstandig, August 4, 2003, Alexandria, Va.; Helms interview; *WP*, May 29, 1983, A17.

16. Kenneth Cribb to Craig Fuller, Re: Information from Drew Lewis on PATCO Situation, March 6, 1981, WHORM Subject File PE001 (000141CA), RRPL; Craig L. Fuller to the President, Re: Air Traffic Controller Negotiations, June 18, 1981, OA 10520, David Gergen Files, RRPL; quotation from Janet Rice to Annelise Anderson, Re: Status of FAA Negotiations with the Professional Air Traffic Controllers Organization (PATCO), March 3, 1981, PATCO Strike File 2, OA 10974, Box 4, Craig L. Fuller Files, RRPL; "1981 Professional Air Traffic Controllers Organization Negotiations," February 7, 1981, PATCO file 4, OA 6850, Robert Bonitati Files, RRPL.

17. Interview with George A. Stohner, December 2, 2010, Washington, D.C.; Leyden and Curran, unpublished book manuscript, p. 122 (in the author's possession).

18. Interview with Mike Rock, August 4, 2001, Las Vegas, Nev.; interview with Brian Flores, July 29, 2002, Washington, D.C.; interview with Kenneth Moffett, August 28, 2001, Washington, D.C.; Katharine Graham, *Personal History* (New York: Alfred A. Knopf, 1997), 519, 526, 529, 543, 554–555, 572.

19. Flores interview.

20. "The Air Controller Bid for More Pay," *Business Week*, May 4, 1981, 55, 58.

21. "Federal Worker Unions Prepare to Strike," *GUC*, October 10, 1980, 3; "PATCO Braced for Long Strike," *GUC*, June 19, 1981, 7; William H. Shaker [of the National Tax Limitation Committee] to Ed Meese, June 9, 1981, WHORM Subject File LA005–013 (029,148), RRPL; Minutes of Executive Board Meeting, May 19–21, 1981, New Orleans, Executive Board Minutes file, Box 399, PATCO; Denholm quotation from Denholm interview, January 28, 2004; letters quoted are Col. John T. Dabinett to Ronald Reagan, June 20, 1981, WHORM Subject File PE001 (030,788), RRPL, and JCH to the President, June 18, 1981, OA 6850, Robert Bonitati Files, RRPL.

22. Poli quoted in "The Air Controller Bid for More Pay," 55; Stohner interview.

23. "The Air Controller Bid for More Pay," 55, 58; Minutes of Executive Board Meeting, May 19–21, 1981, New Orleans, Executive Board Minutes file, Box 399, PATCO; Poli quoted in *WP*, May 24, 1981, A18; interview with Terry Bobell, August 5, 2003, by telephone; Flores interview; Arthur Shostak interview with Bill Taylor, October 18, 1985, File 1, Box 8, Arthur B. Shostak Collection, PATCO/UTA.

24. Ken Cribb to Craig Fuller, Re: Potential PATCO Job Action, May 26, 1981, PATCO file, Subject File OA 10974, Box 4, Craig L. Fuller Files, RRPL; Meese interview; Ken Cribb to Craig Fuller, Re: FAA Contingency Plan in the Event of a PATCO Strike, PATCO file, OA 10974, Box 4, Craig L. Fuller Files, RRPL.

25. Devine, *Reagan's Terrible Swift Sword*, 30–31; Meese interview; quotation from Bonitati interview.

26. Glenn Schleede to Craig Fuller, Re: Air Traffic Controllers, June 5, 1981, PATCO Strike File 2, OA 10974, Box 4, Craig L. Fuller Files, RRPL; Kenneth Cribb to Craig Fuller, Re: 6/5 Meeting on PATCO at Transportation, June 5, 1981, PATCO Strike File 2, OA 10974, Box 4, Craig L. Fuller Files, RRPL.

27. Drew Lewis to Ed Meese, Re: PATCO, June 11, 1981, PATCO Strike File 1, OA 10974, Box 4, Craig L. Fuller Files, RRPL; "Assessment of Controller Strike Potential Impact," June 10, 1981, PATCO Strike File 1, OA 10974, Box 4, Craig L. Fuller Files, RRPL.

28. Stohner interview; "Considerations," n.d. [June 11, 1981], PATCO Strike File 2, OA 10974, Box 4, Craig L. Fuller Files, RRPL; Meese and Lewis interviews; Kenneth Cribb to Craig Fuller, Re: PATCO, June 12, 1981, WHORM Subject File PE001 (029749CA), RRPL.

29. Interview with Alex Hendriks, November 13, 2003, by telephone.

30. Grievance of Dwayne A. Theadford, Employer's Brief, AWE-80–264(20A)-3, n.d., Box 525, PATCO.

31. Lawrence M. Jones, David G. Bowers, and Stephen H. Fuller, "Management and Employee Relationships Within the Federal Aviation Administration," 12;

interview with Charles Bolling, July 23, 2002, Bowie, Md.; Bobell interview; interview with Bill Harding, June 29, 2002, by telephone; quotation from interview with Dick Shaftic, June 18, 2004.

32. Shaftic and Bobell interviews; interview with Mike Powderly, July 29, 2003, by telephone; "Bound and Determined," *Junkyard Press*, February 1, 1980; quotation from interview with Ed Meagher, May 31, 2002, Washington, D.C..

33. Interview with Sid McGuirk, June 18, 2002, Washington, D.C.; interviews with Mike Powderly, July 29, 2003, Robert Mischke Sr., June 24, 2004, and John J. Haggerty, October 11, 2002, by telephone ; Peter T. Durmer to Ronald Reagan, May 29, 1981, WHORM Subject File PE001 (029,225), RRPL.

34. Lewis, Flores, and Moffett interviews.

35. Moffett interview; Poli quoted in Flores interview.

36. Moffett and Flores interviews; Gary Eads to Ronald Reagan, June 15, 1981, WHORM Subject File PE001 (029,587), RRPL.

37. Craig L. Fuller to the President, Re: Air Traffic Controller Negotiations, June 18, 1981, OA 10520, David Gergen Files, RRPL [original of this memo can also be found at: WHORM Subject File PE001 (01,965,155), RRPL].

38. Ted Schwinden to Ronald Reagan, June 15, 1981, WHORM Subject File PE001 (029,225), RRPL; JCH to the President, June 18, 1981, OA 6850, Robert Bonitati Files, RRPL; interview with Donald Devine, August 7, 2003, Alexandria, Va. (notes in the author's possession); Meese interview; "6/20/81, PATCO" [Handwritten notes], OA 10520, David Gergen Files, RRPL.

39. Poli quotation from ABC News Transcripts, June 21, 1981 Sunday, Weekend News Sunday Late, LexisNexis; Stohner interview; Record of Meeting, June 21, 1981, FMCS, Daily Negotiation File, Box 2, Dennis Reardon Collection, PATCO/UTA.

40. Moffett, Flores, and Stohner interviews.

41. Anthony Joseph Skirlick Jr., "Forum: Why One PATCO Man Didn't Strike," *Federal Times*, November 1, 1981; interview with Cheryl Jenni, October 29, 2002, by telephone; interview with Rich Andrews, August 11, 2003, by telephone; interview with Ron Taylor, February 12, 2003, Stewart, Fla.; interview with Terry Bobell, August 5, 2003, by telephone.

42. Calculations based on the work of Edwin M. Wintermeyer, "An Insider's View of the Professional Air Traffic Controllers Organization with Special Emphasis on the Air Traffic Controllers Strike of 1981" (M.A. thesis, St. Francis College, 1989), 27–29.

43. Flores interview; quotation from Reardon's Record of Meeting, June 21, 1981, FMCS, Daily Negotiation File, Box 2, Dennis Reardon Collection, PATCO/UTA; interview with Domenic Torchia, May 23, 2003, by telephone.

44. Flores, Moffett, and Stohner interviews; quotation from Reardon's Record of Meeting, June 21, 1981, FMCS, Daily Negotiation File, Box 2, Dennis Reardon Collection, PATCO/UTA; Poli quoted in *NYT*, June 23, 1981, 16.

45. Haggerty, Bobell, Butterworth, Meagher, Jenni, Ron Taylor, Meachum, and Powderly interviews; interview with Ray Carver, July 27 2003, by telephone; interview with Tom Gaffney, August 8, 2006, by telephone; interview with Craig T. Wood, November 9, 2003, by telephone; interview with Carl Kern, July 22, 2003; and interview with Rich Andrews, August 11, 2003, by telephone.

46. Quotations from Levitan and Noden, *Working for the Sovereign*, 102; Herbert R. Northrup, "The Rise and Demise of PATCO," *Industrial and Labor Relations Review* 37 (January 1984): 176; interview with Jesse Calhoon, August 24, 2001, by telephone; interview with Langhorne Bond, November 2, 2001, by telephone; interview with Donald J. Devine, August 7, 2003, Alexandria, Va. (notes in the author's possession); interview with Ray Van Vuren, March 11, 2002, by telephone.

47. Denholm interview; "Disaster Movies in the Making," *National Right to Work Newsletter*, June 29, 1981, 5; "PATCO Settlement Sets Precedent," *GUC*, July 3, 1981, 6; "FAA-PATCO Negotiations Legality Questioned," *GUC*, July 31, 1981, 1.

48. Lewis and Verstandig interviews.

49. Harding (quotations) and Haggerty interviews.

50. Wintermeyer and Gulbranson quoted in *NYT*, June 25, 1981, 15; Carver, Ron Taylor, and Meagher interviews.

51. Interview with Jim Morin, June 19, 2002, Washington, D.C.; Donna M. Reapp to Robert Poli, June 22, 1981, Contract Negotiations 1981 file, Box 444, PATCO.

52. Torchia interview; *NYT*, June 25, 1981, 15; Siegel quoted in ABC News Transcripts, June 25, 1981, World News Tonight, LexisNexis; interview with David Siegel, June 27, 2003, by telephone.

53. David L. Wright to Fred Fielding, Re: Letter from Richard J. Leighton to Michael Balzano, June 20, 1981, Box 34F, Fred Fielding Files, RRPL; Allen E. Ertel, Geraldine Ferraro, et al. to William French Smith, June 26, 1981, Box 34F, Fred Fielding Files, RRPL; *WP*, June 28, 1981, A9; Richard Leighton to William French Smith, June 30, 1981, Box 34F, Fred Fielding Files, RRPL.

54. Lindley H. Clark Jr., "Reagan: Labor's Love Lost?" *WSJ*, June 30, 1981, 31.

55. Torchia interview; interview with Charlie Campbell, February 11, 2002, by telephone; Memo, Michael Fermon to Executive Board, July 1, 1981, Chicago Meeting file, Box 401, PATCO.

56. Interview with Mike Rock, August 4, 2001, Las Vegas, Nev.; interview with George Kerr, August 17, 2001, by telephone; David Morgan, "Terminal Flight: The Air Traffic Controllers' Strike of 1981," *Journal of American Studies* [Great Britain] 18:2 (1984): 168–169; Wintermeyer, "An Insider's View," 22; Butterworth interview.

57. Kerr interview; *WP*, July 3, 1981, A1; Torchia interview.

58. Lewis, Donahue, Moffett, Stakem, and Meachum interviews.

59. "Air Traffic Controllers Consider Private Company," *GUC*, July 17, 1981, 5.

60. Maher interview, August 8, 2006, by telephone; John J. Seddon, "PATCO, A Perspective," 115–116; quotations from Purpose of this Meeting [Outline], 7/16/81, "Mon." file, Box 1, Dennis Reardon Records, PATCO/UTA; Rock interview, August 4, 2001; Harding interview; interview with John Thornton, August 6, 1998, Washington, D.C.

61. Quotations from Arthur Shostak interview with Bill Taylor, October 18, 1985, File 1, Box 8, Arthur B. Shostak Collection, PATCO/UTA.

CHAPTER 11

1. Poli to Drew Lewis, July 29, 1981, and Lewis to Poli, July 31, 1981, WHORM Subject File PE001 (035825CA), RRPL; Lewis to Craig Fuller, Re: Update of the PATCO Situation, n.d. [July 1981], PATCO file, OA 10974, Box 4, Craig L. Fuller

Files, RRPL; Lewis to Fuller, Re: Up-Date PATCO Situation, n.d. [July 1981], WHORM Subject File PE001 (018740CA), RRPL; Statement by Secretary Drew Lewis, July 31, 1981, OA 10520, David Gergen Files, RRPL.

2. Interview with Donald J. Devine, August 7, 2003, Alexandria, Va. (notes in the author's possession); John Walsh and Garth Magnum, *Labor Struggle in the Post Office: From Selective Lobbying to Collective Bargaining* (Armonk, N.Y.: M. E. Sharpe, 1992), 173–179; interview with Edwin Meese III, February 1, 2005, Washington, D.C.; interview with Vince Sombrotto, June 6, 2003, by telephone; Mike Natoli and Tara Treacy to Annelise Anderson, Re: Postal Service "Strike" Contingency Plan, June 24, 1981, PATCO file, Subject File OA10974, Box 4, Craig L. Fuller Files, RRPL.

3. Quotation from Kenneth Cribb Jr., Conference Report, PATCO Negotiations, July 31, 1981, WHORM Subject File FG006–01 (047,318), RRPL; PATCO Update, n.d. [July 31, 1981], OA 10520, David Gergen Files, RRPL; PATCO Information, n.d. [ca. July 31, 1981], WHORM Subject File PE001 (035825CA), RRPL.

4. Poli to Fellow Members, April 15, 1980, Cluster Concept file, Box 1, PATCO Local 332 Records, PATCO/UTA; Poli to Fellow Members, April 15, 1980, Exhibit G, Application for a Preliminary Injunction in Alexander T. Graham v. Professional Air Traffic Controllers Organization, August 3, 1981, 1981 Strike Legal File 1, Box 331, PATCO; Eads to Tom Ferring et al., June 25, 1980, Cluster Concept file, Box 1, PATCO Local 332 Records, PATCO/UTA; interview with Bill Harding, June 29, 2002, by telephone; interview with Jack Maher, August 8, 2006, by telephone; quotation from PATCOM, n.d. [1980], Box 417, PATCO.

5. Poli to Fellow Members, April 15, 1980, Cluster Concept file, Box 1, PATCO Local 332 Records, PATCO/UTA; Poli to Fellow Members, April 15, 1980, Exhibit G, Application for a Preliminary Injunction in Alexander T. Graham v. Professional Air Traffic Controllers Organization, August 3, 1981, 1981 Strike Legal File 1, Box 331, PATCO; interviews with Terry Bobell (August 5, 2003), Cheryl Jenni (October 29, 2002), Karen Koch (August 8, 2003), John Haggerty (October 11, 2002), David Siegel (June 27, 2003), and Domenic Torchia (May 23, 2002), by telephone.

6. Leyden to All Locals, Re: Questionnaire #2 Results, n.d. [1979], Questionnaires File, Box 400, PATCO; interview with Ron Taylor, February 12, 2003, Stewart, Fla.; interview with Carl Kern, July 22, 2003, by telephone.

7. Survey data from: Minutes of the Board of Directors Meeting, May 12–14, 1979, Box 457, PATCO; Shostak, "Analysis of PATCO Questionnaire Data, Report 1: National and Builder Data, Questionnaires 2 and 3, January 1980," Box 400, PATCO; Shostak, "Analysis of PATCO Questionnaire Data: Questionnaire 5, March 1981," 26, Folder 2, Box 3, Kansas City PATCO Local Collection, PATCO/ UTA. Striker profile from: Bowers, "What Would Make 11,500 People Quit Their Jobs?" 15; Bert A. Spector, and Michael Beer, "Air Traffic Controllers," 27; Jones, Bowers, and Fuller, "Management and Employee Relationships within the Federal Aviation Administration," 16; Wood interview; "Appeal of Diane E. Webster, Hearing Transcripts," Vol. II, September 10, 1982, Box 1, Washington ARTCC Records, Acc. 92–14, PATCO/UTA; Beatty interview.

8. Jack McDuffie and Hank Crawford quoted in *Raleigh News and Observer*, June 22, 1981, 8; Vermont spouse's quotation from Donna M. Reapp to Poli, June 22, 1981, Contract Negotiations 1981 file, Box 444, PATCO; *ATCSO News*, October 1979;

Tundra Flyer, December 1980, Support Organizations file, Box 3, PATCO Local 601 Records, PATCO/UTA; Spouse Support Groups Only, Support Groups file, Box 438, PATCO; quotation from Jeanette Oehrlein to the Friends of the FAA, June 22, 1981, Contract Negotiations 1981 file, Box 444, PATCO.

9. Don Kopsick to Eads, January 13, 1982, Southern Region Incoming Correspondence, Box 401, PATCO.

10. Interview with Dick Shaftic, June 18, 2004, by telephone; Executive Summary of Background Information, n.d. [July 1981], PATCO file, OA 10974, Box 4, Craig L. Fuller Files, RRPL; interview with Ray Van Vuren, March 11, 2002, by telephone; quotation from interview with J. Lynn Helms, May 3, 2002, Westport, Conn.

11. John F. Leyden and Edward Curran, unpublished book manuscript, pp. 159–160 (in the author's possession); Helms interview; Executive Summary of Background Information, n.d. [July 1981], PATCO file, OA 10974, Box 4, Craig L. Fuller Files, RRPL; interview with Mark Knause, June 27, 2003, Washington, D.C.; interview with Alex Hendriks, November 13, 2003, by telephone; interview with Pete Proulx, May 30, 2002, by telephone.

12. Interview with Lee Verstandig, August 4, 2003, Alexandria, Va.; Helms interview.

13. Interview with Ray Carver, July 27, 2003, by telephone; interview with Brian Flores, July 29, 2002, Washington, D.C.

14. Interview with Drew Lewis, June 22, 2004, Schwenksville, Penn.; Verstandig interview; Paul R. Ignatius to Robert E. Poli, May 28, 1981, PATCO File 4, OA 6385, Robert Bonitati Files, RRPL; interview with James Reinke, August 6, 2003, by telephone.

15. Helms interview.

16. Flores and Helms (quotations) interviews; Richard J. Leighton to Robert E. Poli, Re: Helms and Big Business, September 14, 1981, Legal Correspondence File, Box 1, Dennis Reardon Collection, PATCO/UTA.

17. Richard W. Hurd, "How PATCO Was Led Into a Trap," *The Nation* (December 26, 1981): 696–698; R. J. Van Vuren to Mr. O'Brien, June 30, 1981, Box 35, File 26, ALPA; interview with Ray Carver, July 27, 2003; quotation from interview with Ray Van Vuren, March 11, 2002, by telephone.

18. Norm Mineta to Poli, June 1, 1981, PATCO File 4, OA 6385, Robert Bonitati Files, RRPL; Flores interview, July 29, 2002; interview with Paul Hallisay, August 28, 2001, Washington, D.C.; interviews with John Leyden, July 14, 1998, Washington, D.C., and August 4, 2001, Las Vegas, Nev.; quotation from interview with Jesse Calhoon, by telephone, August 24, 2001.

19. Helms and Lewis interviews.

20. Bernard D. Meltzer and Cass R. Sunstein, "Public Employee Strikes, Executive Discretion, and the Air Traffic Controllers," *University of Chicago Law Review* 50:73 (1983): 781; Eugene H. Becker, "Analysis of Work Stoppages in the Federal Sector, 1962–1981," *Monthly Labor Review* (August 1982): 52.

21. Interview with Langhorne Bond, November 2, 2001, by telephone; Meese and Helms interviews.

22. Lewis interview; quotation from Draft of Presidential Statement, August 3, 1981, OA 10520, David Gergen Files, RRPL; Devine interview; "Transcript of Personal Interview with FAA Administrator J. Lynn Helms, conducted by Nick A. Komons

and Edmund Preston, January 23, 25, 26, 1984," FAA Historian's Office (copy in possession of the author), p. 111; Meese and Verstandig interviews.

23. Interview with Kenneth Moffett, August 28, 2001, Washington, D.C. ; interview with George Stohner, December 2, 2010, Washington, D.C.; interviews; Record of Meeting, August 2, 1981, FMCS, Daily Negotiation File, Box 2, Dennis Reardon Collection, PATCO/UTA.

24. Ron Taylor interview; interviews with Bruce Meachum (quotation), July 28, 2003, by telephone; John J. Haggerty, October 11, 2002, by telephone; Karen Koch, August 8, 2003, by telephone; Rich Andrews, August 11, 2003, by telephone; Jim Morin, June 19, 2002, Washington, D.C.; Domenic Torchia, May 23, 2002, by telephone.

25. Rock (August 4, 2001, and August 13, 2001) and Maher (August 8, 2006) interviews. Calculations on the turnout in large facilities are based on a document titled "Category I Facilities," Box 2, KCARTCC Collection, PATCO/UTA.

26. Flores interview; Poli quotation from Record of Meeting, August 2, 1981, FMCS, Daily Negotiation File, Box 2, Dennis Reardon Collection, PATCO/UTA; quotation from Lewis interview.

27. Kern (quotation), Harding, and Jenni interviews; interview with Bob Butterworth, February 1, 2002, by telephone.

28. Quotation from Francis D. Stamm to Ronald Reagan, August 8, 1981, WHORM Subject File PE001 (036,676), RRPL; interviews with Jenni, Ron Taylor, Bobell, Andrews, and Kern; interview with Donna Taylor, April 22, 2003, Washington, D.C.; interview with Jim Stakem, August 7, 2002, Ashburn, Va.; interview with Robert Mischke Sr., June 24, 2004, by telephone; Guy Linn, June 20, 2002, Washington, D.C.; and Sid McGuirk, June 18, 2002, Washington, D.C.

29. Interviews with Charles Bolling, Bowie, Md.; Sid McGuirk, June 18, 2002, Washington, D.C.; Rick Jones, June 24, 2002, Fort Washington, Md.

30. Stohner, Van Vuren, and Helms interviews; interviews with Dick Shaftic, June 18, 2004, by telephone; Mike Powderly, July 29, 2003, by telephone; and Russ Sommer, June 22, 2004, by telephone.

31. System Status Report, 9 a.m., August 3, 1981, OA 10520, David Gergen Files, RRPL; Lewis interview.

32. Meese interview; quotations taken from the notes of David Gergen, 7[8]/3/81 PATCO, handwritten notes, OA 10520, David Gergen Files, RRPL; PATCO Strike—Update, August 3, 1981, 2:30 p.m., OA 10520, David Gergen Files, RRPL. For slightly different account of this meeting by an assistant to Attorney General Smith, see Giuliani, *Leadership*, 200–201.

33. Lewis interview; handwritten notes on Ed Gray to David Gergen, August 3, 1981, OA 10520, David Gergen Files, RRPL.

34. Statement Before the Press, August 3, 1981, 10:45 a.m., OA 10520, David Gergen Files, RRPL.

35. Quotation from Edward Berman, *Labor Disputes and the President of the United States* (New York: Columbia University, 1924), 248–249; Walter Galenson, *The American Labor Movement: 1955–1995* (Westport, Conn.: Greenwood Press, 1996), 54; Reagan quotation from Statement Before the Press, August 3, 1981, 10:45 a.m., OA 10520, David Gergen Files, RRPL.

36. "Minutes of Meeting of the Executive Council of the American Federation of Labor and Congress of Industrial Organizations," August 3–5, 1981, pp. 1–7, 57, Box 18, IAM; interview with Ken Blaylock, June 30, by telephone; interview with Douglas Fraser, October 26, 2001, by telephone; interview with John J. Sweeney, Washington, D.C., December 5, 2010.

37. Sweeney interview; Blaylock interview; Fraser interview; interview with Ken Young, November 30, 2001, Silver Spring, Md.; interview with J. J. O'Donnell, September 7, 2001, by telephone; quotation from interview with Glenn Watts, September 21, 2001, Chevy Chase, Md.; Fraser quotation from *WP*, August 5, 1981, A1.

38. Knause (quotation), Fraser, O'Donnell (quotation), Young, and Watts interviews. On the IAM's response, see "Minutes of IAM Executive Council Meeting," August 6–14, 1981, p. 1, Box 38, IAM.

39. "Statement by the President on the Air Traffic Controllers Strike, with Secretary of Transportation Drew Lewis and Attorney General William French Smith," August 3, 1981, Air Traffic Controllers File, OA 10441, White House Office of Public Affairs Files, RRPL.

40. Interview with Harri Henschler, November 6, 2003, by telephone; Calhoon interview; Phone call count at noon, n.d., OA 10520, David Gergen Files, RRPL; Late PATCO Developments (11:30 a.m. Tuesday), n.d. [August 4, 1981], OA 10520, David Gergen Files, RRPL; quotation from Gordon Spendlove to Ronald Reagan, August 10, 1981, Correspondence file, OA 6848, Labor Strategy file, OA 6845, Robert Bonitati Files, RRPL; Bonitati interview; quotation on martyrs from "Notes from Karna on the strike," OA 10520, David Gergen Files, RRPL.

41. Blaylock, Young, and Leyden (June 14, 1998) interviews.

42. Leyden interview, July 14, 1998.

43. Meachum, Andrews, Stakem, and Ron Taylor interviews; interview with Tom Gaffney, August 9, 2006, by telephone.

44. Seddon, "PATCO, A Perspective," 122; Carver interview.

45. Meagher interview; interview with Anna Mosely interview, August 9, 2006, by telephone.

46. Siegel and Torchia interviews.

47. Sommer, Koch, Meagher interviews; interview with Will Burner, June 26, 2003, by telephone.

48. Interview with Bill Robertson, by telephone; Rock quoted from Rock, "PATCO History," January 10, 1979; Siegel interview.

49. ABC News Transcripts, August 5, 1981, World News Tonight, LexisNexis; Category I Facilities, Box 2, KCARTCC Collection, PATCO/UTA; Butterworth, Bobell, and Powderly interviews; quotation from interview with Pete Kellum, August 10, 2006, by telephone.

50. Wood interview; August 10, 1981, Call PAC, Day 8, Correspondence with PATCO file, Box 1, James D. Wright Papers, PATCO/UTA.

51. Van Vuren and Helms interviews; *WP*, August 5, 1981, A10; PATCO Update, August 5, 1981, OA 10520, David Gergen Files, RRPL; Devine interview; handwritten note, n.d., OA 10520, David Gergen Files, RRPL; quotation from Craig Fuller to Ed Meese, et al., Re: PATCO, August 5, 1981, OA 10520, David Gergen Files, RRPL; Edmund Morris, *Dutch: A Memoir of Ronald Reagan* (New York:

Random House, 1999), 445; Memorandum, August 6, 1981, 3:40 p.m., OA 10520, David Gergen Files, RRPL.

52. Interview with Steve Elliott, June 10, 2003, Leesburg, Va.; *Daytona Beach Morning Journal*, August 6, 1981; interview with Jim Morin, June 19, 2002, Washington, D.C.; Jimmy Breslin, "Hard to Get Emotional over 'Plight' of Striking Air Controllers," *Jackson Daily News*, August 10, 1981, 5, PATCO Strike file, Box 2139, Mississippi AFL-CIO.

53. Morin interview; Sue Baumgartel quoted in *Daytona Beach Morning Journal*, August 6, 1981.

54. Rock (August 13, 2001) and Maher (August 8, 2006) interviews.

CHAPTER 12

1. Memo, Howard Dugoff, Administrator, Research and Special Programs Administration, FAA, to Lynn Helms, August 6, 1981, File 81–29, Entry 14, Box 163, FAA.

2. *CPD*, August 7, 1981, 13A; controller quotation from Mischke interview; spouse quotation from Kathryn Ellis to Gus Yatron, n.d. [1981], Personnel/Labor/General file 81–25, Box 511, FAA Records, FAA; National Transportation Safety Board Special Investigation of the Air Traffic Control System, December 8, 1981, David B. Waller Files, CFOA 701, RRPL.

3. Interviews with Ray Van Vuren, March 11, 2002, and Mike Powderly, July 29, 2003, by telephone; *WP*, September 4, 1981, A7.

4. *GERR*, September 7, 1981, 7; *WP*, August 8, 1981, A1; *WP*, August 3, 1982, A15; Statement by Mary Wunder, Eastern Pennsylvania Chapter, http://www.ninety-nines.org/atc.html (accessed June 9, 2008).

5. Interview with Russ Sommer, June 22, 2004, and Dick Shaftic, June 18, 2004, by telephone.

6. Interviews with Rick Jones, June 24, 2002, Fort Washington, Md.; Charles Bolling, July 23, 2002, Bowie, Md.; interview with Donna Taylor, April 22, 2003, Washington, D.C.

7. Drew Lewis and J. Lynn Helms to "Dear Air Traffic Controller," October 22, 1981, File 81–32, Entry 14, Box 163, FAA; *GERR*, October 26, 1981, 10; *WP*, October 5, 1982, C2.

8. Interview with Lee Verstandig, August 4, 2003, Alexandria, Va.; J. Lynn Helms to All Air Traffic and Airway Facilities Personnel, September 8, 1981, File 81–30, Entry 14, Box 163, FAA; FAA interview with J. Lynn Helms, May 3, 2002 (copy in the author's possession).

9. Economist David B. Richards quoted in *WP*, October 9, 1983, G6; Lawrence L. Burian, President, National Air Transportation Association, to J. Lynn Helms, August 14, 1981, File 81–29, Entry 14, Box 163, FAA; Late PATCO Developments (11:30 a.m. Tuesday), n.d. [August 4, 1981], OA 10520, David Gergen Files, RRPL; *U.S. News and World Report* (August 17, 1981): 21.

10. Interview with Edwin Meese III, February 1, 2005, Washington, D.C.; Republic Airlines' Daniel F. May to Ronald Reagan, August 13, 1981, WHORM Subject File PE001 (036,802), RRPL; American Airlines chairman Albert V. Casey to Ronald Reagan, August 21, 1981, WHORM Subject File PE001 (037,410), RRPL;

Statement, J. Lynn Helms, September 16, 1981, File 81–35, Entry 14, Box 163, FAA; Paul R. Ignatius to Airline Chief Executive Officers, August 6, 1981, file 9, Box 35, Atlanta Field Office Collection, ALPA; Lawrence L. Burian to Ronald Reagan, August 6, 1981, WHORM Subject File PE001 (035,919), RRPL.

11. *WP*, August 3, 1982, A1; interviews with Mark Knause, Washington, D.C.; J. Lynn Helms, May 3, 2002, Westport, Conn.; and Drew Lewis, June 22, 2004, Schwenksville, Penn.; Anne Reilly Dowd, "What Managers Can Learn from Manager Reagan," in Paul Boyer, ed., *Reagan as President: Contemporary Views of the Man, His Politics, and His Policies* (Chicago: Ivan R. Dee, 1990), 62; *WP*, December 6, 1981, F1.

12. Interviews with Rex Campbell, February 24, 2002; Bruce Meachum, July 28, 2003; John J. Haggerty, October 11, 2002; and Carl Kern, July 22, 2003, by telephone; interview with Donna Taylor, April 22, 2003, Washington, D.C.; Bernard D. Meltzer and Cass R. Sunstein, "Public Employee Strikes, Executive Discretion, and the Air Traffic Controllers," *University of Chicago Law Review* 50:73 (1983), 789; Poli to "Dear ____," October 15, 1981, Rep Chron file, Box 347, PATCO; Butterworth interview; *WP*, August 7, 1981, A7; *WP*, September 10, 1981, C13; *WP*, December 12, 1981, B4; United States v. John J. Haggerty, John S. Hynd, II, Terry L. Maxton, and Gary Shields, Defendants, U.S. District Court for the District of Colorado, 528 F. Supp. 1286 (1981); Memo, December 15, 1981, Executive Board Meetings file, Box 223, PATCO; *WP*, December 9, 1981, A2; *GERR*, August 17, 1981, 10.

13. Interview with Domenic Torchia, May 23, 2002; interview with Brian Flores, July 29, 2002, Washington, D.C.

14. Meese and Lewis interviews; Paul Harvey, "PATCO Not Perfect," September 30, 1981, Tickler file, Box 171, PATCO; quotation from Paul Harvey clipping, *Fremont Argus*, September 22, 1981, Post-strike updates file, Box 2, PATCO Local 601 Records, UTA; on Gosden, see Bryan Burrough and John Helyar, *Barbarians at the Gate: The Fall of RJR Nabisco* (New York: HarperPerennial, 1990), 293–294.

15. Quotation from *WP*, September 4, 1981, A3; Verstandig, Helms, and Knause interviews; *GERR*, October 12, 1981, 8; Thomas P. O'Neill Jr. to Patrick L. Doyle, October 14, 1981, unmarked file, Box 471, PATCO.

16. Quotation from Terry E. Bobell, "PATCO: An Insider's View," typescript, n.d. [1996] (copy in the author's possession); Mischke interview; Memo, George Brandon to Regional Vice Presidents, September 2, 1981, "Bankruptcy" file, Box 221, PATCO; George Brandon to David Trick, August 27, 1981, Correspondence file 4, Box 7, George Brandon Collection, UTA; *WP*, August 19, 1981, A9; Robert E. Poli to Editors of all National Newspapers, August 9, 1981, Media Contacts file, Box 221, PATCO; *WP*, September 10, 1981, A12.

17. Interview with James Reinke, August 6, 2003; Harri Henschler, November 6, 2003, by telephone.

18. Interviews with Andy Anderson, June 3, 2004; and J. J. O'Donnell, September 7, 2001, by telephone; interview with Paul Hallisay, August 28, 2001, Washington, D.C.; Document No. 88, June 1981, file 9, Box 35, Atlanta Field Office Collection, ALPA Records; Eastern Airlines Memo, August 3, 1981, file 9, Box 30, Atlanta Field Office Collection, ALPA; A. C. Gibson to All Captains and First Officers, August 7, 1981, file 9, Box 30, Atlanta Field Office Collection, ALPA.

19. J. J. O'Donnell to Members of the Executive Board, June 11, 1981, file 9, Box 35, Atlanta Field Office Collection, ALPA.

20. Tom Sheppard to J. J. O'Donnell, Re: ATC Information Center Report for August 5, 1981, Box 69, Folder 35, ALPA; Sheppard to O'Donnell, August 6, 1981, Box 69, Folder 35, ALPA; Captain Louis M. McNair to Delcoal Local Council Safety Chairman, August 6, 1981, file 9, Box 35, Atlanta Field Office Collection, ALPA; Sheppard to O'Donnell, Re: ATC Information Center Report for August 7, August 9, 1981, file 35, Box 69, ALPA; Sheppard to O'Donnell, Re: ATC Information Center Report for August 8, 1981, Box 69, Folder 35, ALPA; Sheppard to O'Donnell, August 9, 1981, Re: ATC Information Center Report for August 7, 1981, 8/19/81 Mailing file, Box 332, PATCO.

21. J. D. Howell to All Central Air Safety Chairmen, August 11, 1981, file 9, Box 35, Atlanta Field Office Collection, ALPA; Sheppard to O'Donnell, August 11, 1981, file 35, Box 69, ALPA; quotations from Stanley M. Jorgensen to O'Donnell, ALPA, August 21, 1981, File 81–31, Entry 14, Box 163, FAA; Tom Kreamer to O'Donnell, Re: ATC Communication Center Activity Report for Saturday, August 15, 1981, Box 69, Folder 35, ALPA.

22. O'Donnell to Dear Member, September 1, 1981, Box 30, File 9, ALPA; O'Donnell interview; John Burgess, "Air Line Pilots Association Voices Confidence in Control System," WP, August 20, 1981, A9; Transcript of Press Conference, August 19, 1981, file 35, Box 69, ALPA.

23. Quotation from interview with Ron Taylor, February 12, 2003, Stewart, Fla.; Press Release, August 18, 1981, unmarked folder, Box 200, PATCO; NYT, August 20, 1981, p. B11.

24. WP, August 20, 1981, A9; quotations from Transcript of News Conference, August 19, 1981, file 9, Box 30, Atlanta Field Office Collection, ALPA; Delta MEC to O'Donnell, August 24, 1981, Box 35, File 26, ALPA; Delta MEC to O'Donnell, August 24, 1981, file 9, Box 30, Atlanta Field Office Collection, ALPA; Eastern Master Executive Council to ALPA Board Members, October 21, 1981, Box 30, File 9, ALPA; John P. Gratz to Drew Lewis, November 4, 1981, Box 30, File 9, ALPA; O'Donnell to All Members, September 1, 1981, file 9, Box 30, Atlanta Field Office Collection, ALPA; WP, March 8, 1983, p. A11.

25. Telegram, Bill Robertson to Poli, August 5, 1981, General Correspondence Strike file, Box 1, Dennis Reardon Records, PATCO/UTA; WP, August 11, 1981, A1; WP, August 12, 1981, A1; WP, August 11, 1981, A1; WP, August 12, 1981, A1; WP, August 13, 1981, A16; interviews with Bill Robertson, June 10, 2002, and Pete Proulx, May 30, 2002, by telephone; Knause interview.

26. Helms, Lewis, Meese, Proulx, and Robertson interviews; WP, August 12, 1981, A1; W. J. Robertson to Board of Directors, August 31, 1981, 1981 Strike General Correspondence file, Box 331, PATCO; WP, August 17, 1981, A4.

27. Neil Vidler, Under Control: The Story of the International Federation of Air Traffic Controllers' Associations (Montreal: The Federation, 2001), 179–180; IFATCA News Release, September 10, 1981, IFATCA/CATCA file, Box 221, PATCO; Henschler interview.

28. Fred Fielding to the File, Re: PATCO-Proposed Resolution of Strike, August 14, 1981, Box 34F, Fred Fielding Files, RRPL; WP, August 12, 1981, A6; Secretary of

State and Secretary of Transportation to Edwin Meese III, Re: Background—Foreign Reactions to Civil Aeronautics Board's IATA Show Cause Proceeding," n.d. [August 1981], PATCO File, Box 29, Edwin Meese Files, RRPL; Secretary of State and Secretary of Transportation to the President, Re: Foreign Cooperation in PATCO Situation: Proposed Letter to Civil Aeronautics Board, n.d. [August 1981], PATCO File, Box 29, Edwin Meese Files, RRPL; Fred Fielding to the President, Re: Foreign Cooperation in PATCO situation, August 20, 1981, Box 34F, Fred Fielding Files, RRPL; James Ott, "Reagan Backs IATA Antitrust Immunity," *Aviation Week and Space Technology* (August 31, 1981): 30.

29. Interview with Alex Hendriks, November 13, 2003, by telephone; Vidler, *Under Control*, 176–182; Henschler interview.

30. Lewis and Torchia interviews; interview with David Siegel, June 27, 2003, by telephone; *WP*, August 14, 1981, A6.

31. Fred Fielding to the File, Re: PATCO-Proposed Resolution of Strike, August 14, 1981, Box 34F, Fred Fielding Files, RRPL; Fielding to Meese, Re: PATCO, August 14, 1981, Box 34F, Fred Fielding Files, RRPL; interview with Ken Young, November 30, 2001, Silver Spring, Md.; "civilized" quotation from "Minutes of Meeting of the Executive Council of the American Federation of Labor and Congress of Industrial Organizations," September 18, 1981, p. 2, Box 18, IAM; "shooting" quotation from Puddington, *Lane Kirkland*, 127.

32. Interview with Ken Blaylock, June 30, 2003, by telephone; interview with Donald J. Devine, August 7, 2003, Alexandria, Va. (notes in the author's possession).

33. Blaylock interview; Record of Discussion, August 11, 1981, Daily Negotiations Notes file, Box 2, Dennis Reardon Records, PATCO/UTA; Devine interview; *WP*, August 27, 1981, A2.

34. Blaylock and Rock (August 13, 2001) interviews; George Brandon to Dear Member, September 23, 1981, Correspondence file 7, Box 7, George Brandon Collection, PATCO/UTA; Lundie to Russell, August 14, 1981, Box 397, PATCO.

35. Donovan and Lewis quotes in *WP*, August 22, 1981, p. A1; Devine interview, August 7, 2003; *WP*, August 27, 1981, A2; Fuller quoted in Bob Bonitati to Elizabeth Dole, Re: PATCO, August 27, 1981, PATCO file 4, OA 6850, Robert Bonitati Files, RRPL.

36. Seddon, "PATCO, A Perspective," 133–137; Maher interview, August 8, 2006; Meese interview; PATCO Political Action Committee Bulletin, September 25, 1981, Political Action Updates file, Box 223, PATCO; James Lundie to Fellow Strikers, October 1, 1981, General Information File, Box 1, Dennis Reardon Records, PATCO/UTA; Young interview.

37. Kirkland quotation from *Salem Statesman-Journal*, August 7, 1981, Clipping, Box 40, IAM; Leaflet, n.d. [August 1981], file 14, Box 60, Telecommunications International Union Records, Special Collection, Catherwood Library, Industrial and Labor Relations School, Cornell University; teacher quotation from Mel Hilgenberg to Robert Poli, August 11, 1981, Teachers file, Series 100, Box 1, PATCO; Kalamazoo quotation from Jack Roach to Jim Spalding, August 20, 1981, AFSCME file, Series 100, Box 1, PATCO.

38. Meachum, South, Stakem, and Donna Taylor interviews; Thomas Van Arsdale to Lane Kirkland, October 2, 1981, News Articles file, Box 223; Watts interview;

Glenn E. Watts to CWA Local Presidents, August 24, 1981, Communications Workers of America folder, Series 100, Box 1, PATCO; Poli to Hiroki Fujimoto, November 16, 1981, Rep Chron file, Box 347, PATCO; *CAOOAA General Distribution Bulletin*, [Civil Air Operations Officers' Association of Australia], August 18, 1981, CAOOAA file 2, Box 444, PATCO; Sue Panko to Michael W. Fermon, June 12, 1982, Box 510, PATCO.

39. Teacher quoted in *WP*, August 17, 1981, A18; firefighter quotation from Louie A. Wright to Brother Eads, August 6, 1981, Box 2, Kansas City ARTCC Records, PATCO/UTA; basic right quotation from Dennis Cox to Robert Poli, August 18, 1981, Teachers file, Series 100, Box 1, PATCO.

40. *Fighting Worker*, August 23, 1981, Solidarity Day file, Box 438, PATCO; Steelworker quotation from Ron Weisen to Robert Poli, August 6, 1981, Box 417, PATCO; *Longshore-Warehouse Militant*, August 17, 1981, Correspondence with PATCO file, Box 1, James D. Wright Papers, PATCO/UTA; Philadelphia teacher union official Ray Pollard quoted in the *Boston Union Teacher*, November 1981 [thanks to Jennifer Pish Harrison for alerting me to this citation]; Albert Lannon, *Fight or Be Slaves: The History of the Oakland-East Bay Labor Movement* (Lanham, Md.: University Press of America, 2000), 180; *WP*, September 26, 1981, A20; *Cleveland Plain Dealer*, October 1, 1981, p. D1.

41. V. R. Hardy to Dear Sir, August 17, 1981, and O'Murday to R. Poli, n.d. [August 1981], Correspondence folder, Box 307, PATCO; Gordon S. Spendlove to The Hon. Ronald Reagan, August 10, 1981, Blue Collar Correspondence File, Robert Bonitati Papers, RRPL; firefighters William F. Hyde and John Di Pietro quoted in *WP*, August 6, 1981, A8.

42. Officers of CWA Local 12,143 to Lane Kirkland, August 6, 1981, Communication Workers of America file, Series 100, Box 1, PATCO; Chester L. Migden to Ronald Reagan, August 25, 1981, WHORM Subject File PE001 (037,995), RRPL; interview with Robert Bonitati, August 23, 2001, Alexandria, Va.

43. Bonitati interview; Reagan quotations from *NYT*, September 4, 1981, A10; *NYT*, September 4, 1981, A11; Douglas Brinkley, ed., *The Reagan Diaries* (New York: HarperCollins, 2007), 36.

44. Interviews with Thomas Donahue, October 11, 2001, Washington, D.C.; Ken Young, November 30, 2001, Silver Spring, Md.; Ray Carver, July 27, 2003, by telephone; and Glenn Watts, September 21, 2001, Chevy Chase, Md.; text of Steve Wallaert's Speech, Solidarity Day, September 19, 1981, 1981 Strike file, Box 331, PATCO; Bonitati interview.

45. *WP*, October 23, 1981, A1; *GERR*, October 26, 1981, 5 (Lewis quoted, p. 10); Memo, December 15, 1981, Executive Board Meetings file, Box 223, PATCO. On allegations Shanker illegally lobbied FLRA members Leon B. Applewhaite, see *WP*, February 17, 1982, A6; *WP*, February 18, 1982, D9; *WP*, February 27, 1982, A11; *WP*, March 31, 1982, A8. No charges were brought as a result of the investigation.

46. Poli quoted in *Convention Proceedings of the Fourteenth Constitutional Convention of the AFL-CIO, 1981*, 378–379; hotel unionist Charles Lamb quoted, 384; Executive Council resolution, pp. 376, 384.

47. Butterworth and Meagher interviews; "trouble-maker" quotation from Diane Webster, Statement for Reinstatement, December 21, 1981, Box 1, Washington ARTCC Records, PATCO/UTA; Cleveland Center quotation from Albert R. Rubinoski to Reagan, August 12, 1981, WHORM Subject File PE001 (036,950), RRPL; "slaughtered" quotation from Lambrecht interview; "never dreamed" quotation from George LeGrand to Bob [Cameron], March 16, 1982, Correspondence file, series 100, box 8, PATCO.

48. Quotation from Dan B. Russell to Jim Lundie, October 8, 1981, Box 397, PATCO; Mosely interview; Haggerty interview; WP, August 14, 1981, C1; Harding interviews; "Statistical Breakdown of Controllers who have Committed Suicide since August 3, 1981," Suicides File, Box 2, Washington, D.C., PATCO Collection, PATCO/UTA; ChiST, November 22, 1981, 22.

49. Raspberry quotation from WP, December 7, 1981, A15; Jude Wanniski to Drew Lewis, October 14, 1981, File 81–34, Entry 14, Box 163, FAA; Safire quotation from NYT, August 16, 1981, E19; Kemp quotation from clipping, Buffalo News, September 27, 1981, News Articles file, Box 223; Patrick L. Doyle to Jack Kemp, September 28, 1981, Sept. Chron file, Box 311, PATCO.

50. Bob Bonitati to Elizabeth Dole, Re: PATCO, November 9, 1981, Professional Air Traffic Controllers File 2, OA 6850, Robert Bonitati Files, RRPL; "Minutes of Meeting of the Executive Council of the American Federation of Labor and Congress of Industrial Organizations," November 18, 1981, Box 18, IAM; Watts interview.

51. Flexibility quotation from Robert Bonitati to Elizabeth Dole, Re: Vice President's Meeting with Lane Kirkland, December 1, 1981, AFL-CIO Executive Council with the President File, Robert Bonitati Files, RRPL; WSJ, December 2, 1981, p. 3; WP, December 2, 1981, A1; PATCO local leader quoted in WP, December 3, 1981, A18; Jake Garn et al. to Pres. Ronald Reagan, December 2, 1981, File 3711, Entry 14, Box 166, FAA.

52. Elizabeth Dole to Lane Kirkland, December 7, 1981, AFL-CIO Executive Council with the President File, Robert Bonitati Files, RRPL; Fraser and Sweeney interviews.

53. Quotations from Notes, AFL-CIO Executive Board Meeting with President, AFL-CIO file, OA 6841, Box 2, Robert Bonitati Files, RRPL; President PATCO, n.d. [December 1981], AFL-CIO Executive Council with the President File, OA 6841, Box 2, Robert Bonitati Files, RRPL; Fraser interview and Sweeney interviews. In his diary account of the meeting, Reagan barely mentioned PATCO. Brinkley, ed., The Reagan Diaries, 52.

54. Meltzer and Sunstein, "Public Employee Strikes, Executive Discretion, and the Air Traffic Controllers," 781; Bonitati interview.

55. Donald Devine to Edwin Meese III, December 7, 1981, Re: White House Meeting on Air Traffic Controllers, PATCO file, Subject File OA 10974, Box 4, Craig L. Fuller Files, RRPL.

56. Craig Fuller, Briefing Memo on Meeting with Secretary Lewis, December 9, 1981, December 8, 1981, CFOA 741, Presidential Briefing Papers, RRPL; Memorandum for the Director of the Office of Personnel Management, Re: Federal Employment

of Discharged Air Traffic Controllers, December 9, 1981, Professional Air Traffic Controllers File 2, OA 6850, Robert Bonitati Files, RRPL.

57. Taylor quotation from interview with Cheryl Jenni, October 29, 2002, by telephone; "Waterloo" from notes on legal pad, October 2, 1981, Box 1, Kansas City ARTCC Records, PATCO/UTA.

58. Siegel interview; Poli quoted in *WP*, January 1, 1982, D6; *WP*, January 3, 1982, A7.

59. *WP*, January 14, 1982, A1; *WP*, January 15, 1982, A1, A7; *WP*, January 26, 1982, A1; *WP*, January 29, 1982, A16; Ralph James Savarese, "Piecing Together What History Has Broken to Bits," in *American Disasters*, ed. Steven Biel (New York: New York University Press, 2001), 339–381.

60. *WP*, January 17, 1982, A10; quotation from *WP*, March 3, 1982, A2; *WP*, March 4, A30; Willis Nordlund, *Silent Skies: The Air Traffic Controllers' Strike* (Westport, Conn.: Praeger, 1998), 149.

61. A thorough study of Flight 90 was made by one PATCO striker. See Robert E. Lambrecht, "One Strike and You're Out" (unpublished manuscript, 1989), 133–151. Reagan quotations from *NYT*, January 27, 1982, A16.

CHAPTER 13

1. Peggy Noonan, *When Character Was King: A Story of Ronald Reagan* (New York: Random House, 2001); Greenfield quotations in *WP*, March 17, 1982, A25; *WP*, February 15, 1984, A19.

2. Allen quoted in Arch Puddington, *Lane Kirkland: Champion of American Labor* (Hoboken, N.J.: John Wiley & Sons, 2005), 126; Noonan, *When Character Was King*, 375; Safire quoted in *NYT*, August 16, 1981, E19; Edmund Morris, *Dutch: A Memoir of Ronald Reagan* (New York: Random House, 1999), 448; Stephen S. Rosenfeld quoted in *WP*, November 6, 1981, A31.

3. Bruce Schulman, *The Seventies: The Great Shift in American Culture and Politics* (New York: De Capo Press, 2002), 233; Morris, *Dutch*, 792–793; *London Times*, August 7, 1981, 11; *London Times*, Wednesday August 12, 1981, 8; Donald J. Savoie, *Thatcher, Reagan, Mulroney: In Search of a New Bureaucracy* (Pittsburgh: University of Pittsburgh Press, 1994).

4. John C. Armor, "The Right to Strike: Some Basic, But Neglected, Questions," *GUR* 2:3 (Summer 1981), 8; Will quoted in *WP*, November 4, 1984, D8.

5. Gary W. Eads to Jesse Calhoon, April 22, 1982, Correspondence file, Series 100, Box 8, PATCO; Poli quotation from *NYT*, January 17, 1982, F2; George Brandon, "Letter from the Boss," *Metro Update*, January 7, 1982, Southwest Region file, Box 396, PATCO.

6. *WP*, January 5, 1982, D9; Gary M. Fitzgerald to PATCO People, May 14, 1982, Remit Letters file, Series 100, Box 8, PATCO.

7. *WP*, June 12, 1982, A6; PATCO Executive Board Minutes, June 24–25, 1982, Lenexa, Kansas, PATCO Board Minutes binder, Box 1, Kansas City ARTCC PATCO Records, PATCO/UTA; Eads quotation from PATCO Press Release, July 2, 1982, Box 365, PATCO; *WP*, July 3, 1982, C8; *WP*, January 4, 1984, A11.

8. Gary W. Eads to Dear Brothers and Sisters, November 15, 1984, Correspondence File, Box 7, James D. Wright Papers, PATCO/UTA.

9. Katherine Newman, *Falling From Grace: The Experience of Downward Mobility in the American Middle Class* (New York: The Free Press, 1988), 151–152; interview with Antoinette Pole, August 9, 2006, by telephone.

10. "Report on Union Busters, RUB Sheet, National Organizing Coordinating Committee," September 1982, Report on Union Busters file, Box 2575, Series II, AFL-CIO Civil Rights Department Southeastern Region, Southern Labor Archives, Georgia State University; cost estimate in Nordlund, *Silent Skies*, 11.

11. *WP*, August 3, 1982, A1; *WP*, December 23, 1982, A15; *WP*, May 29, 1983, A16.

12. William Welsh to William D. Ford, December 22, 1981, Re: Preliminary Staff Report on Alleged Grade Manipulation at FAA Academy, Mitzner/Schonberger file, Box 108, Usery; Nordlund, *Silent Skies*, Chapter 8; *NYT*, December 21, 1982, A1; *WP*, December 23, 1982, A15; anonymous controllers quoted in *WP*, May 29, 1983, A1, A16.

13. *WP*, May 29, 1983, A1, A16; *WP*, October 9, 1983, G1, G6, G7.

14. *WP*, December 29, 1982, A1; *WSJ*, October 7, 1983, 1, 20; *WSJ*, December 15, 1983, 1, 18.

15. Interview with Leo Perlis, May, 1985, File 1, Box 8, Arthur B. Shostak Collection, PATCO/UTA; Anthony J. Skirlick Jr. to William D. Ford and Hippy Left Winger Ronny Dellums, n.d. [1982], Eads Correspondence file, Series 100, Box 5, PATCO; Memo, Patrick L. Doyle to Members of the Post Office and Civil Service Committee, January 11, 1982, Box 200, PATCO; Anthony J. Skirlick Jr., March 24, 1982, David B. Waller Files, OA 5144, RRPL; Anthony J. Skirlick Jr. to Ronald Reagan, August 11, 1981, David B. Waller Files, OA 5144, RRPL; interviews with Sid McGuirk, June 18, 2002; Terry Bobell, August 5, 2003; Dick Shaftic, June 18, 2004; Noel Keane, June 10, 2003, by telephone; interview with Jim Morin, June 19, 2002, Washington, D.C.; supervisor quoted in *WP*, October 11, 1986, A8; Lewis quoted in *NYT*, March 23, 1982, A11.

16. Interview with Ray Van Vuren, March 11, 2002, by telephone; on the jailing of strikers Gary Greene and Ron May in 1983, see *USATCO National Newsletter*, June 1983, pp. 1–2, Box 7, James D. Wright Papers, PATCO/UTA); *WP*, August 21, 1981, A8; J. Michael Luttig to Fred F. Fielding, January 7, 1982, Re: Postal Service Hiring of PATCO Employees, OA 10019, Box 1, J. Michael Luttig Files, RRPL; *NYT*, August 20, 1982, A17; Barbara M. Singleton to John C. Gauff, August 23, 1991, Correspondence file, 1990–92, Box 1, Washington, D.C. PATCO Collection, Acc. 95–18, PATCO/UTA; *Dallas Morning News*, August 16, 1981, 16A; Ken Guier to David Skocik, September 24, 1981, Media Contacts file, Box 221, PATCO.

17. *WP*, September 24, 1990, A25; Shostak and Skocik, *The Air Controllers' Controversy*, 116.

18. *NYT*, March 23, 1982, A11; *WP*, September 24, 1982, B2; *WP*, May 29, 1983, A17; "Hearings Before the Subcommittee on Public Works and Transportation, House of Representatives," 100th Cong, 1st Sess. (Washington, D.C.: Government Printing Office, 1989), 6; *WP*, March 11, 1987, A12.

19. Fred Fielding to James A. Baker, June 15, 1983, Re: PATCO Clemency Suggestion, OA 11419 Peter J. Rusthoven Files, RRPL; *WP*, May 14, 1983, A1; May 15, 1983, A4; *NYT*, June 6, 1983, A16; quotation from David M. Whynot to Ronald Reagan,

May 24, 1983, WHORM Subject File JL001 (155,928), RRPL; interview with Ray Carver interview, July 27, 2003, by telephone.

20. *WSJ*, April 5, 1985, p. 27; interview with Guy V. Molinari, March 4, 2010, by telephone.

21. Molinari interview; *WP*, July 31, 1986, A6.

22. *WP*, October 9, 1986, A4; *WP*, October 17, 1986, A4; Taylor quotation from *PATCO Lives: The Lifeline* [hereafter *PL*], Vol. 2, No. 5 (September/October 1986), p. 1, The Lifeline file, Box 4, AR 397, PATCO Local 332 Records, PATCO/UTA.

23. *WP*, April 25, 1987, A22; *NYT*, September 25, 1988, LI1, LI16; Molinari interview, March 4, 2010; *PL*, Vol. 6, No. 3, 3rd Quarter 1989, *PATCO Lives* file, Box 4, James D. Wright Papers, PATCO/UTA.

24. Interview with David Siegel, June 27, 2003, by telephone; Leyden to PATCO staff, January 9, 1979, PATCO Memoranda 1979 file, Box 239, PATCO.

25. Helene S. Tanimoto and Joyce M. Najita, *Guide to Statutory Provisions in Public Sector Collective Bargaining: Strike Rights and Prohibitions*, Third Issue (Manoa: Industrial Relations Center of the University of Hawaii at Manoa, 1981), 8–12; Paul Johnston, *Success While Others Fail: Social Movement Unionism and the Public Workplace* (Ithaca, N.Y.: ILR Press, 1994), 55–86.

26. Blaylock quoted in "Air Controllers' Strike," *Facts on File*, Vol. 41, No. 2136 (October 23, 1981), 772; Biller quoted in "Federal Unions Press for Right to Strike," *GUC*, November 20, 1981, 7; "Federal Sector Unions Post Declines in 1981," *GUC*, April 23, 1982, 8–9; *NYT*, August 5, 1984, E2; Pierce quoted in *WP*, May 31, 1987, A1, A23.

27. "Unions Warned of PATCO Effect," *GUC*, November 6, 1981, 5; quotation from James J. Kilpatrick in *CPD*, November 6, 1981, B18; Romulus Mayor William Oakley to Ronald Reagan, August 14, 1981, WHORM Subject File PE001 (036,859), RRPL; Garland Mayor Charles G. Glack to Ronald Reagan, August 21, 1981, WHORM Subject File PE001 (037,377), RRPL; Dyersberg Mayor Bill Revell to Ronald Reagan, August 14, 1981, WHORM Subject File PE001 (036,798), RRPL; Snyder Mayor Milton Ham to Ronald Reagan, August 12, 1981, WHORM Subject File PE001 (036,786), RRPL; Robert M. Sturges to Ronald Reagan, August 17, 1981, WHORM Subject File PE001 (037,191), RRPL; union leader quoted in "Air Controllers' Strike," *Facts on File*, Vol. 41, No. 2136 (October 23, 1981), 772.

28. Jonathan Alter, "Featherbedding in the Tower: How the Controllers Let the Cat out of the Bag," *Washington Monthly* 13:8 (1981): 22, 27; James J. Kilpatrick, "They Struck a Blow for Tyranny," *The National Review* (October 2, 1981): 1132, 1157; Elizabeth Sullivan, "Public Unions Reach a Flash Point," *CPD*, September 7, 1981, p. 7B; Leyden quoted in "Public Employees, Unions Agree: Times Are Tough," *GUC*, January 29, 1982, 1; Henry S. Farber, "Union Membership in the United States: The Divergence between the Public and Private Sectors," Working Paper #503, Princeton University Industrial Relations Section, September 2005, Princeton University, p. 1, www.irs.princeton.edu/pubs/pdfs/503.pdf (accessed July 12, 2010).

29. By 1983, state and local government were paying approximately $66 billion to private contractors to perform public service work. AFSCME, *Passing the Bucks: The Contracting Out of Public Services* (Washington, D.C.: AFSCME, 1983), 9.

30. Johnston, *Success While Others Fail*, 3; David Lewin, "Public Employee Unionism in the 1980s: An Analysis of Transformation," in *Unions in Transition*, ed. Seymour Martin Lipset (San Francisco: Institute for Contemporary Studies, 1986), 247; "Strike Figures Show Unions in Retreat," *GUC*, November 19, 1982, 1; "Strikes Decline," *GUC*, July 30, 1982, 1; "Teacher Unions Strike Less, PATCO Fallout?" *GUC*, November 6, 1981, 8; Richard C. Kearney, *Labor Relations in the Public Sector* (New York: Marcel Dekker, Inc., 1984), 239; Ronald Donovan, *Administering the Taylor Law: Public Employee Relations in New York* (Ithaca, N.Y.: ILR Press, 1990), 205–206.

31. Tiziano Treu, "Labor Relations in the Public Sector: A Comparative Overview," in *Public Service Labor Relations: Recent Trends and Future Prospects: A Comparative Survey of Seven Industrialized Market Economy Countries*, ed. Tiziano Treu et al. (Geneva: International Labour Office, 1987), 1–47; Fort Lauderdale Vice Mayor Robert O. Cox to Ronald Reagan, August 24, 1981, WHORM Subject File PE001 (037,730), RRPL; Donahue quoted in Philip Dray, *There Is Power in a Union: The Epic Story of Labor in America* (New York: Doubleday, 2010), 639; FMCS director Kay McMurray quoted in "Strike Activity Down, Thank Reagan, Says New FMCS Director," *GUC*, August 27, 1982, 2; quotation from *Boston Union Teacher*, November 1981 [thanks to Jennifer Pish Harrison for alerting me to this citation]; interview with Pete Benner, September 23, 2008, by telephone (transcript in the author's possession); Lewin, "Public Employee Unionism in the 1980s: An Analysis of Transformation," 263; Grace Sterrett and Antone Aboud, *The Right to Strike in Public Employment*, 2nd ed. (Ithaca, N.Y.: ILR Press, 1982), 1; "'81 Strike Count Hits 13-Year Low," *GUC*, February 12, 1982, 1.

32. Allan M. Cartter, *Theory of Wages and Employment* (Homewood, Ill.: Richard D. Irwin, Inc., 1959), 117.

33. *Longshore-Warehouse Militant*, August 17, 1981, Correspondence with PATCO file, Box 1, James D. Wright Papers, PATCO/UTA; William J. Lanouette, "Sending Labor a Message," *National Journal*, August 22, 1981, 1516; William Allen White, "Cal Coolidge and the Boston Police Strike," *WSJ*, August 13, 1981, 18 (reprinted from William Allen White, *A Puritan in Babylon: The Story of Calvin Coolidge* [New York: Macmillan, 1938]); "PATCO Will Impact Labor Relations," *GUC*, August 14, 1981, 1.

34. James B. Atleson, *Values and Assumptions in American Labor Law* (Amherst: University of Massachusetts Press, 1983), chapter 1; James Gray Pope, "How American Workers Lost Their Right to Strike, And Other Tales," *Rutgers Law School (Newark) Faculty Papers* 2004, paper 3 (copy in the author's possession).

35. William B. Gould, IV, *Agenda for Reform: The Future of Employment Relationships and the Law* (Cambridge, Mass.: MIT Press, 1994), 185; James L. Dougherty, *Union-Free Management—And How to Keep it Free* (Chicago: The Dartell Corporation, 1972); John Logan, "The Union Avoidance Industry in the United States," *British Journal of Industrial Relations* 44:4 (December 2006): 651–675.

36. I. Herbert Rothenberg and Steven B. Silverman, *Labor Unions—How To: Avert Them, Beat Them, Out-Negotiate Them, Live With Them, Unload Them* (Elkins Park, Penn.: Management Relations, Inc., 1973), 14; W. H. Hutt, *The Strike-Threat System:*

The Economic Consequences of Collective Bargaining (New Rochelle, N.Y.: Arlington House, 1973), 282. Chapter's opening quotation from p. 283.

37. Jason F. Hellwig, "Big Labor in a Small Town: The Hortonville Teachers' Strike," *Voyageur: Northeast Wisconsin's Historical Review* 19:2 (2003): 10–26; McCartin, "Fire the Hell Out of Them"; Michael H. LeRoy, "Regulating Employer Use of Permanent Striker Replacements: Empirical Analysis of NLRA and RLA Strikes 1935–1991," *Berkeley Journal of Employment and Labor Law* 16 (1995): 169–207.

38. Interview with Thomas Donahue, October 11, 2001, Washington, D.C.; on PATCO as a crystallizing event, see Timothy J. Minchin, "Torn Apart: Permanent Replacements and the Crossett Strike of 1985," *Arkansas Historical Quarterly* 59:1 (Spring 2000): 33; Dan Clawson and Mary Ann Clawson, "What Has Happened to the U.S. Labor Movement? Union Decline and Renewal," *Annual Review of Sociology* 25 (1999): 104; Robert Michael Smith, *From Blackjacks to Briefcases: A History of Commercialized Strikebreaking in the United States* (Athens: Ohio University Press, 2003), 120; Puddington, *Lane Kirkland*, 277–278; Robert Schwartz, "Navigating a Minefield: U.S. Workers and the Legal Right to Strike," *Labor Notes* 338 (May 2007): 10–11.

39. Stein, *Pivotal Decade*, 227–231; William Greider, *Secrets of the Temple: How the Federal Reserve Runs the Country* (New York: Simon and Schuster, 1987), 431–456, passim; Lawrence Mishel, Jared Bernstein, and John Schmitt, *The State of Working America, 2000/2001* (Washington, D.C.: Economic Policy Institute, 2001), 237.

40. "Shifts in Auto Industry Employment, 1979–98," *Monthly Labor Review* (September 28, 1999); Charles N. Weaver, "Workers' Expectations About Losing and Replacing Their Jobs," *Monthly Labor Review* 103:4 (1980): 53–54; "Employees on Nonfarm Payrolls by Major Industry Sector: Historical" Table B-1, BLS; B-2; "Average Hours and Earnings of Production or Nonsupervisory Workers on Private Nonfarm Payrolls by Major Industry Sector, 1964 to Date," Bureau of Labor Statistics, tables available at http://data.bls.gov (accessed January 27, 2006).

41. For a discussion of the *Clear Pine Mouldings* case, see James A. Gross, *Broken Promise: The Subversion of U.S. Labor Relations Policy, 1947–1994* (Philadelphia: Temple University Press, 1995), 250–269, esp. 263.

42. Martin Jay Levitt and Terry Conrow, *Confessions of a Union Buster* (New York: Crown Publishers, 1993), 217–220, 235, 248–249.

43. Charles R. Perry, Andrew Kramer, and Thomas J. Schneider, *Operating During Strikes: Company Experience, NLRB Policies, and Government Regulations*, Labor Relations and Public Policy Series, No. 23 (Philadelphia: Wharton School Industrial Research Unit, 1982), 121; quotation from Charles R. Perry, "Plant Operation During Strikes," in *Employee Relations and Regulation in the 1980s*, ed. Herbert R. Northrup and Richard L. Rowan (Philadelphia: The Wharton School, Industrial Research Unit, 1981), 201–202. The Wharton School solicited the help of Drew Lewis in preparing this volume. See Herbert R. Northrup to Drew Lewis, October 21, 1981, File 81–35, Entry 14, Box 163, FAA.

44. John Hicks, *The Theory of Wages* (London: Macmillan, 1932), 141–157. For critiques and revisions of the Hicks approach, see Albert Rees, "Industrial Conflict and Business Fluctuations," *Journal of Political Economy* 60: 5 (1952): 371–382; Allan M. Cartter, *Theory of Wages and Employment* (Homewood, Ill.: Richard

D. Irwin, Inc., 1959), 128; Orley Ashenfelter and George E. Johnson, "Bargaining Theory, Trade Unions, and Industrial Strike Activity," *American Economic Review* 59:1 (1969): 35–49.

45. *WSJ*, June 30, 1983, 18; Jonathan D. Rosenblum, *Copper Crucible: How the Arizona Miners' Strike of 1983 Recast Labor-Management Relations in America* (Ithaca, N.Y.: ILR Press, 1994); Barbara Kingsolver, *Holding the Line: Women in the Great Arizona Copper Strike of 1983* (Ithaca, N.Y.: ILR Press, 1989); *WSJ*, November 4, 1983, 8; November 18, 1983, 6; December 5, 1983, 3.

46. Peter J. Rachleff, *Hard-Pressed in the Heartland: The Hormel Strike and the Future of the Labor Movement* (Boston: South End Press, 1993); Dave Hage and Paul Klauda, *No Retreat, No Surrender: Labor's War at Hormel* (New York: William Morrow and Co., 1989); Steve Babson, *The Unfinished Struggle: Turning Points in American Labor, 1877–Present* (Lanham, Md.: Rowman & Littlefield Publishers, 1999), 158.

47. Timothy J. Minchin, "Torn Apart: Permanent Replacements and the Crossett Strike of 1985," 31–58 (Glenn quotation, p. 33); Timothy J. Minchin, "Broken Spirits: Permanent Replacements and the Rumsford Strike of 1986," *New England Quarterly* 74:1 (March 2001): 5–31; Julius Getman, *The Betrayal of Local 14: Paperworkers, Politics, and Permanent Replacements* (Ithaca, N.Y.: Cornell University Press, 1998).

48. Interview with George Stohner, December 2, 2010, Washington, D.C.; Peter Cramton and Joseph Tracy, "The Use of Permanent Replacement Workers in Union Contract Negotiations, 1980–1989," *Journal of Labor Economics* 16:4 (October 1998): 687; Logan, "The Union Avoidance Industry in the United States," 653; Smith, *From Blackjacks to Briefcases*, 120, 128; Cynthia Gramm, "Employers' Decisions to Operate during Strikes: Consequences and Policy Decisions," *Employee Rights in a Changing Economy: The Issue of Replacement Workers*, ed. William Spriggs (Washington, D.C.: Economic Policy Institute, 1991); Steve Early, *Holding the Line in '89: Lessons of the NYNEX Strike*, (Somerville, Mass.: Labor Resource Center, 1990); Ken Grossinger, "Can Strikes Still be Won?" *Social Policy* (Spring 1989): 4–12.

49. Early, *Holding the Line in '89*, 7; AFL-CIO quotation in Cramton and Tracy, "The Use of Permanent Replacement Workers in Union Contract Negotiations, 1980–1989," 671; Robert M. Schwartz, *Strikes, Picketing, and Inside Campaigns: A Legal Guide for Unions* (Cambridge, Mass.: Work Rights Press, 2006).

50. In 1984, two of America's preeminent labor researchers considered the post-PATCO downturn in strikes a momentary blip. "While there is some downward trend in strike-time lost, the notion that strikes are now diminishing is now recognized to be inaccurate," they wrote. "Strikes remain a part of labor-management relations." See Richard B. Freeman and James L. Medoff, *What Do Unions Do?* (New York: Basic Books, 1984), 237. My data is drawn from major work stoppages registered by the U.S. Bureau of Labor Statistics. See BLS data, http://www.bls .gov/news.release/wkstp.t01.html (accessed May 28, 2009). The data are not without problems. From 1947 to 1981, the BLS cataloged all strikes involving at least six workers. After 1981, it recorded only "major work stoppages" involving at least one thousand workers. Thus, any effort to address patterns over decades before and after 1981 requires a focus on major work stoppages. But according to

the best research on the question, it is reasonable to assume that the pattern of large strikes reflects the overall patterns of strikes. See L. J. Perry and P. J. Wilson, "Trends in Work Stoppages: A Global Perspective," Working Paper No. 47, 2004, Policy Integration Department, Statistical Analysis Unit. Geneva: ILO, available at http://papers.ssrn.com/sol3/papers.cfm?abstract_id=908,483 (accessed May 28, 2009); Bruce E. Kaufman, "Research on Strike Models and Outcomes in the 1980s: Accomplishments and Shortcomings," in David Lewin, Olivia S. Mitchell, and Peter D. Sherer, eds., *Research Frontiers in Industrial Relations and Human Resources* (Madison: Industrial Relations Research Association, 1992), 77–132.

51. P. K. Edwards, "The End of American Strike Statistics," *British Journal of Industrial Relations* 31 (November 1983): 392–394.

52. Susan B. Carter, et al. eds., *Historical Statistics of the United States: Earliest Times to the Present, Volume 2, Part B, Work and Welfare* (Cambridge: Cambridge University Press, 2006), 2–352.

53. Phil Keisling, "Money Over What Really Mattered: Where the Air Traffic Controllers Went Wrong," *The Washington Monthly* (September 1983), 11; David G. Bowers, "What Would Make 11,500 People Quit Their Jobs?" *Organizational Dynamics* (Winter 1983): 6, 16; Paul McNally, *Against the Wind: The History of the National Air Traffic Controllers Association* (Washington, D.C.: NATCA, 2002), 35–43.

54. Tom Berry to Edward V. Curran, October 11, 1981, General Information file, Box 1, Dennis Reardon/PATCO Records, PATCO/UTA; clipping, Aviation Safety Institute *Monitor*, Mid-Sept. 1983, p. 3, in Post-strike Memos and Correspondence files, Box 2, AR 397, PATCO Local 332 Records, PATCO/UTA; *WP*, May 30, 1984, A1, A7.

55. *WP*, July 24, 1984, A12; McNally, *Against the Wind*, 47–49.

56. McElroy, *Against the Wind*, 54–56.

57. *WP*, July 24, 1984, A12; *NYT*, June 13, 1984, A16; McElroy, *Against the Wind*, 58–67.

58. Interview with Barry Krasner, December 10, 2010, Washington, D.C.; *NYT*, November 12, 1985, A1, B4; *NYT*, November 13, 1985, B2; *NYT*, November 23, 1985, 30; *WP*, December 2, 1985, A5.

59. Engen quoted in *WP*, February 8, 1987, A10; *WP*, September 24, 1986, A10; *WP*, July 31, 1986, A9; *WP*, May 29, 1983, A16.

60. *WP*, February 8, 1987, A10, A11; *WP*, June 10, 1987, A15; NATCA quotation from Nancy Risque to Senator Baker, Re: Air Traffic Controllers Union, June 11, 1987, WHORM Subject File JL002 (503868CU), RRPL; *WP*, June 12, 1987, B3; *NYT*, September 25, 1988, LI1, LI16; "Air Traffic Controllers, FAA Reach Tentative Agreement on Three-Year Pact," *Air Transport* 130:4 (January 23, 1989): 66.

61. *PL*, Vol. 3, No. 2, Second Quarter 1987, *PATCO Lives* file, Box 4, James D. Wright Papers, PATCO/UTA; Bill Fauth to Brother, n.d. [1991], Correspondence file, 1985–91, Box 1, Washington D.C., PATCO Collection, PATCO/UTA.

62. *PL*, Vol. 5, No. 1, Second Quarter 1988, *PATCO Lives* file, Box 4, James D. Wright Papers, PATCO/UTA; William Clay and Barbara Boxer to President George Bush, November 11, 1991, Box 1, Correspondence file, 1990–92, Washington D.C., PATCO Collection, PATCO/UTA; interview with Trish Gilbert, December 10, 2010, Washington, D.C.

63. *PL*, Vol. 9, No. 2, Second Quarter 1992, p. 1, *PATCO Lives* file, Box 4, James D. Wright Papers, PATCO/UTA; *ChiST*, February 16, 1993, p. 5.

64. *PL*, Vol. 9, No. 4, Fourth Quarter 1992, *PATCO Lives* file, Box 4, James D. Wright Papers, PATCO/UTA; Bob Harris to Lane Kirkland, January 27, 1994 (copy in possession of the author); *Miami Herald*, May 12, 1993, 14.

65. *USA Today*, February 4, 1993, 4A; *WP*, February 3, 1993, A13; *NYT*, May 11, 1993, A1, A19; *WP*, August 13, 1993, A7; quotation from *StPD*, August 13, 1993, 1A.

66. *StPD*, August 13, 1993, 1A; *CPD*, October 5, 1994, 1; interview with Domenic Torchia, May 23, 2002, by telephone; interview with Paul Rinaldi, December 10, 2010, Washington, D.C.

67. *StPD*, February 20, 1994, 12A; *CPD*, October 5, 1994, 1; *CPD*, October 8, 1994, 6B; *WSJ*, August 25, 1995, 1.

68. McElroy, *Against the Wind*, 156–160; *WSJ*, June 16, 1998, 1; Krasner interview.

69. *PL*, Vol. 10, No. 2, Second Half 1993, *PATCO Lives* file, Box 4, James D. Wright Papers, PATCO/UTA.

BLACK BOX

1. Maher quote from Jack Maher to Past PATCO Members, Friends, and Associates, December 6, 1995 (copy in the author's possession); plow quote from interview with Ray Carver, July 27, 2003, by telephone.

2. James J. Kilpatrick, "They Struck a Blow for Tyranny," *The National Review*, October 2, 1981, 1132–1137, 1157; Richard W. Hurd, "How PATCO Was Led Into a Trap," *The Nation*, December 26, 1981, 696–698.

3. For examples of conflicting interpretations and explanations of the strike, see Herbert R. Northrup, "The Rise and Demise of PATCO," *Industrial and Labor Relations Review* 37 (January 1984): 167–184; Richard W. Hurd and Jill K. Kriesky, "'The Rise and Demise of PATCO' Reconstructed," *Industrial and Labor Relations Review* 40:1 (October 1986): 115–123; Herbert R. Northrup, "Reply," *Industrial and Labor Relations Review* 40:1 (October 1986): 122–127; Richard W. Hurd, "Reflections on PATCO's Legacy: Labor's Strategic Challenges Persist," *Employee Rights and Responsibilities Journal* 18:3 (September 2006): 207–214; Arthur B. Shostak, "Second Thoughts on the PATCO Strike," *Social Policy* 16:3 (Winter 1986): 22–28; Arthur Shostak and David Skocik, *The Air Controllers' Controversy: Lessons from the PATCO Strike* (New York: Human Sciences Press, 1986); Arthur B. Shostak, "Finding Meaning in Labor's 'Perfect Storm': Lessons from the 1981 PATCO Strike," *Employee Rights and Responsibilities Journal* 18:3 (September 2006): 223–229; Art Shostak, "Labor Professor Highlights Lessons from the 1981 PATCO Strike," *Air Traffic Controller* 19:3 (May/June 2005): 14; Willis Nordlund, *Silent Skies: The Air Traffic Controllers' Strike* (Westport, Conn.: Praeger, 1998); Round, *Grounded: Reagan and the PATCO Crash* (New York: Garland, 1999).

4. James W. Ceasar, "The Reagan Presidency and American Public Opinion," in *The Reagan Legacy: Promise and Performance*, ed. Charles O. Jones (Chatham, N.J.: Chatham House, 1988), 184; Johnson, *Sleepwalking Through History*, 193; *WSJ*, February 6, 2006, p. A18.

5. William C. Berman, *America's Right Turn: From Nixon to Clinton*, 2nd ed. (Baltimore, Md.: Johns Hopkins University Press, 1998), 98; "simplistic" quotation from

Parbudyal Singh and Harish C. Jain, "Striker Replacements in the United States, Canada, and Mexico: A Review of the Law and Empirical Research," *Industrial Relations* 40:1 (January 2001): 24; William T. Dickens and Jonathan S. Leonard, "Accounting for the Decline in Union Membership, 1950–1980," *Industrial and Labor Relations Review* 38:3 (April 1985): 323–334; Walter Galenson, *Trade Union Growth and Decline: An International Study* (Westport, Conn.: Praeger, 1994).

6. Sidney Blumenthal and Thomas Byrne Edsall observed, "The acceleration of the decline of the union movement is one of the major political successes of the Reagan administration, as the administration has used the power of the presidency and the federal regulatory apparatus to chop away at labor. The tenor of the antiunion drive was set by Reagan himself when he fired 11,345 striking air traffic controllers in 1981, setting an example that would be widely followed in the private sector, where employer-ordered lockouts, challenges to union collective bargaining rights, and the hiring of nonunion workers during labor disputes proliferated during his administration." Sidney Blumenthal and Thomas Byrne Edsall, *The Reagan Legacy* (New York: Pantheon, 1988), 32–33.

7. Leaflet quoted in *ChiST*, October 22, 1993, 6.

8. Timothy J. Minchin, "Permanent Replacements and the 'Social Accord' in Calera, Alabama, 1974–1999," *Labor History* 41:4 (2001): 372; *NYT*, June 15, 1993, A23; *NYT*, June 24, 1993, A22; *NYT*, July 13, 1994, D12.

9. Ronald Turner, "Banning the Permanent Replacement of Strikers by Executive Order: The Conflict Between Executive Order 12,954 and the NLRA," *Journal of Law and Politics* 12:1 (Winter 1996): 1–61; Chamber of Commerce of the United States, et al. v. Robert B. Reich, 74 F.3d 1322; 316 U.S. App. D.C. 61; Michael H. LeRoy, "Presidential Regulation of Private Employment: Constitutionality Of Executive Order 12954 Debarment of Contractors Who Hire Permanent Striker Replacements," *Boston College Law Review* 37 (March 1996): 229; Roger Pilon, *The Rule of Law in the Wake of Clinton* (Washington, D.C.: The Cato Institute, 2000), 50.

10. Tom Juravich and Kate Bronfenbrenner, *Ravenswood: The Steelworkers' Victory and the Revival of American Labor* (Ithaca, N.Y.: ILR/Cornell University Press, 1999), x; Stephen Franklin, *Three Strikes: Labor's Heartland Losses and What They Mean for Working Americans* (New York: Guilford, 2001); Lichtenstein quoted in *NYT*, August 20, 1997, A1.

11. U.S. Bureau of Labor Statistics, Table 1: Work Stoppages Involving 1,000 or more workers, http://www.bls.gov/news.release/wkstp.t01.htm (accessed December 11, 2010).

12. Steve Early, "Walking Out and Winning," *Against the Current* 124 (September/October 2006): 29.

13. Interview with Ed Gaffney, August 9, 2006, by telephone; *Christian Science Monitor*, August 29, 2005, 2; Frances Florino, "AMFA Settlement," *Aviation Week & Space Technology* 165:15 (October 16, 2006): 19.

14. John Schmitt, "The Wage Penalty for State and Local Government Employees," Center for Economic and Policy Research, May 2010, pp. 1, 3; Jeffrey Keefe, "Debunking the Myth of the Overcompensated Public Employee: The Evidence," Economic Policy Institute, EPI Briefing Paper, #276, September 15, 2010 (copy in the author's possession).

15. Dick Morris and Eileen McGann, "Smash the Union Thug-ocracy," November 8, 2010, http://www.dickmorris.com/blog/smash-the-union-thug-ocracy/ (accessed March 9, 2011).

16. Walker quotations taken from the recording of a prank phone call in which a reporter from a Web publication called the *Buffalo Beast* impersonated a conservative donor in order to engage the governor in a conversation about his conflict with labor. For access to this recording, see http://www.buffalobeast.com/?p=5045 (accessed March 9, 2011).

17. Anonymous controller quoted in Newman, *Falling From Grace*, 169; PATCO strike James D. Wright quoted in, *Newsletter Supplement*, January/February 1985, 5, *PATCO Lives* file, Box 4, James D. Wright Papers, PATCO/UTA; Tony Kelly to PATCO81Yahoo Group, July 18, 2004; Domenic V. Torchia to Bill Taylor, n.d. [1991], Correspondence file, 1990–92, Box 1, Washington, D.C., PATCO Collection, PATCO/UTA.

18. *USATCO National Newsletter*, May 1983, 5, Box 6, James D. Wright Papers, PATCO/UTA; Jenni interview; Bill Fauth to Brother, n.d. [1991], Correspondence file, 1985–91, Box 1, Washington, D.C., PATCO Collection, Acc. 95–18, UTA.

19. Mark A. Cassillas quoted in *Newsletter Supplement*, January/February 1985, 8, *PATCO Lives* file, Box 4, James D. Wright Papers, PATCO/UTA; *PATCO Lives*, Vol. 2, No. 3, May/June 1986, The Lifeline File, Box 4, AR 397, PATCO Local 332 Records, PATCO/UTA; *PATCO Lives*, Vol. 3, No. 3 (Third Quarter 1987), *PATCO Lives* file, Box 4, James D. Wright Papers, PATCO/UTA.

20. Skocik and Shostak, *The Air Controllers' Controversy*; John F. Leyden and Edward Curran, "PATCO Manuscript" (unpublished manuscript in the author's possession); Robert E. Lambrecht, "One Strike and You're Out," (unpublished manuscript, 1989); John J. Seddon, "PATCO, A Perspective: Who Were They? What Were They? And What Could or Should Have Been Done?" (M.A. thesis, State University of New York, Empire State College, 1990); Edwin M. Wintermeyer, "An Insider's View of the Professional Air Traffic Controllers Organization with Special Emphasis on the Air Traffic Controllers Strike of 1981," (M.A. thesis, St. Francis University, 1989); Cathy Langston, *What It Means When God Goes on Strike* (self-published: CreateSpace, 2010); Amos William South, "Miami Tower" (unproduced screenplay manuscript, 2005); Terry Paddack, *Crossing Runways* (College Station, Tex.: Virtualbookworm.com Publishing, 2004).

21. Jack Maher to Past PATCO Members, Friends, and Associates, December 6, 1995 (copy in the author's possession).

22. Ron Taylor to *PATCO81@yahoogroups.com*, July 11, 2004, (copy in the author's possession); Ron Taylor to Jack Seddon, and Jack Seddon to Ron Taylor, April 30, 2004, (copies in the author's possession); http://www.patco81.com/PATCO%20 History.htm (accessed December 11, 2010).

23. Maher interview, August 8, 2006.

INDEX

★